1350

The World Today Series®
Stryker-Post Publications
Harpers Ferry, WV
USA

REFERENCE ONLY

Western Europe

DISCARD

2003

VINELAND PUBLIC LIBRARY

940
WES
2003

by Wayne C. Thompson

TWENTY-SECOND EDITION
NEXT PUBLICATION DATE, AUGUST 2004

D1312115

Graphic Materials Acknowledgments

For their generosity in providing certain visual material for use in this book, and in order of their appearance, special thanks to the following:

European Community Information Services
Delegation of the European Union in Washington
North Atlantic Treaty Organization
The Swiss National Tourist Office
The Government of Liechtenstein
The Government of Liechtenstein
French Cultural Services, New York
The Royal Netherlands Embassy
The Embassy of Belgium

The Embassy of Ireland
The British Embassy
The Embassy of Italy
The Embassy of Malta
The Sovereign Military Order of Malta
The Government of Monaco
The Embassy of Spain
The Embassy of Portugal
The Government of Andorra

First appearing as *Western Europe 1982,* this annually revised book is published by

Stryker–Post Publications
P.O. Drawer 1200
Harpers Ferry, WV 25425
Telephones: 1–800–995–1400 (U.S.A. or Canada)
 Other: 1–304–535–2593
 Fax: 1–304–535–6513
 www.Strykerpost.com
 VISA–MASTERCARD–AMERICAN EXPRESS

Copyright © 2003 by Stryker–Post Publications

All rights reserved. This publication, or parts thereof, may not be reproduced in any form whatsoever without permission in writing from the publisher.

The World Today Series has thousands of subscribers across the U.S. and Canada. A sample list of users who annually rely on this most up-to-date material include:

Public library systems
Universities and colleges
High schools
Federal and state agencies
All branches of the armed forces & war colleges
National Geographic Society
National Democratic Institute
Agricultural Education Foundation
Exxon Corporation
Chevron Corporation
CNN

International Standard Book Number: 1–887985–54–9

International Standard Serial Number: 0084–2338

Library of Congress Catalog Card Number: 83–643780

Cover design by Filar Designs

Cartographer: William L. Nelson

Typography by Barton Matheson Willse & Worthington
Baltimore, MD 21244

Printed in the United States of America by United Book Press, Inc.
Baltimore, MD 21207

Photographs used to illustrate *The World Today Series* come from many sources, a great number from friends who travel worldwide. If you have taken any which you believe would enhance the visual impact and attractiveness of our books, do let us hear from you.

DEDICATION

To the memory of my mother and father

ACKNOWLEDGMENTS

I am especially grateful to the Alexander von Humboldt Foundation, a far–sighted German organization which, since 1869, has persistently nurtured the spirit of intellectual discovery and has sought to tighten the links between Europe and the rest of the world, for having granted me a two–year research fellowship at the University of Freiburg in Germany. Without its aid, I would have been unable to complete the first edition of this book.

No author could possibly write a book with the breadth of this one without the assistance of numerous persons and organizations. Mark H. Mullin, a Harvard graduate who earned an M.A. as a Marshall Scholar, Oxford University, wrote all but the political and economic sections of the chapters on the United Kingdom and the Republic of Ireland. His personal familiarity with Britain and Ireland far surpasses my own.

I wish also to thank my colleagues and acquaintances throughout Western Europe and the U.S. who took the time to read or to comment upon various chapters dealing with their own countries or specialties. They include: David M. Keithly, Richard Laurijssen, Jacky Paris, Philippe Vidal, and Maureen and Peter Ward. I am grateful to my students at the College of Europe who critiqued the chapters on their native countries. They are: Ritienne Bonavia (Malta), Nuno Borges (Portugal), Isabelle Costa (Monaco), Francisco Bossa Dionisio (Portugal), Sylvain Dufeu (France), Gregory Gosp (France), Koen Lenssen (Netherlands), Jean Micallef Grimaud (Malta), Eelco Keij (Netherlands), Nuno Queirós (Portugal), Alejandro Ribo Labastida (Spain), Hélène Stergiou (Netherlands), Sabine Tomordy (Liechtenstein), Tim Van Broeckhoven (Belgium) and Giuseppe Zaffuto (Italy). Renée Maeyaert and Anne Heber-Suffrin, librarians at the College of Europe, Bruges, have consistently given me important assistance in obtaining European newspapers and visuals for this book. Jean-Michel Cassiers and Monika Sapilak provided me in Brussels with information and materials on Belgium's language laws and practices. Catherine Lowe thoroughly read the entire manuscript in order to comb out style, spelling and typographical errors. My wife, Susan L. Thompson, took some of the photographs and carefully proofread some of the manuscript. My daughter, Juliet Bunch, also provided me with photos for this book.

I am grateful to Pro Helvetia, which arranged and financed a week-long study tour of Switzerland, as well as to numerous embassy and foreign ministry officials who provided information and arranged visits to Western European capitals to speak with representatives of parties, parliaments, universities, research institutes and news media about this book. A Fulbright Teaching Fellowship to Estonia in 1995–96 enabled me to visit Finland several times. A second Fulbright professorship in the spring semester of 2001 at the College of Europe in Bruges provided me with intellectual stimulation by top graduate students from all over Europe, in addition to an in-depth look at the BENELUX countries and EU and NATO institutions. My dear friend, the late Philip F. Stryker was without doubt one of the most competent, encouraging and congenial publishers with whom an author could work.

W.C.T.

Lexington, Virginia, June 2003

Wayne C. Thompson ...

Wayne C. Thompson . . .

Professor of Politics, College of Europe, Bruges (Belgium) and Warsaw. Professor Emeritus of Political Science, Virginia Military Institute, Lexington, Virginia. Ohio State University (B.A. in Government); Claremont Graduate School (M.A. and Ph.D., with distinction). He did further graduate study at the universities of Göttingen, Paris/Sorbonne and Freiburg im Breisgau, where he has since been a guest professor. He has studied and researched many years in Germany as a Woodrow Wilson, Fulbright, Deutscher Akademischer Austauschdienst, Earhart and Alexander von Humboldt Fellow. He has served as scholar–in–residence at the Bundestag in Bonn and as a Fulbright professor in Estonia. During the 1999–2000 academic year, he was a visiting professor at the Air War College in Montgomery, Alabama. In the spring semester of 2001 he had a second Fulbright professorship at the College of Europe in Bruges and continues to teach at that graduate institution. In the fall semester of 2003 he is a visiting professor of politics at the American University of Bulgaria. He is the author of *In the Eye of the Storm: Kurt Riezler and the Crises of Modern Germany* (Iowa City, University of Iowa Press, 1980), *The Political Odyssey of Herbert Wehner* (Boulder, CO: Westview Press, 1993), *Historical Dictionary of Germany* (Metuchen, NJ: Scarecrow, 1994), and coauthor of *The Challenges of Change: Redefining Transatlantic Relations* (Manchester University Press, 2003). He has written two other books in The World Today Series: *Canada*, as well as *Nordic, Central, and Southeastern Europe*. He also co–edited *Perspectives on Strategic Defense and Space: National Programs and International Cooperation*, and *Margaret Thatcher: Prime Minister Indomitable* (Boulder, CO: Westview, 1987, 1989, 1994). He has written many articles on European politics, philosophy and history which have appeared in such periodicals as *The American Political Science Review, Western Political Quarterly, East European Quarterly, Journal of Politics, Central European History, The American Review of Canadian Studies, German Studies Review, Current History, The Yearbook on International Communist Affairs, The History Teacher, Armed Forces and Society, Freedom at Issue, Communist and Post–Communist Studies, Contemporary French Civilization, Europe-Asia Studies*, and *Virginia Social Science Journal*. He is currently Editor-in-Chief of Stryker-Post Publications.

Mark H. Mullin ...

Harvard University (B.A. Cum Laude in Government), where he was First Marshal of his class and Ivy League and Intercollegiate Mile Run Champion. He was a Marshall Scholar at Oxford University (B.A., M.A. in Philosophy, Politics and Economics) and studied at The General Theological Seminary, New York (M. Div.). The Reverend Canon Mullin was Dean of the Choate School, Wallingford, Connecticut, where he also taught European History, Assistant Headmaster at the Blue Ridge School, Virginia, Headmaster of St. Albans School, Washington, D.C., and at the Casady School, Oklahoma City. He is author of *Educating for the 21st Century: The Challenge for Parents and Teachers* (Lanham, MD: Madison Books, University Press of America, 1991).

The Mullins chat with Prince Charles

CONTENTS

September 27, 2001: European Commission President Romano Prodi, Belgian Prime Minister Guy Verhofstadt and President George W. Bush

Courtesy: Central Audiovisual Library, European Commision

IRELAND

UNITED
KINGDOM

NETHERLANDS

BELGIUM

LUXEMBOURG

FRANCE

SWITZERLAND

LIECHTENSTEIN

PORTUGAL

ANDORRA

SAN
MARINO

MONACO

SPAIN

ITALY

VATICAN

0   100   200   300 miles

0   200   400 kilometers

MALTA

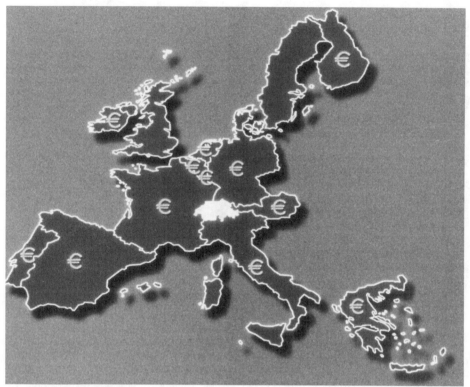

Countries using the euro

"McDonald's? Me? Always!!!"

In 1945 much of Europe lay in ruins, its peoples destitute and demoralized following a war on its own soil more destructive than any conflict in history. Two world wars in the 20th century (World War I from 1914 until 1918 and World War II from 1939 until 1945) had brought Europe's dominance over world affairs to an end and had led to a rise of the United States of America and the Soviet Union as the world's most powerful nations. These wars also ended Europe's colonial hold on much of the world, a hold which, despite some negative effects, had spread European civilization to the Western Hemisphere, Africa, the Middle East and the Far East.

Western Europe is a region rich in diversity, with a population of 382 million persons (if one adds Germany, Austria

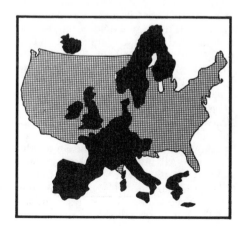

and the Nordic countries). This compares to about 281 million in the U.S.

Geographically, Western Europe is much smaller than the U.S. The entire region is scarcely more than twice the size of Alaska and would easily fit into the continental U.S. west of the Mississippi with much room to spare. Like the U.S., Western Europe offers a very rich diversity of climates and landscapes, from the permafrost and midnight sun of northern Norway to the hot, dry, sunny Mediterranean; from the fog and rain of northern Germany to the warm blue skies of the Azores and to the snows and arctic winds of Iceland, from the Alpine peaks of Austria and Switzerland to the flat and sub–sea level terrain of the Netherlands.

With the collapse of communism in Europe, the unification of Germany, and the dissolution of the Soviet Union, Europeans are faced with the most significant alteration of their continent's political map since World War II. Because two hostile Europes no longer face each other, Europe has doubled its size from 382 to 700 million people. From Moscow to Lisbon and Dublin to Budapest democracies exist in which free elections provide the only legitimate claim to power and which are basically committed to freedom, individual rights, and some variant of capitalism.

Looking eastward, Western Europeans see more than a dozen independent nations emerging, all in difficult economic circumstances, with borders in dispute,

ethnic scores to settle and millions of discontented and frightened citizens who may decide to seek a better future in the West. Most are clamoring for admission to the plentiful Western European table and a place under the Atlantic Alliance's security umbrella. The August 1991 putsch in the former Soviet Union destroyed central authority and dispersed power among its various republics. Western European countries led the way in recognizing the newly independent Baltic states of Estonia, Latvia, and Lithuania, which are reaching out to the West. Moldova, carved out of Romania at the beginning of World War II, may one day find its way back into union with that struggling state.

In this dramatically changed situation, the earlier logic of dividing The World Today Series' two European volumes between West and East no longer applies. As political boundaries on the European continent, which extends from the Atlantic Ocean to the Ural Mountains in Russia, have become less sharp and more open, Stryker-Post Publications has decided to present this diverse continent in three volumes organized along geographic lines. This book on Western Europe includes countries with a total population of approximately 262 million. It extends from the British Isles to Italy and the Iberian Peninsula and embraces the BENELUX countries, France and Switzerland. Russia and the Commonwealth of Independent States (CIS), former Soviet republics (minus the Baltic States) from Belarus, Ukraine and Moldova through the Caucasus to the Central Asian Republics, are presented in a separate volume.

In between is a 500- to 800-mile strip of countries with a total population of approximately 250 million and extending about 2,400 miles from the Nordic countries to Greece in the South. The geographic center of Europe runs through Ukraine. Therefore, all the countries included in the new volume entitled *Nordic, Central, and Southeastern Europe,* are located in the western half of Europe.

Western Europe Today

All look primarily westward for their trade, and almost all feel western in their political and cultural orientation.

In December 1991, Ukrainian voters chose independence, thus paving the way for the creation of an historically conscious sovereign state of 52 million people, the fourth largest in Europe with more territory than France and a sizable armed force. Following the collapse of the Soviet Union later that month, it joined Russia and Belarus to form the CIS, to which all former Soviet republics except the Baltics belong. The CIS is a loose organization to coordinate policies mainly in the economic field, but it also performs limited political and military functions. In the South, Yugoslavia came unglued and became the scene of the first full–scale war in Europe since 1945.

Western Europe still has many cultures and many lands and regions with characters and appearances of their own. However, there are many things which make much of modern Western Europe and the U.S. look more and more similar: large shopping centers, fast-food stores, freeways, modern cities with some skyscrapers and much concrete, many automobiles and everywhere signs of prosperity.

Americans and Western Europeans also face many of the same problems and have many of the same concerns, though in differing degrees: the "generation gap," the role of women in modern society, a declining birth rate, equal rights for women, illegal immigration, the integration of racial and religious minorities, a flood of political refugees, urban violence and terrorism, the protection of the environment and the quality of life, the defense of their homeland and values in the nuclear age, the provision of adequate supplies of energy and raw materials and the maintenance of prosperity and generous social security programs despite the dangers of inflation, unemployment and declining economic growth rates.

NATO Headquarters

Young Americans and Western Europeans have similar cultural tastes for music, films (70% of the film market in Western Europe is from Hollywood), language expressions (especially English ones!) and dress. Jeans, jogging shoes, T–shirts and hairstyles no longer provide accurate clues to nationality; they have become international. Western European students and scientists are strongly attracted to American universities and research institutes, and European businessmen have, on the whole, been very successful in adapting production and management techniques to European conditions. Americans also continue to be drawn culturally, emotionally, politically and economically to Western Europe. In short, the American or Western European no longer enters a "different world" when he arrives at the other side of the Atlantic.

The reader will confront numerous abbreviations and acronyms, and one must understand not only what the letters signify, but also what function the indicated institutions serve. Therefore, in the following pages, these acronyms will be presented in the context of a more general discussion of some of the more important Western European bodies and organizations.

Today, Western Europe is a region that is, on the whole, highly prosperous, though it is relatively poor in natural resources. It has a large industrial base, much capital and know–how and a highly skilled work force. It is also relatively secure militarily. Such prosperity and security are partly due to the countries' high degree of voluntary cooperation, formalized in numerous international organizations. All major Western European countries are full members of the United Nations (UN), and all participate in the many organizations linked to the UN, such as the UN Educational, Scientific and Cultural Organization (UNESCO), the UN Conference on Trade and Development (UNCTAD), the World Court, which sits in the stately Peace Palace built with funds contributed by Andrew Carnegie in the Hague, Netherlands, the International Labor Organization (ILO), the UN Industrial Development Organization (UNIDO), the World Health Organization (WHO), the Food and Agriculture Organization (FAO) and a number of others.

Most Western European countries would be unable to defend themselves alone. Therefore, the majority has chosen to join the North Atlantic Treaty Organization (NATO), also known as the Atlantic Alliance. Created in 1949, NATO links the power of the United States and Canada, and the geographic position of Iceland

A Changing Alliance

Source: *The Washington Post*

(which has no army) with the military resources of Belgium–Netherlands–Luxembourg (BENELUX), Great Britain, Norway, Denmark, the Federal Republic of Germany (FRG or Germany), Italy, Portugal, Turkey, Greece, France, Spain, and (since 1999) Poland, Hungary and the Czech Republic. At its November 2002 Prague summit, NATO invited seven more countries to join in 2004: the three Baltic States (Estonia, Latvia, Lithuania), Slovakia, Slovenia, Romania, Bulgaria. The only major Western European countries that remain neutral are Ireland, Switzerland, Austria, Sweden, and Finland.

When the question arose concerning the organization of a European military combination, France, Italy and West Germany initiated in 1952 a treaty creating a European Defense Community (EDC). It was intended to bring into being an integrated European army under a unified command structure, which would ultimately include troops from West Germany and the BENELUX countries. However, in 1954 the French National Assembly rejected this plan, fearing the possible loss of its sovereignty if it relinquished command over its army.

As a compromise, Great Britain proposed a Western European Union (WEU), composed of the BENELUX countries, France, Italy, Germany, Great Britain, Greece, Spain and Portugal, with headquarters in Brussels. Turkey, Norway and Iceland became associate members. It conducted contingency planning, organized and controlled small all–European military operations (with the possibility of using NATO units and equipment), and attempted to coordinate the defense policies and armaments programs of its members. In November 2000 the European Union (EU), known until 1993 as the European Communities (EC), largely absorbed the WEU.

At the 1991 EU summit meeting in Maastricht, it was agreed that the WEU would be Europe's own defense system, albeit "linked to" NATO. It ceased to exist the end of 2000, and its staff and activities were folded into the EU. At its Helsinki summit in 1999, the EU decided to create a 60,000-strong rapid reaction corps, officially operational in 2003, to act in crises when the U.S. and NATO choose not to get involved. An informal organization within NATO known as the "Eurogroup," composed of all European members of NATO except France, Portugal and Iceland, serves as a forum for some European states within NATO to discuss their special defense needs.

NATO itself has both political and military components. The highest political organ and decision-making body is the North Atlantic Council (NAC). It selects the Secretary General of NATO, who chairs all meetings and seeks consensus among members. By tradition he is always a European. In 1995 ex-Spanish foreign minister, Javier Solana Madariaga, filled the post. In 1999 the EU created a new post of "high representative" to breathe life into the EU's Common Foreign and Security Policy (CFSP) and named Solana to occupy it. To give CFSP a military arm, the EU created the European Security and Defence Policy (ESDP) with a rapid reaction force. This enabled the EU to take command of the small peacekeeping force in Macedonia in 2003. George Robertson, former British defense minister, replaced him as NATO secretary general and served until the end of 2003. Each member country sends a permanent ambassador to NATO Headquarters in Brussels, and these ambassadors meet once a week. Less frequently, the member countries' heads of government, foreign, defense or finance ministers meet to iron out higher-level political problems. All decisions are reached by consensus, not by majority vote. In other words, each member has an actual veto power although such vetoes are seldom cast.

The ambassadors or ministers of all but those nations that do not participate in the integrated defense system (presently France and Iceland) also take part in the Defense Planning Committee (DPC), which is assisted by a variety of committees and working groups. A staff of about 1,000, divided into divisions of Political Affairs, Defense Planning and Policy, Defense Support and Scientific Affairs are in Brussels to assist in the NATO effort.

The highest NATO military authority is the Military Committee, made up of the chiefs–of–defense from all states participating in the NATO military command plus France (since 1995). By tradition it is chaired by a European officer. Although the chiefs–of–defense meet infrequently, their permanent representatives meet regularly in their absence. The Military Committee's primary role is to advise the DPC.

NATO has an integrated system of commands. The Supreme Allied Commander Europe (SACEUR), who by tradition is always an American, heads the Allied Command Europe (ACE). He also commands all U.S. forces in Europe, and his European Command encompasses Russia and all of Africa except the Horn. In 2002 Marine Corps General James L. Jones replaced Air Force General Joseph W. Ralston as SACEUR. Having grown up in Paris, Jones is the first SACEUR to speak fluent French and the first Marine to become SACEUR. He was chosen because he is an innovative thinker who, as a Marine, can help reshape NATO into a more mobile expeditionary military alliance. The Deputy SACEUR is alternately a British or German officer.

ACE is based outside Mons, Belgium, at the Supreme Headquarters Allied Powers Europe (SHAPE). In case of war, ACE is responsible for military operations in the entire European area. A British or a German general alternately commands one of its two top regional subcommands, the Regional Command North, in Brunssum, Netherlands. The Regional Command South in Naples, Italy, is always entrusted to an American admiral. The French advocate turning this command over to a European officer. However, the United States, whose Sixth Fleet provides the most potent naval forces in the Mediterranean area, rejects this suggestion. The other major NATO command is the Allied Command Atlantic (ACLANT), commanded by an American admiral or general and headquartered in Norfolk, Virginia. At its 2002 Prague summit, NATO endorsed a new military command structure that is to be leaner, more efficient, more effective and more deployable. A strategic command for operations will remain in Belgium, while another strategic command will be based in the U.S. with a presence in Europe responsible for continuing transformation of military capabilities and interoperability of allied forces.

North Atlantic Council Meeting, NATO Headquarters ("A Free Spirit in Consultation")

ANIMUS IN CONSULENDO LIBER

Western Europe Today

The European Council and European Commission, Brussels
Courtesy: Central Audiovisual Library, European Commision

Only the U.S. engages in Strategic Arms Reductions Talks (START) or negotiations aimed at limiting nuclear forces in Europe. But Western European members are consulted about any American negotiating positions which might affect European interests. Europeans have developed bodies, such as the NATO Nuclear Planning Group (NPG) and the less formal Special Consultative Group, which serve as channels to inform the U.S. of its allies' views and to keep the latter informed of U.S. objectives. In 1973 most NATO members joined the U.S. in the unsuccessful Mutual Balanced Force Reduction (MBFR) talks, conducted in Vienna with members of the Warsaw Pact, a military alliance that combined forces of the Soviet Union, Poland, East Germany, Czechoslovakia, Hungary, Romania and Bulgaria before the pact was dissolved in 1991.

In 1989 the Conventional Forces in Europe (CFE) negotiations in Vienna replaced the moribund MBFR talks. This culminated in an agreement between NATO and the Warsaw Pact in 1990 to thin out their military equipment in the center of Europe. It did not apply to troops. Several years after the Warsaw Pact collapsed, the terms of the CFE Treaty began to be reexamined, at Russia's insistence, to take account of the fact that Moscow no longer has allies and has potentially serious internal instability.

In 1991 President George Bush announced unilateral nuclear cuts that went far beyond the START agreement reached in July. European allies and Soviet President Mikhail Gorbachev gave Bush's plan unanimous backing. The greatest impact was on Europe, where the only targets for NATO's tactical nuclear weapons were in areas that are no longer enemies, such as Poland and eastern Germany. Officially

endorsed by NATO, the cuts did not make Europe nuclear–free: NATO retains some atomic bombs on dual–capacity aircraft to provide a measure of nuclear deterrence against unknown threats. Also, Britain and France retain some of their nuclear systems. But European defense has become almost entirely non–nuclear.

The sweeping American disarmament proposals, following the disappearance of a clearly identifiable foe, prompted Europeans to try to develop a distinct European Security and Defence Identity (ESDI); this is the NATO term for ESDP and is, in essence, the same thing. A consensus exists that such an identity is necessary, while preserving NATO in one form or the other. No European country wants the total withdrawal of American troops, which had already been drawn down from 320,000 to 100,000 by century's end. Americans have called on Europeans to bear a greater responsibility for their own defense, but not in competition with NATO, which remains the major pillar for American leadership in Europe. One American diplomat said: "Sure, we want the Europeans to do more, but we're always going to be wary of anything that looks like it could push the U.S. out of Europe."

In order to facilitate greater European security independence, NATO in 1998 reduced the number of its command headquarters from 65 to 20, emphasized a multinational approach to the manning of these headquarters, and arranged them in a way that they can support both regular NATO tasks as well as Combined Joint Task Forces (CJTF), authorized in 1994. If certain members, such as the U.S., do not wish to participate in a certain military operation, a coalition of those that do can use NATO units and assets under the

leadership of the WEU as long as NATO is asked first to deal with the crisis. Non–NATO countries can also be included in such Combined Joint Task Forces.

International military groupings that are dedicated to the ESDI concept have proliferated in Europe since the end of the Cold War. Within NATO, a Dutch–German corps under alternate command has been formed; its troops use English. British, German, Dutch and Belgian troops constitute a multinational division with an airmobile brigade. It is part of the ACE Rapid Reaction force. The Dutch navy has merged its naval headquarters with those of Belgium. A corps has been created with headquarters in Szczecin, Poland, that comprises Polish, German and Danish troops and is commanded by a Polish officer. This unit was modeled on the French-German Eurocorps in Strasbourg, France, created in 1992. The Eurocorps now includes BENELUX and Spanish troops and uses English as its common language. In the summer of 2000 this Eurocorps took temporary charge of the NATO-led peacekeeping operation in Kosovo (KFOR). A U.S. combat division serves in a German-led corps, while a German division is part of a U.S.-led corps. Outside NATO, Italy, Austria and Slovenia have created a joint land-based force, and the Spanish, French, Portuguese and Italians have formed a rapid operational force called EUROFOR based in Florence. Many NATO troops serve alongside other European and non-European soldiers in the Stabilization Force (SFOR) to guard the peace in Bosnia Herzogovina, as well as in KFOR.

In 1991 NATO was transformed into a more political organization seeking to reach out to its former enemies. It created a North Atlantic Cooperation Council (NACC, renamed in 1997 the Euro–Atlantic Partnership Council—EAPC) comprising 44 countries at century's end to provide for regular consultations between NATO

EU Members

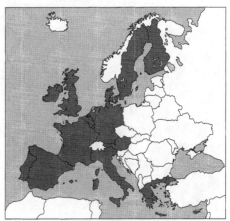

and the former Soviet republics and eastern European nations on subjects ranging from security issues, arms control, and the conversion of defense industries. In 1994 NATO initiated the Partnership for Peace (PFP), which links 27 countries, including Russia, in bilateral treaties with NATO. The purpose is to expand and intensify political and military cooperation and to strengthen stability and peace, primarily through training forces for peacekeeping operations. A special NATO–Ukraine Commission was established to deepen cooperation with that important country.

These nations are also linked in the 55–member Organization for Security and Cooperation in Europe (OSCE, known until 1994 as the CSCE), to which all European states, former Soviet republics, and the United States and Canada belong. It meets irregularly to consider how to defuse threats to peace through mediation, crisis management, and the dispatch of observers.

Many countries regard PFP as a crucial stepping–stone to full NATO membership. In principle, the alliance is prepared gradually to accept new members, on the condition that they have solid democratic credentials, including a firm civilian grip on the armed forces, and can make a genuine military contribution to the common defense. At their Madrid Conference in May 1997 NATO members opened their door and admitted Poland, Hungary and the Czech Republic in 1999. In 2002, seven more were invited to join despite the fact that some NATO planners fear the effects that increases in membership have on already complicated decision–making mechanisms, which require unanimity and consensus. The door remains open to a select group of European democracies.

Russia once opposed such enlargement, especially insofar as former Soviet republics, such as the Baltics, are concerned. To assuage Moscow's fears, the Atlantic allies signed with Moscow in 1997 a NATO–Russia Founding Act. This is not a legally binding treaty, but it states that NATO has no need, intentions, or plans to create additional capabilities or permanently station troops or nuclear weapons in the new member states. NATO also created a Permanent Joint Council (PJC) at its headquarters in which Russian officials could discuss, though not veto, NATO policies and decisions. In the wake of close Russian-U.S. cooperation in the war against terrorism after the September 11 terrorist attacks in New York and Washington, the PJC was upgraded and renamed in 2002 the Russia-NATO Council. This signaled greatly improved relations with the former superpower.

NATO's outdated doctrine of containing Soviet power through "forward defense" and "flexible response" was replaced by one that gives NATO a reason to exist in the changed European environment. Smaller, highly mobile, conventional, and multilateral forces are being created which can be deployed on short notice anywhere within NATO territory, and which can help manage unpredictable crises and instability in eastern Europe, the Balkans, the Mediterranean area and beyond. NATO chose at its 2002 Prague summit to create a multi-national rapid deployment force of 21,000 troops for use against enemies far outside of Europe.

No region in the world has been so successful in creating voluntary economic unions of sovereign states as Western Europe. In 1922 the Belgium and Luxembourg Economic Union (BLEU) was created, which made the two countries a single unit for importing and exporting purposes and established a unified currency. In 1944 the Netherlands joined to form BENELUX, which was later extended to include even non–customs matters.

In order to help the devastated countries of Europe recover economically, the United States offered Marshall Plan aid in 1947, but insisted that all countries receiving such aid sit down together and decide as a group how the money should be spent. Thus, the U.S. provided an important initial impetus for a unified Europe. In response, the Europeans created in 1948 the Organization for European Economic Cooperation (OEEC) for making the decisions and the European Payments Union (EPU) for administering U.S. funds.

In 1960, the U.S. and Canada joined the OEEC which was renamed the Organization for Economic Cooperation and Development (OECD), with headquarters in Paris. Later other Western industrialized nations, and Japan, Australia and New Zealand, joined OECD, which does economic analysis and forecasting for industrialized countries, including estimates of future growth, inflation, unemployment, and Gross Domestic Product (GDP, a measurement of an economy's total production of goods and services. A related and less used term, Gross National Product—GNP—adds to this value citizens' foreign earnings and subtracts foreigners' income within the country.) The OECD also attempts to coordinate members' economic and development aid, and it provided a forum for member states to hammer out an anti–bribery convention in international commerce. All Western European countries belong. Wanting closer contact with the world's industrial leaders, the Czech Republic, Hungary, Poland and Slovakia joined, and Russia decided to enter. With only 16% of the world's population, its 29 members produce two–thirds of the world's economic output.

The Council of Europe was created in Strasbourg in 1949. Its 40 members include all Western European countries and most newly independent countries in eastern Europe. Its assemblies of parliamentarians from the member states serve as a forum for discussing political, economic, social and cultural issues of interest to all European countries. Perhaps its main contribution has been its various conventions, especially its Convention for the Protection of Human Rights and Fundamental Freedoms (known as the European Convention on Human Rights—ECHR), adopted in 1950. Since 1991 it has been particularly active in trying to strengthen democracy and human rights in eastern Europe. It was because of possible human rights violations in Chechnya

European Parliament building, Strasbourg, France
Courtesy: Central Audiovisual Library, European Commision

Western Europe Today

that there was criticism of Russia's entry in 1996. The United States requested and was granted observer status in 1996 in order to be able to promote democracy more effectively in Eastern Europe.

The BENELUX countries, together with France, West Germany and Italy, made in 1951 the first significant move toward transferring a portion of their national sovereignty to a supranational organization by creating the European Coal and Steel Community (ECSC). Many persons could scarcely believe at the time that six countries that had been locked only six years earlier in a bloody struggle would be willing to transfer sovereignty over questions relating to these commodities, which are so crucial for heavy industry. Not only was it bold and far-sighted to share these important goods rather than to fight wars over them, but the ECSC gave these nations the practice in economic cooperation needed to convince the six that a move to create a unified Europe could succeed.

The same six nations signed the Treaties of Rome in 1957 which created both the European Economic Community (EEC, frequently called the "Common Market") and EURATOM, which seeks to coordinate the six countries' atomic research and policy. Both came into existence the following year and merged with the ECSC under the same overall organization. This union provided for the elimination of tariffs and customs among themselves, common tariff and customs barriers toward non–members, the free movement

Italian election poster for the European Parliament: "Your vote for your Europe"

10 giugno.
Elezioni per il Parlamento Europeo.
Il tuo voto per la tua Europa.

of labor and capital within the union and equal agricultural price levels through the establishment of the Common Agricultural Program (CAP). To avoid giving the impression that the three communities were only *economic* in nature and to express the fact that they are managed by common institutions, they were referred to in the singular as the European Community (EC).

The 15 member states (with about 375 million citizens in 2000, one–third more than the U.S.) which now include the BENELUX countries, France, Germany, Italy, Great Britain, the Republic of Ireland, Denmark, Greece, Spain, Portugal, and since 1995 Austria, Finland, and Sweden, have agreed to transfer a portion of their national sovereignty to the union. The irresistible logic of European unity has affected countries all over the continent.

Most European countries formally applied for EU membership. Norway was offered membership in 1972 and 1994, but its voters rejected it both times. In December 2002, EU members invited 10 more countries to join: Estonia, Latvia, Lithuania, Poland, Hungary, the Czech Republic, Slovakia, Slovenia, Malta and Cyprus (despite its continued division). Because of its questionable human rights record, constitution grant of political power to the military, continued Greek opposition, and fear by some Western European countries that a flood of Turkish immigrants would arrive at their doorstep, Turkey was again denied an invitation. However, Romania, Bulgaria and Turkey were promised to be told in 2004 when such an invitation might be forthcoming.

The issue of immigrants and refugees is a very sensitive one. Some Western Europeans fear that they bring in crime and terrorism and overburden their generous welfare states at a difficult time when their economies are suffering under the challenges of the global economy. Controlling the movement of outsiders who have entered Western Europe has been made more difficult by the Schengen agreements of 1985 and 1990 that aim to eliminate Europe's internal border controls. The idea is that one need only go through border formalities when entering one of the fifteen participating countries; then one can pass freely into the other 14, submitting only to occasional spot checks. All EU members except the UK and Ireland have joined, and since the Nordic countries long since abolished internal border controls, Norway and Iceland are automatically included. There are many problems to work out, and not all of the 15 participate entirely in the agreements.

On November 1, 1993, the Maastricht treaty came into force, bringing with it terminological confusion. It created a Eu-

ropean Union (EU), which added common foreign and security policy and cooperation in justice and police matters to the EC. But unlike the EC, the EU has neither a single decision–making process or a legal persona; it cannot conclude international agreements. Although the EC and EU are technically not exactly the same entities, most scholars and journalists now employ the term EU instead of EC. The term EU will be used throughout this book.

It is this political element which had prevented some other European states such as Switzerland from joining the EU, but the EU has successfully dealt with this problem by granting associate membership (which generally excludes agricultural aspects only) to most non–full–member states in Western Europe. Regular contacts are also maintained with 70 African, Caribbean and Pacific (ACP) countries linked to the EU through the Lomé Convention of 1975.

Most of the success the EU can claim has been in the economic field. The record is most impressive. With only 6% of the world's population, the EU accounts for a fourth of the world's economic output, a third of the world's monetary reserves and 36% of the development aid. The EU is the United States' second largest regional export market after Asia, but the U.S. enjoys balanced trade with Europe, which is not the case with Asia. No single country in the world rivals Canada as America's major trading partner, and Mexico is its second largest. The EU countries' investment in the U.S. exceeds that of the U.S. in the 15 EU nations.

Having cornered a fourth of global trade, it is the world's largest trading power. Politically, Western Europe is and will probably remain a region of largely sovereign states, which make their own decisions about the vital matters that affect them.

The EU has a well–developed institutional apparatus. It has a dual executive: the European Council is the major decision–making body and is composed of the heads of state or government; it is called the Council of Ministers when member state ministers with responsibilities for finance, agriculture, etc., depending upon the specific matter which is pending, meet.

The second part of the executive which directs the day–to–day business of the EU is the European Commission which meets in Brussels and which is composed of 20 members, two each from France, Germany, Italy, Spain and Great Britain and one from each of the smaller member states. Each member is chosen by the government of his country for five–year renewable terms. After selection, each commissioner is expected to make decisions based not upon the interests of his home country, but instead on the interests

Old currencies go ...

of the EU as a whole. The commissioners decide issues by a simple majority vote; none has the power of veto. The chairmanship of the Commission rotates on a yearly basis among the member states. A 17,000–member staff, working mainly in Luxembourg, Strasbourg, and the large EU headquarters buildings in Brussels carry out the decision of the Council of Ministers and the European Commission. The highest EU official is the European Commission President, selected by member countries for a ten–year term. The current president is Romano Prodi, former Italian prime minister, who replaced Jacques Santer of Luxembourg 1999.

A 626–seat (rising to 732 in 2004) European Parliament has 81 members from each of the most populous countries (except unified Germany, whose number was raised to 98), 60 from Spain, 25 from the Netherlands, 24 each from Belgium, Greece and Portugal, 16 from Denmark, 15 from Ireland, and six from Luxembourg. The rest go to the organization's three new members—Austria, Finland, and Sweden. It meets seven to eight times a year for one–week sessions. Formerly, the Parliament met in both Strasbourg and Luxem-

bourg. However, in 1981 the Parliament voted to hold all its sessions in Strasbourg. Since 1979 its members have been elected directly in their home countries according to each country's own preferred method of election. Its members do not sit in national delegations, but in party groupings, such as the Communists and Allies, Socialist European People's Party (Christian Democratic), European Progressive Democratic and Liberal and Democratic Groups. There are a few unaffiliated members.

The European Parliament is officially entitled to oversee the work of the European Commission and to approve or reject the EU's budget. Since the SEA was introduced in 1987, the Parliament's power and influence have grown. Some legislation, most importantly that covering measures to bring into effect a unified European market, can be altered or amended by the Parliament. It can now veto the accession of new member states to the EU, as well as new trade agreements with non–EU countries. Finally, it oversees the Commission, a power that was dramatically demonstrated in 1999.

For years it had been asking questions about waste and mismanagement, but the

Commission responded with arrogance and indifference. In January 1999 the Parliament threatened a vote of censure; a two–thirds majority could have removed all the Commissioners. This threat was averted when a panel of five independent experts was appointed to investigate financial impropriety. In March the panel published a devastating report accusing the well–paid Commissioners ($200,000 salary and expenses in 1999) of tolerating widespread fraud, corruption, nepotism, favoritism and mismanagement. All twenty felt compelled to resign. The consequence of this scandal is not only more democratic accountability, but a dramatic alteration of the political balance of power in favor of the elected European Parliament.

Finally, there is a European Court of Justice with its seat in Luxembourg and composed of fifteen justices, each chosen by member states for six–year terms. The Court judges violations of three major documents, the ECSC, EU and Euratom Treaties, as well as all subsequent EU treaties that are collectively called the Treaty of the European Union (TEU). The most recent is the Nice Treaty of 2000, ratified by all 15 in

Western Europe Today

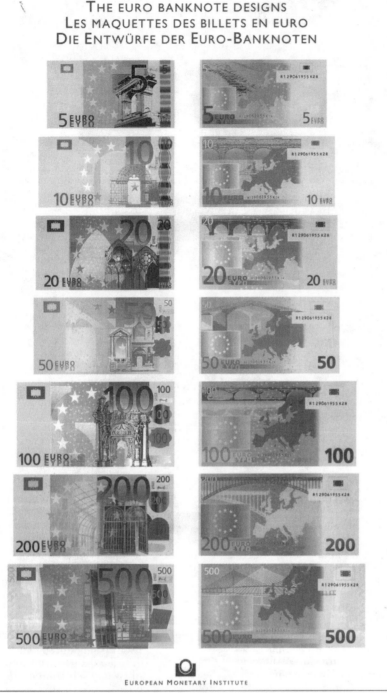

THE EURO BANKNOTE DESIGNS
LES MAQUETTES DES BILLETS EN EURO
DIE ENTWÜRFE DER EURO-BANKNOTEN

EUROPEAN MONETARY INSTITUTE

© EUROPEAN MONETARY INSTITUTE 1997
All rights reserved

... and a new one arrives   Courtesy: Central Audiovisual Library, European Commision

2003. It redistributes national votes, restricts vetoes, revamps certain institutions, limits the number of commissioners and grants the European Parliament more power and seats. The court will also be the final arbiter of a new constitution being drafted in a constitutional convention, chaired by former French President Giscard d'Estaing and attended by 66 representatives from member states and 39 from applicant states. It is intended to be ratified and adopted by the time the 10 new members join in May 2004. Proponents hope that the new constitution will democratize the EU, make its internal structures more efficient, and put teeth in the CFSP.

The SEA amends the European treaties by spelling out certain EU objectives: completion of the European internal market, creation of a great area without frontiers, technological development, progress toward economic and monetary union, improvement of the environment and working conditions, creation of more effective and democratic institutions, and institutionalization of cooperation among member states in the field of foreign policy. The target year 1992 was chosen for its symbolic importance: 500 years after the discovery of the New World.

From 1979 the European Monetary System (EMS) attempted, not always successfully, to coordinate the monetary affairs of certain Western European countries by attempting to link their currencies. At their 1991 Maastricht summit, EU leaders agreed to create a single European currency (called the "Euro") and a European Central Bank (located in Frankfurt, with Dutch banker Wim Duisenberg as its first president). The criteria for joining this Economic and Monetary Union (EMU)—a budget deficit of not more than 3% of GDP and a total national debt not in excess of 60% of GDP—placed enormous political strains on member governments. The inevitable austerity policies were resented by many of their voters. Many Europeans thought that the price to be paid for the euro was not worth it.

In 1998 the governments of 11 members (known unofficially as "euroland") decided to adopt the euro as of January 1, 1999, with Britain, Sweden, Denmark, and Greece waiting until later to join. Danish voters rejected the euro again in a September 2000 referendum, but Greece enthusiastically entered on January 1, 2001. The quoting of stock and bond prices in euros intensified efforts to combine the London and Frankfurt exchanges, until London pulled out in 2000. Stock exchanges in Paris, Amsterdam, Madrid and Milan showed interest in an eventual merger.

The participating countries phased in the euro until it became the exclusive currency of members between January and March 2002. In order not to hurt national feelings, the new euro bills bear generic European designs: Gothic arches, bridges, windows, and a map of Europe. No scene from a particular country is recognizable. The only national concession for paper money was made to Greece, which does not use Roman letters. The word for the currency appears both as "EURO" and "EYPO." The coins are uniform on one side, but each participating country made its own design for the reverse side. Thus 12 different coins circulate but are legal tender throughout the eurozone.

A few countries that are not full members of the EU belong to the European Free Trade Association (EFTA), which was created in 1959 and whose headquarters are located in Geneva. Whereas the EU has a huge bureaucracy and budget, EFTA is a shoe–string operation, with 62 full–time staff, spending only $7 million in 1987. English is the working language, even though no member nation uses it as its mother tongue. EFTA has no political objectives, and its members have not relinquished a shred of sovereignty.

EFTA eliminated tariffs and customs on all industrial products bought or sold from all member nations, but it does not include agricultural or fishing products. All EFTA members have separate free–trade agreements with the EU. EFTA's economic importance declined after Great Britain, Ireland and Denmark left to join the EU in 1972 and Finland, Sweden and Austria in 1995. To restore EFTA's significance, its members—Switzerland, Liechtenstein, Norway, and Iceland—signed a trade agreement with Estonia, Latvia and Lithuania, effective 1996, calling for the free exchange of industrial goods and processed food and fish products. They also concluded cooperation agreements with Egypt, Morocco and Tunisia.

In 1991 the EU and EFTA countries agreed to form a European Economic Area (EEA), which creates a market of 380 million customers extending from the Mediterranean to the Arctic and accounting for over 40% of world trade. Within the EEA, EFTA members enjoy the EU's "four freedoms": of goods, services, capital, and people, but EEA does not include agriculture, fish, energy, coal and steel. EFTA members live under many

EU rules although they have no voice in their writing; this lack of representation gives them added incentive to join the EU as full members. In 1991 the European Court of Justice rejected certain juridical aspects of the accord, and Swiss voters decided in 1992 not to join this single market.

All Scandinavian countries are in the Nordic Council, which meets regularly to discuss non–military problems that they have in common. Eleven nations belong to the European Space Agency (ESA) which, with American assistance, launched the first European Spacelab into orbit at the end of 1983. On board this Spacelab was the first European astronaut to travel into space with Americans—Dr. Ulf Merbold, a German physicist. In 1988 ESA also joined with the U.S. and Japan to begin construction of the Space Station Freedom.

Western European countries are also active in such international economic treaties or organizations as the General Agreement on Trade and Tariffs (GATT), the World Trade Organization (WTO), which since 1995 attempts to resolve disputes relating to the GATT Treaty, the International Monetary Fund (IMF), which provides funds for countries with balance–of–payments problems, the International Bank for Reconstruction and Development (World Bank), and the European Bank for Reconstruction and Development (EBRD). Headquartered in London, the EBRD was created after the collapse of communism to help Central and Eastern European countries make successful transitions to free–market economies.

The International Energy Agency (IEA) exists to insure that all industrialized nations have minimally sufficient energy supplies in times of crisis. No European country belongs to the Organization of Petroleum Exporting Countries (OPEC), whose headquarters is in Vienna. Nevertheless, those Western European countries which export large quantities of oil, such as Great Britain and Norway (from the North Sea), note what is charged by the OPEC countries before setting their own prices. Interpol, headquartered in Paris, provides some coordination in fighting international crime. Europol, based in The Hague, shares intelligence among national police forces and cooperates in a limited way with the U.S. Eurojust coordinates the EU countries' prosecuting authorities. Following the September 11 attacks in the U.S., EU governments rapidly accepted a single European arrest warrant to facilitate the struggle against terrorism.

This high degree of cooperation and organization explains in great measure the tremendous growth of the economy of Western Europe. In a sense it may be

likened to the United States, which, after discarding the Articles of Confederation and creating the present Constitution two centuries ago, abolished tariffs on goods shipped between the states and laid the groundwork for ever–closer cooperation among formerly sovereign entities. The EU is in the process of drafting its own constitution. Through the many organizations they have formed and joined, Western European nations are better equipped and prepared to face the complicate problems of today.

For the United States, the world changed dramatically on September 11, 2001, when fanatical Islamic al-Qaeda terrorists, trained and financed by Osama Bin Laden and sheltered in Taliban-ruled Afghanistan, hijacked four American commercial airliners and crashed three of them into the twin towers of the World Trade Center in New York and the Pentagon in Washington, killing more than three thousand persons from 81 different countries. More British and French citizens perished that day than in any previous terrorist attack. Americans' feeling of invulnerability from outside threats went up with the noxious smoke from the buildings' rubble. Any temptations to pursue a unilateralist—not to mention an isolationist, North America-focused policy—disappeared, at least temporarily. A shaken America looked for help from its friends, and the most steadfast of them were Europeans and Canadians. They responded with emotion and resolve. Within 36 hours of the attack, NATO offered to invoke the mutual defense clause, Article 5, for the first time in its half-century history.

EC President Romano Prodi called an emergency session the next morning. After a moment of silence for the victims of the attacks, he decided to send "the strongest possible signal of European solidarity with the American people" and to "call for a common European approach to all aspects of this tragedy." In moving language he announced, "this barbaric attack was directed against the free world and our common values. It is a watershed event, and life will never be quite the same again…. In the darkest hours of European history, the Americans stood by us. We stand by them now." In a poll taken a week after the attack, Europeans showed a strong willingness to support a US military assault: 80% in Denmark, 79% in Britain, 73% in France, 58% in Norway and Spain, and half in Germany. The EU called for a three-minute silence on September 14, and from Finland to Italy and Berlin to Paris, businesses and stock exchanges, buses and shoppers stopped to honor the dead and reflect upon their world that had changed so suddenly.

The United Kingdom of Great Britain and Northern Ireland

with Mark H. Mullin

Political power's most coveted address: 10 Downing Street, residence of the Prime Minister

Area: 89,038 sq. mi. (230,609 sq. km., slightly smaller than Oregon).

Population: 59.4 million (estimated).

Capital City: London (Pop. 7 million, estimated, including the city's sprawling suburbs).

Climate: Mild and temperate, rarely above 86° F (30° C) or below 14° F (−10° C).

Neighboring Countries: Ireland (a short distance across the Irish Sea to the west); France, Belgium and the Netherlands (a short distance across the English Channel or North Sea to the east).

Official Language: English.

Other Principal Tongues: About a fourth of the population of Wales speaks Welsh, and about 60,000 Scottish speak a form of Gaelic. Both are Celtic dialects.

Ethnic Background: Angle, Saxon, Celtic and Nordic.

Principal Religion: In England—Church of England (Anglican) 49%, Roman Catholic 7%. In Scotland—Church of Scotland (Presbyterian) 19%. In Wales—Church in Wales. Methodist, Jewish and other.

Main Exports: Finished and semi-finished manufactured products, oil and gas, foodstuffs, chemicals, motor vehicles.

Main Imports: Manufactured goods, foodstuffs, fuels.

Main Customers: EU 57.2%, U.S. 15.7%, Germany 12.1%, France 9.9%, Netherlands 8%, Ireland 6.5%.

Currency: Pound sterling.

National Day: Celebration of the birthday of the Queen is in June, although she was actually born on April 21.

Head of State: Her Majesty Queen Elizabeth II, b. 1926. Married Lieut. Philip Mountbatten (Prince of Greece and Denmark) on November 20, 1947; he had been created Duke of Edinburgh on the preceding day and (in 1957) Prince of Great Britain. Queen Elizabeth II succeeded to the throne on the death of her father, George VI on February 6, 1952; her coronation took place on June 2, 1953.

Heir Apparent: His Royal Highness Prince Charles (b. Nov. 14, 1948), Prince of Wales. His son, Prince William of Wales (b. June 21, 1982) is second in succession to the throne.

Head of Government: Tony Blair, Prime Minister (since May 1997).

National Flag: The Union Jack—a dark blue charged with the white cross of St. Andrew (for Scotland), the red cross of St. Patrick (for Ireland), surmounted by the red cross of St. George (for England) bordered in white.

No country in the world has closer ties with the United States in language, history, shared assumptions and emotion than does the United Kingdom. In the capital of each country there stands a prominent statue of one of the greatest leaders of the other. Abraham Lincoln gazes at the Houses of Parliament in London, and in a prominent section of Washington, Winston Churchill (himself half American) stands giving his famous "V" for victory salute. Although the British influence on the United States is not surprising, what is remarkable is the influence that the United Kingdom has had on the rest of the world. It is striking that a moderately–sized island off the coast of Europe should achieve first a piv-

The United Kingdom

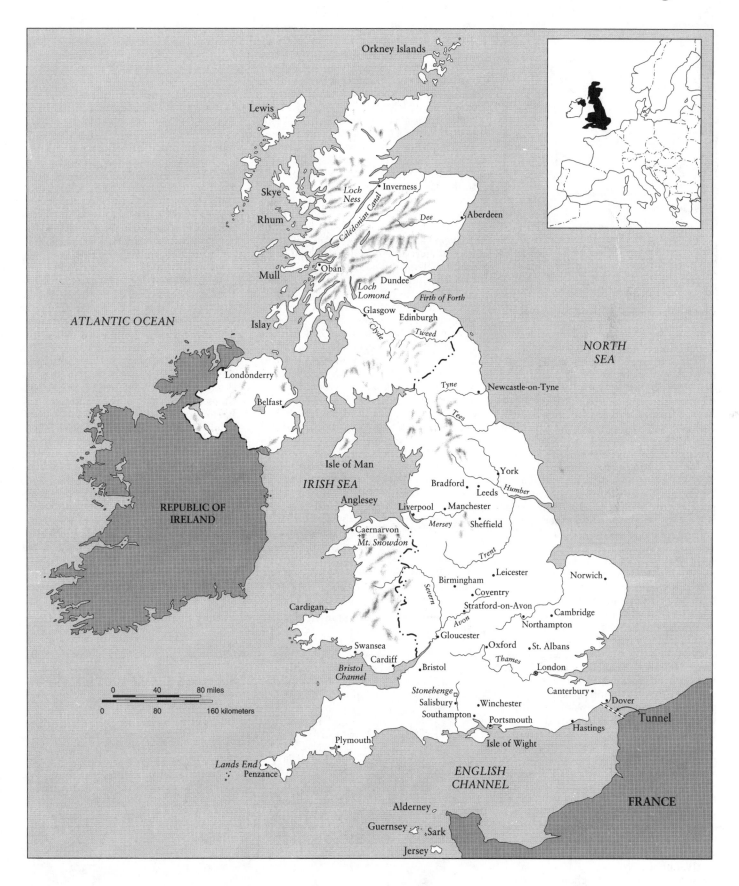

The United Kingdom

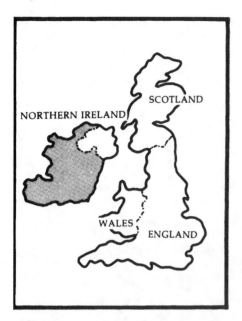

otal role in European affairs and then domination of much of the entire globe.

Britain is blessed with a moderate climate, despite its northerly location, due to the warmth of the Gulf Stream, which after originating in the Caribbean Sea crosses the Atlantic. Its waters provide a warmer, albeit moister, climate than would otherwise be the case. Rain is frequent, but not over–abundant. The sun shines in most parts for one out of four to eight daylight hours during the winter. The mountains of the west modify this pattern, condensing the clouds into rainfall, which is more abundant there.

The climate is not suited to plant life needing heat, but it is ideal for water–seeking crops, particularly grasses. With a population density of about 640 persons per square mile, much of Britain is urbanized. In spite of the fertile soil, it is an importer of foodstuffs. The industrial revolution, for which Britain is renowned, resulted in a particularly dense type of city building construction. Wales is a mixture of industry, agriculture and herding. Virtually all sheep and cattle are consumed within the country; the sheep support production of fine woolens, few of which are exported. Scotland, about one quarter the size of England and Wales, consists of a small area of lowlands and the larger highlands, which actually reach a maximum height of only 4,400 feet. The cities of Glasgow on the Clyde River and Edinburgh on the Firth (Bay) of Forth are seats of heavy industry and highly urbanized. The mountains are widely interspersed with valleys where intensive sheep–raising supports the production of world–famous Scotch tweeds and plaids, treasured by tailors throughout the world.

While Roman remains can be found in various parts of England today, the most important architectural work is virtually invisible. London, located at the spot closest to the sea where the Thames could most easily be bridged, was walled and became a Roman center, even though the Celtic name was retained. It became the hub from which spokes of roads headed out to other parts of the island. This pattern still shapes the roads and rails of Britain. The city today extends far beyond the boundaries of the original wall.

Natural resources that were important in the early Industrial Revolution in the late 18th and 19th centuries have been a second blessing. Its island location has protected it from invasion for more than 900 years and encouraged it to use the sea for commercial and political gain. But its greatest blessing has been a relatively stable history that developed quite early in a tradition of freedom and representative government. Americans are sometimes confused by the various names applied to Britain. Its official name is The United Kingdom of Great Britain and Northern Ireland. Four areas combine to make up the country: England, Wales, Scotland and Northern Ireland. The word "Britain" encompasses the first three. The last is composed of the six northern Irish counties. Because England is the site of the capital and over the centuries came to control the other areas, the term "England" or "the English" is sometimes (but inaccurately) used to describe the whole country. Residents of Wales, Scotland and Northern Ireland prefer to use the term "Great Britain" or "British."

The growth toward world leadership and representative democracy in Britain has not been smooth or steady, but the history of Britain has been a stage on which royal pageantry has combined with remarkable commercial, industrial and political success of more humble citizens.

HISTORY

The Early Period

It must have been quite a shock for the Roman legionnaires who left the brilliant sunshine of Italy, marched across Gaul, and then made the short but perilous crossing of the English Channel. They arrived in a land of soft greens, frequent rains and fearsome warriors who painted themselves blue and drove chariots armed with sharp blades at the axles. These Celts had come to the island during the Iron Age, spoke a dialect known as Brythonic, and thus their land was known as Britain.

Julius Caesar led two expeditions to Britain in 55 and 54 B.C., but it was not until 43 A.D. that the Roman Emperor Claudius began to establish settlements. The campaign to stamp out Celtic Druid beliefs, with all of their mysticism, that have faded into the mists of time, produced the first of the great British queens, Boadicea, who managed to kill several thousand Romanizing Britons before finally being captured and committing suicide. While the popular image has always seen the British as chauvinists in their men's clubs, the fact that in the 1980s both the throne and the office of prime minister were occupied by women is less surprising when one remembers that the first resistance leader and the monarchs with two of the greatest reigns in English history, Elizabeth I (1558–1603) and Victoria (1837–1901) were women, however different they were. The first was an astute monarch, who is reported to have utilized amorous affairs to advance the affairs of state. The latter was

The prehistoric ruins of Stonehenge on the Salisbury Plain which scholars date from 1800 to 1400 B.C.

conservative, conventional, prudish and astute, devoted only to her husband Albert. Indeed, rightfully or wrongfully, an entire age is known by the name of each in the English–speaking world.

Celtic tribalism continued in the mountains of Wales and Scotland. Hadrian's Wall ran for miles to seal off the northern borders of the Roman area since the people in the mountains there were beyond conquest. No attempt was made to invade Ireland.

The Early Christian Era

Roman soldiers and merchants brought Christianity with them to the island. Their persecution by Emperor Diocletian produced the first Christian martyr of the island, St. Alban. But after Emperor Constantine legalized Christianity in the empire, the Church began to flourish in Britain.

The Romans occupied England for about 400 years, but as the empire collapsed inward, barbarian pressure on England increased. Angles, Saxons and Jutes, Teutonic tribes from what is now northern Germany and Denmark, filled the vacuum left by the Romans. Now it was the Celts leading their tribal lives in Wales, Scotland, Ireland and Cornwall, who kept alive the light of Western civilization and Christian culture.

King Arthur may be more legendary than historical, but his story represents the urge to restore Christian order during the dark period that lasted for two centuries. In 597 the monk Augustine (named for the more famous St. Augustine of Hippo) was sent from Rome to convert the English. He established Canterbury as his see and became its first archbishop. As Roman Christianity spread, it came into contact and then into conflict with Celtic Christianity. The synod of Whitby, meeting in 664, decided that Roman Christianity would prevail. This proved to be a most significant decision, for England was thus brought once more under the influence of Rome; its culture, its politics and religion would be shaped by events on the Continent. Nearly 900 years later, when England turned away from Roman Christianity, the effects would be even more important. During the 8th century, English culture flourished. The first English historian, Venerable (later Saint) Bede, wrote his *Ecclesiastical History of the English People*; the great Anglo–Saxon epic Beowulf was written; and the Saxon monk Alcuin of York was a leading intellectual of Charlemagne's court.

Viking Invasion and Expulsion

By the 9th century, Vikings (Norsemen, Northmen, Normans) from Norway and

A castle in Wales

Denmark attacked and then conquered much of the British isle. In response, the only English king to be known as "the Great," Alfred of Wessex, whose capital was at Winchester, organized an army, developed a navy, founded schools and stopped the growth of Norse–Danish power. It is ironic that the Norsemen then invaded France, where their region became known as Normandy. Almost two centuries later, one of their leaders would head the last successful conquest of England. Although Alfred died in 899, his son, Edward the Elder, conquered the remaining Danish–controlled areas and thus became the first King of a united England.

For the next 100 years, Anglo–Saxons and Norsemen merged during a golden age of relative peace. As the English historian Trevelyan said, "Had it not been for the Scandinavian blood infused into our race by the catastrophes of the ninth century, less would have been heard in days to come of British maritime and commercial enterprise." Again ironically, at about the same time, the Scandinavians were invited to Russia to establish order among the belligerent, disorganized Slav warlords.

By the start of the 11th century, a weak king, Ethelred the Unready, allowed his kingdom to fall into confusion. The Danish king, Canute, invaded the island in 1016 and England became part of

an empire that included Denmark and Norway. Canute was followed by his two sons, each of whom died shortly after ascending the throne. Ethelred's son, Edward the Confessor, who was half Norman and had lived in Normandy during the reign of Canute and his sons, was placed on the throne. He made two decisions with far–reaching consequences. He founded Westminster Abbey outside of London, starting the separation of the government from the city. Because he was childless, he promised his cousin, William, Duke of Normandy, that the throne would one day be his.

The Final Conquest and the First Plantagenets

The year 1066 is to the English school children what 1492 is to Americans. In that year, Edward the Confessor died. The Witan (national council) elected his brother–in–law, Harold, as his successor. A Norwegian invasion in Yorkshire called Harold to the north. Seizing the opportunity, William landed a Norman force in the south of England. Harold raced south to meet his death—at the Battle of Hastings he was killed by a sword blow, and William established himself and his Norman lords as rulers of England.

William chose to rule by a rigorous system of feudalism. He established

The United Kingdom

Normans loyal to himself as lords of all the great manors. But they were tenants on the land; ownership was the King's right. The most important lords made up the Great Council, the forerunner of parliament. William also placed Normans in the most important positions in the church hierarchy and ruled that clergy would be tried in ecclesiastical, rather than secular courts.

All over England, Norman buildings characterized by massive rectangular towers, showed that the conquerors had come to stay. The most notable were the Tower of London and Westminster Hall. Scores of parish churches, castles and monasteries dotted the landscape. William dispatched Norman legal scholars to go among the people and inquire by what laws (including customs which were virtually laws) they lived. These were organized into the Common Law—the law of the people, which were to be used in secular courts. This greatly pacified the conquered people, since they corresponded with what had prevailed before the Norman conquest. Writs were established which were an intriguing combination of Latin, Anglo–Saxon and French— *Assumpsit, Trespass Quare Clausum Fregit, Indebitatus*, etc.

William's great–grandson, Henry II (the first of the Plantagenets), came to the throne in 1154. He asserted the power of the king at the expense of the barons by tearing down unlicensed castles, creating a militia instead of depending upon the nobility for armed troops, and created traveling judges. The decisions of these judges were based on the Common Law, which operated by establishing written precedents rather than a codified law. Henry II also invaded Ireland, and, with the permission of the Pope, established himself as King of England's western neighbor. No one could possibly foresee what enormous consequences this would have for England in the years to come—consequences that affect Britain to this day.

Henry might have foreseen the consequences for which he is most remembered. He got into a dispute with his Archbishop, Thomas à Becket, over the issue of whether the clergy should be tried in Church courts or civil courts. Whether Henry ordered that Becket be killed, or merely hinted that it would please him, will never be known. But Becket's murder turned him into a martyr and Canterbury into a shrine. Henry's two sons, Richard and John, were low points in the history of the English monarchy. Richard (who came to be known as the Lion–Hearted) spent most of his reign out of the country as a crusader, trying to wrest Jerusalem and Israel from the Arabs. His absence did

England little good, but it did provide that great scene in stories and movies where, when he did return to England, he reveals himself to Robin Hood.

John was not only ineffective but also very unpopular. He lost English possessions on the Continent, including Normandy, and ran up such a debt that the barons were able to force him to sign the *Magna Carta* in 1215. This document was not the forward–looking cornerstone of freedom that it is sometimes portrayed to be, but rather it guaranteed the rights that the nobility and the Church expected. At the same time, it established the principle that there are limits on the powers of the monarch, and thus it was a first step toward the largely unwritten constitutional monarchy of today.

The 13th century was a time of intellectual growth. Groups of scholars gathered at Oxford, and a splinter group later moved to Cambridge. Roger Bacon was a leading teacher stressing scientific experimentation. The King's Council was expanded to include representatives of shires and boroughs; thus the way was prepared for a representative House of Commons. At the end of the century, Edward I epitomized the medieval monarch. Physically imposing, he aided the growing spirit of nationalism by checking the power of the barons and the Church, and by increasing English power in Wales and Ireland. However, unsuccessful attempts to invade Scotland led Edward into financial difficulties, and in 1297 he was forced to sign a confirmation of the Magna Charta. He agreed that the King could not impose taxes without the consent of the newborn parliament.

Edward's grandson, Edward III, attempted to reassert English power on the continent. In 1337 the Hundred Years War began. At first, success came to the English and the war strengthened the nation. However, in 1348 the Black Death (Bubonic Plague) swept the country and nearly half the population died. The country sank into economic depression, and by the time the king died in 1377, all the lands he had conquered in France had been lost except for a small area around Calais.

The period produced the first great work of literature in primitive English, Chaucer's *Canterbury Tales*. For centuries, Latin had been spoken by the Church and French by the nobility, but now the nation was uniting with the use of the English language.

The War of the Roses and the House of Tudor

Among Edward's sons were John of Gaunt, Duke of Lancaster, and Edmund, Duke of York. During the first half of the 15th century, the Lancaster branch held the throne, but in 1455 the Wars of the

Roses, symbolized by the red rose of Lancaster and the white rose of York, subjected the country to a brutal civil war. Shakespeare puts the words "Uneasy lies the head that wears a crown" in the mouth of Henry IV, the first of the Lancastrian kings. The instability of a monarch's life continued throughout the 15th century. Perhaps the best example was Richard III of the House of York, who gained the crown by allegedly having two of his nephews, young princes, murdered in the Tower of London, and lost his own life in a battle against Henry Tudor of the House of Lancaster. Despite the battles for the throne, the 15th century was one of growing prosperity for England, especially in wool and foreign trade. To this day, the Lord Chancellor's seat in the House of Lords is a woolsack.

With the arrival of the Tudors, the medieval world drew to a close. During the first Tudor reign (Henry VII), Columbus sailed for the New World. The wealth that Spain acquired there provided constant problems for the Tudors, and it was not until their successors, the Stuarts, that English colonies were firmly established. Soon the winds of the Reformation would bring even greater changes to England. Henry arranged for his eldest son, Arthur, to marry Catherine of Aragon, daughter of the king of Spain. This was a particularly important match for diplomatic reasons, because Spain controlled the Netherlands through which much of English trade entered the continent.

Arthur died in 1502 before his father. Despite both scriptural and canon law injunctions against marrying one's brother's widow, the Pope granted a dispensation allowing Arthur's brother, Henry, to marry the young widow. Henry's sister, Margaret, married the King of Scotland, thus providing England with marital allies on several sides. When Henry VIII assumed the throne after his father's death, he realized the importance of a male heir. But his union with Catherine only produced a daughter, Mary. It is important to note that Henry was initially loyal to Roman Catholicism, and because of a work he authored attacking the doctrines of Martin Luther, the Pope granted him the title "Defender of the Faith." It is ironic that his non–Roman Catholic descendants still carry that title.

Because Henry realized that Catherine would not produce a son, and because he was lusting after the attractive, dark–haired Anne Boleyn, he asked the Pope to grant him an annulment of his marriage to Catherine, claiming that it was illegal in the first place. Unfortunately for Henry, Catherine's uncle, Charles V, of the Holy Roman Empire had his troops in Rome at the time. When the

King Henry VIII

Anne Boleyn

Pope refused to grant Henry's request, in an unprecedented move, Henry had himself declared Head of the Church in England. His marriage to Anne Boleyn, however, produced only a daughter, Elizabeth, and Henry then proceeded through four more wives, making six in all, only one of whom produced a son, Edward. Every student learns to keep track of Henry's wives by the saying "Divorced, beheaded, died, divorced, beheaded, survived."

Edward VI followed his father to the throne in 1547 at eleven years of age. His guardians moved the country rapidly in the direction of Protestantism. But the sickness–prone boy died six years later (he was possibly murdered), and the first of Henry's daughters, Mary Tudor, assumed the throne. Had Mary wanted to move England back to the religious position of her father, she probably would have lasted. But she felt a calling to return the nation to full Roman Catholicism and further alienated her subjects by taking Philip of Spain as her husband.

Although the number of resisting Protestants who were burned at the stake was actually quite small, there were enough prominent bishops ignited to earn the Queen the historical title of "Bloody Mary." The words of one of these bishops—"Be of good cheer, Master Ridley, we shall today light such a candle as will by God's grace never be extinguished in England" proved to be prophetic. At

Mary's death after only five years on the throne, her half–sister, Elizabeth I became queen, and with her, one of the great ages in English history began.

The Elizabethan Period

Since the Catholic Church considered Elizabeth illegitimate, she moved the country back toward Protestantism. It was a moderate protestant position, with the old forms of worship retained in English and no vigorous attempt to be overly scrupulous in matters of doctrine. As Elizabeth put it, "We shall make no window into any man's soul." At this time, Elizabeth's cousin, Mary Stuart, abdicated the throne of Scotland in favor of her son, James, and fled to England. For years, Roman Catholic attempts to oust Elizabeth flurried around Mary, who was Catholic. Despite "that divinity that doth hedge a king," (or queen), Elizabeth finally yielded to the advice of her court and had Mary beheaded in 1587.

That same year, Sir Francis Drake, having already stolen Spanish gold from the New World, raided the port of Cadiz. In reprisal, the next year Spain sent a Great Armada to invade and conquer England. But a "Protestant wind" and English naval tactics carried the day; less than half of the Armada managed to limp back to Spain. England had established itself as a ruler of the seas, a position it would continue to enjoy for almost 400 years.

The Elizabethan Age was a flowering of English culture and the brightest blooms were uses of the language that still affect our thought and speech. Although William Shakespeare was the most magnificent of the blossoms, others, such as Spenser, Drayton, Donne and Marlowe bloomed in the sunshine.

Thomas Cranmer produced a Book of Common Prayer in 1549 whose magnificent collects shaped the way the English–speaking world addressed God and whose words start the most important ceremony in most people's lives: "Dearly beloved, we are gathered here together in the sight of God and in the face of this company to join together this man and this woman in holy matrimony: which is an honorable estate instituted of God, signifying unto us the mystical union that is betwixt Christ and His church." The musical liturgy of the book was done with assistance from Lutherans, who had retained Catholic plain song chant traditions in German; they were adapted to English. Further, harmonized Anglican chant was first produced. All of this is preserved with little change in many churches to this day.

In the last part of Elizabeth's reign, William Shakespeare began to write his plays. Their plots shape our view of history, or romance, and of humor, and his phrases fill our speaking and our reading, even when we do not know the source of the words. Finally, shortly after

The United Kingdom

Elizabeth's death, the language of the Book of Common Prayer and the language of Shakespeare came together in the most influential of all English books, the King James Bible. Until recently, it was read by more people than any other book in the English language, and for many Americans on the frontier, it was their only book in the English language. It has been only in the past five decades that serious attention was paid to any of the "modern" English translations.

The Tudor monarchs were able to dominate England by their political skill and by the force of their personality. All except Edward and Mary enjoyed considerable popularity, and if those who followed them had enjoyed similar success, the parliament might have melted out of British life. But the Stuarts, of whom it could be said, "They learned nothing and forgot nothing," tried to push the doctrine of the Divine Right of Kings farther than the English wished to have it carried. When Elizabeth died unmarried in 1603, James Stuart, King of Scotland, became James I of England and the whole island was united under one monarch.

The Stuarts Brief Tenure

The second of the Stuarts, Charles I, came to the throne in 1625. He soon began to have trouble with Parliament over taxation, and his inflexibility and demands for royal absolutism only angered the democratic movement within the country. Moreover, Charles was a "high"

churchman, with Roman Catholic leanings, and most members of Parliament were Puritan protestant in inclination (i.e. a full, chanted eucharistic service with all ceremonial acts, including incense, holy water, etc. vs. three hymns, a psalm, lessons and sermon). For 11 years Charles managed to rule without Parliament and his persecution of Puritans led to the founding of the colonies in New England. In order to raise revenues, Charles reconvened Parliament in 1640 and soon civil war broke out in England. Catholics, high churchmen, the nobility and the rural people of the north and west supported the King; Puritans, people of trade and commerce and most important, Londoners, supported Parliament.

Religious and Civil Turmoil

Unlike the Wars of the Roses, the Civil War of the 17th century was not simply a fight over who should occupy the throne, but an ideological struggle to determine the very nature of English society. Oliver Cromwell emerged as leader of the parliamentary forces after Charles had been captured. Cromwell purged Parliament of all but his loyal supporters, abolished the House of Lords, and in 1649, had Charles beheaded. He was the only English monarch to die for religious reasons, and the last to be killed for political reasons. Whether Charles was a martyr for the causes of royal stability and the Anglican Church or whether he justly died for opposing the representatives of the peo-

ple depends on one's viewpoint—and perhaps both views are true.

The Commonwealth Period and Return of Monarchy

Cromwell had hoped to rule in a liberal and democratic way, but continued factionalism and the threatening anarchy in English society caused him to assume absolute power as Lord Protector. This period was known as the Commonwealth. When Cromwell died in 1658 and the monarchy was restored in 1660, Charles II, the son of the dead king, returned from the continent to which he had escaped and was greeted by a joyful people.

During Charles' reign, English culture extricated itself from the heavy burden of Puritanism and flourished again; Bunyan, Milton and Pepys were the most famous writers. The great fire of 1666 destroyed much of London, but allowed such master architects as Christopher Wren to rebuild a new and even more glorious city. On another continent, the Dutch were driven out of North America and New Amsterdam became New York.

James II followed his brother to the throne, but did not renounce his faith in Roman Catholicism. The English then turned to William of Orange, a grandson of Charles I, who came to England and later defeated James in the July 1690 Battle of the Boyne in Ireland. From then on, the fact that England was Anglican (not Roman Catholic or Puritan) was settled. But both William of Orange and his wife

Queen Mary I

Queen Elizabeth I

were childless. The most logical successor was Queen Anne, daughter of James II, but she died childless in 1714. What was the answer for a people accustomed to a monarchy?

The House of Hanover (later Windsor) and Parliament Power

Britain turned to George of Hanover (a great–grandson of James I, and a Protestant) to become king. The fact that he could speak no English (only German) was of immense importance. It meant that the king had to leave many of his powers in the hands of the chairmanship of his council, and that person was the leader of the Whig Party, with a majority in the House of Commons. Thus, England developed the tradition of having a Prime Minister preside over a Cabinet that grew out of parliament.

During the middle part of the 18th century, the first British Empire took shape. English forces defeated the French for control of much of India and the defeat of the French forces at Quebec in 1759 meant that Canada and the area west of

the thirteen colonies were brought under British rule. In 1760, George III succeeded to the throne. Since he believed a king should rule the country, he suspended the cabinet government, intending that the king and the "king's friends" would rule.

As the British Empire expanded with Captain Cook's discovery of Australia, relationships with the thirteen American colonies deteriorated. By 1782 they had been victorious in their revolution and the period of the First British Empire was largely over. With the disaster in North America came the return of the cabinet system to England as William Pitt the Younger became the new Prime Minister. For the next 50 years the Tories would lead the country and maintain a steady and conservative posture while the French Revolution and then the armies of Napoleon forced Britain once again to demonstrate its mastery of the seas.

Nineteenth Century Change

At the turn of the century, the Act of Union dissolved the Irish Parliament and incorporated Catholic Ireland into the

United Kingdom. Tragically, religious persecution of the Catholics kept the Irish from full integration into British society and thus, the Union was doomed from the start.

But change was occurring in England. The Industrial Revolution, gradual at first, gathered momentum. Early machines made of wood were replaced by stronger and more efficient ones of iron. James Watt's inventions harnessed the power of steam. Reforms in agriculture improved food production, but caused many farmers to leave the land. Thus, as industry and commerce were growing, along with the wealth and power of those who controlled them, so, too, there was a growing urban class kept in degrading poverty. As populations shifted, parliament became less representative.

In so–called "rotten" boroughs, a few voters could control who was elected to Parliament. In one district in Cornwall a single voter could elect two members! It is coincidental, but symbolic that in 1830, the Reforming Whigs Party obtained a majority in parliament and the first railroad line on which the Rocket whizzed along at 35 miles an hour was opened.

The Whigs were able to get their Reform Bill through Parliament in 1832. This most important piece of legislation abolished many "rotten" boroughs, gave representation to the new towns and significantly lowered the property qualifications necessary to be a voter. Many observers think that this Reform Bill saved the country from revolution, which had become so popular in the rest of Europe. Certainly, it gave new power to the middle classes, and was an important step toward mass democracy.

Victoria

In 1837 the 18–year–old Victoria began the longest reign in British history. As the last half of the 17th century had belonged to Elizabeth, so the 19th century belonged to Victoria. During Victoria's reign, reform acts gradually increased the number of people enfranchised and gave protection to the lower classes. The repeal of the "Corn Laws" and free trade not only stimulated industry, but also reduced the cost of living for the poor. Thus, under the leadership of such greats as Palmerston, Gladstone and Disraeli, Parliament found a course that kept England moving toward democracy without being caught up in the excesses that racked so much of the continent. By 1846 Canada had been made self–governing, and within a few years, Australia and New Zealand were given internal self–government. Thus, the concept of the Empire of free countries bound to the mother country by loyalty to the Queen was born.

George III (1738–1820)

17

The United Kingdom

John Constable's *Hay Wain* (1821)

National Gallery, London

Two great events marked the reign of Victoria. The great Exhibition of 1851 demonstrated British industrial might and middle class prosperity, whereas the Golden Jubilee of the Queen in 1887 marked the high point of the Empire. The claim that the sun never set on the British Empire was indeed true. Its members included Canada in North America, British Guiana in South America; the United Kingdom in Europe; South Africa, Kenya, Somaliland in Africa; India and Ceylon in Asia; and Australia and New Zealand in the Pacific. The greatest problem, however, was closest to home, and various attempts to solve the Irish problem through Home Rule were unsuccessful.

Until 1900 the roar of the British lion could be heard throughout the entire world. Britain controlled over one-fifth of the earth's land surface and ruled a quarter of the world's population. Its flag flew on every continent and the largest and most powerful navy in the world protected its magnificent empire. At the same time, Britain was invulnerable to foreign invasion. This meant that, unlike many other nations with frontiers instead of shorelines, it could leisurely develop a democratic form of government. Nations under the constant threat of attack often could not afford the luxury of a relatively inefficient and cumbersome governmental order that involved parliamentary meetings, long debates, votes, press coverage and criticism. As a nation equally invulnerable, the Americans shared this advantage with their English forebears.

Also, Britain did not need to maintain a large standing army. As the history of many countries indicates, ambitious soldiers, led by prestigious officers close to the political heart of the country sometimes cannot resist meddling in the political affairs of a nation. The British never had difficulty in maintaining control over their military; a military putsch is unthinkable in the British context. Fortunately, the tradition of civilian supremacy over the military was passed on to many

(though not all) of its former colonies, including in the United States.

Political Power Struggles and Social Change

A watershed year in the growth of power of the House of Commons was 1911. The Liberal Party government had proposed a land tax, and although tradition had it that only Commons controlled finances, the House of Lords rejected the bill. The parliament bill of 1911 deprived the Lords of any control of finance and limited their power over other bills to a two–year delay. In a move to make the Commons more responsive to the popular will, the maximum life of a Parliament was reduced from seven to five years. When it appeared that the Lords would veto this bill, George V threatened to increase the number of Lords and pack the Upper House with those favorable to the bill. The Lords yielded to the threat and thereafter the House of Commons gained virtual total control of legislation. In the same year, members of the House of Commons began to receive pay, and thus, those without independent incomes could be in Parliament.

World War I not only devastated a generation of Englishmen—it helped to produce changes in society. As recognition for their part in the war effort, women received the vote in 1918. Because they involved so much of the population, both World Wars did much to further popular democracy and reduce the differences between social classes. Shortly after World War I, the southern part of Ireland left the United Kingdom and achieved dominion status as the Irish Free State. Protestants living in the north clung tenaciously to their membership in the United Kingdom and their loyalty to the crown, but their conflict with Catholics living alongside them has not been solved to this day.

Following World War I, trade unions grew in power and were able to call a general strike in 1926. But the great depression of the 1930s significantly reduced the power of the Labour government, and the Conservatives led the country in the years before World War II. The last crisis to affect the monarchy occurred in 1936. Edward VIII ascended the throne, but within months he abdicated so that he could marry the divorced Wallis Simpson, an American.

The Hitler Threat and World War II

As Hitler began to threaten more and more of Europe, Prime Minister Neville Chamberlain practiced a policy of appeasement. This only whetted the German appetite; after an attack on Poland in September 1939, Britain joined France as allies in World War II. In May of the next

THE
BRITISH NAVY
guards the freedom of us all

year, Winston Churchill became Prime Minister. His courage and his words epitomized the best of the British spirit and inspired the nation to withstand withering aerial attacks from bombers and rockets. With tremendous assistance from the U.S., Britain and its allies were victorious, but prostrated and devastated by the end of the conflict in 1945.

The Postwar 1940s and 1950s

Two world wars in the 20th century brought enormous changes. These included revolutions in many European countries, the rise of the United States and the Soviet Union as the most powerful countries in the world and the relative decline of the traditional global powers, including the United Kingdom, in terms of political and military significance. As a victorious ally, Britain gained a veto right in the United Nations Security Council, but it had to liquidate most of its foreign investments to finance its own recovery; these foreign investments had once paid for a third of British imports. The merchant marine was depleted and factories and equipment were either destroyed or obsolete.

The negative economic consequences of the wars reduced Britain's ability to be a global power and stimulated in many British colonies the desire for independence. By proclaiming the Truman Doctrine, the U.S. assumed from Britain the burden of economic and military aid to Greece and Turkey and relieved the U.K. of its responsibility for supporting the struggle against communist forces in the Greek civil war. The British also found themselves in the crossfire between Jews and Arabs in Palestine and Hindus and Moslems in India and were forced in 1947

to abandon both important regions. In 1952 it lost control of Egypt. When Egypt seized the Suez Canal in 1956, Britain, supported by France and Israel, attempted to re-conquer that important waterway. However, stiff joint United Nations, U.S. and Soviet opposition to this move, which seemed like the last gasp of colonialism, forced the British, French and Israelis to back down.

In 1959 Britain still ruled over 53 countries with a population of 81 million, and 86,000 British troops were deployed around the world outside of Europe. But the floodgates opened, and by the 1960s a tidal wave of separations swept through Africa, the Middle East and Asia. Having lost most of its Asian empire in the late–1940s, the British recognized the inevitability of African independence. Fortunately, Britain had trained many Africans as capable administrators and had established there a relatively efficient system of local administration. Therefore, when they gradually relinquished their hold, well–trained Africans were usually able to take their places. An exception was Rhodesia, whose tiny white minority took power in 1965 and held it for years before finally handing the reins of power to the new black–ruled state of Zimbabwe.

Britain spearheaded the international U.N. boycott of Rhodesia. But the U.K. was in the throes of such economic distress that it was not only unable to steer events in Africa, but it was also forced in 1971 to terminate most of its military and political responsibilities "East of Suez." This withdrawal was unfortunate for the U.S., which was trapped at the time in the quagmire of Vietnam. The U.S. felt compelled to assume Britain's prior responsibility for maintaining "stability" in the Middle East. It thereby became embroiled in one of the world's least stable regions. This untimely responsibility prompted American administrations in the 1970s to help build up the Shah's power. The hope was that a modernized and well–armed Iran could maintain order in the oil–rich Persian Gulf region and keep the Soviet Union's power and influence out of the area. The Americans paid heavily in the 1980s for this gamble.

Elizabeth II succeeded her father, George VI, on the British throne in 1952. Thirty generations separated her from her ancestor, William the Conqueror, and she began her reign in a nation struggling to find a new role in the modern world. The Empire became a Commonwealth of independent nations, bound together by language, democratic principles and a residue of loyalty to the person (but not the power) of the British monarch. De-colonization had a serious negative economic impact on Britain by depriving

it of many protected markets, sources of raw materials at low prices and cheap food. The resulting economic difficulties harassed the United Kingdom for a quarter of a century following the Second World War.

Domestic Politics before Thatcher

On July 5, 1945, voters delivered a dramatic blow to the Tories by electing the first Labour prime minister with a clear majority of 145 seats in the House of Commons, Clement Attlee. Although the British deeply admired Churchill as a great wartime leader, they associated his Conservative Party with the soup lines and unemployment of the prewar depression. Labour had ably guided the home ministries in the national government during the war. It had impressed the British as being the best team for creating full employment, housing and better social security and health care for a people that had just sacrificed so much in the war effort.

Although ideologically divided, as always, between more pragmatic and radical wings, the Labour Party moved boldly to make many sweeping economic changes, including the nationalization of the Bank of England, hospitals, railways, aviation, public transport and the gas, electrical, coal and steel industries. Unlike France and Italy, though, the newly nationalized industries were placed under the direction of autonomous corporations (subsidized from the state treasury), rather than government agencies and ministries. In 1946 the National Insurance Act and National Health Service Act were the prime examples of popular social welfare legislation which strengthened or created old–age pensions, unemployment compensation, education, social insurance and free health service. No sooner were these innovations in place, though, than the Labour government began losing popularity. It was badly divided, British influence abroad was noticeably eroding, the pound was losing its value, and economic recovery was painfully slow.

At age 77 Winston Churchill was returned to power in 1951, and his Tories ruled until 1964, the longest period of continuous party government in modern British history. His government returned the iron and steel industries and road transport to private ownership, although Labour renationalized iron and steel in 1967. However, accurately sensing the sentiments of the British nation, the Tories did not make a radical U–turn. It accepted the national welfare and health services, as well as the commitment to full employment.

Following a stroke, Churchill was finally persuaded to step down in 1955. His successor was his long–time foreign minister

The United Kingdom

Horse Guardsmen leaving their barracks for duty at Buckingham Palace

Anthony Eden. After only a year Eden had to resign in the aftermath of the Suez crisis of 1956. He was followed by Harold Macmillan, who optimistically predicted a turnaround in Britain's economic fortunes (for which reason he was dubbed "Supermac"!). There was a short–lived economic boom in the late–1950s, and the living standards of some British rose. But inequalities of wealth remained which the government could not alleviate because of a rising imbalance of payments and a serious sterling crisis. Britain was obviously not keeping up with its international trade competitors, and management and trade unions were not inclined to introduce more efficient and modern methods of production. In an attempt to protect the value of the pound, the government had to introduce an unpopular wage freeze and raise the bank rate. Macmillan sought to halt the growing economic malaise and increase British industry's competitiveness by leading Britain into the EU, but French President Charles de Gaulle vetoed its entry in 1963.

Following this humiliation came the coup de grace for the Macmillan government: a lurid sex scandal involving Secretary of War John Profumo. He was alleged to be involved with a call girl who had been asked by the Soviet naval attaché to

gather information from him on the UK's nuclear weapons. No government could possibly benefit from such a spicy and embarrassing affair. But what forced Macmillan to demand Profumo's resignation was not so much the illicit activity itself as the fact that he had insulted parliament by lying to it about his

Churchill

involvement. He thereby dragged both himself and the prime minister down.

The colorless Sir Alec Douglas–Home replaced Macmillan in the fall of 1963. Home (pronounced Hume) was a rare example of a prime minister being drawn from the House of Lords, even though he scrambled to win a by–election seat to the

Commons. Home could not quiet the growing desire for a change, and with only a razor–thin majority he could not prevent Harold Wilson's Labour Party from winning power in October 1964.

A former Oxford University economics don (lecturer), Wilson was from the more conservative, reformist wing of the Labour Party. Faced with daunting economic problems, he not only pared down the UK's military commitments abroad, but he applied the traditional conservative policies of increasing taxes and reducing government spending. These unpopular economic policies widened ideological divisions within his own party, sparked industrial unrest and strikes and brought Wilson into a head–on collision with the trade unions. Widening trade imbalances, another devaluation of the pound, and a renewal of strife between Catholics and Protestants in Northern Ireland, all spelled disaster for Wilson in the June 1970 elections, when the Tories, led by Edward Heath, returned to power.

Heath's government knew little happiness, aside from Britain's entry into the EU in 1973. His bitter confrontations with the assertive coal miners brought serious economic disruptions and forced the prime minister to declare states of emergency five times. The crippling coal strike in the winter of 1973–4 destroyed what credibility remained for the cabinet. Voters brought Wilson's Labourites back to power in February 1974 on the assumption that they would have better relations with the powerful unions.

Wilson had only a miniscule majority. He expended precious energy and patience fending off an ambitious radical left wing within his own party which sniped at him constantly and openly advocated such unpopular policies as a "socialist transformation" of British society, massive nationalizations of large companies, the abolition of elite institutions such as the House of Lords and private schools, withdrawal from NATO and the EU, and unilateral disarmament. These leftist antics ultimately drove some moderates out of the party and led to the formation in 1981 of the now defunct Social Democratic Party (SDP).

It is hardly surprising that Wilson was unable to improve the economic situation. The sky–rocketing price of oil resulting from the 1973 OPEC embargo hit the struggling British economy hard, despite the discovery of oil in Britain's own sectors of the North Sea. Inflation rose to dizzying levels, and for the first time since the war unemployment reared its ugly head. These problems made hopes for harmonious labor relations a pipe–dream, as the spate of disruptive strikes indicated.

In 1976 an exasperated and tired Harold Wilson turned the keys to Number 10 Downing Street over to his foreign minister, James Callaghan. The new prime minister was no more successful than Wilson had been in controlling the unions, improving the overall economy, and coping with rising violence in Northern Ireland and growing separatist movements in Scotland and Wales.

It has been said that the world stands aside for a man who knows where he is going. By the spring of 1979, the British voters were prepared to do just that, with one historical twist: they brought to power the first woman prime minister in British politics, Margaret Thatcher. She acted with such determination and decisiveness that by January 3, 1988, she had become the longest continuously serving British prime minister in the 20th century. Ruling over a country with the highest economic growth of any major economy, low inflation, declining unemployment, a rising pound, and tamed unions, she had every reason to believe that she would remain at the helm into the 21st century and perhaps even overtake the record of Sir Robert Walpole, whose 21 consecutive years of service as prime minister began in 1721.

Attitude and Political Change

Terrorism related to the unsolved problem of Northern Ireland, along with rising crime in Britain, helped shift British voters' view of the world in an important way. It helped many of them shape a tough–minded attitude and become more receptive to political appeals based on "law and order," replacing the compromise politics of the 1960s.

The parliamentary elections of 1979 and 1983 took many foreign observers by surprise because they revealed that the political landscape in Britain had dramatically changed. Upon closer scrutiny, it can be seen that these changes are the consequence of important changes in Britain's economy and society in the course of the decade of the 1970s. Those changes broke down much of the class structure of Britain, which traditionally had shaped British politics to such a large extent.

Public opinion polls and election analyses continually confirm that fewer and fewer British spontaneously identify with a particular class, and that class–consciousness has and is declining markedly. Class itself has become only one of many factors shaping individual attitudes and preferences. It has become harder to classify Britons by class, which has increasingly become more a matter of taste and culture, rather than of income and occupation. With less than a quarter of workers in manufacturing jobs, fewer

than two workers in five belong to a labor union. Two–thirds of all British own or are buying their homes; even one of three unskilled manual laborers is a home–owner. Also, leisure is no longer the privilege of a few; instead, almost all full–time workers receive four weeks of leave. In short, more workers have become middle–class. Young people from all economic strata mingle more easily and are more likely to intermarry than they used to. Since Britons have become more individualistic, their social attitudes and political behavior have become less predictable. These changes are bound to have a negative effect on political parties whose appeals have traditionally been heavily class–based, especially the Labour Party.

Since 1979, Britain's population has barely grown, but the size of the electorate increased from 39.3 in 1970 to 42.2 million in 1983. The voting age was dropped to 18 in 1970, but the number of pensioners has grown, so the average voter today is actually older than in 1970. He is also more highly educated, more likely to be divorced and live alone or in small households, own his own home, and, despite high unemployment, have a higher standard of living than in the 1970s. Disenchantment with unions (see Economy) and changes in social patterns (see Culture) that were occurring in the 1970s set the stage for dramatic political shifts in Britain. After 1979 these effectively altered much of the conventional wisdom about British politics and realigned the structure.

Although the diminishing numbers of unionized workers in the mines and factories retained their traditional loyalty to the Labour Party and the managers remained steadfast to the Conservative Party, their diminishing numbers hoisted the flag of change on the pole in the 1970s. Soaring inflation and rising unemployment, accompanied by increasingly strident union demands alienated the people. Their revulsion at the excessive "un-elected power" which union bosses wielded boiled to the surface in "the winter of discontent," 1978–9, when coal and transportation strikes threatened to paralyze the entire nation.

These changes led to conditions whereby a party leader would advocate a policy based on the notions that the best help was self help, that initiative deserved rewards, than an economic pie must be baked before it is divided, that welfare could not produce prosperity, that private business is better than nationalized industries, that the problem of inflation is more important than the problem of unemployment, and, finally, that the government cannot control the economy. In other words, traditional Keynesian economics

The United Kingdom

(see Economy) was no cure for British problems, but was part of the disease. That leader was Margaret Thatcher, leader of the Conservative Party (Tory) since 1975, who was elected prime minister in 1979. Leading a changed party, she captured the mood of an altered society and spoke for the new social realities.

Return to the Conservative Party

When she moved into the prime minister's office, she promised "three years of unparalleled austerity," and for three years the pain of Thatcherism was far more evident than the benefits. Unemployment rose and economic conditions worsened. She was unable to cut government spending significantly because of greater numbers on welfare and pay raises for government workers to bring them into equity with the private sector. Nevertheless, the "iron lady," as she began to be called, held firm to her monetarist policies (restricting the money supply) and vowed, "I will not stagger from expedient to expedient." By 1982 her party was well behind the Labour Party in the polls and she seemed to be heading for sure defeat in the next elections when the unexpected occurred.

The Falklands War

Argentine troops invaded and captured a small group of off–shore islands that had long been settled and ruled by the British. Mrs. Thatcher galvanized the nation with her firmness and resolution in organizing the recapture of the Falklands Islands. The British basked again briefly in imperial glory, and an overwhelming majority of them applauded their leader for her ability to deal with a crisis, winning back control of the islands, albeit at a tremendous financial cost. The Falklands War boosted her party's popularity, and the economy fortuitously began to revive at the same time, with inflation shrinking to the lowest level in 15 years. The electorate became convinced that her economic medicine had been a harsh necessity and that she was a true leader. Sensing the political winds blowing briskly at her back, she took advantage of the prime minister's privilege to set an election whenever it suits his or her party. It was called for June 1983 and demonstrated beyond doubt that the party landscape had greatly changed and that a new Conservative Party had become the dominant force in British politics by the mid–1980s.

Her astonishing electoral triumph in June 1983, which made her the first Conservative prime minister in the 20th century to be reelected to a second term, revealed both her leadership image, established in the Falklands War, and the extent

to which most social and economic groups in Britain accepted her diagnosis of the nation's problems. Most voters did not even blame her for the country's most pressing problem: continuing unemployment, which shot up from 5.4% to 13.3% during her four years of rule. They clearly patted her on the back for bringing inflation down.

"The Iron Lady"

She was a fundamentally cautious politician, whose bark was often more powerful than her bite. She did take modest steps to return some of the nationalized industries to private hands, but she did not precipitously withdraw the public from the economy; in 1988 government spending amounted to 42% of GNP, about the same as in 1979. Nor did she dramatically reduce public employment, welfare assistance or taxes; she disliked spending what she did not have. Therefore, most voters did not see in her a fanatic ideologue who wished to turn the clock backward.

She never enjoyed "popularity," as her many nicknames reveal: "Leaderene," "Attila the Hen," "Rhoda the Rhino" and "Nanny," to mention only a few of the "kinder" ones. Many saw her as uncaring, cold and obsessed. But she had authority and respect because of what she accomplished and what she represents. She strode firmly forward to remake her country in her own self–image: brisk, hard–working, frugal and self–sufficient. She combined some of the best 19th century values with 20th century energy. She was a strong leader who entered office with a sense of mission: to make Britain great again. Of course, she bene-fited from an opposition that was in disarray.

Part of Thatcher's appeal was that she represented a new kind of Conservative Party that had emerged. The image of the party as the preserve of the landed gentry, bankers or high–level civil servants,

which could display charity when needed toward the lower classes, and which assembled in prayer in the Church of England, has changed.

The attitude of most citizens, an overwhelming majority of whom are baptized protestant, is now indifference toward religion—its traditional role in politics has all but vanished. Tory leaders cannot count on the support of the Church of England, containing many clergy bitterly opposed to its policies.

Thatcher was an example of the "new" kind of Tory, who worked her way up in the world. The daughter of a dressmaker and grocer from Grantham, Lincolnshire, she lived with her family in an apartment above the shop and worked all her childhood in her father's store. She studied chemistry at Oxford, where she led the Conservative student organization and held off–campus jobs. She later acquired a law degree after marrying a successful businessman, Denis Thatcher, who served as the nation's "First Gentleman," staying a discreet half pace behind the prime minister. She was never an insider in "the establishment," and, like Ronald Reagan, she harbored a bias against the party elite. She served only four years in the early 1970s as Education Secretary before gaining the party leadership in 1975.

Having emerged from the middle class herself, she was well able to forge an alliance between skilled workers and the middle class, in a society which is becoming more and more middle class. She capitalized on the dream of owning one's home by giving residents of government–built houses the opportunity to buy them at bargain prices. About a half million gratefully did so. This was the greatest transfer of wealth to the British working class in history. By the time her Tory party was voted out of power in 1997, 68% of all housing units were owner–occupied, a higher percentage than in the United States or elsewhere in Europe.

Mr. Denis Thatcher and former Prime Minister Thatcher

She benefited from a transformation within the party, which extends from the grass–roots all the way up to parliament. Its seats are no longer occupied primarily by traditional local notables, but increasingly by insurance agents, housewives, teachers, salesmen and self–made middle management types. Perhaps as good an example of the new kind of Tory as Thatcher herself was a Speaker of the House, Bruce Bernard Weatherill, a former tailor who always carried in his pocket a thimble to remind himself of his humble background. It is said that when he entered parliament, one aristocratic Conservative MP was overheard saying to another: "I don't know what this place is coming to, Tom: they've got my tailor in here now!" The point is that the tailor to whom they were referring was a Tory!

GOVERNMENT

Simplicity and Flexibility

Speaking of his country, the great Victorian prime minister, Benjamin Disraeli, stated: "In a progressive country, change is constant, and the great question is, not whether you should resist change which is inevitable, but whether that change should be carried out in deference to the manners, the customs, the laws and the traditions of the people." Americans often imagine the British as a conservative nation. In fact, Britain has skillfully adjusted to change for centuries, and today it confronts fundamental shifts in its society, economy, political system and place in the world. The British genius is to combine astonishing continuity with necessary change; they excel in pouring "new wine into old bottles."

Great Britain remains a monarchy with a noble class that still enjoys certain privileges. However, Britain is the birthplace for the most durable democratic model of government in the world. Unlike the complicated American democratic system, which has almost never been successfully adapted to other societies, the "Westminster model" not only fits the British people and circumstances, but it can quite easily be made to fit other nations as well. Its secret lies in its simplicity and its flexibility. It can be modified and tailored to other peoples' needs and circumstances without losing its essentially democratic character.

British politics operates according to an unwritten constitution that prescribes the "rules of the game" and places limits on the rulers. In Britain voters elect 659 members of the House of Commons, the lower house of parliament. The leader of the party that wins a majority of the seats (or has more seats than any other party) becomes the prime minister,

the most powerful political figure in the land. The monarch is the chief of state, but her role is largely symbolic; she makes no important political decisions. The prime minister selects other ministers, who are also experienced parliamentary leaders in the party, to sit in the cabinet.

Together the prime minister and cabinet are called "the government" which rules "collectively." This means that all members of the government must publicly support its policies or resign from office, in great contrast to the United States. Further, the entire team assumes responsibility for the overall policy. The government rules as long as it maintains a majority in the House of Commons. Thus, it rules until it loses a "vote of confidence" on an important bill. The prime minister must call a new election at least five years after the preceding election, but she or he can call one earlier if that would be to the party's advantage.

Contrasts with U.S.

Unlike the United States, where both houses of Congress are equally powerful, the British upper house, the House of Lords, has far less power than the House of Commons. Also, unlike in the United States, there is neither "separation of power" among the executive, legislative or judicial branches, nor a distribution of political powers among the national government and many state governments. Executive and legislative powers are fused, and the prime minister is both the chief executive and the chief legislator of the land. Through party discipline the prime minister controls the House of Commons. Further, political power is concentrated in the central government. Britain is a *unitary*, not a *federal* state, so he/she does not have to contend with separate states that wield constitutionally granted powers of their own. No court in the country can judge a law unconstitutional. Parliamentary supremacy is the fundamental principle of British government.

This set–up is the basic model for most democracies in the world. Even the founders of the American government, whose political views had been shaped by British political ideas but who had consciously sought to depart from that model, adopted more from the British system than many Americans care to remember. After all, what the founders had deemed to be so unjust and tyrannical was the fact that Americans had been "denied their rights as Englishmen." Even the arguments and wording of the Declaration of Independence bore striking resemblance to the work by the 17th century English philosopher, John Locke, entitled *The Second Treatise of Government*,

an important blueprint and philosophical foundation for British government.

The American founding fathers were certainly aware of their debt to Westminster when they included in the American constitution such provisions as the necessity of senatorial confirmation of cabinet ministers, congressional election of the president in the event that no candidate wins a majority in the electoral college, and the possibility for the national legislature to impeach and remove a president. It is indeed fitting that the statue on the top of the Capitol faces toward London, symbolic of the extent to which the American government, the political habits, and the thinking of its people have been shaped by Great Britain.

The Unwritten Constitution

As the British political system is more closely examined, perhaps the first striking aspect is the fact that the country's constitution is *unwritten*; that is, there is no single document, as in the United States. One must refer to one or all of five sources to know what is constitutional: first are particularly important documents, such as the Magna Charta (1215), the Habeas Corpus Act (1679), The Bill of Rights (1689) which, unlike the American Bill of Rights, defines rights of parliament, not rights of individual citizens, the Parliament Act of 1911, and the Statute of Westminster (1931). Then there are interpretations of courts of law and principles of common law (which has itself been in a constant state of change). For example, basic individual liberties, such as the freedom of assembly, speech, and religion are all derived from common law. There is the Law and Custom of Parliament, which deals with the special privileges which parliament and each Member of Parliament (known as MP) enjoy.

Finally there are wholly unwritten elements, known as conventions. These include such practices as: parliament must meet at least once a year, the government must resign if it loses a vote of confidence, the monarch cannot attend cabinet meetings or enter parliament without permission. However, the monarch always opens parliament with a speech from the throne. She is there in all her finery, displaying the majesty and royal tradition that stretch back continuously over so many centuries. Yet, she is surrounded by members of parliament, freely elected by the people and operating within the context of an effective multi–party system. Her speech does not contain her own ideas, but puts forward the program of the prime minister and the government which holds a majority in the lower house of parliament. Members of the opposition party, often

The United Kingdom

Her Majesty Queen Elizabeth II opens Parliament in the House of Lords

called the "Loyal Opposition," listen to it. Because the monarch delivers the speech, tradition requires that even critics refer to it as "the gracious speech." For example, opposition leader John Major responded to Prime Minister Tony Blair's text read by the Queen in May 1997 as follows: "The road to hell is paved with good intentions, and this gracious speech is very full of good intentions."

Perhaps no other idea has been a more important gift of the British to the growth of free government than the concept of the "Loyal Opposition." That someone may be opposed to the present government in its policies and yet still be loyal to the country and not subject to political punishment is incomprehensible in totalitarian or one–party states.

No politician could violate these conventions without touching off a serious political crisis. The well–informed and respected *Economist* described Britain's constitution as a "contraption, stuck together from old laws, bits of precedent, scraps of custom and practice and blind faith in the steering ability of its driver, the prime minister of the day. The machine is notoriously short on brakes: the checks and balances which are a feature of written constitutions."

Why does a nation of 59 million persons have no written constitution? One reason is that Britain is one of the few democracies in the world to enter the democratic age without a revolution. After successful revolutions, winners are far more inclined to put in writing the kind of guarantees and rights that had been denied them by the former rulers. The outlines of the British regime were established before the industrial revolution in the 19th century. Therefore, the economic and social conflicts which that revolution sparked could ultimately be reconciled within the system. Also, the British aristocracy had the foresight to make concessions to the middle and working classes, prompting the latter to realize that they could achieve change and satisfaction through reform, rather than rebellion. This is one reason why Marxism was never as potent a political force in Britain as it was on the European continent. Further, Britain is not a federal state, so there is no need for a careful delineation of jurisdictions between various governments, as in the U.S.

Most important, however, is the kind of political culture one finds in Britain. There is widespread agreement on basic political values, and the population broadly supports the leading institutions. This consensus has meant that disagreements over policies have (except under Cromwell) never led to fundamental challenges to the regime and constitution. The

British have changed their political system only gradually. Important changes usually only occur after much dialogue and after the major parties have reached general agreement on them. The British also are a law–abiding people, a fact that makes it especially shocking to read about bombings or racial riots in that country. They tend to be moderate and pragmatic and are remarkable for their unwillingness to mount the barricades over abstract or idealistic principles.

They are inclined to boil political disputes down to conflicting interests rather than to conflicting morals or ideas, and this makes compromise much easier. Finally, there is a widespread acceptance of democracy and pluralism. Any foreigner who needs a reminder of the fact that there are many different groups or viewpoints which have a right to exist and be heard in Britain can go to Hyde Park on any Sunday morning to hear the soap–box speeches of dozens of advocates.

The Monarchy

Britain is a monarchy, and in theory the Queen or King has sweeping powers. She theoretically appoints the prime minister, assembles or dissolves parliament, approves of all laws, makes foreign policy, commands the "Armed Forces of the Crown," and appoints officers who hold their rank by "Royal Commission." The trappings of political power would seem to confirm this. The "Queen's government" contains "Ministers of the Crown," who propose laws which always begin with the following words: "Be it enacted by the Queen's Most Excellent Majesty, by and with the consent of the Lords Spiritual and Temporal and Commons in this present Parliament assembled …" She is the temporal head of the Church of England, the country's official religion, and she appoints the leading priests. Also, in theory, sovereignty resides not in the people, but in the "Crown," which is not the person of the monarch, but rather the symbol of supreme executive power.

Actually, she no longer exercises any of the above powers. She "reigns but does not rule." The "Glorious Revolution" in 1688 established parliamentary supremacy and spelled the end of any monarchical pretense to rule absolutely. The last exercise of royal veto power was in 1707. Walter Bagehot wrote in 1867, "the greatest wisdom of a constitutional king would show itself in well-considered inaction," and Queen Elizabeth II has obeyed this dictum. By the 20th century, the real reason why "the Queen can do no wrong" is that the government never permits her to make any important decisions. In the case of Elizabeth, she does not even express

her opinions publicly. This does not mean that the monarch does not perform any important functions whatsoever. She retains the right "to be informed, to advise and to warn." This right confers no power, but it does provide influence. As constitutional expert Ivor Jennings notes, "she can be as helpful or as obstreperous as she pleases: and she is the only member of the Cabinet who cannot be informed that her resignation would assist the speedy dispatch of business."

In unusual circumstances or in times of crisis, the monarch could actually exercise considerable influence. If a prime minister dies or resigns and a successor has to be appointed from the same party, or if an election yields no majority, the Queen could wield authority, so long as she would not act according to personal preference. For instance, in 1957 when Anthony Eden resigned, it was not clear who would replace him until Queen Elizabeth named Harold Macmillan. The monarch holds other significant "reserve powers," such as dissolving parliament or rejecting requests for dissolution. The ultimate guarantee that the monarch will not overstep her bounds is the British people, who are sovereign in reality, if not in theory. Prince Charles admitted this fact frankly, saying, "something as curious as the monarchy won't survive unless you take account of people's attitudes. I think it can be a kind of elective institution. After all, if people don't want it, they won't have it."

Much more importantly, she symbolizes the unity of the nation and the continuous thread through a millennium of English history. She is thus the focus of national pride. Politics touches not only the mind, but also the heart, and she helps to provide her subjects with an emotional attachment to their country. She is therefore an important cornerstone for the kind of low–keyed, but deeply–rooted, patriotism most Englishmen share. Finally, because of her dual position as head of state and defender of the faith, she helps to link governmental with religious authority in the minds of many Englishmen.

In his brilliant book published in 1867, *The English Constitution*, Walter Bagehot distinguished between the "dignified" and "efficient" parts of government. The "dignified" parts, especially the glittering monarch and nobility, were useful in securing authority and loyalty for the state from the citizenry, while the "efficient" parts actually used the power and resources of the state to rule. In his book, The Body Politic, Sir Ian Gilmour argued that "legitimacy, the acceptance by the governed of the political system, is far better aided by an ancient monarchy set above the political battle than by a transient president, who has gained his position through

The United Kingdom

The Order of Succession to the Throne

Her Majesty Queen Elizabeth II and His Royal Highness Prince Philip the Duke of Edinburgh

—— *The Heir Apparent, eldest son of The Queen.*

1. His Royal Highness The **Prince CHARLES Philip Arthur George,** Prince of Wales and Earl of Chester, Duke of Cornwall and Rothesay, Earl of Carrick, Baron of Renfrew, Lord of the Isles and Great Steward of Scotland, b. November 14, 1948. Married Lady Diana Frances Spencer (3rd daughter of the 8th Earl Spencer) July 29, 1981.

> The Prince and Princess of Wales separated in 1992 and were divorced in 1996. Diana, Princess of Wales, died from injuries received in a car crash in Paris on August 31, 1997.

—— *The sons of that union,*

2. His Royal Highness **Prince WILLIAM Arthur Philip Louis of Wales,** b. June 21, 1982.
3. His Royal Highness **Prince HENRY Charles Albert David of Wales,** b. September 15, 1984.

—— *The second son of The Queen,*

4. His Royal Highness The **Prince ANDREW Albert Christian Edward,** Duke of York. b. February 19, 1960. Married Miss Sarah Margaret Ferguson July 23, 1986. They separated in 1992 and were divorced in 1996.

—— *The daughters of that union,*

5. Her Royal Highness **Princess BEATRICE Elizabeth Mary of York,** b. August 8, 1988.
6. Her Royal Highness **Princess EUGENIE Victoria Helena of York,** b. March 23, 1990.

—— *The third son of The Queen,*

7. His Royal Highness The **Prince EDWARD Antony Richard Louis,** b. March 10, 1964. Married Miss Sophie Rhys-Jones June 19, 1999.

—— *The daughter of The Queen,*

8. Her Royal Highness The **Princess ANNE Elizabeth Alice Louise,** Princess Royal, b. August 15, 1950. Married (1) Captain Mark Anthony Peter Phillips, November 14, 1973. The marriage was dissolved April 23, 1992. Married (2) Commander Timothy James Hamilton Laurence, RN, December 12, 1992.

—— *The son and daughter of her first union,*

9. **PETER Mark Andrew Phillips,** b. November 15, 1977.
10. **ZARA Anne Elizabeth Phillips,** b. May 15, 1981.

—— *The sister of The Queen,*

11. The son and daughter of the union of Her Royal Highness The late-Princess MARGARET Rose, Countess of Snowdon, b. August 21, 1930, d. February 10, 2002. Married Mr. Antony Charles Robert Armstrong–Jones, May 6, 1960, later created Earl of Snowdon. The marriage was dissolved July 5, 1978.
12. **DAVID Albert Charles,** Viscount Linley, b. November 3, 1961. Married Hon. Serena Alleyne Stanhope (only daughter of Viscount Petersham, son and heir of the 11th Earl of Harrington) October 8, 1993.
13. Lady **SARAH Frances Elizabeth Chatto,** b. May 1, 1964. Married Daniel Chatto July 14, 1994.

—— *The son of that union,*

14. **SAMUEL David Benedict Chatto,** b. July 28, 1996.

—— *The first cousin of The Queen,*

15. His Royal Highness **Prince RICHARD Alexander Walter George,** Duke of Gloucester, b. August 26, 1944. Married Miss Birgitte Eva Van Deurs (of Denmark) July 8, 1972.

—— *The son and daughters of that union,*

16. **ALEXANDER Patrick Gregers Richard,** Earl of Ulster, b. October 24, 1974.

Buckingham Palace

17. **Lady DAVINA Elizabeth Alice Benedikte Windsor,** b. November 19, 1977.
18. **Lady ROSE Victoria Birgitte Louise Windsor,** b. March 1, 1980.
—— *The first cousin of The Queen,*
19. His Royal Highness **Prince EDWARD George Nicholas Paul Patrick,** Duke of Kent, b. October 9, 1935. Married Miss Katharine Lucy Mary Worsley, June 8, 1961.
—— *The first son of that union,*
   GEORGE Philip Nicholas, Earl of St. Andrews, b. June 26, 1962, is no longer in line of succession having married a Roman Catholic, Miss Sylvana Palma Tomaselli, January 9, 1988.
—— *The son and daughters of that union,*
20. **EDWARD Edmund Maximilian George,** Baron Downpatrick, b. December 2, 1988.
21. **Lady MARINA-CHARLOTTE Alexandra Katharine Helen Windsor,** b. September 30, 1992.
22. **Lady AMELIA Sophia Theodora Mary Margaret Windsor,** b. August 24, 1995.
—— *The second son of the Duke of Kent,*
23. **Lord NICHOLAS Charles Edward Jonathan Windsor,** b. July 25, 1970.
—— *The daughter of the Duke of Kent,*
24. **Lady HELEN Marina Lucy Taylor,** b. April 28, 1964. Married Timothy Verner Taylor, July 18, 1992.
—— *The sons of that union,*
25. **COLUMBUS George Donald Taylor,** b. August 6, 1994.
26. **CASSIUS Edward Taylor,** b. December 26, 1996.

—— His Royal Highness **Prince MICHAEL George Charles Franklin of Kent,** b. July 4, 1942, brother of the Duke of Kent married a Roman Catholic, Baroness Marie Christine von Reibnitz, June 30, 1978, and under the terms of the Act of Settlement of 1701, he is no longer in line of succession to the Throne. The son and daughter of that union, however, remain in the line of succession:
27. **Lord FREDERICK Michael George David Louis Windsor,** b. April 6, 1979.
28. **Lady GABRIELLA Marina Alexandra Ophelia Windsor,** b. April 21, 1981 (known as *Lady Ella*).
—— *The sister of the Duke of Kent,*
29. Her Royal Highness **Princess ALEXANDRA Helen Elizabeth Olga Christabel of Kent,** born December 25, 1936. Married the Honourable Sir Angus James Bruce Ogilvy (second son of the 12th Earl of Airlie), April 24, 1963.
—— *The son of that union,*
30. **JAMES Robert Bruce Ogilvy,** b. February 29, 1964. Married Miss Julia Caroline Rawlinson, July 30, 1988.
—— *The son and daughter of that union,*
31. **ALEXANDER Charles Ogilvy,** b. November 12, 1996.
32. **FLORA Alexandra Ogilvy,** b. December 15, 1994.
—— *The daughter of the union of number 29,*
33. **MARINA Victoria Alexandra Mowatt,** b. July 31, 1966. Married Paul Julian Mowatt, February 2, 1990. They were divorced 1997.
—— *The son and daughter of that union,*
34. **CHRISTIAN Alexander Mowatt,** b. June 6, 1993.
35. **ZENOUSKA May Mowatt,** b. May 26, 1990.

The United Kingdom

Hyde Park Corner, London

that battle … . Modern societies still need myth and ritual. A monarch and his family supply it; there is no magic about a mud–stained politician."

Bagehot had written, "we must not let daylight in upon magic." But in an age of non–deferential journalists and citizens in Britain, royal indiscretions have completely exposed that "magic." In the wake of lurid reports in the tabloid press about marital breakdowns and infidelity within the royal family, the succession to the throne and the very future of the monarchy in Britain are being questioned. The concept of a family monarchy, a Victorian–era notion that granted a symbolic and public role to royal offspring and consorts as well as to the king or queen, has been severely shaken.

Three of Queen Elizabeth II's four children have been unable to sustain a stable first marriage. The year 1992 saw the formal separation of Prince Charles from Diana, a superstar princess who overshadowed the estranged crown prince until her tragic death in Paris in 1997. In 1999 he began appearing in public with his long–time love, Camilla Parker Bowles. In 2001 he deliberately kissed her publicly. No one can predict whether the people would ever accept her: a 1998 MORI poll revealed that only 53% of the public thought he should be allowed to become king if he married her, and a mere 19% were prepared to accept her as queen. Prince Andrew is divorced from Sarah Ferguson. In 1992 Princess Anne, who divorced her first husband, Mark Phillips, became the first top–ranking British royal since King Henry VIII to divorce and remarry. She wed a divorced naval commander, Timothy Laurence. The ceremony had to be held in Scotland because

the Church of England does not condone second marriages. In November 2002 she suffered the indignity of becoming the first member of the royal family to be convicted of a criminal offense since Charles I was beheaded for treason in 1649. Her loose English bull terrier, Dotty, bit two children in Windsor Great Park. Although she drove the kids to the hospital and apologized for her dog's behavior, a judge fined her $620 for violating the Dangerous Dogs Act. Edward waited until 1999 to announce his engagement to Sophie Rhys–Jones, whom he married.

Personal revelations about the royals are dangerously corrosive because an un-elected institution in a democracy depends on the popular will for its legitimacy. Despite this bad publicity, an April 1997 MORI poll revealed that 62% of respondents oppose removing the monarch's constitutional powers, and only 19% support it. A MORI poll in 1996 had already confirmed that the royals still enjoy considerable trust: when voters were offered a choice among 13 candidates for an elected president, the clear favorite was Princess Anne. A 1997 poll taken September 7, the day after Diana's moving funeral and an outpouring of grief that saw 60 million bouquets placed around the royal palaces, revealed that the mood toward the monarchy had changed: 73% of respondents (82% if Diana's eldest son William were to be the next monarch) favored its retention (down from 85–90% a decade earlier); fewer than half thought it would survive the next 50 years; and 39% now think less of the royal family.

An increasingly hostile mood had been shown in the reaction to a fire that caused $90 million worth of damage to Windsor

Castle in 1992. The royal family had invented its name Windsor after this favorite castle in 1917 in order to shed its German name (Saxe–Coburg & Gotha) during the war against Germany. Popular outrage greeted the government's decision to pay the costs of the repair, which were completed beautifully in 1998.

The flames re-ignited the debate over whether the monarch should pay taxes and whether the state should provide annual incomes to the members and staffs of a very wealthy royal family. To quiet the fury, Queen Elizabeth announced that she would pay income taxes amounting to about $4 million annually and about $1.9 million to most members of her family out of her own fortune. She noted in 1997 that the cost of operating the monarchy had fallen by 39% since the beginning of the decade and that the royal yacht, "Britannia," had been decommissioned for financial reasons. It is understandable that on the fortieth anniversary of her coronation she publicly described 1992 as an *annus horribilis*.

Princess Diana's death was one of the few times the Queen was ever personally criticized by the media; she felt obliged to share her grief publicly and to lower the flag at Buckingham Palace to half-mast. After Diana died the royals made a real effort to be more accessible and open. They hired pollsters to help them come closer to the people and to read the public's message. As Elizabeth II admitted: "Read it we must." It appears to be working. In 1996 only 41% of Britons thought that Charles would make a good king; by 1998 that had risen to more than 60%.

The year 2002 was the Jubilee to celebrate Queen Elizabeth II's half-century on the throne. But it was also a year of death. On February 10 Princess Margaret died, and she was followed on March 30 by the most popular royal, the 101-year-old Queen Mother. The splendor of her burial showed that the British public still likes

Prince William

monarchical dignity and theater. But the funeral could not stifle the noisy national debate about the role of an inherited monarchy in a nation that champions democracy and meritocracy. BBC received many critical calls complaining about its cancellation of normal programming. One caller said: "The Queen Mum had 40 people waiting on her, and we taxpayers had to cough up 600,000 quid [ca. $900,000] to support it. What did she do to deserve it, except marry the right bloke 80 years ago?" The family can no longer hide behind the Queen Mother's popularity. As Richard Stott wrote in the *Sunday Mirror*: "They have some painful decisions to make involving money, palaces, lopping off minor royals. The alternative is that within two generations the royal family will be no more."

Parliamentary Government

The seat of power was once the House of Commons, which elected and controlled the prime minister and the cabinet. It debated the great issues of the day and shaped the laws of the land. It was supreme, and no political institution in the entire kingdom can block its will. A century later this was no longer true. The rise of powerful mass parties firmly controlled by party leaders had largely converted the majority in the House of Commons into the tail wagged by the dog in Number 10 Downing Street, the residence of the prime minister. Observers gradually stopped speaking about parliamentary government and began talking first of cabinet government, then prime ministerial government.

The prime minister is not all–powerful. He must face a powerful civil service (collectively called Whitehall), sometimes count his votes carefully in the Commons, and deal with a multitude of quasi–governmental and interest groups. In theory, the British political process is simple; in practice, it is surprisingly haphazard. British governments do at least as much "muddling through" as they command. The need to persuade, coax, beg, threaten or compromise with so many groups and institutions, all with independent standing of some sort, changes the traditional picture of British government, which is centered on the prime minister and cabinet, who can do anything they want. In truth, British government has never been exactly as it appears to be on the surface. While clothed in basically the same institutional garb, the reality of British politics is always changing.

The House of Commons

The House of Commons has 659 Members of Parliament (MPs) elected at either general elections, which must be held at least every five years, or at by–elections, held when a seat falls vacant because of the death or resignation of a member. From the Great Reform Bill of 1832 until the electoral reform of 1970, the suffrage was gradually expanded until all men and women 18 years and older can vote. Also, all citizens of the Republic of Ireland who reside in the United Kingdom are allowed to vote. Compared with American elections, British campaigns are very short.

Usually only about four weeks elapse between the time the prime minister sets the date for new elections and the polling day. Many voters complained that the six–week campaign in 1997, the longest in 70 years, was much too long. The threat of sending MPs out on the hustings with very little notice is a powerful tool of persuasion in the hands of the prime minister. The MP does have certain advantages over the U.S. Congressman at election time: the parties pay the bulk of the campaign expenses. Also, since the MP's constituency has only one–seventh the number of inhabitants as an American congressional district, he or she is able to canvass the voters at their doorstep and get the full blast of public opinion face to face.

MPs are elected by a system that is very simple and controversial: the single–member constituency. The candidate with the most votes in each of the 659 constituencies is elected, even if he or she won fewer than 50% of the votes. This electoral system has the advantage of preventing many parties from gaining seats in parliament. By bolstering the two–party system, proponents say it enhances political stability. Since one or the other of the large parties usually has a majority in the House of Commons, there has never been the need for a formal coalition to rule.

Opponents say that it is undemocratic and unfair because it favors the larger parties by enabling them to win a far higher proportion of parliamentary seats than the percentage of votes they won nationally. For example, in the 1997 election, the Labour Party won 43.1% of the total vote, but received 63.4% of the seats. By winning 30.6% of the vote, the Conservative Party gained 25% of the seats. The Liberal–Social Democratic Alliance, with 16.7% of the total vote won only 7% of the seats. This was nevertheless twice the number of constituencies it had captured in 1992 even though its percentage of the total votes had dropped from 17.9%. It is increasingly common for MPs to be elected with the support of fewer than half the voters; in the House of Commons elected in 1997, 312 of 659 are in this situation. In 1992 a Liberal Democrat, Sir Russell Johnson, won his Inverness constituency with only 26% of the votes.

It is no surprise that the Alliance is strongly in favor of a proportional representation (PR) system, which would award seats in proportion to the total votes won. A 1997 MORI poll revealed that two–thirds of voters agree. The question is: exactly how could this be done?

Virtually every other Western European democracy has some form of PR. Prime Minister Tony Blair confessed before his

House of Commons. View of the Chamber showing the Speaker's Chair, seating for Clerk of the House and assistants.

The United Kingdom

party won a huge majority in 1997, "I personally remain un-persuaded that proportional representation would be beneficial for the Commons." Aside from the obvious fact that his party benefited from the old system, he points out that a fair electoral method must not only reflect opinion, but "it must also aggregate opinion without giving disproportionate influence to splinter groups." This is "particularly important for a parliament whose job is to create and sustain a single, mainstream government." The British political system needs an electoral system that offers voters a clear choice between the governing party, whose performance can be judged, and an opposition party, whose promises can be weighed and considered. The clear distinction between the two sides necessarily discourages third parties and splinter groups from developing.

In 1998 Prime Minister Blair appointed a commission under Lord Jenkins to examine the electoral system but with two stipulations: that the need for "stable government" should be kept in mind and that the link between MPs and their constituencies should be preserved. The conclusion was that a "lack of democracy" would have to be accepted at the national level in the interest of retaining stable, one–party government, while proportional representation could be practiced at the regional and local level. That is exactly what was done in regional elections in Scotland, Wales and Northern Ireland.

The very organization and physical structure of the House of Commons depends upon a government and an opposition, without a wide spectrum of opinion. The House of Commons is arranged in rows of benches facing each other rather than in seats facing the podium. This arrangement encourages debate and questions because members of the opposing parties sit facing each other across an aisle. By ancient custom, and for good reason, the aisle is wide enough so a man may not reach across it with a sword and skewer his opponent during debate. The government sits on the front row to the right of the speaker's throne, and the leaders of the opposition (known also as the "shadow cabinet") sit on the first row to the speaker's left. Because of the massive Labour majority after May 1997, some of its members had to sit on the opposition side. MPs on the lower end of the pecking order in their respective parties sit higher up on the back rows and are therefore called "backbenchers."

The speaker, who since 2000 is Michael Martin, a former sheet-metal-worker, directs the debate. By tradition the speakership alternates between the two main parties, and the new speaker resigns from his

The funeral cortege of Diana, Princess of Wales, proceeds through Hyde Park toward Westminster Abbey.

Photo: Edward Jones

party. But like his predecessor, Betty Boothroyd, Martin is a Labour MP. A former shop steward and son of a stoker, he grew up in poverty in Glasgow. He observed the tradition of feigning reluctance to assume the post and having to be tugged to the speaker's chair, a throwback to the days when speakers were occasionally beheaded because of their uncomfortable position between the Commons and the monarch. When he strides into the chamber, his aides call for the long–standing ritual of respect: "Hats off, strangers!" The speaker has little control of the Commons' business. The Leader of the House, who belongs to the cabinet, organizes this. However, a skillful speaker can protect the prerogatives of the House against the government.

Unlike in the United States, the opposition party in Britain has an alternative cabinet that is pre–selected and ready to assume office at a moment's notice. Indeed, a major strength of British parliamentary democracy is that talented leaders in a government which loses an election still retain their front–row seats in parliament and are therefore kept in reserve until a later date when the electorate's moods change and their services are again desired. This shadow government leads what is known in Britain as "her Majesty's loyal opposition," a concept grounded in the notion that two persons of good will can disagree agreeably on an important issue. In contrast to America, though, the "loyal opposition" has no means of delaying governmental action through filibuster in parliament.

In theory, parliament checks and controls the executive (the prime minister and the cabinet). In practice, it is normal-

ly the other way around. Parliament lacks the facilities to watch over the government competently, and MPs are underpaid, understaffed and under–informed. Despite some recent pay increases, MPs still earn far less than their American counterparts. In 1996 they raised their salary to £43,000 (ca. $67,000), plus $72,000 for secretarial and research assistance. MPs do receive expenses for travel, phoning, postage and housing allowances (if they must maintain two homes). After the 2001 elections the salary for a cabinet minister was raised to the equivalent of about $155,000 and that of the prime minister to the equivalent of $220,000.

Two–thirds continue working at their normal jobs. For centuries until 2002 the hours of the parliamentary sessions had been set from 2:30 p.m. to 10:30 p.m. in order to accommodate that need. Now parliamentary business starts at 11:30 and must be concluded no later than 7:30 p.m. in order for MPs to have a more "family-friendly" schedule. One–third even work for private lobbying firms and other businesses with interest in legislation, something forbidden for U.S. congressmen. They have inadequate office space and receive only a modest sum for secretarial and research assistance while the average American congressman has 16 aides and the average senator 36. With such minuscule staffs, ordinary MPs have great difficulty acquiring sufficient information to challenge the government, which has the entire civil service to provide it with facts.

Unlike the U.S. Congress, the House of Commons does not have a well–developed committee system to do the detailed work which cannot be done on the floor of the House. The ad–hoc "standing committees" have too little expertise and are too large to be truly effective. The smaller "select committees" have a relatively permanent membership, are often chaired by an opposition MP, and do play a more important role. In 1980, new committees were set up to oversee the work of specific ministries and to deal specifically with Scottish and Welsh affairs. There is considerable discussion of reforms to improve the committee structure in the House, but in the absence of successful reforms, it is likely to remain more a forum to debate the important issues of the day than a powerful law–making body. In 1988 the Commons voted to allow television to record its often rowdy deliberations.

It remains the government's job to determine what will be the law of the land. All important legislation, including the budget, is drafted by the government and Whitehall. Since the government determines the order of parliamentary business, its proposals always take priority over those of private members or the opposition. Parliament can make amendments and must give its approval, but the government has numerous ways to insure that its policies will be accepted. First, all MPs are party members, and they jeopardize their careers if they defy their party leaders. Renegades are seldom reelected. Second, as many as 110 MPs are actually members of the government, and all are expected to vote with the government.

Finally, since the very survival of the government depends upon maintaining a majority, MPs are under far greater pressure from the cabinet to support the government than is the case in the U.S. Rigid party discipline on most bills has always been essential in order to make the political system work. MPs are permitted to "vote their conscience" on moral issues, such as abortion, capital punishment, and gun control. The demand for the latter became very strong after a deranged man charged into a Scottish primary school in Dunblane with four high–powered rifles in 1996 and massacred 16 children and their teacher. Prime Minister Blair announced in May 1997 that Labour MPs would be free to vote on this question as they think right.

Control by the government is much less effective than it once was. From 1945 to 1970 no government lost a vote of the full House of Commons. The 1970s brought a significant change. The Conservative government of Edward Heath suffered defeat in parliament six times. Before 1970 it would have been unthinkable for a government so defeated to remain in office, but he returned to the 19th century practice of resigning only upon losing a declared vote of no confidence. The

Labour government that ruled from 1974 until 1979 suffered 23 such defeats, and Thatcher was defeated twice. The fact that the MPs can now often vote against the government without bringing it down encourages backbenchers to revolt without severely endangering their careers. The days are over when the backbenchers automatically vote as their leaders order.

The House of Lords

Great Britain is a monarchy, and it should therefore not be surprising that its aristocracy continues to enjoy certain political privileges. These are institutionalized in the upper house of parliament, the House of Lords. Of the 1,164 members (known as the "peers") 650 had hereditary titles until 1999. This meant that all the offspring of these peers who inherited the titles would automatically be entitled to a seat in the House of Lords. These titles range, in order of precedence, from Duke, Marquess, Earl, Viscount and Baron, all except Dukes being commonly addressed as "Lord." Some of these peerages have ancient origins, such as the Marquis of Salisbury or the Duke of Norfolk, but half the hereditary peerages were created in the 20th century "for services to the nation." No new hereditary peerages were created after 1964 until Prime Minister Thatcher ennobled senior minister William Whitelaw and retiring Speaker of the Commons George Thomas.

A law of 1958 creating "life peers" set an irreversible trend. Such peers are appointed for their learning or their distinguished public service. However, after they die, their heirs cannot claim their seats. Among the life peers named in 1997 was composer (now Baron) Andrew Lloyd Webber. Sir Paul McCartney (now

a knight) and "Dynasty" star Joan Collins (now an Officer of the Order of the British Empire) were not awarded peerages. The House of Lords in 1999 consisted of 650 peers by inheritance, about a dozen law lords (who form the highest appellate court in the land), 26 Church of England Bishops and 514 life peers. Among the life peers are 67 peeresses, compared with 120 women in the House of Commons after the 1997 elections.

As the democratic wave caused a steady expansion of the franchise in the 19th and 20th centuries, the powers of the House of Lords came under increasing attack. In the Parliament Acts of 1911 and 1949, its veto right was taken away; now the only kind of bill it can veto is one to prolong the life of parliament beyond five years. Also, its power to delay legislation was reduced; it can now hold up bills for 13 months at the most (only 30 days for a financial bill). Until the Thatcher era, it seldom exercised its power out of fear that if it fully used its powers, it would ultimately lose them.

The Labour Party has long sought "to abolish the undemocratic House of Lords as quickly as possible." One of Labour's most influential leftists even renounced his title of Viscount Stansgate, giving up his right to sit in the House of Lords. He also shortened his name from Anthony Wedgewood Benn III to the more proletarian Tony Benn. One cannot say, however, that he "put his money where his mouth is" because he did not renounce his considerable fortune.

Labour's dislike for this body was understandable in view of the fact that the Conservative Party enjoyed a permanent majority in it. However, when one looks only at the 300 or so peers who regularly

Queen Elizabeth II with six former prime ministers celebrate the 250th anniversary of 10 Downing Street as the official residence of the Prime Minister.

The United Kingdom

attend the sessions and do the actual work, the Conservative majority is only about five to four. An even closer look at those Tory lords reveals that many of them are what Thatcher derisively called "wets": those in her party who disagreed with many of her hard–line economic policies on the grounds that they widened the gulf between rich and poor. A prime minister has no control over them.

In normal times, opposition to the prime minister's policies is exercised in the House of Commons. But Thatcher so dominated that body until 1990 that another institution performed that function: the House of Lords. Said one Labour Lord in 1988: "It hurts to admit it, but on many issues we are the government's only real opposition." A Liberal baroness added: "As an un-elected body, it would obviously be quite improper for us to try to kill a bill outright. But there is nothing to stop us from being an utter nuisance to the government. We call it playing Ping–Pong—holding up a bill for so long that the government is compelled to accept our amendments just to get the thing passed." In fact, by 1988 Thatcher had suffered 107 defeats in the House of Lords, compared with only two in the House of Commons!

Why is such a privileged house, to which no one is elected, retained in a democratic country? In fact, debates in the House of Lords are at least as well informed and much less partisan than in the lower house. In order to demonstrate this fact, debates in the upper house began to be televised in 1985. The lords' main job is to examine and to revise bills that have proceeded too hastily through the House of Commons. With such experienced peers, the most active of whom had already distinguished themselves in all walks of life outside parliament, the lords perform an important function in improving legislation. Also, the fact that the most active lords are persons of great prestige and influence in British society means that no government systematically ignores the House of Lords.

Supported two–to–one in a 1997 MORI poll, Tony Blair's Labour government moved swiftly to enact its campaign promise to remove "the absurdity of the hereditary element." He appointed a royal commission that produced a white paper in 1999. It recommended that the hereditary peers' right to sit and vote be removed, that the nomination of life peers be accomplished through an independent appointments committee (not the prime minister), that some be indirectly elected by bodies such as the new regional assemblies, and that longer–term reform be considered.

To move this reform through the legislative process, Blair agreed to a compromise with the Tory leader in the House of Lords: 92 hereditary peers were permitted to stay until a final second–stage reform of the house could be undertaken; over 500 life peers retained their seats. In 2003, his government tried to complete the reform, but it failed. The prime minister favored an all-appointed House of Lords as the best way of insuring that it would not challenge the primacy of the all-elected House of Commons, and the lords supported this 335 to 110. But the House of Commons rejected all seven different options, ranging from a wholly elected to an entirely appointed body, with various hybrids in between. The only thing that was clear was that most MPs want a large elected component in the second chamber even though they narrowly rejected a fully-elected House of Lords by 289 to 272. Lacking any consensus, the question was sent to a joint committee of both houses to try to find a way forward.

Prime Ministerial Government

The nerve center of British politics is "the government," a collective term to describe the prime minister, the 16 to 23 cabinet ministers and the parliamentary secretaries or junior ministers, a team which may total from 70 to 110 members.

In theory, the prime minister is the 'first among equals' within the governing team. But as a senior Whitehall official noted at the end of the 20th century: "The idea that the prime minister is primus inter pares is wrong. The prime minister is not pares. He's way above that. Like Caesar he bestrides the world like a colossus." The prime minister is the leader of the party that has a majority (or at least a plurality) in the House of Commons. Thus, the holder of this highest office is a MP who has worked his or her way upward through the legislative system. The average prime minister has served a quarter of a century in the House of Commons. It is virtually inconceivable that a stranger to the national capital, such as Jimmy Carter, Ronald Reagan, Bill Clinton, or George W. Bush, could become prime minister. In actuality, the powers of the post are so great that the description 'first among equals' is misleading.

The prime minister's powers, which are almost nowhere clearly spelled out in statute, strike the American as sweeping. As the nation's chief executive, chief legislator and chief administrator he is the primary focus of political attention. After the election, he is rather free to appoint and dismiss cabinet members, thereby largely determining the broad political direction the government will take. The convention of 'collective responsibility' prevents his ministers from criticizing him in public, and the tradition of secrecy

shields many of his decisions and actions from the public eye. He decides on the agenda for cabinet meetings and appoints the cabinet committees, which prepare government policies or deal with crises and carry out most ministerial business. For example, in 1982 Thatcher formed a 'war cabinet' to manage the Falklands crisis; she also had influential committees for economic, foreign and defense, domestic, and legislative policy. Such grand committees have subcommittees. There are no votes taken in cabinet meetings, and the prime minister interprets the sense of the cabinet.

Regardless of how the debate in the secret cabinet meetings might have gone, he can always announce the meaning in a way which conforms to his own views. As ex–Labour cabinet member Richard Crossman revealed, any prime minister who is subordinate to the cabinet is "consciously refusing to make use of the powers which now constitutionally belong to the office." In practice, most issues are decided either in Whitehall or in cabinet committees and are not even discussed in full cabinet meetings, which are normally held twice a week, including each Thursday morning. The modern cabinet is increasingly a reporting and reviewing body and less and less an executive one. Crossman was correct. Collective decision-making has been replaced by a system in which ministers have been reduced to agents of their leader, forced to deal with him bilaterally rather than as part of a collectively responsible group.

The prime minister selects new peers to the House of Lords. He directs the nation's sizable civil service. He determines the country's foreign and defense policies and can commit Britain to a policy that the cabinet and Commons can do little to alter. He can even enter treaties with foreign nations that need not be approved by parliament; foreign policy was a 'royal prerogative' which was never passed to parliament, although a prime minister does customarily discuss with it treaties and declarations of war. Finally, as leader and chief strategist for the national party, he alone can decide the date of the general election and thus determine when the entire government and Commons must face the voters. He is burdened neither by separation of powers nor by a federal structure. No American president wields such power.

Limitations on the Prime Minister

A closer look at the contemporary British political system reveals that the prime minister's power is far more restricted that initially meets the eye. Although he appoints and dismisses the cabinet members, he can hardly lord over them. Unlike most American cabinet members, the British ones are highly experienced and influential parliament members with whom the prime minister has usually worked for many years. He cannot scout the country for talented individuals whose main responsibility is to carry out the chief executive's policy; he can only choose from his close colleagues in parliament who have powerful political bases of their own in the party and in the nation. He thus does not deal with minions, but with powerful political office–holders, who would be far less afraid to stand up to him in private.

He must retain the confidence of the most important factions within the parliamentary majority party. He must inevitably take into the cabinet some persons who disagree with him on some fundamental issues. This has tended to weaken the convention of cabinet solidarity. In the 1970s Labour prime ministers suspended it twice so that certain ministers could express themselves freely. Thatcher had to cope with scarcely concealed criticism from those within her own cabinet whom she dubbed "wets." John Major lost the 1997 elections in part because he never succeeded in silencing Tory colleagues who opposed his policy toward Europe. Finally, since 1999 he must deal with regionally–elected parliaments in Scotland, Wales, Northern Ireland, and since 2000 a Greater London Assembly.

It is often argued that the prime minister enjoys the advantage of not having to direct huge ministries, as cabinet members do. Therefore, he is freer to deal with larger political questions. To some extent, this is true, but the other side of the coin is that he lacks manageable administrative backing. He has no department to provide him with independent analyses and advice. His "private office" at his residence, Number 10 Downing Street, is too small. More valuable to him is the "cabinet office," headed by a top civil servant, which organizes the agenda for cabinet discussions. Thatcher established a "policy unit" at Number 10 composed of some expert advisers. Yet these specialists were no match for the massed expertise available to departmental ministers. Thus, the quality of the prime minister's information is not generally better than that of his cabinet members.

He must deal with a complicated network of ministries and departments with diverse views and a good deal of autonomy in their own areas of responsibility. By American standards, there is virtually no "spoils system" in British politics. The prime minister is able to send to each ministry only one minister and one to three parliamentary secretaries. But when

they arrive, often with little or no detailed experience in the particular areas of responsibilities and with no staffs of their own, they are faced with a permanent secretary, the senior civil servant of his department with several decades of experience. He and his subordinate civil servants have the facts at their fingertips and brief the minister.

Although it is his job merely to give technical advice and let the minister set the political direction, it is but a short step from persuasively "giving the facts" to actually determining departmental policy. Usually continuity, not change, wins out. New policies must be negotiated with these bodies, not simply imposed upon them. Nevertheless, if the minister comes to clear, firm decisions, then his officials will almost always carry them out.

Bureaucracy and the Civil Service

As in all advanced countries, much of the work which used to be done by leading politicians has now been delegated to the civil service, which numbers about 640,000 bureaucrats. Most do not actually work in Whitehall, that small area in London where the chief administrative buildings are located. Britain is fortunate to have civil servants who generally work efficiently, who are almost entirely uncorrupted and whose decisions usually arise not from personal or political reasons, but from good administrative ones.

Personnel are frequently criticized because they, the top people, come from too narrow a social background and because they operate under a blanket of secrecy. It remains essentially true that the top 3,500 administrators are drawn heavily from the "Oxbridge" (Oxford and Cambridge) universities after having received a generalist's education, despite the fact that the three–class hierarchy was replaced in 1971 by a single, open structure. The recruitment system remains largely unchanged.

Not only the cabinet, but the top 3,500 or so civil servants must take oaths of secrecy. Among cabinet ministers, this convention is breaking down somewhat, as they leak information to the press or write revealing memoirs. The civil servants' oath makes it a crime to disclose any official information, whether it is classified or not; he is bound to remain silent for life.

A vigorous campaign has been launched by a variety of groups to punch some holes in this screen of secrecy by adopting a law similar to the U.S. Freedom of Information Act. One hole appeared in 1991 when for the first time the newly appointed chief of the MI5 counterespionage service, Stella Rimington (the first woman ever to occupy the

post), was identified by name; this agency, as well as Secret Intelligence Service (SIS, formerly know as MI6), which deals with foreign intelligence, has long inspired the imagination of thriller writers. When a disgruntled former MI6 agent, Richard Tomlinson, put the names of more than a hundred British secret agents on the World Wide Web in 1999, British security officials conceded that the Internet is so far–flung that no government can control the flow of information on it.

Despite the Official Secrets Act and tradition, the British news media have always been an important check on governmental power. Britain has more newspapers per capita than any other country. Nevertheless, Prime Minister Blair has vowed that his government will introduce a Freedom of Information Act, a reform with the backing of three–fourths of the population, according to a 1997 poll.

Acts of parliament usually merely establish the basic principles of law, and the civil service fills in the details. Bureaucratic regulations now vastly outnumber actual laws, as is the case in the United States. Traditionally, the Treasury, led by the Chancellor of the Exchequer (Treasury minister), has been the main coordinator of the many departments and ministries. Since it was responsible for the budgets of the various departments, it gained the right to comment on any policy proposal from any department. There is some skepticism about the Treasury's ability to oversee and review all policy effectively. But if anybody is master of Whitehall, it is the Treasury and not the cabinet as a whole.

In addition to the huge bureaucracy, the prime minister must deal with a maze of so–called "quasi–autonomous non–governmental organisations," mercifully shortened to "quangos." Depending on how wide the net is thrown, these organizations number up to 5,521 and include such bodies as the Arts Council, the University Grants Committee, the Commission for Racial Equality, the BBC, Trustees of National Museums and the nationalized industries. Many are purely advisory, but some dispense large sums of money. All consider themselves to be more or less autonomous, but most are financed, and most members are named, by the central government, usually by a department of Whitehall. The government can sometimes force these "quangos" to comply with overall policies by giving or withholding grants, but it frequently faces stiff opposition and must often modify its policies in order to win compliance. They have taken over many services formerly performed by local authorities.

Alongside the "quangos" are especially important interest groups that have

The United Kingdom

semi–official status with the government or with various ministries. They include the Church of England, the universities and the umbrella organizations for the unions and industry—the Trade Union Congress (TUC) and the Confederation of British Industry (CBI). The latter is the largest employers' association in the world, with a highly professional bureaucracy. Sometimes the government is driven to very close negotiations with one of these. From 1974 to 1978 the Labour government agreed to a "social contract" with the unions, swapping legal concessions and price restraints for limits on wage increases. More often, the government tries to conduct "tripartite" negotiations with both the TUC and the CBI to maintain economic stability. The fatal flaw in this effort is that the CBI and the TUC (whose constituent unions are autonomous and therefore negotiate their own wage agreements and decide when to strike) cannot bind their members to whatever agreements are reached under the auspices of the government.

The Judiciary

Another limitation on the government's power, which has long been one of the chief cornerstones of British liberty, has been an independent judiciary. Political leaders are forbidden to obstruct the judicial process, even though judges make decisions that significantly influence politics. As with most other aspects of the British public life, the legal structure is fragmented and complicated. There are different court systems: one for England and Wales, one for Northern Ireland and one for Scotland, which has always retained its own separate, Roman–based legal system. There are different layers of courts. At the pinnacle are the 10 to 12 Lords of Appeal (known as the "Law Lords"), who sit in the House of Lords and who, constituted as the Judicial Committee of the Privy Council, can even hear appeals from some parts of the British Commonwealth.

Usually the Law Lords' hearings are dry and poorly attended; they involve less pomp and ritual than does the U.S. Supreme Court. But the eyes of the world were on them in 1998–9, when former Chilean leader, General Augusto Pinochet, went to Britain for medical treatment. While there, Spain and other European countries demanded his extradition because of his alleged international human rights violations. He claimed immunity as a former head of state and current member of the Chilean senate, so the Law Lords were asked for a ruling. Normally these jurists do not have reputations for their political leanings, as do American Supreme Court justices, but

View of London across the Thames, with "Big Ben" (right)

their politics became an issue in the long legal battle. In the end, they rendered seven judgments that revealed differing interpretations on points of law. Nevertheless, they ruled that Pinochet could be extradited to Spain to face charges of torture, but only for those acts committed after December 1988 when Britain implemented the 1984 Torture Convention.

Much of criminal law and most civil law in Britain does not come from acts of parliament, but instead from "common law." Unlike "civil law," which most European democracies have, "common law" is based on tradition, a slow development of rules based on previous cases ("precedents") which are reported in writing, indexed and published in an elaborate system for reference. It is law made by judge and jury. In order to make legal language more comprehensible for litigants, civil courts eliminated Latin legal terms from proceedings in 1999, replacing them with plain English.

Britain's tradition of parliamentary supremacy excludes the possibility of "judicial review," such as exists in the United States. This would permit the courts to overturn acts of parliament on the ground that they were unconstitutional. This was theoretically impossible since no body could be superior to parliament. That ended in 2000. A kind of individual bill of rights went into effect by incorporating into British law the European Convention for the Protection of Human Rights and Fundamental Freedoms (often referred to as "the European Human Rights Charter" or EHRC). This convention includes such protections as rights for criminal defendants and freedom of speech, religion and assembly. These are rights that have been recognized for centuries under common law. To these freedoms is now added a defendable right of privacy.

A half century earlier, British jurists had played a leading part in drafting the charter, and it has applied to British citizens since the UK entered the EU in 1973. But it was not enforceable in British courts. That has changed. Parliament should not make laws that violate the EHRC. Judges still do not have the right of judicial review, that is, the right to strike down legislation. However, they can now make a "declaration of incompatibility" when British laws conflict with the EHRC. Parliament or the government must determine whether the "incompatible" statue can remain. The government can by-pass parliament by amending the law by statutory instrument. Although the legislative and executive branches have the last say, political pressure is very strong to bring any law in line with the European charter.

Only a small part of the governing of Britain is carried out by parliamentary acts. Ministers, civil servants, local government authorities and "quangos" must use discretion in applying general laws to concrete situations, and it is precisely this discretion that can be checked by the courts. In the 1970s a group of parents took the minister responsible for education to court on the charge that the way in which he had applied the school reform was illegal, and the court ruled in their favor. In order to deal with concrete cases, judges must decide what the laws mean. It is in such interpretation that judges have most of their power; the whole thrust of a law can be changed or bent by judges. One might ask "who needs judicial review?" when judges have this kind of power.

As in the United States, there is much controversy over the question of whether the courts have too much power and whether they are, in fact, political. There can be no question that judges' ability to assess the propriety of ministerial actions opens up another course of action to persons who oppose the government's policy. Of course, if parliament does not like what the courts are doing, it could make new laws that are clearer and more specific, but parliament has taken that step only once since 1945. It is far too busy to monitor the judges' use of their discretionary power. Whether one likes it or not, the impact of judicial interpretations will remain political and will continue to place limits on governmental power. However, judicial restraint still prevails in Britain to a greater degree than in the United States.

Local Government

Largely because of historical circumstances, the United Kingdom is a unitary, not a federal state. That is, it is not a collection of "united states." Unlike the United States of America, the UK was not consciously created by sovereign states that carefully retained important powers. The English conquered Wales militarily in the 12th century; it was politically integrated with England in 1536. The thrones of England and Scotland were united in 1603, and the process of union was completed in 1707. The question of succession to the throne led to Anglo–Scottish conflict in 1715 and 1745, which culminated in the occupation of Scotland by English armies. Ireland was simply taken by force, and the six northern counties remained in the United Kingdom in 1922, when the southern 26 counties became independent.

Therefore, the British government is, in theory, freed from the problems of getting its policies accepted by powerful states or provinces. This centralization would seem to fit well with the land and its people—it is a small country, no bigger than the state of Oregon, with a population of 59 million. It is highly urbanized, with 40% of the population living in only seven urban centers that account for less than 4% of the total land area.

London, with a population of seven million (over 15% of the United Kingdom's total), is seven times larger than the second largest city, Birmingham. Only four other cities have more than half a million inhabitants: Liverpool, Manchester, Sheffield and Leeds. Unlike Washington, New York, Ottawa or many national capitals, London is simultaneously the center of government, finance, the mass media and the arts. Nearly three–quarters of the people who earned a place in Who's Who live within a 65–mile radius of London. Half the MPs never resided in their constituencies before their election, and many of these are from London. Further, most ambitious civil servants climb the career ladder in London.

Nevertheless, unitary government does not mean that orders from Number 10 Downing Street, Westminster, or Whitehall are automatically carried out in all corners of the UK. There are many institutions that give much scope for local resistance to central authority. Let us look first at local government.

It is not a surprise that, like most other British political and legal institutions, the structure of local government is diverse and highly complicated. In 1974 a reorganized structure of local government came into effect in an attempt to produce a fairly uniform pattern throughout the entire kingdom. This reform scarcely made the structure of local government easier for the foreigner to understand. To begin with, local government still differs in England, Wales, Scotland and Northern Ireland. In the first three, there are two tiers of administration, each with elected councils, taxing authority and its own powers. The top tier (composed generally in England of metropolitan or county councils, and in Scotland of nine regional councils) and the lower tier (composed of borough, or district councils) together provide schools, local roads, government–owned housing (known as "council housing"), and an array of services, such as buses, garbage pickup, libraries, swimming pools and (except in London) police protection.

These two tiers often clash with each other, especially in metropolitan areas. To muddle things even more, there is usually even a third tier composed of parish or community councils with powers of their own. In all, there are more than 14,000 local governments in Britain! These local units provide for about half of their own expenses through local property taxes (known as "rates") and fees for services. They employ almost three million people (over 12% of the total work force), far more than the central government.

Former Prime Minister Thatcher locked horns with local authorities. In 1988 she sought to abolish the existing system of local taxes, based on the size and value of personal property, and to replace it with a flat–rate levy, or community charge, which would spread the tax burden to residents of all incomes. Opponents said this was regressive and unfair, while she said that by spreading taxes evenly, the new tax would bring pressure to bear on local councils, many of which are dominated by Labourites, to reduce their budgets. Thus, a motive to modernize the tax system was mingled with one to reduce the opposition's power even further. So unpopular was this flat–rate levy that it helped lead to her downfall in 1990.

She also moved to abolish the metropolitan councils, at least in part because some of them had become centers of leftist power. These included the Greater London Council (GLC) and what was sometimes derisively referred to in Tory circles as the "Socialist Republic of Yorkshire." While eliminating the GLC in her 1986 reform, the elected councils in London's 32 administrative areas, such as Kensington and Chelsea, Westminster, and Lambeth and Hackney, continued to exist. Within days of assuming office in May 1997 Prime Minister Blair proposed a referendum for Londoners to create an elected government and mayor.

In 1998, 72% voted in favor of a directly-elected mayor, and in May 2000 self-proclaimed socialist Ken Livingston, running as an independent, was elected

Feeding the pigeons, Trafalgar Square, London

The United Kingdom

Siambr y Tŷ

Dyluniwyd Siambr bresennol Tŷ'r Cyffredin gan y diweddar Syr Giles Gilbert Scott ac fe'i hagorwyd ym 1950. Cymerodd le'r Siambr a ddyluniwyd gan Syr Charles Barry, a ddefnyddiwyd gyntaf gan Dŷ'r Cyffredin ym 1852, ac a ddinistriwyd gan fomio'r Almaenwyr ym 1941. Cafodd aelodau Tŷ'r Cyffredin eu cartref parhaol cyntaf ym 1547, pan neilltuwyd Capel San Steffan ar eu cyfer. Fe'i defnyddiwyd gan y Tŷ tan 1834, pan gafodd ei ddinistrio gan y tân a ddifaodd Balas San Steffan bron yn llwyr. Gorosoedd rhan isaf capel San Steffan y tân, ac fe'i hadnabyddir bellach fel 'Capel y Crypt'. Ar yr union safle hwn y lleolir Neuadd San Steffan, y bydd ymwelwyr yn cael mynediad trwyddi i'r Cyntedd Canolog, ac mae hi'r un maint â'r hen Siambr.

O ran ei ffurf a'i maintioli mae'r Siambr bresennol bron yn atgynhyrchiad o Siambr Barry, er bod ei haddurniadau'n llai cywrain, a bod orielau mwy wedi'u darparu ar gyfer ymwelwyr. Ehangiad yw trefniadau eistedd cyffredinol y Tŷ mewn gwirionedd ar y trefniadau eistedd a ddefnyddid bedwar can mlynedd a rhagor yn ôl yng Nghapel San Steffan, pan fyddai'r Aelodau'n eistedd yn eisteddleoedd y côr a phan safai Cadair y Llefarydd ar risiau'r allor. Mae 650 o Aelodau Seneddol; ond ceir eisteddleoedd (gan gynnwys yr orielau ochr) ar gyfer 437 yn unig. Mae'r cyfyngiad hwn yn fwriadol; nid fforwm ar gyfer areithiau gosod mo'r Tŷ; i raddau helaeth mae'r trafodaethau'n ymddiddanol yn eu hanfod; ac ar gyfer llawer ohonynt – rhai arbenigol dros ben o ran themâu, neu o natur rigolaidd – ychydig o Aelodau a fydd yn bresennol, a llawer o'r lleill yn brysur â dyletswyddau Seneddol eraill ym Mhalas San Steffan. Gan hynny mae Siambr fach ac agos atoch yn fwy cyfleus. I'r gwrthwyneb, ar achlysuron o bwys, pan fydd y Tŷ yn llawn a phan fydd rhaid i'r Aelodau eistedd yn y rhodfeydd neu ymgasglu o amgylch Cadair y Llefarydd, ger y Bar ac yn yr orielau ochr, cryfheir drama'r Senedd ac yng ngeiriau Syr Winston Churchill, ceir 'ymdeimlad o dorf ac o frys'.

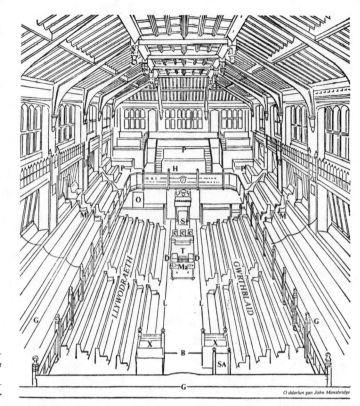

O ddarlun gan John Mansbridge

Ymgorfforwyd mwyaduron yn y gwaith coed yng nghefn pob mainc. O bwyso yn ôl ychydig yn hytrach na phwyso ymlaen gall ymwelwyr glywed yn well.

Arddangosir gwybodaeth am yr hyn sy'n digwydd yn y Tŷ ar setiau monitor teledu yn ymyl y ffenestri yn yr Orielau ochr.

Gellir cael ffurflen archebu ar gyfer prynu Adroddiad Swyddogol (Hansard) eisteddiad y dydd drwy'r post oddi wrth y Porthorion neu o'r Swyddfa Archebion Mynediad.

Os oes arnoch angen rhagor o wybodaeth ynglŷn â'ch ymweliad, neu am waith y Tŷ'n gyffredinol, ffoniwch y Swyddfa Hysbysrwydd (01-219 4273).

S	Mr Llefarydd	T	Bwrdd y Tŷ	SA	Rhingyll Arfau
P	Orielau'r Wasg	D	Blychau Gohebiaeth	M	Orielau'r Aelodau
H	Gohebwyr *Hansard*	Ma	Brysgyll †	G	Orielau'r Ymwelwyr
O	Blwch Swyddogion y Llywodraeth (ymgynghorwyr a Gweinidogion)	L	Llinellau ‡		
C	Clercod y Tŷ*	B	Bar y Tŷ		
		X	Meinciau Traws		

*Pan fydd y Tŷ'n Pwyllgora, bydd y Llefarydd yn ymadael â'r Gadair a'r Cadeirydd yn eistedd yng nghadair Clerc y Tŷ, sef yr un ar y chwith.   † Pan fydd y Tŷ'n Pwyllgora, rhoddir y Brysgyll "islaw'r Bwrdd" ar fracedi.   ‡ Llinellau nad oes hawl gan Aelodau gamu drostynt tra byddant yn siarad o'r meinciau blaen.

Welsh description of House of Commons

London's mayor. He is known as "Red Ken" because of his outspoken opposition to Thatcher and his earlier policies as GLC head of declaring the capital a nuclear-free zone, making common cause with IRA supporters, and backing gay rights. He vowed to rid Trafalgar Square of pigeons, which he described as "rats with feathers." In 2003 he launched a revolutionary program to diminish central London's traffic congestion, among the world's worst. Every private automobile and truck driving into an eight-square-mile area in the heart of the city on weekdays between 7 a.m. and 6:30 p.m. must pay an equivalent of $8 per day for the privilege. The proceeds are spent on public transport projects. Even Blair had called him and his colleagues as a "ragbag of Trotskyists" and threw him out of the Labour Party a couple months before the election. The Labour and Conservative parties each won nine seats in the new 25-seat Greater London Assembly.

Sometimes strong–armed measures toward local governments do work, depending largely on the skill and determination of the prime minister. Nevertheless, it would be more accurate to describe the overall relationship in terms of bargaining between interdependent levels of government.

Island Governments

The United Kingdom includes certain island groups, such as the outer Hebrides, Orkney and Shetland, which have more local authority than county, district or metropolitan county councils on the mainland. For instance, Shetland controls oil developments in its own territory and has launched a strong movement toward total internal autonomy. The Isle of Man in the Irish Sea and the partly French–speaking bailiwicks of Guernsey and Jersey off the French coast already have autonomous legal status, Norman–based legal systems, their own parliaments and governments which control domestic, fiscal and economic policy. They are quaint anomalies in that they are not part of the UK, but are Crown dependencies.

The Channel Islands had been occupied by 30,000 Germans during World War II. In 1993 embarrassing evidence was released that islanders had collaborated with, profited from, or slept with the German masters. In one notorious incident in 1942, local authorities helped the Germans identify 2,100 Jews and English–born residents to be deported to camps in Germany. These revelations reopened old wounds and prompted Britons to think about how they might have reacted if Hitler's forces had overrun the entire country.

Wales, Scotland and Northern Ireland

The three large regions on the outer fringe of the United Kingdom comprise less than a fifth of the UK's total population: Wales (2.9 million), Scotland (5.1 million) and Northern Ireland (1.6 million). These populations compare with 48.7 million in England. Until 1999 all were, in varying degrees, Celtic in background and relatively poor economically. All three were ruled by departments of the central government: the Wales Office, the Scottish Office and the Northern Ireland Office, each with a mini–Whitehall at its disposal. The prime minister appointed a secretary of state for each, and these politicians, who never come from the areas they control, sat in the cabinet.

H.R.H. The Prince of Wales

Although these regions' relations with London have rarely been smooth, regionalism was seldom a major factor in British politics. The differences were masked by a common language, the facade of unitary government and economic prosperity. This changed dramatically in the 1970s. Strapped with a disproportionate number of dying industries and unhappy with the remoteness of central government, nationalist parties in Wales and Scotland grew. At the end of the century Westminster transferred important powers to these regions. "Devolution," which resulted in all three having their own elected parliaments in 1999, represents a historic shift in the way Britain is governed.

Wales

Wales is technically a principality whose titular ruler is the Prince of Wales, who is always the heir apparent to the English throne. It lost all traces of political identity through the Act of Union with England in 1535. However, its social integration with England proceeded much more slowly. English was the language of the government after 1535, but until the 19th century the Welsh language, which is a Celtic dialect related to Irish, Scottish and Breton, was spoken by a majority of the people. Now only one–fifth of the Welsh population speaks it, mainly in rural areas and small towns in North Wales, but one–third claims to have "some understanding" of the language. Welsh speakers form a majority in outlying areas in the West inhabited by only 10% of the population.

Unlike Scotland, it was the preservation of the language, more than independence from England, which fired the Welsh

nationalist movement in the 1970s. Lacking its own aristocracy, the Welsh always tended to be somewhat more egalitarian in their outlook. The coal mining and basic industry, especially in the more populous South Wales have always made it a Labour Party stronghold. In 1978 London offered both Wales and Scotland regional assemblies whose powers would have fallen short of American state legislatures. But in a 1979 referendum, Welshmen rejected such an assembly by a margin of four–to–one, largely because of the revulsion English–speaking Welshmen felt toward the pretensions of the Welsh–speaking minority.

To help satisfy Welsh nationalist urges, Welsh–language schools were established, and by 1984 they numbered 344 primary and 36 secondary schools. The result is that for the first time since reliable statistics have been taken, the proportion of children who speak Welsh is rising: Between 1982 and 1996 the proportion of children aged three to 15 who speak Welsh grew from 18% to 24%. Second, a separate Welsh–language television channel was established (*Sianel Pedwar Cymru*—channel four—S4C), which, due to the small viewing audience, is one of the most expensive television channels in the world. Finally, the Welsh Language Act of 1993, which declared that Welsh and English were to be considered "on a basis of equality," enabled Welsh speakers to be more insistent that Welsh be spoken more. Language disputes are nevertheless mild compared with Belgium or Quebec.

Welsh nationalism is alive though not robust. A nationalist party, *Plaid Cymru* (pronounced "Plide Cumry"), founded in the 1920s amid anti–English feeling, no longer talks much about an independent Wales with a seat in the United Nations since most citizens do not want that. A pressure group, the Independent Wales Movement, was organized in 2000 outside Plaid's ranks. It is more exuberantly nationalist, forcing Plaid leader, Ieuan Wyn Jones, to speak of "full national status" for Wales. He explains that this means the same standing as Ireland has within the EU. It settled for the referendum leading to an elected Welsh Assembly. In 1997 a razor–thin majority in Wales, with only half the eligible voters participating, voted in favor of its first elected parliament in nearly 600 years. Its powers are more limited than those of the new Scottish Parliament. It cannot change acts of Westminster, pass its own laws, nor raise taxes. It can decide how to spend the budget formerly administered by the Welsh Office, including for health and education, and scrutinize and alter the administration of Wales.

In May 1999 the first elections were held, and the Labour Party captured 35.4% of the votes and 28 of the 60 seats. *Plaid Cyrmu* garnered 30.5% and 17 seats, while the Tories won 16.5% and nine seats and the Liberal Democrats 12.6% and six seats. It used a new electoral system modeled on that of Germany: each voter has two votes, the first for his preferred representative (called Member of the Welsh Parliament—MWP) in the 40 constituencies and one for the party of his choice. Thus it is a combination of Britain's "first–past–the–post" system and proportional representation. Secretary of State for Welsh Affairs Alun Michael of the Labour Party handed over his powers to himself in his new capacity as first secretary of the Welsh Assembly. In 2000 Labour's popular Rhodri Morgan was elected as first minister.

In the May 2003 Welsh elections, the first since devolution, voters decided that Labour still best represented their interests, giving it 36.6% of their votes in a low turnout of 38.2%. *Plaid Cymru* slid downward by 10.8%, winning only 19.7% and 12 seats. The Conservatives almost overtook the Welsh nationalists, winning 19.2%, and the Liberal Democrats garnered 11.7%. The weakened *Plaid Cymru* has shelved the question of ultimate independence and will deal with it at a later date, perhaps at a constitutional convention.

Scotland

Scotland, which is still a kingdom in its own right, joined England by agreement in 1707. Although the Scottish parliament voted itself out of existence at that time, other institutions remained intact, such as the legal system, based on Roman law, a distinctive educational system and a Presbyterian Church of Scotland. By long–standing custom, the Queen worships as a Presbyterian in Scotland and as an Episcopalian in England! One should therefore not wonder at the fact that the Scots have a secure sense of separate national identity that has survived union with England.

Scottish nationalist feeling has simmered for two and a half centuries, but the intensity and strength surged furiously in the 1970s when oil was discovered in the North Sea off Scotland's coasts. The Scottish Nationalist Party (SNP), founded in 1928, argued that "It's Scotland's Oil!" and that it would make this relatively poor region in the UK wealthy and capable of independence. In the 1974 parliamentary elections, its vote surged to 30%. In the face of such rising nationalism in their traditional party stronghold, the ruling Labour government offered to create a popularly–elected Scottish assembly if such a move were approved by a majority in a referendum.

The United Kingdom

Such an instrument of "direct democracy" means that between parliamentary elections, the people, not parliament, decide. Because of the tradition of parliamentary supremacy, there were no referendums in Britain until the 1970s. Parliament did stipulate that at least 40% of the eligible Scottish voters had to approve the transfer of powers to the region (a process known in the UK as "devolution"). The referendum was held in March 1979, and 51.6% of the voters approved of the assembly; however, only 33% of the eligible voters participated, so parliament repealed the devolution act for Scotland. The Labour Party, which had always won most of the Scottish seats, reasserted itself in Scottish affairs and picked up the torch of devolution.

The 1990s witnessed a resurgence of Scottish nationalism and the SNP. Polls in 1992 indicated that 80% of Scots wanted either a Scottish parliament or outright independence. One native son, actor Sean Connery, compared Scotland to the independent Baltic states. This was quite a role reversal for "James Bond," who on screen risked everything to serve the British crown. The hit movie "Braveheart" in the mid–1990s also boosted the movement for greater Scottish independence. Even more Scotsmen began saying: "We're not free. We need a William Wallace." This feeling helped fuel a huge upsurge of interest in learning Scotland's Gaelic language, which had declined to only 80,000 speakers. Still there is no language motive to Scottish nationalism, as in Wales. Nor are there religious ones, as in Northern Ireland, or ethnic motives, as in eastern Europe. Former SNP leader Alex Salmond remarked, "we are a mongrel nation."

In the 1997 elections the SNP, which captured six seats, did not come close to overtaking Labour, which won 56 of 72 seats in Scotland in 1997 and for the first time in Scotland's history drove the Tories out completely. With Labour dominating Westminster again, a devolution of powers to Scotland and Wales came back on the agenda. A referendum in Scotland in September 1997 paved the way to a democratically elected assembly in 1999. Voters overwhelmingly approved a 129–seat parliament, Scotland's first in 300 years, with wide powers over such local matters as health, education, municipal government, economic development, housing, criminal and civil law, fisheries and forestry. They also voted for the right to raise or lower income taxes by up to 3% and to levy charges, such as road tolls. The polling set the stage for the most important constitutional change in British government in modern times. It also signaled the peaceful rebirth of a nation in an extraordinary way: no guerrilla army, separatist terrorists, civil disobedience, or even mass demonstrations.

On May 6, 1999, voters elected their first Members of the Scottish Parliament (MSP). Using the same mixed single–member constituency/PR electoral system as the Welsh, they favored Labour, which received 33.8% of the votes and 56 seats. The SNP was second, with 27% of the votes and 35 seats. The Conservatives got 15.4% of the votes and 18 seats, while the Liberal Democrats won 12.5% and 17 seats. This result was a setback for the SNP's independence cause. In the 2001 British parliamentary elections, Labour captured 43.9% of the Scottish votes and 56 seats, the SNP 20% and 5 seats, the Liberal Democrats 16.4% and 10 seats, and the Tories 15.6% and a single seat.

In 2000, Labour's leader, Donald Dewar, died of a brain hemorrhage. This was not only a personal tragedy, but it was a blow to those like him who advocate autonomy rather than separation from Britain. Polls were showing that the separatists, though still a minority, were gaining ground. Nevertheless, before stepping down as leader of the SNP, Salmond had concluded that an election victory in Scotland would no longer be a sufficient mandate for independence. It would need to be followed by a referendum before an SNP government could enter negotiations to remove Scotland from Britain. Scots appear to want to see how devolution works before leaping into independence.

In its first opportunity to test its voter appeal in Scottish assembly elections since devolution, the SNP discovered that it had fallen in favor, sliding in May 2003 down from 35 to 27 seats and 20.9% of the votes. Labour gained support to win 29.3% of the votes, with the Tories winning 15.5%, the Liberal Democrats 11.8%, the Greens 6.9%, and the Trotskyite Scottish Socialist Party (SSP) 6.7%. The SNP, led by John Swinney, had clearly failed to persuade voters that it would be a plausible government and that full independence would be a good thing. The party is now divided between those want to return to being a protest party and those who believe that a gradual accumulation of power by the Scottish parliament is the best route to go.

Northern Ireland

The UK's most serious regional problem by far is Northern Ireland. The Irish island can be said to be England's oldest colony, having been invaded by the English in the 12th century and ruled as a colony until 1800, when it received its own parliament. Ireland remained legally a part of the United Kingdom until 1922, when the 26 predominantly Catholic southern counties formed what is now the Republic of Ireland. The Protestant majority in the six northern counties rejected "home rule" (independence from Britain). The British at the time pledged that no change in the link between Northern Ireland and the United Kingdom would occur without the consent of the majority of the people. Every subsequent British government has held firmly to this commitment.

The largely Presbyterian and Church of Ireland Protestants are descendants of Scottish immigrants who began arriving in the 17th century. Their loyalty to the English crown is based upon the monarch's historical status set forth in the 1689 Bill of Rights, as "the glorious instrument of delivering this kingdome from Popery and arbitrary power." It is not surprising that this historical attitude, along with the Protestants' rejecting unification of the two parts of Ireland, has always antagonized the Catholic minority in Northern Ireland (who comprise 42% of the population of 1.6 million). Although Northern Ireland is officially a secular (i.e. non–religious) state, in actual practice the friction between Catholics and Protestants dominates politics there.

Northern Ireland has been in turmoil since 1968, when a Catholic civil rights movement organized internationally publicized street demonstrations to object to Protestant discrimination in housing, jobs and electoral representation. British governmental pressure on the Northern Irish parliament (which has existed since 1921 and is known as "Stormont" because it met in Stormont Castle) to meet many of the Catholic demands created a Protestant backlash. Peaceful street demonstrations in 1969 gave way to open violence, and British troops were sent to reestablish order.

The Irish Republican Army (IRA) sprang to life again and launched a modern terrorist campaign to remove the British from the territory and to reunify the entire island. It has received money and arms from overseas sources ranging from Gadhafi in Libya to the Irish Northern Aid Committee—NORAID—in the United States. Due to bad publicity, IRA fund–raising in the U.S. became more difficult. It found a lucrative substitute: extortion and racketeering in Northern Ireland itself. Because it also seeks the overthrow of the Dublin government, it had been banned in the South since 1936.

In retaliation, some Protestants in the North organized illegal forces. The best-known illegal Protestant paramilitary group, known for its violence, is the Ulster Volunteer Force (UVF). This illegal unit should not be confused with the Ulster Defence Regiment (UDR—the British army in Northern Ireland), the Royal Ulster

Constabulary (RUC—the mainly Protestant police force) or the Ulster Defence Association (UDA—a moderate and legal Protestant paramilitary group). In 1993 Protestant gunmen murdered more people than did the IRA.

The British disbanded Stormont in 1972 and resorted to the unpleasant task of ruling the region directly, through a Secretary of State for Northern Ireland. Successive British governments have sought earnestly for ways to devolve governmental power to the Northern Irish themselves. The problem was always how to protect the Catholic minority's interests against a perpetual Protestant majority. This difficulty revealed a major weakness of the English model of parliamentary democracy, which presents great power to any political group that commands an electoral majority: the model does not work well in societies which are divided religiously, ethnically or racially, because minorities can be voted down so easily.

Realizing this, the British government had to reject in 1975 a proposal by the leaders of the Protestants that a constitution be drawn up for Northern Ireland that would copy British parliamentary practice. Instead, British governments sought some form of "power–sharing" arrangement that would guarantee the minority Catholic parties a place in any Northern Irish executive. This idea infuriated the two Protestant political parties, the Ulster Unionists and the Democratic Unionists.

The IRA, a dedicated and ruthless band of 400 to 500 paramilitaries operating in small cells called "active service units," is divided into two groups: the "official" IRA was formerly Marxist, but now it seeks power through elections; the "provisional" IRA (Provos) was strictly nationalist, but it shifted to armed struggle to convert Ireland into a Marxist state. This shift was one reason why Irish–Americans became less generous toward the IRA. Both these wings face some competition from the smaller, but more radical Irish National Liberation Army (INLA, the paramilitary wing of the Marxist Irish Republican Worker's Party).

From 1976 to 1982 the IRA campaigned for special treatment as "political prisoners." After the failure of such tactics as refusing to wear prison garb and smearing the walls of the cells with their own excrement, they resorted to hunger strikes. The deaths of ten IRA hunger strikers in Maze Prison in 1981 sparked renewed militant Catholic nationalism. Shortly before his death, one of the hunger strikers, Bobby Sands, even managed to win a seat in the House of Commons, while he was still in prison.

In response, the British government tried again to restore a measure of devolved government by means of the 1982 Northern Ireland Act. Elections for a 78–seat Northern Ireland Assembly and an executive branch were held in 1982. This new body was to have the power to make proposals to the British government on how to return to self–government. It failed. Neither the mainly Catholic, moderate and law–abiding Social Democratic and Labour Party, nor the militant Sinn Fein (the political arm of the IRA, pronounced "Shin Fane," receiving only 10% of the total votes), took their seats in it. The Ulster Unionist Party also walked out and vowed that it would not return until security had been restored in Northern Ireland.

That is exactly what the British tried to do. In 1975 it ended the detention of both Catholic and Protestant terrorist suspects without trial, and it refused to declare martial law in the violence–torn area. Because of the risk of intimidation against jurors, non–jury courts (known as "Diplock Courts") were created for those accused of terrorist–related offenses. The British have always contended that the fundamental principles of British justice— a fair trial, the onus on the prosecution to prove guilt, the right to be represented by a lawyer, the right of appeal if convicted— are maintained for all.

The most effective anti–terrorist measure undertaken by the government in 1983 was the granting of pardon or lenience to onetime terrorists if they would tip off the police (in Northern Irish slang, 'to grass') on the whereabouts of active terrorists. The testimony of such 'supergrasses' led to a dramatic number of arrests in both the IRA and Protestant Ulster Volunteer Force. These organizations were so paralyzed that terrorist deaths in Northern Ireland dropped by half in one year, from 97 in 1982 to about 50 in 1983. IRA terrorists did give British Christmas shoppers a grisly indication they were alive in 1983, however, when they exploded a bomb outside of the bustling Harrods Department Store in London, claiming still more innocent lives (including an American teenager, a fact that hurt IRA fund–raising in the U.S.) in their ruthless struggle.

The Brighton bombing of 1984 was another grim reminder of the IRA's intent to wreak as much havoc as possible, this time by assailing the highest levels of British government itself. Having organized into "cells," the IRA became more difficult for police to combat. The violence prompted the Irish Republic to ratify the European convention on terrorism, which requires the extradition of terrorists.

By 2003 the toll stood at over 3,600 since 1969. In doing its bloody work the IRA

Mr. Gerry Adams
President, *Sinn Fein*

had the tactical advantage over the 30,000 security forces, which were kept on the defensive by the IRA's meticulous planning and constant shifting of tactics. To minimize its own losses, it increasingly struck at "soft targets," such as bands, military hospitals, off–duty RUC officers, and civilian firms that supply goods and services to the security forces. It also acquires state–of–the–art equipment; for example, it has surface–to–air missiles to use against army helicopters.

Democracy still existed at the local level in Northern Ireland, and voters send 27 MPs to the House of Commons in London. Protestants win a majority of these seats. Catholics would take more if the competing SDLP and Sinn Fein would unify in constituencies with predominantly Catholic populations. In the 1997 elections the two Catholic parties captured an unprecedented 40.2% of the votes.

The Protestant Unionist parties also have trouble working together, with Ian Paisley's hard-line Democratic Unionists taking five seats and David Trimble's larger Ulster Unionist Party winning six. Sinn Fein traditionally refused to take any seat in the British parliament, whose authority it does not recognize and which would require them to swear allegiance to the Queen. In 2002 Adams and three other party members took a historic step by going to the House of Commons and signing up to use all of the facilities except actually occupying a seat. Adams emphasized: "There will never ever be Sinn Fein MPs sitting in the British houses of parliament."

In the 1997 elections it won an all–time high of 16% of the votes in Northern Ireland. Two of its candidates, Gerry Adams and Martin McGuinness (an IRA leader who has served jail sentences), won

The United Kingdom

seats, which remained vacant. Sinn Fein does occupy seats in local councils on both sides of the Irish border and in the Northern Ireland Assembly. In 2002 it decided to run for seats in the Irish Republic's elections and it won five. In June 2002 Sinn Fein won control of Belfast, and Alec Maskey became lord mayor. Northern Ireland's Protestant majority has almost vanished.

There has been some progress in addressing the problem of social and economic discrimination; unemployment in Northern Ireland declined to 11.6% by 1996. Nevertheless, a Catholic man was still two and one-half times more likely to be unemployed than a Protestant man, and the jobless figure exceeded 70% in some ghettos of Belfast and Londonderry, where the terrorists do most of their recruiting. Northern Ireland has failed to attract large new investment deals, but many tourists are returning to the province, which surprisingly has the lowest rate of violent crime in the UK.

In 1985 former Irish *Taoiseach* (prime minister) Garrett FitzGerald and British Prime Minister Thatcher signed an Anglo–Irish agreement on Northern Ireland. This marked the first time the British government formally permitted the Irish Republic involvement in Northern Ireland's affairs, a concession many Northern Irish Protestants could not accept. It is regrettable, but perhaps not surprising, that all groups in Northern Ireland condemned this landmark act, despite the fact that its first article stated that no change in the province's status would come about without the consent of a majority of its people.

Peace Talks in Northern Ireland

In 1993 optimism was ignited by a joint declaration by the British and Irish prime ministers offering Sinn Fein a seat at the bargaining table to discuss Northern Ireland's future if the IRA renounced violence. Former Prime Minister John Major, who admitted that his government had conducted secret contacts with the IRA, promised that Britain would not stand in the way of a united Ireland if a majority of Northern Ireland residents supported such a step. His Irish counterpart pledged that there would be no change in the six counties' status without majority consent.

The following year President Bill Clinton, betting that the IRA wants peace in Northern Ireland, made a risky decision to grant a visa to Sinn Fein leader Gerry Adams to come to the U.S. Although the British government criticized him for this, it triggered a series of historic events. On August 31, 1994, the IRA declared a cease-fire, which prompted the Irish government to begin meeting with Sinn Fein

leaders. Six weeks later Protestant loyalists also declared a truce. While paramilitaries on both sides continued to terrorize their own communities, inter–sectarian violence and IRA attacks on British forces stopped. As a result, the British government relaxed its security measures in Northern Ireland and began drawing down its 18,000 troops. In December London opened direct talks with Sinn Fein and, later, with the Protestant paramilitaries. In February 1995 the British and Irish governments issued a "Framework for Agreement," outlining their proposals for Northern Ireland's future.

The U.S. government did its part to keep the momentum going by permitting Sinn Fein to open an office near Dupont Circle in Washington in 1995 and to raise money legally in the U.S. Much to London's displeasure, Clinton invited Gerry Adams to a St. Patrick's Day party in the White House honoring Ireland's *Taoiseach* (prime minister). In May the U.S. also organized a Northern Ireland Investment Conference in Washington that brought together more people from more different Northern Irish parties under one roof than ever before. It was also attended by top government officials from the UK and Ireland and was the venue for the first meeting between Gerry Adams and Britain's ex–Secretary of State for Northern Ireland Patrick Mayhew. This was the highest–level meeting between British and IRA leaders in 75 years and a giant step toward Adams' goal of receiving the same recognition and treatment accorded to Northern Ireland's other political leaders.

Clinton gave another powerful boost to the peace process in November 1995 by paying the first visit to Belfast ever made by an American president. It was a triumph. The very approach of his historic visit helped dissolve a stalemate in the talks and revitalized cooperation. Hours before his arrival the Irish and British prime ministers met and agreed to a breakthrough: preliminary all–party talks, led by former U.S. Senator George Mitchell, would be held while an international "decommissioning commission," led by former Canadian chief–of–staff and ambassador to Washington, General John De Chastelain, sought a way around the weapons impasse.

John Major admitted that Clinton's coming helped "concentrate the mind." Greeted everywhere in Belfast by cheering crowds waving American flags, Clinton addressed over 100,000 people, the largest throng in memory to gather in the square of Belfast City Hall. He appealed to everyone to put aside "old habits and hard grudges" and to seek peace. One witness said: "I've never seen anything

like this before. Everybody's come together." His American optimism reportedly made a deep impression. He met with all major leaders in the conflict and invited them to a reception at Queen's University; most came, which would have been unthinkable earlier. It was a very different Belfast that he saw: gone are the soldiers on the hunt, the countless roadblocks and the barbed wire. Although the ugly wall topped with razor wire separating Protestants and Catholics, inaptly called the "peace line," still stands, most of the blockaded streets have been reopened in Belfast.

There is little support in Northern Ireland or elsewhere for immediate reunification of Ireland. But not since 1969 have there been so many grounds for optimism that "the troubles" can end and that the Northern Irish can discuss their future peacefully. As a symbol of returning normalcy with Britain in 1995, Prince Charles became the first member of the royal family to make an official visit to the Irish Republic since 1922. Also in 1995, David Trimble, leader of the Ulster Unionist Party, the main Protestant group, traveled to Dublin and met with the Irish *Taoiseach*. This was the first time since 1922 a Unionist leader was received in Dublin.

In February 1996 the IRA ended an 18–month cease–fire and launched a bombing campaign in Britain and Northern Ireland. Tony Blair's Labour government, which for the first time appointed a woman—Marjorie "Mo" Mowlam—as Secretary of State for Northern Ireland, departed from the previous government's policy of not admitting Sinn Fein to multiparty talks until the IRA ended its violence campaign. Sinn Fein insisted that there could be no preconditions to its participation in negotiations, which resumed in June 1997.

Since the Labour government is not dependent upon Unionist MP's from Northern Ireland to win important votes in parliament, as John Major was, it has more political flexibility on Northern Irish issues. A couple of weeks after becoming prime minister, Blair lifted the ban on official contacts with Sinn Fein in order to explain London's position and to assess whether the IRA was really prepared to renounce violence. Gerry Adams accepted the offer. Blair dropped London's insistence that terrorists disarm before joining peace talks. He visited Northern Ireland on May 16, 1997, in order to demonstrate that he is willing to take risks for peace in the six counties.

To continue the negotiation process, he invited Gerry Adams to a meeting in Downing Street in December. This was the first visit by an Irish Republican leader to the prime minister's private residence in 76 years. It was a richly symbolic encounter, with the meeting over tea held in the cabinet room, the target of an IRA mortar attack only six years earlier. A month later, in January 1998, Adams returned to Downing Street to hear from the prime minister that the peace process is an "absolute priority" and that "the status quo is not an option." To balance his gesture to Sinn Fein, Blair told Protestants that "none of us ... , even the youngest, is likely to see Northern Ireland as anything but a part of the United Kingdom."

Talks, involving eight Northern Ireland parties and the British and Irish governments continued, despite the outbreak of renewed violence following the assassination of a Protestant terrorist, Billy Wright, in Maze prison just after Christmas. American George Mitchell emphasized the importance of the negotiations: "We're talking about, literally, people's lives, the possibility of the resumption of the terrible conflict that enveloped this society with fear and anxiety. So, frustrating and tedious as it seems—and it is—you have to be patient and recognize how tough it is for them to move."

Good Friday Agreement

In the early morning hours of Good Friday, 1998, after a series of marathon sessions, all parties at the table reached an historic agreement: a new 108–member Northern Ireland Assembly would be elected using the Irish Republic's system of proportional representation with the transferable vote. To protect Catholics from being permanently outvoted on sensitive "cross–community" issues and to necessitate consensus, a majority of both Catholic and Protestant blocs or an overall "weighted majority" of 60% would be required for decisions. The cabinet would consist of 10 seats distributed proportionally to the four largest parties. The assembly would share power with a new North–South Ministerial Council, composed of ministers from the Republic and Northern Ireland. This gives the Irish Republic its first formal role in Northern Ireland's affairs. In return, Ireland's leaders agreed to give up the Republic's claim to the North. All parties pledged to use their influence to persuade armed groups to turn in their weapons within two years, and imprisoned members of those armed groups would be released within two years as well.

On May 22, 1998, referenda were held on both sides of the border, and 71% of Northern Irish and 94.4% in the Republic approved of the Good Friday settlement. The following month, the first elections to the new assembly were held, and David Trimble's UUP came out on top with 28 seats. John Hume's SDLP (later led by Seamus Mallon) was second, with 24 seats. For their indispensable role in the entire peace process, Trimble and Hume shared the 1998 Nobel Prize for Peace. Hume had declared that "we finally decided that agreement for the whole community is more important than victory for one side." Other seats went to the DUP (20), Sinn Fein (18), the Alliance (6), the UKUP (5), Independent Unionists (3), and the Women's Coalition and PUP two each. The great number of parties winning seats demonstrated the effect of the propor-tional representation electoral system. Trimble became First Minister, and the body met for the first time in the traditional Stormont building on July 4.

This being Ireland, an island with so much history and so many memories, things were not destined to go smoothly. In August a fringe Catholic organization calling itself the "Real IRA" exploded a car bomb in the Northern Irish city of Omagh, killing 28 people. The public was so repelled by this grisly act that the "Real IRA" apologized and announced a permanent cease–fire on September 12. This was soon broken, and the IRA was forbidden from raising money in the United States. After the BBC named four men it said were involved in the attack, three were arrested in October 2000. In 2002 the first was convicted to 14 years in jail. Colm Murphy, a wealthy pub owner and building contractor, was found guilty by a three-judge panel in a special criminal court in Dublin. The group was also the prime suspect in the September 2000 rocket attack against the London headquarters of MI6, Britain's foreign intelligence service. To maintain his credibility in the Protestant community, Trimble called for a beginning of "decommissioning" (turning in) of weapons even before the creation of a Northern Ireland cabinet. Noting that this precondition had not been in the agreement, Sinn Fein balked at completing the peace process.

Endless haggling over paramilitary groups laying down their arms threatened the peace deal. However, both sides began taking cautious steps to implement the agreement. On December 1, 1999, a new coalition government in Ulster was formed that shared power devolved from Westminster in London. It included both the party of hard-line Protestant, Rev. Ian Paisley, and former IRA commander, Martin McGuinnes, as minister of education. However, this government was suspended in February 2000 after the IRA failed to meet the Unionists' deadline for starting turning in its arms.

Power-sharing was reestablished in May 2000 when the Unionists accepted an IRA pledge to put its arsenal "beyond use" and to allow limited inspections by international observers to verify that that the promise is being kept. Such visits were conducted in June and October 2000, and the arms dumps were reported to have a substantial amount of military material that was safely stored. For a year and a half the IRA dragged its heels. As a result David Trimble, leader of Northern Ireland's power-sharing government, quit in the summer of 2001, and things came to a standstill.

In November 2001 the IRA finally began destroying some of its weapons under international supervision. In quick response to this breakthrough, Britain began demolishing military installations, including army watchtowers overlooking regions with high IRA support. Trimble led his Ulster Unionist Party back into the assembly and was narrowly reelected first minister with the help of the Alliance Party, which had steered a middle road between unionists and republicans. Peace was back on track.

Genuine struggles remain on such emotional symbolic issues as flying flags over official buildings and reforming and

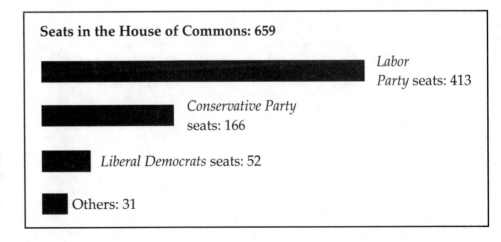

Seats in the House of Commons: 659

Labor Party seats: 413

Conservative Party seats: 166

Liberal Democrats seats: 52

Others: 31

The United Kingdom

renaming the Royal Ulster Constabulary (RUC), which is 93% Protestant. A top American law enforcement official, Tom Constantine, former head of the Drug Enforcement Administration (DEA), was appointed as "oversight commissioner" to scrutinize changes in the RUC. But progress is undeniable. The bloodletting has subsided although armed dissidents abound. Maze prison, just outside of Belfast, was emptied and closed in September 2000. Ex-prisoners had played a role in the peace process; they were crucial in the maintenance of their various organizations' ceasefires. The British closed six bases along the Irish border and looked forward to reducing the number of bases from 64 to no more than 20 and of troops from 13,500 to 8,000.

In July 2002 the IRA stunned everybody with an expression of "sincere apologies and condolences" for all the persons it had killed in the Northern Irish sectarian violence. The "troubles" appeared to be close to an end when a spy scandal at the heart of the Northern Irish government broke in October 2002. After raiding Sinn Fein homes and offices at the Northern Ireland Assembly, British authorities charged three members of gathering intelligence from Britain's Northern Ireland Office that could be used for terrorist operations. Police found sensitive political material, including minutes of conversations between Blair and his Northern Ireland secretary of state, and names, home addresses and license plate numbers of many provincial police officers and British security personnel. It was feared that some of the information could be used for assassinations.

Sinn Fein leaders denied the allegations and claimed the police had orchestrated a frame-up. The British suspended the assembly, and Protestant leaders vowed that they would not resume participation unless the IRA renounces violence unmistakably. The IRA then broke off all contact with the independent panel established to oversee disarmament, which had already supervised the destruction of two caches of IRA weapons. One Sinn Fein leader, Martin McGuinness, announced that he had abandoned his fight with Britain and was committing himself to preventing the deaths of any more people. "My war is over." Nevertheless, the peace process had suffered its most serious blow since the Good Friday Agreement five years earlier.

In April 2003 President George W. Bush visited Blair and Irish Prime Minister Bertie Ahern in Belfast to lend his endorsement to the peace plan. The president had aroused the ire of the British government when Gerry Adams was invited to a White House St. Patrick's Day

party in March, this when IRA operatives had been arrested while traveling undercover in the U.S. Although Blair sensed that breaking the stalemate was "frustratingly close," all his efforts to get the IRA to make a crystal-clear statement that it had given up paramilitary activities like gathering intelligence, threatening and attacking adversaries and acquiring weapons failed. Adams' statement that there would be "no activities which will undermine in any way the peace process or the Good Friday Agreement" was not enough. The atmosphere became even more strained when the head of London's Metropolitan Police released evidence in April that agents working for the British army had worked with death squads in Northern Ireland, including the 1989 murder, before his family's very eyes, of Belfast lawyer, Patrick Finuncane, who had represented IRA terrorists. Blair postponed assembly elections scheduled for May 29, a decision protested by both Sinn Fein and the Irish government. He asserted, "we are at the point where people have got to go to the absolute, definitive, completed position of forswearing violence in all its forms."

Today's Political Parties

Like any modern democracy, the British system could not function without parties. They recruit and select candidates, define issues which are important, educate voters about them, finance and fight electoral campaigns, put up governments which rule at all political levels, and provide well–organized opposition which continually remind the electorate of the government's shortcomings. For the government, the party is an essential tool for maintaining a parliamentary majority, and for the individual politician, it is the ladder to power. For the political activist it is an important means for putting his ideas into practice. For the voter, it is an indispensable label for a set of politicians, policies, sympathies or interests.

British parties bear some similarities to those of America, but there is a striking difference which stems from a fundamental difference in the two political systems: the real power in American parties is at the bottom of the hierarchy; a national party in America is nothing more than a loose coalition of state and local parties. By contrast, in Britain the real power within the party is at the top.

Basically, all British parties have a similar organization. At the lowest level are party units in the wards, which are grouped together into 659 constituency parties, each of which struggles for a seat in the House of Commons. These ward or constituency parties raise funds (part of which must be passed up to the national

party), recruit members, campaign at election time and select candidates.

National parties rarely try to overrule constituent parties' choice of candidates, although the national parties clearly influence the selection. The most obvious evidence is that about a half of all MPs do not reside in their constituencies before their election to parliament. Unlike the U.S., there is no legal requirement for this, and the national party leaders search all over Britain for "safe seats" for important MPs. Constituency party leaders often decide that national party interests override their own local desires. All constituency parties are grouped into regional organizations, which, except Wales and Scotland, have little importance.

At the national level, each party organizes an annual conference to which each constituency sends representatives. This large conference debates and adopts the party's overall policy (which is never binding on the party if it is in power) and, in the case of Labour, elects the party's leadership. At the national level, two other party organizations also exist. The central bureaucracy assists the party at all levels. The parliamentary party consists of the MPs and members of the House of Lords belonging to it.

All British parties are coalitions of differing interests and ideologies. It is often assumed that British parties are class parties. While this, to some extent, is true of the Labour Party, the Conservative Party has always had an appeal which cuts across class lines. In terms of policy, the major parties have normally been far closer together than is often assumed. From 1945 until the early 1970s, there was a large measure of consensus among the major parties. All were agreed on a welfare state, the mixed public–private economy which permitted much state intervention in the economy and employer–union–government collaboration (sometimes referred to as "corporatism").

Some observers even spoke of the "end of ideology" in Britain. That broad consensus collapsed in the 1970s, and both the Conservative and Labour parties became more ideologically oriented. By the 1983 elections the major parties had become more polarized than they had been in a half-century. Margaret Thatcher's embrace of market–oriented economics and rejection of state intervention, of "welfarism," and of "corporatism" was matched by revived class–warfare rhetoric in the Labour Party. Its moderate wing found itself placed on the defensive by the left–wing, which demanded radical changes in Britain's social, economic and political power structures. Sir Winston Churchill's observation was no longer correct that "four–fifths of the two major

British parties agree about four–fifths of the things that need to be done." But four defeats in a row from 1979 to 1992 prompted Labour to move toward the political center. The payoff exceeded its wildest expectations.

The Conservative Party

The Conservative Party is conscious of its heritage, which it traces back to the 17th century. Its pragmatic approach has always enabled it to appeal to British from all classes, even though its strongest appeal could be found among those who were well–off economically. At the heart of the Tory Party, as it was formerly known, is the unity of the whole nation. It has always preferred voluntary effort to public assistance, and this stems from its insistence on free enterprise in industry, advocacy of the profit motive and of indirect (sales) taxes rather than direct (income) taxes.

It has never argued that the state has no role in the economy, and it even nationalized industries under certain circumstances, such as the Central Electricity Board in 1926 and Rolls–Royce in 1971. Nor has it ever rejected the notion that the state should provide social welfare services sensibly. In her 1987 campaign Margaret Thatcher said that all decent people want to help the ill, the unemployed and the aged, but that a healthy economy is needed to provide the level of services which the British want.

There has, of course, always been division within Tory ranks between proponents of more state intervention and those who favor less regulation and a much freer market economy. Some of the differences in political orientation within the party are reflected in well–established pressure groups: they include the Bow Group, which presses for policies which benefit all classes, the Monday Club (the old right), the Tory Reform Group (progressives) and the Charter Movement, who want to democratize the party.

It was publicly known in 1975 when Thatcher defeated Edward Heath for the party leadership that the new leader represented a different Toryism than Heath. After she became prime minister in 1979, those persons in her cabinet who loyally supported her views were dubbed "dries." Those who had doubts about her medicine, especially about how it would affect millions of citizens and their families, were dubbed "wets." In a cabinet reshuffle after the 1983 and 1987 elections, she dismissed the "wets" in her cabinet.

Thatcher's stunning victory in the 1987 elections revealed that although she was an unpopular and unloved leader, British voters respected her no–nonsense competence and will. They grudgingly accepted

The Rt. Hon. Iain Duncan Smith, MP Leader of the Conservative Party

her bitter economic medicine of sound money, hard work, and standing on one's own two feet. She was the first prime minister to win a third consecutive term in modern British history and surpassed Winston Churchill and H.H. Asquith as Britain's longest serving prime minister in this century. Why did she win?

The first reason is that her opposition was severely divided. Second, the prime minister had won considerable stature and influence in the international arena. She could boast with justification that "we have put the Great back into Britain." The main reason for her victory was the undeniable economic success her government had achieved.

Thatcher's Fall

The willingness of France and Germany to relinquish more sovereignty to Europe widened the chasm between the UK and its continental partners. Thatcher's cabinet had been rocked by high–level resignations stemming from disagreements over Europe. In 1986 Michael Heseltine stormed out because he wanted a European consortium, not one from the U.S., to purchase a British helicopter company. In 1989 Nigel Lawson left because he wanted to include the pound in the European Monetary System (EMS). The fatal resignation—and the catalyst for her downfall—was that of Sir Goeffrey Howe, the last surviving member of her original 1979 cabinet and an architect of "Thatcherism." He charged in parliament that her obstruction in Europe carried "serious risks for our nation."

The devastating speech led to a successful challenge to her leadership in November 1990. After an historic eleven–year rule, the longest prime ministership since the Victorian era and the longest consecutive one since the Napoleonic age, Thatcher

resigned. The events leading to her fall related to Europe, but the reason why 45% of her parliamentary party colleagues voted against her was that she was guiding her party toward defeat in the next elections. For 18 months her party had trailed in the polls a Labour Party that had become more moderate, had overthrown its suicidal commitment to nuclear disarmament, and had embraced the EU. Her country was experiencing high inflation, a growing trade deficit, a slow–down in economic growth, and intense domestic opposition to her poll tax for local governments.

With her passing, the UK entered a period under John Major, Britain's youngest prime minister in this century, until Labour leader Tony Blair evicted him from Number 10 Downing. Major was a self–made man from a very humble background and with no university education. His father had been a circus performer and minor league baseball player in the U.S. Major was the Iron Lady's protegé and hand–picked successor. Nevertheless, he backed away from strident Thatcherism, abolishing the hated poll tax in 1991. He buried the grudge Thatcher had borne against both the EU and Germany and became a more cooperative European. Like Thatcher, he benefited from an unexpected war, this time in the Gulf in 1991, which went very well for Britain and its allies.

He entered the 1992 elections with the highest popularity rating of any British prime minister in three decades, but nobody expected his stunning victory in the midst of Britain's worst recession in a half century. He led his party to a 21–seat majority, based on 42% of the votes and 336 seats (down from 376).

The Tory party was deeply divided, especially over Britain's role in the EU. Major's government was sometimes held hostage by several dozen vocal "Euroskeptics" in his own party, including Thatcher herself, who were determined to sabotage all moves to closer European union. Not only did the government appear to be at war with itself. It was also dogged by a succession of scandals and sleaze, as well as the fall–out from the "mad–cow disease" debacle, which the government handled ineptly. Voters were tired of Tory rule after 18 years. Even the party's most significant achievement—a booming economy and unemployment half as high as when Major took office in 1992—played in the opposition's favor since voters seemed to think they could afford the risk of voting Labour.

The 2001 elections brought the second devastating defeat in a row for the Conservative party. It climbed from 30.6% of the votes to 32.7% and to 166 seats (up

The United Kingdom

from 165). The party won only one constituency in Scotland and none in Wales. It has become a regional party confined to the English countryside. Party leader William Hague resigned immediately. His replacement is Iain Duncan Smith. He was selected by a new kind of primary election: first the parliamentary party voted on the contenders. The top two candidates then were submitted to a vote by all party members in the UK (average age: ca. 70).

Demoralized after its two worst election defeats since 1906, and in opposition for the second time since 1979, the Conservative party faces a difficult task of rebuilding. This is especially true after Smith assembled a shadow cabinet more purely Euroskeptic than any of his predecessors. They had tried to balance the party's differing factions, but he surrounded himself with people who agree with him. The Tories were jolted again in 2002 by stories of another sensational sex scandal, this time involving John Major. Miffed that he had not mentioned her in his autobiography and had not given her a cabinet post during his prime ministership, former Education Minister Edwina Currie and later talk-show host revealed in her published diaries that she and Major had had a four-year affair from 1984–8. She had indirectly alluded to this in her 1997 novel, *A Parliamentary Affair*. This lapse of judgment blemished both Major's reputation for honesty and the wisdom of his 1993 campaign, "back to the basics," calling for strict moral values. Most Tories supported Prime Minister Blair's decision to participate in the war against Iraq in 2003, but this did not help the party in the polls. It remains so internally divided that Duncan Smith warned: "We have to pull together or we will simply hang apart. My message is simple and start: unite or die."

The Labour Party

Although its roots extend far back into the 19th century, the Labour Party was officially founded in 1900. Under the influence of the small but well–connected Fabian Society, which sought to reform British society gradually from above rather than through violent revolution or labor union agitation from below, the party adopted in 1918 a new constitution which transformed it officially into a socialist party. It proclaimed that the goal of the party is to "secure for the producers by hand or by brain the full fruits of their industry and the most equitable distribution thereof that may be possible upon the basis of common ownership of the means of production and the best obtainable system of popular administration and control of each industry and service."

Rt. Hon. Tony Blair, MP, Prime Minister of the United Kingdom, and Leader, *Labour Party*

That purely Marxist objective helped prevent the Labour Party from sharing the fate of many socialist parties in Europe that split apart in the aftermath of the Russian Revolution. However, it became the source of continuous intra–party friction ever since. During most of its history the party was in reality more moderate than its constitution might indicate. It sought to "democratize" the economy by nationalizing key industries and regulating others, to distribute wealth more equally, to expand social welfare services and to eliminate class differences.

During the Thatcher government Labour took a leftward lurch and embarked upon an almost suicidal political course. Grossly underestimating Britain's first woman prime minister and the public support for her economic austerity policies, the Labour Party committed itself to radical promises: unilateral nuclear disarmament, withdrawal from the EU, massive nationalization of industries and huge increases in public spending.

This led to an electoral disaster, and in the 1983 elections, it suffered its worst defeat in 60 years. Its 27.6% was Labour's lowest popular vote since 1918 and was 20 percentage points lower than in 1966. Almost a quarter of those voters who had identified themselves consistently with the Labour Party abandoned it.

It failed to win a majority of the votes among the working class or among labor union members. This was a severe setback for a party created by and organizationally linked to the unions; it seriously hollowed out the party's claim to be the party of the worker. Only the traditional

working class remained more loyal: that segment which worked in nationalized or "smokestack" industries or which lived in council housing, Scotland, Wales or the North of England. This represented the most significant basic shift in the social basis of British politics since World War II.

Within hours after the polls had closed, the move to replace the ineffective Labour leader, Michael Foot, began. The choice was Neil Kinnock. He began immediately to mend the gaping, intra–party split between the left and right which had led to electoral disaster and the massive drop in party membership between 1979 and 1983 to a level comparable to that of 1945. He moderated his party's views on the EU, defense and the status of capitalism. With a sharp eye on the social changes which have occurred in Britain, Kinnock announced that Labour must appeal to the "newly well–off" and should be a party which appeals to the haves, as well as the have–nots.

Going into the 1987 elections, he recognized that if Labour were to be electable and to regain the initiative in British politics, which it had lost in 1979, the party would have to shy away from extremism. The platform it prepared purged the earlier pledges to abolish the House of Lords (which has been critical of some of Thatcher's policies), to nationalize much more industry and to control the country's banking system. It accepted the principle of selling public–owned houses, and it no longer opposed the UK's membership in the EU.

The party clung to some of its old cures: more public spending and borrowing, higher taxes for the "very rich," and restoration of trade union immunities by repealing Tory legislation. An enormous electoral liability was Kinnock's decision to stand by his party's unilateral nuclear disarmament position. The electoral effect was suicide. The party suffered its second worst defeat in more than a half-century, capturing only 32% of the votes and 229 seats.

The 1992 elections showed that the Labour Party continued to suffer from an image problem: voters worried about extremism within the party, and they had doubts about its defense and economic policies and, in general, its competence to rule the country. It faced important social changes which worked against it: its traditional support base—trade–union members, manual laborers and tenants of state–owned housing—is shrinking.

Party leaders conducted a thorough rethinking of its positions. In order to be able to present a credible challenge to the Conservatives, Labour had to develop a moderate, non–socialist program. It unveiled its new policy, which scrapped unilateral nuclear disarmament, as well as

View of London from St. Paul's Cathedral

vote–losing calls for withdrawal from NATO, removal of U.S. military bases in Britain, scuttling the Trident nuclear submarine program, and state ownership of industry. It reconciled itself to the market system.

The year 1992 seemed ideal for a Labour victory, but voters handed Labour its fourth consecutive defeat, even though it climbed to 35% of the votes and 271 seats. Voters were still unwilling to trust Labour with power and continued to associate it with crippling strikes, chaos, and economic decline. Kinnock had begun to introduce the kinds of changes that would ultimately lead his party to victory in 1997, but he had failed at the time to persuade his countrymen that Labour's transformation and pragmatism were genuine and lasting.

Kinnock resigned as leader and was replaced by John Smith, whose untimely death of a heart attack in 1994 forced his colleagues to select another leader who could bring the party victory. They turned to Tony Blair. The son of a life–long Conservative, Blair was educated at a private boys' school and studied law at Oxford. He took no interest in student politics and spent his spare time singing in a rock band called "Ugly Rumours." He entered parliament in 1983 representing a traditional Labour constituency in the North. He bears no scars of Labour's dismal rule in the 1970s, and he is its first leader with no roots in the labor movement and with no grounding in traditional socialism.

This made it easier for him to complete the process of modernizing his party. He lessened its dependency upon and identification with unpopular unions. In the 1960s, union money made up 80% of the party's budget; by 1995 that figure was 50% and then 30% by 1998. He remained silent during a 13–week railway strike in 1994, breaking a long tradition of unfail-

ing party support for the unions' actions. He curbed the voting power of union leaders, who had controlled large blocks within the party. Their power was diluted by changes in the complicated rules governing party voting and policy making. He persuaded the powerful NEC to accept his revision of Clause IV of the party constitution, setting aside the party's 1918 commitment to public ownership of key industries. This had been a major obstacle to its return to power. Blair confessed later that scrapping Clause IV had "shown me what I intuitively thought but wasn't sure of: that the party was actually behind change." Since it was a democratic process every step of the way, he was sure that most of the party's rank and file had changed and were behind the reform.

Through his patience, charm, and power of persuasion, he reversed the radicalism within the party and opened it up to fresh ideas. He led Labour toward the political center. He ceased regarding Labour as a tribal party focusing on the working class. By enhancing its appeal

among the middle class in the heavily populated south of Britain, he aimed directly at the bedrock of the Tories' support. He is highly confident, disciplined, focused, energetic, and quick to master a brief. He is also sometimes accused of being brutally autocratic when it comes to bringing his party in line with his reforms, a quality Margaret Thatcher is said to admire in him. Unlike Thatcher, though, who relished battering her opponents into submission, Blair prefers logical argument and persuasion.

In the 1997 elections he demonstrated what a skillful campaigner he is. He can orchestrate a tightly organized campaign, present himself convincing in two television debates with his opponent (an innovation in British campaigns), "work a crowd" very effectively, and inspire voters without promising too much. His main challenge was to convince voters that his party had indeed shed the heavy baggage of the past. He stuck to a single message: that his party was now "New Labour." "The old ideologies are dead. New Labour is offering a new and different form of politics. ... There has been a revolution inside the Labour Party. We have rejected the worst of our past and rediscovered the best. ... We have made ourselves fit to face the future."

He distanced his party from the "outdated ideology" of high taxes financing expensive government programs, from powerful unions, and from unilateral nuclear disarmament. He established friendly relations with business leaders. He vowed neither to renationalize industries nor raise income taxes. Instead, he pledged to keep inflation low, to spend no more than the Tories had already budgeted, but nevertheless to improve the struggling National Health Service and the school system, to introduce a minimum wage, to combat crime, and to reform the constitution.

Vote new Labour

new Labour new Britain

'New Labour has the vision – and the energy – to build a strong dynamic economy breathing new life into Britain'

Labour

Campaign brochure for Charlotte Atkins, April 1997

The United Kingdom

Seeing too little difference between his program and that of the Tories, some observers dubbed him "Tony Blur." He responded by arguing, "I do not think everything that has happened in the last 18 years has been bad. My attitude is: keep what is working and change what is not." Clearly Britain's economy was already working well, with unemployment at a 10–year low of 6.2% on election day. This fact persuaded even more voters that there was little danger in voting for a Labour Party that promised not to tamper with one of Europe's most robust economies. Blair assured his countrymen within hours after his victory: "We ran as New Labour and will govern as New Labour."

The electoral payoff for Labour was historic: it won 418 of 659 seats on the basis of 43.1% of the votes. Its majority of 179 seats was its best performance ever. It wiped the Tories out of Scotland and Wales altogether and made deep inroads into Tory strongholds in southern England and London, capturing even Margaret Thatcher's north London Finchly constituency. In a stunning turnaround women flocked to Labour, which won 53% of their votes (compared with 30% who voted Tory). The number of women with seats in the House of Commons shot up from 63 to 120, and 101 of them were from Labour. Most of the nine ethnic minorities, including a wealthy Muslim, elected to parliament ran on the Labour ticket. Blair's cabinet also contained many firsts: five women, a blind man (David Blunkett, Education and Employment Secretary), and an openly gay man (Chris Smith, National Heritage Secretary).

In the June 2001 elections, which saw a startling 12% drop in turnout to 59%, the lowest since 1918, Labour slipped to 42% and lost six seats. Nevertheless, with 413 seats it still commanded two-thirds of the seats in the House of Commons. This was the first time in its century of existence that it had succeeded in being reelected to a second full term. Blair immediately proceeded to reshuffle his cabinet; the most dramatic change was former Home Minister Jack Straw's replacing Robin Cook as foreign secretary. Cook became Leader of the House of Commons until he resigned in 2003 in protest against Blair's decision to go to war in Iraq.

The Liberal Democrats

In reaction to the Labour Party's earlier swing to the left, a group from the party bolted and in 1981 formed the Social Democratic Party (SDP). This new grouping sought to occupy the center ground of the British political spectrum, which had opened up because of the polarization between the two larger parties. Its strategy was to align with the older Liberal Party of the center.

The Liberals had been one of the two major parties during the 19th century, but it had not been in power since the Labour Party eclipsed it just after World War I. Their heaviest emphasis has been on individual freedom, and it speaks for decentralization of state power, for a greater focus of local political issues and for workers' (not union) councils sharing control with management. Both the Liberals and the SDP strongly support European integration and reform of the electoral system in favor of proportional representation.

Just how important such a change would be for the SDP–Liberal Alliance was demonstrated in the 1983 elections. It won 25.4% of the vote, the best performance of center parties for 60 years. Its remarkably even support across the entire class spectrum proved that it was not merely a fashionable "wine and cheese" grouping, as critics had charged. But it won only 23 seats in the House of Commons. The SDP was reduced to a tiny rump within parliament. Most of the former Labourites who had switched their allegiance to the SDP, including two of its four founders, were swept from office. The SDP's share was only six seats. Under the popular leadership of David Steel, the Liberals improved their standing, winning 17 seats.

The Alliance did even worse in 1987, falling to 22% of the votes and only 22 seats. It had hoped to gain a surge of new support from voters in the political center, but all it managed to do was to split the opposition vote with Labour.

Many analysts had believed that the Alliance could supplant the Labour Party and that the new Social Democrats and the traditionally independent, undisciplined Liberals could forge a partnership that could "break the mold of British politics." But the Alliance had failed to establish itself as an electable non–socialist alternative. Therefore, in 1988 the SDP dismembered itself. It merged with the larger Liberal Party to form a new party, the Social and Liberal Democrats, led by Paddy Ashdown. The prospect of a hung parliament in 1992, meaning that neither of the large parties would win a parliamentary majority, buoyed the party's spirits. It could then play the "king–maker role" and demand the introduction of proportional representation as the price for entering a governing coalition with one of the large parties. This would have secured its own future and decisively changed British politics. But its hopes were dashed, as the Tories won a majority.

Doubling their seats to 46 (from 26 in 1992) on the basis of 16.7% of the total votes (down from 17.9%), the Liberal Democrats registered in 1997 the best performance by a third party in three generations. Party leaders and members were elated. But the magnitude of the Labour victory meant that their 46 votes in the House of Commons could not be employed to enhance their party's political influence as many Liberal Democrats had hoped. Ashdown stepped down as leader in 1999, having accomplished in his 11 years most of what he had wanted. He had rescued his party from the splits and name changes of the 1980s. He had put it close to the center of power. Former journalist Charles Kennedy replaced him and led the party in the June 2001 elections, in which they captured an impressive 18.8% of the votes and 52 seats. The party's temporary boost in the polls from opposing the 2003 war in Iraq evaporated as the quick victory made the military action popular in Britain.

RECENT FOREIGN POLICY AND POST–COLONIAL PROBLEMS

Today the sun technically does not set on the British Empire. Ten dots on the map are still ruled by Britain: Pitcairn in the south Pacific Ocean; Bermuda, British Virgin Islands, Caymans, Leeward Islands, Turks and Caicos in the Caribbean area; the Falkland Islands, St. Helena in the south Atlantic Ocean; Gibraltar in the Mediterranean; and Diego Garcia in the Indian Ocean. Yet it must still deal with many problems that stem from its colonialist legacy. They have included both foreign policy problems and domestic political difficulties, such as how to control and treat millions of immigrants from the former colonies (see Culture).

The Commonwealth of Nations is a loose, voluntary association of the former ruler and the ruled, and the head is the British monarch, even though some of its members are republics. Member states regularly confer at Commonwealth gatherings, and sometimes Britain must assume additional, unwanted responsibilities under the aegis of the Commonwealth, such as in helping to arrange a transition to democracy in the tiny Caribbean island of Grenada after four years of totalitarian rule and an invasion by the United States and six other Caribbean island states.

Britain also faces terribly complicated problems with the smaller enclaves it rules because local inhabitants there fear their larger neighbors and look to Britain for protection. It has declared that the principle of self–determination must not be violated and that a neighboring land can absorb subject peoples only by their consent. The principle is an admirable one, but it has a high cost. The 2,200 inhabitants of the Falklands, located off the Argentine coast, called upon Britain to defend them from Argentina in 1982. Britain's military victory did not convince Argentina to renounce its claims to the islands. No doubt Buenos Aires also has its eye on the Falklands' potential offshore oil reserves of two to five billion barrels, larger than those of the North Sea. As a deterrent, London stations 2,000 troops on the islands. Although Britain still refuses to discuss its sovereignty over the islands, it has established friendly relations with Argentina. President Carlos Menem received a warm welcome in London in 1998, where he laid a wreath to the Britons who died in the war. Prince Charles visited Argentina the following year.

The 31,000 inhabitants of Gibraltar cling to their rock and are largely self–ruling. But they rely on the protection of 5,000 British troops stationed there because they are afraid of becoming a part of Spain. In 1985 the border between Gibraltar and Spain was reopened, and discussions over its sovereignty and eventual disposition continue.

Painstaking negotiations with the People's Republic of China (PRC) over Hong Kong resulted in an agreement that gave the PRC sovereignty over the colony in July 1997. But it committed China to guarantee Hong Kong's capitalist economy and lifestyle for 50 years.

Special Relationship with United States

Britain's foreign policy involves close cooperation with the United States and a primary focus on Europe. As separate sovereign states with their own interests, the Americans and British sometimes have different views on issues, ranging from the British–French invasion of Suez in 1956 to the American invasion of Grenada in 1983. But many people on both sides of the Atlantic still talk of a "special relationship" between the two countries stemming from their common language and heritage, as well as from their alliance during two world wars. They cooperate closely on defense, intelligence gathering and nuclear technology. In a 2001 poll, 59% of British respondents believed the U.S. is their most reliable ally in a crisis, vs. only 16% the EU is and 15% the Commonwealth.

This relationship does not exclude disagreement. Ex–Foreign Minister Geoffrey Howe spoke in 1983 of the "special intimacy and a special mutual confidence that we're able to talk with each other with the candor which one would normally expect only between one's own ad-

British students celebrate the special relationship

visers." But some Europeans suspect that Britain is a sort of Trojan Horse for American objectives on the continent. This, among other things, influenced former French President Charles de Gaulle to reject Britain's first attempt to join the European Community.

No country's leader seized the moment more decisively after the September 11, 2001, terrorist attacks against the U.S. than did Tony Blair. They claimed 100 British lives and thereby became the worst terrorist strike against British citizens in history. He flew to America immediately after the disaster, visited "ground zero" where the World Trade Center once stood, listened to President Bush's speech to the nation from the gallery of the House of Representatives, and offered stirring words to the Americans and his own people: the terrorists "have no moral inhibition on the slaughter of the innocent. If they could have murdered not 7,000 but 70,000, does anyone doubt they would have done so and rejoiced in it? There is no compromise possible with such people, no meeting of minds, no point of understanding with such terror. Just a choice: Defeat it or be defeated by it. And defeat it we must. To the Americans, we were with you at the first. We will stay with you to the last." The Queen awarded former New York Mayor Rudolph Giuliani an honorary knighthood for his leadership in the aftermath of the crisis.

Blair put his country's money where its mouth was. Within two months Britain

had sent 4,200 troops to the war zone in and around Afghanistan. In the opening salvos against the Taliban regime, British submarines fired cruise missiles at key targets and put special forces and Royal Marines on the ground to assist the opposition's push to rout Taliban forces. In 2002 its commandos joined the Americans and other allies on search-and-destroy operations aimed at remnants of al Qaeda and Taliban forces. For a half-year it commanded the international peacekeeping forces in Kabul trying to stabilize the traumatized country. The American president and people benefited greatly from Blair's support, and the two leaders developed a close personal relationship. But the prime minister was mocked in left-leaning British media as the "president's poodle." He is criticized at home for getting too little in return.

The March-April 2003 war in Iraq offered a further opportunity for Britain to act as a transatlantic bridge; it provided 45,000 well-trained troops, 15% of the total. With a sensitivity to growing European concerns about the U.S. role in the world, Prime Minister Blair stood up for a disliked and distrusted American president and repeatedly condemned anti-Americanism, reminded his countrymen of past American contributions to their security, and warned that opposing the U.S. would merely reinforce American tendencies toward unilateralism. He did this at considerable temporary damage to his popularity at home, and even 139 of his own Labour MPs voted against the war, one of the largest rebellions in parliamentary history. He tirelessly argued the case for military action against Saddam Hussein's dictatorship and withstood merciless heckling and a strange British form of disagreement toward speakers—slow hand clapping.

His eloquence and persuasiveness paid off; at the beginning of 2003 only 13% of Britons thought their country should go to war against Iraq; by the time war began, 56% were in favor. He was able to demonstrate that America did not stand alone in the world and that the transatlantic divide ran down the middle of Europe rather than through the Atlantic. The result was a strengthening of the "special relationship" and an elevation of British influence in the world. One senior Bush administration put it this way: "The special relationship had become a cliché which was being constantly trotted out, but all of a sudden it is very real. It is very deep and very operational." He continued: "This kind of partnership makes the United Kingdom a world player." For his part, Blair reminded his party comrades at Labour's October 2002 conference: "For

The United Kingdom

all the resentment of America, remember one thing. The basic values of America are our values too....My vision of Britain is not as the 51st state of anywhere, but I believe in this alliance, and I will fight long and hard to maintain it because alliance with America is in the interests of this country."

Defense

For centuries Britain was a global power, whose interest in Europe was merely to prevent any one power or combination of powers from upsetting the military balance there and dominating the entire continent. Now its primary focus is on Europe.

This shift of focus is best seen in defense. It was a founding member of NATO, and until 1990 it organized its defense on the assumption that the chief threat was the Soviet Union. It therefore channeled the bulk of its resources into strengthening NATO rather than defending British outposts elsewhere. In 1971 it abandoned its defense commitments east of Suez.

The "NATO–first" policy necessitated fundamental changes in defense structure. Britain converted the once–mighty Royal Navy into a specialized force whose purpose was primarily to assist the American navy and to defend against submarines. In the 1970s it phased out its attack aircraft carriers. The Falkland Islands war in 1982 revealed how this change in force structure could affect Britain's commitments outside of Europe. It had to lease luxury liners and merchant vessels just to transport its troops and equipment to those faraway islands. The conflict prompted Britain to bolster its capabilities to project military power in the world by canceling the scheduled deactivation of an aircraft carrier and the Royal Navy's last two amphibious assault ships.

The heart of the British defense effort today is the army. It has thousands of soldiers on station in Northern Ireland. It deploys a diminishing number of troops on the European continent, mainly in Germany. The costs for this force are great, especially since Britain has a volunteer army. With the disappearance of the Soviet threat to Europe, NATO faces fundamental restructuring that affects the British military. In 1991 the allies decided to establish a sizable rapid reaction force to confront unforeseen threats anywhere in Europe. This new force is stationed mainly in Germany and is commanded by a British officer.

Within Britain itself, the most controversial aspect of British defense was its nuclear arsenal. Aside from France, the UK is the only European country to possess atomic weapons. The Thatcher government decided to replace the aging Polaris vessels (each carrying 16 missiles) with more modern submarines, capable of firing ultra–modern American–made Trident missiles, each of which could attack eight separate targets. As part of its nuclear modernization program, the UK also equipped Tornado jets with the capability of delivering nuclear bombs. The new Labour Party, which took power in May 1997, dropped its long–standing opposition to Britain's nuclear force. But in post–cold war Europe, nuclear weapons have become largely irrelevant. The UK decided in 1998 to halve the number of its nuclear weapons at sea to 200 on four Trident submarines.

Although nuclear targeting is coordinated with the United States, only the British prime minister can order the use of Britain's nuclear weapons. The willingness of the British government since the 1950s to permit the deployment of American nuclear weapons on British soil, which are not under the direct command of the British prime minister, reflects NATO's importance in British defense planning. "Dual–key" safeguards were considered unnecessary because the UK had a firm agreement with the U.S. (which has never been published) that no American nuclear weapons could ever be launched from Britain without the approval of the British government.

In 1991 Britain's participation in the war to drive Iraq out of Kuwait was solidly supported at home. The UK sent a powerful contingent of land, air and naval forces serving under the overall command of American General Norman Schwarzkopf, whom the Queen knighted after the successful campaign. In 1998 it dispatched an aircraft carrier back to the Persian Gulf to show its solidarity with the American and UN efforts to force Saddam Hussein to open his weapons facilities to international inspectors.

No sooner were the warriors home than the government began a steady reduction. In the decade to 2000, it cut the army from 156,000 to 113,500, the navy and marines from 63,000 to 43,700, and the RAF from 89,000 to 55,200. Infantry battalions sank from 55 to 40 and front-line tanks from 699 to 304. The British Army of the Rhine was halved to 20,800. However, Britain built up its special operations forces to 2-3,000. The navy retains its three small (a fourth the size of America's larger ones) but expensive aircraft carriers and four ballistic-missile submarines (especially the Tridents). But its fleet of 28 attack-submarines was cut to 12, and its 48 frigates and destroyers to 35. The RAF lost nine of its 30 front-line combat squadrons; its total front-line fighters and bombers sank

from 630 to 500, some of which are flown by women. The draw-down continues. By 2000 total forces had declined to 212,400.

Defense spending was cut by a fifth from 1990 to 1999, to 3% of GDP, the lowest since the mid–1930s. Critics charge that such a slimmed–down force would never be able to respond to another crisis as big as the invasion of Kuwait in 1990, especially since the UK has increasingly assumed peacekeeping responsibilities. It deployed several thousand troops to Bosnia in a peacekeeping role. It also sent 35 combat aircraft, eight ships and 6,600 troops to participate in the air war over Yugoslavia in 1999.

The ruling Labour party produced a long overdue Strategic Defence Review published in 1998. It emphasized mobility, flexibility, sustainability, interoperability, and rapid reaction. It called for a nimble British military capable of going quickly "to the crisis, rather than have the crisis come to us." To back this up, the navy will receive two new full–sized aircraft carriers (the first in 30 years). The army will get an air cavalry brigade, complete with American Apache attack helicopters and paratroop regiments. The air force will acquire giant transport aircraft and sophisticated air–to–ground surveillance systems.

The Labour government shows an increased interest in a European defense capability that could, when necessary, operate without the U.S. The prime minister met with French President Jacques Chirac at St. Malo in December 1998 to give his blessing to the European Security and Defence Policy (ESDP), which decided a year later to build a European rapid-reaction force that can act when NATO chooses not to do so. The government also wants more competitive European defense production. To that end, British Aerospace and Daimler-Chrysler Aerospace decided to merge.

ECONOMY

Britain for almost two centuries has been a highly industrialized and developed nation. It led the Industrial Revolution in the 18th and 19th centuries, but after World War II it enjoyed less efficiency than some of its newer rivals. Only a fourth of the present gross domestic product now comes from manufacturing (a fifth from industry), while service industries provide 73.7% and agriculture 1.4%. In terms of employment, a fourth is in industry and 73% in services. Although agriculture employs only 2% of the working population, it produces more than half of the country's food requirements. Two-thirds of Britain's agricultural land is used for grazing; the main field crops are

wheat, barley, oats, potatoes and sugar beets.

Because of the extraction of oil and natural gas from the North Sea, Britain became self–sufficient in these sources of energy in the 1980s. It became the 10th largest oil producer in the world. It is the biggest coal producer in Western Europe. At the present rate of extraction, Britain's coal supplies could last for another 300 years. Nuclear power provides 23% of Britain's electricity.

Temporary Decline in Economic Performance

Most manual workers have shared in the general growth of affluence since the war. This was partly due to the primary political focus from 1945 to 1979 on income redistribution, rather than on high production and profit. In 1949 the top 10% in terms of income received a third of the nation's productive wealth, but by 1976 this had fallen to only one fourth. Wealth, on the other hand, remained very concentrated, with the richest fifth possessing three–fourths of all personal wealth, principally inherited.

Economic and social shifts in Britain helped to bring important changes in some fundamental assumptions. From 1945 to 1970, it had generally been assumed (and was broadly the case) that despite temporary ups and downs, the economy would always continue to improve, that inflation was unimportant, that full employment was normal and that if the economy got a little out of kilter, it could be put back on course by reducing or raising demand through taxes and public spending (classic economic methods of the late British economist, John Maynard Keynes). It was therefore widely accepted that governments should regulate the economy in order to maintain employment while expanding the welfare state out of ever–increasing national prosperity. By 1975 state spending amounted to more than 60% of national income.

The Keynsian assumptions, which more or less enjoyed an acceptance by both major parties, were torn asunder in the 1970s. At the beginning of the decade inflation began to rise, reaching the stratospheric level of 25% annually in the mid–1970s and 22% in 1980. Unemployment began to rise steadily, and the old cure did not seem to work any more.

As economic growth slowed to a standstill, governments were faced with an unpleasant dilemma: demand for welfare services continued to grow while the national income to pay for them did not. British economic discussions began to be preoccupied with "managing decline." The nationalized industries (most of

The United Kingdom

which had passed to public control in the immediate postwar years) were performing poorly and were becoming an increasing drain on the nation's productivity, thereby discrediting the very idea of public ownership. Everywhere people began talking about the "English disease."

The Thatcher Revolution

Margaret Thatcher brought dramatic economic changes during her prime ministership from 1979 to 1990. Neither the Tory government of John Major nor Tony Blair's Labour government, which took office in 1997, moved to undo her reforms in any fundamental way. She denationalized more than a third of Britain's nationalized industries, including Rolls–Royce, British Airways and the British Gas Corporation. The sale of these brought more than $40 billion into the state treasury, eliminated the need for taxpayers to subsidize them, and reaped handsome annual tax revenues. In 1987 the government began selling shares of British Petroleum. In 1988 plans were announced to privatize the electric industry in England and Wales. British Telecom was sold, and in 1996 its merger with the American MCI was made public. Thatcher's large–scale privatization program included two-dozen major companies. Nevertheless, state spending still accounts for 39% of GDP (compared with 30% in the U.S.), roughly the same percentage as when she took office.

Thatcher had argued that the state was overspending, and the shortfalls were being covered by public borrowing and expanding the money supply, rather than by taxes. These expedients stimulated inflation and absorbed the capital that was desperately needed to finance industrial innovation. The cure, she argued, was to restrict the money supply and cut public expenditures, which would both reduce inflation and free investment capital. To create economic incentives, income taxes should be cut. Finally, trade union power had to be curbed.

Her pride and her optimism were borne out by the facts: Since the country began pulling out of recession in 1981, productivity increased at an annual rate of 3.5%. The economy grew at an annual rate of 3%. Inflation was down from a high of 24.2% to 3.3% in 1995. Taxes had been reduced slightly, and the average voter's real pre–tax income had increased by 25% since 1979. From 1971 to 1994 real disposable income grew by almost 50%, and spending on social benefits increased by 168%. Britons live more prosperous lives. Nevertheless, it is the only EU country in which working hours have increased, to 43.4 hours.

Unemployment was higher than the 4.3% when she took office. Nevertheless,

a million new jobs had been created under her rule, in part because of incentives to small enterprises. Also, the jobs of those who were employed seemed far less threatened than in the early 1980s. Interest rates were falling, and the pound was much stronger. Its stock market was booming, and the UK had again become a leading creditor nation. Public borrowing had fallen to 1% of national income. Most important, she had restored morale and seemed to have ended decades of relative economic decline.

After her 1987 victory, London's *Sunday Times* pronounced that Thatcher has brought about Britain's "biggest transformation since the Industrial Revolution." Indeed, her economic performance has profoundly changed her country. She has created what she calls a "property–owning democracy," in which "every earner shall be an owner." Two–thirds of Britons now own their homes, compared to 50% in 1979, and car ownership has risen from 54% to 66%. In 1979 four times as many Britons belonged to trade unions as owned shares in the stock market. But by 1989 the number of stock–holders had tripled from 7% to 21%. As a result of a fall in union membership by one–fourth to nine million, the number of union members and stock–holders are now equal.

Thatcher enormously reduced the power of the once–mighty labor unions, which had been able to topple the governments of her two predecessors. She introduced laws that limit unions' legal immunities. They restrict picketing rights, ban secondary picketing and political strikes, make national unions financially responsible for the actions of their members, and require unions to have a secret balloting of members before declaring a strike. She rooted out one of the main causes of the "English disease" by taking on the bosses of the most powerful unions and crushing them: the steel workers in 1980, the coal miners in 1985 and the teachers in 1986. By 1987 strikes were at a 50–year low; workdays lost to union disputes declined from 29.5 million in 1979 to 1.9 million in 1986.

The reduction in the number and length of strikes was, in part, due to workers' and employees' fear of losing their jobs and to their realization that real earnings for those with work has risen almost 35% between 1980 and 1987. There has also been a change of attitudes: many workers associate unions with strikes and therefore have increasingly turned their backs on the unions, whose membership has continued to decline. An important result for the overall economy is that the unions are no longer able to block the introduction of state–of–the–art technology in

order to protect jobs. Thus, while from 1974–80 output per worker in British manufacturing did not increase at all, from 1981–7 it grew by 40%. So powerful had the unions been that many people wondered: "Who governs?" After she was finished, no one would suspect that it was the union bosses.

More and more workers became homeowners (43% by 1983 and one–third of even unskilled laborers by 1988) thanks in part to Margaret Thatcher's policy of selling many state–owned council houses to their occupants. By the time her party finally left power in 1997, 68% of all households own their own homes. It is not surprising that the percentage of Britons who consider themselves to belong to the middle class increased from 30% of the population in 1979 to roughly 50% in 1987. Their lifestyles became more and more like those of the middle class; this was given added impetus by the education changes in the 1970s that largely did away with the several schooling tracks and brought most British schoolchildren together in one school. The massive occupational shifts and break–down in elite–structure in the educational system fostered increasing social mobility. It is no wonder that persons who lived in several classes in their own lifetime ceased to use class as a major political reference point. It is quite simply no longer accurate to speak of "two Britains," one a deprived working class and the other a traditional upper class.

Thatcher created a more prosperous and productive Britain. But her chief economic legacy was one of the mind. The pursuit of comfort and wealth had become marks of bad form. But she made prosperity an acceptable goal and free–market capitalism morally defensible. Tony Blair's Labour Party not only embraces both, but he won the 1997 elections by promising that his government could manage Thatcher's economy even more competently. By the 1990s anybody working in Britain's offices and factories could see that they are much better and more productively run than was the case two decades earlier. Industrial relations have improved dramatically.

Labor Unions

Public sympathy and enthusiasm for labor unions gradually eroded in the 1970s and early 1980s. In order to gain wage restraint from the powerful unions, Labour governments made so many concessions to them that many persons began to blame the unions for high prices and many of the economic problems. Their revulsion at the excessive "un-elected power" which union bosses wielded boiled to the surface in the 1978–9 "winter of discontent," when coal and transportation strikes threatened to paralyze the entire nation.

Both the economic recession and the Conservatives' broadside attacks against the Labour Party in general and the unions in particular greatly weakened the latter. Between 1979 and 1992 their membership dropped from 12 to 8 million. In 1979 more than half the workforce was unionized; 38% was in 1990 and 29% in 2002. By election time in 1983, almost three–fourths of all Britons favored stricter laws to regulate unions; an astonishing three–fifths of all trade unionists also favored legal curbs on union power. Union popularity declined further as the result of a protracted coal miners' strike in 1984–5. Union leader Arthur Scargill fanned the flames of anti–unionism with public pledges to bring down Thatcher's government. He failed, and her ability to break trade union power is her most lasting legacy.

In the 1990s strikes were at their lowest level in more than a half-century. In 1979, 29.5 man–days were lost to strikes; in 1995 that figure had fallen to 4.15. One expert noted: "It's much more risky to strike now. If you don't do it right according to the law, you end up in court." The 1.9 million lost workdays were the lowest figure since 1963, a fourth of the average in the 1980s and six times lower than the average in the 1970s. Unions affiliated with the TUC lost a third of their members after the Tories came to power in 1979. Even within the Labour Party the unions' influence has been drastically reduced, though not eliminated, thanks to the efforts of Prime Minister Tony Blair.

By 2002 only 18% of American workers belonged to unions, compared with 29% in the UK. The gap between the working and middle classes has also been narrowed by the changing composition of the labor unions. The increase in the number of civil service employees, the growth of the service sector within the economy, and the rise of computer–related and other high–technology industries in the south of England and especially around London and Cambridge prompted the growth of so–called "white collar unionism." That is, union members were no longer exclusively manual workers in factories and mines, but they could be teachers, engineers in a nationalized industry, secretaries in Whitehall, etc.

With rising inflation and talk of "paring down the public sector," these white–collar unions even became quite militant in pressing their demands. Thus, Britain began to experience a different breed of striker, from nurses and hospital personnel to civil servants. This militancy among the white-collar employees has helped even more to bridge the social gap between workers and employees and to break down class divisions.

Of course, there are still workers concentrated in large manufacturing or mining industries living in rented council housing in working class sections and remaining in a largely isolated social environment. They confront employers and managers whose political attitudes are also traditional and are diametrically opposed to those of their workers. These groups are far more likely to retain a strong loyalty either to the Labour Party or the Conservative Party and a strong class–consciousness. However, these kinds of workers and managers are becoming a diminishing minority in Britain's more service–oriented economy. Union members in the service sectors work in an environment that brings them into contact with all other classes, a factor that reduces, rather than sharpens class-consciousness. As a consequence, their voting behavior is far less class–bound. They can be attracted to parties that portray a new, non–class image and seem capable of overcoming the old social divides.

Britain and Europe

In 1973 the UK entered the EU, a move that has had a dramatic impact on its economy. The EU now buys 43% of British exports, compared to 31% in 1972. The high prices for food, fixed by the EU's common agricultural policy, have been a boon for British farmers. Still, many British remain critical of their country's entry into the EU.

In practice, British governments have tended to put British interests ahead of European interests. They have been cool on a common EU energy policy, a directly elected European Parliament and European Monetary Union (EMU). Britain has shown little interest in expanding European integration, and Thatcher tried hard to reduce the British contribution to the EU budget. In 1989–90 she remained suspicious of "deepening" EU unity on the grounds that it would undermine national sovereignty and that it is no time to create new bureaucracies and weaken national parliaments just when Eastern European nations are digging themselves out from underneath their bureaucracies and breathing new life into their legislatures. Not all British, even all Tories, agreed with her foot–dragging, and this contributed to her fall.

At the historic 1991 summit in Maastricht, Britain agreed to greater economic and political union on the condition that the UK could "opt out" of an eventual single European currency, which it chose to do when the Euro was introduced in 11 EU countries in 1999. It also rejected moves to make an EU "social policy" mandatory for all members. Despite much resistance from many Tories, Parliament finally accepted the treaty in 1993.

The Labour government is more supportive of British membership in a more united Europe although Prime Minister Blair promises to put British interests first. Thanks to the economic accomplishments of his predecessor, the UK does not have to worry about meeting the criteria for EMU. Its budget in 2002 had a deficit of .8% of GDP, and overall public debt stood at 40% of GDP. One of Blair's first acts as prime minister was to transfer the power to set interest rates from the Chancellor of Exchequer (Gordon Brown) to an unelected panel of the Bank of England. Greater independence for central banks is one of the EU's prerequisites for participation in the common currency. EMU remains unpopular in the UK. In 2000 only 27% favored the Euro, while 56% opposed joining. The Blair government decided that the UK would not join the first wave of monetary union, and the prime minister found it publicly expedient to announce in 2000 that "people don't want Europe interfering in every aspect of people's national lives." But he continued to steer a course toward Europe and the euro, with his sights on a referendum.

The British and French finally agreed to construct a twin–bore, 32–mile channel tunnel (dubbed "Chunnel") through which an auto–rail link between the two countries passes. Road vehicles are loaded on trains at terminals on both sides of the Channel and whisked at a speed of 100 miles per hour from one side to the other. The Channel became what Napoleon had described as "a ditch that will be leaped whenever one has the boldness to try." The two nations' leaders shared not only a bold vision of the future. This multi–billion-dollar project created many jobs and made a sizable dent in the unemployment problems that plagued both countries. In 1990 the burrowing French and British crews linked up under the Channel, and the Chunnel opened in 1994.

In November 1996 a dangerous fire broke out on a truck–carrying rail car, raising serious questions about the safety of the system. Miraculously no one perished in the inferno, but 800 yards of tunnel were ruined, and one of the system's two transport tubes had to be closed for more than a half year. Traffic in the other tube continued. Despite the accident, the Chunnel is extremely popular, carrying half a million passengers and nearly a quarter of a million tons of freight each

The United Kingdom

The 600–foot long boring machine which led others in clawing through 7.5 million cubic meters of chalk–marl one mile beneath the sea which divides Britain and France.

month. It has captured 45% of the lucrative cross–channel market. Nevertheless, it is mired in serious financial difficulties, having cost twice as much to build as projected. Repayment of the $13.5 billion debt had to be suspended while its finances were restructured.

The United Kingdom has been heavily involved in overseas trade for many centuries, and the importance of that trade continues to grow. In the last 50 years, the export of goods and services has moved from being one–fifth of the gross domestic product to one–third. Of these exports, 43% go to the EU, 17% to the rest of Europe and 11% to North America.

After the U.S., Britain is the world's largest investor abroad. In 1998 it was actually the largest because of British Petroleum's (BP) purchase of Amoco for $61 billion. Many well–known "American" brands are now British: Brooks Brothers belongs to Marks and Spencer, and Diageo owns Burger King and Pillsbury. In 1995 it surpassed Japan to become the largest source of foreign direct investment in the U.S. By 1999 the UK directs 30% of its direct investment to America, while the U.S. sends a fifth of its foreign direct investment to Britain. At the turn of the century only the U.S. and China attract more money from foreigners than does Britain. In part, this is due to the fact that Britain's labor costs (about $14 per hour in 1997) are the lowest of any major industrialized country.

The City of London (a small area within greater metropolitan London) is of immense significance in international finance. It has the world's largest insurance market, the lengthiest listing of overseas securities, the highest proportion of the Eurodollar market, and the biggest foreign exchange market. In 1986 a "big bang" occurred in the London financial world: the financial markets were largely deregulated, and foreign companies were permitted to trade in British financial markets for the first time. The overall effect has been to make London the world's most important financial center. Each day, 600,000 people go to work in 580 banks; that is more than the total population of Frankfurt. Big American banks have their continental headquarters there, and London's traders have grown to control 30% of global foreign exchange trading. Britain's financial institutions are fully competent in dealing with the Euro, even though its political leaders are not yet ready for it.

Prime Minister Blair inherited an economy that no one calls "diseased" any more. Its growth rate was 1% in 2002. At 5.1% in 2003, unemployment is one of the lowest of any major country in western Europe and is about half the EU average. Inflation is 3.1%. The budget deficit was

1.9% in 2003, considerably lower than that of other large European nations. Roughly a quarter of all foreign direct investment flowing into the 15 EU nations goes to the UK.

Productivity is a problem, lagging 37% behind that of the U.S. in 1998, and 25% behind that of Germany and France. It is higher in foreign multinational firms, which employ two million Britons, primarily because they invest more. The Blair government introduced the country's first minimum wage law. But the current economic success is also due to less cumbersome business regulations, cost effectiveness, and a flexible labor market. Privatization is also well advanced.

In September 2002, 400,000 rural Britons marched in London to dramatize what they called a "crisis in the countryside." It suffers from a depression in agriculture, made worse by the disastrous handling of the foot-and-mouth disease. Since the mid-1990s farm incomes have halved, and weekenders and 100,000 Britons resettling in rural Britain each year have driven house prices so high that many locals can no longer afford to live where they grew up. The positive side of this real estate inflation is that the value of farmers' assets has risen by ca. 40% since 1992. Thus the average farmer possesses an average net worth of 700,000 pounds (ca. one million dollars).

Britain is the fifth most popular tourist destination in the world, attracting 25 million foreign visitors annually. The 125,000 mostly small tourist businesses employ 1.75 million people, more than agriculture, food production, coal mining, steel, car and aircraft manufacturing, and textiles combined. In the 1990s it was responsible for creating a sixth of the new jobs.

CULTURE

The impact and pervasiveness of British culture on the rest of the world has been out of all proportion to the size and population of the United Kingdom. While those who participated in the Beatlemania of the 1960s might disagree, two British gifts to world culture stand out as most important. First, the achievement of English writers in producing a magnificent body of literature has influenced the way people think around the world. And within English literature, certainly Shakespeare and the King James Bible have been most important.

Second, the development of a constitutional, parliamentary democracy set an example to all the world of how men and women may live in freedom and guide their own destinies, and how compromise and civility rather than coercion are the

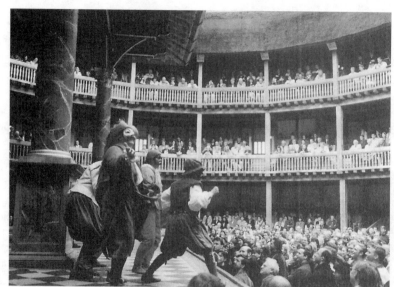

Globe Theatre

best ways to pull together the social fabric. In a world in which the majority of human beings do not enjoy political or individual freedoms, and other countries that attempt democracy are unable to achieve stability, the United Kingdom stands a worthy example of a free society living under laws.

The widespread knowledge of English as a first or second language throughout the world speaks for itself, be it the Americanized or British version. It has become the language of scientific expression almost worldwide. English is not spoken throughout England, Wales, Scotland and Ireland in an identical fashion. Local expressions and local pronunciations vary widely. The urbanized lower classes of London traditionally speak "Cockney" English, which the average American can seldom understand. Language has traditionally been a key to identifying the social class of a British person. The reason lies partly in the educational system.

Education and Class in Britain

The traditional school system had been tracked in such a way that a child's educational program was more or less fixed at age eleven. After the crucial "eleven–plus exam," some children went into trade or commercial schools. Others went into the more elite, state–supported grammar schools or the independent, privately endowed "public schools" (the most prestigious being Eton, Harrow and Winchester). "Public Schools" were especially geared to preparing pupils for the few seats in universities, especially at Oxford and Cambridge (known collectively as "Oxbridge"), which held the keys to success in politics, industry and scholarship. In a 1992 study of the top 100 persons in

Britain's elite, *The Economist* found that two–thirds had attended public schools, and more than half had studied at Oxford and Cambridge. Only a decade later, in 2002, those percentages had fallen noticeably to 46 public school and 35 Oxbridge graduates. The number of women had climbed from four to a mere five. The loosening hold of public school and Oxbridge alumni reflects the growth of competition, especially in business, that has resulted from deregulation and globalization. Life in Britain's larger and more multinational companies is no longer as cosy as it used to be. Ambitious products of the country's expanded university system have claimed top positions once reserved for the well-bred and those from famous schools.

Critics had long charged that the traditional educational system actually hardened and perpetuated class lines in British society. That is a major reason why the old grammar and secondary modern schools were fused into "comprehensive" secondary schools, in which all pupils learn under one roof. State-sponsored schools can no longer select for ability, and state scholarships to the coveted private schools were eliminated. About a tenth of all pupils attend the fee–paying "public schools." Some say that these reforms actually lowered educational standards, and the gap between rich and poor people's education has in fact widened. However, to make the testing easier, less intimidating, and fairer, the old A-levels taken in the pupil's final year of secondary school, which were crucial for university admission, were changed. They now take "Advanced Subsidiary," or AS-level, exams in their second-to-last year in school, and they are permitted to retake some of those tests to improve their grades. They then

take the more difficult A2 exams at the end of their last year. Their final grades are based on the results of the two years combined.

Over a third (35%) of university–age Britons (up from 5% in 1960 and one–eighth in 1980) study in one of the 90 universities or polytechnic schools. The Labour government wants to raise this to 50%. This dramatic increase in enrollment broke the budget and required that students contribute to the cost of their education. Many of these students were distressed by the Labour government's decision to end tuition–free higher education and to levy a £1,000 (ca. $1,700) yearly tuition charge. Those from lower–income families pay less, and the lowest 30% pay nothing. This is on top of the roughly $2,600 room and board costs, much of it borrowed or obtained through grants, including from local governments. Although Britons with a university education earn 17% more over a lifetime, there is resentment over such tuition and any talk of raising it to a level needed to cover the annual cost of a student (£10,500, according to Imperial College). Some enterprising British universities attract large numbers of foreign students and charge them American–level tuition.

The educational system remains a target of criticism. Critics argue that spending for it was cut by 10% in real terms under Thatcher. Even her Minister for Information Technology, Geoffrey Pattie, had complained, "schools are turning out dangerously high quotas of illiterate, delinquent unemployables." In 2002, spending on higher education was a mere 1.1% of GDP, compared to 2.3% in the U.S.

In 1993 the government introduced an Education Bill to parliament that took school reform another step forward. But after haphazard and under funded reforms under Thatcher and Major, British

Eton boys

The United Kingdom

schools still reflect the social stratification of the country. A majority of pupils leave full–time education or training at age 16, as John Major had done in 1959. As a result, less than half the work force is classified as skilled, compared with 85% in Germany and 75% in France. Tony Blair's campaign appeals in 1997 for higher academic standards and lower class sizes fell on sympathetic ears. The feeling is widespread that British schools are not fully prepared for the challenges of the 21st century.

While there is considerable dissatisfaction with the educational system, there is little doubt that Britain's establishment and class system have changed dramatically in the last decades. Of course, intelligent and ambitious individuals have always been able to succeed in Britain, whose society has long been less rigid than in many other countries. But in the UK today, status is largely earned, not inherited. BBC producer Nick Guthrie speaks of a revolution in the class system and argues, "it's not so much your family that matters; it's what you've achieved, and of course how much money you've got." Chancellor of the Exchequer Gordon Brown agrees, noting that on corporate boards, "titles are out, for the most part. Today it's not who you are, but what you have done....The old class system is not dead. But it is much weaker than ever before." An example of the new kind of establishment, based on money, athletic prowess or celebrity, is the knighthood conferred in 2002 on Sir Michael Jagger. The musical superstar asked meekly, "does this mean I'm part of the establishment?" Considering his global reputation, massive wealth and elegant country estate, the answer is yes.

Religion

Polls in 1990 revealed that 71% of Britons believed in God (77% in 1965), 44% in life after death, and 30% in the devil. Although the Anglican Church of England (in Scotland the Presbyterian Church of Scotland) is the official state religion, claiming up to 30 million members on paper, only a fifth of religiously active Britons belong. Church attendance has fallen dramatically in the Church of England. In 1960, 2.1 million attended on Easter Sunday, a figure that had fallen to 1.3 million by 1994. It is estimated that it lost about 1,000 church–goers every week during the 1990s. Polls in 2002 indicated that barely one in 50 British families say grace regularly before meals, compared with close to half in the U.S.

Most worshipers are drawn to religions that are better able to satisfy the thirst for spirituality: immigrant religions (mainly Islam, Sikhism and Hinduism), cults, Pen-

WORLD BUSINESS NEWSPAPER

FINANCIAL TIMES

Monday March 24 2003

www.ft.com

WAR IN IRAQ
9 pages of news and analysis

● US General Tommy Franks: Taking Vietnam's lessons to heart Page 13
● Hour of revenge at hand for Iran Khairallah Khairallah, Page 15
● Our military experts assess war strategies www.ft.com/tactics

PLUS Russia fights its risky reputation, FTfm

IRAQI RESISTANCE AT NAJAF ● UK WARPLANE DOWNED BY PATRIOT MISSILE ● US TROOPS ADVANCE ON BAGHDAD

Allied forces shaken by setbacks

Test ahead after early relief among investors

Oil and financial markets have reacted to the first days of the war with something close to euphoria, writes Alan Beattie.

A Truly European Newspaper

tecostal or charismatic Christian churches, or new age, non–mainstream faiths. In an attempt to lure worshipers back to the Church of England, its General Synod voted in 1992 to ordain women, a decision which had to be approved by parliament and the Queen in 1993. In protest, traditionalist Anglicans threaten to split away from the Church, and some may migrate to Catholicism.

The Media

Britain has 11 country-wide newspapers, and London boasts both high–quality titles, such as *The Guardian*, *The Times* and the *Financial Times*, as well as the more popular *News of the World*, *Daily Mirror* and *Sun*. Two–thirds of the papers sold are conservative; in order of circulation, they are the: *Sun*, (which nevertheless en-

dorsed Labour's Tony Blair in 1997), *Daily Mail*, *Daily Express*, *Daily Telegraph*, *Daily Star*, and *Times*. Fewer than 10% are non–aligned: *Today*, *The Independent*, and *Financial Times*. Only a fourth are left–leaning, chiefly the *Daily Mirror*, and *The Guardian*. With one of the world's most competitive and irreverent presses, Britain sells 14 million newspapers a day. However, most newspapers face financial problems, and they are losing readers. Since 1990 overall national readership has fallen by a fifth. Most troubling is that young people are not buying newspapers as their parents did and have not developed the habit of reading a daily at the breakfast table. Instead they are getting their news from TV, radio or online.

The news wire service, with particularly good international coverage, Reuters, is

renowned for its meticulous accuracy and avoidance of editorializing. In spite of the fact that ownership of these London dailies is concentrated in a few hands, they keep a sharp eye on Downing Street, Westminster and Whitehall. Bringing the important political news to all corners of the country, they do not stifle the lively regional press. They are also reinforced by widely–read weekly news magazines, such as *The Economist* and *The Observer*.

The written media is supplemented by radio and television, which are controlled by two public bodies, the British Broadcasting Corporation (BBC), whose directors are nominated by the government, and the Independent Broadcasting Authority (IBA), which permits private advertising. Both are expected to remain politically impartial (in stark contrast with commercial American television), and both vigorously resist being used by the government in power. For instance, when the American TV film *The Day After*, portraying the effects of a nuclear war was shown in 1983, the Minister of De-

fense, Michael Heseltine, demanded the right of reply on BBC. His demand was refused. The BBC also rejected Tory charges that it had presented a biased and unprofessional picture of the American bombing raid on Libya in April 1986, an attack made possible by British permission to use FB–111 aircraft stationed in Britain.

Since multi–channel TV came to Britain in 1990, a flood of American shows began to appear on screens. BBC struggles against losing its audience. It launched a 24–hour news service, News 24, to compete against Sky News and CNN. Its best defense is to continue producing its high–quality programs, which Americans like to watch on public television.

Ethnic Changes in Britain

A basic change in British society is ethnic—it had for 900 years experienced almost no immigration, except from Ireland. Now it is no longer a racially homogeneous society. As a consequence of decolonization, Asians and blacks poured into Britain from India, Pakistan, Africa and the Caribbean. The population is 7% non–white (half of them Asians of Indian, Pakistani, and Bangladeshi descent), a percentage that is likely to grow because of the declining birth rate of white Britons. In 2003 the Muslim population constituted 2.7% of the total.

By 1992 half of all West Indian babies in the UK were born out of wedlock (compared with 29% of whites), and two of five marriages in Britain ended in divorce. Since more than two–thirds of single parents are on welfare, and a child raised by only one parent is five times as likely to be poor, many more non–whites seem destined to poverty.

Immigration has been reduced. The 1981 British Nationality Act restricted it, and the inflow was reduced to a trickle. The number of successful applicants for British citizenship in 1993 was the lowest in more than a decade. Britain is now faced with the extremely difficult problem of integrating large groups of non–white minorities, who tend to be concentrated in the decaying inner cities, even though there is less residential segregation by race in Britain than in the U.S. Such concentration gives the impression that the minority presence in the UK is far greater than it actually is. A fifth of London's population belongs to an ethnic minority, and that figure will rise to a third by the year 2010. They often speak little or no English, worship religions that are quite unfamiliar to most British, dress or groom themselves in very different fashion from the rest of the population.

Ethnic minorities suffer the most from any economic downturn, especially un-

The United Kingdom

Statue of Martin Luther King

employment. In 1998 the jobless rate for blacks was around 22%, compared with under 7% for whites. The comparable figures in the U.S. were 11% and 5%. It is even higher among Pakistani and Bangladeshis: 27%. British blacks have not penetrated the top levels of business, the professions, judiciary, or the cabinet, as the American black elite has. Only 1% of soldiers are minorities (compared with 27% black in the U.S.), 2% of the police (3.3% in London) and 5% of civil servants. This may change as a result of an increase in non-white enrollment at British universities; 12% of students are from ethnic minorities, double their representation in the overall population. In London 29% of nurses, 31% of doctors, and more than 20% of civil servants are already from ethnic minorities.

The British began to become uneasy about being swamped by immigrants. When in 1981 dramatic racial riots occurred in such non-white ghettos as Brixton and Southall in London and Toxeth in Liverpool, they began to fear for their own protection. These violent outbreaks were the result of youth unemployment and disillusionment, poor living conditions, racial discrimination and inefficient police practices. The unarmed "Bobbies," who always seemed to symbolize British tact and tolerance, were severely criticized for alleged racism, arrogance and brutality. They still are regarded with distrust and suspicion in many non-white areas. In an effort to improve their public image, the London Metropolitan Police has recruited more black policemen.

The riots helped raise the awareness of the extent to which racial problems fester in a society in which many citizens have not yet accepted the fact of a multi-racial Britain. There is no consensus among Britons about race relations. Laws aiming to improve race relations were passed in 1965, 1968 and 1975, mainly modeled on American legislation, except that the provisions for judicial enforcement are much weaker. Also there is no official affirmative action. The government-sponsored Commission on Racial Equality combats discrimination, but its tools are mainly investigative and conciliatory, rather than prosecutive.

Young white gangs of "skinheads" and the "punk-rock" and "heavy metal" set derive morbid amusement from "Paki-bashing." Those whites who want to exploit the rising racial tensions, such as the neo-Nazi British National Party, seldom find favor with the voters. But in 1993, promising "rights for whites," it won a municipal council seat in London's East End.

In some ways Britain is a more integrated society than is the U.S. There is more dating and intermarriage between white and black men and women. According to a 1997 survey, half of Afro-Caribbean men born in Britain and a third of women born in the UK have a white partner. This is lower among British-born Indians, but the figures still show progress: 20% for men and 10% for women. In the U.S. only 4% of black men and 2% of black women have a white spouse. Tolerance for inter-racial marriage is strong: 74% respondents said in a 1997 poll that they would not object to one of their close relatives marrying a black, and 70% said the same about an Asian. Bangladeshis, Pakistanis and Indians remain more to themselves, though; fewer than 5% live with whites. Perhaps the most visibly integrated group in Britain was the female rock group Spice, five sassy young ladies exuding "girl-power."

A glowing example of integration is Trinidad-born V.S. Naipaul, who won the 2001 Nobel Prize for Literature. He graduated from University College at Oxford in 1953 and remained in England. An eternal outsider, he is a prickly critic of religious extremism. The panel praised him for transforming "rage into precision" in such books as *Among the Believers*.

A combination of tough anti-immigration policies, unusually detailed laws against racial discrimination, and the fact that legal immigrants have always been treated not as migrant workers but as permanent settlers, with automatic rights to vote, to run for office, and to claim social security benefits, has prevented the spread of kind of anti-immigrant sentiment and support for racist parties seen on the continent in the 1990s. Nevertheless, the number of racially motivated attacks doubled in Britain between 1989 and 1995. Serious ethnic rioting broke out again in 2001.

The immigration issue, so explosive in the 1960s and 1970s, has ceased to have any great significance at election time. Nevertheless, white fears worked politically more in favor of the tough-minded Conservatives than of the Labourites. On the other hand, Labour, which has always presented itself as the party of the underdog, receives the overwhelming majority of non-white votes. In the 1987 election, 27 non-whites ran for office, and for the first time since 1922, non-whites took seats in the House of Commons. In 1992 six non-whites were elected to parliament, including one Tory, and in 1997 there were nine. In 1993 there were more than 100 non-white local councilors.

Prior Tory attempts to bid for black votes sometimes backfired. For instance, in 1983 the largest of many ethnic minority newspapers, the *Caribbean Times*, refused to print a Tory advertisement displaying a neatly dressed black and the slogan, "Labour says he's black, the Conservatives say he's British," on the grounds that it was "insulting, obnoxious and immoral." In fact, 75% of blacks in the UK are British citizens, and most of the rest are Commonwealth citizens who can vote in Britain.

It has been difficult to integrate blacks and Asians into the political process, except in direct defense of their own interests. But there has been progress. Non-whites in the UK have visible positive role models in sports, the arts, business and the professions. There are grounds for optimism that the lauded English tolerance and gradualism will lead more British to accept the immigrants and their children as non-white Britons. It is symbolic that in 1998 a statue of Martin Luther King was placed in the last remaining niche above the Great West Door of Westminster Abbey.

FUTURE

During 18 years of Tory rule, power was increasingly centralized in the cabinet's hands in London, and the system's already weak institutional checks and balances withered. In reaction, a lively discussion on constitutional change is taking place. Will Hutton, whose book, *The State We're In*, was a bestseller in 1995, wrote that "once the courtesies of a 19th-century debating chamber have been observed, the government can make laws almost at will ... Monarchical power has passed in effect to the majority party in the House of Commons." Another bestseller, *Ruling Britannia: The Failure and Future of British Democracy*, offered a similar critique. Charter 88, an organization advocating broad structural changes in British government, grew by 1,000 supporters a month.

Polls in 1995 revealed that half the adult population thought the political system is out of date; 79% agreed that a written constitution and a bill of rights to protect individual liberty are needed; 77% favored adopting a referendum system. It is small wonder that Tony Blair wrote a half year before becoming prime minister that "changing the way we govern, and not just changing our government, is no longer an optional extra for Britain. ... The challenge facing us ... is to take a working constitution, respect its strengths, and adapt it to modern demands for clean and effective government while at the same time providing a greater democratic role for the people at large." The prospect for significant constitutional change came with the landslide Labour victory in 1997. Blair's win was a personal triumph for the prime minister, who had remolded his party into New Labour.

He wasted no time in announcing an ambitious legislative program, including constitutional reform. With its huge majority in the House of Commons, most of the government's proposals are enacted. Devolution in Scotland and Wales was begun by referenda to establish parliaments there and culminated in elections to them in 1999. His government is working hard on a settlement in Northern Ireland, which devolved power to that violence-stricken area. Limited self-government was introduced for London, and a leftist former-Labour politician, Ken Livingston, was elected mayor in May 2000. Referenda will be used more often to allow British to express their desires between elections. For example, a referendum to decide whether Britain should adopt the euro is likely within the next few years. An ad by euro opponents, depicting a Hitler look-alike giving the Nazi salute and proclaiming "One people! One state! One euro!" sparked a storm of indignation in Britain as "bad taste". Although Blair remains in favor of the euro, public opinion remains strongly opposed. In June 2003 the government postponed a decision. Reform of the House of Lords by completely eliminating hereditary peers and finding an acceptable mix of elected and appointed seats is delayed since the House of Commons could not agree upon a formula in 2003.

The government changed the raucous "prime minister's question time" in the House of Commons by converting it into a more serious, once-a-week half-hour session in which more questions from opposition backbenchers are allowed. The leadership confrontations with the opposition leader, which tend to be the sharpest, most entertaining and sometimes most embarrassing interchanges for the prime minister, have not disappeared, but opposition leader Iain Duncan Smith is no match for the eloquent and agile Blair.

Seeking answers to the question of how government could do more with less, its overall goal has been to take a welfare state built for the Britain of the 1940s and reform it for the Britain of the 21st century. The rising costs of welfare are unsustainable, and the electorate finds them unjustifiable. Blair designed a welfare-to-work plan in an attempt to move young and long-term unemployed workers off the government rolls. This bold move ignited a noisy revolt within his own party.

Britain remains Europe's healthiest large economy. Many Britons do not yet feel like they live in the new prosperous Britain, especially outside of London and the relatively prosperous enclaves in southern England. In fact, the gap between the prosperous Southeast and the poorer North continues to get wider. The North's industry is still mainly traditional, while that in the South tends to be newer, such as communications and electronics, which spend more on innovation. Nevertheless most of the doubt about Britain's future that surfaced in the bitter debates over joining Europe is gone.

Blair, who turned 50 on May 6, 2003, is not a confrontational politician and prefers to build coalitions across traditional class and political divides. Entering the March-April 2003 war against Iraq, he faced a rebellion of 139 of his party's MPs, and he told the *Sun* in a postwar interview that he had directed his aides to draw up resignation papers in case the outcome of a Commons debate went against him. Labour MPs know that he is the best guarantor of future Labour victories. As he had reminded a trade union meeting in 1995, before winning power: "I did not join the Labour Party to protest. I joined it as a party of government, and I will make sure it is a party of government." His standing with the public rose rapidly with the fall of Saddam Hussein, and it temporarily rewarded him for his principled stance on the war. By May 2003 his own approval rating had returned to the high levels he had enjoyed when taking office in 1997. But nagging questions about his use of intelligence information to justify going to war had by July 2003 dragged his party's popularity to below that of the Conservatives for only the second time in 11 years. Nevertheless, he is likely to lead Britain longer than Margaret Thatcher, who served more than 11 years. However, Blair had promised after the 2001 elections to restore the country's decrepit public services. He commented that the 2001 election results were "a mandate for reform and investment in the future, and it's also, very clearly, an instruction to deliver." This remains his challenge: to harness his new authority to improve public services and enact public service reforms. He must assert at home the kind of clarity and decisiveness he has shown on the international stage.

The Prime Minister: *Labour Party* leader Tony Blair with his wife, Cherie, and children, from left to right, 9–year–old Kathryn, 11–year–old Nicky, and 13–year–old Ewan, outside his local polling station in Trimdon, northeast England, Thursday, May 1, 1997, after casting their votes in Britain's national election.   AP/Worldwide Photo

The Republic of Ireland

with Mark H. Mullin

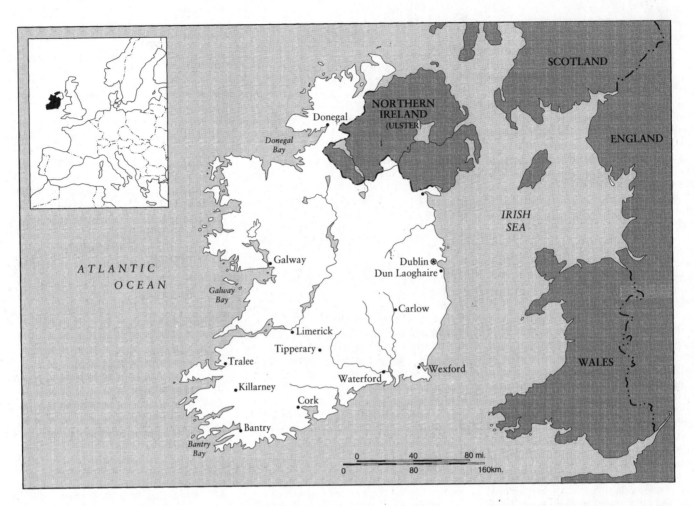

Area: 27,136 sq. mi. (70,262 sq. km., slightly larger than West Virginia).

Population: 3.8 million (estimated).

Capital City: Dublin (Pop. 650,000, estimated).

Climate: Cool and damp (rarely above 65 | SDF or below 40 | SDF).

Neighboring Countries: Great Britain lies a short distance eastward across the Irish Sea.

Official Languages: Irish (Gaelic), English, which is the first language of 98% of the population.

Ethnic Background: Celtic (some Norman and Norsemen).

Principal Religion: Roman Catholic (93.1%). 2.8% are Church of Ireland, .4% Presbyterian, and 3.7 other faiths.

Main Exports: Machinery and transport equipment, chemicals, foodstuffs and tobacco, high-tech equipment.

Main Imports: Machinery and transport equipment, chemicals, foodstuffs, petroleum and other fuels.

Currency: Euro.

Major Customers: EU 62,8% (including United Kingdom 19.8%), United States 17.1%, Germany 11,3%, France 7.7%, Netherlands 5.6%, Belgium and Luxembourg 4.8%.

Former Colonial Status: "Given" to England in 1155 by the Pope, turbulent English control until 1922; its own parliament, diminishing control until independence.

Independence Dates: December 6, 1921. (Dominion status); April 18, 1949, independent republic.

Chief of State: Mary McAleese, President (since October 1997).

Head of Government: Bertie Ahern, *Taoiseach*, pronounced "Tea–such," or Prime Minister (since June 1997).

National Flag: Three vertical stripes of green, white and orange.

Green fields, white–washed thatched cottages, leprechauns and men sitting in front of a peat fire spinning tales that are part fact and part fiction are images of Ireland that the first–time tourist seeks. This scene is also found in St. Patrick's Day cards, framed in green. While the tourist may miss much of what is new in Ireland, both the green fields and the confusion of fact and fantasy are still there for him to find. And both are largely the result of Ireland's location—it lies at the spot where the warm air and water of the Gulf Stream confront their cold rivals

of the northern latitudes. This produces a climate in which temperature variations are rare; it is an unusual day when the temperature is more than slightly warm or cold.

The confrontation of warm and cold produces air that is frequently moist—thus the lushness of the green, and skies that are always changing—gray and sad one minute, brilliant and joyful the next. If the sky is not constant, why should reality be constant? And, perhaps it is the soft, moist air that blurs fact and fantasy. George Bernard Shaw wrote of Ireland to an English friend, "You've no such colors in the sky, no such lines in the distance, no such sadness in the evenings. Oh the dreaming! The dreaming!"

If one may generalize about the people of a nation, the Irish people reflect their climate. There is a gentleness about the Irish, an essential sadness punctuated by flashes of sparkling wit. And there is a willingness to let the line between reality and dream be as indistinct as that between the distant mountains and the evening sky.

If its location has shaped the green beauty of Ireland and the character of its people, its location has been more responsible for shaping its history. Ireland is not merely an island; it is an island off the coast of another island. While its contact with the continent has usually been indirect, its subjugation to England has been of paramount influence. Being one step removed from the mainland has kept continental armies, and the cultural influences that they brought, out of Ireland. Roman legions never tramped across its fields. Although Norsemen settled on the east coast and raided many other areas, Irish culture achieved a flowering of learning and artistic brilliance while the rest of Europe slipped into the Dark Ages.

As nation–states developed on the continent, Ireland was involved in European dynastic wars only when England had a stake in the contest. The last continental troops to be in Ireland made an unsuccessful attempt to export the French Revolution. Ireland even managed to be one of the few European countries to be neutral during World War II. As the English, century after century, negotiated and fought rivals on the continent, they did not want to have to worry about the island on their other side. The English always felt a domination of Ireland was essential to their security. The Irish Sea, after all, varies in width from 120 miles to only 11 miles, thus the fates of England and Ireland have been intertwined for the past 800 years.

Ireland is like a small bowl floating in the Atlantic. Its mountains ring the coastal region; they seldom reach more than 3000 feet (914 km.) into the sky. But the steepness with which they meet the sea gives them the appearance of considerable height. The center of the island is relatively flat, with the Shannon River flowing from north to south like a fine crack in the bottom of the bowl. West of the Shannon, peat bogs provide much of Ireland's fuel. East of the Shannon, the plains are rich grasslands, superb for cattle or horses. In fact, the Curragh, the finest stable and racetrack in the land, has 5000 acres of grass uninterrupted by either a tree or a fence. But even in the center of Ireland, one is never far removed from the sea, for the whole island is only 150 miles wide and 275 miles long.

Ireland is a beautiful and gentle land. Tragically, its history has not always been so.

HISTORY

The Early Period

The earliest remains of humans in Ireland date from about 7000 B.C. These hunters and food gatherers lived along the coasts and near the rivers. By 3000 B.C. Neolithic settlers had introduced agriculture and pottery. Their most spectacular accomplishments, elaborate Megalithic burial chambers, can still be seen today. At Newgrange one may enter the massive chamber by crawling through a tunnel 62 feet long. It is so constructed that only at the summer solstice does sunlight come down the tunnel and illuminate the interior chamber.

About 300 B.C. the Gaelic Celts used their knowledge of iron weapons to gain control of the island. Celtic Ireland was divided into some 150 local kingdoms under the loose control of the Kings of the Five Provinces. Although Meath later became part of Leinster, the four provinces of Ulster in the north, Leinster in the southeast, Munster in the southwest and Connacht in the west have retained fairly similar boundaries to this day.

Saint Patrick

One of the High Kings who ruled at the Hill of Tara from 380 to 405 A.D. was Niall, an ancestor of the O'Neills, an important family in Ulster until the 17th century. Niall's troops attacked both Britain and Normandy. On one raid, a young Briton named Patrick was brought back as a slave. After several years in Ireland, Patrick escaped to the continent where he entered a monastery. In 432, after being consecrated as a Bishop, Patrick returned to Ireland. He spent Lent in prayer at the top of Croagh Patrick, a mountain overlooking the Atlantic in County Mayo. Bound by age–long tradition, even now, more than 50,000 people a year make the strenuous 2700-foot climb to the top. And it is typical that some do it as an adventurous outing and some do it as a religious penance. In fact, thousands climb over the rough stones with bare, and therefore bleeding, feet. The story is told that two young men were climbing and one of them saw some attractive girls up ahead. He said, "Let's hurry and catch up with those girls." The other one replied, "Oh, I wouldn't dare. It's for too much foolin' with the girls that I'm havin' to make the climb."

Certainly Patrick was one of the most successful missionaries of all time. Within a few years after his death, the whole island was Christian. Celtic Christianity developed in unusual patterns. Instead of the Bishop and his Diocese being the chief authority, the Abbott and the monastery were the center of ecclesiastical life. The emphasis on monastic life had three major effects on cultural developments.

First, monks often practiced extremes of asceticism. To this day, Irish Christianity has maintained an emphasis on self–denial and penance that affects the Irish character. Second, while the rest of Europe

The ruins of Rocktown Castle, County Limerick

Ireland

descended into darkness, Irish monasteries kept the light of western culture burning. Piety, painting and learning were combined into one art form: the illuminated manuscript of the scriptures. Flights of imagination turned the letters of holy books into fantastic geometric shapes and celestial beings. The most famous illuminated manuscript, the Book of Kells, may be seen today in the Library of Trinity College, Dublin.

Third, because monastic orders thought beyond the geographic boundaries of the Diocese, Irish missionaries carried Celtic Christianity to Britain and the continent. The Irish St. Colombo established a famous monastery at Iona off the coast of Scotland. But perhaps the most interesting missionary was St. Brendan—medieval manuscripts describe how he and a group of monks sailed in a leather boat from the coast of Kerry. They visited a land of sheep, then an island occupied by giant blacksmiths working at their forges, and later an area of great fog. Finally, they reached a new land of beauty and richness that was divided by a large river. Brendan returned to Ireland just before he died. The story has usually been dismissed as a fanciful legend. In 1977, however, a group of men built a leather boat and sailed from Brendon's creek in Kerry. They were blown to the outer Hebrides (where there are many sheep), wintered in Iceland (where volcanoes might be confused with giants' forges), were becalmed in the fog off the Grand Banks, and finally, in 1978, washed ashore in Canada. Perhaps Brendan, not Leif Ericson or Christopher Columbus, was the first European to reach the New World!

Viking Raids and Norse Settlements

Unfortunately, the very success and more particularly the wealth of the monasteries brought trouble. Beginning in the 9th century, Viking raiders began to attack monastic and other settlements, plundering them for gold and valuables. Inevitably, the monks sought refuge in remote places. The most spectacular of these is Skellig Michael, a tiny island off the coast of Kerry. Today, those who brave the four miles of rough seas in an open boat can climb the steps cut into the stone face by monks over a thousand years ago and visit the remains of the bee–hive huts perched 550 feet above the water.

By the 10th century, the Norsemen began to plan settlements. The Vikings established the first cities in Ireland near the mouth of important rivers. Dublin, Waterford, Cork and Limerick all began that way.

At times the Celtic Irishmen intermarried with the Norse and at times they

Skellig Michael

tried to drive them into the sea. Brian Baru, after defeating the Norsemen in Munster, established himself as High King of all Ireland in 1002. Brian married the beautiful Gormflath whose six feet of height was crowned with flaming red hair. Unfortunately, as so often happened in Irish history, treason destroyed a chance for national unity. Gormflath's half–Danish son by an earlier marriage plotted with his mother, his uncle and other Danish chieftains to attack Brian. At the Battle of Clontarf in 1014 in which 20,000 men took part, Brian's forces were victorious and broke the Viking domination of Ireland. Tragically, at the end of the battle, a Danish soldier broke free and killed Brian in his own tent. Even more tragically, neither Brian's brief unification of Ireland nor his freeing it of foreign domination, proved lasting. No clear successor to him was able to establish control, and strife between local warlords continued as an Irish tradition. Because of these rivalries, new invaders arrived within a hundred and fifty years.

The name Dermot MacMurrough has been a black one in Irish history for eight hundred years. It was he who invited British troops into Ireland. But it is easier to see the tragic consequences of his act in retrospect than it would have been in the 12th century. In fact, it was the Pope himself, Adrian IV, the only Englishman ever to be Pope, who set the stage. Wishing to bring the practices of Celtic Christianity into conformity with the rest of Roman Christianity, Adrian issued the Papal Bull *Laudabilitier* in 1155 that granted Henry II of England permission to control Ireland. For twenty years, Henry did not make a move across the Irish Sea. However,

when Dermot MacMurrough lost control of the Kingdom of Leinster, he asked for help from the Normans who had then been ruling England and Wales for a hundred years.

Norman–Anglo Saxon Invasion and Control

In 1170 Strongbow, Earl of Pembroke, led a group of Normans into Ireland. He married MacMurrough's daughter and for a while it appeared that an independent Norman kingdom might be established. A year later, however, Henry II himself brought a large force of British Normans into Ireland. With the murder of Thomas à Becket less than twelve months behind him (see The United Kingdom), Henry may have thought it was a good time for some foreign travel. He not only established Normans loyal to himself as local rulers, but did away with the Celtic form of worship and brought Irish Christianity under the control of the Roman Church.

Two legacies of the Normans are still plentifully evident in Ireland. Many of the great names of Ireland came with the Normans: Joyce, Fitzgerald, Barry and Burke. These names can still be seen on many store and pub fronts. A person driving through Ireland also still sees the remains of castles, the prototypes of which were built by the Normans. These are usually rectangular stone towers three or four stories high. Most are in ruins, but a few such as Bunratty, Blarney, Dungory, Cahair and Knappogue have been restored and are open for visitors or popular medieval banquets. Over 300 castles still stand in Ireland.

As the Anglo–Normans became settled in Ireland, they adopted more and more of the Irish ways. The old saying is that "They became more Irish than the Irish themselves." Eventually, of course, such assimilation began to threaten the rule of the British crown. The attitude of the English was shown in the statutes of Kilkenny in 1366. These provided a punishment of the loss of lands for any Englishman who spoke Irish, married Irish people or adopted Irish customs.

English authority was strongest in the area around Dublin, known as "The Pale." Outside this region, local rulers paid only nominal homage to the British Crown and British ways. Thus the expression "Beyond the Pale" as a term of derision expresses things from the English point of view. While they had only small loyalty to Britain, the Irish rulers could hardly be described as ardent nationalists. Ireland was so fragmented politically that the idea of allegiance to Ireland itself was not an effective alternative. Rather, each local lord simply looked after his own interests.

Religious Intolerance After the Reformation

It is interesting, but futile, to speculate what would have happened to relationships between Britain and Ireland if the Reformation had not come to England. Perhaps Ireland would have gone the way of Scotland and Wales and become part of the United Kingdom. But the Reformation drove an irreconcilable wedge of hatred and mistrust between the English and the Irish.

England vacillated between Roman Catholicism and Protestantism through several monarchs, but with the crowning of Elizabeth I, the English were ready to try to export the Reformation. For the next four hundred years, religion and nationalism would be intertwined in Ireland. In 1579, armed rebellion arose in the southwest of the island. As a reprisal against the rebels and as a reward to her soldiers, Elizabeth confiscated vast areas of land from the Irish and gave them to Englishmen. On one such parcel of land, Walter Raleigh planted the first Irish potato. It was a crop well suited for growing by the Irish and they soon became dependent on it, much to their regret during the potato famine 275 years later, one of the greatest tragedies in Irish history.

By 1588 Elizabeth's rule was strong enough that as the ships of the Spanish Armada wrecked against the rocky shores of Ireland, the Irish obeyed her orders and slaughtered the would-be invaders. Only in Ulster in the north were the Spaniards spared. This was ironic; because Ulster held out against English rule, a sequence of events began that led in the 20th century to the north being the one area of Ireland loyal to the British crown.

At the end of the 16th century, Hugh O'Neill led a rebellion in Ulster. He embarrassed Elizabeth's current favorite Essex, but finally in 1601 was defeated at Kinsale by Mountjoy. In 1607 he and other Ulster chiefs fled to the continent in "the flight of the Earls." James I filled the vacuum by sending Scots Presbyterians to settle in Northern Ireland. These are the antecedents of today's Protestants in Northern Ireland loyal to the British. It is significant that the only Protestants in Ireland were imported.

Upheavals in the British monarchy brought violence to Ireland in the 17th century. Oliver Cromwell beheaded Charles I and in 1649 landed in Ireland. His purpose was to establish his brand of Puritanism in Ireland and end the possibility of rebellion. Tens of thousands of Irish were killed or driven into exile. Irish landlords in the fertile east were given the choice of death or migration to the rocky areas of the west. "Hell or Connacht" are still remembered as the only options open to them. By 1660, only one quarter of the country was owned by Irish Catholics.

When James II, a Catholic, came to the throne of England, there was a chance of reconciliation. But there was an immediate rebellion of Protestants against James, who chose William of Orange, a Netherlands Protestant as King of England; the decisive battle was fought in Ireland in 1690. Protestants in Ulster still celebrate the anniversary of the Battle of Boyne, fought on Irish territory, where William defeated the forces of James. This greatly irritates their Catholic neighbors.

As retribution for support of James, the English confiscated more areas of Irish land and imposed the Penal Laws. These forbade Catholics to vote, to hold office, to send their children to anything but a Protestant school or to have wealth above a set limit.

The Georgian Era

Much of Dublin and many beautiful country homes were built by the Protestant aristocracy during the Georgian era of the 18th century. The vast majority of the population, Catholic peasants, subsisted on potatoes grown on tiny plots of land. The success of the American and French revolutions inspired hopes among the down-trodden people. The ideals of equality and fraternity were imported from the continent. Theobald Wolfe Tone founded the United Irishmen, a group that sought to include those of different religions in the establishing of a Republic. In 1798 a French force with Tone in attendance landed in Mayo on the west coast. The British commander, Cornwallis, was more successful than he had been at Yorktown, and the French–Irish forces were soon defeated.

The English now tried to have Ireland conform to the pattern that Scotland and Wales had followed years earlier. The Act of Union, passed in 1800, abolished the Irish Parliament and gave the Irish representation in the British parliament at Westminster. Robert Emmet tried an unsuccessful revolution in 1803; his statue stands today in Washington, D.C., but his words were engraved on the heart of

The ancient mansion of Sir Walter Raleigh, Youghal

Ireland

every Irish revolutionary who came after him: "When my country takes her place among the nations of the earth, then and not till then let my epitaph be written."

Further Attempts at Freedom and the Potato Famine

Two names dominate Irish attempts for freedom in the 19th century: Daniel O'Connell and Charles Stewart Parnell. But their periods of influence were separated by the most terrible tragedy Ireland ever knew. In the first half of the century, Daniel O'Connell worked to improve the position of Catholics. He won election to the House of Commons in 1828 even though, as a Catholic, he could not take his seat. A year later, the Penal Laws that accomplished this were replaced. In the 1840s O'Connell developed a large following that demanded the repeal of the Act of Union. However, when he obeyed an order by the British government to cancel a mass meeting in Clontarf, his political support soon failed.

By the 1840s more than half the people of Ireland were dependent on potatoes as their principal source of food. In the wet summer of 1845, blight attacked the crop, and it appeared again in 1846 and 1847. Famine and death spread across the stricken land. The relief efforts of the British government were too little and too late. In a population of 8.5 million, 1 million starved and another million fled their country. English–speaking countries around the world, particularly the United States, received a transfusion of Celtic, Catholic blood that would, in turn, help shape their destinies. Even as the famine subsided, immigration continued and for the next forty years, 1% of the population left each year. Many found their way to America, where by the onset of the 21st century 44 million persons claim Irish descent, nine times as many as inhabit the whole island of Ireland. One hundred years after the great famine, the population was only one–half what it had been before the blight struck.

As Irish immigrants prospered abroad, many did not forget the cause of Irish independence. Money and occasionally arms or leaders flowed back into Ireland and supported various movements. The Fenians, a secret society favoring armed revolution and also known as the Irish Republican Brotherhood, was founded in 1856 in Ireland and the United States. In 1879, the Land League was founded by Michael Davitt and was supported by American money. It worked through parliament to achieve land reform. Charles Stewart Parnell became the leader of the Irish Parliamentary Party. He controlled enough seats in the British parliament to tip the balance of power at various times.

His Home Rule Bill passed the House of Commons, but was defeated in the House of Lords. His next try for home rule might have been successful, but in 1890 a scandal broke when Parnell was the cause of a divorce between Kitty O'Shea and her husband. Although Parnell married Kitty, neither Victorian England nor Catholic Ireland would forgive him. How ironic it was that one man's illicit love of a woman

delayed the possibility of home rule until it was too late to be effective.

In 1912, after severely limiting the power of the House of Lords, the House of Commons finally passed a Home Rule Bill, but by that time the Protestants in Ulster were afraid of being controlled by a Catholic majority. Sir Edward Casson organized the Ulster Volunteers, a military group armed with German guns to

The potato famine struck a severe blow to Ireland

oppose the move. The next year the Irish Republican Brotherhood and the *Sinn Fein* (pronounced "Shin Fane," meaning "Ourselves Alone") formed the Irish Volunteers to oppose the Ulster Volunteers.

But the outbreak of World War I caused Britain to postpone home rule for the duration of the war. With British attention focused on the continent, the Irish Volunteers and the Irish Citizens Army staged an armed rebellion. On Easter Monday, 1916, rebels captured the center of Dublin. At the General Post Office, they proclaimed the Irish Republic: "We declare the right of the people of Ireland to the ownership of Ireland and to the unfettered control of Irish destinies to be sovereign and indefeasible. The long usurpation of that right by a foreign people and government has not extinguished the right nor can it ever be extinguished except by the destruction of the Irish people. In every generation for centuries the Irish people had and have asserted their right to national freedom and sovereignty. Six times in the past three hundred years they have asserted it in arms. Standing on that fundamental right and again asserting it in arms in the face of the world, we hereby proclaim the Irish Republic as a sovereign, independent state, and we pledge our lives and the lives of our comrades in arms to the cause of its freedom, of its welfare, and of its exultation among the nations."

Within a week the rebellion was crushed; because the British were at war, they reacted to the rebellion as treason, and with great severity, executing most of the leaders. Eamon deValera was spared because he had been born in the United States. Those executed instantly became heroes and martyrs to the Irish people, and hatred toward England became even deeper.

When World War I ended, the Sinn Fein again proclaimed an Irish Republic. Eamon deValera was President and Michael Collins led frequent terrorist raids on British installations. The British fought back with the Auxiliary Cadets (former officers) and the Black and Tans (former enlisted men). Both sides practiced atrocities, murders, burnings and lootings. The Irish desire for freedom received world–wide publicity when Terrence McSwiney died in a British prison after a 74–day hunger strike. This strategy would later be used in the fight by India for its freedom from Britain and again in Ulster in the 1980s and 1990s.

Strife and Freedom

The three years of fighting are still known by the Irish as "The Troubles," though many years in Irish history could

The Counties of Ireland

qualify for that title. Parliament passed the Government of Ireland Act in 1920 that allowed for two types of Home Rule, one for the six counties in the north and another for the rest of Ireland. In early 1922 the Republican Government led by Arthur Griffith and Michael Collins accepted a treaty that made twenty–six counties a free state within the British Commonwealth, and left the six northern counties a province of the United Kingdom. DeValera refused to accept the treaty, and for a year and a half led a civil war against his former friends. Collins was killed in a battle and Griffith died, but deValera was forced to give up his fight. William Cosgrave became head of the Irish Free State; the boundary between the Free State and Northern Ireland was accepted in 1925.

Eamon deValera returned to power in 1932 as head of the Fianna Fail ("Warriors of Destiny") Party that held a majority for sixteen years. In 1937 a new constitution declared Ireland to be "a sovereign, independent, democratic state." Only formal ties with Britain remained. Ireland was officially neutral during World War II, but many Irishmen served in the British armed forces. Further, it was an important refueling stop for transatlantic military aircraft during the strife.

In 1949, a coalition government led by John Costello took Ireland out of the Commonwealth and made it an independent Republic. DeValera served as *Taoiseach*, (pronounced "tea–such"), a Prime Minister, several times, but in 1959 he gave up leadership of the Fianna Fail and was elected President of the Repub-

Ireland

By the sea in County Cork

lic. During the 1950s, Ireland began a major push toward industrialization. Foreign capital was invited into the country and given tax incentives. By the mid–1960s, industrial output was growing at over 5% a year. Ireland joined the EC in 1973, which gave a great boost to both its agricultural and industrial production. The improved economic situation brought about a rising standard of living. Automobiles and televisions became commonplace.

POLITICAL SYSTEM

A Written Constitution Derived from an Unwritten One

The Republic of Ireland (Eire) is Europe's newest independent state, having been founded in 1921 and having separated itself completely from Britain in 1949. It devotes much attention to strengthening a sense of Irish national identity, and the resentment resulting from recent British occupation is still very strong. Because of its long domination by Great Britain, it is hardly surprising that the Irish political system so closely resembles that of its former conqueror. Before Ireland gained its independence, many Irishmen had served in the British House of Commons. Therefore, they had not only gained their parliamen-

tary experience in Britain, but had also contributed to the very development of the British political system.

In some important ways, however, Irish democracy differs from the "Westminster model" of Great Britain. The Republic of Ireland has a written constitution that it adopted in 1937. Article 2 of that document mandated the eventual reunification of Ireland: "The national territory consists of the whole island of Ireland, its islands and the territorial seas." This article was removed in 1998 as a contribution to a daring Northern Ireland settlement.

The Catholic Church

The constitution also pledges to support the teachings of the Roman Catholic Church. Except for the Vatican itself, Ireland has traditionally been the least secular state in all of Europe. The Catholic Church maintains considerable influence in social affairs. It controls all but 462 of the 3,940 primary and secondary schools. Senator Donal Lydon once noted, "the Church has contacts at every level of society, in every corner. Its influence is everywhere. Any politician who ignores the views of the Church would need to be crazy." Many younger Protestants in Eire left; of the 115,000 Protestants who remain, most are elderly.

In recent years, the church's political influence has declined significantly, as a younger generation is more reluctant to accept Catholic teachings. In the 21st century only six in ten Catholics regularly attend Sunday mass, down from 87% in 1984 and 91% in 1974. Only 38% of Irish Catholics regularly take communion. Contraceptive devices are now legal, but that does not prevent a fifth of all children from being born out of wedlock. Following referenda in 1992 and 1995, Irish women are permitted to have abortions abroad; they may be performed in Ireland if the life of the mother is threatened. By 2002 about 7,000 women were going to Britain to have an abortion, up from 578 in 1971. This would be as if 500,000 American women had to go to Toronto each year to obtain an abortion. Ireland remains the only western country, except Malta, where abortion is banned, not only by law, but by the constitution. In a March 2002 referendum Irish voters rejected by the narrowest margin (50.4% vs. 49.6%) a proposal to tighten abortion laws.

As a result of a close vote in 1995 (50.2%, with urban support outweighing rural opposition), couples are allowed to divorce after a four–year separation. The 60% yes vote in Dublin swung the result. All the parties and most of the media supported it. The campaign was bitterly fought: opponents' posters read "Hello Divorce, Goodbye Daddy!," while proponents, irreverently referring to the spate of revelations about child–molesting and sexual transgressions by priests, waved signs reading "Let the bishops look after their own families!" These scandals involving clergy have shaken respect for ecclesiastical authority. The government became involved in 2002 by ordering the police to set up a special team of detectives to investigate every case of sexual abuse involving priests ever reported. It also reached an agreement with 18 religious orders indemnifying them against abuse claims at state-financed schools they operated. Thousands of victims are expected to receive as much as $1 billion total.

The referenda manifest an open revolt against the Church's dominance. Former President Mary Robinson spoke of the country's "new pluralism," which "means the movement of a predominantly Catholic country, where the Catholic moral code and doctrines had a very significant place, to a society still influenced by the role of the Church but having other voices and having a sense of space between legislators and the Catholic Church." In the spirit of the times, the 30–year censorship ban on *Playboy* magazine was lifted in 1996.

Whereas Protestants in Northern Ireland outnumber Catholics by about 58% to 42%, in the Republic they constitute only about 3% of the population. Since Independence their numbers have declined by two–thirds. Nevertheless, they have played and continue to play a role out of proportion to their size. They were important in creating modern Irish nationalism, from Wolfe Tone and his United Irishmen at the end of the 18th century to Charles Stewart Parnell and the home rule movement in the 19th. The Republic's first president, Douglas Hyde, was one, as were great Irish writers like W.B. Yeats, Samuel Beckett and Oscar Wilde. They were products of the Dublin Protestant middle class. Ireland's premier university, Trinity in Dublin, was opened to Catholics only in recent years. Protestants created even such recognizable Irish products as Jameson whiskey and Guinness stout.

Two Languages

The constitution recognizes two official languages: English and Irish, the latter of which is a Celtic language, closely related to Scottish, Gaelic and more distantly, to Welsh. It was spoken by a majority of Irishmen until the first half of the nineteenth century when it rapidly lost ground to English. Irish is now "used frequently" by only about 5% of the people and is spoken as a native language by only about 2% (about 70,000 people) in seven small pockets along the western seaboard, an area known as The Gaeltacht. There are three dialects, and the speaker of one will not necessarily understand everything said in the other two.

As the twentieth century closes, Ireland is experiencing a resurgence of the Irish language. In 1996 polls, more than a million claimed "some proficiency" in it, and a half million said they are "fluent" or intend to become so. These numbers justified the creation of an Irish–language television station, called *Teilifis na Gaeilge* (literally "Irish TV"), which broadcasts home–grown soap operas and news and sports programs aimed primarily at educated and urbanized Irishmen. They also prompted the education ministry to create a dozen new all–Irish primary schools.

With state policy to promote the use of Irish, it is a required subject in the schools. Only recently did it become possible to receive a school leaving certificate without passing an examination on the Irish language. Parliamentary documents are translated into it, and parliamentarians sometimes begin their speeches in the language. After a few sentences, though, they usually switch to English with the words "As I was saying ..." Also, some persons wonder what good a sign does which reads *Roinn na Plandeolaiochta. Aonad an Leicteron Mhiocrascóip'*, when the following words must be written underneath it to make it comprehensible: "Department of Plant Science. Electron Microscopy Unit."

The Supreme Court

As in most countries, a written constitution also calls for the Supreme Court to uphold that fundamental document. The Republic has a Supreme Court consisting of a Chief Justice and five others. It is empowered to decide on the constitutionality of laws if the President of the Republic asks for an opinion. This provision, known in the United States as "judicial review," is, of course, not present in Great Britain because there is no written constitution. However, English legal concepts and common law did replace the ancient Irish law (known as the Brehon law) by the 17th century. Thus Irish justice does bear an unmistakable British stamp. The Supreme Court demonstrated its power in 1993 by declaring hundreds of EU directives unconstitutional because they had bypassed the Irish Senate.

The President

The most notable divergence from the "Westminster model" is that the Republic of Ireland does not have a monarch and all links with the British crown were severed in 1949. Instead of a monarch, the Republic has a President, elected by the whole people for a seven–year term. This term can be renewed only once. The office is chiefly ceremonial, but unlike the British king or queen, Irish presidents have been leading political figures who continue to exercise considerable influence within the system, even if their powers are restricted.

The first woman president in Irish history, Mary Robinson, was elected in 1990. For years she had opposed Catholic positions on contraception, divorce, and homosexuality. Her election signaled an important change from traditional social

President Mary McAleese

attitudes. She became one of the most popular presidents in Irish history, enjoying a 93% approval rating in 1996. Not inclined to shy away from controversy, she unofficially met Sinn Fein leader Gerry Adams in 1993 and shook his hand in public in 1996, a political act that won her countrymen's praise. She became the first Irish chief of state to meet a British monarch. The fact that she is married to a Protestant manifests tolerance on this religiously torn island. In 1997 she became UN High Commissioner for Human Rights.

Her successor is Mary McAleese, a Belfast lawyer and vice–chancellor of Queen's University, who was the candidate of Fianna Fail. A resident of Northern Ireland, she is the first British subject to be elected president of Ireland. Under the Irish constitution, residents of the six "partitioned" counties of the North are considered citizens of the republic. She is a conservative Catholic who opposes the legalization of abortion and divorce, but she favors the ordination of women. She admits that she is an unabashed nationalist. She was not helped by the fact that Gerry Adams said during the campaign that she would make a fine president and by the fact that she has a cousin serving a life prison term for an IRA murder. She disavows any links with Adams or Sinn Fein and pledges to stand above

Ireland

politics, to "seek to heal the hurt of divided Ireland," and to "build bridges."

The Parliament

Despite the differences described, the Irish political system developed by using Britain as a model. Irish government is parliamentary. This means that there are no checks and balances among three equal branches of government as in the United States. The Lower House of parliament is supreme because unless the government can find a majority in it to carry forth its policies, that government must resign. Parliamentary government in the Republic of Ireland has usually been stable and durable. Conflict in the Republic now takes place almost entirely within the parliamentary traditions and standards of conduct left by the British.

The Irish Parliament (called the *Oireachtas*—pronounced "or–rock–tas") is bicameral. The Upper House is the Senate (*Seanad*) composed of 60 members, 11 of whom are named by the Prime Minister and six by the universities. The remaining 43 are selected from five panels of nominees representing the national language and culture, agriculture and fisheries, organized and unorganized labor, industry and commerce, public administration and social services. The Senate has the power to delay legislation for up to 90 days in order to try to amend bills. However, the lower house can always outvote it.

One might ask why such a weak body should even exist. Upper houses usually have the greatest importance in federal states where regional interests must be represented within the national government. However, the four traditional Irish provinces (Ulster in the north, Connacht in the west, Munster in the south and Leinster in the east) are not political units. Further, the 115 local authorities are supervised by the National Department of Environment. Local budgets are financed partly by grants from the national government, since local property taxes (known as "rates") cannot possibly provide enough revenue. In other words, the Republic of Ireland is a unitary state, and political authority rests largely with the central government. This centralized system exists even though local concerns are very important to Irish politicians. Thus, the Senate's purpose was never to represent provincial interests, but instead to give some political power to certain groups which could not win it in free elections before the whole people.

Political power is centered in the Lower House of Parliament known as the *Dáil* (pronounced "Doyle"). This House is composed of 166 members known as *Teachtái Dála*, or TD for short), elected from 41 constituencies. Elections must be held at least every five years. The prime minister (called the *Taoiseach*—pronounced "Tea–such") may choose to hold earlier elections if he desires to reestablish or widen his party's majority in the *Dáil*. For instance, in late 1982 the third election in 18 months was held because the government could not maintain its majority. The *Taoiseach* is by far the most important political figure in the Republic. With his cabinet, which is composed of from 7 to 15 members, he establishes the country's policies and dominates his party in the *Dáil* in order to get his government's bills through parliament.

Electoral System: Proportional Representation

In any democratic system, parties usually play a key role, presenting candidates and policy issues as alternatives from which to choose. They educate the voters, wage election campaigns and, above all, rule or prepare to rule. Political parties are especially important in the Irish Republic because interest groups are far less tightly organized than in most other European countries. Thus, Irish parties are particularly important channels for interest groups expressing their concerns and wants at high policy levels.

Parties seek seats in the *Dáil* by means of a particularly complex electoral system—a form of proportional representation system involving what is known as a single transferable vote in multi–member constituencies. The voter marks his ballot by placing the number 1 opposite the name of the candidate of his first choice and may then place the figure 2 opposite the name of his second choice, and continues on until he has numbered all the candidates. Thus the voter is able to say in effect, "I wish to vote for A, but if he does not need my vote or if he has no chance of being elected, transfer my vote to B. If B in turn does not need my vote, or he has no chance of election, transfer my vote to C," and so forth.

Thus, the system reflects more completely the voters' preferences for the three to five seats filled by each constituency. This makes it easier for smaller parties and independents to win parliamentary representation. At the same time, it is designed to prevent fringe politicians and a high number of small parties from winning seats in the *Dáil* and thereby adversely affecting the stability of the parliamentary system. It is therefore one of the better proportional representation systems in Europe. However, this complicated system enormously slows down the tabulation of the votes, and it often takes several days to determine the final results of an Irish election.

The Republic's electoral system affects Irish politics in several important ways. By permitting voters to discriminate among candidates of the same party (as does the American primary system), it pits members of the same party against each other. Thus, the individual candidate's appeal must veer from the policy of the national party and be far more closely tailored to local concerns. Politicians compete with each other to perform a variety of services for local constituents, and this strengthens an important characteristic of Irish politics: personality and personal ties become far more significant than national policy issues.

Moreover, the local political clubs, not the national parties (which have very small staffs), recruit candidates and wage campaigns. Although it is not required by law, *Dáil* members almost always come from the constituency in which they are elected. Also, most TDs continue to hold local political office at the same time. All of these factors represent a strong decentralized tendency in Irish politics: politicians show strong loyalties to their local constituencies, but at the same time the national party leadership needs to maintain strong party discipline as it seeks a majority in the *Dáil*. Without such discipline, no government could possibly survive.

Political Parties

Irish political parties are noticeably different from British parties whose bases were traditionally rooted in different social classes. The Republic of Ireland is a more homogeneous country, and it has historically been economically underdeveloped. It has no major national, regional, religious or racial differences that could become the basis for different parties. There are, of course, social cleavages, but these do not have the overriding significance that they do in many other European countries. It is more likely that the dividing line between the two major parties is determined by the position one's father or grandfather took on the signing of the Anglo–Irish treaty in 1921, which divided the island and created the Irish Free State. In 1932, after a bloody civil war followed by intense domestic political rivalry, the party that had accepted the treaty (now the *Fine Gael*, pronounced Finna Gwail, meaning "Family of Irish") suffered an election defeat and relinquished power to the Fianna Fail (pronounced Fee–anna Foil), which had originally opposed the treaty. The 1932 elections firmly established democratic government, which stands or falls on the parties' willingness to alternate power peacefully, in response to the wishes of the voters.

The "pro" or "anti" distinction between the two major parties does not mean very much today. But the importance of family ties in Irish politics inclines Irishmen to vote as their fathers and grandfathers did, and it encourages political activists to become leaders in those same parties. It is hardly surprising that parties that are not formed along class or religious lines are not very ideological in their orientation.

North Americans who observe the two major Irish parties have the same difficulties distinguishing between them that Europeans express about American parties. Perhaps the 1960s saying of George Wallace about the American mainline parties applies to their Irish counterparts: "There's not a dime's worth of difference between them." Both parties in the Republic are catch–all parties that attract voters from all social groups. Both are rather conservative, anti–secular, nationalistic and predominantly male. Both are what one would call Christian Democratic parties elsewhere in Europe.

The Irish party system has developed into two more or less stable blocs. In the past three decades, the government has alternated between the Fianna Fail and a coalition combining Fine Gael and the Labour Party. Traditionally Fianna Fail did not enter coalitions, but it must often rely on support from small parties, making its governments more fragile. Fine Gael–Labour coalitions were made easier by the fact that there is very little ideological distance between them.

Fianna Fail has governed most of the time since 1932. It is moderate to conservative on economic matters; it still has a slightly anti–British attitude although it has eliminated many of the more militant elements in the aftermath of a party split in 1970 over the question of Irish unification. It attracts considerable support from businessmen and professional people as well as parts of the urban working class. However, its greatest strength remains in the rural western regions. The native Irish–speakers solidly support it because it has stamped itself as a party seeking restoration of the Irish language (at least nominally). It often sees itself as a grass roots party and demonstrates populist tendencies.

Fianna Fail was able to stay in power after 1989 only by forming a historic coalition with its most bitter political enemies, the Progressive Democrats. This was the first time ever that Fianna Fail has shared power while ruling. In 1992 Charles Haughey was finally forced out after it had been revealed that he had been aware of police bugging of two journalists' phones. He was replaced as *Taoiseach* by Albert Reynolds, a self–made pet–food tycoon.

Two days after taking office, Reynolds entered an ethical minefield that took him to the root of what kind of society Ireland is and aspires to be. With abortions forbidden in Ireland, his government got a court order to prevent a 14–year old rape victim from going to Britain to end her pregnancy, as several thousand Irish women do annually. This decision triggered a barrage of international criticism and an emotional national debate, which continued even after the court later overturned the decision to ban her from traveling to the U.K. In 1992 voters overwhelmingly decided in referenda to permit women to obtain information and to have abortions abroad, though not in Ireland. In 1995 this passed in parliament and was affirmed by the Supreme Court. In March 2002 voters rejected a government effort to reverse a Supreme Court ruling that permits a pregnancy to be terminated when there is a risk that the mother may commit suicide.

After calling his own Fein Gael coalition partner "reckless, irresponsible, and dishonest," Reynolds lost a vote of no–confidence in 1992 which prompted a snap election. Fianna Fail suffered its worst electoral setback in 50 years. Reynolds emerged from the polling badly wounded and had to enter Fianna Fail's first coalition with Labour in order to stay in office. With 100 seats, the coalition had the biggest *Dáil* majority in Irish political history until a crisis broke it apart in 1994 and forced Fianna Fail out of the government. Bertie Ahern became party leader.

Ahern led the party to victory in the June 1997 elections, winning 39.3% of the votes and 77 seats. Together with its small ally, the Progressive Democrats, the government has 81 seats and can maintain an unstable majority only with the votes of a handful of independents. As usual, it took weeks of haggling and deal making before the new prime minister could go to the elegant Phoenix Park residence of the president and ask for permission to form a government. A populist Dubliner from a lower class background who is separated from his wife and lives openly with his girlfriend, Ahern vowed to "cut taxes, cut crime and work for peace in Northern Ireland." Although reputed to be "green" or pro–Catholic on the volatile subject of Northern Ireland, he has pushed hard for progress in the peace talks. This has cost him the support of a few independents' votes.

Ahern had a frail grip on parliament, and his government was shaken by scandals. Only five months after taking power, his foreign minister, Ray Burke, had to resign for accepting a campaign donation from a man who wanted to develop land in Burke's constituency. The cloud of

Hon. Bertie Ahern
Taoiseach of Ireland

financial scandal was already looming over the party when a judge found former *Taoiseach* Charles Haughey guilty of accepting gifts of almost $11 million from business interests while in office and then stashing it away in offshore bank accounts, presumably in order to hide it from the tax collectors. He paid $1.4 million in back taxes in 2000, and in 2003 he was required to pay another $5.3 to tax authorities. Ahern had been a close colleague of both men for many years, and their sins greatly embarrassed him and his government.

Riding on a tide of popular contentment with the economy in 2002, Ahern's Fianna Fail became the first government in more than 30 years to be re-elected. It won 42% of the votes, but because of proportional representation it garnered 49% of the seats, or 81 (up from 77). This enabled Ahern to form a comfortable majority coalition with his old partners, the Progressive Democrats, who doubled their seats to eight. Together the two parties command 89 of 166 seats.

Fine Gael is a traditional establishment party that draws a disproportionate share of its votes from the upper and middle classes and from farmers with large holdings. Its leaders also tend to be drawn from somewhat higher social strata. Although it tends to be moderate to conservative on economic matters, the party has moved slightly to the left to accommodate the Labour Party. Fine Gael is the most centralized and hierarchically organized in the Republic. Led by John Bruton, a wealthy rancher with long governmental experience, Fine Gael slipped in 1992 to less than 25% of the votes and 45 seats. Nevertheless, Bruton was able to form a center–left governing coalition with the Labour and

Ireland

**Hon. Mary Robinson
UN High Commissioner for
Human Rights**

Democratic Left parties in 1994 and become *Taoiseach*.

In June 1997 Irish voters continued a tradition maintained since 1969: never reelect a government no matter how good its record. Despite the fact that the Fine Gael government presided over the strongest economy in the 75–year history of independent Ireland, with the fastest growth rate in the EU that won it the nickname, "Celtic Tiger," and living standards that were near the EU average, it was thrown out of power. It captured 27.9% of the votes (up from 24.5%) and 54 seats (up from 46). But its partner, the Labour Party, collapsed in the voting booths. The two parties were rudely reminded of an old saying in Irish politics: No good turn ever goes unpunished. In 2002 Fein Gael experienced near collapse, falling from 54 to only 31 seats and only 22.5% of the votes. The defeat was so severe that its party leader, Michael Noonan, resigned before the votes were tallied. Its humiliation signals a realignment of Irish politics, as the votes of the two traditional rival parties dropped from 84% in 1982 to only 64% in 2002. The Irish party divide may now develop along left–right lines, as is typical in the rest of Europe.

Unlike in Britain, the Labour Party in Ireland has never articulated socialist or Marxist ideologies. In fact, by western standards, it is hardly a party of the left although it does have a left–wing minority. It had been virtually excluded from urban politics in the eastern part of the country, and most of the working class voted for one of the two major parties, especially the Fianna Fail. But its leader, Dick Spring, an astute rugby–playing lawyer with a wife from Virginia, brought Labour more into the public eye. Labour's

main electoral support is found among rural, agrarian workers. Its importance in Irish politics was greatly enhanced by the fact that until 1997 it had been an essential part of any ruling coalition led by either Fine Gael or Fianna Fail. Mary Robinson's election as president in 1990 forced Ireland's leaders to take a fresh look at Irish society, which has proved to be more receptive to change than most had realized. She became Ireland's most respected politician and helped pave the way for 20 women to win seats in the 1992 elections.

▌ Bertie's bowl

Seats in Irish parliament, 2002 *(1997)*

Fianna Fail 81 *(77)*

Fine Gael 31 *(54)*
Labour 21 *(21)*
Progressive Democrats 8 *(4)*
Greens 6 *(2)*
Sinn Fein 5 *(1)*
Socialists 1 *(1)*
Independents 13* *(6)*

*A recount is pending in one constituency

Source: *Irish Times*

Source: *The Economist*

Labour triumphed in 1992, becoming the king–maker in Irish politics. In 1994 it entered a governing coalition with Fine Gael, with Spring as deputy prime minister (*Tánaiste*) and foreign minister. However, it slipped badly in 1997 to 10.4% of the votes (from 19.3%) and only 17 seats (down from 32). It finds itself in the opposition. It experienced disaster in 2002, winning only 10.8% of the votes and 21 seats. Even Spring was defeated by a Sinn Fein candidate, a former convicted gunrunner.

Minor Parties

Despite the proportional representation electoral system, which usually permits many parties to enter parliament, small parties had almost entirely disappeared from Irish parliamentary politics. Ten representatives of minor parties and six independents did win seats in the 1997, elections. The Democratic Left won 2.5% of the votes and four seats (down from six). It was in the governing coalition from 1994 to 1997. The ecological Greens won 2.8% of the votes and two seats in 1997, and it grew in 2002 to 3.8% and six seats.

The most significant development in the 1987 elections was the rise of a new center–right party, the Progressive Democrats (PD). The PD had broken away from Fianna Fail in 1985 in protest against its hard–line Northern Ireland policy. It temporarily displaced Labour as third largest

party, a position that Labour had occupied since 1922. The PD appeared to break the mold of Irish party politics; it supplanted Labour as Fine Gael's favorite coalition partner, although Fine Gael and PD still are likely to compete for the same kinds of voters. In 1993 Mary Harney was elected to replace Desmond O'Malley as party leader. She is the first woman to head an Irish party. In 1997 PD received the same percentage of votes as in 1992 (4.7%), but it lost half its seats, capturing only four. It won them back again in 2002, securing 4% and eight seats and entering the government.

The Marxist–oriented Communist Party of Ireland seeks to unify the entire island under an orthodox communist regime. It plays no significant role whatsoever in Irish politics. The Trotskyite Socialists captured one seat in 1997. The Workers' Party took that name in 1976 following a split six years earlier among the ranks of the small Sinn Fein Party, which was the political arm of the Irish Republican Army (IRA). The split resulted in two distinct groups: the first is a "official" IRA, whose political arm—the Workers Party—has for years competed in parliamentary elections in the Republic and has accepted the few seats which it has won.

The second group is the "provisional" IRA (Provos), which is has become Marxist and remains fervently nationalist. Until 1987 it refused to recognize the Dublin parliament as a legitimate Irish parliament, and it therefore refused to participate in elections, except for town councils in which it occupies a few seats in both parts of Ireland. Its suspicions that it would win precious few votes were confirmed in the 1997 elections, when Sinn Fein won a paltry 2.5% of the votes. Caoimhghin O Caolain became the first member of Sinn Fein ever to win a seat in the Irish parliament since independence in 1922. But the Fianna Fail–led government did not seek his support. The result underscores two facts: although polls indicate that two–thirds of Eire's population believes ideally that Ireland should one day be a unified nation, the overwhelming majority abhors the violent attempt to unify Ireland by bullets and bombs.

It is precisely to try to overcome its isolation that leader Gerard (Gerry) Adams ended the party's boycott of the Irish (though not of the British) parliament. As he stated: "We've lost touch with the people for the simple reason that we have not been able to represent them in the only political forum they know. To break out into the broad stream of people's consciousness, we have to approach them at their own level." To many traditionalists, this approach smacked of betrayal. As one die–hard remarked, "when you lie down with the dogs, you get up with the fleas." Nevertheless, Sinn Fein made dramatic gains in 2002, capturing 6.5% of the votes and five seats, nearly winning three more. It is the only party with parliamentary seats in both parts of Ireland (and in London although it refused to occupy its Westminster seats). Analysts concluded that Sinn Fein's success was not primarily due to a rise of nationalist sentiment in the republic. Instead its young candidates exuded dynamism and concern in poorer areas on the island.

Foreign and Defense Policies

A central reality in the Republic of Ireland's foreign and defense policy is that the Irish live on a politically divided island and are a politically and religiously divided people. Few foreign policy issues can be treated entirely separately from these facts. Most Irish citizens and politicians in the Republic want to see these divisions overcome, and no Irish Republican government has ever recognized the division of the island as permanent. Most people in the Republic do not use the term "Republic of Ireland." which implies permanent division, but instead refer to their state almost exclusively as "Ireland." But the unification issue is no longer as important in Irish politics as it once was. Younger leaders with no direct memories of the bloody struggle and with far greater interest in Ireland's economic development replaced the old revolutionary elite who fought for independence against Britain.

The Republic of Ireland lived for a long time in the shadow of Great Britain although it has become a much more confidant nation and is no longer obsessed by its ancient hatred of the British. Because of Britain's part in Irish history and the continued presence of the British in Northern Ireland, the Republic is inclined to remain neutral in conflicts where Britain is involved. It remained neutral in World War II—in fact it even refused to observe black–outs in its cities at night. Thus German bombers were able to orient themselves by regrouping in the skies over Dublin and then flying in a direct line toward such British cities as Liverpool. In 1982, the Republic also refused to go along with EU sanctions against Argentina when Britain, a fellow member, was engaged in an armed struggle for control of the Falkland Islands.

Ireland's policy of neutrality does not mean that the Republic is ideologically neutral or politically indifferent. It shares the basic democratic, political and economic values of other countries in Europe and North America. However, it is only

one of four EU countries that have not joined NATO. This fact does cause disputes sometimes. For instance, when the *Dáil* debated the ratification of the EU's Single European Act (SEA), which calls for majority votes in the EU Council of Ministers and a completely free market, some members questioned how the Republic could remain neutral and still take part in the security and foreign policy cooperation for which the act called. The Supreme Court found that the ESA's political cooperation section was unconstitutional and therefore ruled that a referendum on amending the constitution was necessary. In the voting in 1987, 70% voted in favor of it and 30% against.

Ireland's long–established policy of military neutrality is increasingly irrelevant since the country cooperates on European security matters, and Irish and British troops coordinate the fight against the IRA. In 1999 it decided to establish formal links with NATO through the Partnership for Peace (PfP). Following the September 11, 2001, terrorist attacks against the United States, Ireland offered its airspace and airfields to American military planes. In 2003 about 30,000 American soldiers passed through Shannon Airport during the military buildup around Iraq. However, Taoiseach Ahern declared, "Ireland cannot engage in support of military action because we work under the U.N. resolution." It had served a two-year term on the UN Security council from 2001–2.

The Republic is so enveloped by the military forces of the Atlantic Alliance that it is able to keep its own defense forces very small. Internal security rests almost entirely with the unarmed police, the 10,000 strong *Garda Siochana*. External defense is the responsibility of the permanent defense forces that number 11,500, about 9,300 of whom are land forces. The Navy has 1,100 personnel and seven coastal and patrol vessels. The Air Force has 1,060 troops and is composed of less than 40 aircraft, including helicopters. Military service is voluntary, and there is also a reserve defense force of 14,800 that could be mobilized in time of crisis. Ireland has contributed troops to UN peacekeeping units throughout the world, including in southern Lebanon, Bosnia, Croatia, Cyprus and Western Sahara. In 1991 the Irish government supported UN policy toward Iraq. Although Ireland played no direct role in the war, it did permit U.S. military planes to refuel at Shannon Airport, thereby prompting many domestic critics to cry that its neutrality had been breached.

Out of sheer economic necessity, Ireland joined the EU in 1973, at the same time that Britain entered. Ireland stood to benefit from EU regional aid and the Common Agricultural Program (CAP), which in 2002 accounted for 4% of its GDP or $1.5 billion. In three decades, such assistance has totaled over $32 billion. EU aid helps modernize Ireland's infrastruc-

Ireland

ture. For a few years CAP funds were a boon to Irish farmers, but their benefits were not lasting. Adjusting to CAP, western Ireland has been forced to change from its traditional dairy and beef farming economy to tourism and forestry. In 25 years its forestry industry is expected to be as important to the economy as its food industry is now. Its trade volume with Britain (to which a fifth of its exports still go) remains very high. Three decades of EU membership have helped raise the people's income-per-head from about 60% of the EU's average to 122% in 2002.

EU membership has served to shift Irish foreign trade and political attention away from Britain to a broader view of the rest of Europe. Former President Robinson argued, "it lifts the burden of the relationship with our close neighbor. We are now partners with them in Europe. The history is still there, but it is less a tight connection and burden between us." For centuries Ireland had defined itself in relation to Britain, as a victim. That is far less prominent now. Today it is more inclined to define itself in relation to Europe and the EU, in which it is recognized as an equal. It distinguishes itself from Britain and benefits from being the most pro–European anglophone country in the EU. This foreign policy reorientation has not altered the fact that hundreds of thousands of Irish still live and work in Britain, where they enjoy the same political, legal and social welfare rights as British citizens.

Some Irish worry that increasing integration with Europe may have negative effects on Irish culture. Arts Minister Sile de Valera, granddaughter of Eamon de Valera, said during a visit to Boston that EU regulations and directives "often seriously impinge on our identity, culture and traditions." Ahern's deputy prime minister, Mary Harney, has also warned against a more centralized and bureaucratic Europe. She claimed that spiritually Ireland is "probably a lot closer to Boston than to Berlin."

In a June 8, 2001, referendum marked by massive abstention and indifference, a majority of Irish slapped the EU in the face by rejecting the Nice Treaty, which had laid out the process for enlarging the community. Many Irish were smarting from an earlier EU rebuke of the country's economic policy, were fearful of losing EU funding if a dozen poorer countries were admitted, and were uneasy that its neutrality was being threatened by Europe's acquisition of its own defense and security role. A second referendum was held in October 2002, and this time the government spent ten times more on the referendum campaign than it had the first time. Voters overwhelmingly endorsed the Treaty of Nice, with a turnout of 48.5%,

giving the green light to EU institutional reform and enlargement and causing a sigh of relief throughout the community. In 2002 Ireland gained more visibility in the EU when Pat Cox was elected president of the European Parliament.

Reunification

The vast majority of the citizens of the Irish Republic and virtually all of its political leaders share the goal of reunifying all 32 Irish counties. But they eventually wish to see this accomplished peacefully and with the consent of the Northern Irish. In Northern Ireland, about a million Irish Protestants outnumber the half million Catholics, so Irish unity must take a form palatable to the Protestants. As it is, most southern Irish probably secretly abhor the idea of having to deal directly with Northern Irish Protestants as fellow citizens until fundamental changes in attitudes have occurred. Violence spilled over from Northern Ireland to the South. The Irish government outlawed the provisional IRA; government raids and arrests provide frequent reminders that the IRA can expect no tolerance within the Republic. In 1982 a Dublin court convicted an Irishman for possessing explosives, even though the crime was committed in Britain. This was the first application of a 1976 law that was part of an ongoing Irish–British cooperation against terrorism in both countries.

In 1981 a U.S. court convicted the Irish Northern Aid (NORAID) committee for failing to list the IRA as its principal foreign agent. The Irish government ordered its diplomatic representatives in the United States to boycott the 1983 annual St. Patrick's Day parade in New York City because the organizers of the parade had chosen an IRA supporter as Grand Marshal. In explaining its decision, the Irish government noted that the IRA's actions, which include collecting money from unsuspecting Irish–Americans to finance violent operations in Northern Ireland, "have deepened the wounds of our troubled history and continue to postpone the day of Irish unity and reconciliation." Dublin has frequently appealed to Americans not to support violence in Ireland. Funds from NORAID declined, and the IRA sought to fill its coffers by means of extortion and racketeering in Northern Ireland.

The Irish government realizes that unification can be accomplished only in cooperation with Britain and Northern Ireland. This has brought the Irish and British Prime Ministers together for periodic high-level meetings to discuss the developments in the area. Former Prime Minister FitzGerald proposed to change the Irish Republic's constitution in a way that would calm Protestant fears by presenting a less stridently Catholic image.

Mr. David Trimble
Leader, Ulster Unionist Party

FitzGerald's objectives were not easy on an island where so much blood has been spilled and where so much bitterness has already been created. Nor was it easy for a country whose population is still deeply Catholic and whose religious values are reflected in its laws and constitution. FitzGerald alluded to his preferred path to unity when, with an eye on the Northern Irish Protestants, he said: "If we could create a state down here which they could accept, and they could find the civil and religious liberties in which they believe, they would be willing to think again about this."

A "New Ireland Forum," which he sponsored, issued a report containing proposals to achieve better understanding between Northern Irish Protestants and Catholics, Dublin and London. However, the proposals, which called for a joint Irish British panel, were criticized by Catholics, who found them too conciliatory, by Northern Irish Protestants, who reject any notion of reunification and finally, by the Thatcher government itself. Mrs. Thatcher was no doubt responding in part to the grisly IRA bombing in 1984 of the hotel in Brighton where she was staying. She narrowly escaped death, and several Tory leaders were killed or wounded. The bombing enflamed anti–Irish sentiments to a height unequaled since the IRA murdered Lord Mountbatten in 1979, and it set back progress towards peace. By 1985 FitzGerald's initiative was dead.

Nevertheless, consultation between representatives of Eire and the UK continues within the rubric of the 1985 Anglo–Irish accord. For the first time, this permitted Dublin some say in Northern Ireland's affairs. The agreement enjoys majority support in the Republic. In 1990 the Pope appointed Bishop Cahal B. Daly, a fierce critic of IRA terrorism, as Ireland's primate. In 1993 optimism was ignited by a joint declaration by the British and Irish prime ministers offering Sinn Fein a seat at the bargaining table to discuss Northern Ireland's future if the IRA renounced violence. Prime Minister John Major promised that Britain would not stand in the way of a united Ireland if a majority of Northern Ireland residents supported such a step. *Taoiseach* Albert Reynolds pledged that there would be no change in the six counties' status without majority consent.

As a symbol of returning normalcy with Britain in 1995, Prince Charles became the first member of the royal family to make an official visit to the Irish Republic since 1922. Also in 1995, David Trimble, leader of the Ulster Unionist Party, the main Protestant group, traveled to Dublin and met with *Taoiseach* Bruton. This was the first time since 1922 a Unionist leader was received in Dublin.

A couple of weeks after becoming British prime minister in 1997, Tony Blair lifted the ban on official contacts with Sinn Fein. He visited Northern Ireland in May 1997 in order to demonstrate that he is willing to take risks for peace in the six counties. To continue the negotiation process, he invited Sinn Fein leader Gerry Adams to a meeting in Downing Street in December. This was the first visit by an Irish Republican leader to the prime minister's private residence in 76 years. In January 1998, Adams returned to Downing Street to hear from the prime minister that the peace process is an "absolute priority" and that "the status quo is not an option." On November 26, 1998, Blair became the first British prime minister since Ireland's independence to speak to the Irish parliament.

Talks, involving eight Northern Ireland parties and the British and Irish governments, continued despite sporadic outbreaks of violence. American George Mitchell emphasized the importance of the negotiations, which he chaired: "We're talking about, literally, people's lives, the possibility of the resumption of the terrible conflict that enveloped this society with fear and anxiety. So, frustrating and tedious as it seems—and it is—you have to be patient and recognize how tough it is for them to move."

In 1998 a majority in Eire backed the deletion from their constitution of the mandate to unify the island. As a result of the 1998 Good Friday Peace Agreement, followed by dramatic "yes" referenda votes for the accord in both the Republic (94.4%) and Northern Ireland (71.1%), Ireland reached the doorstep of peace. Trimble and his Catholic counterpart, John Hume, received the 1998 Nobel Peace Prize for their role in reaching an historic peace agreement in Northern Ireland that year. Optimism is greater than

it has ever been that "the troubles" will soon end.

Endless haggling over paramilitary groups laying down their arms threatened the peace deal. However, both sides began taking cautious steps to implement the agreement. On December 1, 1999, a new coalition government in Ulster was formed that shares power devolved from Westminster in London. It included both the party of hard-line Protestant, Rev. Ian Paisley, and former IRA commander, Martin McGuinnes, as minister of education. However, this government was suspended in February 2000 after the IRA failed to meet the Unionists' deadline for starting turning in its arms. Power sharing was reestablished in May 2000 when the Unionists accepted an IRA pledge to put its arsenal "beyond use" and to allow limited inspections by international observers to verify that the promise is being kept. For a year and a half the IRA dragged its heels. As a result David Trimble, leader of Northern Ireland's power-sharing government, quit in the summer of 2001.

In November 2001 the IRA finally began destroying some of its weapons under international supervision. In quick response to this breakthrough, Britain began demolishing military installations, including army watchtowers overlooking regions with high IRA support. Trimble led his Ulster Unionist Party back into the assembly and was narrowly reelected first minister with the help of the Alliance Party, which had steered a middle road between unionists and republicans. Peace was back on track, especially after the IRA stunned everybody in July 2002 with an expression of "sincere apologies and condolences" for all the persons it had killed in the Northern Irish sectarian violence.

That ended when a spy scandal at the heart of the Northern Irish government broke in October 2002. After raiding Sinn Fein homes and offices at the Northern Ireland Assembly, British authorities charged three members of gathering intelligence from Britain's Northern Ireland Office that could be used for terrorist operations. Police found sensitive political material, including minutes of conversations between Blair and his Northern Ireland secretary of state, and names, home addresses and license plate numbers of many provincial police officers and British security personnel. It was feared that some of the information could be used for assassinations.

Sinn Fein leaders denied the allegations and claimed the police had orchestrated a frame-up. The British suspended the assembly, and Protestant leaders vowed that they would not resume participation unless the IRA renounces violence unmistak-

ably. The IRA then broke off all contact with the independent panel established to oversee disarmament, which had already supervised the destruction of two caches of IRA weapons. One Sinn Fein leader, Martin McGuinness, announced that he had abandoned his fight with Britain and was committing himself to preventing the deaths of any more people. "My war is over." Nevertheless, the peace process had suffered its most serious blow since the Good Friday Agreement five years earlier.

In April 2003 President George W. Bush visited Blair and Taoiseach Ahern in Belfast to lend his endorsement to the peace plan. The president had aroused the ire of the British government when Gerry Adams was invited to a White House St. Patrick's Day party in March, this when IRA operatives had been arrested while traveling undercover in the U.S. Although Blair sensed that breaking the stalemate was "frustratingly close," he failed to get the IRA to make a crystal-clear statement that it had given up paramilitary activities like gathering intelligence, threatening and attacking adversaries and acquiring weapons. Adams' statement that there would be "no activities which will undermine in any way the peace process or the Good Friday Agreement" was not enough. Blair postponed assembly elections scheduled for May 29, a decision protested by both Sinn Fein and the Irish government. (See United Kingdom)

ECONOMY

In the last half century, Ireland has undergone an economic revolution. The influx of foreign investment as a result of generous incentives and the increase in trade have added significantly to the prosperity of Ireland. More than 800 foreign firms employ close to half of all Irish workers involved in manufacturing. Foreign companies are also responsible for 80% of the country's non–food exports. It has also acquired an impressive high–technology industry. By 1986 it had already achieved the highest ratio of high–tech to total exports of any EU country. At the turn of the century this tiny land is the 19th richest country in the world.

Growth and prosperity in Ireland have been dramatic. Less than 30% of all households are rented. The Irish entered the 1990s with a 50% gap between their living standards and those of the EU average. By 1998 income in Ireland had caught up with the European mean and surpassed Britain in per capita GDP for the first time in history. If measured by GDP adjusted for purchasing power, the difference became even greater by the turn of the century. Also a variety of social welfare indicators in Ireland are as good or better

Ireland

than in Britain. Life expectancy is about the same, and Ireland spends a higher percentage of its GDP on public education. Per capita consumption rose 10.5% from 1990 to 1996, twice the average rate of increase in the rest of Europe. Sustained economic growth, low inflation, a hard currency, a healthy trade surplus, and declining unemployment (3.7% in 2001) cohabit with a growing income gap between rich and poor.

About a fifth of the population is marginalized from the mainstream economy and barely benefits from the upsurge in prosperity. Competing successfully in the global economy has cost Ireland the kind of low–wage, unskilled jobs other countries do more cheaply. *The Economist* spoke of a "tale of two economies." One is a still–backward, unproductive and labor–intensive one owned by the Irish. The other is an extremely productive, capital–intensive and modern one owned by foreigners, including companies like IBM, Intel, Fujitsu, and Motorola, as well as banks and financial institutions, like Citibank, Merrill Lynch, and Daiwa.

By 1998, 40% of all American electronics investments in Europe and a third of all American overall investment in the EU were going to Ireland. A third of the personal computers sold in Europe were being made there. Many of its unskilled laborers are joining an idle underclass, and drug use and drug–related crime are rising. The problem of organized, drug–related crime in the country was highlighted in 1996 of a gangland assassination in 1996 of a courageous investigative reporter, Veronica Guerin, who had put the spotlight on ruthless mobsters. Nevertheless, Ireland still has one of Europe's lowest crime rates, with a murder rate one–seventh as high as the United States.

Agriculture has declined in importance in the last four decades—the percentage of the working force employed in farming dropped from 43% to 8%. Almost a fifth of the country's workers still is directly or indirectly involved in producing food. Agriculture now accounts for only 5% of GDP, compared with industry's share of 45%. Services account for half. The agricultural life of Ireland benefited from EU membership, although income from the CAP helped fuel the rapid growth of welfare spending and thus contributed to the country's debt problem. Income in the farm sector has doubled in the past three decades, and today one–half of the value of agricultural production is exported. However, family farming remains relatively unsophisticated, and food processing has not developed as far as in most EU countries.

Two other sources of revenue are important to Ireland: tourists and pubs. By

2000 Ireland was the fastest growing tourist destination in Europe, growing by 12% during the 1990s. Each year 5.5 million tourists (that is more than the number of Irishmen there are to receive them) visit the nation despite the fact that Ireland is the only EU nation not directly linked to the continent since the opening of the English Channel "Chunnel" in 1993. Americans account for 14% of the total, although they tend to spend more than other visitors. They drink in over 11,000 pubs; the ratio of one pub for every 300 people is even more striking when one knows that half the population is under age 25, and thus the ratio of pubs to those old enough to drink is even higher. Annual alcoholic consumption per Irish adult jumped from 10.6 quarts of pure alcohol in 1985 to nearly 15.8 quarts in 2000, compared with the EU average of 9.5 quarts, despite high taxes on wine and spirits. This is the highest increase in the EU and has brought with it more social problems, such as higher absenteeism on the job, auto accidents and medical care costs. Despite the unrest, 1.25 million tourists visited Northern Ireland in 1993, and that number is growing as violence ends.

The Irish economy is very dependent on events outside of the country because of the important roles that trade and foreign sources of energy play in the life of the island. It is a land that must import many essential raw materials. It does have a large quantity of zinc ore, as well as copper, sulphur, baryte, gypsum and dolomite. Its only valuable energy source is peat, or turf bogs, which cover parts of the Central Plain and large areas along the south, west and northwest coasts. It lacks sizable coal deposits, but it extracts natural gas near Kinsale Head. Although recent discoveries on the ocean shelf may produce oil for Ireland, at this time the country has very little. Yet 70% of its energy needs are supplied by oil. Thus, the Irish economy was drastically affected by changes in oil prices, while remaining dependent upon unstable world trade for its strength. It generates no nuclear power.

Almost 90% of Ireland's GDP is generated by trade. Manufactured goods account for well over half the value of exports. Since almost a third of these go to the United Kingdom (and the percentage is steadily declining) and another third to the continental EU members (a percentage which has steadily risen since 1973), Ireland is very vulnerable to economic ups and downs in those industrialized countries. In an attempt to reduce that vulnerability somewhat, the Irish severed the link between the British and Irish pound in 1979 and tied its currency later to the European Monetary System. In 1999

it joined 10 other EU nations in adopting the Euro, to be fully introduced by 2002. Ireland presents an image of financial stability that foreign investors like.

By 1999 the total public debt stood at 55% of GDP (down from 131% in 1987), and its 1997 budget deficit was only 1.2% of GDP, well below the 3% limit required to meet the EU's convergence criterion for the European currency. In 2000 it enjoyed a fiscal surplus of 3.3%.

Taxes are kept low for foreign firms in order to attract them to invest in Ireland, making it the EU's biggest tax haven. New investors receive tax breaks, and overall corporate tax rates are 12.5%, far below the EU average of more than 30%. Therefore, wage and salary earners bear a heavy income tax burden (including a 21% VAT, Europe's highest). For example, a single man with no allowances sees two–thirds of his pay disappear through taxes and deductions. It is no wonder that tax cheating has become rampant.

The economic growth that Ireland has enjoyed since the mid-fifties continues. In 2000, the rate was 8.5% of GDP, after averaging 6% from 1993–8, and in 2003 the economy was growing at 3.2%. From 1994 to 2000 Ireland had the EU's fastest growing economy. Inflation at 4.1% in 2001 is a worry. The economy has speeded ahead so rapidly that Ireland has not had time to revamp its infrastructure. Roads are often clogged, hospitals are overcrowded, and housing is tight and expensive. Dublin real estate prices shot up 40% in 1998; in some suburbs prices have quintupled in one decade. Elsewhere, housing prices rose by 20% a year in the last years of the 1990s. Inflation might be even higher were it not for a "social partnership" created by government, labor and business to slow wage-rate increases and secure labor peace. Its 3.7% unemployment is far lower than the 20% posted at the low point of the 1980s and about half the EU average of 8.8% in 2000. It continues to decline steadily. This is partly due to more than three-quarters of a billion dollars in annual investment by offshore companies, creating directly or indirectly more than 300,000 jobs. Also, as a formerly poor member of the EU, Ireland still gets structural and CAP funds from Brussels, amounting to 4% of its GDP or ca. $1.5 billion annually, although these monies are bound to diminish over time.

As the country with the EU's highest sustained growth in population and labor force, the Republic must provide jobs for those Irishmen who continue to move back to Ireland and from the agricultural into the manufacturing and service sectors, but it must also provide work for the growing number of young persons and women who are entering the labor market. The economic boom is also attracting other EU nationalities, including British. At the turn of the century, immigration to this once-poor island exceeds emigration. The government's strategy to create jobs for the EU's youngest labor force has been through rapid industrial development.

In the past high unemployment set in motion a disappointing wave of emigration. Almost a fourth of Ireland's adults have lived abroad at some point in their lives. The impressive economic growth reversed the population flight, and skilled workers are returning to Ireland. Labor became scarce in such sectors as electronics, computers, information technology, and building. American firms advertise in American newspapers to fill vacancies in their Irish businesses. In 2000 the government calculated that Ireland needs 200,000 foreign workers by 2005 and therefore loosened up restrictions on immigration. The state training agency (FAS) conducts worldwide recruitment, known as Jobs Ireland, to fill vacancies. The republic's population had soared to 3.8 million in 2001, the highest in 120 years, although its fertility rate has plummeted and is below the level required for a stable population.

The tradition of spirited trade union activity has remained in Ireland. This is reflected in the 94 member unions of the Irish Congress of Trade Unions (ICTU), which have affiliates in Northern Ireland. About 60% of working Irishmen are members of unions, which were among the strongest and most militant in the world.

CULTURE

Ireland's culture, like its history, reflects the problem of a native people being dominated by a more powerful neighbor. For centuries the natives spoke Gaelic (usually called Irish); the Norman invaders spoke French; but as the English Anglicized them, they came to speak that language as it had evolved in the 14th century. As so many of the Irish–speaking people died or immigrated after the Potato Famine in the mid–19th century, English came to be the predominant language. Despite efforts to require school children to learn Gaelic, only 2% of the population (located primarily in the rural areas of the west) speaks Irish as a first language. The fact that road signs and official government publications are still in Gaelic is quaint, but hardly necessary. In fact, it is so difficult to find someone who speaks it that fluent speakers can wear a lapel pin called a *fainne* to invite others to address them in Irish.

Because of the poverty in which they lived for many centuries, the Irish developed world–wide recognition in only one art form; it required no capital investment—the use of words. The Irish have always prided themselves in their ability to talk and write. Celtic history is rich in legend and folklore, and more recently, a number of authors, poets and dramatists have achieved international prominence. Whenever one thinks of masters of the English language, the names of Irishmen come to mind. Jonathan Swift, Thomas More, James Joyce, Oliver Goldsmith, John Millington Synge, Sean O'Casey and Brendan Beehan are influential in all of literature. And four Irishmen, William Butler Yeats, George Bernard Shaw, Samuel Becket, and in 1995 Seamus Heaney, have won the Nobel Prize for Literature. Born in Belfast the son of a potato farmer, Heaney's poetry is stamped by the simplicity and nature images of his boyhood farm. With his characteristic modesty, he said that he is a mere "foothill of a mountain range" compared to Yeats and Becket. In the 1990s writers like Colm Toibin, Dermot Bolger, Mary O'Donnell, Evelyn Conlon, and Nuala Ni Dhomhnaill are being widely–read.

The Irish are indeed a musical people, but their music has most often taken the form of widespread participation rather than special expertise of outstanding composers or professional performers. The Celtic harp, along with the shamrock, is one of the most frequently used symbols of Ireland. Harp playing is heard wherever there are groups of expatriate Irish. Many American pioneer songs, bluegrass and country music (but not western) have Irish roots. In rural Ireland, amateur nights where performers display a variety of talent are still popular. Even today, a visitor to a rural cottage may be told, "Now you mustn't leave until we have a little sing–song." Then all those present will sing together, usually unaccompanied by any musical instrument. The Cork jazz, Wexford opera, and Waterford light opera festivals attract thousands of visitors.

Among the most famous Irish musicians was U2, a successful rock group and winner of two Grammy awards in 1988. Although three out of four are Protestant, their unmistakable Irishness is revealed by the political content of some of their texts, which deal with fighting and dying on their island. The repertoire of the popular Irish–American rock band, Black 47, is also overtly political, as the title of its debut album, Fire of Freedom, indicates. Other musicians, such as Moving Hearts, Fleagh Cowboys, and Mary Coughlan, mix musical styles like rock and traditional and demonstrate that Ireland is still fertile ground for creative music. Ireland is also producing world–class films.

Celtic dancing (rhythmical patterns formed by four or eight dancers using rapid foot movements, with the arms usually held down at the sides) has spread around the world. Irish step dancing has burst out of the local parish hall and onto a world stage. The dance show–musicals, Riverdance by Bill Whelan and Lord of the Dance starring Chicagoan Michael Flatley and Jean Butler, are performing before packed audiences everywhere and are receiving global acclaim. After one performance, an observer claimed, "the speed and coordination took my breath away!" Another noted that Irish vernacular is being married to "American razzmatazz." These dance sensations are part of a larger cultural phenomenon in the 1990s. The Irish are becoming more urban, secular, experimental, self–confident, and less attached to nationalist certainties. Their once rural–based arts are being transplanted to Dublin, where they find a new cosmopolitan expression and no longer serve a nationalist agenda.

Irish art in both Celtic and medieval times displayed a wild imagination with brightly colored swirls and fantastic figures best represented in the illustrated manuscripts. Until recently, Irish art has tended to copy work being done in England or on the continent. But in the last quarter century, there has been a revival of crafts that have used the old

Aerial view of Dublin

Ireland

U2

Credit: Anton Corbijn

Gaelic and medieval symbols to create the beginnings of an indigenous modern art.

Until the 20th century, Ireland had only one university, Trinity College in Dublin, which was founded in 1591 by Queen Elizabeth I. Only recently was it opened to Catholics. In 1908 the National University of Ireland was founded. It has branches in Dublin, Cork, Galway and Limerick. Education is free and compulsory for children through the age of fifteen. The system pays its teachers more in relation to average earnings than any other land in the OECD. It produces a well–educated work force, especially at the upper end. This and the use of the English language are very appealing to foreign investors.

Both the postal and telephone services are operated by the government, which claims that 90% of all letters mailed reach their destination within one day. There are seven daily newspapers, five in Dublin and two in Cork. An autonomous public corporation operates radio and television broadcasting; licensing fees are charged and advertisements also produce revenue.

Dublin, whose graceful Georgian buildings are now falling into the shadow of taller concrete and glass structures, continues to dominate the life of Ireland. Eighteen percent of the population lives within the city's boundaries, and a third of Eire's population lives in greater Dublin. This reflects the fact that Ireland has become much more urban than it once was. It also means that some of Eire's poverty, which was largely confined to rural areas, is now more visible in the capital city. Dublin is the center of the nation's cultural, financial and political life.

FUTURE

The major problem that still faces Ireland is its relationship with Ulster.

Until recently, every patriot and every successful politician preached the necessity of unifying the whole island. But the violence and economic depression in the North made most citizens of the Republic wary of unification. Election battles have been fought on economic grounds and not the Ulster issue.

For 800 years, Ireland was dominated by a foreign power. Those who led the country from the 1920s to the 1950s were men who had helped to expel the British. For the next 25 years, Ireland was able to forget its past and make dramatic strides in modernization and industrialization. Now the people face the challenge of maintaining their new prosperity. But they may be proud that Robert Emmet's vision has come true—his country has taken its place among the nations of the earth.

Ireland has acquired the new nickname, "Celtic Tiger." It has undeniable economic strengths. Its growing standard of living during the past 50 years reached that of the EU, and for the first time in history it overtook that of Britain. Small wonder that when Prime Minister Ahern visited China in 1998 the mayor of Shanghai told him: "If there were more Irish here, I think development would be much faster." This wealth and success have significantly increased the expectations of the Irish people and their demands on the government for continued prosperity.

The failure of any party to gain a majority in parliament and the frequent elections point to the difficulty any government will have in satisfying these aspirations. With typical Irish wit, FitzGerald said before the 1982 election, "Whoever wins the election should have first choice on going into opposition."

By electing two female presidents in a row, including British subject from

Northern Ireland Mary McAleese, voters signaled a receptivity to reforms which enabled the country to enter the 21st century as a modern European nation. In 1994 a bill was passed "without a ripple of controversy" legalizing homosexuality. Abortion and divorce are also legal now in certain circumstances. The traditional bastions of power and paternalism—state, church, and family business patriarchs—are under assault as never before.

Ireland's overall political course has not changed under the Ahern government, reelected in 2002 with a comfortable majority coalition with the Progressive Democrats. Ahern faced his biggest challenge when he returned to voters in October 2002 to seek approval for the EU's Nice treaty. Without Irish approval, the EU could not reform itself and enlarge to include ten more members. The government campaign succeeded, and Irish voters overwhelmingly supported the treaty this time. Ireland is justified in being optimistic about its own future.

Ireland's culture is attracting attention far beyond its borders. When leaving for Paris in 1939, Irish dramatist Samuel Becket claimed that he preferred France at war to Ireland at peace. His country has changed dramatically. Frank McCourt, whose best-selling *Angela's Ashes* describes his youth in a poor and hide–bound Ireland before and during the Second World War, said about Ireland in the late–1990s: "When I go back I see it in a way the kids walk. The confidence. It's almost saucy. We have entered the age of Irish sauciness. God help us all."

A new generation of Irish youth, Kinsale

The French Republic

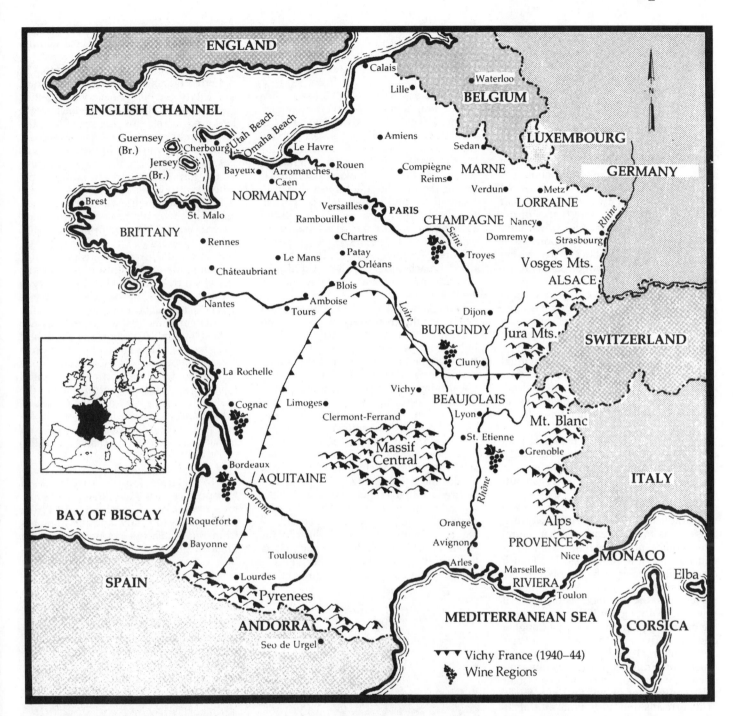

Vichy France (1940–44)
Wine Regions

Area: 211,208 sq. mi. (547,026 km.) This is the largest country in Western Europe, four fifths the size of Texas and four times the size of New York State.

Population: 59.2 million. Average annual growth rate 0.37%.

Capital City: Paris, population 2.4 million within city limits, 9.1 million within Metropolitan Paris.

Climate: Pleasant, rather temperate, except in the south, where the weather resembles that of Florida.

Neighboring Countries: Belgium, Luxembourg, Germany (North and Northeast); Switzerland (East); Italy and Monaco (Southeast) Spain and Andorra (Southwest).

Official Language: French.

Ethnic Background: Indo–European, of diverse origin.

Principal Religion: Roman Catholic (83%), Muslim (5%), Protestant (2%), Jewish (1%), Unaffiliated (13%).

Chief Commercial Exports: Capital equipment, consumer goods, automobiles, agricultural products, including wine and spirits.

Main Imports: Capital equipment, consumer goods, automobiles and transport equipment, energy, foodstuffs.

Major Customers: EU (62.5%), Germany 15.1%, UK 9.8%, Spain 9.7%, Italy 8.9%, U.S. 8.8%.

Currency: Euro.

National Holiday: July 14, anniversary of the storming of the Bastille Prison in Paris in 1789, the spark that brought the French revolution to an explosion.

Chief of State: Jacques Chirac, President (since 1995).

Head of Government: Jean-Pierre Raffarin, Prime Minister (since May 2002). Unlike many nations where the presidency is merely ceremonial, France has a Chief Executive with broad pow-

France

ers; the Prime Minister concerns himself primarily with the daily workings of the government, and he also can wield great power if he is from a different party than that of the president.

National Flag: The tricolor—three broad vertical stripes, blue, white, red.

France is a land of visible contrasts. In many ways it appears divided. Within the past two centuries, during which time the United States has had one continuous political system, France has experienced three monarchies, two empires, a half dozen republics and more than a dozen constitutions; its history is strewn with revolutions, counter–revolutions and *coups d'etat*, and its political party system is extremely fragmented. General de Gaulle, the founder of the present French Republic, once asked in exasperation how one could ever rule a land that has more than 300 different cheeses! Yet there is an underlying stability in contemporary France and a strong consensus concerning the importance of respecting individual rights and of maintaining a republican, democratic form of government. Indeed, France is one of the few stable democracies in the world and is therefore a haven for political refugees.

France also is highly centralized politically, economically and culturally. The predominance of Paris is undeniable. No successful revolution ever began outside of Paris. King Henry IV's famous statement in 1593 justifying his conversion to Catholicism, that "Paris is worth a mass," was an early reminder that control over France must emanate from Paris and not from the provinces. The French capital often seems to be the place where French history is made and then merely presented to the provinces as the finished product. With a population as great as the entire continent of Australia (roughly one out of five Frenchmen lives in Paris or its suburbs), it is the residence of a fourth of France's civil servants and doctors, a third of its students and half of its university professors, two thirds of its artisans and authors, a fifth of its factory workers and factories employing more than 25 persons and two–thirds of its company and bank headquarters. Efforts since 1955 to decentralize the French economy have met with little success.

At the same time, France is a land of great diversity in terms of religion, landscape, language, customs and styles of living. Such ethnic minorities as the Basques, the Alsatians, the Bretons, the West Indians and the Corsicans preserve their own languages and cultures, but only in Corsica is there a movement for autonomy that enjoys any appreciable popular backing.

In general, ethnic diversity does not threaten the present French state to the degree that it does other European countries such as Ireland, Belgium and Spain.

France, it has often been said, is "weighed down by history." Frenchmen have a long memory for their own past, although they do not always agree about its high and low points. Yet, far from being a country exclusively living in the past, contemporary France is a highly dynamic and forward–looking nation. It is among the wealthiest, most technologically advanced and influential countries in the world. Clearly, France has a future, but Frenchmen would say that they have a *destiny*. From the time of the Crusades, the first of which was practically an entirely French affair, to the present day, Frenchmen have felt a sense of mission to civilize the world.

Perhaps no one expressed this mission better than the great realist de Gaulle, who opened his war memoirs with the following words: "All my life I have had a certain idea of France. This is inspired by sentiment as much as by reason. The emotional side of me tends to imagine France, like the princess in the fairy stories or the Madonna in the frescoes, as dedicated to an exalted and exceptional destiny. Instinctively I have the feeling that Providence has created her either for complete successes or for exemplary misfortunes .... But the positive side of my mind also assures me that France is not really herself unless in the front rank; that only vast enterprises are capable of counterbalancing the ferments of dispersal which are inherent in her people; that our country, as it is, surrounded by the others, as they are, must aim high and hold itself straight, on pain of mortal danger. In short, to my mind, France cannot be France without greatness."

The General, who once admitted that he preferred France to Frenchmen, disdained the petty squabbling of everyday politics. He denied that the essential France was to be found in the yawning provincial bureaucrat, the scandalous French president (Felix Faure) who died in the presidential palace while making love to his mistress, or the impetuous Parisian pamphleteer who plots to bring down the regime. He believed that one must inhale the heady air of the mountain peaks in order to see the true France: "Viewed from the heights, France is beautiful."

France is at the same time an Atlantic, Continental and Mediterranean country, and it is territorially the largest country in Europe west of Russia. The country is somewhat hexagonal in shape with rather regular contours. It stretches roughly 600 miles (960 km.) from north to south and west to east. Through it flow five great rivers, the Seine, Loire, Garonne, Rhône and Rhine, which originate in the central land mass (Massif Central) or in the mountains of the Alps and the Pyrenees. It faces three seas (the North Sea, the Atlantic Ocean and the Mediterranean), and has a coastline of more than 1,200 miles (1,930 km.).

In the North, there are no natural barriers to separate France from northern Europe. Elsewhere, the Rhine River separates France from Germany, the Alps from Switzerland and Italy, and the Pyrenees from Spain. The geographical relief of France begins from the coastline to the valleys, and then rises to plateaus, highlands and finally to mountains, the highest be-

From atop Notre Dame Cathedral, a stone gargoyle stares vacantly over the Seine River and the rooftops of Paris to the distant Eiffel Tower   Courtesy: Jon Markham Morrow

ing Mont Blanc in the Alps (15,777 feet, 4,809 meters) and Mont Vignemale in the Pyrenees (10,804 feet; 3,293 meters).

Although France is large, it has the lowest population density in the European Union (EU). Its total population and economic riches are very unevenly distributed geographically. If one were to draw a line on the map of France from the northern port of Le Havre to Grenoble and then on to Marseilles, one could see two halves of a country as different from one another as northern Italy is from southern Italy. The western half of France contains 56% of the territory, but only 37% of its people, and is steadily losing population. It tends to be less industrialized, and its agriculture is based on small farms and is therefore less efficient. East of the line one finds 80% of France's industrial production and three–fourths of the industrial employees. Economic development is particularly rapid in the northeast of France, and recently in Rhône–Alps and Marseilles regions. Farming tends to be more intensive and efficient, and a far smaller percentage of inhabitants live agriculturally.

Geographic and demographic statistics can hardly convey the beauty that for centuries has been called *la belle France*. The visitor invariably finds himself charmed by the smell of rich vines heavy with grapes, by the rolling green countryside studded with more castles than one finds in any other country, by the towering cathedrals whose bells resound throughout the countryside, by the warm beaches along the Riviera and by the majestic, snow–capped peaks. As one begins to realize how this beauty blends with the Frenchman's proverbial *joie de vivre* ("joy of living"), one sees why the Germans have always described the good life as "living like God in France."

HISTORY

The Early Period

Although France has played a prominent role in European history for at least 1500 years, it did not become a national entity or even approximately achieve its present shape until the 16th century A.D. The legend of French unity goes back to Vercingetorix, the chief of a Gallic tribe called the Arverni, who led a coalition in an uprising against the Roman occupiers in 52 B.C. Although he placed his foot soldiers in a hopeless strategic position and squandered his cavalry before the critical phase of the battle had begun, resulting in his troops' and his own capture, he is seen as the first patriot and resistance hero of French history.

The French profess a close kinship to the Gauls. But the latter were a people

who left no literature, no language, no laws, who worshipped many gods and practiced human sacrifice, and who, according to the Roman arch at Orange, fought naked, their hair buttered and in a long looped knot, with drooping mustaches and long narrow shields. It is doubtful that such a race had a profound impact on the French people and their civilization. Frenchmen today are very amused by the caricature of the early Gaulois in the popular *Asterix* comic books.

They no doubt owe far more to the Romans, who occupied for centuries much of what is now France. The Romans built towns, roads, aqueducts and theaters. They provided examples of centralization, efficient bureaucracy, written law and a periodic census. They brought education and culture to France and gave the French an appreciation of abstractions. They also left a tradition of grandeur, spotting France with statues and monuments. Finally, their language—vulgarized by common usage, later developed into French.

Even before the fall of the Roman Empire in the 5th century, France had become an invasion ground for tribes from all over the known world: Visigoths, Burgundians, Alemans, and Franks (Germans who eventually gave the country its name). In the 8th and 9th centuries, Charlemagne, the warrior king who established himself as "Emperor of the West," absorbed what is now France into a huge political unit encompassing much of present Europe, from Saxony to the island of Elba, including Bavaria and most of Lombardy in Italy. This great empire, however, did not survive his death in 814 A.D., and France again became fragmented.

The Capets Claim Paris

Not until a century and a half later did conditions begin to develop which were favorable to unity. In 987 the Capet family, which owned large tracts of land around the region now called the *Île de France*, raised a claim of dynastic leadership over France. The Capetians chose as their capital a small town nearby, which had been established in 100 B.C. on a five–acre island in the middle of the river Seine by a curly headed Celtic tribe of fishermen and navigators called *Parisii*. The Romans had named this city Lutetia and had built it up to a town of from 6,000 to 10,000 inhabitants. The city had also served as capital for the Frankish King Clovis, who had defeated the last remnants of the retreating Romans in 486.

The Capetians adopted *Francien*, a Latin–based dialect spoken around Paris, as their official language. Hugues Capet, born in 938, was the first Frankish king who could speak no German, and as a result of the Capetian example, German

and Latin soon disappeared from the early French court. French became the language of the elite, both at the court and abroad (for example, Marco Polo wrote about his travels to China in French!), and the political and military successes of the French dynasty gradually led to the language's adoption by all the people. This language became a powerful agent in the forma-tion and expansion of the French nation and civilization. For that reason, few peoples in the world try so hard to preserve and spread their language as do the French.

Crusades

The first Crusade in the 11th century, sponsored by the French Pope Urban II, and organized by the French cleric Peter the Hermit, was conducted almost exclusively by the French knights. While building castles in Lebanon and establishing a Kingdom of Jerusalem (which endured at least in name until the 15th century), they showed a zealous sense of mission in extending French civilization, which they tended to see as embodying Christian values. This became a major rationale for most French military and colonial enterprises in the centuries to follow.

A crucially important by–product of the Crusades was the weakening of the feudal bonds which tied serfs to their lords. French noblemen were often left penniless by the military expenses they bore, and many times they obtained needed money by freeing serfs and selling charters to cities. By the 13th century, serfdom had almost disappeared in France, and cities had sprung up everywhere, partly because of the trade the Crusades had created. Spices and textiles from the Orient were highly desired by the Europeans, and cities became the crossroads for such trade. France prospered.

Another indirect example of French expansionism occurred when William (the Conqueror) invaded England in 1066, conquering the Anglo–Saxons by 1070. Although initially French largely displaced Anglo–Saxon, at least at the court, the latter soon revived, and the two languages were combined, enriching each other. Court decisions and proceedings by the twelfth century were written in a curious combination of English, French and Latin. But William retained his holdings in Normandy, Maine, Touraine and Anjou within what is now France; this later became a source of friction between the French and the English. William's great–grandson, the incompetent King John of England, lost many of the French territories in the early 13th century.

By the end of the 12th century, France, especially Paris (which by that time was

France

Crusaders and Saracens in Battle
(From a 12th century stained-glass window)

the most populous city in Europe) was considered to be the world center of science and culture, having replaced Athens and Rome. By the 14th century one–half of the people in the Christian world lived in what is now France.

Disorganization and Weak Monarchs

Despite the establishment of a unique language and a French dynasty, French history, until the 16th century, continued to be characterized most of the time by weak kings struggling against foreign rulers and by powerful, rebellious French noblemen, who often did not hesitate to ally with foreign powers against their king. Such division exposed France to the danger of absorption into a large kingdom dominated by England because of its control over much of France. But in the 13th and 14th centuries, three powerful French kings, Philippe Augustus, Louis IX (canonized in 1297 as Saint Louis) and Philippe IV (the Fair), succeeded in wresting control of some of the English

domains in France. They began the slow process of patching France together, sometimes by legitimate feudal claims, often by intermarriage, and very often by war. However, England maintained its huge foothold in Aquitaine, acquired in 1154 and encompassing most of southwestern France below the Loire River; England was also allied with the Burgundians north of the Loire. In the 14th and 15th centuries, the French kings waged a "Hundred Years War" to finally drive the English out of France.

Joan of Arc

In the midst of this struggle, a female savior emerged from the small village of Domremy in Lorraine. At the age of 16, Joan of Arc, the daughter of a French shepherd, claimed to have heard the voice of God commanding her to free the besieged city of Orléans and to have the French King crowned in Reims. Having persuaded a French captain to give her a horse and an armed guard, and flying a

white flag, she set off to find the King. She told a distrustful Charles VII that she would drive the English out of France and be "the lieutenant of the king of heaven who is king of France."

Dressed in a man's armor, and displaying remarkable skill in improving offensive military operations, she liberated Orléans, defeated the enemy forces at Patay and Troyes, and amidst enthusiastic crowds, proceeded to Reims to have the 26–year–old Charles VII crowned on July 17, 1429, in the way traditionally prescribed for French kings. Whenever she addressed the crowds as "Frenchmen," the response indicated that a new nationalism mingled with a divine mission was emerging.

Short–lived was the fortune of this girl. Dressed in men's clothing and violating the feudal law barring women from combat, she was distrusted by the clergy, the nobility and even the newly–crowned king. Mounted on a beautiful horse, she led her forces in a vain attempt to storm Paris and Compiègne, and though wounded by an arrow, she tried unsuccessfully to rally her troops. She was captured in May 1430 and delivered to the Duke of Burgundy, who was allied with the English and who sold her to them for a high fee. She was tried in Rouen by a French ecclesiastical court and, despite her own eloquent defense, was pronounced guilty of heresy. On May 30 she was burned at the stake in Rouen's marketplace, without the ungrateful king having made the slightest effort to save her.

Centuries later there is still no consensus in France concerning the legacy she had left. A monarchical France before 1789 had little use for saviors from the masses, and her mystical, religious aura made her out of place in an enlightened, revolutionary France. Nevertheless, Napoleon had a beautiful statue of her erected in Orléans in 1803, and the process to have her made a saint was initiated in 1869. Not until the humiliating defeat of France at the hands of the Prussians in 1870 was she embraced as a symbol of vengeance toward an outside power that had taken her native Lorraine. She was finally canonized in 1920.

Joan of Arc is to many Frenchmen the ideal symbol of patriotism: a pure lady warrior with a sense of mission who placed God solidly on the side of the French. She is undoubtedly the Madonna in de Gaulle's memoirs who incorporated France, since the great French leader also adopted the cross of Lorraine as his own symbol. His stubborn, righteous defense of France's destiny moved an exasperated Englishman, Sir Winston Churchill, to remark that "of all the crosses I have had to bear, the heaviest was the Cross of Lorraine."

France

Joan of Arc triumphantly enters Reims

Further Union Followed by Religious Wars

By 1453 the English had been driven from France, except for a tiny foothold in the northern port city of Calais. The "Hundred Years War" had nevertheless been a cruel disaster for the French people. Within a century, the war and the plagues that had struck at roughly the same time had reduced the population by almost one–half. In the closing years of that century Brittany, which had been independent, was integrated into France. Anne of Brittany, who in 1491 married the French King Charles VIII, sealed the union. She took her native Brittany as a dowry. Upon his death she married the next French King, Louis XII, in 1499 in order to preserve this union. Though France had made impressive strides toward territorial unity in the 15th century, the century to follow was not to be one of peace and unity.

In 1519 a minor German priest named Martin Luther courageously raised a chal-

lenge of faith to the powerful Catholic Church and began the Reformation that spread throughout the Christian world. A Frenchman, John Calvin, also developed a religious doctrine hostile to the Church and was forced to flee to the Swiss city of Geneva, which he soon shaped into a Protestant "capital." He left behind a France seriously divided into two sects: the Huguenots (Protestant) and the Catholics. From 1559 until 1598, the Wars of Religion raged in France; this was a chaotic period dotted by eight distinct wars, assassinations and massacres. These unfortunate events were related to the issue of the king's and other nobility's respective powers, as much as to theological matters.

The situation became particularly grave in 1572 when 4,000 Protestants gathered in Paris for the wedding of the 19–year–old King Henry of Navarre to Charles IX's sister. Henry, whose life was under threat, had announced his conversion to Catholicism, ostensibly to heal fanatical religious

divisions in France. The Protestants were massacred on orders of the French king, and they promptly responded to this "St. Bartholomew's Day Massacre" by announcing that such a treacherous king was no longer to be obeyed. Henry quickly reassumed the Protestant faith and the wars raged on. When all involved finally realized in 1598 that the strife was without any redeeming value, Henry, upon becoming king, issued the Edict of Nantes, which promised Frenchmen religious freedom. Nevertheless, the religious issue continued to gnaw away at the unity of France for more than three centuries.

The French Century

The 17th century became "the French century" in all of continental Europe. This was a period when forceful French kings and brilliant royal advisers succeeded in reducing much of the French nobility's powers and in establishing the present borders of France. The glitter of the royal court soon dazzled Europe.

When in 1624 Louis XIII chose an ambitious cardinal to be his chief adviser, he gained at his side a tireless servant of the French crown and the French state. Cardinal Richelieu was not a man given to courtly debauchery, theological hairsplitting or listening for voices from God. "Reason must be the standard for everything," he said, and "the public interest ought to be the sole objective of the prince and his counselors." Raison d'état ("reason of state"), the interests of the community, became for him the overriding concerns.

Since Richelieu was convinced that only absolute monarchical authority could elevate his country to the highest rank in the world, he proceeded to neutralize any powers that could challenge the central authority of the King. He had torn down all castles not belonging to the King that could be used to resist royal authority. In a swash–buckling era presented so vividly in Alexander Dumas' *The Three Musketeers*, Richelieu dared to ban dueling, a favorite pastime of the nobility, on the grounds that weapons should be drawn only against enemies of the state. While not attacking religious principles, he whittled away at the privileges granted in 1598 to Protestants, believing that a free, powerful Protestant party in France could easily undermine the centralized power of France.

At the same time he sent money and troops to support the Protestants in the Thirty Years War that ravaged Germany from 1618 to 1648. His reasons were simple: although Austria and Spain were fighting in the name of Catholicism, their victory in the struggle would have strengthened these great powers and thus

France

presented a greater threat to France. Further, by sending French troops southward, eastward and northward, France acquired territory along the way. France's borders thus moved outward. Clearly, the Cardinal did not think religiously; he thought *French*. When he died in 1642 (followed in death a few months later by Louis XIII), he left behind an almost unchallenged central authority, a powerful French army, a small but effective fleet and a highly organized professional diplomatic service. He also established French as the new diplomatic language for the world, a position it enjoyed for more than 250 years. Above all, he left a tradition of total dedication to the power and glory of France.

Louis XIV, Cardinal Mazarin and Anarchy

This renowned monarch became king in 1643 at the age of five. He was able to build on the great works of Cardinal Richelieu and on the works of another Cardinal who, though extremely unpopular, held France together against an angry and dangerous storm until the young king was ready to assume the reins of government. Cardinal Mazarin was a wealthy Italian, whose love of money did not prevent him from energetically serving the young king's mother and regent, Queen Anne, with whom Mazarin reportedly had more than just cordial relations.

Picking up where Richelieu had left off, Mazarin led France to victories over Austria. The Treaty of Westphalia in 1648 and subsequent victories over Spain left France the foremost power in Europe. Austria was seriously weakened, and Germany was fragmented, depopulated and exhausted. French strength and German "weakness" through division remained a cornerstone of French politics until 1990. Indeed, Frenchmen have always liked to say ironically, "we like Germany so much that we want there to be many of them."

Having achieved a position of power in Europe, France became seriously weakened internally. From 1648 to 1653 it was rocked by a complicated series of civil disturbances which threatened the young king's hold on the throne, and which in some ways anticipated the French Revolution which came a century and a half later. The parliament, the bourgeoisie (a class of persons who had risen socially above the level of peasants and manual laborers, but who had no titles of nobility), and the Parisian mobs, all for their own reasons, created such an anarchical situation in Paris that the king and his mother were forced to flee to the palace of St. Germain, where they lived at Mazarin's personal expense.

Some French nobles invited the Spanish troops to reenter France, and Parisian mobs erected barricades and took law into their own hands. In the prolonged confusion, battles raged in the countryside and the streets of Paris, and finally Mazarin was forced to flee to Germany. However, after all order had disappeared, the key figures of this uprising, known as the *fronde* (named after the French word for slingshot, used by rioters to smash windows in Paris) surprisingly lost their nerve, and this revolt against the centralized monarchy and the unpopular Mazarin gradually collapsed.

The 14–year–old Louis led his loyal troops in 1652 into a tired and shamed Paris. Louis never forgave the rebellious city and wasted little time in removing himself from the clutches of this beautiful, but tempestuous and unfaithful mistress. The rupture between the king and Paris would later have disastrous consequences for the monarchy.

Louis Comes of Age

Immediately after Mazarin's death, the young king called a meeting of all the court's advisers and announced: "Now it is time that I rule!" No one questioned this. By then, the 23–year–old monarch's imposing physical dignity and his polished manners, combined with an unhesitating decisiveness, rapidly brought him respect within France, which sometimes bordered on worship. France was weary of chaos and was ready to kiss the hand that ruled with firm authority. His prodigious lovemaking at the court, which has certainly lost nothing in the telling, greatly irritated his mother, but it did not prevent him from being a hard–working and effective king. Almost no state affairs escaped his attention; in 1661 he commanded his ministers not to sign or seal any order without his permission.

The entire kingdom increasingly felt the impact of the royal government. When the affairs of state became too great for one man to handle, he developed a bureaucracy and efficient procedures to enable his government to absorb the workload. All aspects of French foreign affairs, defense, finance, commerce, religion and the royal household were channeled through the king's court. He appointed officials to secure royal control over all activities in the various regions in France. He supervised all major appointments in his bureaucracy and the army. Though there is no evidence that he ever really said "I am the state," there was no question that he would have readily agreed with such an assertion. He actually worked very hard to live up to his rather arrogant motto: *Nec pluribus impar* ("None his equal").

As a symbol of his magnificence, the "Sun King" ordered that a royal palace be built in Versailles, which would not only be at a safe distance from Paris, but would be unsurpassed in all of Europe for its beauty and dignity. For 20 years he had this gigantic structure, with its surrounding gardens, fountains and smaller palaces, built and rebuilt. His finance minister, Colbert, was exasperated by the project, which almost emptied the royal treasury and which could only be financed by selling many of the state's treasures. However, once finished, this palace became the assembly point for much of France's ambitious nobility. There Louis could keep an eye on them and busy them with ritual duties, such as buttoning his coat or escorting the servants who brought his food to the royal table. Louis' preeminence was

Paris in the 17th century

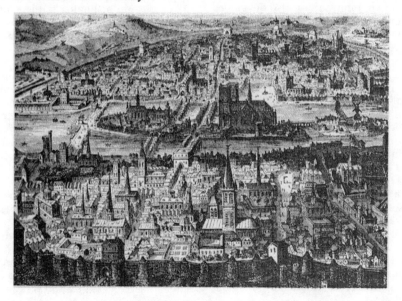

France

Louis XIV, the "Sun King." Probably painted at about age 55+, it indicates he had lost his teeth, was overweight, had bunions from wearing high heels, and a double chin.

Stirrings of Discontent

The "Sun King" long outlived all of his children, and upon his death his five–year–old great–grandchild was crowned Louis XV. The new King ruled until 1774, when Louis XVI, a good man who never wanted to be king, succeeded to the throne. Both were rather weak and increasingly unpopular kings who were unable to guide their country's adjustment to the changes that occurred in French society during the 18th century. This was a formula for revolution. Greatly contributing to and benefiting from France's prosperity, the bourgeoisie resented its exclusion from political responsibility, which was almost entirely in the hands of the aristocracy. The rural peasantry, which comprised 80% of the population and owned 40% of the land, resented the aristocracy's rights to hunt on their land, its local police power and its near monopoly over rural mills, bakeshops and wine presses. The manorial lords appeared to live well without performing an obviously useful function.

The dissatisfaction with the aristocracy was fed by the enlightened ideas of the time. In the course of the 18th century, thinkers such as Montesquieu, Voltaire and Diderot had brilliantly chipped away at the foundations of aristocratic society. An irreverent Frenchman named Jean–Jacques Rousseau had written in his bombshell book, *The Social Contract*, that "man was born free, but everywhere he is in chains," and he had proposed provocative ways of breaking these chains and creating a society of free and equal human beings. Rousseau was driven from France because of these ideas, and died in 1778.

Events in America that same year caused revolutionary ideas to pour in that brought the soup to a boil. A young revolutionary named Thomas Jefferson from Virginia had written, "all men are created equal and are endowed with unalienable rights." In rapid succession, the 13 colonies began to produce democratic constitutions, which were translated almost immediately into French and avidly read by intelligent persons grown weary of social hierarchy and inherited privilege. Benjamin Franklin, who was sent to France to persuade the government to help the American colonies in the struggle against the English, was lionized by France's high society. His rustic, egalitarian wisdom was the talk of Paris. Most importantly, he persuaded France's leaders, who had lost their colonies in North America to the English in the Seven Years' War (1756–1763), to enter the struggle against the British. French assistance to the rebellious colonies was a very important contributing factor in the American victory; without the French army and

such that nobles competed for the honor of performing even the most menial functions at his court. For instance, the Princess of Ursins, who later became the Queen of Spain, was considered one of the luckiest persons at the Court of Versailles because she performed the task of handing the king his dagger and night pot each evening as he retired to his private bedroom.

Under the conscientious guidance of Louis XIV, France achieved an incomparable political, military and cultural ascendancy. The arts bloomed, and France was the richest and most populous country in Europe. It also acquired the most powerful army on the continent, and Louis was more than willing to use it. He conducted almost continuously destructive wars. He thereby was able to establish France's pres-ent borders, but he ultimately converted almost every country in Europe into an enemy of France. He ordered that the Palatinate in the western part of Ger-

many be burned, resulting in the destruction of Heidelberg, Mannheim, Speyer, Worms and hundreds of smaller towns. His soldiers ripped the bones of earlier Holy Roman emperors out of their graves in Speyer, a sacrilege that was not soon forgotten in Germany. The Treaty of Utrecht finally established an uneasy peace in 1713, two years before the king's death.

Even if France gradually exhausted itself financially and physically through almost continuous warfare, it was certainly well administered. Louis' powers were broad, and he used them with great energy. However, he could by no means be called a dictator in the modern sense. He had to deal with a limited national treasury, an absence of a national police force, ineffective and slow means of communication and regions that still jealously guarded their remaining powers. All in all, he gave Frenchmen an era which they still proudly call "the grand century."

France

navy, perhaps the ill–equipped and militarily untrained colonists would never have prevailed against their masters.

While the French government slapped its traditional enemy in the face, it had unknowingly allowed the bacillus of freedom to enter France through the back door. Some officers and many non–commissioned officers returned to France deeply moved by the events in America of which they had been a part, and they were very sympathetic and supportive of revolutionary movements in their own country. The world now had a concrete model of a large country ruling itself in a republican way.

Financial Woes Lead Toward Revolution

Another unforeseen consequence of France's aid to the Americans was that it brought France to the brink of bankruptcy; it doubled the national debt and consumed more than one–half of the crown's income. It was not an extravagant court that caused France's desperate financial situation; only 5% of the public expenditures were devoted to the entire royal establishment. The French Revolution did not spring from a naive, spendthrift Queen Marie Antoinette (called by the people "Madame Deficit") who was re-

ported (incorrectly!) to have asked why the peasants did not eat cake if they had no bread.

One–fourth of France's budget was devoted to war costs, and a whopping one–half was needed to service France's debts. Other countries, such as England, had similar expenditures, but France's financial crisis could not be solved because of its archaic and unequal tax system. The aristocracy and the wealthy bourgeoisie either evaded or won exemptions from taxation. The Church also refused to pay taxes, so the tax collectors could turn only to the poorest French citizens. Thus, although the country was generally prosperous, the public treasury was empty.

Louis XVI, who like his predecessor had often opposed the aristocracy and sought strength from the bourgeoisie, well understood the problem, but he was so weak and unpopular that he could do nothing about it. In desperation, he convened an Estates General in May 1789, the first such meeting in a century and a half. However, the class antagonism in France was such that the three classes assembled (clergy, aristocracy and bourgeoisie) simply could not work out reform in cooperation.

On June 17, 1789, the bourgeois element (the "Third Estate") decided to declare it-

self the "National Assembly." When the king panicked and closed the hall in which the Third Estate met, the latter moved to a nearby indoor tennis court and proclaimed in the "Oath of the Tennis Court" that it was the true representative of the people and that it would not disband until it had produced a constitution for France. This was a revolutionary step, unleashing explosive events that an irresolute king could not control. It was the first act in the French Revolution, which went through many stages and lasted ten years. Whether or not these events represented "the end of history," as the Prussian philosopher Friedrich Hegel maintained, neither France nor the world would thereafter be the same.

Revolution

The events at the Versailles meetings stirred up crowds in Paris, which began to look for weapons in arsenals and public buildings. On July 14, 1789, a crowd went to the Bastille, which, like the Tower of London, was a stronghold built during the Middle Ages to overawe the city and to provide a place of detention for influential prisoners. When the official in charge of the stronghold refused to distribute any weapons, the crowd successfully stormed the fortress. The mob, infuriated that almost a hundred persons had been killed, slaughtered the guards who had surrendered. They then beheaded the commanding official with knives and paraded around Paris with the heads of their victims on spikes. This bloody skirmish and macabre display was a harbinger of ferocious acts to come. Nevertheless, Frenchmen celebrate July 14 today as their major holiday.

The unrest and violence spread to the countryside as manorial lords saw their properties sacked and burned by bitter peasants. The more fortunate escaped with their lives, but royal power vanished quickly. The Marquis de Lafayette, a revolutionary–minded aristocrat who had served on George Washington's staff during the American War of Independence, was given command over the guard in Paris. He designed a flag for the new France to replace the blue and white fleur de *lis* ("lily flag"). He combined the colors of the city of Paris, red and blue, with the white of the House of Bourbon. Thus, the tricolor, which is France's flag today, represented a fusion of the new and old regimes.

The sudden acts of violence had frightened the ruling group into granting important concessions. On August 4, 1789, the nobles relinquished their feudal rights, and on August 27 the National Assembly promptly proclaimed the Declaration of the Rights of Man. The U.S. ambassador to France and author of the American

The Palace at Versailles

France

LA MARSEILLAISE.

and in September 1792 suspected royalists were hunted down and massacred in prisons, monasteries and elsewhere. In December the king was tried and convicted of conspiring with the enemy (a charge which was no doubt true), and he was beheaded one month later. Scarcely had the king's head fallen into the basket of the guillotine before France found itself at war with all the major monarchies of Europe.

Faced with a frenzied, imperiled nation, the moderates were pushed aside by the radical Jacobins, a revolutionary club which had met regularly since 1789 in the Jacobin Convent in the Rue Honoré and which was led by the fanatical Robespierre. A Committee of Public Safety was formed to cope with enemies abroad and at home. On October 10, 1793, the new revolutionary leadership declared that the government of France must remain "revolutionary until the peace." In clear text, this meant a "reign of terror," and political "trials" were begun at once.

On October 16 Queen Marie Antoinette was guillotined, followed by all the Girondists who could be arrested. For the next nine months the guillotine would never cease from doing its grisly work. Until Robespierre and his followers' own execution in July 1794, France was subjected to a dictatorship in the hands of fanatically self-righteous people who asserted, "terror is nothing else than swift, severe, indomitable justice; it then flows from virtue."

Enlightened democrats make no claims to know absolute truth and therefore tolerate other men's views and weaknesses. By contrast, the ideologues who controlled France in those bloody days had such an abstract conception of liberty that they lost sight of man. Out of love for humanity and the truth, they would have eradicated the human race.

The noted French author, George Sand, wrote that "during the terror, the men who spilled the most blood were those who had the strongest desire to lead their fellow men to the dreamed-of golden age, and who had the greatest sympathy for human misery ... the greater their thirst for universal happiness, the more relentless they became." Charles Dickens was no doubt correct when, in the opening sentence of his *A Tale of Two Cities*, he referred to the French Revolution: "It was the best of times, it was the worst of times, it was the age of reason, it was the age of foolishness ..." Perhaps at no other time could one see so clearly the worst and best in man.

Although Frenchmen today tend to remember mostly the noblest aspects of the Revolution, the terror made it difficult then and now for persons outside of France to have a unified opinion of this

Declaration of Independence, Thomas Jefferson, had been asked to read and improve this French equivalent before its publication, a request that he declined for diplomatic reasons. This French document was one of history's most eloquent assertions of equality before the law, of the opening of public service to all classes and of freedom as an unalienable individual right, limited only by the freedom of others. An enlightened constitutional monarchy was established. The king was forced to return to the Tuileries palace in Paris. There he would be under the watchful eye of France's new, moderate regime, guided by the aristocrat Count de Mirabeau, who, like many aristocrats, had concluded that the future lay with the Third Estate.

Revolution Out of Control

It is always a great misfortune when moderate and democratic revolutionaries cannot control the beast of revolution once it has been un-caged. As in Russia a century and a quarter later, a more radical "second revolution" often overtakes the first one, wiping away many of the democratic gains in the process. This misfortune befell the French Revolution.

The first signal for such a change came on the night of June 21, 1791, when the king and his family attempted to escape to Germany. Caught at Varennes, close to the border, two days later, they were brought back to the Tuileries without glory and locked up in their palace. After this clumsy move, the king's commitment to the new order was no longer credible, and the people's loyalty to the king, which had already been eroded, disappeared entirely.

This new situation greatly angered the other monarchies of Europe, especially those of Prussia and Austria. The moderate "Girondists," members of a revolutionary club whose name derived from the department (state) of Gironde and who had gained a majority in the National Assembly in 1792, responded to what they saw as a clear external threat to the Revolution. They declared war on Austria. It went badly for France, but it quickly added a new element to the Revolution. Seeing the "fatherland in danger," the citizens took up arms, and patriotism rose to fever pitch. Nationalism and revolution joined hands as the French national anthem, the Marseillaise, indicates.

The newly unleashed popular tide became extremely difficult to control. The Tuileries palace was stormed by a mob and forced a humiliated king to wear a red hat of the Revolution and to drink with them from a common bottle. The constitutional monarchy was overthrown,

83

France

first great European revolution. No doubt, many of the 17,000 victims of the terror were in fact enemies of the new republic. Only 15% of the executions took place in Paris, and more than half took place in western France, where the resistance to the new order was the greatest. Only 15% of the victims were aristocrats or clergymen. To some extent, then, the terror was a defensive measure. However, the number of innocent persons who were caught in the grinder was so great that the new republic disgusted highly respected friends abroad. Also, although France's foreign enemies were ultimately defeated, the French Revolution was knocked off its democratic path, and it was almost a century before France was able to return to relatively stable, republican government.

Napoleon

Robespierre was overthrown and beheaded on July 27, 1794. That date fell within the month of Thermador in the revolutionary calendar, which had been introduced on August 18, 1792, the date the constitutional monarchy began. The notables who assumed power moved rapidly to restrict suffrage and eliminate the masses from political influence in a tired, internally paralyzed France. In 1795 they created a Directory, led by five Directors, but this new form of government could not create order in France.

In the midst of such instability, a brilliant young general saw his great opportunity. Born into an Italian family from Corsica in 1769, Napoleon Bonaparte had been educated in French military schools and had gained notoriety by suppressing an uprising against the Directory shortly after its founding. An ingenious innovator of lightning military tactics combined with effective use of field artillery, he understood how to win the unswerving devotion of his soldiers. He achieved great victories in Italy, and in

1799, while his troops were conducting a major campaign in Egypt, he returned to Paris and seized power at bayonet point.

For the next 15 years, France followed this man, who though slight of stature (barely five feet tall), was a great leader in many ways. He clearly preferred order to liberty, and he quickly moved to establish order in France. Despite his authoritarian style of rule, he was an immensely popular leader who quickly showed that he was, at least to some extent, a child of the Revolution. He introduced financial reforms and tightened the centralized administration of France. He promulgated a new constitution and a civil code which reflected the major accomplishments of the Revolution: popular sovereignty, underscored by Napoleon's practice of submitting every constitutional change to a plebiscite; trial by jury and equality before the law; a citizens' army; office holding based on competence; abolition of feudal privileges; freedom of religion; and freedom of speech and press (at least in theory). Though they had often been ignored in practice during the ten years since 1789, liberty and equality had within a decade become so embraced in principle that they have remained permanent elements of French public life.

Napoleon may appear today as a greater friend of monarchy than of the Revolution. He signed a Concordat with the Catholic Church in 1801, reintroduced slavery in French colonies in 1802 and allowed émigrés to return to France and reclaim their unsold properties. In 1804 he crowned himself "Emperor of the French," and during his reign he divorced his wife Josephine in order to marry an Austrian princess. He also placed his brothers, son and marshals upon thrones throughout Europe as he proceeded from conquest to conquest. Nevertheless, in his own day, the other peoples of Europe saw him as a very embodiment of the Revolution who carried its ideals to every part of Europe. These principles were always among his most effective weapons.

Napoleon remained a great military leader who sought both to secure France's "natural borders" and to pacify Europe under French leadership. This was essentially accomplished by 1802. However, his ambition was to be more than a peacemaker, and his lack of moderation not only sapped his own country's vigor, it ultimately doomed him to defeat. In May 1803 he began an endless series of wars aiming far beyond the mere protection of France's frontiers. Due to stunning victories, French domination by 1806 extended from Holland and the German North Sea coast to the Illyrian Provinces along the east coast of the Adriatic Sea.

Italy was completely under French control, and some territories (including Rome itself) were annexed to France. But his very successes helped to bring about his downfall.

His invasions stimulated nationalism outside France, and the other governments of Europe felt compelled to imitate France by making popular reforms and raising citizens' armies. Soon Napoleon discovered that he faced opposition, not just from hostile governments and ruling groups, but from entire nations in Europe. He fought an unsuccessful guerrilla war in Spain, and in 1812 his Grand Army suffered a disastrous wintertime defeat in frigid Russia. The following year he was defeated at the "Battle of the Nations" in Leipzig that pitted France and its allies, chiefly the Rhineland Germans, against Prussia, Austria, Russia, Sweden and England. His enemies pursued his disintegrating army into the heart of France, capturing Paris itself on March 31, 1814.

Napoleon was forced to flee to the island of Elba, where the victors erected a small kingdom for him, but in less than a year he returned to France in order to regain his empire. Though exhausted from long sustained warfare, the French succumbed once more to Napoleon's magic. In a hundred days he prepared a new army, but his dreams were crushed by a united Europe on the Belgian battlefield of Waterloo on June 18, 1815. This time he was held as prisoner on the small British island of Saint–Helena in the South Atlantic while the victorious European powers gathered at the Congress of Vienna to reconstitute Europe.

Napoleon died in lonely exile in 1821, but this "little corporal," as he was often called, still casts a giant shadow in the memories of Frenchmen. He brought France pride, and he rests in magnificent glory in the Invalides, a military hospital in Paris, where the mutilated from his Grand Army were cared for. To this day, the elite professional officers of the French army descend at midnight to their knees at the foot of Napoleon's giant illuminated statue to receive their commissions at St. Cyr, the military academy he had created.

The Monarchy Returns

In 1815, with 150,000 occupation troops on French soil, the Bourbons were again placed on the throne. Although one spoke of a restoration and although 70,000 returned from exile abroad, few believed that the clock was to be turned back before 1789. The royal family was compelled to live in Paris under the eyes of a population that had never made the kings' lives comfortable. The new King, Louis XVIII, the brother of the ill–fated Louis XVI, wanted no part of the revolutionary flag,

At the Court of Napoleon I

He did not pursue glory, a fact the poet Lamartine lamented: "France is a bored nation." Although an admirer of the king, even Victor Hugo wrote in that great work of fiction about post–Napoleonic France, *Les Misérables*, that "his great fault was that he was modest in the name of France … His monarchy displayed excessive timidity which is offensive to a nation that has July 14 in its civil traditions and Austerlitz in its military annals."

An economic crisis in 1846 made the voteless urban workers in Paris nervous, and the middle classes wanted an end to the narrow elite composed of a few thousand noblemen and upper bourgeoisie. The influence of the extremely unpopular premier, François Guizot, who was reputed (incorrectly) to have advised those in power to "enrich yourselves," helped fan the republican and democratic revival which was gaining momentum. On January 27, 1848, Alexis de Tocqueville, who had gained a great reputation for his perceptive study Democracy in America, told the French Parliament, "I believe that at this moment we are sleeping on a volcano." The volcano erupted in Paris only a few days later. Wanting no bloodbath on his conscience, Louis–Philippe abdicated and departed for England.

The Second Republic, More Anarchy and another Napoleon

The Second Republic was declared immediately, and a highly idealistic government under Lamartine's leadership proceeded to introduce universal male suffrage, to abolish slavery in the colonies again and and to guarantee every citizen a job by establishing national workshops at the state's expense. To the new leaders' surprise, their government suffered a crushing defeat in the first parliamentary elections in the spring of 1848. A new legislative majority eliminated the costly socialist experiments, most notably the national workshops. This action provoked desperate workers and idealists again to erect barricades in the streets of Paris and to resist the reaction that always follows each radically democratic experiment in France. In four bloody "June Days" of street fighting in Paris, General Cavaignac crushed the rebels, killing 1,500 and arresting 12,000 in the process; 3,000 persons were hunted down and executed later.

The frightful events in Paris set off rebellions in capitals all over Europe. French workers were left bitter and smoldering, and class hatred in France was hardened, feelings which remained a part of French life for the rest of the century and which, to a limited extent, continue to exist in France today.

After the June convulsion there was a widespread desire for a return to order.

the tricolor. He did accept a constitutional order which left things more or less as they were before 1815; feudal customs and special privileges of the nobility were not reintroduced, and France's law code, formalized under Napoleon, the tax system, personal freedoms, centralized administration and the principle of equality before the law remained.

Louis' other brother, who was crowned Charles X in 1824, showed that he had learned little about France since 1789. He believed in the divine right of kings to rule, and he tried to restore the earlier authority of the Catholic Church. His men sought revenge against former Jacobins and Bonapartists, and the ultra–royalists demanded restitution of their properties. In 1830 he made his final mistake by suspending liberty of the press, dissolving the French legislature and so restricting the electorate that practically only noblemen could vote. While the oblivious king was hunting in Rambouillet, dissidents publicly waved the tricolor and erected barricades in the streets of Paris, some of which reached a height of up to 80 feet. One nobleman, sensing danger, noted to his friend: "Things look bad. They are singing La Marseillaise!"

Three days of bitter street fighting (known as the *trois glorieuses*) convinced Charles that he could not master the situation, so he set sail immediately for Scotland. No Bourbon ever ruled France again; their last King had failed to notice that although the French population had

grown tired of revolution and war, it nevertheless continued to take equality and liberty seriously. However, unlike the Americans, the French did not experience one successful 18th–century revolution which established a new democratic political order once and for all. The French Revolution had to be re-fought at intervals, and each revolution left France divided. It remained a country with a seed of civil war.

Another monarchy was established in 1830. The new King was the 57–year–old Duke of Orléans, Louis–Philippe, the son of the renowned Philippe *Egalité* ("equality"), who had voted for the beheading of Louis XVI and who soon thereafter was also beheaded in the name of the Revolution. Louis–Philippe had fought for the Revolution at Valmy and Jemmapes and then had gone into exile, visiting the United States at one time. Despite his romantic past, the new king was an uninspiring man. He was intelligent enough to disavow the divine right of kings and to proclaim himself the "citizen's king." He restored the revolutionary tricolor as the nation's flag, lifted censorship and doubled the suffrage (although only about 200,000 in a nation of 32 million had the right to vote).

He was a moderate, business–oriented king who brought France more prosperity at home and peace abroad. But the fact that he was the target of more than 80 assassination attempts indicated that his rule was not universally acceptable to Frenchmen.

France

A new constitution was written, calling for presidential elections by universal male suffrage. In elections held late in 1848 the winner by a landslide was a man who in the past had not displayed any political talent. He was not a dashing figure. He was short and rather paunchy, and his appearance was once described as that of a "depressed parrot." However, he enjoyed two immense advantages: his name was Louis Napoleon Bonaparte and he was the nephew of the former emperor.

He had been raised in Germany and always spoke French with a slight German accent. He had served as a captain in the Swiss army and had participated in revolutionary events in Italy. In 1836 and 1840 he had made two almost comic attempts to overthrow the dull regime of Louis–Philippe. In his trial in 1840 he had cried: "I represent before you a principle, a cause, a defeat. The principle is the sovereignty of the people; the cause is that of the Empire; the defeat is Waterloo!" Though he did not persuade the court, he managed to associate his name in the minds of many Frenchmen with the Napoleonic legend, which had been experiencing a rise in popularity at the time. Streets in Paris had been named after Napoleonic victories, the Arch of Triumph that Napoleon I had ordered had been

finally completed, and the "little corporal's" remains had been brought back to France and solemnly transported through the city before the wet eyes of thousands of nostalgic Frenchmen.

For his revolutionary activities in France, Louis Napoleon had been imprisoned for life in the fortress of Ham, where he spent his time in luxurious confinement, writing tracts on such topics as "The Extinction of Poverty." One morning early in 1846, Louis Napoleon slipped into workman's clothes and with a pipe in his mouth and a board over his shoulder walked out the front gate of the fortress. He was in England the next day, where he awaited his opportunity. In May 1848 his chance came, and he returned to France; by the end of the year he had been elected France's president.

Louis Napoleon invoked the revolutionary principle of popular sovereignty, but he left little doubt that his would be an authoritarian regime. He once remarked: "I do not mind being baptized in the water of universal suffrage, but I do not intend to live with my feet in it." With his four–year term of office approaching its end, and with a hostile parliament that refused to change the constitution so he could succeed himself, he sent his troops to occupy Paris the night of December 1–2, 1851, and to arrest most of his oppo-

nents. When Parisians awoke the next morning, they learned that a *coup d'état* had just effectively put an end to the Second Republic.

In characteristic post–1789 style, Louis Napoleon asserted the sovereignty of the people as the first law of the land and promised a referendum on all constitutional changes. Also, in characteristic fashion, the Parisian population refused to accept this change without a fight. The barricades went up again; at one across the Boulevard de Montmartre near the Saint–Denis Gate, a military column panicked under the insults of the mob and opened indiscriminate fire on the fleeing citizens. Two hundred persons lay dead as a result of this unfortunate carnage. Although a terrified Parisian populace did not rise up again for 20 years in 1871, Louis Napoleon's hope for a bloodless takeover was dashed; the December massacre was never forgotten or forgiven. Years later his wife Eugénie confided to a friend: "A *coup d'état* is like a convict's ball and chain. You drag it along and eventually it paralyzes your leg."

Observing the usual practice, Louis Napoleon proceeded rapidly to rewrite the constitution. He created a weak legislature and a strong president who could appeal directly to the people by means of plebiscites. After a year, he could no

Foyer of the Paris Opera

longer resist one last temptation: on the first anniversary of his *coup d'état*, he submitted a referendum to the people asking whether they favored "restoration of imperial dignity." Almost eight million votes indicated yes against only a quarter of a million who said no. On December 2, 1852 he was proclaimed Napoleon III, Emperor of the French.

For all his talk of restoring France's glory, Napoleon III desired above all to establish order and to make it a prosperous, industrially advanced country. He expanded credit and stimulated new investment. Everywhere new industry and railroads sprang up. He liberalized trade, which boosted French commerce. Overall, French industrial production doubled under his rule; signs of dynamism were everywhere.

Perhaps the most lasting of his public works can be seen in the large cities such as Marsailles and Paris. Napoleon III appointed Baron Haussmann to administer the department of the Seine in which Paris is located. Haussmann completely transformed the city. He built the Paris Opera. He destroyed the narrow, medieval streets and laid wide boulevards and broad squares (such as the Place Étoile) with radiating avenues. It was noticed immediately that such wide boulevards would make barricade building, a periodic Parisian pastime, almost impossible and would facilitate military mobility inside the city. Nevertheless, these changes were badly needed to accommodate the capital's rapid growth and to make it a more modern, livable and beautiful city. During the Second Empire Paris was a prosperous, carefree and culturally active city that attracted admirers from all over the world.

In the first decade of his rule, Napoleon III restricted political parties and freedom of the press. He was a very popular ruler in France, however, and seeing that he had nothing to fear he introduced greater political freedoms in the 1860s. He even took what at the time seemed to be a very radical step: he legalized trade unions and granted workers the right to strike. His regime certainly did not come to an end due to domestic resistance. Instead, he shared the fate of his uncle, falling victim to foreign policy entanglements. He conducted a very active colonial policy in Africa, the Near East, China and Indochina, bringing the latter under French control in the 1860s.

In 1861 he decided to take advantage of the United States' preoccupation with its own Civil War by trying to establish a monarchy in Mexico dominated by France and ruled by Archduke Maximilian of Austria. In 1863 French troops entered Mexico City and placed the Archduke on the newly-created throne. But he never

developed popular backing and as soon as the American strife ended in 1865, the U.S. invoked the Monroe Doctrine and demanded that France get out of Mexico. Napoleon III complied, and when by 1867 no French troops were left in Mexico, the naive Maximilian, who had decided to remain with "his people," was executed by a firing squad. The Mexican adventure was a blunder that greatly diminished Napoleon III's prestige at home.

The fatal blow to the Second Empire was delivered in 1870 when the emperor tried to enforce France's long–standing policy of keeping Germany permanently divided. Provoked by the Prussian Chancellor Otto von Bismarck, who sought to create a unified Germany under Prussian domination, the French government declared war against Prussia. Napoleon calculated that the southern German-speaking states would not support Bismarck and might even side with France, but he had made a grave miscalculation; southern Germans were swept up in the new tide of German nationalism.

War and Defeat

France entered the war extremely unprepared. Prussia had a far superior general staff, supply system and strategy. Also, because of their faster mobilization, the German soldiers outnumbered the French two to one. Smashing through Lorraine, the Prussian Army cut Paris off from the two main French armies and delivered a devastating blow to the French at Sedan on the Belgian border. Napoleon III and more than 100,000 French soldiers were captured there, and the Empire came crashing down. In Paris, a republic was declared and the Parisians prepared for a long siege. The new government's 32–year–old leader, Léon Gambetta, escaped from the surrounded city of Paris by balloon and tried to raise a new army in the Loire area. However, the capture of the last trained French army in Metz in October 1870 demoralized the remaining untrained troops in France. In early 1871, after every last scrap of food in the capital had been consumed, including the rats in the sewers and the animals in the zoo, and after the trees in the Bois de Boulogne and the Champs Elysées had been chopped down for fuel, Paris and the troops in the provinces surrendered.

A humiliated France looked on as the German Empire was proclaimed in the Hall of Mirrors at the Versailles Palace. Germany then proceeded to set a very bad precedent by imposing a harsh peace on a prostrate France: Alsace and most of Lorraine, with their rich iron deposits and industry, were annexed by Germany. Further, France was required to pay the victor a very large reparations sum and

to allow German occupation troops to remain in France until the sum was paid. For the next half century, French policy would revolve around undoing these terrible losses. Referring to the lost provinces, Gambetta told his countrymen: "Never talk about them, always think about them."

France Drifts

While a new government under Adolphe Thiers saw no alternative to accepting this bitter peace, hundreds of thousands of Parisians saw the matter differently. They had suffered the most during the war and had been humiliated both by the Prussians' triumphant entry into Paris and by the transfer of the French capital to Versailles. Further, this traditional hotbed of republicanism resented the monarchist sentiment that dominated both the provinces and the newly elected National Assembly. Finally, Parisians greatly resented the new government's termination of the wartime moratorium on rents and debts and of all payments to the National Guardsmen, who had defended Paris, and who, because of France's financial collapse, were now out of work and without subsistence. Again, Paris became a powder keg.

On March 18, 1871, the government sent cavalry troops commanded by two French generals to remove the guns from the promontory of Montmartre that overlooks the city. An angry mob attacked the cavalry and lynched the generals. Violence spread throughout the city, prompting the government's troops to withdraw hastily. Recalling the radical days of 1793, a new Commune of Paris, composed of radical republicans, socialists and National Guardsmen was formed. However, this strange mixture of idealists and rowdies spent more time debating socialist and political experiments than in preparing for their own defense. The government immediately besieged the city and, reinforced by French prisoners of war whom the Germans had released for just that purpose, prepared to storm the city.

The troops struck on May 21, and for one bloody week the street battle raged. In the closing days of the struggle, the Communards, as the dissidents were called, shot their hostages, including the Archbishop of Paris, and set fire to many public buildings, including the Tuileries palace and the Palais Royal. Finally the remaining Communards were trapped in Père–Lachaise Cemetery, where they were executed against the Mur des Fédéré (now highly revered shrines for socialists and communists all over the world).

The government's vengeance was severe: any person caught wearing a National Guard uniform or army boots

France

was shot immediately without trial. In all, about 20,000 Communards were killed in battle or executed without trial. Thousands more were imprisoned or driven into exile. Both sides, fired by hatred, had fought literally like animals. Reflecting on the events, the French novelist Flaubert wrote: "What an immoral beast the mob is, and how discouraging it is to be a human being." Karl Marx, in his widely read pamphlet *The Civil War in France*, made a legend of the Commune, and these violent events widened the gap created in 1848 between the workers and the political left, on the one hand, and the rest of France on the other. A constant reminder of this gulf is the beautiful white Sacre Coeur (Sacred Heart) church that overlooks Paris from the top of Montmartre. Built to commemorate the suppression of the Commune, it remains for the French left a prominent and hated symbol of a reactionary France.

For a while a monarchist majority in the National Assembly pressed for the restoration of the monarchy, and Bourbon, Orléanist and Bonapartist pretenders waited for the call. There were very good prospects for the aging Bourbon pretender, the Count de Chambord, who would rule as Henry V. But the Count quickly showed how little he had learned about his own country. He insisted that the king have absolute authority, unrestrained by any constitution. He also insisted that the old *fleur-de-lis* flag of the old monarchy replace the revolutionary tricolor. Even the most die-hard royalists could see the folly of such demands.

Meanwhile the French people, who in the past 100 years had experienced about every conceivable regime and who were growing tired of provisional governments, pressed for a decision. In 1875 important constitutional laws were adopted calling for the establishment of a two-house parliament and a weak president. The wheel that always alternates in France between a strong parliament and a strong executive had again come full circle. This Third Republic lasted until 1940, longer than any French scheme of government since the Revolution.

The capital was moved back to Paris from Versailles in 1880; July 14 was established as the national holiday and *La Marseillaise* was made the national anthem. Paris began to bustle with artistic creativity. By the time the Eiffel Tower was unveiled at the World Exposition in 1889, it had assumed the place, in many foreigners' minds, as the intellectual and artistic capital of the world, of which one often said: every person in the world has two capitals—his own and Paris. One can scarcely imagine contemporary culture without the creative contributions of

Renoir's *The Luncheon of the Boating Party* (1881)

artists, writers and scholars in Third Republic France: impressionism in music and art (e.g. Renoir, Monet, Degas, Debussy) and the reaction to it (e.g. Bracque, Picasso, cubism or fauvism); the positivism of Auguste Comte, the *"élan vital"* of Henri Bergson, and the discoveries of Louis Pasteur in medicine or Pierre and Marie Curie in physics.

Stung by its territorial losses in 1870, France, with Bismarck's encouragement, sought to reestablish a world empire such as the one it had lost a century earlier. It created French Equatorial Africa and protectorates in Tunisia and Indochina (presently Vietnam, Cambodia and Laos). Thus, by 1914 the tricolor flew in most of North, West and Equatorial Africa, in Madagascar, in several West Indian and South Pacific islands and in small holdings elsewhere. Such a policy was not universally popular in France, but a colonial empire offered France the opportunity to resume expansion of its culture overseas. It also offered some economic benefits to France, which was experiencing a slower rate of population growth and economic progress than Germany and Britain.

Many French industries remained small, family-owned and cautious, a situation which persisted in France until after World War II. At the same time, there was considerable worker unrest and violent strikes during the Third Republic. Legalized trade unions tended to remain dedicated to direct, sometimes violent action, rather than to pursue gains through the parliamentary political process. Such "syndicalist" tendencies (to which French

trade unions are still attracted) reveal that the deep wounds of the Paris Commune never healed entirely.

At the beginning of the Third Republic, more than half of the population lived in rural areas, and this number had declined to only about one-third by 1940. While the visitor to France has always been struck by the amount of acreage that is cultivated, many farms remained small and relatively inefficient. In the 1870s plant lice threatened the wine industry with extinction. Only by importing American plant grafts was this precious jewel saved. Thus, in a certain sense, French wine is actually American wine!

Third Republic Politics

The Third Republic was seriously rocked by religious disputes, parliamentary instability, scandals, a world war and economic depression. The new republic moved in traditional French revolutionary fashion to reduce the influence of the Catholic Church. Its anti-clerical policies included the permission to divorce and the loosening of the Church's grip on the school system. The result was a total separation of church and state in most of France by 1905.

The absence of party discipline and the distrust of any president who tried to play a guiding role in French politics (Third Republic presidents were said to be merely "old men who wore evening clothes in the afternoon!") produced a constant rotation of weak parliamentary coalitions. The resulting "parliamentary game" inclined French citizens to view politics with increasing cynicism and decreasing trust. Representatives rarely hesitated to vote themselves frequent and large salary increases. At the occasion of one such increase in 1905, a socialist member of parliament was heard to say "my indignation is matched only by my satisfaction."

Scandals further shook the confidence in France's political institutions. In the 1880s a dashing general named Boulanger was reputed to have wanted to put an end to the republic after gaining power legally. When he was summoned to the Senate in 1889 to answer to charges of conspiracy against the state, he lost his nerve and fled to Belgium, where he committed suicide two years later. Scarcely a year after his death, another scandal came to light, Since the 1870s a private French company had been attempting to build a canal across the Isthmus of Panama. Unwise engineering and yellow fever bankrupted the company in 1889, but its directors bribed politicians and press in order to secure public subsidies for the project. The revelation of such bribery in 1892 helped convince many Frenchmen that all politicians were corrupt, an attitude which has by no means disappeared from France today. The French still tend to be far less shocked by political scandals than is the case in the United States.

A further scandal convinced many Frenchmen that it was not only politicians who could not be trusted, but military leaders as well. In 1894 Captain Alfred Dreyfus, the first Jewish officer to be assigned to the French general staff, was convicted of selling military secrets to the Germans and was sent to the infamous Devil's Island off the northern coast of South America. Later, probing journalists, aided by a skeptical army officer, discovered that the documents presented by the military had been forged and that Dreyfus had been framed. The army, seeing its honor at stake, refused to reopen the case, and many French conservatives and clergymen openly supported the army. Dreyfus was later pardoned, promoted to lieutenant–colonel, and awarded the Legion of Honor. But for more than a generation this sordid affair, with its implications for anti–Semitism, the army, the Church and democracy in France, weakened the republic. Not until 101 years later, in 1995, did the French military formally and publicly acknowledge that the army had been wrong. On January 13, 1998, the 100th anniversary of Emile Zola's sensational headline article, "J'accuse" (I Accuse) in L'Aurore newspaper, Prime Minister Lionel Jospin laid a wreath on Zola's tomb in the Pantheon and called the Dreyfus affair "one of the founding events in the history of our country."

The Café concert by Edward Manet

Until the 1890s Germany's Chancellor, Bismarck managed to keep France diplomatically isolated in Europe. However, after the Chancellor's fall from power in 1890, France was able to improve its relations with Italy and in 1894 to forge a military alliance with Russia. France's intense colonial activity led it into frequent conflicts with the greatest colonial power of the time, Britain. Nevertheless, after the turn of the century France gradually settled its differences with England, and military and political cooperation between the two countries became much closer. Thus emerged the outlines of the Triple Entente alliance against Germany and Austria–Hungary before and during the First World War. Eventually, crises in Morocco and then in the Balkans brought about the devastating explosion which Bismarck had predicted shortly before his death in 1897: "One day the great European war will come out of some damned foolish thing in the Balkans." It did (see Austria, history).

World War I

The outbreak of World War I in August 1914 unleashed an outburst of patriotic sentiment in all major countries of Europe. Even workers rallied to the French cause, and trainloads of enthusiastic troops left their hometowns in railroad cars with words "à Berlin" written on the sides. Although not openly avowed, many French undoubtedly viewed the affair as an opportunity for revenge of the dismal defeat of 1870 and recovery of the "lost provinces." Never since that time did France experience such unity of purpose.

The British and French armies were able to stop the German advance within heavy artillery range of Paris. Thereafter, the ar-

mies faced each other during four weary and bloody years of trench warfare. This unimaginative method of fighting made it exceptionally difficult for either side to win. The enthusiasm faded quickly as 300,000 French soldiers lost their lives in the first five months. Colonel de Grandmaison's axiom that "there is no such thing as an excessive offensive" produced untold carnage on battlefields such as Verdun, where a half million soldiers were slaughtered in the spring of 1916. A young second lieutenant named Charles de Gaulle, who was wounded and sent to a German prisoner–of–war camp for two years, noted: "It appeared in the wink of an eye that all the virtue in the world could not prevail against superior firepower."

The defeatism and demoralization which such mindless frontal assaults produced led to large–scale mutinies on the French front from April to October 1917. Miraculously, the Germans never heard about them at the time. They also produced a frame of mind which the novelist Jules Romains described in his book, Verdun, which first appeared at an unfortunate time—1938: "Men in the mass are seen to be like a school of fish or cloud of locusts swarming to destruction. The individual man is less than nothing—certainly not worth worrying about . . . My most haunting horror is not that I see men now willing to suffer and act as they do, but that having so seen them, I shall never again be able to believe in their good intentions."

Ultimately a million fresh American troops in France tipped the balance, and on November 11, 1918, the exhausted and starving Germans saw no alternative to capitulation. France had technically been victorious, but it was left breathless and demoralized; 1.3 million Frenchmen had been killed and more than a million crippled. Northeastern France, the country's most prosperous industrial and agricultural sector, was largely devastated. France's enormous human and material losses inclined French leaders to demand a heavy price from Germany in the Treaty of Versailles.

Germany and its allies were branded as solely responsible for the war, and Germany was therefore required to pay exorbitant reparations. France regained Alsace and Lorraine, established temporary control over the German Saar, stationed its troops in Germany west of the Rhine and obtained mandates in the former German colonies of Togo and Cameroons, and in Syria and Lebanon as well. While France's demands were somewhat understandable, they played into the hands of a future German rabble–rouser named Adolf Hitler, who promised to undo the

France

hated treaty. The settlement is a glaring example of the fact that policies that may be righteous are not always wise.

The Post–World War I Era

The French expected to rebuild their land with the reparations from Germany, but when it became apparent that an impoverished Germany could never pay the sums demanded, the French set about to do the work themselves. Displaying remarkable resilience, the French had, by the mid–1920s, cleared away the rubble, rebuilt homes, factories and railroads, and achieved a measure of prosperity which exceeded even that of Britain. Unfortunately, many of the economic gains were wiped away by the great depression that spread to France by 1932. The last European country to be affected by "Black Friday" on Wall Street, France was so jolted that when democracies all over Europe toppled, France tottered also.

The Nazi seizure of power in Germany in 1933 further destabilized France by pumping new life into right–wing and, in some cases, openly fascist groups in France. The best–known was the *Action Française*, which had emerged from the Dreyfus controversy, and whose leader, Charles Maurras, powerfully and eloquently railed against Jews, Protestants, foreigners and the French Republic generally. Offshoots and competitors of *Action Française* such as the *Camelots du Roi* or the *Francistes*, bullied people in the streets, dressed like Hitler's storm troopers, and ceaselessly pointed to the difference between the vigor and effectiveness of the dictatorships in Italy and Germany and the tired, ineffective parliamentary system in France. Royalist and fascist groups, supported by thousands of students and some communists gathered on February 4, 1934, at the Place de la Concorde and stormed the National Assembly, located just across the Pont de la Concorde. The police stopped the assault, but 21 persons lay dead and more than 1,600 were injured in this violent action against the feeble republic.

Storm Clouds and Paralysis

As storm clouds gathered over Europe, France had only short–lived, stop–gap governments that could not begin to cope with the mounting crises. In desperate economic straits, no French government could propose military increases to counter the dictators. Also, the memories of the First World War were so horrifying in the minds of many Frenchmen that they could not tolerate the thought of participating in another war, for whatever cause. *Surtout pas la guerre* ("Above all, no war!") was the slogan of *Action Française*. It was uttered with all the energy of "Hell no, I won't go!" in the America of the 1960s and 1970s.

Pacifism was widespread and was manifest in the writings of many of France's literary figures. In a letter to a friend, novelist Roger Martin du Gard wrote: "I am hard as steel for neutrality. My principle: anything, rather than war! Anything, anything! Even fascism in Spain ... even fascism in France! . . . Anything: Hitler rather than war!" The highly respected writer, Jean Giono, dared to write: "I prefer to be a live German than a dead Frenchman!" Even the Minister of Public Works, Anatole de Monzie said publicly, "I prefer to receive a kick in the behind than a bullet in the head." French patriotism after World War I had become tinged with the fear that the costs of war were simply too great.

A state of mind jelled which prepared France for defeat in the next war. As noble as it may seem sometimes, pacifism usually plays into the hands of the world's bullies, as France was soon to see.

With the fascist leagues active in the streets of France, the parties of the left began to speak of unified action for the first time. In 1935 the Socialists and Radicals formed a Popular Front that won a great victory in 1936 parliamentary elections. Under Léon Blum, the first Jew and first Socialist to serve as Prime Minister of France, the Popular Front, with the parliamentary support of the communists, proposed a forty–hour work week, paid vacations, collective bargaining and the partial nationalization of the Bank of France. Blum was unable, however, to find a solution to the problem of lagging production, and in 1938 the government fell.

France was the helpless observer of an aggressive German government which in the mid and late 1930s reoccupied the Rhineland, sent troops and squadrons to Spain to fight for Franco in its Civil War, absorbed Austria and occupied part of Czechoslovakia. After World War I, France had not only constructed the Maginot line, it sought to protect itself by surrounding Germany with enemy powers. It forged military alliances with Belgium, Poland, Czechoslovakia, Romania and Yugoslavia. Hitler merely pointed to this encirclement to justify his own aggressive policies.

In 1930, before Hitler came to power, just 12 years after the end of World War I, the French Parliament voted funds to build an allegedly impregnable defensive line against invasion from Germany. The Maginot Line consisted of an elaborate system of underground bunkers, fortifications and anti–tank devices and extended all the way along France's border with Germany. It was based on a conclusion drawn from the previous war that all advantages lie with the defense. Colonel Charles de Gaulle disagreed. He warned at the time in his controversial book, *The Army of the Future*, that modern warfare requires great mobility with tanks and aircraft. Regrettably the book was read only by the German commanders, who reportedly carried it with them when they invaded France in 1940. Unfortunately the designers of the line forgot one of the basic principles of fortress–building: protect all sides.

This shield–mentality naturally meshed with the pacifist feelings in the French population and political circles. Léon Blum, who apparently believed in the power of a strong world conscience that hated war, opposed the extension of military service from one to two years and continued to speak of the need for France to take unilateral steps toward disarmament, as if such a French policy could incline Hitler to be more peaceful. As his government fell, France was literally frozen with fear. Political parties and alliances were such that the country was ungovernable. Complicating the scene was journalism at its lowest. Most political parties and groups printed their own newspapers that propagated untruths daily about opposing parties, groups and people. There were 39 regularly published in Paris alone.

World War II

Thus, when Germany invaded Poland on September 1, 1939, and when France reluctantly and finally felt compelled to declare war three days later, France entered a disastrous conflict militarily and emotionally unprepared and half–consciously aspiring more to an armistice than to a victory. Germany and the Soviet Union quickly partitioned Poland, but Hitler delayed military action against France for three–quarters of a year. In France, one spoke of a "phony war" or a *Sitzkrieg*, and precious little was done to prepare for a future onslaught. The German tank commander, Guderian, later wrote, "the relatively passive attitude of the French during the winter of 1939–40 incited us to conclude that the adversary had little inclination for war."

On May 10, 1940, Hitler unleashed his armies against France. Invading the Netherlands and Belgium (thereby avoiding the face of the Maginot Line which was unprotected from the rear) German forces used lightning warfare (*Blitzkrieg*) tactics against a French army that was poorly and lethargically led and in some respects technologically outdated. French leaders refused to withdraw troops from the Maginot Line to confront actual German advances to the north, and their ad-

France

German troops enter Paris, 1940

ministrative confusion prevented badly needed French aircraft and artillery from being transferred to the actual front. This produced such disastrous reversals that the French government was forced to abandon Paris within one month. British Prime Minister Winston S. Churchill testified that French soldiers fought valiantly, but that their political and military leaders were so quickly seized by defeatism that the French cabinet could not muster the tenacity or eagerness to persist after the shock of initial defeats.

Britain pleaded urgently that France both honor its earlier agreement not to seek a separate peace and even consider a political union of the two countries. The latter proposal was understandably unwelcome to a country that had spent centuries ridding itself of English domination and influence. A demoralized French cabinet, under the influence of the First World War hero, aging Marshal Pétain, chose instead to surrender on June 22, 1940, barely 40 days after the German attack. The degree of French resistance to the onslaught can be seen today in French cities and towns that have memorials to soldiers who died in the two World Wars. The names of World War I victims outnumber those of the subsequent conflict by uncounted numbers.

The surrender terms were very harsh. The northern half of France, including Paris, and the whole of the Atlantic coast to the Spanish border, were to be occupied by German troops at French expense. The rest of France was to be ruled by a French government friendly to Germany. This government was to supply its conquerors with food and raw materials needed for the German war effort. The French army was to be disbanded and its navy placed in ports under the control of the Germans and the Italians.

The fate of the French navy especially distressed the British. They were unaware that the French naval commander–in–chief, Admiral Darlan, had secretly ordered his fleet commanders to scuttle his ships if the Germans or Italians tried to seize them by force. When the British tried to take control of the French Atlantic squadron in Mers–el–Kebir in Algeria, the French commander resisted. The British destroyed the squadron, an action that caused a wave of anti–British feeling in France. This sentiment played into the hands of the cunning Premier Pierre Laval and the 80–year–old Pétain, who had long opposed the Third Republic as a decadent, inefficient regime.

They quickly abolished the Third Republic and established a repressive Vichy Republic (named after the spa in France where the new government established its seat of power). Without prompting by the Germans, they denied Jews and Freemasons the protection of the law. In all, 76,000 of the 330,000 Jews in France at the beginning of the war were, with the help of the French police, deported during Vichy, and only 2,500 returned. Foreigners who had come to France to escape Hitler's persecution were penned up in French concentration camps and, unless they were able to escape, were later returned to Germany where an uncertain, usually fatal, future awaited them. In fact, most Jews deported to Germany had been new arrivals in France who had fled Nazi persecution elsewhere.

Many Frenchmen were relieved to have achieved a peace at any price; nevertheless, they felt a numbing feeling of humiliation and an awareness that this was a tragic debacle which had befallen the French nation. What followed was as much a French civil war as a war against the Germans. For the next four years there were two Frances, one fighting against the Germans and one trying to ignore the conflict and to minimize damage to the French population. The individual Frenchman could find sound patriotic reasons for supporting each, and it was up to the individual to decide which France was his. France still has not fully recovered psychologically from the terrible tension of the Vichy years. A poll in 1992 showed that 82% of Frenchmen considered the Vichy government to be guilty of "crimes against humanity," and 90% thought that their country should admit it.

In 1994 the trial of Paul Touvier captivated France. Convicted of murdering Jewish hostages in 1944, he became the first Frenchman charged and convicted of a crime against humanity. This was also the first time a French court blamed Vichy for its role in the Nazis' Final Solution. In 1995 Jacques Chirac became the first president to accept the responsibility of the French state for the arrest and deportation of Jews during Vichy. In 1997 the Bishop of St. Denis admitted for the first time the French Catholic Church's guilt in "acquiescing by its silence" in the persecution of the Jews: "We beg God's pardon and we ask the Jewish people to hear our words of repentance."

Maurice Papon was a police supervisor in Bordeaux from 1942–4, who, according to documents first revealed by the satirical *Le Canard Enchaîné*, was instrumental in the arrest and deportation of 1,690 Jews; very few returned. Still defiantly maintaining that he had been a loyal member of the resistance, he became de Gaulle's post–war police chief in Paris, member of the National Assembly, Gaullist party treasurer, and budget minister under President Giscard d'Estaing. He

Gen. Charles de Gaulle, London

91

France

was found guilty in 1998 and sentenced to ten years in prison, becoming the highest-ranking Frenchman ever convicted of complicity in crimes against humanity. His trial had been the longest and most expensive in modern French history, and it forced the country to confront a part of its past that many still try to forget. Vowing that he would "go into exile" rather than spend his last years behind bars, Papon fled to Switzerland. He was quickly apprehended. In 2000 President Chirac rejected his plea for release. Nevertheless, in September 2002, less than three years into his sentence, Papon was discharged under a law allowing early release for the ill and aging. He sparked anger when he walked unassisted from jail after the doctors had determined he was lacking in mobility. Experts must periodically reexamine him to verify that he still qualifies for freedom.

France has a respectable record in returning assets seized from Jews. A study in 2000 found that about the equivalent of $1.3 billion had been taken: 80,000 frozen bank accounts, 6,000 safe-deposit boxes, 38,000 confiscated apartments, 50,000 "aryanization" cases to seize businesses and homes, 100,000 works of art. About 90% of these were compensated in some form within a decade of war's end. Some were never reclaimed. France still

has about $3 billion in unclaimed funds, earmarked for a "National Foundation for Memory" to keep alive the awareness of the Holocaust. In 2003 the government-appointed Commission for the Compensation of Victims of Spoliation recommended that the government and French banks pay Jews an additional $84 million.

While working together with the Germans, the Vichy government introduced what it called a "National Revolution." Although this was, in some cases, fascist in inspiration, it sought among other things to strengthen the role of France's regions, to introduce economic planning at the highest political level, to concentrate small agricultural holdings into larger, more efficient farms and to stimulate population growth through family allowances for children. Postwar France actually built on some of these Vichy innovations.

The Vichy government's powers were drastically reduced at the end of 1942 when the Germans, in response to Anglo–American military landings in North Africa, occupied all of France. Vichy's prestige declined rapidly and when Frenchmen were sent to Germany involuntarily in order to work in German war industries, the ranks of the resistance began to grow.

French resistance leader Jean Moulin

By 1943 command over the entire French resistance movement had been gathered into the hands of General de Gaulle, who had fled to Britain in 1940 and who had organized there the Free French Movement. He reminded his countrymen by radio, "France has lost a battle,

Allied invasion of Normandy, June 6, 1944

but not the war." His claims to be the legal French government in exile and the sole spokesman for France greatly irritated Churchill and Roosevelt, who, for a time, found it politically wise to maintain diplomatic recognition of the Vichy government. Further, when Admiral Darlan was assassinated three weeks after he scuttled the French navy, Britain and the United States recognized another French General as "chief of state" in French North Africa. Roosevelt greeted him warmly in Washington, which infuriated de Gaulle. His wartime experiences with the British and Americans did not leave him with a strong admiration for the two countries, and his resentment was to disturb these two nations' relations with France even after 1958 when he became France's leader.

The French resistance fighters helped protect unfortunate Allied pilots and often provided useful military intelligence and other support to the Allies. There is no doubt that resistance against the Germans was very dangerous business. De Gaulle later estimated that 20,000 French resistance fighters had been executed and more than 50,000 deported from France before the Allied landings in Normandy. But German documents reveal that this movement had not constituted an effective military threat to the Germans, as had the resistance movements in the Soviet Union and Yugoslavia. Still, when the Allies landed on the Normandy beaches (which are sobering and moving sites for visiting and reflecting today), the French resistance played an important part in destroying bridges, assembling paratroops for action and providing Allied units with useful information. Also, French military units that had been organized in London under de Gaulle's overall command fought side by side with the Americans, British and Canadians.

Local resistance forces and delegates from de Gaulle's headquarters in London assumed political control in liberated France, arresting or executing Vichy officials. On August 19, 1944, resistance fighters rose up in Paris against the German occupiers. Six days later, Free French units commanded by General Philippe Leclerc took control of the city, which a disobedient German commander had saved from senseless destruction by refusing to burn and destroy as ordered by Hitler. De Gaulle arrived with the French troops, and the following day he led a triumphant march down the broad Champs–Elysées.

The Vichy government fled to Germany, and for the next year and a half, de Gaulle's provisional government exercised unchallenged authority in liberated France. The resistance movement had brought together persons from all backgrounds and political convictions, and de Gaulle hoped that this predominantly young, patriotic, idealistic, but at the same time practical core of Frenchmen would provide the spark for national revival and change. He announced during the war, "while the French people are uniting for victory they are assembling for a revolution."

His movement also encompassed French communists although he was always suspicious that his desired revolution was not the same as theirs. French communists displayed undeniable courage and commitment after Germany had attacked the Soviet Union in 1941, "but never, as an army of revolution, losing sight of the objective, which was to establish their dictatorship by making use of the tragic situation of France … I was quite as decided not to let them ever gain the upper hand or by–pass me, or take the lead." He successfully blocked their efforts to gain a ministry controlling foreign affairs, defense or the police. French Socialists and other groups also learned then and later what a mixed blessing cooperation with communists can be.

The End of Conflict and the Beginning of Bickering

De Gaulle engaged in feverish diplomacy in order to reestablish France's position in world affairs: he traveled to Moscow in November 1944, helped create the United Nations, fought successfully for a permanent French seat on the Security Council and secured a French occupation zone in Germany as a victorious power. He also initiated a program of nationalizing the nation's coalmines, electrical production, natural gas, some banks and other basic industries, such as the Renault auto company. Since many French business leaders had collaborated with the enemy during the Vichy years and since a national effort to rebuild the French economy was so obviously necessary, few people opposed such a policy.

Frenchmen shared an almost universal desire for the creation of a Fourth Republic, but they split on the perennial French dispute concerning the kind of republic that was appropriate for France. De Gaulle stood aloof from these controversies, although it was widely known that he preferred a strong executive and a weak parliament. "Deliberation is the work of many men. Action, of one alone!" Sensing that the old bickering party and parliamentary activity was about to re–emerge, that his coalition was collapsing and that his views on the future republic were not gaining support, he announced in January 1946 his resignation as temporary president. He apparently expected a wave of popular support to swell in his favor, allowing him to strengthen his hand in shaping the new republic, but such a movement failed to materialize. For seven years he tried to return to power, but in 1953 he withdrew completely from direct involvement and lived for the next five years in the political desert, awaiting a crisis that would direct his countrymen's eyes again on de Gaulle, the savior.

In 1946 that kind of political regime was created which de Gaulle had most feared: a parliamentary system with a weak president—practically a restoration of the Third Republic which, in his eyes, had so thoroughly discredited itself and France in 1940. In the plebiscite of late 1946, a bare majority voted in favor of the

Gen-Leclerc and his troops preparing to capture Paris

France

new constitution, an ominous sign for the new Fourth Republic. There was no clear majority, either in the parliament or the nation, so subsequent political instability was hardly surprising. There were ten governments in the first five years, and by 1958 Frenchmen had witnessed no fewer than 25 governments. A coherent policy was very difficult to achieve, and the "parliamentary game" appeared more and more to be divorced from the pressing needs of the public.

The governments of the Fourth Republic were faced with many crises in economic, foreign and colonial policy, some of which they mastered and most of which weakened or destroyed them. Nevertheless, it is a great mistake to view France from 1946 until de Gaulle's return to power in 1958 as a hopelessly paralyzed country. France had a resilient population, a rather competent and dedicated bureaucracy and a few leaders with sound judgment.

Economic Growth and European Cooperation

France set about very quickly to repair the destruction from the long war and to reestablish economic strength. The results, with massive assistance of the United States' Marshall Plan, were impressive. Between 1949 and 1957 its GNP increased by 40%, and from 1952 forward, its growth rate was more than 10% a year, consistently among the highest in Europe. Frenchmen poured into the urban areas from the countryside, thereby dramatically changing the face of French society. Fortunately, French industry was able to absorb them. At the same time, agricultural production increased by 24% from 1949–1957. Government financial subsidies for families with children, coupled with the people's increasingly optimistic view of the future, helped bring about one of Europe's highest birth rates, a welcome development for a country which for more than a century had experienced relatively low population growth.

France's rapid economic growth was greatly aided by economic planning, which, in contrast to planning in communist countries, is entirely non–compulsory. These periodic plans set targets and suggest investments to French industry, with a view to making the economy as efficient and modern as possible. Perhaps most important, such planning has helped Frenchmen believe strongly in the possibility of progress. The Marshall Plan assistance which the United States gave to France and other Western European countries encouraged such planning and even had a further long–term benefit for Europe: a condition for aid was that European countries discuss and agree among themselves how such help should be used. These discussions opened possibilities of European cooperation that laid the foundations for the creation of NATO and the EU.

The fruits of this were not long in coming. In 1950, France's brilliant Foreign Minister, Robert Schumann, proposed an imaginative European Coal and Steel Community, which within two years provided a common market for these two critical commodities among West Germany, France, the BENELUX countries and Italy, a step unthinkable five years earlier. Seven years later, Schumann and his countryman, Jean Monnet, de Gaulle's wartime representative for economic negotiations with Washington and London, and from 1946 to 1952 chief of France's General Planning Commission, were key figures in the creation of the EU by the same six powers. The French were not inclined to transfer any French sovereignty to the EU; indeed, de Gaulle later reiterated that this was to be a "Europe of Fatherlands," i.e., of entirely sovereign nation–states. Yet

De Gaulle leaves Notre Dame Cathedral after the liberation of Paris   Courtesy: Central audiovisual Library, European Commission

they have clearly recognized that French interests are best served in a cooperative, democratic Europe and they have strongly supported such a Europe.

At one time France sought to extend European cooperation into the military sphere as well. When the Korean War began in 1950, there was fear in Europe that the Soviet Union might be considering an aggressive assault against Western Europe. When the United States suggested that West Germany be permitted to rearm, the French became uneasy. Therefore, the government proposed a European Defense Community (EDC) that would integrate German soldiers into an overall European command. There would be no German general staff. However, Britain refused to join and French public opinion also gradually turned against it. In 1954 the parliament, not wanting French troops to be under supra–national control, rejected the proposal. After the vote the Gaullist and communist deputies stood up and sang the *Marseillaise*. France, however, remained a member of NATO, which had been formed in 1949 and which West Germany also joined in 1955.

The Empire Crumbles

While France's economic recovery and contribution to a unified Europe, which included former enemy powers, were glittering successes of the French Fourth Republic, the government was brought to its knees by the painfully traumatic disintegration of the colonial empire. The two world wars had stimulated a desire in colonies all over the world for independence, but many Frenchmen believed it was impossible to restore French power, prestige and prosperity without aid from the colonies.

The first disaster occurred in Indochina, which the Japanese had occupied during the war. When the French attempted to reestablish control after liberation, a powerful native communist resistance movement called the Viet Minh and led by Ho Chi Minh opposed them. Fighting broke out in December 1946 and all French political parties, including the communists, initially supported the war effort. However, eight inglorious years of fighting without victory created powerful domestic opposition to continuation of the conflict. The United States refused in principle to help the French in a colonial war although it did provide about $1 billion in financial assistance. When in 1954 France sought a quick solution to the war by asking that the U.S. use atomic bombs against the Viet Minh, the request was turned down. After the Viet Minh captured the French stronghold of Dien Bien Phu in 1954, the French agreed to a temporary division of Vietnam and to a permanent withdrawal after free elections. For complicated reasons, such elections were never held.

Jean Monnet Courtesy: Central Audio-visual Library, European Commission

Having had no time to recover from the shock of loss of Indochina, the French had to turn their attention immediately to a rebellion in Algeria that erupted in November 1954. Algeria was a much more complicated problem. Legally it was not a colony, but an integral part of France, as Hawaii is part of the U.S. Located directly south of France, it (unlike Indochina) had an immediate strategic importance for the country. Further, there were more than a million French settlers living there, some of whose families had been in Algeria for more than three generations. Many were farmers, producing semi–tropical food-stuffs for France.

The Algerian rebellion shook France to the core. It unleashed conspiracies against the government, assassinations and ill–fated military *coups d'état*. A half-million troops were sent to Algeria to suppress it. It was a struggle that prompted the French military, which was left more or less to its own devices, to conduct unconventional warfare and atrocities against an enemy that often used terrorist methods and melted into a sympathetic population. In response, French methods were sometimes unsavory. In 2001 a former French general in the secret service, Paul Aussaresses, wrote a book, entitled *Special Services in Algeria 1955-1957*, in which he described in a matter-of-fact way how he and other French military routinely tortured and executed suspects, noting that as many as 3,000 suspects had simply "disappeared." He admitted having executed 24 suspected guerrillas himself and claimed to have only "followed orders." The book was a sensation in that he showed no remorse,

and it reflected a "cold tone, lacking any hindsight and any humanity," in the words of the judge who fined him for "complicity in justifying war crimes." France has never officially apologized for its conduct during the war, which claimed the lives of 30,000 French men and women and at least a half million Algerians.

The war brought an aging man out of retirement from the eastern village of Colombey–les–deux–églises: Charles de Gaulle. When the French military seized power in Algeria's capital city, Algiers, in May 1958, and soon thereafter on the island of Corsica, Napoleon's birthplace, many, especially French generals, believed that only de Gaulle could save Algeria or protect the country from civil war.

De Gaulle haughtily said that he would respond to the call of his fellow citizens only on his own terms: that he be granted unrestricted authority to cope with the crisis. In mid–1958, he was appointed Prime Minister, and he quickly went to Algeria and gave an enthusiastic French throng the highly ambiguous assurance "I have understood you!" He undoubtedly knew the situation was hopeless. In late 1958 an electoral college of notables elected him President of the Republic. This spelled the death knell of the Fourth Republic and the birth of the present Fifth Republic.

The de Gaulle Years in Power

Always a realist under his mantle of magnificence, de Gaulle was convinced that Algeria could no longer be held by force, but he proceeded very cautiously in seeking a settlement of the crisis. He did not want to provoke a military *coup d'état* in France itself. He shrewdly allowed all groups to think that he shared all of their own objectives. Sensing that the right time had come, he announced a referendum for early 1961 to decide whether Algeria should be granted self–determination. Fifteen million said yes; only 5 million said no. He thus had received a free hand to pursue negotiations with the Algerian National Liberation Front (FLN), and he directed France's Prime Minister, Georges Pompidou, to lead the negotiations.

This was an extremely unstable time in both France and Algeria, and de Gaulle felt compelled to assume sweeping emergency powers to master the situation. The cloud of a military takeover loomed over the country. Indeed, some French officers regarded the President's policy as "treachery" and formed the Secret Army Organization (OAS) with the aim of keeping Algeria French by any means possible, including terror, bombings and assassinations. De Gaulle himself barely escaped three assassination attempts in 1962.

A breakthrough occurred in March 1962: France granted Algeria full sover-

France

eignty in return for the Algerian promise to respect the French settlers' lives and property, as well as French oil interests in the Sahara and military interests in a port city. Ninety percent of the people approved this settlement in a referendum, and three–quarters of a million French settlers from Algeria (known in France as *pieds noirs*—"black feet" since many had been farmers) left for mainland France. The promise regarding oil interests was not fully kept by the Algerians.

De Gaulle had already offered all the other French colonies the option of becoming independent while retaining cultural ties with France. By 1960 all had accepted this option, with the exception of Guinea, which rejected all ties with the French Community that was to be established. Thus, by 1962 the French empire had practically ceased to exist. It now possesses five overseas departments (Guadeloupe and Martinique in the Caribbean, French Guiana in South America, Réunion in the Indian Ocean, and Saint–Pierre and Miquelon in the Atlantic near Newfoundland) and five overseas territories (New Caledonia, French Polynesia, Wallis and Futuna in the South Pacific, Mayotte in the Indian Ocean and a smattering of islands in the Antarctic in the southern part of the earth). The inhabitants are French citizens with a right to vote and economic subsidies that enable them to enjoy a standard of living comparable to that of metropolitan France. Far from weakening France, the shedding of the colonial burden freed its hand for a more assertive foreign policy in Europe, the Middle East, and elsewhere and it eliminated the searing domestic division that stemmed from unpopular colonial wars. In the years that followed, de Gaulle was able to show his countrymen that it was possible to have a measure of grandeur without a colonial empire.

Prosperity and Social Benefits

While de Gaulle provided France with a constitution that could maintain a greater measure of political stability, he also sought to eliminate the bases of social conflict by introducing needed social reforms. The often enigmatic, but always pragmatic General was a point of intersection between two seemingly contradictory forces. He was an agent of French modernization and also the guardian of the idea of French mission and grandeur. His task was to change France without discarding her glorious tradition. Among his followers were traditionalists, technocrats, social reformers, French nationalists, dreamers and realists.

He continued work begun before 1958 to expand education opportunities, thus facilitating greater mobility, especially for workers and other formerly underprivi-

leged groups. He stabilized France's currency and helped bring about a rise in real wages. He expanded the social security net that protects Frenchmen against ill health, unemployment and old age. He also proposed that large firms distribute a portion of their shares to employees and include workers in the firms' decision–making practices, which some companies such as Renault actually adopted.

In general, he furthered efforts to provide his countrymen with prosperity and higher common consumption standards shared by all. He could write with pride, "once upon a time there was an old country hemmed in by habits and circumspection . . . Now this country, France, is back on her feet again."

Foreign Affairs—Estrangement from U.S. Hegemony

With social peace and economic prosperity at home, de Gaulle could turn full attention to that which was undoubtedly his major interest: foreign affairs. He had been greatly displeased with France's position in the world when he came to power. Colonial wars had sapped almost all of France's attention and military strength. What was worse, the fate of Europe had been determined by the Soviet Union, the U.S. and Britain, and after the advent of the Cold War in 1946–7, French security had fallen almost exclusively into the hands of NATO, with an American general in command. That is, France's security was basically in the hands of the U.S., a friendly, but foreign country, which in his words, "brings to great affairs elementary feelings and a complicated policy."

De Gaulle and all his successors knew that the Soviet Union posed a threat to Western Europe, which ultimately needed American protection. He also knew that the United States' tolerance level toward its European allies was high. He therefore decided that France needed and could achieve foreign policy independence. He unquestionably also had bitter memories of what he considered a personal snub by Churchill and Roosevelt during the struggles of World War II.

His first step was to develop French atomic weapons. When he was informed in 1960 of the successful French explosion in the Sahara, he exclaimed: "Hurray for France!" This nuclear capability, known in France as the force de frappe has come to be supported by most of the French political parties, including the Communist Party.

Seeking to strengthen the center of Western Europe, he signed a treaty with West Germany in 1963. It basically called for regular consultation and semi–annual state visits between the leaders of these two European powerhouses. A disappointed de Gaulle later referred to this treaty as a "faded rose" because it had failed to persuade the West Germans to loosen their own ties with the U.S., as he had hoped. Nevertheless, it was an extremely important and imaginative policy observed by all his successors. For example, the first meeting President Mitterrand had with a foreign political leader after his election was with the West German Chancellor. Further, Helmut Kohl's first foreign visit after becoming German Chancellor in 1982 was to Paris. De Gaulle had provided an enormous boost for a develop-

M. RENÉ COTY S'ADRESSE AU PARLEMENT

LE FIGARO

Bas Néamat-7 *sans couture* — EDITION DE 5 HEURES

Le Gaulois — 20 francs

132ᵉ ANNÉE Nº 4270 depuis la Libération

« Sans la liberté de blâmer, il n'est pas d'éloge flatteur. »
BEAUMARCHAIS

VENDREDI **30** MAI 1958

150ᵉ JOUR DE L'ANNÉE

DIRECTEUR : Pierre BRISSON

APRÈS UNE HEURE D'ENTRETIEN AVEC M. COTY

LE GÉNÉRAL DE GAULLE ACCEPTE

TOURBILLONS

Dans un message au Parlement le Président de la République avait déclaré :

« Je demande au général de Gaulle de bien vouloir venir conférer avec le chef de l'État, et examiner avec lui ce qui, dans le cadre de la légalité républicaine, est nécessaire à un gouvernement de Salut National »

Aujourd'hui, M. René Coty consultera lui–même les chefs de groupe

Le général est reparti pour Colombey

TUNIS : J.-F. CHAUVEL

Tension persistante en Tunisie

LE PANTHÉON DE L'EUROPE

Remise des prix aux gagnants de notre référendum–concours dans les salons du « FIGARO »

96

ment which few Europeans would have considered possible in 1945: for the first time in European history, the idea of a war between France and Germany had become unthinkable.

In 1967 he announced an "opening to the East" which amounted to direct French contact with the Soviet Union and actual participation in the era of détente. In 1967 when war broke out between Israel and its Arab neighbors, de Gaulle, unfettered by a colonial policy in North Africa, chose to adopt an openly pro–Arab position. Although many Frenchmen were displeased by his anti–Israel (and occasionally unconcealed anti–Jewish) remarks, this policy was not reversed by his next two successors, who were only too well aware of France's dependence upon Arab oil. Mitterrand promised a more even–handed policy toward Israel and the Arabs.

The U.S. reluctantly honored de Gaulle's demand that American troops (whom he called "good–natured but bad mannered") be withdrawn from French soil, a move that greatly increased NATO's logistical problems. This was a logical step to follow his announcement a year earlier that France would withdraw from NATO's integrated command (although not from NATO itself). He did not oppose the presence of American troops elsewhere in Europe because he did not want to remove France from the NATO shield. It was always assumed that France would support NATO in the event of a Warsaw Pact attack against Western Europe. This assumption was underscored by the fact that France continued to maintain 70,000 troops in West Germany and participates in many joint military exercises. De Gaulle was convinced that in case of a ground war in Europe, Frenchmen would be more willing to make sacrifices to defend Europe because they would see this as primarily a French defense effort, not an American one. Thus, in his opinion, the Western alliance would be strengthened, not weakened.

American leaders in 1967, bogged down in a hopeless Vietnam War, had little understanding for such logic. Many Americans remembered that there are possibly more American soldiers buried in France as a result of World War II than there are French who fell during that conflict. However, after 1968, the White House had far more admiration for de Gaulle's character and policy. Kissinger noted in his memoirs that de Gaulle's policies "so contrary to American postwar preconceptions, were those of an ancient country grown skeptical through many enthusiasms shattered and conscious that to be meaningful to others, France had first of all to mean something to herself."

The changes were by no means universally supported in France at the time, but by the early 1970s they had been embraced by all political parties, including the communists. The basic Gaullist goal to create an independent Europe under French leadership, and thereby to diminish U.S. influence in Europe, has not been accomplished. Nevertheless, his design to create an independent French foreign policy has been followed by his presidential successors, despite some changes in emphasis and style. He gave France a role of which it could be proud, and he ultimately won the world's respect for his country. Kissinger recalled that the General "exuded authority " and told of de Gaulle's attendance at a reception given by former President Nixon on the occasion of General Eisenhower's funeral in Washington: "His presence ... was so overwhelming that he was the center of attention wherever he stood. Other heads of government and many senators who usually proclaimed their antipathy to authoritarian generals crowded around him and treated him like some strange species. One had the sense that if he moved to a window, the center of gravity might shift and the whole room might tilt everyone into the garden."

The "Events of May" and de Gaulle's Exit

Under de Gaulle, France had not become a land of complete satisfaction and harmony. Many Frenchmen grew weary of his paternalism. His preoccupation with foreign affairs gradually slowed down the reformist impulse. Some notice that while most Frenchmen shared in the increasing prosperity, income differences had actually widened during the Fifth Republic. Further, despite the educational reforms, only 1% of the children from the working class families entered the universities. Class stratification was not breaking down as much as some would have liked. At the same time, some Frenchmen, especially the young and the educated, were becoming afraid that the new consumption–oriented society was not good for France; it became apparent that France's traditional schizophrenia about change and modernism had not been entirely erased.

Before departing for a state visit to Romania in May 1968, de Gaulle announced that France was an "island of calm" in a very troubled world. Scarcely had he arrived in Budapest when a furious storm erupted in France that brought the Fifth Republic to the brink of extinction.

"... the whole room might tilt everyone into the garden."

France

Student unrest at the new University of Nanterre, a slogan–besmeared concrete complex located at the edge of Paris, spilled over to the Sorbonne and to other universities in the country. Many small groups of anarchists, Trotskyite and Maoist students believed that the university was the ideal place to launch a revolution against the capitalist society. Trying to reestablish order, the police violated an old taboo by entering the university grounds. This tradition stemmed from the time when the universities actually exercised the privilege of ruling themselves, a privilege long since revoked by a highly centralized French regime.

With vivid pictures of the Paris Commune in their heads, students erected barricades in Paris, and night after night they battled police with bricks from the cobblestone streets for control of the Latin Quarter. (For this reason, Parisian authorities later paved over all of the city's cobblestone streets, thereby eliminating this arsenal of projectiles!) Miraculously, the chaos claimed only two dead.

De Gaulle's number-two man, Prime Minister Georges Pompidou, was very conciliatory toward the students, but before he could restore order, French workers were on strike and the French economy practically came to a standstill. The Paris Stock Exchange was burned and the threat of civil war was in the air.

De Gaulle developed a bold plan of action. He quietly flew by helicopter to Baden Baden, the headquarters of the French Forces in Germany, in order to assure himself that the French military no longer bore grudges against him and would help him in the crisis. Returning to Paris, he announced new parliamentary elections in a radio speech that reversed the entire situation.

The campaign that followed was one of the shortest (19 days) and crudest in France since 1945. De Gaulle presented the basic issue as a choice between himself or anarchy. He successfully raised the specter of a communist danger to France. He also freed the remaining OAS prisoners in order to placate the army and right–wing elements. Opposition collapsed when the communists decided that it was not yet time for a revolution in France and advocated a return to order. The elections held in June 1968 were a virtual landslide for the Gaullists. The left lost half its seats and found itself in utter shambles.

The "events of May" had so shaken de Gaulle's grip on power he decided that he needed to restore his authority. He announced a referendum for April 1969, and, as usual, warned that if his recommendations were not accepted, he would resign. He combined a rather unpopular reform (a change in the election of senators), with a more popular measure designed to strengthen the French regions. It was clear, however, that the chief issue was de Gaulle's popularity and his continued presidency, and on election day 53% voted against him. The General was thus handed the first referendum defeat in French history—a stinging rebuke.

Never tempted by dictatorship over his country, he resigned immediately and returned for the last time to his estate in Colombey–les–deux–églises in eastern France. Many Frenchmen asked whether this would be the end of the Fifth Republic, but they soon saw that he had not left a political void. He had left a sturdy constitution, in many ways well tailored to French needs, and had left a successor who easily won the presidential elections and whose greatest contribution to France was that he showed how the Fifth Republic could survive its creator.

Georges Pompidou and Valery Giscard d'Estaing

The new president, Georges Pompidou, had been educated at one of France's elite *Grandes Ecoles* and had quietly taught French literature in a Paris *lycée* during World War II. He was characteristic of many successful French political leaders, including Mitterrand: highly literate and intelligent, with a humanistic education and a sharp, practical sense for the realities of modern and political economic life.

In foreign policy, Pompidou was only slightly less Gaullist than de Gaulle himself, although he was always more modest and less abrasive than the General had been. He did break with his predecessor's policy by allowing Britain to enter the EU. He stressed continued industrial growth and the protection of French economic interests in the world. He also sought to modernize Paris by constructing urban freeways and skyscrapers in the city. However, Frenchmen, who are always sensitive to any alterations of their capital, widely condemned this "Manhattanization" of Paris, and his successor therefore abandoned this face–lifting operation.

Pompidou died in 1974 and was succeeded by Valery Giscard d'Estaing, who won a razor–thin victory over Socialist leader François Mitterrand. A product of the super–elite *Ecole Nationale d'Administration* (ENA) and a former finance minister, Giscard, who possessed distinguished aristocratic looks and a logical and photographic mind, had emerged as leader of a cluster of parties in the center and moderate right of the French political spectrum which came to be known as the Union for French Democracy (UDF).

Giscard entered the presidency determined to establish a more relaxed style in the Elysées Palace. Calling himself a "conservative who loves change," he wore a business suit instead of formal wear to his inauguration and after the ceremony walked instead of motored down the Champs–Elysées. He allowed himself to be photographed in a V–necked sweater and took a ride on the Paris Metro. For a while, he even ate monthly dinners in the homes of ordinary Frenchmen, and once he invited a group of Parisian garbage men to breakfast in the presidential palace. But he, like U.S. President Jimmy Carter, discovered that his people did not necessarily respect folksiness in their highest leaders. Soon he withdrew to the dignity of his office and eventually assumed such an aloof and aristocratic air that his political opponents were always able to score points with voters by attacking his "monarchical" style.

Giscard did introduce some social changes. During his term the minimum voting age was lowered from 21 to 18, divorce laws were liberalized, abortion was legalized, a minimum wage was made available to agricultural workers, and most of the emigrants housed in embarrassing shanty towns, known as Bidonvilles," on the periphery of France's metropolitan areas, were resettled in newly–built public housing.

In foreign affairs he observed the basic Gaullist principles of French independence and active presence on the international scene. He modernized France's *force de frappe*, sent warships to the Persian Gulf to underscore French interests in the area and took an active hand in Zaïre (Congo) and the former French West Africa. About 6,000 French troops, including Foreign Legionnaires, are stationed in Africa, where about 300,000 mainland French still live. The largest units are in Djibouti, Senegal, Ivory Coast and Gabon.

He sent French troops in 1977–8 to Shaba (formerly Katanga) Province in Zaïre to halt an invasion of Angolan and rebel forces. While France continued to sell arms to Libya, Giscard approved French military operations against Libyan moves in Mauritania (1977 and 1979) and Tunisia (1980). He joined anti–Libyan efforts in Chad. He also approved the use of French soldiers in 1979 to help depose the butcherous leader of the Central African Republic, Jean Bedel–Bokassa, a man who figured in one of Giscard's most embarrassing and damaging scandals: while finance minister under Pompidou, he had accepted gifts of diamonds from Bokassa.

Giscard prided himself for his support of European cooperation. He increased France's role in NATO planning and exercises although he never hinted at any willingness to lead France back into full participation. Sometimes, though, he chose to act alone, reaping condemnation not only from France's western allies, but from many French as well.

Giscard's main objectives were to reorder in a systematic and long–term way French industrial priorities. Industries such as textiles or steel that could no longer compete in international markets were denied government subsidies and were therefore often forced to reduce their operations. Future–oriented sectors, such as telecommunications, micro–electronics, nuclear and aerospace technology and seabed research, which could compete successfully, were granted support. To reduce French energy dependence on oil from over one–half of energy needs to less than a third, Giscard supported an atomic energy policy that made France Europe's largest producer of nuclear power.

On the whole, France was more prosperous and economically prepared for the future than when Giscard entered office. But his effort to strengthen the economy by making firms more competitive put many Frenchmen out of work. This, combined with growing revulsion of Giscard's aloof and aristocratic manner and the scandals that surrounded him and his family, convinced a majority of the French voters in 1981 that it was time for change. Power passed to the Socialists.

GOVERNMENT IN THE FIFTH REPUBLIC

In his famous Bayeux Manifesto of 1946, de Gaulle had repeated the rhetorical question posed by the ancient Greek thinker Solon: "What is the best constitution?" He answered: "Tell me first for what people and during which period." De Gaulle suggested to his countrymen "Let us take ourselves as we are." He asserted that French political parties, as indeed most individual Frenchmen, traditionally obscured the highest interests of the country and thereby created confusion in the state. He admitted that a parliament is necessary, but that it could not be entrusted with the destiny of the French nation. Due to its very nature, France requires a powerful, popularly elected president who stands above the parties, focuses on the "national purpose," and wields the supreme power of the state.

The constitution of the Fifth Republic, adopted in 1958 and still in force, reflects these convictions. It contains a workable compromise between the need for national unity and the legitimate expression of many political ideas, social classes and interests; between the need for a strong executive and a representative parliament; between lofty politics and common, day–to–day politics. It also incorporated the Napoleonic practice of involving the

Subway entrance, Paris Photo by Susan L. Thompson

citizens directly in the political process. Beginning in 1962, they directly elected the president for a seven–year renewable term, lowered to five years in 2000. Through referenda, they are called upon occasionally to give opinions on major national policy issues.

The Presidency
The French president's constitutional powers are immense, and the character of the presidents since 1958 expanded these powers far beyond the letter of the constitution. He appoints the prime minister and cabinet, chairs all cabinet meetings and actively directs the work of the cabinet ministers. Within any one-year period, he may dismiss the National Assembly (lower house of the parliament) for whatever reason he chooses and call new elections. He may question the constitutionality of any law and require parliament to reexamine any piece of legislation. He may submit any issue to a referendum, but he is not bound by the results, except insofar as constitutional amendments are concerned.

These infrequently held referendums almost always demonstrated confidence in

the president and therefore invariably strengthened him with respect to the parliament. He is commander–in–chief of the nation's military forces, and he negotiates and ratifies all treaties. He may not issue decrees. But if, in his opinion, the Republic is in danger, he can assume emergency powers that enable him to wield full executive, legislative and military authority. He is formally obliged to seek the advice of the Constitutional Council and is not permitted to dismiss Parliament during this time. There is no provision for terminating such emergency powers. In effect, the French president determines domestic and foreign policy and has veto power over every imaginable aspect of policy, including constitutional amendments. Unlike his American counterpart, though, he cannot veto an act of parliament. He can be removed from office only if he is convicted in a special tribunal (not by the parliament!) of high treason.

De Gaulle in 1964 described the presidency which he had created in breathtaking terms: "It must of course be understood that the indivisible authority of the State is confided in its entirety to

France

Hon. Valery Giscard d'Estaing

the President by the people who have elected him, that no other authority exists, neither ministerial nor civil nor military nor judicial, which is not conferred and maintained by him ..."

Clearly this is hardly presidentialism of the American type! The U.S. president must deal with 50 powerful states and what has become the most powerful and assertive legislature in the world. One foreign minister complained that in matters involving the United States he had to deal with 535 secretaries of state! The French president traditionally appoints the prefects (governors) in the 96 departments (states) and until 1986 faced neither serious regional resistance nor a powerful legislature. Whereas the American president must deal with such non-constitutional checks as an influential, independent and often fiercely investigative press and electronic news media, the French president faces a meeker press. Until 1984, radio and television networks were controlled by the government and were hesitant to attack the president openly.

In contrast, the American president must operate in an environment in which the Freedom of Information Act and various "sunshine" laws have made more visible the working of government. The French traditional cult of secrecy and more impenetrable bureaucracy are a haven for the chief executive. The public appears to be more used to viewing the state as something that is walled off.

Some prefer to describe French presidentialism as monarchy, in which the incumbent's whims and favors are crucially important. The French satirical magazine *Le Canard Enchaîné* ("The Chained Duck") once put it: "There's the President, and under him there's a vast void. And after-

wards there is a nothing. And below that, nothing. But finally one stumbles over the government." Edouard Balladur asked: "In which other democracy is the president in charge of the executive and the legislature and the judiciary; in charge of the order of business in parliament, where by intimidation, force or a reverential majority he gets the votes he wants; in charge of the promotion of magistrates and of the public prosecution that sends them cases; in charge of a government that moves only at his whim?" The powers of the presidency grew so much that President Mitterrand pledged to reduce them and to pass back to parliament some of the powers it had lost. He had always been a vocal critic of the Fifth Republic's constitution, as the title of his 1964 book indicated: *The Permanent Coup d'Etat*. In office, he did nothing to diminish presidential powers.

In order to reduce the risk of seeing the same person occupy the presidency for 14 long years, 73.5% of the voters in a 2000 referendum opted to reduce the term of office to five years with no limit on the number of times to be reelected. All the major parties supported this reform. Even though only about one out of three eligible voters bothered to go to the polls to record their opinion, this change could dramatically alter the balance of power in the political system. The unusually long tenure of seven years had been designed to create a powerful chief of state who could provide France with the kind of stability that had been lacking in earlier republics. By the end of the century France had achieved that stability, so an imperial presidency is no longer needed. The special aura of the magisterial presidential office will decline. The reform will also reduce the periods of power sharing with parliament, known as "cohabitation." By making presidential and parliamentary elections coincide more frequently, France could gain more coherent governments. Referring to such a significant shift by means of a referendum, political analyst Dominique Moisi said this "ends Gaullism in a very Gaullist way."

The Prime Minister and Cabinet

The prime minister and the cabinet ministers (the "government") have usually been drawn from all the parties in the president's majority coalition, although some have belonged to no political party. They are forbidden from having seats in the National Assembly. Ministers, including prime ministers, must give up their seats to substitutes, and if they later leave the government, they can reclaim their seats only by persuading the substitutes to stand down and by winning a by-election. If the prime minister and

Hon. Jacques Chirac
President of the French Republic

president are from the same party, the former is responsible for explaining and gaining support for the president's policies and for insuring that the president's overall directives are carried out in practice. The prime minister executes the laws. He supervises the drafting of the budget, which is submitted to the parliament for overall approval, but which parliament rarely alters. Finally, he determines the agenda of parliament; government legislation always takes priority. He is the president's lightening rod and is dependent on him; from 1958 to 1991 only one prime minister resigned voluntarily and none survived a full five-year legislative term.

If the president's party does not have a parliamentary majority, then the president must select a prime minister whose party or coalition can get a majority of votes in the National Assembly. In this case, the prime minister is a very powerful political figure who establishes the main lines of French domestic and economic policy and shares with the president responsibility for foreign and defense policy. He appoints and instructs the top officials in the foreign ministry.

Parliament

The parliament has two houses; the Senate and the 577-seat National Assembly. Deputies to the National Assembly are elected for five years by universal suffrage. The president can call new elections before the end of the five-year term. The Senate has 260 members elected for nine-year terms by municipal counselors and members of the National Assembly. One–third of its members are elected every three years.

Both houses of Parliament have essentially the same powers with two exceptions: the National Assembly has the privilege of examining the government's budget first. Further, only the National Assembly can force the government to resign by assembling a majority against an important piece of government legislation. However, the Fifth Republic's constitution places severe limits on this latter practice, which in past republics had been abused and which therefore brought a merry–go–round of governments with extremely short life spans. Such a vote may be submitted only once during any legislative session, and all abstentions or blank ballots count automatically for the government. Also, if such a vote succeeds, the National Assembly is dissolved immediately and new elections are called. This latter provision takes the fun out of the former "parliamentary game" of shooting down the government for the most trivial reasons and makes such a vote of censure a much more serious step for the parties and the individual deputies.

An additional limitation of the parliament's powers is that much of what is considered "legislation" in other democratic countries is defined in the French constitution as "rule–making." The president

has the right to issue decrees on the latter, thereby circumventing the parliament altogether. Finally, the number of parliamentary committees (which enable a parliament to develop the expertise to challenge the executive) is limited to six, and even these few committees are not permitted to amend a government bill before it comes to the floor. Such an increasingly weak parliament has been called "a device to provide majorities." There is little public interest in its debates, and people turn to their mayors rather than to their local deputies to pursue causes and grievances.

A final striking innovation in the constitution is the Constitutional Council, composed of nine members appointed by president of the Republic and the two houses of Parliament for nine–year terms. This body was designed to guard the constitution, and upon request of the three above mentioned presidents or the prime minister it can review the constitutionality of laws, treaties, elections and referendums. The Council cannot be compared to the far more prestigious United States Supreme Court, which possesses the power of unlimited judicial review. From 1986 to 1988, though, when for the first time since 1958 the prime minister came from a different party than the president, the Council of State was called upon to make important judgments concerning which powers and responsibilities belong to each

office. It became the ultimate referee in the political system. A Council of State also exists to deal with administrative and public law.

Political Parties

It has always been difficult to rule France from the center, long referred to as the "swamp." Since the founding of the Fifth Republic there has been a steady reduction in the number of parties with any hope for electoral success. There has also been an obvious polarization between parties of the political left and right, although the Socialists have moved closer to the center. The major parties on the right are the UMP, the UDF and the National Front. On the left are the Socialists and the Communists.

Union for a Popular Movement (UMP)

After numerous name changes, including the Rally for the Republic (RPR) until 2002, the Gaullist Party renamed itself the Union for a Popular Movement (UMP), with former Prime Minister Alain Juppé as its first chairman. The UMP is a federation of parties that grew out of Jacques Chirac's successful electoral alliance in 2002, then called the Union for the Presidential Majority, with the same acronym. It merged several conservative and centrist groups, including the Liberal Democrats (DL), the free–market quasi–Thatcherite party of Prime Minister Jean-Pierre Raffarin. For the first time in the Fifth Republic, the French right can reasonably claim to be united in a single party.

Founded in 1976, the RPR and its successor seek to preserve the fundamental Gaullist values: foreign policy independence, caution toward a more united Europe, maintaining the institutions of the Fifth Republic and economic and social expansion and progress. Even a third of a century after his death, de Gaulle basks in widespread approval. His predictions seem to have come true in the 1990s: the collapse of communism and the USSR, upheaval in Eastern Europe, the unification of Germany, which Frenchmen accepted with only a little uneasiness, an emergence of a Europe more independent of the superpowers. "Europe from the Atlantic to the Urals" was his concept before Mikhail Gorbachev picked up on it. In 1990, to celebrate his famous call for resistance on June 18, 1940, the obelisk at the Place de la Concord was draped with a 35–meter high radio model blaring popular songs of the time and coded messages from London to the Free French.

In May 1995 Jacques Chirac was elected president. But he was reduced almost to the status of a figurehead after the 1997 parliamentary elections, when the RPR crashed from being France's largest party

The asparagus vendor

France

Prime Minister Jean Pierre Raffarin

with 258 seats to a minority with only 134 seats. In 2000 the party picked the first female leader of a major French party, Michele Alliot-Marie, a law lecturer. The RPR struggled to unify itself and to find a new identity more compatible with the rise of a global economy and the EU and the reduced French role in the world.

Chirac and his party faced the 2002 presidential elections in serious trouble. They suffered a defection of a Gaullist nationalist and former interior minister, Charles Pasqua, who leads the breakaway Rally for France (RPF). They were also mired in scandals that are coming perilously close to Chirac himself. During the 18 years Chirac was mayor of Paris (1977–1995), fictitious jobs were created at the taxpayers' expense, and grateful public-works contractors made contributions to parties, especially the RPR. In September 2000 a video-tape surfaced in which a deceased property developer described illicit RPR fund raising, including a $660,000 cash payment in Chirac's presence. The president called such allegations "abracadabra," but three-fourths of the public thought he should tell what he knows. François Bayrou, leader of the UDF, spoke menacingly of "a moral and political crisis without precedent."

Chirac and his party did well in the 2002 elections. He won a massive reelection as president thanks to voters' revulsion against his chief opponent, Jean Marie Le Pen. He then organized a conservative grouping broader than his RPR to win the June 2002 parliamentary elections—the UMP. It decimated the left, winning 355 seats, up from the RPR's 1997 showing of only 134. He greeted an end to cohabitation with the Socialists as well as massive defections from the RPF and the UDF.

The Union for French Democracy (UDF)

Former President Giscard d'Estaing had founded his own Independent Republican Party in 1966, renamed the Republican Party (PR) and then Liberal Democra-

cy (DL), which joined the UMP in 2002. In order to enlarge his electoral and parliamentary base, he forged in 1978 a larger, loosely–knit group of parties called the Union for French Democracy (UDF), which is more pro–Europe and free–market oriented than the UMP. The UDF has several thousand direct members who strive to unify all disparate groups within the umbrella organization.

In addition to diverse centrist political groups, the UDF includes The Democratic Force (FD), formerly the Center of Social Democrats (CDS). Now centrist, devolutionist and strongly pro–European, this is the last remnant of the postwar reformist Popular Republican Movement (MRP), which had played such an important political role in the Fourth Republic. It also includes the Radical Party, a pro–Europe social democratic product of 19th century liberal tradition and one of France's oldest parties. During the Third Republic it almost dominated French politics and led a particularly determined campaign against the power of the Catholic Church in politics and society. This always undisciplined party shrank in importance after World War II, and in 1971 its more leftist–oriented members broke away and formed the Leftist Radical Movement (MRG), a tiny party which closely cooperated with Mitterrand's Socialist Party. A final party in the UDF is the pro–European Popular Party for French Democracy (PPDF).

The UDF was never a sufficiently powerful political base for Giscard, although it was constructed around him. Conservatives were always plagued by divisions and bickering. In 1996 the former president retired from politics. In the 1997 elections the UDF captured 108 seats, down from 206 in 1993, and entered the opposition. François Bayrou assumed the leadership in 1998. To make it look fresher, the party's name was officially changed in 2000 to *Nouvelle UDR* (New UDF). But it is a difficult task to make this loose collection of disparate parties into a credible political force. It was torn by a dispute over whether local party leaders should deal with the National Front; three regional leaders were expelled for doing so. Finding itself in disarray, it formed an Alliance of various conservative groupings in 1998 to present a unified image for the 1999 European elections and beyond. But this experiment did not succeed. In the 2002 parliamentary elections it lost many of its voters and members to Chirac's new UMP. But it managed to capture 29 seats on its own.

The National Front

The phenomenal rise of the extreme right–wing National Front (FN), led by

the former paratrooper, Jean Marie Le Pen, was the 1986 election's biggest surprise. Foaming against France's 4.2 million immigrants, whom he accused of being responsible for high unemployment and crime, Le Pen's party won 9.7% of the votes. It did particularly well along the Mediterranean coast, where there is much hostility to North African immigrants.

The timely abolition of proportional representation in 1988 practically eliminated the party from parliament. This time its 9.7% of votes translated into only one seat. But its 14% showing in the 1988 presidential balloting and 15% in 1995 indicate that racist fears and resentments on which the party feeds are strong in French society. Its high vote (*eg.* 28% in Marseilles) in regions, towns and suburbs with large concentrations of immigrants, unemployed, and crime is a warning to the government to eliminate the seeds of discontent that keep the National Front alive.

Although Le Pen insists he is not a racist, a court ordered him to pay a fine of FF900,000 (ca. $180,000) to nine French deportee organizations for his reference to Nazi gas chambers as a mere "detail of history." Because of this remark the European Parliament, in which he won a seat in 1994, lifted his immunity, clearing the way for the prosecutor's office in Bavaria to proceed toward an indictment of Le Pen. He also found himself convicted in court for assaulting a Socialist politician at a 1997 rally; he was banned from voting or holding office for most of 1999. He complains repeatedly about Jews having excessive power in the French media, a view that, according to a poll, was shared by 88% of the delegates at the party's 1990 congress. The other conservative parties have refused to deal with this overtly racist, xenophobic party, which opposes greater European unity. A populist, he presents himself as a supporter of the "little guy" against a corrupt establishment. Le Pen's supporters are predominantly young, urban, poor and unemployed. Le Pen captured 15% of the votes in the first round of the 1995 presidential elections. In 1997 the party also won 15% of the votes in the first round, but because of the electoral system it received only one seat in parliament, which it lost in a by-election in 1998.

In 1999 Le Pen's number two, Bruno Mégret, a well–educated man with a master's degree from Berkeley, launched an intra-party putsch against him. Mégret sought to turn the party into an acceptable mainstream party although his political views differ little from those of Le Pen, who expelled him and 19 other leading party officials from the party. Mégret then called a congress of 2,000 disaffected party members that included about half the

Le Pen: The People. National Front campaign poster

party's elected politicians and officials, had himself elected the new president (and Le Pen named as "honorary president"), and sought to carry off the party under his own banner. However, a court ruled that only Le Pen had the right to use the name, National Front, and declared null and void the January vote by Mégret's splinter group to take control of the party. The party has been left in tatters, and Mégret formed a new party, the National Republican Movement (MNR), which captured 2.4% of the firstround votes in the 2002 presidential elections.

In 2000 Le Pen had been stripped of his last official post, his seat in the European Parliament, as a result of a court ruling banning him from public office after being convicted of assaulting a Socialist politician. He got it back, however, and after his phenomenal second-place finish in the first round of the 2002 presidential elections, displacing then-Prime Minister Lionel Jospin, he was drowned out by jeers and boos when he tried to deliver a speech to the European Parliament. He was trounced four-to-one in the second round, and his party was unimpressive in the parliamentary elections that followed. It won only 11% of the votes and lost its only seat. His youngest daughter, Marine Le Pen, is maneuvering to become his political heir. Reportedly toning down her father's notoriously aggressive rhetoric, she is trying to improve the party's image and broaden its electoral base.

The party faces a serious danger in the Chirac government's 2003 change of the electoral system for regional councils and the European Parliament. By raising the thresholds for winning any seats to 10%

in the first-round of regional elections and 5% in eight regional areas for the European Parliament, the National Front and a host of small parties may find themselves locked out. The result, Chirac claims, will be "stable majorities" of the UMP or the Socialists.

The Communists

The main reason why the left had difficulty assuming power in France is that it has always been fragmented, with two parties particularly prominent: the French Communist Party (PCF) and the Socialist Party (PS). The PCF was founded in 1920 when delegates to the Socialist Party congress walked out to join the Comintern, the external arm of the Soviet's party. It converted the Socialist newspaper, *L'Humanité*, into an organ through which the new party consistently advocated a hard–line, class–conscious revolutionary policy, closely attuned to the aims of the Soviets. In 1936 the PCF refused to join the Popular Front because Socialists dominated the coalition, and it loyally supported Stalin's non–aggression pact with Hitler, which was the prelude to the devastating German attack on France in 1940. Once the Soviet Union was invaded by Germany, though, the PCF joined the resistance to Hitler's Germany and fought valiantly, thereby winning the admiration of such diverse persons as de Gaulle and Mitterrand.

When the Cold War poisoned relations between the West and the Soviet Union, the PCF did not hesitate to orient itself toward the latter. The Soviet suppression of uprisings in Eastern Europe in 1953, 1956 and 1968 all ultimately won the PCF's approval. In the 1970s a thaw in the party began to occur. It officially disavowed the

Marxist–Leninist concept of "dictatorship of the proletariat" and accepted in 1972 Mitterrand's offer of a common program of the left, including both socialists and communists. The course was an entirely new concept for Western European socialists, who had seen clearly what happened in Eastern Europe after socialist and communist parties had agreed to cooperate.

The PCF, led until 1994 by former steelworker Georges Marchais, showed itself to be a difficult partner. Mitterrand's PS could count on only about 5% of the vote in 1972, whereas the PCF consistently received over a fifth of the vote in any election (and a third of all workers' votes). Therefore the PCF believed that it would soon be able to control its "junior" member. It was badly mistaken. During the decade the PS grew very rapidly in voter appeal and eventually overtook the PCF. Not wishing to be the smaller member of a parliamentary majority, the PCF torpedoed the chances for a leftist victory in the 1978 parliamentary elections.

The PCF had second thoughts about its Eurocommunist course. It openly supported the Soviet invasion of Afghanistan and was returning to its pro–Soviet position. This was disastrous. To halt its stunning erosion, the PCF saw no alternative in 1981 to joining forces with the Socialist Party, but this alliance collapsed within three years. The PCF has suffered a steady decline in votes and membership, especially among the young and intellectuals. By 1991 it had little more than 100,000 card–carrying members. The Socialists overtook the Communists in the traditional "red bastions" in the north. The PCF declined to where it stood a half century ago.

In 1997 it managed to climb from 24 to 38 seats. Led until 2003 by Robert Hué (assisted by another government minister, Marie-George Buffet, who became a second national secretary in 2001), a jovial former male nurse and judo champion, the PCF shed such dogmas as the pledges to "abolish capitalism" and "nationalize the means of production." It remains staunchly opposed to Europe's single currency and the Maastricht Treaty, which many French identify with the government's austerity measures. Nevertheless, it entered the Socialist Party's governing coalition in 1997 and had four ministerial posts.

The party is struggling to avoid disappearing completely and is trying to reinvent itself. If it modernizes its policies to adjust to a market-oriented new world not understood by Marx and participates in governments, it loses many of its core voters. If it does not do this, it becomes irrelevant and seals itself off from new

France

Worker's party demonstrators at Mur de Fédére, Paris   Photo by Michael Bunch

voters. The results of its dilemma are obvious. In the 2002 presidential election Hué won only 3.37% of the votes. In the first round of the parliamentary elections in June 2002 the PCF captured a record low of 4.8%. It wound up with only 21 seats, down from 86 in 1978. Hué himself lost his seat. Calling the outcome "catastrophic," he turned the leadership over to Buffet in April 2003. The PCF's steady downward slide continues.

It lost most of its votes to other leftist groupings, which together captured 11% of the votes in the 2002 presidential elections. They include such parties as the Workers' Struggle (Trotskyite), the Revolutionary Communist Party, the Workers' Party (Trotskyite), and the Radical Party of the Left, led by Christiane Taubira, Guiana-born Euro-MP, the only candidate who is both black and female.

The Greens
The French public now focuses greater attention on environmental protection because of such highly–publicized problems as the Chernobyl nuclear accident in the Ukraine, chemical factory accidents which polluted the Rhine and Loire rivers, depletion of the ozone layer, global warming and deforestation. They are also untainted by scandals, which have shaken other parties. French Greens are on the left of the political spectrum, although they advocate protecting the high

material standard of living, rather than radically changing the structure of French society. They call for restraints on foreign capital in France and the preservation of small neighborhood stores, which are increasingly threatened by supermarkets. The *Verts* (Greens), led by Dominique Voynet, who was environmental minister,

"For a Sixth Republic in a Federal Europe". The Greens

captured seven seats in 1997. A Citizens' Movement also won seven seats in 1997.

Because of France's electoral system and because it lacks a tradition of pacifism, nuclear protest or respect for the environment, the Greens do not have the political clout that their German counterparts do, even though both are in their respective national governments. Desiring to overtake the Communists as the second–largest party on the left, they chose as their standard–bearer in upcoming elections a German citizen, Daniel Cohn–Bendit. Known earlier as "Dany le rouge" (Dany the Red), he had been expelled from France for playing a leading role in the 1968 student rebellion. Known for his pugnacity, charisma and rhetorical skills, he is an outspoken Europhile who already represented the German Greens in the European Parliament. He is the first foreigner to head an electoral campaign in France. He could not rescue the party in 2002, when it won only three seats; the most prominent victim was Voynet.

The Socialists
The chief opposition party is the Socialist Party (PS). After it lost its parliamentary majority in 1993 and the presidency in 1995, Lionel Jospin took the reins of the party and has breathed new life into it. He imposed his authority on this fractious party and was successful in having a new program adopted in 1996 that he calls a "new New Deal." Like its American forerunner in the 1930s, this aimed to "break with the blindness and sterility of conservative policies which dominate the western world and are threatening the European social model." It called for the creation of jobs for young people, a reduction of the work week from 39 to 35 hours with no pay reduction, improvement of housing and decaying inner cities,

Former Premier Lionel Jospin

Mme. Martine Aubry

and the cancellation of recent tax cuts and privatizations. Also, women candidates would be presented for at least 30% of the parliamentary seats.

The PS, entered a new period of cohabitation after the 1997 parliamentary elections, when it won a resounding victory, electing 253 members (including 12 Radical Socialists) to the National Assembly, up from only 63 four years earlier. The new parliament doubled its female membership to 11% thanks to the PS's policy of fielding women for nearly a third of the seats. This compared with an EU average of 17% and 11% in the U.S. House of Representatives and 7% in the U.S. Senate. In French local government, 6% of the mayors and 12% of regional councilors are female. Of ex-Prime Minister Lionel Jospin's 27 ministers, 30% were women. They included Martine Aubry, his second-in-command, and Elisabeth Guigou, France's first justice minister.

Disaster befell the Socialists in the 2002 parliamentary elections. Penalized by the voters' perception that they had failed to address the twin problems of crime and growing insecurity, they fell precipitously from 241 to only 140 seats. Many prominent heads rolled, including that of Martine Aubry, the creator of the 35-hour workweek. Seven cabinet members were swept out of parliament. Jospin relinquished leadership of the party, which faces a difficult and divisive future.

Socialist Past

The PS was created in 1971 from the staunchly anti-communist French Section of the Workers' International (SFIO,) François Mitterrand's own Convention of Republican Institutions and various other socialist elements. Its rapid growth was partly due to the decline in some social groups which traditionally supported parties of the right: farmers, small shopkeepers, wealthy bourgeois families and non-workingwomen. But the Socialist Party's success can be attributed mainly to the work of a man who was both far-sighted and persistent, but who, like de Gaulle, was also mysterious, elusive and unknowable: François Mitterrand.

He was born into a piously Catholic bourgeois family in the Cognac region of France in 1916. His father was a railway stationmaster who inherited a thriving vinegar business. Brought up on Balzac's panoramic novels, Lamartine's romantic poetry and Barrè's patriotic fiction, he acquired a love for literature; which remained his primary passion. He authored ten books himself and certainly ranks with Léon Blum and de Gaulle as one of the most literary figures in French politics. His career did not always follow a consistently left-wing course. At age 18 he joined the youth group of the far-right *Croix-de-Feu* (Cross of Fire) and wrote for right-wing journals.

He studied law and political science at the Sorbonne in Paris. A sergeant in the army, he was wounded in the chest at Verdun in 1940 and was sent to a POW camp after his capture. After two unsuccessful attempts to flee, he finally succeeded. Asked many years later why he thought he could win the presidency after two unsuccessful attempts in 1965 and 1974, he noted that in 1941 he had succeeded in returning to France only on his third try! He became a civil servant and admirer of Marshal Pétain. He was awarded the highest honor given by the Vichy state, the *Francisque* in 1943, and from 1986 to 1992 he lay a wreath on Pétain's tomb every Armistice Day. He also maintained personal contact with a number of collaborators, such as René Bousquet, who had overseen the deportation of French Jews. Joining the resistance movement under the cover name of "Morland" in 1943, he gained respect for French Communists and a strong distaste for de Gaulle, who had demanded that he subordinate his activity to the General's leadership.

Mitterrand was hardly a new face in Fifth Republic politics, having occupied many ministerial seats during the Fourth Republic under diverse governments. His political views continued to be very changeable, leading to charges that he was a political opportunist. In the Fifth Republic, though, he was a consistent and ferocious opponent of Gaullism and a man determined to unify the left in order to take control of France's destiny.

His first task was to establish a program acceptable to his own heterogeneous party. He set a clear leftist course for the 1981 elections. However, he never mentioned the word "Marxist" in the campaign, even though the party's program does contain some Marxist references and principles. In the campaign, Mitterrand hammered away at the rising unemployment rate, the many inequalities in French society and Giscard's unpopular style. He presented himself as the "tranquil force" which France needed. His countrymen listened.

Mitterrand's 1981 Election

Mitterrand's triumph was the first time that an entire generation of Frenchmen had experienced a transfer of presidential power from right to left. One of his first acts in office was to dissolve the National Assembly and to call new elections. This reveals a fundamental characteristic of the French political system. Despite the extremely powerful office of the presidency, no incumbent had been able to rule long in the face of a determined, reasonably cohesive opposing majority in the National Assembly because of its budgetary and legislative approval powers. For the first time in the history of the Fifth Republic, a president faced a hostile parliamentary majority. The elections in June produced a landslide victory for the PS, which won an absolute majority with 288 out of 491 seats in the assembly.

The new government wasted little time in seeking legislation for the most far-reaching of its proposed reforms: the

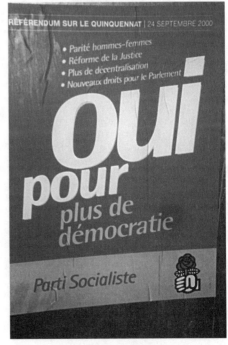

"Yes for more democracy"
Socialist Party

France

nationalization of certain industries and the decentralization of the French political system. Although Mitterrand's plan to extend state control over more of the French economy appeared at first glance to be a radical move, three things had to borne in mind: first, France has a long tradition of extensive state intervention in the economy, at least since the time of Louis XIV. Laissez–faire economics (believing that the government should intervene as little as possible) never really took hold in France, and for a long time the government has heavily subsidized industries for one reason or another. Second, 12% of the French economy had already been nationalized before Mitterrand was elected. The state–owned sector was already France's largest employer and responsible for 30% of all industrial output.

Third, the French state has supervised economic planning since the end of World War II. Managers, union representatives and government officials have always drawn up "Le Plan," and parliament debates and approves it. It usually extends for a five–year period and sets economic targets, investment priorities, statistical analyses of past, present and future economic performance and needs. The aim is to sustain balanced economic growth; under Mitterrand it clearly was designed especially to increase employment. Traditionally, there have been no coercive measures associated with the plan, but the state has always offered industries many incentives to participate: it provides useful statistics and analyses, grants tax relief and tariff concessions, awards government contracts or provides loans for investment funds.

Decentralization

The second fundamental reform was the decentralization of the political system. Since at least the 17th century, French national leaders consistently strengthened the powers of the central government at the expense of the regions and communes. Napoleon I divided France into 96 departments, each headed by a prefect, a powerful and uniformed official appointed by and answerable to the national government. The prefect oversaw the work of locally elected mayors and councils in the 37,500 municipalities. For economic and administrative purposes, 22 regions, whose borders roughly approximate those of France's ancient provinces, each headed by a regional prefect, were created. The essential fact is that all important initiatives had either to originate or be approved in Paris. For example, the designs for school cafeterias, soccer fields, swimming pools and other public facilities had to clear numerous bureaucratic and political hurdles in Paris.

Reading a good novel

Photo by Susan L. Thompson

This not only required personal connections and caused serious delays, but many Frenchmen feared that it was creating excessive visual uniformity in a land admired for its rich diversity. Many observers also believed that centralization stifled individual civic action and stimulated suspicion toward the French state. Mitterrand took seriously his pledge to reduce the power the central government and the prefects had over sub–national political units and to allow popularly elected regional and local assemblies and executives to handle their own affairs. Within two years, his government announced ten devolution laws and 50 decrees designed to decentralize France. Perhaps the most significant change was that the prefects, renamed "Commissioners of the Republic," were stripped of many of their administrative, financial, judicial and technical powers. During the 1980s local governments were granted more autonomy in spending, taxation, and borrowing. The result was more local activity to build new airports, wider streets, pedestrian zones, museums, concert halls, and stadiums. However, the shift of power from civil servants to local politicians also brought a higher level of local indebtedness and corruption.

A political problem which devolution presented to the Mitterrand government was that his conservative opponents did very well in local and regional elections after 1982. Regional assembly presidents, such as Giscard d'Estaing (Auverne) and Jacques Chaban–Delmas (Aquitaine), emerged as powerful provincial barons. Further, the National Front, which was traditionally untouchable in the National

Hon. François Mitterrand

Assembly, bolstered its power in the regions, where its votes were vital in electing five conservative presidents. Thus, Mitterrand created a troublesome territorial set of checks and balances that provide departmental and regional restraints on the Paris government.

A More Conservative Outlook

The Socialists promised France in 1981 fundamental changes, but few persons expected to see France emerge as a more pragmatic, conservative country with a more robust brand of capitalism. In his first year, Mitterrand nationalized some industries that the conservative government began to undo in 1986. Other reforms, such as a reduced workweek and retirement age and increased minimum wages and paid annual vacation of all Frenchmen, are reforms which no future government dares undo. But after it was clear by 1983 that his socialist revolution had failed, the Mitterrand government pursued a more austere economic course and stressed modernization, rather than socialization of France.

As an intellectual force, Marxism became far less popular than it once was. Partly because of Mitterrand's maneuverings, the Communist Party became practically impotent and is locked in a steady decline. The trade unions, a traditional pillar of the PCF, have almost never been weaker in modern France, partly because of the scourge of unemployment.

As French Socialists began to talk about modernizing France and going "back to the basics" in schools, French society was beginning to manifest more conservative

changes as well. Support for government–subsidized Catholic schools was so great that the Mitterrand government had to back down from efforts to restrict their independence. The government grip on the airwaves was also loosened, as private radio and TV stations sprung into life.

Cohabitation—1986 to 1988

The 1986 electoral results created something entirely new since the beginning of the Fifth Republic in 1958: a president whose party is a minority in the National Assembly. The traditional conservative parties won a whisker–thin majority. Therefore, Mitterrand was compelled to appoint a conservative prime minister, Jacques Chirac.

Chirac had studied international relations at Harvard, paying his way by working as a waiter at Howard Johnson's. During the Algerian War he served in the French Foreign Legion, after which he entered the prestigious *Ecole Nationale d'Administration*. His subsequent political rise was meteoric, working, as always, so energetically that Pompidou gave him the nickname "the Bulldozer." From 1974–76 he had served as Prime Minister under Giscard. However, believing that he was given too little leeway to pursue his own policies, he became the only prime minister in the Fifth Republic to quit due to disagreements with the president.

Observers coined the word "cohabitation" to describe the relationship between a strong president and an equally strong prime minister who is not willing merely to execute the will of the president. This relationship changed the basic rules of the

French political game from 1986 to 1988. It also showed that the institutions of the Fifth Republic are more adaptable and resilient in democratic politics than even de Gaulle had ever imagined.

The president's actual powers diminished somewhat, but they nevertheless remained formidable. "Cohabitation" was not a return to the parliamentary politics and "games" of the Third and Fourth Republics because the powers the president lost fell to a powerful prime minister, not to parliament. Nevertheless, it was a difficult relationship with which the French had almost no experience. Both the president and the prime minister had an interest in making this power–sharing succeed. French politics has traditionally been characterized by polarization between the left and the right; the new experiment proved could find common ground and cooperate with each other in the interest of the French nation. In fact, by election time in 1988 it had helped diminish the ideological gulf separating the major parties. Therefore, it actually strengthened French democracy. "Cohabitation" proved to be a workable alternative, and 70% of the French found it to be good.

As soon as Mitterrand appointed Chirac prime minister, the latter declared that he would play an active role in French foreign and defense policy, fields traditionally reserved for the president. Although Chirac and Mitterrand thought almost alike on these issues, their struggle was over constitutional power, not policy substance.

In domestic affairs, Chirac moved extremely quickly, hearing loudly and clearly the count–down to the 1988 elections. His government probably put through the largest number of reforms by any French government since 1958. He abolished the proportional representation electoral system, which Mitterrand had intentionally introduced in order to reduce the Communists' parliamentary seats and to prevent any party from winning a majority. An unfortunate by–product of this system had been that it enabled the National Front to win 35 seats and thereby reduced Chirac's usable majority to only two deputies, even though the right, as a whole, had won 55% of the vote.

Although Mitterrand initially balked at some of the conservative government's initiatives, he could not stop a single policy the prime minister wanted to pursue. He was the first Fifth Republic president to have his wings clipped while still in office. He watched most of his power drain away from the Elysée to the Matignon palace. However, by knowing how and when to assert his residual authority, he succeeded in halting the trend. Having pre-

Autumn in Paris ... Susan and Wayne Thompson

France

served his authority, his popularity soared. By standing above the political fray and focusing on the nation's interests, he let Chirac, who was in the trenches doing day–to–day combat, acquire some serious political bruises. Mitterrand thereby enhanced his own chances of reelection in 1988 and diminished Chirac's chances to win the presidency.

1988 Elections

The strength of de Gaulle's constitution had been demonstrated by the two–year "cohabitation" experiment, which coupled a Socialist president with a conservative prime minister. The 1988 elections led the country into yet another untested experiment: a minority government.

Chirac garnered only 46% of the votes to Mitterrand's 54%. Ignoring statements he had made during the campaign, the re-elected Mitterrand called for parliamentary elections in June, expecting to see the momentum of his victory produce a solid Socialist majority in the National Assembly. His plan backfired as the PS fell 14 votes short of a majority. He appointed a popular and capable rival within his party, Michel Rocard, as prime minister with a cabinet containing some non–Socialists.

The minority government had to work with other parties to make the system work. But this is nothing unusual in Europe, where most major democracies have coalition or minority governments. The constitution had been designed in 1958 to enable a country with a fractious parliament to enjoy stable rule. No new elections can be called for 12 months, and governments cannot be brought down unless a majority unites against it. In other words, it is the opposition, not the government, which needs a majority. Rocard went far in introducing non–socialist ideas on how an advanced economy should be run. He deserves much of the credit for transforming the PS from a party of doctrine to one of government.

In many ways Mitterrand had done more to transform French society and politics than de Gaulle. No one would have expected that he would be so able to convert the French to an acceptance of a market economy and the need for stable and rigorous economic management. In foreign policy he swept away some of the most important cornerstones of Gaullist foreign policy by nurturing a more trusting relationship with the United States and by championing greater European integration, including in the field of defense. It was in the context of greater European integration and closer Franco–German relations that he sought to contain an enlarged, unified, and dynamic Germany within a Europe whose map is being redrawn.

He also oversaw the most ambitious building program in Paris since Haussmann remade the capital more than a century earlier. I.M. Pei's glass pyramid in the court of the Louvre had shocked Parisians at first, but it gave new life to one of the world's finest museums. The Grand Arch at the heart of the suburb of La Défense, completed for the bicentennial in 1989, is a majestic, modern, 360–foot steel–and–glass version of Napoleon's Arc de Triomphe. The Bastille Opéra, opened in 1989, has been less successful in winning public admiration, but numerous other *Grands Travaux*, such as a new National Library, leave Mitterrand's stamp on Paris.

1993 Parliamentary Elections

Mitterrand's party, which had been in power too long and had run short on vision, ideas, and energy, was swept from power in the most devastating defeat in modern French electoral history. It was a hard verdict, but it was not an ideological one, since the Socialist Party had already shed most of its socialist ideology. Before stepping down in May 1995, Mitterrand admitted that with all the formal powers a French president has, he had "underestimated the ponderous nature of society, the slowness of its wheels, the weight of its traditions. You don't change society by an act of legislation."

The conservative victors captured 80% of the seats in the National Assembly, and for two years France again experienced rule by cohabitation. The conservative government of Edouard Balladur advanced resolutely toward greater European unity. The latter goal was a challenge after a hair–thin 51% voted *Oui* for the Maastricht treaty in a 1992 referendum. The narrowness of that margin in one of the EU's founding nations was a stinging blow to France's political elite.

1995 Presidential Elections

Balladur's government was embarrassed by charges of American industrial espionage in France and subsequent expulsion of four U.S. diplomats. This was the first time France had publicly sought the removal of alleged American agents from its soil. It was also a setback for the two countries' intelligence cooperation, which had been instrumental in France's 1994 capture in the Sudan of the world's most wanted terrorist, known as "Carlos the Jackal." The government's handling of the spy affair widened a serious breach in the cabinet between Balladur's supporters and those of party leader Jacques Chirac. The latter had put Balladur into the prime ministerial hot seat to free himself to run for the presidency, which had eluded him twice before. Boosted by

temporary popularity, Balladur's ambition grew, and he decided to make a bid for the presidency himself. Chirac felt double–crossed, and the stage was set for a tense race.

In the second round in May, neither Chirac nor Socialist Lionel Jospin agreed to bargain with Le Pen, who had received 15% in the first round, even though unemployment and immigration were the dominant issues on the minds of voters. Chirac campaigned energetically under the banner, "France for All," to try to show that he stood above party politics. He repeated in his standard stump speech that French society "is more divided and dangerous than ever." With a turnout of 80%, Chirac won 52.6% of the votes, doing best among farmers, business people, shop–keepers, artisans, and the professions, such as doctors and lawyers. For the first time, a conservative candidate won a majority of voters under age–35, as well as more than 40% of blue–collar workers and French describing themselves as under–privileged. Since a record 6% of blank ballots was cast, he actually won only 49.5% of the votes cast, making him the first president to be elected with fewer than half the total votes.

Chirac's victory left the right in control of the presidency, 80% of the seats in the National Assembly and two–thirds in the Senate, 20 of 22 regional councils, four–fifths of the departmental councils, and most of the big cities. Never in the history of the Fifth Republic has there been such a concentration of power.

Growing public cynicism toward the political establishment emboldened journalists to break hallowed taboos against reporting on politicians' private lives. In 1994 the weekly *Paris Match* published a cover photo of Mitterrand in public with his daughter born from an extramarital affair two decades earlier. Mistress and daughter had been housed in government guesthouses and had traveled at taxpayers' expense. Although the magazine was sold out within hours, there was an outcry among public figures that it had crossed the line. Unlike in the U.S., this harmed neither Mitterrand, who made no attempt to conceal his daughter's paternity, nor his party. At his funeral in January 1996 his wife, Danielle, stood for the first time with his daughter out of wedlock, Mazarine Pingeot, and her mother Anne Pingeot. He died of prostate cancer. He had been informed of this condition several months after his election in 1981, but he ordered that it be kept secret. On the first day of his presidency Chirac traveled to Colombey–les–Deux–Eglises to emphasize his political roots by laying a wreath at the burial site of

French National Assembly elections: 577 Seats
The pendulum of French politics: left, right, left

1988

Others
UDF (Giscard)
Socialists
RPR (Chirac)
Communists

1993

Others
UDF (Giscard)
Socialists
RPR (Chirac)
Communists

1997

Others
UDF (Léotard)
Socialists
RPR (Chirac)
Communists

his mentor, Charles de Gaulle. On the following day, he lunched with German Chancellor Helmut Kohl in Strasbourg to underscore the importance of France's ties with its powerful neighbor. He promised a less monarchical presidency than that of his predecessor. He promptly ordered that the fleet of military jets and helicopters at the disposal of the president and cabinet be disbanded and that ostentatious signs of power, such as motorcades with screaming sirens and motorcycles racing through the streets, be banned.

During his campaign, Chirac promised "profound change" and an attack on unemployment as his "priority of priorities." As it became obvious that Chirac could not fulfill his campaign promises of lower taxes and bountiful jobs, his approval rating plummeted. Without preparing the public, he suddenly announced an abrupt reversal of his economic policy from creating jobs to cutting the deficit in order to ensure that France would be able to join Europe's monetary union in 1999.

The sense of betrayal over the unexpected U–turn from job creation to austerity ignited in 1995–97 the worst strikes since 1968, involving millions of citizens, from civil servants and truck drivers to students, actors and doctors. Unlike in 1968, though, there is no unified political idea behind the unrest. Demonstrators in 1968 had risen up against materialism and an allegedly soulless affluent society. Many French now revolted, not just because they refused to relinquish treasured welfare benefits and special privileges, but also because they had a feeling that life is getting worse and worse and that affluence and security might be slipping away from them. This is why strikers today enjoy strong public support and why the government caves into them so often.

1997 Parliamentary Elections

In the June 1997 final round of elections, control of the National Assembly changed

hands for the fifth straight parliamentary election in 16 years. Tired of Chirac's broken promises made only two years earlier, voters turned back to the Socialists, led by Lionel Jospin, a former diplomat, economics professor, and education minister.

They believed in Jospin's promises to create 700,000 jobs for the young—half of them in the public sector, to create more jobs by reducing the work week from 39 to 35 hours with no loss of pay, and defending the welfare state without raising

France

taxes. While not entirely disavowing the common currency, Jospin pledged to allow neither it nor global market forces to condemn France to the "cruelties of 19th century capitalism," which many French identify with American–led economic reforms sweeping the industrialized world. The Socialists captured 253 seats (including 12 Radical Socialists) in the 577–seat Assembly. Since that is short of an absolute majority, the government formed by Prime Minister Jospin had to rule with the support of the Communist Party, which won 38 seats, and the Greens, which got seven. President Chirac, who disastrously misread the mood of the French public, was obligated to accept cohabitation for the third time in 11 years.

2002 Elections

France was reeling after the 2002 presidential elections. With 16 candidates running in the first round and with an unprecedented 28% of the voters too disillusioned even to vote, Chirac won just under 20% of the votes, the lowest ever for an incumbent president. Socialist challenger, Prime Minister Lionel Jospin, fell to a disgraceful third place, with about 16% of the votes, behind Le Pen, who won almost 17%.

In the campaign Jospin had come unhinged, venting his frustration by questioning Chirac's age and stamina and thereby violating an unspoken rule against negative campaigning. Even though he had presided over a growing economy and falling unemployment, he failed to recognize early enough that the real issues for French voters were crime, which had risen to American levels in such categories as armed robberies and car theft, and fear of foreigners, whom many French blame for the ascending crime rate. He was also handicapped by an electoral system that allowed many other candidates to compete for the left, which together won a respectable 44% of the total votes. Even one of his former cabinet members, Jean-Pierre Chevènement, created a breakaway party, Citizens' Movement, that won 5% of the votes and thereby deprived Jospin of the crucial margin that would have put him into the second round and perhaps into the presidential office. All together the two largest parties, the RPR and the Socialists, gathered only 35% of the votes.

It was Le Pen and his National Front who benefited from the sense of insecurity that had gripped the country, especially in the aftermath of the September 11, 2001, terrorist strikes against the U.S., which fueled fears of Arab terrorists moving within France's large Muslim mi-

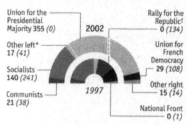

The swing to the right

Seats in the French parliament, 2002 *(1997)*

Union for the Presidential Majority 355 *(0)*
2002
Rally for the Republic† 0 *(134)*
Other left* 17 *(41)*
Union for French Democracy 29 *(108)*
Socialists 140 *(241)*
Communists 21 *(38)*
1997
Other right 15 *(14)*
National Front 0 *(1)*

*Includes Radical Party of the Left, 7 *(12)*; Greens, 3 *(7)*
†In 2002 it was absorbed into the Union for the Presidential Majority
Sources: French interior ministry; *The Economist*

nority. This feeling of insecurity was exacerbated by the physical attacks by Arab immigrants on French Jews and synagogues. He said, "I want to reestablish security throughout the territory." Despite the country's strict gun control laws, more and more crimes now involve firearms, including pistols, machine guns and grenade launchers. This was brought home again by a man who went berserk and burst with guns blazing into a meeting in a Paris suburb, killing eight city councilors before leaping out a window to his death. Le Pen was thus a symptom of a wider political malaise, including the fear of globalization, ugly xenophobia, and gloomy declinism. He spoke of France as a country "in regression": in its economy, its public safety, and its morality. The endless series of corruption scandals surrounding the political class, including Chirac, whom a nightly satirical television show routinely lampooned as "Super Liar," had sickened many French, especially the "little people" to whom Le Pen appealed.

The shock to the nation caused by Le Pen's success in the first round brought millions of Frenchmen of diverse political persuasions into the streets demanding a massing show of opposition to Le Pen in the second round two weeks later. These were anti-Le Pen rallies, not pro-Chirac ones. The most common slogan for the demonstrations was "Vote for the Crook, Not the Fascist." The usually neutral French media broke with tradition and endorsed Chirac. *Le Figero* carried a banner headline, "For France."

This worked. In the second round, Chirac captured an unprecedented 82% of the votes with a turnout of 80%. He faced the anomaly of having been elected by the largest margin in French history, outdoing even his hero Charles de Gaulle, but having very weak support from the public. A Harris poll revealed a day after the tally that only 13% of voters supported him because of his program; 75% gave as their main reason to shut out Le Pen. Pending the parliamentary elections in June,

Chirac appointed Senator Jean-Pierre Raffarin as interim prime minister. He is from the provinces with a reputation as a popular speaker with a sensitive ear for what he terms "France down below."

Chirac's newly-formed conservative Union for the Presidential Majority (UMP) dominated the parliamentary elections that followed on the heels of his presidential landslide. The right captured 399 of 577 seats, leaving only 140 for the humiliated Socialists. This victory not only left the right in control of the Senate and local government, but it ended cohabitation of a conservative president and a Socialist government. Voter abstention was a record 40%. Promising all things to all voters—tax cuts, subsidies to help women and the young to find employment, more police on the streets—he appointed a diversified 39-minister cabinet that included 10 women and one Muslim.

FOREIGN AND DEFENSE POLICIES

German unification in 1990 led many French to fear that their country would be overshadowed by Germany and would be driven to the margins of international politics. That has not happened. France plays an important role as a medium–sized power willing to use its force abroad. It preserves its independence and has not rejoined NATO's integrated command structure, although it has intensified its contacts with the alliance. For example, in 1994 it began attending NATO defense minister meetings again. In 1995 it rejoined NATO's military committee, which brings the service chiefs together, and its officers began working more closely with SHAPE. It did not join the Defense Planning Committee, which in 2003 became the forum for a NATO decision to send support to Turkey in the face of fierce French opposition.

In part because of defense cuts in all European countries, the French now talk of creating a European defense pillar within NATO, rather than in competition with it. President Chirac's meeting with British Prime Minister Tony Blair at St. Malo the end of 1998 agreed on a blueprint for such a new European defense.

The wars in the Persian Gulf and the former Yugoslavia convinced France that it could not do much in military operations without NATO assets and American help. It put some of its ships and aircraft under American control in the Balkans. Its troops that enforce the Bosnian peace settlement serve in a NATO force. France dispatched the largest foreign contingent—4,000 troops—to Bosnia to play the leading role in the UN Protection Force, led initially by a French general. Its combat pilots helped enforce the "no–fly zone" over that war–torn country. When NATO created a rapid–reaction force in 1995 to protect UN peacekeepers in Bosnia, France contributed 1,500 elite troops and assumed overall command. France was a major participant in the Implementation Force (IFOR) in Bosnia, assuming responsibility for maintaining peace in the most complicated spot imaginable: Sarajevo. Its troops remained after IFOR ended.

Many of the country's leading intellectuals embraced the cause of direct military intervention in the Balkans, fearing that "ethnic cleansing" could spread across Europe. This mood reflects a sharp break with the pacifist traditions of French intellectuals. That support continued in 1999 when France contributed 61 combat aircraft and five ships to conduct an air war against Yugoslavia in a NATO attempt to stop ethnic cleansing in Kosovo. France's pragmatic Atlanticist ex-Foreign Minister Hubert Védrine noted in April 1999, "in contrast to Bosnia, there's been no major disaccord at any point among Europeans or between Europeans and the United States. It doesn't happen often, but this time we've had a remarkable identity of views on the cause of the problem and what to do about it."

What has replaced antipathy toward America is fear of the sole remaining superpower's domination of world affairs. Polls reveal consistently that a majority dislikes this, and most French discount the idea that American policy abroad, including in the Balkans and Iraq, is motivated by ideals of human rights and democracy. Védrine, who referred to the U.S. as a "hyperpower," remarked, "without a counterweight, there is a danger of a unilateralist temptation, a risk of hegemony. So, depending on the situation, we will be friends and allies of the United States; but sometimes we will need to say No without acrimony, in the name of our legitimate interests or those of Europe."

France often disagrees with the U.S. In 1996 Paris proposed reforms in the NATO command structure as a price for its further reintegration into the alliance. Specifically, it demanded that the Southern Command headquartered in Naples be led by a European officer, preferably by a Frenchman. The U.S., whose Sixth Fleet comprises the main military force in the Mediterranean, refuses. The French government believes that France's reintegration into NATO must be contingent upon a European's receiving that southern command. The strong Gaullist antipathy toward a more united Europe is gone.

Another important departure is a dramatic increase in France's military cooperation with Germany. The two neighbors created an experimental joint brigade, whose command alternates between French and German officers. In 1991 they agreed to expand that unit to a corps size—35,000 troops. The French eased some of America's and NATO's fears by conceding that this "Eurocorps," which also includes troops from Spain and the Benelux countries, could operate under NATO for international peacekeeping and in time of war. The creation of Combined Joint Task Forces (CJTF) allows some of NATO's European assets to be used in military operations where the U.S. has no interest in participating. The concept is meant to work within NATO and not against it.

In the aftermath of the 2003 Iraq war, which both France and Germany opposed, the two countries joined with Belgium and Luxembourg to create a joint rapid reaction unit built on the existing French-German brigade. Belgium would contribute commandos and Luxembourg a reconnaissance team. In addition, the four said they would set up a multinational headquarters and a separate military center in Belgium in 2004 to command and plan EU military operations when NATO is not involved. President Chirac emphasized, "we are not questioning the transatlantic alliance. We want to reinforce it. But in order to have a balance, we have to have a strong Europe, as well as a strong U.S." The four invited other European nations to join their effort, but sensing that the real purpose of this effort was to weaken the transatlantic alliance, none did. The four did not pledge to raise their defense spending to cover the costs of these innovations, and it is uncertain whether this initiative will ever get off the ground.

France seeks to tighten its already close links with the FRG. Bilateral ties, EU integration and NATO tether Germany securely to the West. German unity made Germany, not France, the leader of a strengthened Europe, and France seeks to act with Germany's support in the name of "European interests." When Gerhard Schröder became chancellor in 1998, French leaders worried about his talk of tighter links with Britain and feared that this might destroy the special relationship between Paris and Berlin. The French had a host of disagreements with the new German government ranging from financial contributions to the EU, possible German cancellation of nuclear reprocessing contracts, and Germany's questioning of the NATO nuclear "first-use" doctrine. By 1999 French fears of a new Berlin-London axis were quieted, but some of the warmth that had once characterized Franco-German collaboration at the top disappeared.

In January 2003 the two neighbors celebrated the fortieth anniversary of the Franco-German friendship treaty in grand style. President Chirac and Chancellor Schröder met at the Elysée Palace, and 603 German parliamentarians joined 577 counterparts in the palace of Versailles. The next day, the two leaders met in Berlin. In their "Elysée Declaration," the two leaders agreed to increase the frequency of their special meetings to every six weeks, to appoint in each other's capital a "secretary-general for Franco-German cooperation" who would coordinate, prepare and follow up their common European policies, to dispatch the relevant minister to the other country's cabinet meetings when discussing a subject of interest to the other, and to propose common Franco-German legislation to each other's parliaments. They hope that such integration at the top, along with partner relationships between cities and combined military units, will help warm their citizens' hearts toward the other. The reality is that French and Germans are not particularly attracted toward each other. One can see that in the choice of languages schoolchildren take. Fewer than a million French secondary pupils learn German, and only 5% of German children are still learning French in their final year.

Typical World War I monument seen in every French village

France

French recruitment poster

Military Forces

The end of superpower confrontation meant that France had to reexamine the three pillars of its defense policy—its nuclear forces, its draft army, and its operational independence from permanent alliances. Without a Soviet threat it had problems defining a clear purpose for its atomic *force de frappe*. It became difficult to maintain its expensive triad of forces, which in 1991 consumed a fifth of total defense spending.

Its underground nuclear test series in 1995–96 unleashed a violent world outcry, especially in Asia and the Pacific, where they took place. Taken aback by the world–wide protest, Chirac swore that these tests were needed to perfect computer simulation programs that would make further testing unnecessary. They enabled France to sign an international treaty banning nuclear testing in 1996. In 1991 the French had finally signed the nuclear Non–Proliferation Treaty to emphasize the need to stop the spread of atomic weapons.

France continues to maintain the largest and most diversified military capability on the Europe continent outside of Russia, as well as a credible nuclear force. Despite the changed security environment in Europe following the end of the Cold War, a consensus remained to maintain as the ultimate security guarantee a minimal nuclear force posture for the purpose of "dissuasion," the French version of deterrence. A significant change is that these nuclear weapons are to be linked to European security, not just the defense of French territory and interests. The French

are aware that there is little current interest in Europe for such a link and that the establishment of a European defense identity would be a precondition.

The consequence of France's decision to maintain only a minimal dissuasion policy is that major reductions in its nuclear force posture and infrastructure became possible. In the course of the 1990s, France reduced its nuclear spending by more than 50%. It started eliminating its 18 land–based nuclear missiles on Plateau d'Albion (to be completed by 2005), reduced to four its planned new ballistic missile submarines, and began closing its plants at Pierrelatte and Marcoule that produce fissile material for atomic weapons, to be completed by 2002. Of the five nuclear submarines in use the end of the century, four are always operational and two at sea. One sub has 16 M4 missiles, each carrying six warheads. Four new strategic subs carrying upgraded missiles have or will enter the force: "Le Triomphant" in 1996, "Le Téméraire" in 1999, "Le Vigilant" in 2002, and the final one in 2007. This submarine force represents four–fifths of the French nuclear arsenal. An airborne component remains: three squadrons of Mirage 2000 N planes are equipped with ASMP missiles; and two fleets of Super Etendards, equipped with ASMPs, are stationed on aircraft carriers.

The aircraft carrier "Clemenceau" was decommissioned in 1997, and the following year it was announced that the aged "Foch" would also be withdrawn from service. Coming on line in 2000 after a four-year delay was the "Charles de Gaulle." This is the first French carrier constructed

to be interoperable with U.S. Nimitz–class carriers. It has compatible catapults, can receive U.S. aircraft, and carries U.S.–built Hawkeye planes flown by U.S.–trained pilots that control the airspace around the carrier and guide planes to their targets. Plagued by troubles, including the loss of a propeller during a shake-down cruise, the Charles de Gaulle must spend four months a year in port for maintenance. A second carrier has been order to accompany it.

The 1991 Gulf War revealed that France's conventional forces were not equipped or structured to cope with faraway crises. Its draftees could not be sent out of France, and its equipment was found wanting. The war reinforced the case for a more professional army. Consequently, France began in 1996 to phase out its 10–month conscription and to create an all–volunteer army. By 2000 France had a total force of 317,300 troops (drifting upwards to about 330,000 by 2003), including 22,790 women. It also has 419,000 reservists. Over a five–year period, it disbanded 38 of its 180 regiments, including 12 in Germany, where only 3,300 soldiers remain. Army manpower was reduced from around 400,000 to 178,300, which includes 31,000 marines, 8,200 foreign legion, and 13,490 women. France has trained 1,450 special operations forces, and these elite troops have fought with the Americans and other allies in Afghanistan. The navy has 62,600 sailors, including 2,900 naval marines, 3,500 naval air, and 3,000 women. Its air force consists of 76,400 troops, including 6,300 women. There were cuts in the land–based nuclear deterrence force, military bases, schools and hospitals, and civilian defense contractors; 16 warships are being decommissioned. The professional officer corps remains at 38,000.

France spends more than most European countries on defense: 2.6% of GDP in 2003. The newly elected center-right government, with the country's first female defense minister, Michele Alliot-Marie, embarked in 2002 on a costly defense modernization plan and shifted France's strategy toward creating a force that can be projected anywhere in the world. It ordered a second aircraft carrier, new spy satellites, reconnaissance drones, 50 new Airbus A400M heavy-lift transport planes, 34 helicopters, and 57 Rafale combat aircraft. By 2008 it is hoped that total armed forces, including the paramilitary gendarmerie, will rise from 437,000 to 446,000. The goal is to catch up with Britain's armed forces in terms of professionalism, equipment and global reach. It aims to improve France's inter-operability with allies, but at the same time to protect its ability to act alone "should it be necessary" and to "assume the role of lead nation" in any coalition.

Its independent stance had been challenged by the reality of emerging European defense identity, which the French government advocates. More than any Western country, France was rocked by the break–up of the old world order. It can no longer pose as an independent force between two superpowers—such a state of affairs has ceased to exist. But it hopes to put itself in a position of leadership in Europe with the future possibility of heading a counterweight to American predominance in a more multipolar world. For that it needs more military muscle and mobility.

Response to Terrorism and War in Iraq

When terrorists high jacked four commercial airliners and flew three of them into the World Trade Center and the Pentagon in 2001, killing 3,000 persons, including many French, France did not hesitate to help. It shed its usual hesitation toward collaboration with the U.S. President Chirac was the first foreign leader to visit Washington after the attacks. He told the American president that France stood in total solidarity" with the United States and "our forces will take part. We will assume our role in a spirit of solidarity and responsibility." Prime Minister Lionel Jospin also declared, "the struggle against terrorism calls for solidarity and cooperation. Our solidarity is first with America, the ally to which we owe victory over Nazism, the friend with whom we jointly affirm the ideal of democracy." French public opinion backed these stands.

As military action against Afghanistan began, it had a refueling ship and an Exercet-rocket launching frigate patrolling the waters close to the war zone with the American and British navies. It quickly put intelligence agents on the ground to work with the Afghani opposition and dispatched special forces. It deployed 2,000 on three naval vessels, as well as combat and reconnaissance aircraft; it stationed some of its fighter-bombers in neighboring Tajikistan. It also sent some of its AWACS airborne control aircraft to the Balkans to relieve NATO AWACS planes for use in protecting the U.S. East Coast. French leaders regarded America's turning to its friends as inevitable. Said one of Chirac's senior advisors: "America's power in the world may be unrivalled in military, political and economic areas, but in the era of globalization even a superpower cannot disregard the need for allies."

In 2003 the French government fiercely opposed war against Saddam Hussein's Iraq, with which France had long enjoyed lucrative commercial ties. Chirac and his

Les Etats-Unis haussent le ton contre la France

La mise en place de l'UMP se heurte aux ambitions des ex-RPR

Cours particuliers : le marché de l'angoisse parentale

FESTIVAL
Flaming Lips aux Festins d'« aden »

La France dit non à l'ultimatum

dynamic Foreign Minister Dominique de Villepin argued that UN arms inspectors needed more time to complete their work and that such a conflict would breed even more terrorism and easily spill over into France itself, especially given its large Muslim population, which solidly supported Chirac on this question. President Chirac, who enjoyed overwhelming backing within his own country and majority support in public opinion elsewhere on the continent, believed that the crisis offered him an ideal opportunity to enact his version of the earlier Gaullist doctrine: that Europe must act as a counterweight to a much too powerful United States and

France

that France, with German backing, must be the directing force in Europe. Whereas British policy aimed to promote unity with Washington rather than trying to rein it in, French policy sought the recreation of a multipolar world in which Europe, led by France, could stand up to the sole superpower. The UN Security Council would be the sole source of legitimacy for countries' going to war. With its veto power, it could stop or limit the use of American military force whenever it chooses to do so. In the process, France's diplomatic weight and prestige would be greatly enhanced and its interests served.

This grand design ran into almost immediate difficulties. Chirac's tactless remarks at an EU summit meeting caused unexpected indignation throughout Europe that undermined any chances of placing France at the forefront of a united Europe. After 18 European governments, including most of those in central and eastern Europe, signed letters supporting U.S. policy toward Iraq, he hinted in frustration that France might veto the application by former communist countries to join the EU. He said that they "have not been very well behaved and have been rather reckless of the danger of aligning themselves too rapidly with the American position." Referring to Romania and Bulgaria, who were still waiting for an invitation to join, he stated, "if they wanted to diminish their chances of joining the EU, they could not have chosen a better way." The new partners in the East were furious. His policy also poisoned France's relations with many of its other allies, including the U.S. When he declared on March 10 that he would veto "in all circumstances" any new resolution to bring about Iraqi disarmament, he unwittingly had called an end to all chances for a diplomatic settlement of the crisis. The U.S. and Britain proceeded to defeat Saddam's regime in three weeks without France's support, even though the French government permitted coalition warplanes to use its airspace.

In France's own press and elsewhere, it began to sink in that France might have overreached its capacities. His condescending treatment of central European governments had split and weakened Europe, rather than uniting it. The EU's nascent Common Foreign and Security Policy (CFSP) was left in shambles, thereby destroying any hope for a European pole dominated by France. France's dogged resistance to war had paralyzed the UN Security Council, thereby possibly weakening the only body in which France has equal standing with the U.S. France was left on the sidelines in a new post-Saddam Middle East, and it faced a difficult task in repairing its relations with the United States and Britain. Chirac phoned

President Bush after the short war was over, expressing his pleasure that Saddam's government had been demolished and offering to be "pragmatic" about postwar reconstruction. He dropped France's long-standing resistance to NATO's formal assumption of command over the international security force in Afghanistan.

Activism in Foreign Policy

France always tried to remain largely independent of other western industrialized nations in its dealing with the "third world." In 1984 it created a 47,000–man "Rapid Action Force" (FAR). This mobile force was designed not only to plug holes in NATO defenses in Western Europe, but also to be sent to trouble spots anywhere in the world to back up French interests, such as in Africa.

No other country of comparable size maintains as big a military presence abroad; it has more than 60,000 soldiers stationed in some 35 countries and territories. The French maintain military bases in six African ex–colonies and have troops in more in order to protect French interests and citizens, who number about 130,000 in Sub–Saharan Africa. They station 4,000 troops in Djibouti on the East coast and smaller forces in West and Central Africa. France also sends two–thirds of its foreign aid to Africa, making it the continent's major patron. Since 1990 it encourages the trend toward democracy in Africa by linking its aid to democratic reforms.

Until 1994 it provided 13 African countries belonging to the *Communité Financière Africaine* (CFA), also called the "franc zone," with the benefits of a hard currency pegged to the French franc. Then it decreed that such pegging would cease; this caused widespread African hardships. The establishment of a common European currency further weakened what was left of French support of African currencies.

Although it convenes a Franco–African summit each year, it decided to trim its costs on that continent. Its military interventions have become rarer, although in 1992 it joined other allies to participate in the UN humanitarian relief operation in Somalia. It was the only European country to send troops to Rwanda in 1994. Its 2,500 soldiers managed to interrupt the first round of genocide and save thousands of lives. In 1997 its troops in the Central African Republic were used against mutinous local soldiers who opposed the local president and who had killed two French soldiers.

In 1997 the Socialist government called for a complete rethinking of France's policy in Africa. It ordered a reduction in

French troops permanently stationed in Africa from 8,400 to 6,000 in 1999 and declining further to 5,000. Two bases in the Central African Republic were closed, and military cooperation agreements with 23 countries were reviewed. President Chirac reiterated at a Franco–African summit in 1998: "The period of outside interference is over."

That declaration had to be put aside in 2002–3 when French forces were rushed to the Ivory Coast, a former French colony that was once a model of stability in West Africa. A bloody and confusing uprising got out of control, endangering 20,000 French nationals and prompting the rescue by French soldiers of 191 American school children trapped in the crossfire. Paris mediated a peace pact in January 2003 establishing a government of national unity, but it was rejected in the Ivory Coast for giving too much power to rebels in control of the North and West. By April 2003 there were 4,000 French troops, including Foreign Legion and elite reconnaissance forces, and 1,200 West African peacekeepers trying to protect the government and enforce the oft-violated ceasefires. Feeling itself trapped in an increasingly impossible situation, France called on to the UN to become more involved. Chirac's free hand in Africa was demonstrated once again in February 2003 when he invited Robert Mugabe, Zimbabwean president, to a Franco-African summit in Paris even though the EU had declared a travel ban against Mugabe.

France has long–standing interests in the Middle East. It sent a powerful 12,600–man air, naval and ground contingent in 1991 to help drive Iraq out of Kuwait. This was a bold move, considering the large Arab population in France and the fact that Iraq had been France's best Middle Eastern customer, and owes France $3 billion. In doing this it violated one of de Gaulle's most basic teachings: French troops should never be under U.S. command. Former President Mitterrand answered critics, saying "we are linked, we are allies, and we intend to do what we are committed to do."

Other countries look to France to take the lead in deciding how to respond if Algeria, to which France annually provides $1 billion in aid, becomes a fundamentalist Islamic republic. France is torn between the desire to prevent Muslims from coming to power and fear of making irreconcilable enemies out of potential rulers of Algeria. It supports the military junta in power, reinforced by its election, even though it has outlawed the popular Islamic Salvation Front (FIS). This policy creates problems within France itself. To punish France, the Armed Islamic Group renewed it terrorist activities within

France, using bombs, which killed four innocent bystanders in ugly carnage at the Montparnasse underground rail station in 1996.

France's nervousness is understandable. By 1995, a third of the 78 foreigners killed in a year and a half of Algeria were French, and the threat of violence on French soil had become real. Out of a total of about five million Muslims in France, over 1.5 million persons of Algerian origin live in France, and authorities believe that fundamentalists wield influence over a small but growing minority of them. This was demonstrated in 1994, when terrorists hijacked an airliner in Algiers, intending to blow it up in the skies over Paris. It was intercepted in Marseilles when police stormed it. After the September 11, 2001, terrorist strikes, French security services note an especially strong Algerian influence within terrorist groups in Europe.

In March 2003 President Chirac made the first ever state visit to Algeria since independence four decades earlier, and he was welcomed with enthusiasm. The government in Algiers treated this high-profile visit as a momentous event in its postcolonial history. Its purpose was to redefine the tortured relationship with Algeria, gripped by a deadly civil war that had claimed at least 120,000 deaths. It was time for reconciliation. Chirac, who had served there as a second lieutenant during the Algerian war, said that that conflict had been "a painful moment in our common history that we must not and

cannot ignore, but it is time now to move forward." He signed a "declaration of Algiers," forerunner to a formal treaty underscoring a "special partnership" between the two nations. Everywhere he went he was greeted with cries of "visa, visa!". He promised to improve visa procedures, while his interior minister at home vowed to crack down on the large increase in visas issued.

France's pro–Arab foreign policy, driven in part by domestic considerations, has put the country in conflict with the U.S.'s basically pro–Israel leaning. Its viewpoint has been reflected in 1996–7 by "shuttle diplomacy" calculated to resolve differences between Israel and the militant Islamic Hezbollah. It refused to support U.S. air strikes and an expansion of the "no–fly zone" in Iraq in 1996.

Corsica

France also must deal with domestic terrorism from Corsica. Since the 1970s Corsicans have suffered an average of 400 explosions a year by various and divided nationalist groups, who finance their operations by extorting "protection money" from local businesses. Supported by no more than one Corsican in ten, these groups do not agree among themselves about whether they are seeking independence or more autonomy. But in 1996 they took their struggle to the French mainland, bombing a courthouse in Aix–en–Provence and the Bordeaux office of the prime minister. The Corsican National Liberation Front (FNLC)

claimed responsibility for the multiple explosions.

In 1998 the troubles escalated on "the impossible island." France's prefect, Claude Erignac, was murdered, and the assassins were never found. Bernard Bonnet replaced him and was given *carte blanche* to crack down on separatist terror, corruption, organized crime and clan vendettas. He succeeded in reducing bomb attacks to 96 in 1998, armed robbery fell by two–thirds, and scores of separatist extremists were arrested. Dozens of local politicians and dignitaries were placed under investigation in some 80 corruption scandals.

Then in April 1999 five paramilitary gendarmes from an anti–terrorist squad were sent to burn down a beachfront restaurant. They bungled the job and were caught after fleeing. They claimed they had been sent by the island's top gendarme, who in turn explained that he had acted under orders from the prefect himself. All were put in prison awaiting charges and trial; this was the first time in the history of the Fifth Republic that a prefect had been fired or jailed. In 2002 Bonnet was convicted of arson and given three years in prison, two of them suspended, for ordering policemen to burn down the restaurant. Prime Minister Jospin had to admit that it was a "very serious and unacceptable affair." In 1999 alone, 210 bombs exploded on the island, and 22 persons were murdered. This situation contrasts sharply with France's Basque region, where a majority favors creating a separate department or administrative area, but oppose independence.

In 2000 the French government sought to end the violence by recognizing the island's unique identity and history and by offering Corsica a limited form of self-government. Responsibilities would be transferred in two stages. If peace prevailed and the terror stopped by 2004, the French constitution would be amended to grant some legislative powers. However, the parliament in Paris would have to approve of any laws recommended by the Corsican assembly. Islanders would have more authority over culture, education, economic development and the environment. The teaching of the Corsican language would be required in all nursery schools. In December 2000, a large majority in the island's legislature approved this plan for greater autonomy.

However, some Frenchmen regard the decentralization plan as nothing short of heresy. Spokesmen from the right reacted with fury, decrying this "tearing apart of the French republic." Former Socialist Interior Minister Jean Pierre Chevènement resigned in protest, saying: "There is a po-

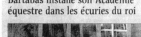

www.lemonde.fr

59ᵉ ANNÉE – N° 18072 – 1,20 € – FRANCE MÉTROPOLITAINE –   DIMANCHE 2 – LUNDI 3 MARS 2003   FONDATEUR : HUBERT BEUVE-MÉRY – DIRECTEUR : JEAN-MARIE COLOMBANI

SUPPLÉMENT
Le Monde
ARGENT
Charmes et dangers
de la « love money »
Marché de l'art

AUTRICHE
Schüssel reconduit
la coalition avec
l'extrême droite   p. 3

RÉPUBLIQUE TCHÈQUE
Vaclav Klaus,
nouveau président p. 3

THAÏLANDE
Guerre contre la
drogue : plus de 1 000
morts en un mois   p. 6

VERTS
Affaiblis et toujours
divisés   p. 7

DÉCENTRALISATION
Raffarin a présenté
son projet   p. 8

PARFUMERIES
Bataille entre Sephora
et Marionnaud   p. 10

LUTTE ANTI-DOPAGE
Réunion à Copenhague
pour définir

France-Algérie, les retrouvailles

C'EST LA PREMIÈRE visite d'État d'un président de la République française depuis l'indépendance de l'Algérie. Du 2 au 4 mars, Jacques Chirac se rendra à Alger puis à Oran, et les autorités algériennes lui ont organisé un accueil exceptionnel. Pour Paris, il s'agit, après les dix années de guerre civile qui ont dévasté l'Algérie, de regarder désormais « vers l'avenir » et de « relancer » les relations entre les deux pays. Lundi, devant les parlementaires algériens, M. Chirac devrait souligner la destinée commune de la France et de l'Algérie, plaider pour la démocratie et la relance de réformes économiques aujourd'hui en panne. Histoire et mémoire seront également présentes lors de ce voyage. M. Chirac se rendra au Monument des martyrs algériens de la guerre d'indépendance et dans un ancien cimetière français. Cette visite devrait également relancer les relations économiques entre les deux pays, la France étant le premier partenaire commercial de l'Algérie.

► La première visite d'État d'un président français depuis 1962

► Une déclaration solennelle signée par Jacques Chirac et Abdelaziz Bouteflika

► Dans un discours devant le Parlement, M. Chirac devrait faire l'éloge de la démocratie

► ONG et familles de disparus s'inquiètent

Lire pages 2 et 3 et l'éditorial page 11

Alger, la ville, le jour, la nuit

AVANT la visite de Jacques Chirac, une équipe de journalistes du Monde s'est promenée à Alger en toute liberté.
Lire notre dossier pages I à VIII

La guerre inéluctable de Washington

À L'ISSUE d'une réunion technique avec des experts des Nations unies, l'Irak a annoncé que la destruction des missiles prohibés Al-Samoud 2, réclamée par les inspecteurs, commencerait samedi 1ᵉʳ mars. Toutefois, le porte-parole de la Maison Blanche a présenté cette décision comme un élément du « jeu de tromperie » pratiqué

changement de régime à Bagdad. Pour l'administration américaine, l'Irak a annoncé que la destruction des missiles en question ne sont que la « partie émergée de l'iceberg ». Pour sa part, le ministre français des affaires étrangères, Dominique de Villepin, a estimé que la décision de Bagdad « confirme que les inspections donnent des résultats ». C'est également l'avis

► Bagdad annonce la destruction de ses missiles

► Une « tromperie » selon les Américains

PATRIMOINE

Bartabas installe son Académie équestre dans les écuries du roi

France

litical current that wants to see decentralization and a move to a federal constitution. It's against the history of France!" In the 2002 presidential elections, he received only 5% of the votes and was consigned to irrelevance. Unfortunately the reform proposals did not bring peace; in 2001 alone there were 28 killings in the murky world of separatists and gangsters. There was also scant interest in Corsica among the electorate. The Senate objected to the devolution of legislative powers. Finally the Constitutional Council ruled in 2002 that it was unconstitutional to give Corsica limited autonomy. It determined that other parts of the reform, such as teaching the Corsican language in local schools and giving tax incentives for regional investment, were all right.

Greater autonomy for Corsica is on hold. Prime Minister Raffarin visited Corsica in 2002 to announce that his approach is identical to that of his predecessor except that Corsican devolution would be placed into an overall policy of greater decentralization in all of France. The government's plan is to take some powers from the central government and give them to the regions, which would be authorized to bypass Paris on some aspects of tax collection and spending. The constitutional description of France as "an indivisible, lay, democratic and social republic" would be amended to add the words, "its organization is decentralized." Thus Corsica, which is to receive close to $2 billion in development aid over 15 years, would become a "precursor" for this re-

France welcomes the euro

form. But 51% of Corsican voters rejected this plan in a July 2003 referendum.

ECONOMY

After World War II France experienced an economic miracle no less impressive than that of West Germany. The U.S. Marshall Plan, economic planning, membership in the EU and de-colonization were important factors in this success. It possesses enough raw materials to supply about half of its overall needs, and it has a diversified and modern industrial base and a highly skilled labor force, 25% of which is employed in industry and 74% in services (producing 71% of GDP). Women constitute 43% of the work force, compared with 36% in 1968. With its cultural riches and geographic beauty, France employs many people in its tourist industry; it is the world's most visited country, just ahead of the U.S., Spain and Italy. It had 60 million visitors in 1996, but the French do not reciprocate. With more second homes than any other nation, 90% of them stay in France for their holidays.

By 1995 it had become the fourth richest country in the world, despite the fact that it has only 1% of the world's population. Household assets doubled from 1970 to 1995. Overall production rose threefold between 1946 and 1966, after having only doubled between 1889 and 1940. In the two decades following 1967, its economy grew an average of 3.3% per year. Its trade surplus continues to grow, and its high–tech industries in aerospace, transportation, electronics, telecommunication, and software are among the most competitive in the world.

At 2.6% in 2003 its inflation was the lowest in four decades. By contrast, unemployment, while slowly declining, stood at 9.3% in 2003 (more than twice that among the young and 22% and rising for unskilled workers). One major reason for the problem is the high cost of French labor ($17.10 per hour on average in the manufacturing sector). Employers must pay a minimum wage of ca. $1,100 per month, plus an added 40% in benefits. It is politically impossible to create new jobs by cutting the pay and benefits of those working. Half the households in France pay no income tax. To strengthen incentives to invest and to produce, the government in 2000 lowered the tax rates. The top personal rates dropped from 54% to 52.5% and corporate rates to 33.3%. Low-paid workers pay lower social-security contributions, and the car license tax was abolished. Trumpeted by the government as the most dramatic tax cut in a half century, the changes still leave the French with a higher tax bill than most of their competitors: 45% of GDP. Government

spending accounts for over 53% of GDP, far above the OECD average of 38% and 30% in the U.S.

The workweek was lowered to 35 hours for private companies with more than 20 employees beginning in 2000 (smaller companies a few years later). After fighting hard against the new law, employers discovered that by averaging the hours over 52 weeks they now have more flexibility to increase hours in busy periods and reduce them during slower times. They can respond better to seasonal demands. Thus workers find themselves doing shift work at awkward hours and six–day weeks. Also coffee breaks do not count in the 35 hours. Although wages are seldom cut, they are often being held down. It became clear that the new law would not create new jobs. These unintended results disappointed many employees, who did what frustrated French workers always do: many went on strike against the 35–hour week!

France has usually had relatively peaceful labor relations. In part, this is because France's social security programs have taken much of the heat out of the issue of unequal income distribution. Only 8% of the work force in the private sector belongs to labor unions (compared with 9% in the U.S.), and membership continues to decline. However, in the public sector the share is about one-fourth (compared with 37% in America). This gives France the least unionized work force of any industrialized country. Nevertheless, its unions are socially and politically strong in spite of their numerical weakness. The reason is that they have an ensconced place in positions of power. They and employers are joint managers of the health, retirement and social-security organizations, dominate company employee committees, and belong to every labor tribunal. Unions representing public-sector workers are a mighty force, and they insist at a minimum on preserving what their members already have. The Communists dominate the largest union, the General Confederation of Labor (CGT). The French Democratic Confederation of Labor (CFDT) displays moderation, as does the leftist but anti–communist Workers Force (FO). The powerful National Education Federation (FEN) and the Confederation of Supervisory Grades (CGC) organize teachers and engineers and skilled technical personnel. Some non–unionized French, especially in the public sector, belong to so–called "coordinations," ad hoc bodies that serve as liaisons between competing unions or spring up in protest at the unions' inattention.

Its economy is still troubled by certain traditional structural weaknesses, such as an over centralized state bureaucracy.

It has a clumsy system of distribution due partly to the relatively large number of small retail shops. In 1973 parliament passed a law giving locally elected officials and representatives of commerce and crafts the right to veto the opening of new supermarkets. Not until 1989 did supermarkets do more business than small neighborhood stores.

Although many signs of the old France remain, the economy is being modernized at an impressive rate. The Jospin Socialist government privatized far more of the country's industry than its center-right predecessors had done, leaving about 1,500 companies (compared with 3,500 in 1986) in which the state has a controlling share. In 2003 the state also continued to hold large shares of some of France's key industries: 25% of Renault, 22% of Thomson Multimedia and 55% of France Télécom. One sign of the ascendancy of the "new economy" is the fact that half the graduates of the elite Ecole Polytechnique now goes into private business, rather than into the civil service or large corporations. The result in the 21st century is an undeniable boom.

The Socialist government also quietly legalizing practices that once raised ideological red flags: Stock options for young companies were legitimized in 1999, and private pension funds, heretofore illegal, are being discussed under the innocuous heading, "workers' savings plans." Nevertheless, fewer than 13% of French own shares, compared to 23% of Britons.

The Socialists were unable to introduce a major reform of France's unsustainable "pay-as-you-go" pension system, whereby current workers are taxed to pay pensions of today's retired people. With a birthrate of only 1.9 children per woman, the French face a demographic time bomb: whereas there are two workers today supporting one pensioner, by 2040 there will only be one. The conservative government made reform of the complex pension system a major campaign promise in 2002. They cannot duck the issue even though the president and prime minister are aware that it was street demonstrations that had brought down the earlier center-right coalition in 1997. Public sector workers can retire after 37.5 years with a full pension (an income of 97% of the working population), private-sector after 40 years. This means that many can retire at age 55 with a full pension, in some cases at 50. Only 16% of French citizens aged 60–65 are still working. Health care, costing 10% of GDP, remains among the best in the world, and the poor receive free treatment.

Agriculture

1% of Frenchmen are now employed full-time in agriculture (compared with more than a third in 1945); they produce a mere 3.3% of GDP. France is self–sufficient in all foodstuffs except tropical produce, and it is the major agricultural country in the EU, producing 21% of the Community's total output (before enlargement to 25 members). It is the world's fourth-largest producer of cereals and meat. Only the U.S. exports more food and drink products.

France remains one of the world's leading producers of wine although by 2002 its wine industry was unable to sell all it produces. Winegrowers in Beaujolais, Burgundy and elsewhere face ever stiffer competition from aggressive wine-exporting countries like Australia and Chile. However, the main reason for declining wine revenues comes from a dramatic reduction in wine consumption in France itself. Sipping wine throughout the day has gone out of fashion in France. The average Frenchman today drinks fewer than 60 liters of wine a year compared with 120 in the mid-1960s. Desperate winegrowers even resorted in 2002 to suing the government over its campaign against drunk driving, claiming that it is illegal to discriminate between products, even those that make one intoxicated and those that do not.

As in other European countries, the farm lobby wields influence out of all proportion to its numbers. French farmers get a fourth of the EU's agricultural subsidies (CAP). The combined EU and French gov-

French bread for euros

Courtesy: Central Audiovisual Library, European Commission

ernment subsidies account for half the farmers' income, but they are distributed very unevenly. A fifth of the largest and richest farmers, especially the grain growers, receive 80% of the funds. Some, such as wine producers, were traditionally able to compete well on the world market and therefore had no need for the assistance.

The importance of agriculture, not only for the French economy but for the country's emotional rural roots in *la France profonde*, was demonstrated in the farmers' violent reaction to a compromise reached in 1992 between the EU and the U.S. regarding GATT limits on agricultural subsidies. They took their tractors and manure to the streets of France, targeting not

A farmyard near Tours

France

only the National Assembly and the European Parliament, but also Coca–Cola plants and the 790 McDonald's restaurants, each of which serves 1,000 to 1,500 customers per day. All of them use only French farm products. However, the facts that Coke had cornered half of the soft drink market by the mid–1990s and McDonald's continued to grow steadily gave them symbolic value.

The emotion and fury of their clashes with the police underscored their intense concern about the effects a slash in subsidies would have on rural France. President Chirac was able to persuade the German government to postpone full-scale reform of CAP until well after EU enlargement in 2004. Agriculture Minister Hervé Gaymard vowed in 2003 to continue protecting farmers from free trade. He argued that one must start from the premise that "farm products are more than marketable goods." Farming is part of France's culture. Since they are literally rooted in the land, farmers cannot be transferred from one location to another like factories. The main issue is protection of France's farm interests, not of its consumers. Food constitutes only 16% of an EU family's budget compared with over 50% when CAP started in 1968.

Already barely surviving economically, many farmers would be forced off the land and into crowded cities, leaving depopulated regions behind them. From 1970 to the end of the century the number of farms declined from 1.6 million to 700,000, of which only half were run by full–time farmers; 40,000 farms go out of business each year. Cattle farmers and consumers were jolted by the discovery of "mad cow disease" (BSE) in French herds, with the possibility that BSE-tainted beef had to be sold in grocery stores. If only one animal is discovered to be infected, the entire herd must be destroyed. French beef was banned in several European countries, and panic spread in France.

Energy

France is concerned about its future energy sources. Its energy consumption doubled during the 1970s. It is heavily dependent upon the importation of fossil fuels. It imports 96%. It obtains roughly half its needs from Persian Gulf countries, one–fourth from Mediterranean countries and one–eighth from Black Africa. It imports 90% of its natural gas. Some is produced in the southwestern region of Aquitaine, but these wells are rapidly being depleted.

By September 2000 the high tax levied on fuel (75% of the price) drove gasoline prices to about $4 per gallon, and diesel at the pump had climbed 50% since the beginning of the year. This sparked severe

MARS 1990: 32ᵉ RECENSEMENT DE LA POPULATION POUR PRÉPARER L'AVENIR DE LA FRANCE.

Toi, moi, lui, tout le monde compte.

RECENSEMENT RÉALISÉ PAR VOTRE MAIRIE ET L'INSEE

Poster for the French census

demonstrations in strike-prone France. Truckers, joined by farmers, ambulance and taxi drivers, and Paris tour-boat operators, stopped work and blockaded oil refineries and fuel storage depots. Paris and other cities were partially brought to a standstill. The government stated that it would not give in, but then it reduced diesel fuel taxes after all. This capitulation helped spark similar outbursts elsewhere in Europe. The events underscored that while the "new economy" has contributed much to France's economic boom, the old economy remains very much alive.

Nevertheless, France produced about half the total energy it needs. The reason is that it launched a full–scale program to develop nuclear power, especially fast breeder reactors. Now Europe's largest producer of nuclear power, producing half the EU's nuclear energy, it is the world's fourth richest country in uranium, with 10% of all known reserves. Its Eurodif enrichment plant at Tricastin represents a third of the Western world's capacity and feeds a third of the world's nuclear reactors. By 2001, 77% of France's electricity (compared with 19% in the U.S., 28% in Japan, and 33% in Europe as a whole) was generated by 56 nuclear reactors. In 1994 it fired up the world's only working fast–breeder reactor, which creates plutonium while it generates electricity. Nuclear power provides the country with the EU's cheapest electricity, except in Denmark. France even has an overcapacity in electrical generation that allows it to export about 13% of its production.

There are critics who argue that France has become overly dependent upon a sin-

gle energy source and that such heavy use is unsafe. But its reactors are among the safest in the world. Its decision to build a single standard reactor design not only reduces construction costs but enables technical personnel to be used interchangeably in all the sites, rather than being trained to work only in one site. Because of violent local opposition, it has still not succeeded in finding a deep–storage site for nuclear waste. In the meantime, low–level waste is stored above ground, while high–level waste is stored in vitrified form in both steel canisters and concrete pits at La Hague and Marcoule.

CULTURE

The French have long fought what some critics see as a futile battle to preserve the purity of the French language, which is spoken as a native tongue by about 90 million persons throughout the world. This struggle is waged particularly against the powerful onslaught of the English language. One author even wrote a book with the provocative title *Parlez–vous Franglais?*, "franglais" being a combination of the words meaning French and English. The number of pupils learning English in school quadrupled in the 1980s. French scientists find it increasingly necessary to publish their works in English, and they often choose to deliver their lectures in English at international conferences held in France.

Ordinary Frenchmen have adopted English words so quickly that in 1975 the parliament passed the Bas–Lauriol law requiring that trade names, advertising material, product instructions and receipts use only the French language. The text of the law even specified French replacements for such common expressions:

French model

"savoir–faire" (for "le know–how") "boutique franche" (for "le duty–free shop"), "mini–marge" (for "le discount"), "aéroglisseur" (for "le hovercraft"), "credit–bail" (for "le leasing"), "matériel" (for "le hardware"), "grosporteur" (for "le jumbo jet"), "astronef" (for "le spacecraft"), "boteur" (for "le bulldozer"), "retrospectif" (for "le flashback"), "spectacle solo" (for "le one–man show"), "palmarès" (for "le hit parade"), "baladeur" (for "le Walkman"), "mercatique" (for "le marketing"), and "zonage" (for "le zoning"). Some words escaped the sharp eyes of the language legislators: "le football," "le shopping," "le parking," "le living," and "le footing" (a word which is gradually being replaced in common usage by "le jogging"!).

Economic–Cultural Influences

Whether "le come–back" of pure French will succeed depends in part on "le marketing" of American investors in France. In 1983, the state's High Committee of the French Language stepped in to ban English words in the audio–visual field. Thus, "cameraman" and "close–up" became "cadreur" and "gros plan," and "drive–in theater" gave way to "ciné park." It also banned Anglo–Saxon terms in all government publications and speeches, legal contracts and schoolbooks. The counterattack has been generally successful in the computer field, such as "logiciel" (software) and "la Toile" (the web), despite the persistence of a few terms such as un batch of data or un floppy disk.

In 1996 the High Committee sued the American sponsors of an English-only site on the World Wide Web because the material is not also available in French. It was thrown out of court in 1997 on a technicality. President Chirac argued, "the stakes are clear. If, in the new media, our language, our programs, our creations are not strongly present, the young generation of our country will be economically and culturally marginalized." The government has created a process to prevent this from happening. Seven committees, including one in the Economy Ministry, suggests French replacements for English terms. These suggestions are sent to the Academie Française. If it and the Economy Ministry approve the changes, their use becomes mandatory for public bodies and law courts.

The French government wages a difficult battle. By 1995, 83% of high school pupils in EU countries learn English (84% in France itself), compared with 32% learning French and 16% German. Only in Romania do more secondary-school pupils learn French than English. In an editorial, the *Washington Post* spoofed the apparent obsession with enforcing language purity by imagining a bureau in Washington sending a disk jockey a letter like this: "It has come to our attention that you have repeatedly used the word 'taco' to describe the comestible for which the officially sanctioned word is 'corn meal crispette.' Please be advised that ..." *A Dictionary of Official Terms* contains 3,500 new French words for advertising, broadcasting, public notices, official documents and those dealing with goods, services and conditions of work. All international conferences held in France must allow participants to speak in French if they want and must provide French translations of foreign–language speeches and documents.

French is the mother tongue of about 90 million people in the world and the occasional language of another 60 million. As such, it ranks only ninth in the world, behind English, Spanish and Portuguese. The French insist that it remain one of the two official languages in most international bodies, but only a tenth of the documents produced by the UN Secretariat are in French. In an attempt to promote use of

France

the language worldwide, France also foots the bulk of the bill for Francophonie, an assortment of 53 countries from Congo to Cambodia who enjoy "a shared use of the French language." Since French need not be the country's dominant or official language and since the membership includes such lands as Egypt and Moldova, it is doubtful that this organization is effective in achieving France's lingual goals.

The government's policy of rejuvenating France's cultural life did not work well, despite a doubling of the Culture Ministry's budget since 1981. The number of French feature films exported declined even though subsidies to the film industry were increased by 800%. Fifty percent of the films French cinema fans went to see in 2001 were American, almost double the proportion a decade ago, but down from 63% in 2000 and below the EU average of 70%. In 1991 the top ten films in terms of attendance were all American. In 1995 audiences in France for French films were half as large as a decade earlier, while audiences for American films had not changed. This worried many French: in a 1996 poll, 70% of the respondents feared that American culture has an "excessive" influence in TV, and 59% in movies. By 2002 this had changed. In 2001 41% of ticket sales were for French films, up from 28.5% in 2000.

The French still make more films than do their European neighbors. In 1990 French filmmakers put the swashbuckling and poetic classic, *Cyrano de Bergerac*, on screen, staring Gérard Depardieu, who won the best actor award at the Cannes Film Festival and was nominated for an Academy Award. In the 21st century the lead has been taken by a new wave of creative directors who are products of French film schools and criticism: Olivier Assayas, Catherine Breillat, Claire Denis

and Erick Zonca. The 2001 blockbusters, *Le Fabuleux Destin d'Amélie* (The Fabulous Destiny of Amelie) and *Le Pacte des Loups* (The Pact of the Wolves), were smash hits in France and drew large crowds abroad. French films are making a comeback.

Television has been influenced even more strongly by America. The most popular soap opera in 1992 was called "Santa Barbara," and a French clone of the game show, "Wheel of Fortune," topped the popularity charts. "Who Wants to Be a Millionaire" and "The Weak Link" became the new hits. Reality TV made its debut in 2001 with "Loft Story," which drew one of the largest TV audiences ever and divided France between millions of viewers who love such low-brow entertainment and incensed critics who dismissed such trash television as the dumbing-down of French society. Ratings for American programs are as high as for French ones. About 70% of foreign TV shows purchased are from the U.S. Nevertheless, by law, 60% of TV programming must be European (of which two–thirds French); 40% of songs on FM radio must be French, instead of less than 20% before the law was passed. Many of the teeth were extracted from this law in 1995 when the Constitutional Council ruled that it conflicted with freedom of expression.

Anti–Americanism still exists. De Gaulle's humiliation during World War II is no longer relevant, and thanks in part to the writings of Alexander Solzhenitsyn the Soviet model fell from grace in French eyes. *Le Nouvel Observateur* even criticized anti-Americanism as "socialism for imbeciles." The dethroning of French as the world's cultural leader has hurt many Frenchmen. However, as ex-communist and singer Yves Montand remarked, "if America has succeeded in invading us culturally, it is because we like it."

Perhaps "invasion" is the wrong word: a 1991 poll revealed that whereas two–thirds of U.S. respondents believed French culture was important to America, only 44% of the French repaid the compliment. In 1999 two–thirds of French respondents said they "do not feel close to the American people," and 60% believed the U.S. is too influential culturally. These feelings were strongest among young and educated. One sign of America's acceptability was the hard–won contract negotiated by a Socialist government to build a $4 billion Disneyland 20 miles east of downtown Paris. It opened in 1992 promising to create 12,000 new jobs. The only saving grace for hard–line Americanophobes is that Disney, himself, is of French lineage; the family's name was not Disney at all, but *D'Istngy*!

In 1999–2000 the reaction against American popular culture was perhaps symbolized best by the antics of José Bové, a farmer who became something of a national hero for trashing one of McDonald's many new restaurants in the southern town of Millau. Using tractors, he literally brought down the roof. This act, along with protests at 40 other McDonald's establishments around France, was ostensibly in protest against the American decision to levy high tariffs on certain luxury foods imported from France, such as Roquefort cheese and *pâté foie gras*, in retaliation for the EU's and France's decision to ban American hormone-treated beef. By linking French culture with the protection of its food, Bové enormously widened his support within French society. President Chirac joined in by announcing that he "detests McDonald's food," and Prime Minister Jospin also went on record that "I am personally not very pro-McDo," as the chain is called in France.

In order not to turn Bové into a martyr, McDonald's decided not to take civil action against him. Instead it launched a publicity campaign stressing that the franchises in France are owned by French, employ thousands of French workers, and use French products almost exclusively. Nevertheless, he was tried in July 2000 for his destructive acts and sentenced to several months of prison. Over 40,000 of his fans came to Millau to cheer him as he went to court. In 2002 France's highest court upheld his conviction and six-week jail term; he exhausted all appeals. In 2003 the court ordered him to serve an additional 10 months in prison for damaging fields of genetically modified rice in 1998.

Bové's crusade taps into far deeper issues gnawing at the French, including fear of globalization, a general annoyance with the vigor of the American economy, and nostalgia for a bygone way of life, including long lunches. French voters on

Trompe l'oeil: false painted storefront in Lyon. Which are the real pedestrians?

both the left and right instinctively mistrust globalization, which erodes French sovereignty and smacks of unrestrained free markets and American hegemony. The conventional wisdom is not that globalization should be prevented, but that it should be regulated. A 2000 poll found 12% of respondents who admired the United States, 46% who were either critical of or worried by it, and 75% who favored less American influence on "economic and financial globalization."

Academie Française

Since 1635 the "Academie Française" has striven, in the words of its first patron, Cardinal Richelieu, to "preserve the purity of the French language." The body itself selects individually forty distinguished literary figures known as "immortals." They meet every Thursday in order to compile a French grammar book (finally completed in 1932) and a dictionary that is to serve as a criterion for good usage rather than as a list of all the words in the French language. Each word proposed for inclusion is first brought up before a special committee and then is voted on by the Academy as a whole. In 1986 the Academy added 912 new words; three-fourths of them were based on English or technical terms.

Such great French writers as Voltaire, Racine and Victor Hugo were members, but no female writer, such as Madame de Staël or George Sand (pseudonym for Aurore Dupin, later Baroness Dudevant), ever managed to break the Academy's all-male tradition. Finally, in 1980 it chose Marguerite Yourcenar, who at age 16 had begun to publish her string of poems, novels and historical works, culminating in her monumental Memoirs of Hadrian. When World War II broke out, she decided to join the faculty of Sarah Lawrence College in New York, and she became an American citizen in 1947. After teaching ten years, she moved to a wood frame house on Mount Desert Island in Maine, where she could escape the literary circles and gossip of Paris and New York, which she detested.

In 1989 the French Academy found itself in the midst of a storm over a proposal to simplify French spelling by, for example, eliminating the circumflex accent in such words as être, replacing the "x" on the end of plurals such as bureaux with a simple "s," writing "f" instead of "ph" (thus filosofes!), and doing away with unexpected double consonants in words like traditionnel when the noun is tradition. A government survey had revealed that about 20% of the adult population is functionally illiterate, twice the percentage in Britain. One poll of teachers revealed that 90% favor making French easier to write in order to combat both such illiteracy and

to enable French to hold its own as a world language.

Proponents of simplification point out that French has in the past been changed by decree and that another change is long overdue since the last one came in 1832 when King Louis–Philippe ordered all public servants to conform strictly to the French Academy's dictionary. As expected, the opposition to change is strong and furious. One teacher warned his colleagues acidly to "keep your filthy hands off our language." Therefore, the Academy ruled in 1991 that changes should not be enforced, but should instead be subject to the "test of time." They have been blithely ignored.

The language watchdogs were stirred again in 1998 when the Academie Française, whose members wear green medieval costumes and carry swords when they meet, stoutly resisted female government ministers having themselves referred to as "Madame la Ministre" (the word being masculine). The "immortals" cringed when the education ministry declared that all women's job titles should be linguistically feminized: a female member of parliament should be a "députée," a lawyer an advocate, an inspector an inspectrice. Just how much the French admire their wordsmiths was revealed again on November 23, 1996, when André Malraux, a wartime hero, adventurer, and writer was re-interred in the Panthéon. The ceremony was televised live on national TV, and his creative career was discussed exhaustively in the other media.

Although all citizens of France can speak French, there are many tongues spoken by ethnic minorities, primarily on the periphery of the country. These languages include Provençal, Breton, Corsican, Italian, Catalan, Basque, Flemish and Alsacian. In 1993 the government faced protests because of its refusal to sign the European Charter on Minority Languages, adopted in 1988 by the European Parliament. In 1999 the Socialist government adopted only 39 of the Charter's 98 clauses and again set off a wave of nationalist passion. The youngest member of the Academie Française, Jean-Marie Rouart responded defensively: "At the very moment that our language is being bastardized by Anglo-Saxon expressions, it is to be undermined from within by having to compete with local dialects!"

Immigration and Ethnic Minorities

France's World Cup championship soccer team in 1998 demonstrated how multicultural France has become. Of 22 players, eight were non–white (most of whom born and bred in France), another four of recent Armenian, Argentine, Kalmyk or Spanish descent, not including the Bretons

and Basques on the team. France has always been a magnet for foreigners, and today a third of all Frenchmen have at least one foreign grandparent. In 1991, 11% of residents were foreign–born. Six percent of the population had foreign passports in 1994. This is the same percentage as 25 years ago, but then three–fourths were Europeans compared with only 40% now; 39% of foreigners come from North Africa and 6% from Sub–Saharan Africa.

Partly as a result of frightening unemployment, non–European immigrants face growing rejection and violence in communities where they live in large numbers. Except for music and sports, non–whites are noticeably underrepresented in business, politics, media and the professions. In parliament some non–whites represent overseas French colonies, but only one had a seat from metropolitan France. That seat was lost in the conservative electoral landslide in 2002, when a black presidential candidate, Christiane Taubira, an economist from French Guiana, won 2.3% of the votes. Only one out of 36,560 mayors and none of the regional parliamentary members is not white. Yet they are visible in the streets. Blacks official number about 1.5 million, but the unofficial number is higher.

Mosques spring up next to empty churches, and exotic North African commercial establishments are everywhere. Some Muslim girls wear scarves to school, igniting emotional debates about whether such headgear should be permitted in secular schools. Violence has escalated in crowded schools and bleak housing blocks heavily occupied by North African immigrants; in 1998 alone 8,000 cars were burned by rampaging youths. Eight in ten Frenchmen said in 1999 that urban violence has reached "unprecedented proportions," and many blame foreigners and call on the government to act.

Called Beurs, a term that North Africans do not consider derogatory, French–born Arabs sometimes face resistance from their own families when they try to integrate into French society. The animosity toward them has helped far–right parties, such as the National Front, to make significant electoral gains in those areas. In their defense, an anti–discrimination lobby, SOS–Racisme has emerged. It is needed, as a 1993 poll indicated: 94% of the French regard racism to be widespread, and 42% confess to be "a bit" or "quite" racist themselves.

France has the largest Muslim population in Europe: ca. five million or 7% of the total are Arab or Muslim, a figure that climbs in Marseilles to about 10% Arab and 17% Muslim. Half are French citizens. France is very vulnerable to a spillover of

121

France

Parakeets for sale, Paris
Photo by Susan L. Thompson

violence from the Middle East. This occurred in 2002 when conditions of warfare and suicide bombings prevailed in Israel and Palestine. This is a major reason why President Chirac was determined that France not become embroiled in the 2003 war in Iraq; French Muslims cheered the president for his decision to abstain.

France also has Europe's largest Jewish population (650,000, the fourth largest after the U.S., Israel and Russia), which becomes a soft target to Arab radicals in times of tension. Despite the prime minister's plea that "passions that flare up in the Middle East must not flare up here," an appalling desecration of Jewish graves occurred at Carpentras, a synagogue was gutted by fire in Marseille over Passover, and attacks on Jewish sites dramatically increased. Violent hate crimes quadrupled in 2002 to the highest level in a decade, and more than half were aimed at Jews, mainly perpetrated by Muslims. Muslim leaders in France condemned the violence but could not prevent it. These attacks fed the existing fear of rising crime and a feeling of vulnerability to global terrorism since September 11, 2001.

With its large Muslim population and colonial history in North Africa, France is a kind of bellwether in Europe for dealing with a Muslim population. The center-right government elected in 2002 seeks to create a model Muslim citizenry, which would be French-speaking and law-abiding, would honor the 1905 French law establishing separation between church and state, would incline females not to wear veils at work or school, and above all to consider themselves French first and Muslim second. The government adopted a two-prong strategy to achieve this: give Muslims a "place at the table" while at the same time regulating their activities through, for example, French intelligence monitoring of Friday sermons in mosques and prayer centers and deporting radical imams (clerics) who do not have citizenship.

To help integrate Muslims into French society, the government created in 2003 a French Council of the Muslim Faith, with members elected by representatives of the country's mosques and prayer groups. It is a platform for discussions with local and national governments about such things as building more mosques and Muslim cemeteries and wearing veils in schools. Catholics, Protestants and Jews have had such councils for decades. Participation was high, with 992 of 1,200 eligible mosques voting. The authorities were not entirely pleased with the outcome of the elections since fundamentalist Muslims in the Union of Islamic Organizations in France came in second and won a strong voice alongside moderate groups. This prompted the government to warn that it would deport immigrant Muslim leaders if they espoused violence or anti-Semitism.

There is widespread uneasiness over the presence of an estimated 5 million immigrants, the majority of whom Arabs and blacks. A 1998 poll revealed that almost 60% of respondents thought there were too many Arabs in France (down from 71% five years earlier); over a quarter believed there were too many blacks (down from almost a half), and 15% said there were too many Jews. Four out of ten admitted to being "racist" or "fairly racist," almost twice as many as in Germany, Britain or Italy. Other polls revealed that half no longer feel "at home" in France and want a "large number" of immigrants to leave. Half expressed a belief in the "inequality of the races."

Earlier immigrant groups are often among the opponents of the new arrivals. Portuguese– and Spanish–born workers in the Marseilles area are among Le Pen's most fervent supporters. But the polls show that racist feeling goes far beyond the 15% who vote for the National Front. About 28% of those who say they are "racist" or "fairly racist" vote for leftist parties. Le Pen's ranting against "invading Muslim hordes" who allegedly threaten Frenchmen with the same fate as America's "Red Indians—annihilated by immigration," prove so seductive that the leaders of more respectable parties borrowed from his xenophobic vocabulary. Chirac once criticized their "odor" and "noise." Giscard d'Estaing warned of an "invasion" and called for nationality laws based on blood to replace the statutes that grant French citizenship automatically to anyone born on French soil. By 1996, almost a half of respondents said they share some of Le Pen's ideas although two-thirds claimed to have been "shocked" by his comments that races are unequal and that the French national soccer team was not "representative" of the country since so many of the players are non–white.

There is positive news, though. A study in 1998 showed that six in ten white Frenchmen say they have friends among "minority groups." The same number says they would not try to stop their child or sibling from marrying a Muslim. In fact, half of boys and a quarter of girls of Algerian origin in France have their first steady relationship with a white. Fremainville, a tiny farming hamlet just outside Paris, even adopted a black Marianne, the potent bare–breasted symbol of French republican liberty springing from the French Revolution.

The government responded by declaring that France "can no longer be a land of immigration." It introduced policies to stop the influx of foreign workers, refugees, and their families, as well as to tighten citizenship rules, while buckling down to speed the integration of foreigners already there. The number of asylum–seekers was reduced from 61,000 in 1991 to 20,000 in 1996 (only 3,000 were accepted), and the number of other foreign immigrants was cut by a third. However, once they arrive, most illegal immigrants are unlikely ever to leave. For instance, close to 44,000 foreigners were ordered to leave in 2000, but only 9,230 were expelled. From 400,000 to a million illegal aliens remain underground, despite a dramatic increase in forced deportations. By 1999 the Jospin government had awarded legal status to 80,000 of them.

France's law-and-order interior minister, Nicolas Sarkozy, carefully explained: "France needs immigrants, but France cannot and should not welcome all immigrants." Determined to crack down on illegal migrants and people-smuggling networks, the center-right government that took power in 2002 made a decisive move the end of that year. Under pressure by Britain, it closed an overcrowded and uncontrollable refugee camp at Sangatte on the north coast set up by the Red Cross three years earlier. Located near the entrance to the "Chunnel," it had attracted thousands of immigrants who were trying to enter Britain illegally and who were willing to risk their lives to hop the fast-moving trains or follow the tracks through the darkness to the other end.

Religion

Almost nine out of ten Frenchmen are baptized Roman Catholic, and two–thirds describe themselves as Catholic. Since 1905 churches in France have been separated from the state, except in Alsace,

Lorraine and the Moselle Department, which then belonged to Germany. In these areas, church–state relations are governed by the Concordat which Napoleon I signed with the Vatican in 1801. Protestants constitute barely 2% of the population, but their influence far outweighs their numbers in business, the civil service and intelligencia. Three of 14 prime ministers, including Lionel Jospin, Michel Rocard and Couve de Murville, are Protestants. In the French public mind, Protestantism is almost synonymous with austerity and moral rigor.

Fewer than one in ten French still goes to Mass regularly. A 1997 poll by the Catholic newspaper, *La Croix*, indicated that two–thirds of the youth believe that the church has little influence on their lives. Because of the principle of "secularity," whereby the state must be strictly separated from religion, the government's involvement in the Pope's visit to France in 1996 sparked months of controversy and hostility. Also, many French resent any attempt by the Catholic Church to interfere in their private lives. Contraception is widely practiced, and abortion is common.

By 1994 the number of weddings had fallen to 254,000, which was 40% fewer than in 1972, and only half those weddings took place in church, compared with almost all of them only a quarter century earlier. France had the lowest marriage rate in Europe after Scandinavia, but by 2002 marriage was experiencing a strong resurgence. In 1998, one in seven couples lived together without marriage, a number seven times higher than a couple of decades ago and double the proportion a decade ago; only 7% of French respondents found such an arrangement "living in sin."

The Socialist government decided in 1999 that it was time to offer some legal recognition to the new kinds of unions although it refused to call them "marriages." It introduced "civil solidarity pacts" (PACs) allowing couples, of the same sex or not, to enter into a union and be entitled to the same rights as married couples in such areas as income tax, inheritance, housing and social welfare, though it does not grant homosexuals the right to adopt children. Any two people sharing a home can sign a contract before a court clerk, and any partner can revoke it by giving the other person three-months advanced written notice. Charging that this law further undermines the family, the Catholic Church, half the country's mayors, and 200,000 irate marchers in the streets of Paris vigorously protested against it. A poll taken in 2000, one year after the PACs were introduced, revealed that 70% of respondents favor them. The

opinion survey revealed other evidence of attitudinal evolution: As many French favor homosexual marriage as oppose it. Two years after the introduction of the PACs there was no discernible effect on the number of weddings since most of the 45,000 PACS were between gay couples.

With the average French woman bearing only 1.8 children in the mid–1990s, there was fear that the country faced the prospect of a declining native population. But by 2002, the fertility rate had risen to 1.9%, the highest in Europe, surpassing Ireland at 1.89. More than 40% of all babies are now born out of wedlock, the highest rates in Europe outside the Nordic countries. Clearly illegitimacy no longer carries a stigma. When President Chirac proudly announced in 1996 the birth of his first grandchild, no one seemed to care that his daughter Claude was not married to the child's father, an ex–judo champion turned television presenter.

EDUCATION

Control over the school system is concentrated in Paris. Education is free and compulsory between the ages of six and 16, and approximately five out of six children attend public schools. Mitterrand stirred up much controversy by promising to do away with private schools, which receive state subsidies, and to create a unified, secular school system. A half million persons protested in the streets against this policy, the largest public demonstration in French history. Such widespread protests prompted him to withdraw the contentious private school bill in 1984.

From ages five to 11 children attend elementary school, and then they spend four years in an "intermediate school," called a "college." After this, they proceed to a high school, called a "lycée," which provides either vocational training or a baccalaureate degree leading to university study. In 1998, 75% were still in school pursuing the "bac," double the proportion only a decade earlier. Over half pass it. The examination for the baccalaureate is a traditional intellectual one, and France is one of the few countries that still includes philosophy as one of its obligatory high school subjects.

About 700,000 students are enrolled in the 57 universities or special advanced schools, and about a third of these students are in the 13 universities in the Paris region. In 1968 a fourth of 18–year–olds and 4% of 20–year–olds were in a school or university; in 1990 the comparable figures stood at 55% and 22%. The rapid growth of enrollment has brought severe overcrowding. Graduates find that their degrees are now worth less and that there are too few jobs for them after graduation.

The unemployment line never threatens graduates of the elitist *Grandes Ecoles*, who are selected by highly competitive nation-wide examinations (*concours*) following two further years of intensive preparation in the Lycée after the "bac." Many students at the universities still suffer from a sort of second–class status, as they watch the best jobs being filled by graduates from the *Grandes Ecoles*. Some of the best university students are admitted to these highly selective institutions, which are very prestigious and produce an elite in teaching, industry, government and the armed forces. Three-fourths of the Jospin government and half of the top 200 business bosses had attended a *Grande Ecole*.

Following the military debacle of 1870, the *Ecole des Sciences Politiques* (called "Sciences–Po"), which offers advanced training in political science and economics, was created to improve the quality of senior civil servants. In 2001 *Sciences-Po* caused a stir by introducing a kind of affirmative action plan to create a special admission track for secondary school students in seven poor neighborhoods whose population contains large concentrations of Arab and African immigrants. Such pupils would be exempt from the stiff competitive entrance exams other applicants must pass and would one day make up about 15% of the student body. Although race is not specifically mentioned, the effect would be to have a more racially balanced school. No one disputes that the *Grandes Ecoles* have always recruited almost exclusively from a limited sociological pool of white, well-connected and wealthy families. There is a growing minority of students from farm and working-class families.

After the defeat in 1940 and the shame of Vichy, the *Ecole Nationale d'Administration* (ENA, whose graduates are called *Enarques*), which accepts 120 students (a fourth to a third female) by examination from the other *Grandes Ecoles* each year for the 27–month program, was set up to train elite administrators who would put the interests of the state above their own. All were in Paris until 1992 when ENA was moved to Strasbourg. Study at ENA is particularly important to those persons aspiring to top civil service positions.

Presently about two–thirds of such offices are held by *Enarques*, who form a highly useful informal network of contacts for each other. Among its graduates were all the major contenders for the presidency in 1995—Jacques Chirac, Lionel Jospin, and Edouard Balladur—as well as former President Valery Giscard d'Estaing. Prime Minister Lionel Jospin and five out of seven of his predecessors are *Enarques*. The mayor of Montpellier spoke bitterly of the influential Enarques:

France

"France is still run by civil servants. There is no difference between a socialist Enarque and a neo–Gaullist *Enarque*. They are intelligent, incorrupt and absolutely convinced they are right. The country is run by thousands of little Robespierres." One conservative politician, Alain Madelin, even said in 1997: "Ireland has the IRA, Spain has ETA, Italy the mafia, but France has ENA." However, the glory of ENA is fading somewhat. Between 1995 and 1999, applications for its notoriously difficult entrance exams declined by 30%. *Sciences–Po*, which supplies 90% of the external exam's successful candidates, has a special program to prepare students for the entrance test, but aspirants enrolling in that program have dwindled from 1,000 per year a decade ago to 200 now. A major reason is that in France's changed economic environment, it is the private sector, not the civil service, which beckons ambitious young people.

In addition, there are two *Ecoles Normales Supérieures*, one in Paris—Rue d'Ulm, which concentrates on classical subjects—and another in Lyon, which also teaches such subjects as history and geography. They train the top Lycée and university professors, who must pass a rigorous final examination called the *Agrégation*. Finally, there are the *Hautes Etudes Commerciales*, (HEC) and other business–oriented schools, the *Ecole des Mines*, and similarly specialized schools, such as the military academy at Saint–Cyr. In 1794 the military *Ecole Polytechnique* was established to train top public officials. Cadets begin with one year in the military to undergo officer training and then spend two years doing top-level engineering and scientific study.

In protest against under funding, overcrowding, decrepit buildings, insufficient security at inner–city schools, and bleak employment prospects, especially in non–technical fields, thousands of lycée and university students again took to the streets in 1998 and engaged in pitched bloody battles with the police. One 15–year–old demonstrator was killed. The education minister admitted that the system is "archaic," but he pleaded for patience until reforms could be enacted. Teachers sympathize because half their classes have over 30 pupils, and some have over 40. One result is that one in four teachers requests a transfer or job change every year.

The American film, *Dead Poets Society*, which portrayed a rebellion against a hidebound educational system, had a profound effect on debates in France concerning reform of the school system. The government proposed reforms to humanize the grueling "bac." A major stumbling block for change has been the resistance of powerful teaching unions. In the meantime, many French ask why their once excellent educational system is soaking up

Le Monde

www.lemonde.fr   58ᵉ ANNÉE – Nº 17794 – 1,20 € – FRANCE MÉTROPOLITAINE –   JEUDI 31 JANVIER 2002   FONDATEUR : HUBERT BEUVE-MÉRY – DIRECTEUR : JEAN-MARIE COLOMBANI

George W. Bush désigne ses nouveaux ennemis

Le président américain menace l'Iran, l'Irak, la Corée du Nord et les mouvements islamistes

EN ILE-DE-FRANCE
aden
Tout le cinéma et une sélection de sorties

DIDIER SCHULLER
Assigné à résidence à Saint-Domingue p. 11

MONDIALISATION
Contre à Porto Alegre, pour à New York. Le FMI accusé   p. 2 et 3

UNION EUROPÉENNE
Bruxelles contre les déficits allemands   p. 6

PIERRE BOURDIEU
Les points de vue de Jacques Bouveresse et Yves Charles Zarka   p. 15

RAVE PARTIES
A Reims, le premier procès   p. 10

COLLEGE OF EUROPE
18 FEB. 2002
Library - Bruges

Insécurité : les solutions des candidats

Le Monde

www.lemonde.fr   58ᵉ ANNÉE – Nº 17749 – 1,20 € – FRANCE MÉTROPOLITAINE –   DIMANCHE 17 - LUNDI 18 FÉVRIER 2002   FONDATEUR : HUBERT BEUVE-MÉRY – DIRECTEUR : JEAN-MARIE COLOMBANI

Tension entre Paris et Washington

Divergences sur l'« axe du Mal » dénoncé par Bush, convocation de l'ambassadeur de France

SUPPLÉMENT
ARGENT
Les fausses promesses des fonds garantis

PRÉSIDENTIELLE
Lionel Jospin pourrait se déclarer candidat dimanche 24 février   p. 6

JUSTICE
Alègre face à sa seule victime survivante   p. 7

LES PRISONNIERS
DU 11 SEPTEMBRE
▸ Guantanamo : la polémique entre Europe et Etats-Unis
▸ Enquêtes : retour à Mazar-e-Charif ; vies de prisonniers
▸ Droits de l'homme et terrorisme

Le Monde

www.lemonde.fr   58ᵉ ANNÉE – Nº 17739 – 1,20 € – FRANCE MÉTROPOLITAINE –   MERCREDI 6 FÉVRIER 2002   FONDATEUR : HUBERT BEUVE-MÉRY – DIRECTEUR : JEAN-MARIE COLOMBANI

Le gigantisme militaire de Bush

Le budget américain de la défense pour 2003 augmente de 48 milliards de dollars. Ces crédits atteignent 379 milliards et représentent plus du double des dépenses militaires européennes

PRIX DE LA PEUGEOT 206

AUTOMOBILE
Bruxelles stimule la concurrence   p. 2

MONDIALISATION
Réunions antagonistes à New York et Porto Alegre   p. 4 et 22 et notre éditorial p. 18

PRÉSIDENTIELLE
Le débat Mamère-Le Pen   p. 8

SYNCHROTRON
A Saclay, Soleil produira sa première lumière en 2006   p. 25

Entreprises à hauts risques

CINÉMA
George, Julia et les autres

Didier Schuller : « De quoi ont-ils si peur ? »

HOMOPARENTALITÉ

124

I.M. Pei's glass pyramid at the Louvre   Photo: Susan L. Thompson

matter of time until private television was permitted. More than 800 private radio stations exist already, providing a voice for all kinds of minority interests. Eventually, about 80 local TV stations will be set up around the country. In 1987 the government took another momentous step by selling the largest of the old state networks (TF1) to the private sector. This was the first sell–off by any government of a state–owned TV network. The state kept two of the six channels. To strengthen Franco-German familiarity with each other, the two countries started a joint satellite TV channel called Arte. However, its total audience had by 2003 stagnated to about 13 million viewers, nine million of whom in France. Many judge Arte as too high-brow and tend to associate it with Paris elites.

The Arts

France continues to be a land rich and creative, and performing arts, although no longer occupying indisputably primary position in the world, are topnotch. Its artists have also declined from their pinnacle, but their past greatness is preserved for the world to admire in such great French museums as the Louvre, the Musée d'Orsay, the Beaubourg, and the Picasso Museum. Traditions date back hundreds of years in literature, art, music and the theatre. The writings of Voltaire and Rousseau are landmarks in rich French enlightenment. The music of father and son François Couperin were classic; that of Frederic Chopin, Jules Massenet, Camille Saint–Saens and Claude Debussy richly romantic. During the Third Republic before World War I, Paris was enriched by

more and more resources and producing students with less knowledge.

The Press

Financial difficulties have steadily reduced the number of daily newspapers to less than a hundred. The most widely read are the conservative *France Soir* and *Le Figaro*, and the moderately leftist, intellectual *Le Monde*, all from Paris, and *Ouest–France* published in Rennes. In order to halt the growing concentration of the French press and, as critics charge, to limit the influence of conservative publishing magnate Robert Hersant, who died in 1996, the Socialist government approved in 1984 a law prohibiting publishers from owning both Parisian and regional newspapers, and from controlling more than 15% of either Parisian or regional circulation. Many educated French read certain political and economic weeklies, such as *L'Express, Le Nouvel Observateur, Le Point, L'Evenement du Jeudi* and *Le Canard Enchaîné*, which offer more in–depth analysis, criticism and, in the case of *Le Canard Enchaîné*, satire. Many French have turned increasingly to television and radio for news.

As a result, newspaper readership has dropped over three million since 1970. Even *Le Monde*, founded in 1944 at the instigation of General de Gaulle to provide journalism untainted by Vichy, was rapidly losing money and circulation. It is owned and operated by its employees and improved in sales and financial condition by 1985, making its format more attractive and by selling and leasing back its headquarters building near the Opera. However, this newspaper, renowned as rigor-

ously intellectual and overwhelmingly serious, received a black eye in 2003 when two journalists published a book, *The Hidden Face of Le Monde*, charging it of bias, conflicts of interest, hypocrisy, and business mismanagement. They argued that *Le Monde* twisted facts to cover up scandals, influenced French politics without declaring its interests, and hide the newspaper's financial weakness. The paper rejected the charges as an amalgam of "errors, lies, libels and calumnies."

Until 1984 the state had a monopoly on television and radio. Radio programs are produced by Radio–France, and French government holding companies partially own three independent radio stations (Radio Luxembourg, Europe No. 1 and Radio Monte Carlo), which broadcast from outside of France. Radio–France and the state–owned television companies are financed by annual license fees paid by those persons owning sets.

Critics charge that these companies, although nominally independent and responsible for their own programming, have been manipulated from the Elysées Palace. Mitterrand proposed reducing government influence over them by placing control into the hands of an independent board of directors that would include government officials, media specialists and private citizens. In fact, little has changed in the management of the state–owned media.

The big changes in 1984 came with the legalization of private radio and television stations. So many private radio stations had cropped up that they could no longer be controlled. By legalizing them, the state broadcasting monopoly had been so irreparably punctured that it was only a

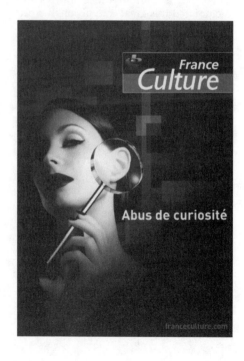

France

impressionism in art, e.g. Renoir, Monet, Degas, and the reaction to it (Bracque, Picasso, cubism or fauvism). During the same period there was the positivism of Auguste Comte, the *élan vital* of Henry Bergson, in medicine the discoveries of Louis Pasteur and in physics the discoveries of Pierre and Marie Curie. In 1988 Maurice Allais became the first Frenchman to win the Nobel Prize for economics, for his study of markets and efficient utilization of resources.

The job of French minister of culture is one of great influence and patronage. Today, the arts in France, as almost everything else, receive state subsidies and are highly concentrated in Paris. To try to spread French cultural activity into the provinces, de Gaulle's minister of culture, André Malraux (himself a leading French writer and art critic, who incurred the wrath of Parisian traditionalists by ordering that all public buildings in Paris be sandblasted to eliminate centuries of soot which had accumulated on them) created cultural centers in ten provincial cities, financed and operated jointly by the central government and the municipalities. These centers are designed to promote artistic creativity and to bring the performing arts into the provinces. They also serve as places for discussions on contemporary problems. Despite such attempts, many persons still speak with some justification of "Paris and the desert."

FRENCH REVOLUTION IN RETROSPECT

The year 1989 marked the 200th anniversary of the French Revolution, and 5,000 events around the country commemorated this great convulsion. It created the opportunity for Frenchmen to look both back into their past and forward into their future. Not all Frenchmen cherish the spirit of 1789, as was shown by Catholic counter–demonstrations to remember martyrs in the Place de la Concorde on August 15, 1989, the production of a movie called "Vent de Galerne" that depicts the savage repression of peasant rebels in the Vendée, the tracing of descendants of the 3,000 persons executed in Lyons by the Jacobins, and the widespread apathy in many parts of the country.

There has been a fundamental rethinking of the causes and meaning of the revolution, and many simplistic explanations have been replaced by a much more complex picture. Some myths were corrected: only seven prisoners were freed at the Bastille; execution by guillotine often took several "chops," and only 10% of those beheaded were nobles; most of the revolution's victims were shot, burned or drowned, rather than beheaded; the

statement attributed to Marie Antoinette, "Let them eat cake!", appeared in Rousseau's Confessions at least two years before Marie arrived in France in 1770.

Frenchmen have even become more ambiguous about their heroes and villains. Polls indicated that the era's most revered character is the Marquis de Lafayette, who broke with the Jacobins and fled France. Also, a televised re-enactment of Louis XVI's trial with the ending left open so that viewers could decide his guilt or innocence produced astounding conclusions: only 27% of viewers favored beheading him, versus 55% who voted to acquit him. It is therefore not surprising that the government decided to focus as little as possible on the bloody elements of the past and almost exclusively on the idealistic achievements of the revolution that have undeniable relevance for France's future, such as the Declaration of the Rights of Man and the Citizen. This focus on human rights and the question of what it means to be a citizen in a free and modern republic relates directly to France's future as a multi-racial, multi-cultural society. Some citizens are also beginning to ask whether France needs to have such a brutal national anthem, which calls on them to "drench our fields" with the enemy's "tainted blood." According to a July 14, 1992, poll, 40% of the French find the lyrics too bloodthirsty, but 75% are staunchly opposed to altering the hallowed verses.

FUTURE

All past attempts to put France on a leftist course failed, as did Mitterrand's. Former Prime Minister Lionel Jospin was elected on a left–wing platform, but he pursued a social–democratic course he called "left–wing realism." The Socialist government found itself politically limited by global competition and by France's commitments to the EU, which require a tight hold on the budget deficit. The Raffarin government admitted in 2003 that its budget deficit of 3.4% of GDP would exceed the permitted 3% limit for countries using the euro. The EU estimated that France's budget deficit would actually exceed 3.7% and ordered it to offer a plan by October how it would get it down to 3% by the end of the year. The defiant prime minister, who had promised a tax cut and increase in defense spending during his campaign and who must confront the problems of growing unemployment and pension reform in the face of determined union opposition, proclaimed, "I won't conduct a policy of austerity." A clash with Brussels is inevitable.

Most French view American capitalism as the law of the jungle; even conservative

President Chirac declared: "I do not want that model." In 1998 Jospin traveled to the U.S. He returned saying that "my view of the United States has changed" and that France could learn much about America's economic dynamism, research and innovation, competitive spirit and capacity for renewal.

France faces the perennial challenge of corruption. In its 2002 report, Transparency International, a Berlin-based organization that campaigns against corruption, ranked France 25th in order of perceived lack of ethical cleanliness, equal with Portugal and behind all other EU countries except Italy and Greece. French voters seem unmoved by this. Jospin entered office promising open and honest government, and the judiciary was energetic in investigating the kind of corruption that Frenchmen used to consider acceptable on the part of politicians. After all, Mitterrand's son, Jean–Christophe, had run the president's Africa office; ex–Culture Minister Jack Lang had employed his own wife as his official adviser, and President Chirac's daughter is paid as his chief publicist. He is dogged by allegations of corruption from the time he was mayor of Paris, but the courts ruled that he has immunity from prosecution as long as he is in office. The judge who led the main investigations was removed from the case and resigned from the bench, saying that his investigation had been sabotaged at every turn: "I've had my eyes opened. People who make off with large sums of money escape justice or get insignificant sentences, while the thief who steals a handbag on the subway gets six years. We have a two-speed justice system."

A former prime minister and two ex–ministers were tried in 1999 in connection with a scandal over HIV–contaminated blood, and one of the ministers was convicted of criminal neglect. France's first female prime minister and one of the country's two members of the European Commission, Edith Cresson, engaged in such blatant misconduct (such as hiring her dentist as her "science adviser") that the European Parliament ultimately prompted a mass resignation of all Commissioners in Brussels. Another former prime minister and current chairman of the UMP, Alain Juppé, was investigated for charges that he let public money be used illegally to pay salaries of dozens of Gaullist party officials.

Roland Dumas, former head of the Constitutional Court, the supreme guardian of France's laws and institutions, was placed under investigation and had to step down in the face of charges that he had received more than $10 million in gratuities from the former state oil giant, Elf, while he was foreign minister. Saying "we absolutely needed French politicians who supported us," the former chairman of Elf testified in 2003 that the company paid about $5 million to French political parties during his leadership. Almost all the money went to Jacques Chirac's Gaullist party until then President Mitterrand insisted that the funds be spread around among other parties. Dumas' funds were allegedly channeled to him through his mistress, Christine Deviers–Joncour, who described the sordid affair in her best–selling book, *The Whore of the Republic*. Dumas was convicted of corruption and sentenced to six months in prison and a $130,000 fine, while Deviers-Joncour was fined $300,000.

It is very difficult to change France. President Chirac, who was reelected to another five-year term in May 2002, had seen his responsibilities shrink to little more than foreign and defense policy under the cohabitation with the Socialists. He spoke in 1997 of the "extreme difficulty of changing anything at all in a profoundly conservative and fossilized country." His victorious government in the June 2002 parliamentary elections is hard-pressed to fulfill all his campaign, promises to reduce taxes, create jobs for women and young French, put more po-

lice on the streets, and balance the budget by 2004.

Determined to show the country that it is responding to a wide-spread feeling that France is experiencing a wave of crime, especially violent crimes against innocent victims, the government enacted a sweeping anti-crime bill. The urgency for this was underscored in October 2002 when a Muslim assailant, who said he is opposed to homosexuals and politicians in general, stabbed Paris Mayor Bertrand Delanoë, the city's first Socialist mayor, during an all-night festival at the City Hall. The new legislation expands police powers to search vehicles and take DNA samples of suspects, criminalizes begging and "vagabondery," and prohibits prostitutes from engaging in either active or passive soliciting. Any woman whose dress or attitude gives police officers the impression that she is soliciting money for sex faces a fine of 7,500 euros or six months in jail.

The most serious challenge for the center-right government will be the explosive issue of pension reform. It decided in 2003 to confront the unions and try to push through the painful but long overdue reform. Prime Minister Raffarin noted:

"Conceived more than 50 years ago, our retirement system no longer corresponds to the current and future demographic reality." The plan is to bring public sector works in line with the private sector by 2008, requiring all persons to work 40 years (42 by 2020) in order to get a full pension. Government support for early retirement will be phased out, and tax incentives will be introduced to persuade workers to invest in company-based savings programs like those in the U.S. Finally, a pension bonus would be offered to those who work beyond 40 years. The battle lines with the unions are clearly drawn, as one union leader made clear: "This isn't reform of the pension system—it's the destruction. Our determination to act is stronger than ever." Massive street demonstrations and strike action are a near certainty.

A charmed Chirac escaped an assassination attempt July 14 when an assailant fired at him while he was passing in the annual Bastille Day parade. The 2002 event was dedicated to Franco-American friendship and featured marching West Point cadets and 75 relatives of victims of the September 11 attacks on the World Trade Center.

Finally, Notre Dame's gargoyles … possibly pondering the mysteries of French politics

Courtesy: Jon Markham Morrow

The Principality of Monaco

Aerial view of Monaco showing the Port of Monaco

Area: .575 sq. mi. (1.95 sq. km.).
Population: 31,700 (estimated).
Capital City: Monaco–Ville.
Climate: Mild Mediterranean.
Neighboring Country: France.
Official Language: French.
Other Principal Tongues: Italian and Monégasque (a mixture of French and Italian) are also spoken.
Ethnic Background: French (50%), Italian (15%), native Monégasques (ca. 4,500), and diverse other European peoples.
Principal Religion: Roman Catholicism is the state religion.
Major Industries: Banking, tourism, postage stamps, gambling, small industries, such as cosmetics, chemicals, food processing, precision instrument manufacture, glassmaking and printing.
Main Customers: France, Italy.
Currency: Euro.
Year of Independence: 1338.
National Day: November 19.
Chief of State: His Serene Highness Prince Rainier III (b. 1923).
Heir Apparent: Prince Albert (b. 1958).
Head of Government: Minister of State in Charge of Foreign Affairs.
National Flag: Red and white horizontal stripes.

The Principality of Monaco is one of the smallest sovereign countries in the world. A densely populated, hilly city overlooking the Mediterranean Sea, Monaco is surrounded on three sides by the French Department of Alpes–Maritimes. The French city if Nice is nine miles (15 km.) to the west of Monaco and the Italian border is five miles (8 km.) to the east. Three picturesque settlements are now unified into one city, and its older section, situated on top of a steep rock, has maintained its medieval flavor. Overlooking crowded Riviera beaches and some of the most luxurious tourist resorts in the world is the 13th century Genoese palace, which was remodeled in the 16th century in Renaissance style. Here resides the Prince of the House of Grimaldi, whose family has ruled Monaco, with periodic interruptions, since 1297. On January 8, 1997, Prince Rainier launched a year–long, $270 million celebration of his family's 700–year reign, the longest of any European dynasty.

Evidence of Stone Age settlements has been found within the present borders of Monaco. Founded much later by the Phoenicians, the city was known to the ancient Greeks and Carthaginians. Under the domination of the Romans (who called the city Herculis Moenaci Portus), Monaco was quite prosperous, and it was from Monaco that Julius Caesar set sail for his campaign against Pompeii. Its wealth was destroyed by the invading barbarians, who brought the once–mighty Roman Empire to its knees. In the 7th century Monaco became a part of the Lombard Kingdom. Later it was absorbed into the Kingdom of Arles and was also subjected to a period of Mohammedan control. In 1191 the Genoese took control of Monaco, but they ceded domination in 1297 to the reining Grimaldi family.

As a minuscule land in a restless world, the independent principality of Monaco always needed the protection of a stronger power in order to survive. It allied itself first with France. In 1524 it accepted Spain's protection instead, but it returned to French safety in 1641. In 1793 the radicalized French National Convention dispossessed the wealthy and aristocratic Grimaldi rulers and annexed the entire Monacan domain to France. After Napoleon's fall from power, the Congress of Vienna awarded Monaco to the Kingdom of Sardinia as a protectorate in 1814. France repossessed the principality in 1848 and after greatly reducing its territory, granted independence to the present tiny remainder in 1861.

France today continues to assume responsibility for Monaco's defense, and a 1918 treaty stipulates that Monaco's policies must conform to French political, military, naval and economic interests. A further treaty of 1919 stipulates that Monaco would be incorporated into France if the reigning prince dies without an heir. To prevent this, the palace made constitutional provisions in 2002 permitting one of prince Rainier's daughters to assume the throne in the event that the bachelor crowned prince dies childless.

The Principality of Monaco

Prince Rainier III married the late American actress Grace Kelly in 1956. She epitomized American affluence and Hollywood glamour and attracted the world's attention to the ruling Grimaldi family, but she met an untimely death in an automobile accident on the hilly roads of Monaco in 1982. Their offspring insure survival of the principality for at least another generation and probably more. Prince Rainier has intimated that he may one day abdicate in favor of his son, Prince Albert, a graduate of Amherst College in Massachusetts. Albert attends government meetings and is already preparing for the transition. Rainier, who is in ill health, has made it known that before handing power over to Albert, he would like the unmarried crown prince to produce an heir "because that is essential for the future of our principality." Albert was a member of Monaco's bobsled team in the 2002 winter Olympics in Salt Lake City.

Since 1865, an economic union with France governs customs, postal services, telecommunications and banking. The principality even used the French franc until it adopted the euro when France did in 2002. Although it is not in the EU, it was permitted to mint its own euro coins with its own motif on the back. Monaco refuses to tax its own citizens, who number only about 20% of the principality's residents. Most of the rest are French. These 4,500 Monégasques also receive housing subsidies and preferential employment. They are guaranteed government service jobs, and all companies must make their first job offers to them. Most Monégasques go to France for higher education, but thanks to the principality's healthy economy, they return.

More than half the residents are French, many of whom chose to reside and to locate their businesses in Monaco in order to avoid French taxation. French protests of this situation in 1962 unleashed a serious dispute. Nevertheless, a compromise was worked out in 1963; all French companies that do more than 25% of their business outside of the principality were brought under French financial control. In 2000 verbal warfare broke out again when France threatened to punish the principality unless it took effective measures against money-laundering, tax evasion and drug barons. It demands that Monaco impose a wealth tax on French residents and disclose details of bank accounts. Compliance would make the principality less attractive. Prince Rainier was not pleased, calling the French attitude "incongruous" and demanding a renegotiation of its treaties with France "to give Monaco back to the Monégasques." The principality likes to portray itself as a secure haven for the well-behaved rich. Per capita GDP in 1999 was $27,000, a third higher than in France. In response to EU pressure, Monaco agreed in 2003 to collect taxes on foreign accounts and to return 75% of the levy to the country of residence without revealing account holders' names.

Monaco has undergone a remarkable economic transformation in recent decades. When Prince Rainier took the throne in 1949, at age 26, his realm was seen, in the words of Somerset Maugham, as "a sunny place for shady people." It was a glitzy but sleazy gambling center. The prince sought to upgrade its image in order to attract wealthy, respectable visitors, depositors, and residents, and to

provide long–term employment opportunities for native Monégasques.

His main achievement was to stimulate the local economy by creating thriving banking and tourist industries. Benefiting from tax advantages, banks have doubled in number since the early 1980s to nearly 40. It is estimated that there is one cashier for every 400 residents! Tough laws permitting the seizure of profits from drug operations were introduced in 1993 in an effort to keep the banks' money clean. The principality now attracts 4 million visitors a year, 3 million of whom are day-trippers from Italy and France. The annual Grand Prix auto race attracts 150,000 alone. Tourist spending amounts for 25% of GDP. Monaco also has experienced a blooming of commerce and light industry.

In 1967 Prince Rainier won a long struggle with the Greek shipping magnate, Aristotle Onassis, over control of the famed casino of Monte–Carlo. Monaco's native citizens are not permitted to gamble in the casino, and contrary to popular belief, less than 5% of the principality's revenues are derived from its gambling royalties. Still, the social life of Monaco centers around the Place du Casino, with its lovely gardens. The Monte Carlo Philharmonic is one of the world's most recorded orchestras. The principality also boasts first–rate opera and ballet companies, as well as 55 galleries and 50 open–air sculptures.

Monaco's present constitution, which was promulgated December 17, 1962, reduced the prince's powers somewhat and increased parliamentary powers. Executive power is vested in the hereditary prince, who rules through his appointed Minister of State. The latter official must be a French citizen and must be selected from a slate of three candidates put to the principality by the French president. Three state counselors (one of whom must be French) and palace personnel who are appointed by the prince assist the Minister of State. France supplies senior civil servants, judges, policemen and firemen. The French judicial system applies in Monaco, and two Parisian judges form the Court of Appeal. Prisoners must serve their sentences outside the principality, usually in France, since its only jail can accommodate suspects awaiting trial, but not convicted criminals.

Legislative power rests with an 18–member National Council elected by universal suffrage for five–year terms. The prince shares the legislative powers in that he retains the right to initiate legislation. Although four political parties are now active in Monaco, one party, the National and Democratic Union (UND), dominated for four decades and controlled all 18 National Council seats. That

Prince Albert and His Serene Highness Prince Rainier III

The Principality of Monaco

ended with the 2003 elections, when the Union for Monaco coalition won an overwhelming majority.

France controls Monaco's foreign relations, and the principality is included in the EU through its customs union with France. Since 1993 it is a full member of the United Nations, and it serves on several UN specialized agencies. It also maintains four embassies (in Paris, Brussels, Bern and Rome) and 110 consuls of its own, including ones in Washington and New York. In 1994 it signed a cultural convention under Council of Europe auspices. But because it is not considered to be either completely democratic or independent, it has never formally asked nor been invited to join the Council of Europe.

Monaco has no newspapers of its own, but there is a private radio station (Radio–Monte–Carlo) with programming in French, Italian and Arabic. Also, Trans–World Radio has a seat in Monte–Carlo and broadcasts in four languages. One private television station (Tele Monte–Carlo) transmits programs in French and Italian.

FUTURE

As the 20th century closed, Prince Rainier could look back on a half century of rule in his mini–state. With an heir to the throne and an active program of home–based economic diversification, this minuscule 700–year–old principality can expect not only to exist, but to prosper in the coming years.

Monaco mints its own euro coins

Courtesy: Central Audiovisual Library, European Commission

The BENELUX Nations

NORTH SEA

NETHERLANDS

GERMANY

BELGIUM

FRANCE

LUXEMBOURG

that have provided standards of living and social welfare systems for their populations that are almost unmatched in the world. Their central location and access to the sea made them prosperous trading nations, and the ports of Rotterdam and Antwerp are the largest and most active in Europe. With relatively small populations and high prosperity, these countries are heavily dependent upon trade, and, therefore, upon economic and political conditions beyond their borders. Roughly half of these countries' GDP results from foreign trade. This heavy volume is an economic blessing as well as a possible liability for the future.

To help secure their trade, they were pioneers in economic unions. In 1922 Belgium and Luxembourg formed the Belgium Luxembourg Economic Union (BLEU), which made the two countries a unit for importing and exporting purposes. It also established a unified railway, customs area and currency for the two countries. Luxembourg coined and printed money below one hundred francs for local circulation, but Belgian currency remained dominant until the euro in 2002. The three countries' governments–in–exile in London in 1944 formed a customs union called BENELUX, which was later extended to include even non–customs matters. Because of the striking difference in postwar recovery, BENELUX did not come into effect until January 1948.

In 1952 they were founding members with France, West Germany and Italy of the European Coal and Steel Community (ECSC), with headquarters located in Luxembourg. Not only was it a farsighted idea to share these commodities, so crucial for heavy industry, rather than to risk fighting over them, but the ECSC gave these nations the practice in economic cooperation needed to convince the six that a bold move to create a united Europe could succeed. The six signed the Treaty of Rome in 1957 and in 1958 the European Economic Community (Common Market) came into existence. Later the Community grew, and its name was changed first to European Community (EC) and then in 1993 to European Union (EU) in order to emphasize that the union was someday to become a political one, as well as an economic one. None tried harder than the BENELUX countries to keep the idea of a united Europe alive in the 1960s, when the six were seriously split over the question of British entry.

All three countries are constitutional, parliamentary monarchies, whose monarchs are relatively popular, though not powerful. As modern constitutional monarchs, they "reign but do not rule." In contrast to the monarchy in Great Britain, which can be traced back more than a

Belgium, the Netherlands and Luxembourg are located at the crossroads of Western Europe. Although they are collectively called "BENELUX," a word derived from the first letters of each country's name, these small countries have developed differing traditions, national characters and problems. Still, they have many things in common, and it is no accident that they cooperate with each other more closely than any other nations of the world. In fact, their example of international cooperation and their steady encouragement of tighter European integration have made them the core and motor for greater unity. The vast majority of the EU's institutions are located in Belgium and Luxembourg.

All three countries are very small and have no natural frontiers that could serve as barriers to unwanted intruders. They have therefore suffered recurrent invasion by all the great European powers. For a century and a half they tried to keep themselves out of the grips of the major

powers by declaring a policy of neutrality. But two disastrous world wars in the 20th century, which spared only the Netherlands from 1914 to 1918, left such a policy and the three countries in shambles. No one can easily forget the lines which the poet John McCrae wrote after visiting the Flemish battlefields: "In Flanders fields the poppies blow between the crosses, row by row … ."

Having paid a heavy price for their neutrality, all three countries became founding members of NATO in 1949. Its political headquarters are now located on the outskirts of Brussels, and its military headquarters, the Supreme Headquarters of the Allied Powers in Europe (SHAPE), is located outside of Mons, Belgium.

The Netherlands and Belgium have the highest population density of all Europe. All three have great numbers of foreign workers who bring both needed labor and social problems with them. These countries are not particularly rich in raw materials, but they have productive economies

The BENELUX Nations

thousand years, the BENELUX monarchies are young. The oldest, in the Netherlands, dates back to 1813. Throughout the centuries these small countries have been tossed back and forth among the great powers of Europe and have sometimes been forced together and sometimes split apart. A quick glance at their history shows why they have so much in common and are nevertheless different from each other.

Early History

The early history of these three countries is so intertwined that it is best considered by grouping them together.

About a half-century before Christ, after a long and destructive campaign, the Roman legions conquered the tenacious Celtic tribes, including the Belgeai and Treveri. In his commentary *The Gallic Wars*, Julius Caeser used the name "Belgium" to refer to all the territory we now call the BENELUX countries. This area, especially what is today Belgium and Luxembourg, was dominated for more than 300 years by the Romans, who built roads and villas and introduced agriculture, especially vineyards and fruit orchards. They also brought Christianity to the area, but this did not begin to flourish until the 6th and 7th centuries.

When Attila the Hun invaded what is now Germany, Germanic tribes were thrown into the Low Countries (the Netherlands) in about 300. Two centuries later another Germanic tribe, the Franks, invaded the area and established a linguistic frontier that exists today in the middle of what is now Belgium. North of the line the Germanic tongues evolved into the Dutch language and into Flemish, a Dutch dialect spoken in northern Belgium. South of the line, vulgarized Latin, which developed into French, was spoken. Thus in Belgium the Latin and Germanic worlds met face to face and presented Belgium with a problem which many centuries later threatened to tear the country apart.

In the 8th and 9th centuries the entire territory that had been fragmented into many duchies, principalities and other political units, became a part of Charlemagne's empire. This was the time when the political center of gravity in Europe shifted from the Mediterranean to the northwestern regions. His great empire fell apart soon after his death, and for several centuries the BENELUX people saw their land converted into a constant battlefield between French and German contenders for control. During this time the crusades opened up trade with the Orient, and especially Belgium experienced a flowering of trade and urban development. The beautiful canal city of Bruges

became a wealthy city of trade and the arts. In the 15th century, the Dukes of Burgundy, who were among the most powerful in Europe, began to acquire control over what is now Belgium and Luxembourg by means of conquest, marriage or land purchase.

Only the Netherlands was able to resist the Burgundian encroachment. As a country whose development had been retarded by its preoccupation with fighting back the sea, the Netherlands was not a very tempting target for Burgundian expansion anyway. At the end of the 15th century the last descendent, Mary of

The Holy Roman Emperor, Charles V

Burgundy, married Maximilian of Austria, and the Burgundian holdings in the area passed into the Hapsburg family. Their son, Philip the Handsome, married the Spanish princess, Juana of Castile; Spain and Spanish America also came under Hapsburg control.

A son born of this union in 1500 in the Flemish city of Ghent was destined to become one of Europe's greatest rulers. He became King of Spain in 1516 and the Holy Roman Emperor in 1519. He was Charles V, and by 1543 he had unified all of what is now the BENELUX area, except the county of Liège, which led a separate existence until the 18th century. Charles ruled his far–flung empire from Brussels, a city established in 979 on the islands of the Senne River, which was then called "Bruocsella." His reign was a time of great economic prosperity, artistic and intellectual bloom for the "Seventeen Provinces," as the Luxembourg area was then called. This was the time of the great humanist, Erasmus of Rotterdam, of Mercator, the most widely known cartographer in the world, of the painters van Eyck and Pieter Breugal.

The unity of the Seventeen Provinces might have survived if the Reformation which Martin Luther unleashed in 1519 had not divided Europe and with it the Low Countries. Charles V abdicated in 1555 in favor of his son, Philip II who had been raised in Spain; he decided to rule the empire from Madrid, leaving the administration of the Seventeen Provinces to governors. He was, however, determined to defend the Catholic faith, and he was cruel and inflexible in attempting to suppress the Protestant movements, which in its Calvinist form, was particularly strong in the Netherlands. William of Orange–Nassau led Protestant resistance in the northern provinces. Because Spain was so severely weakened by its continuous struggles against England and France during the second half of the 16th century, the Netherlands was able to secure its independence in 1581.

Until Napoleon's conquests in the 1790s the Dutch took control of their own destiny, while the Belgians and Luxembourgers continued to be dominated by other powers. In order to give the latter a sense of autonomy, Philip gave the southern provinces to his daughter, the Archduchess Isabella, and her husband, the Archduke Albert of Austria. This was a relatively happy time when the painter Peter Paul Rubens reached the height of his creativity. When Albert and Isabella died childless, the provinces reverted to Spain in 1621, and until 1713 the Hapsburgs fought over control of the area.

In one campaign in 1695, the French Marshal Villeroy, under orders of Louis XIV, bombarded the beautiful Grand Place in Brussels with its majestic town hall, built around 1400; it survived only with its tower and its thickest walls. This disaster merely stiffened the courage and determination of the Brussels population, which began the very next day restoring the structure. The best artistic and architectural talent in the city joined in recreating one of man's greatest architectural treasures. Jan Van Ruysbroeck, the city's master mason, rebuilt the town hall. Wishing to retain the foundation and porch of the old bell tower while extending the new walls as far as possible, he placed the

main portal of the town hall off center with the central axis of the tower. Legend wrongly has it that he threw himself to his death when he discovered the error, but the "error" was in fact intentional. The Grand Place remains the vibrant heart of the city and has always been a favorite subject for painters and poets. It is a place for open–air markets, public meetings, political assemblies, royal receptions and coronations. Earlier it was the favorite place for launching revolutions and for public executions. Each year on a summer evening the Grand Place is transformed into its medieval setting for a historical procession called the "Ommegang."

Both Luxembourg and Belgium passed into the hands of the Austrians, who renamed Belgium the "Austrian Netherlands" and who ruled over these provinces until 1794–95, when French troops snatched them away. The Austrians had exercised a benevolent dictatorship, but some Luxembourgers, Flemings and Walloons were infected by the fever of revolution emanating from France and welcomed the changes that came with the French republican troops. Belgium fell to the French in 1794 and the following year French revolutionary forces conquered Luxembourg and the Netherlands, which had been greatly weakened by its series of wars against England.

The French occupation brought fundamental changes to the Netherlands, which had been ruled by an enlightened oligarchy, with a high official called a *stadholder* (not a monarch!) at the top. Although it was not a modern democracy in that leaders who were exercising power had been elected by universal suffrage, the Dutch republic had nevertheless been one of the most democratic countries in Europe with the possible exception of Switzerland. The old republic had been highly decentralized, with each province stressing its independent powers. The new regime that the French created and called "The Batavian Republic," named after one of the tribes which had populated the country in the Roman period and which had revolted against Roman domination, was highly centralized in conformity with the French constitution.

The Napoleonic Code of laws and the selection of members of parliament on the basis of limited but free elections were also introduced. The Dutch grew restive under French control, especially after the Batavian Republic was abolished and Louis Napoleon, the brother of the French Emperor, was made King of Holland in 1806. Quarrels with his brother forced Louis to abdicate in 1810, but only after he had tried unsuccessfully to have his son, who later became Napoleon III of France,

crowned in his place. The Netherlands was annexed directly into the French Empire in 1810. Again, Napoleon's reversals gave the Dutch the chance to reassert their independence. In 1813, after Napoleon's defeat in the Battle of Leipzig, the son of the last Dutch *stadholder* who had fled to England, landed at Scheveningen, not far from the Hague, and was proclaimed William I of the House of Orange–Nassau, King of the Netherlands. For the first time the Netherlands became a monarchy with a Dutch monarch on the throne. Dutch troops took an active part in the final defeat of Napoleon.

In late 1794 French troops besieged the fortress of Luxembourg, which did not fall until mid–1795. It was annexed to France in the fall; French rule was very unpopular at first, but Napoleon was gradually able to smooth out many problems. When the French left the Duchy in 1814 they had left many positive and lasting gifts behind: the idea of equality, centralized and efficient administration and the Napoleonic Code.

The French were at first widely greeted in Belgium as liberators, and the introduction of the Napoleonic Code and an efficient, centralized administration was generally seen as an improvement over the old regime. Almost no one seemed to have realized at the time that decentralization would have helped Belgium's language groups to live together more harmo-niously in a unified Belgian state. But the seemingly endless Napoleonic wars soon sapped the Belgians' enthusiasm. After Napoleon began suffering disastrous reversals, especially in Russia in 1812, the Belgians joined the enemies of France. It was outside Brussels near a small town named Waterloo that the little dictator was defeated for the last time.

When the great powers of Europe met at the Congress of Vienna in 1814–15, they combined the Netherlands, Belgium and Luxembourg to form the "Kingdom of the United Netherlands," with the monarch William I as King. European leaders, who suspected that they had supported the French too enthusiastically, distrusted the Belgians. They believed that the Belgians, therefore, needed to be controlled by the Dutch King. Further, the East Belgian cantons of Eupen, Malmedy and Saint Vith were ceded to Prussia, whose borders had been moved as far west as possible in order to prevent any future eastward French expansion.

The union of the three countries did not last long. In 1830 the sparks of revolution flying from Paris landed in Brussels. The overwhelmingly Catholic Flemings and Walloons (Belgians who speak French) sensed religious discrimination by the predominantly Protestant Calvinist Dutch,

The BENELUX Nations

despite the tradition of religious tolerance in the Netherlands.

Although it was the only thing that drew Flemings and Walloons together, Catholicism was enough to unify them against the Dutch. Such religious unity was later to prove the weakest of glue to hold the state of Belgium together. The use of Dutch in the Flemish area of the north and in Brussels had been resented by the economically and culturally more influential French–speaking Walloons in the South. This determination to elevate the French language above Dutch also was later to create extremely serious problems for this bilingual country. The eruption occurred in 1830 after the performance of an opera with a liberation theme—after a brief skirmish in Brussels, Dutch troops withdrew and a provisional government proclaimed independence within three months. Seeing the usefulness of a buffer state on the European continent, the British announced that they would thenceforth guarantee Belgium's neutrality.

A liberal constitution, which is still in force, was proclaimed placing sovereignty in the people and providing for a constitutional monarchy. A German prince, Leopold I of Saxe–Coburg who happened also to be a British citizen, became king in 1831. Since sovereignty was placed in the hands of the people, there was no doubt that the Parliament, as the representative of the Belgian people, would be superior to the monarch. French was also declared to be the new country's official language.

The Dutch reacted to these events by attempting to invade Belgium, but the French and British announced their determination not to allow the Dutch to reassert their control. At a London Conference of 1831, a border between the Netherlands and Belgium was drawn, but this settlement pleased neither the Belgians, who claimed about half of Luxembourg, nor the Dutch, whose king wanted no settlement at all which would reduce the size of his kingdom. Finally, the Treaty of Twenty–Four Articles, signed in London in 1839, granted the Dutch a slice of northern Belgium. Belgium, in turn, was compensated through a grant of about half of Luxembourg's territory. Further, the great European powers guaranteed the neutrality of Belgium and Luxembourg. This settlement finally satisfied all but the Luxembourgers, who saw their already tiny state reduced to about one–fourth of its pre–1815 size.

The Congress of Vienna had made Luxembourg an autonomous Duchy with the Dutch King as the Grand Duke, but Luxembourg lost all its territory east of the Moselle, Sure and Our Rivers. The congress also made Luxembourg a member of the German Confederation and granted the Prussians the right to man the fortress in the capital city in order to be able to keep a closer eye on the recently defeated French. This arrangement meant that Luxembourg was wide open to Dutch royal ideas, Prussian military demands and Belgium's liberal cravings.

At first the Dutch King ruled in a rather authoritarian way, and when the Belgians rebelled against Dutch rule in 1830 most Luxembourgers outside the capital city also arose. Although they were unable to establish their independence, Luxembourgers were gradually able to establish separate institutions and administrations. Political autonomy was granted in 1839 and in 1848 the country received a liberal constitution similar to that of Belgium. The Dutch became more benevolent rulers and cooperated in Luxembourg's movement toward democracy and independence. Finally, in 1867 the Treaty of London, drawn up in an attempt to reconcile differences between Bismarck of Germany and Napoleon III of France, proclaimed Luxembourg an independent and neutral country. Only a year later Luxembourg adopted a constitution that in revised form remains in force. Upon the insistence of Napoleon III, the Prussians withdrew from the Duchy and the fortress was razed.

The only disappointment for the Luxembourgers was that the Dutch King remained the Grand Duke. However, when in 1890 there were no male heirs to the Dutch throne, Adolf of Nassau, whose family was related to the Dutch ruling family, became the Grand Duke of Luxembourg and chose to reside in Luxembourg City. Nevertheless, the close historical ties with the Netherlands continue to be symbolized by the fact that the two countries have almost exactly the same flag.

From 1890 on, all three BENELUX countries have been fully independent and sovereign states. Proximity, economic interests and political values continue to bind these three democracies very closely together.

The Monnaie Theater, Brussels, where the torch of liberation was lit

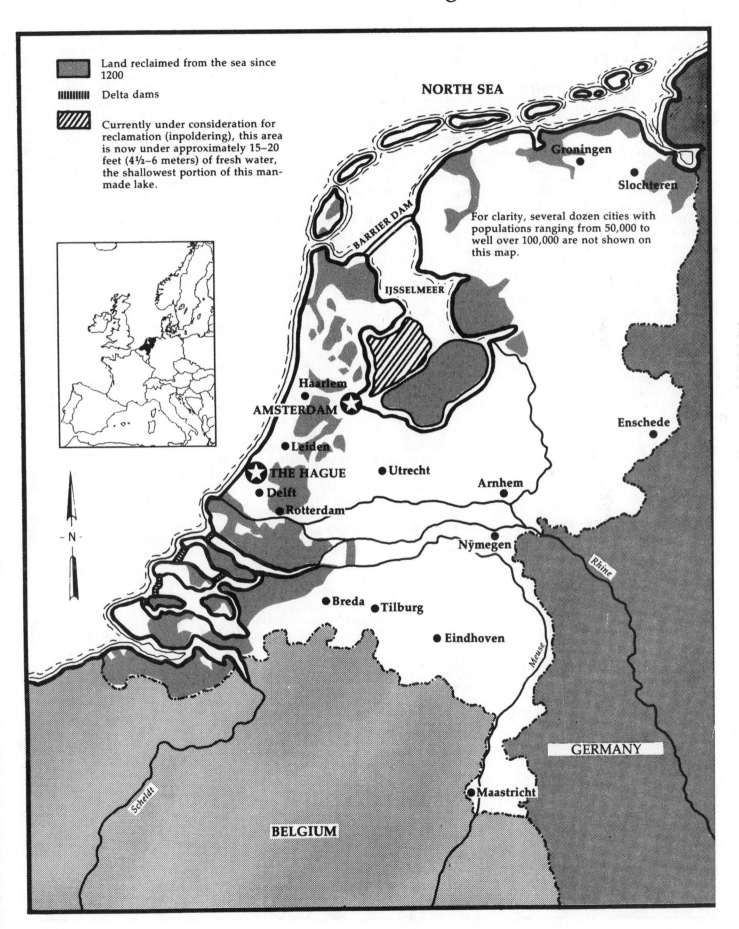

The Kingdom of the Netherlands

Land reclaimed from the sea since 1200

Delta dams

Currently under consideration for reclamation (inpoldering), this area is now under approximately 15–20 feet (4½–6 meters) of fresh water, the shallowest portion of this man-made lake.

NORTH SEA

BARRIER DAM

IJSSELMEER

Groningen

Slochteren

For clarity, several dozen cities with populations ranging from 50,000 to well over 100,000 are not shown on this map.

Haarlem

AMSTERDAM

Enschede

Leiden

THE HAGUE

Utrecht

Delft

Arnhem

Rotterdam

Nÿmegen

Rhine

– N –

Breda

Tilburg

Eindhoven

Meuse

GERMANY

Scheldt

Maastricht

BELGIUM

The Netherlands

Area: 16,163 sq. mi. (41,863 sq. km., twice the size of New Jersey and one-half the size of Virginia).

Population: 16.2 million.

Capital City: Amsterdam (Pop. 1,000,000, estimated). but the seat of government is The Hague (Pop. 530,000, estimated).

Climate: Temperate, with mild winters, cool summers.

Neighboring Countries: Germany (East); Belgium (South); England (West, 90 miles across the North Sea).

Official Languages: Dutch, Frisian.

Other Principal Tongues: English, German.

Ethnic Background: Frisian in the North, Saxon in the East and central part of the nation, Frankish south of the rivers.

Principal Religions: Roman Catholic (about 40%), Dutch Reformed-Lutheran (about 36%). About 24% profess belief in no religion.

Main Exports: Machinery and electronics, agricultural products, largely dairy, processed foods, fish and fish products, chemicals and plastics, petroleum products and natural gas.

Main Imports: Machinery, chemicals, fuels, clothing and cotton, base metals and ores, pulp, pulpwood, lumber, feed grains, edible oils.

Major Trading Customers: EU (77%), Europe as a whole (85%), Germany (26%), Belgium (12%), UK (10.8%), France (10.5%). The U.S. provides 10% of imports.

Currency: Euro.

National Day: April 30th, Official birthday of former Queen Juliana, mother of Queen Beatrix. Liberation day, May 5th, is celebrated every year.

Chief of State: Her Majesty Queen Beatrix (b. 1938), married Claus George Willem Geert von Amsberg on March 10, 1966, a German diplomat who was proclaimed H.R.H. Prince of the Netherlands a few weeks before the wedding.

Heir Apparent: His Royal Highness Crown Prince Willem-Alexander (b. 1967).

Head of Government: Prime Minister.

National Flag: Three horizontal stripes of red, white and blue, almost identical to the flag of Luxembourg, which has a pale blue stripe.

Benjamin Franklin once said: "In love of liberty and in the defense of it, Holland has been our example." Indeed, when the Dutch declared their independence from Spain in 1581, they justified their act in words which in some ways are very reminiscent of those which Thomas Jefferson wrote in the American Declaration of Independence almost 200 years later: "As it is apparent to all that a prince is constituted by God to be the ruler of the people ... and whereas God did not create the people slaves to their prince, to obey his commands, whether right or wrong, but rather the prince for the sake of the subjects ... . And when he does not behave thus, but on the contrary oppresses them ... they may not only disallow his authority, but legally proceed to the choice of another prince for their defense ..." Although their independence was not recognized internationally until 1648, the Dutch had already taken command of their own destiny and established a republic based on the ideas that government should be limited and directed exclusively toward the well-being of the people.

A thousand-year struggle against the sea helped to shape a people who are hard working, persistent, efficient and imaginative. It is a fact of history that nations have expanded their borders at the expense of other nations. The Netherlands, which even the Dutch call "Holland" though North and South Holland were traditionally merely the richest two provinces in the country, is one of the few nations whose expansion has been at the expense of the sea, not of other peoples. According to an old Dutch saying, "the Lord made heaven and earth, but the Dutch made Holland!" For centuries the Dutch built and strengthened dunes and dykes to hold back the sea. Since the 15th century they constructed windmills everywhere to convert the sea winds into energy to pump water back into the sea. Today, almost one-third of the country is below sea level, and if the Dutch were not constantly vigilant, about one-half of the country would disappear under water or become unusable for any purpose. It is precisely in that half that more than 60% of the Dutch live and work and that most of Holland's industry is located. The visitor flying into Holland can scarcely imagine that Schiphol Airport, near Amsterdam, where he would probably land, is the only airport in the world that was once (in 1573) the scene of a naval battle!

Despite the almost miraculous land reclamation the Dutch have achieved, there is still too little land. The Netherlands is the most densely populated country in Europe, with an average of almost a thousand people per square mile. If the United States were as densely populated, it would have about three billion inhabitants. Of course, density is even greater in the horse-shoe shaped megalopolis surrounding a "green heart" of lakes and woods, called the *Randstad* (literally "rimtown"), which encompasses the capital city of Amsterdam, The Hague (the seat of the government and now the royal residence), Rotterdam (the trade center and the largest port in the world), as well as the cities of Delft, Leiden and Utrecht. Its population density is twice that of Japan. Almost half the country's popula-

HOLDING BACK THE SEA: DUNES, DIKES, DAMS

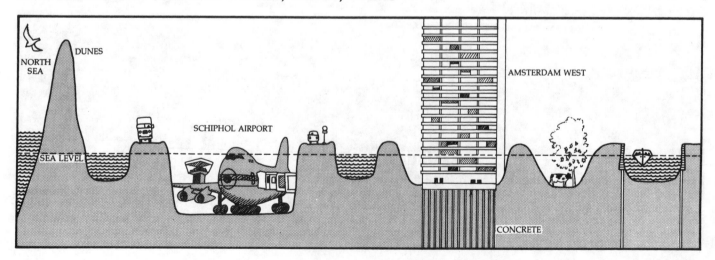

The Netherlands

The Barrier Dam under construction

. . . and completed in 1932

tion lives in this area, which covers only about one-fifth of the total land area. Such concentration has made urban difficulties the most pressing of all Dutch problems although the *Randstad* provides a model for meeting the needs of its seven million inhabitants. In 1997 it created a new metropolitan government to make it easier to manage itself.

The Netherlands is located on the North Sea at the mouth of three large rivers—the Rhine, the Meuse and the Scheldt—and with the large port in Amsterdam as well, it truly deserves the name "Gateway to the heart of Europe." It has a predominantly low-lying, flat landscape, crisscrossed by lakes and waterways, which cover a total of 10% of the country's land area, about half of which consists of polders—land surrounded by dykes and drained artificially. There are many hundreds of such polders because in earlier times the areas were pumped by windmills, which were not powerful enough to drain them. Now, with modern technology, much larger polders can be created. Dutch hydraulic engineers have been among the most ingenious in the world and have successfully tackled projects one can only call gigantic in scope. In this century the Zuyderzee and Delta projects have attracted particularattention.

The Zuyderzee Project was begun in 1920, with the expectation that it would

be completed within 40 years. The idea was to seal off the Zuyderzee Bay in the northern part of the country from the North Sea by means of a 20-mile dam called the Barrier Dam. This created a large, freshwater lake, the IJsselmeer, parts of which have been pumped dry and converted into farmland and recreation areas. If needed, residential areas for Amsterdam also could be created. The Barrier Dam was completed in 1932, and four out of five of the planned polders were created. Extremely high costs, environmental worries and disagreements concerning how the reclaimed land should best be used prevented the fifth from being completed.

In the 1950s a much larger project dramatically claimed a higher priority in the minds of the Dutch. On February 1, 1953, flood waters from the North Sea surged into the Delta area in the southwestern corner of the country, covering many of the islands there and killing almost 2,000 persons. An audacious plan was promptly adopted to close off most of the waterways of the Rhine, Scheldt and Meuse rivers from the sea by a chain of dams and artificial islands. These would shorten the coastline by 440 miles, and reverse the increasing salinization of the inland waterways. They would also enable the Dutch to claim an additional 25,000 acres of land from the sea, if they ever choose to do so.

Only one dam across the Eastern Scheldt was left to be completed when a violent verbal storm erupted over the effect such a dam could have on the plant and animal life in the estuary. The environmentalists' influence was so great that parliament decided to build a costly storm-surge barrier instead of the planned solid dam. This change, which would better protect the ecological system, added more than a billion dollars to the costs, delayed completion until 1986, required entire new technology and could result in a barrier that might not last more than 50 years.

Queen Beatrix officially opened the Oosterscheldedam, assuring her subjects that "nature is under control but not disturbed." Indeed, this two-mile dam is "the ultimate insurance policy." This barrier, costing $5 billion, is the most expensive maritime project in the nine centuries since the Dutch have been building dykes to hold back the sea. It is a movable barrier, anchored by 65 concrete piers as large as grain elevators, which lowers 62 gigantic steel gates at the touch of a button to block off the rampaging North Sea whenever a serious storm threatens. Unless they are lowered, the tides continue to flow into the Rhine estuary as usual. This "compromise barrier" was a victory for the vocal Dutch environmental lobby. Large, man-made changes in the Nether-

The Netherlands

lands' geography on the scale of the past are more difficult. But in 1997 the Dutch completed a storm surge barrier to protect Rotterdam.

Experts calculated that these gates will need to be closed only once every five years or so. When another storm like that in 1953 raged again in February 1995, forcing a quarter of a million Dutch to evacuate their homes, this kind of dam could mean the difference between survival and total disaster for the inhabitants of Zeeland.

In 1995 the Dutch were caught looking the wrong way. Having focused on the North Sea, they were struck this time by man-made perils along the Rhine and Meuse rivers. Marshes and floodplains once acted as sponges, soaking up surges of water. But in order to create residential and industrial property, people all the way along the river have dried out, asphalted and cemented, and buttressed with embankments the earlier water-logged land. Changes in farming practices have also reduced the land's capacity to absorb rainwater. Worst of all, stretches of the Rhine have been straightened, reducing the meander to the sea and doubling the water's speed from Basel. This lessens the river system's ability to accommodate floodwaters. Holland's dykes held in 1995, but they were weakened by what many called "the flood of the century." Alarm bells were rung alerting the Dutch, more than a third of whom live below sea level, that they must again mobilize for a renewed campaign to salvage their lands.

The Netherlands is still a country where the old can be seen alongside the new. Windmills are plentiful, although they no longer serve their original purpose. For centuries the flowerbed of Europe, Holland in April almost seems like a gigantic bouquet of tulips, daffodils, narcissuses and hyacinths. In a few isolated villages one can find men in baggy pants and wooden shoes and women in floppy hats and bustling skirts. Yet the Netherlands is an extremely prosperous and heavily industrialized country, with a people whose dress is now more casual and modern. It is a dynamic country whose modern look prevails over the traditional.

HISTORY

The Emergence of the Netherlands

Protestant leaders in the northernmost provinces of the Spanish empire signed, in 1579, the Declaration of Utrecht swearing to defend liberty and religious freedom. Predictably the Catholic Spanish King was unwilling to accept such freedom in the area he controlled, so in 1581 the northern provinces declared their complete independence of Spain. William, Prince of Orange-Nassau, also known as William the Silent, became the first head (*Stadholder*) of the newly born Dutch Republic. He was assassinated by order of Spanish King Philip II, but the young Republic was able to resist Spanish efforts to reassert control. Aided initially by the English and by a fortuitous storm which decimated a mighty Spanish naval armada in 1588, the Dutch conducted a brilliant land campaign, led by Prince Maurice, son of William the Silent, and forced the Spanish to vacate the Netherlands in 1595. Although more wars with the Spanish followed, the Peace of Westphalia internationally recognized Dutch independence in 1648.

The 17th century was one in which the Dutch were involved in almost constant war, but it was for them also one of commercial success, naval supremacy and cultural bloom. It was the Netherlands' "Golden Age," and Dutch confidence and prosperity were vividly recorded in the paintings of the Dutch masters. It was the century in which Amsterdam quadrupled its population to 200,000 inhabitants and became a major point of departure for the entire world. It was also a city that even at that time was constantly *moving inland* as more and more land was reclaimed from the sea. In 1609 the Bank of Amsterdam was established, 85 years before the Bank of England, and Dutch financiers were among the most influential in the world. It was also a time of philosophical and scientific discovery.

Trade and Colonization

By the middle of the 17th century the Dutch had 16,289 seagoing vessels and 160,000 seamen. Their traders could be found in every corner of the globe, most often representing huge private companies such as the Dutch East and West India Companies, which had been chartered by parliament, called the States General. They traded virtually all over Europe, and their activities extended to Central Asia, where they had obtained the first tulip bulbs in the 16th century, India, Ceylon (now Sri Lanka), Japan, Formosa and Indonesia, where they established a colony which they controlled until 1949. In 1652 they established a colony at a

Aerial view of the Oosterscheldedam

Photo: Aerocamera-Bart Hofmeester

Manhattan Island about 1627 . . . and today

good stopping-off place on the southern tip of Africa.

This Cape Colony was snatched by the British in 1806, but the Dutch descendants packed their belonging in 1836–8 and moved in a "Great Trek" into the interior of what is now the Republic of South Africa and established the Afrikaaner colony of Transvaal in 1852 and the Orange Free State in 1854. Ultimately these Dutch (together with French Huguenot descendants), who speak a dialect of Dutch called Afrikaans, became the predominant white group in the Republic of South Africa that was created from a union of Dutch settled areas and British colonies. Until well into the 20th century the Dutch retained great sympathy for their Afrikaaner relatives, who had created an economically prosperous state in an inhospitable land and who had successfully resisted cultural assimilation by

the British who previously had political control of the area as a colony. However, the Dutch gradually turned against the Afrikaaners because of the latters' policy of racial segregation known as apartheid, an Afrikaans word meaning "separate." Until majority rule was introduced in 1994, the Dutch were among South Africa's most determined foes.

In 1609 a navigational failure brought the Dutch to North America. In that year Henry Hudson, an English sea captain in the service of the Dutch, sailed westward in search of a passage to the East Indies and China. He failed in his mission, but he bumped into what is now New York and sailed up a hitherto unknown river that now bears his name. It was the fate of America in its earliest days to be visited by seamen who actually wanted to get somewhere else! Hudson's contact with America resulted in the establishment of

the Dutch West India Company and in subsequent settlement of the New World.

Six years before the Pilgrim fathers landed, in 1614 the Dutch established Fort Nassau on an island just below the present-day city of Albany, New York, a city which the Dutch incorporated in 1652 as the town of Beverwych. In 1625 an even more important fort and town had been founded on Manhattan Island, and five family farms were established to supply the soldiers and merchants. The name of the town was Nieuw (New) Amsterdam, and it was soon to become the most important city in the Dutch North American Colony, called New Netherland. Only a year later the Dutch Governor made the famous deal with the local Indians, buying the whole of Manhattan Island for 30 guilders' worth of merchandise, which by today's exchange rates is worth only about $12, but which was worth considerably more

The Netherlands

in 1625. It was nevertheless an extraordinarily favorable exchange for the Dutch.

In the next two decades New Netherland continued to grow, but at a much slower rate than the British colonies in New England and Virginia, whose populations outnumbered the Dutch settlers by at least four to one. New Amsterdam had a population that did not exceed 700 by 1647. Its boundaries, if one looks at a present-day map of New York City, extended to Pearl Street and to the northern wall, called *de wal*, which gave the name to what is now perhaps the richest street in the world, Wall Street. Under the last Dutch governor, Pieter Stuyvesant, the city grew to 1,500 (1664) and boasted two windmills and one church. It was a very cosmopolitan city in which reportedly 18 languages were spoken. In strict accordance with Dutch West India policy, religious or other discrimination was forbidden. It was therefore much more tolerant than the Massachusetts Bay Colony to the north. It was also much more fun to live in New Netherland. There were many inns for drinking and dancing, and sports were a favorite activity. One such sport imported from Holland was called kolf, which developed into modern golf.

The Dutch continued to found cities in their colony. Among them were what is now the Bronx, Staten Island, Breukelen (Brooklyn), Haarlem (Harlem), Bergen (now Jersey City), Hackensack and Ridgewood. But the growth of New Netherland was halted abruptly by one of the three wars Holland fought against England in the 17th century. When British ships of war sailed into the harbor of New Amsterdam in 1664, Governor Stuyvesant saw no alternative to surrendering the colony to the English.

Although the Dutch won the colony back for a year in 1673–4, the Dutch foothold on North America was lost. They also lost their settlements in Brazil, although they managed to hold on to Dutch Guiana (since 1975 the independent nation of Suriname) on the northern coast of South America and to a handful of Caribbean islands known as the Netherlands Antilles, which still belong to the Dutch. But Dutch influence did not totally disappear from North America. Governor Stuyvesant returned to his beloved city, renamed New York, to live on his farm on Manhattan Island. His *Bouwerij*, the Dutch word for farm, gave the name for a famous, but now rundown area in New York City known by its Americanized name—the Bowery.

Holland and the United States

In 1775 the Netherlands was the first foreign nation to fire a salute to the newly—designed American flag, and in 1782 it was the second country formally to recognize the independence of the U.S. It was America's major source for loans, although it must be said that Dutch lenders at the same time provided loans to the British.

The Netherlands also left influences in the New World that became a part of American history and culture. Many famous Americans, including James Madison, Martin van Buren, Zackery Taylor, Ulysses S. Grant, Jefferson Davis and Theodore and Franklin D. Roosevelt descended from Dutch settlers. Also, some words such as skate (from *schaats*), cookie (*koekje*), cole slaw (*kool sla*), cruller (*krullen*), halibut and pickle, as well as such seafaring expressions as skipper, marline, hoist and yacht entered English through the Dutch language. Perhaps the most famous, however, was the corruption of the popular Dutch name in the 17th century, Jan-Kees, which came to be applied to all persons from the United States: "yankees." The first serving American president to visit the Netherlands was George Bush, who in July 1989 paid tribute to the contributions made by the Dutch in America, especially their strong spirit of freedom.

Decline and Political Change

In the numerous wars during the 17th century, particularly against the English, the Dutch did not always fare badly. One time during the reign of Charles II of England, as Samuel Pepys described in his diary, the Dutch Admiral de Ruyter sailed up the Thames, burning British warships at Chatham right outside of London harbor and putting the city into a panic. This event was a high point in Dutch history and is still commemorated in Holland. The Dutch were also able to frustrate the plans of Louis XIV to conquer the Netherlands.

Nevertheless, Holland was exhausted by almost continuous war, and it became clear by the end of the 17th century that the Netherlands had assumed a position in the world that was out of proportion to its resources and size. It was propped up to some extent in the 18th century by a close tie with England. When James II of England decided to remain a Catholic, parliament offered the throne in 1688 to the Protestant Dutch *Stadholder*, Prince William III of Orange-Nassau, who had fought the English only ten years earlier. William reigned with his wife, Mary, the daughter of the deposed James II. The childless couple ruled until 1702, and it was after them that the College of William and Mary in Williamsburg, Virginia, was named, as well as Nassau Hall at Princeton University. The 18th century was for Holland one of political and cultural decline. When the French came again in 1795 the Dutch were unable to offer serious resistance.

The Netherlands for the first time in 1813 created a monarchy of its own. In 1848 the revolutionary tide in France, Belgium and elsewhere in Europe reportedly converted King William I into a "liberal overnight," and he accepted a constitutional revision which made the government responsible to parliament rather than to the king. Thereafter, the Dutch monarch reigned but no longer ruled and became merely the first citizen of the kingdom. This was in effect the same position the Princes of Orange had earlier occupied as Stadholders of the Dutch Republic and remains essentially true today.

After 1848 the Netherlands was confronted with tensions arising from industrialization. Though it came later than in Belgium or England, it nevertheless spawned a trade union and socialist movement. Holland also was confronted with struggles between the churches and the state, particularly over the creation of religiously affiliated schools that would be financed by the state. Not until 1920 was the present system of full state subsidies for parochial schools established. In all of these disputes, the Dutch displayed their characteristic willingness to abide by established rule of the democratic game and to find harmonious solutions to conflicts and differences.

The World Wars

During World War I, the Netherlands remained neutral and unoccupied. Sniffing the winds of change this mighty conflagration released, the Dutch did introduce universal suffrage for men in 1917 and for women in 1919. Because it had not joined Germany's enemies, the last German Kaiser fled to Holland after his abdication, living there until his death in 1941. The war radically disrupted the trade on which Holland has always been so dependent, and after the war its prewar prosperity did not return. The economic depression of the 1930s created greater unemployment, which stimulated radical movements on the left and right.

When the German army was hurled westward again in May 1940 the Dutch were unable to remove themselves from the melee. The Dutch army was facing east. The Germans flew around to the western part of Holland and attacked them from the rear. In the first large-scale aerial bombardment of a densely populated city, German dive-bombers destroyed 90% of Rotterdam's

The Netherlands

city center within 40 minutes. The German attempt to capture Queen Wilhelmina and the Dutch government by dropping crack paratroop units over The Hague failed, and the Queen, Crown Princess Juliana and the cabinet managed to escape to London; they worked during the entire war to bring about a German defeat.

Holland fell within 5 days and a Nazi-appointed Dutch Reich Commissioner, an Austrian named Seyss-Inquart, ruled the country for the remainder of the war. This was an especially hard time for the Dutch, especially for Jews. Although its true authorship had been placed into question, the *Diary of Anne Frank*, whose setting is Amsterdam during the Nazi occupation, remains a moving testimony to the suffering inflicted upon the chief victims of Nazi racial theories and policies. Unfortunately, some Dutch people were among the persecutors. As late as 1980, an art-collector, Pieter Menten, was imprisoned and fined for his role in the murder of 20 to 30 Jews in Poland in 1941. In 2000, compensation payments totaling $240 million were offered to about 35,000 Jews for damages they or their relatives suffered in the Netherlands.

Thousands of Dutch were active in the resistance movement against the occupation forces although many did collaborate with the German occupation forces. Despite the successful Allied landing in Normandy in June 1944, because of strong German resistance north of the Rhine and Allied policy to drive toward Berlin, that part of Holland north of the

Rhine was not liberated until May 1945; the area south of the Rhine was freed in September 1944. When the horror was over, the Netherlands was left with 280,000 civilian dead, vast expanses of flooded areas, wrecked harbors and industries, and an economy close to total collapse. Dutch memories and emotions remain strong, which is one reason why a West German chancellor's trip to Holland in December 1987 was only the third official visit there in a quarter of a century.

Recovery

The very popular Queen Wilhelmina returned to Holland in 1945 amid enthusiastic cheers of her people, and the Dutch set about to mend their physically broken country, a task they were able to complete surprisingly quickly. In 1948, Wilhelmina abdicated in favor of her daughter, Juliana, and all would have gone well if the Netherlands had not been forced to face the same searing problem which was plaguing several other European powers at the time: decolonization.

The jewel of the colonial empire was Indonesia. In 1619 the Dutch East India Company had created a city it called Batavia (now Jakarta) on the island of Java. From this base the Dutch extended their control over most of the 3,000 or so islands of the Indonesian archipelago; for more than 300 years they retained firm control over the colony, but their policy of drawing a rather distinct line between themselves and the native population was a major factor which fanned the flames of

an independence movement in the 20th century. The islands were an attractive target for Japanese expansion after 1940. The Dutch government, which was trying to maintain a policy of neutrality in the Pacific war, could not organize a credible defense. Indonesia was captured in February 1942.

Decolonization

When the Dutch returned at the end of the war in order to reclaim what they believed was theirs, they found that they were not wanted by a native population whose leaders had declared the islands' independence in August 1945 immediately after the Japanese surrender. After four years of tension, military conflict and American pressure, a settlement was reached which recognized an independent Indonesia within a kind of union the Dutch equated with the British Commonwealth of Nations.

This agreement by no means settled all the difficulties. The Dutch had insisted on retaining full control of their economic investments, which at the time accounted for almost 15% of their national income. Indonesia's flamboyant and unpredictable President Sukarno solved the problem single-handedly by simply nationalizing all Dutch properties in 1957. Relations between the two countries also remained sour because of the Dutch retention of West Irian, part of the island of New Guinea, which the Indonesians claimed. Finally, in 1962, an American mediator proposed the face-saving procedure of turning West Irian over to the UN, which seven months later transferred sovereignty to Indonesia.

After a painfully drawn out severance from Indonesia, the Netherlands was more than cooperative in aiding its other colonies to gain their own independence. In 1975, Suriname was freed in the midst of widespread fears among the Surinamese that such independence would lead to violent racial measures against the whites and East Indian Hindustani. More than a quarter of the population fled to Holland in the final days before independence. In order to help Suriname adjust to its new status, the Netherlands promised it aid amounting to $100 million for each of the following ten years, certainly one of the most generous foreign aid programs on a per capita basis in history.

However, because of the Surinamese government's flagrant human rights violations, the Netherlands suspended its assistance programs in 1983. The Netherlands notified the six islands in the Netherlands Antilles that they must prepare for their independence. They organized themselves into four self-governing communities: Aruba, Bonaire, Curaçao

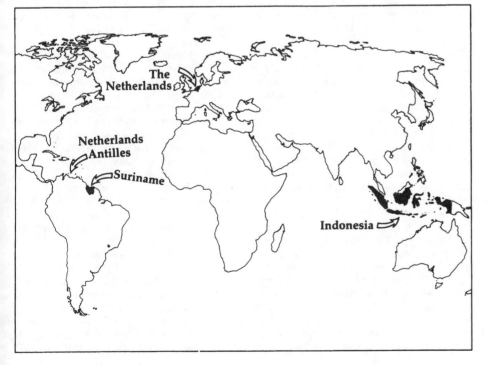

The Netherlands

Prince Constantijn, H.M. Queen Beatrix, H.R.H. the late Prince Claus, Crown Prince Willem–Alexander, Prince Johan Friso

Photo by Vincent Mentzel

and the Leeward Islands (southern portion of St. Maarten, St. Eustatius and Saba). The island of Aruba became an independent state in 1986, and in 2000 voters on the island of St. Maarten opted to break away from the Dutch Antilles federation and become a separate country within the Kingdom of the Netherlands. Amsterdam came to fear that the islands would not be able to find a long-term alternative to economic dependence on Holland. Therefore, Dutch officials opposed St. Maarten's independence, believing that it would be a bad precedent for the other islands.

POLITICS AND GOVERNMENT

The Monarch

The Netherlands is a constitutional monarchy whose character is prominently visible during the investiture ceremony when a new king or queen begins to reign. The monarch takes an oath of allegiance to the constitution. Also, the royal crown is not placed on the head of the new ruler (for which reason the ceremony is called an investiture, not a coronation), but it and the other symbols of royal authority-the orb and the scepter—are arranged on a table around the constitution.

The royal family is the House of Orange-Nassau, whose descendants are inseparably tied to the Netherlands' entire history as an independent state. This is one reason why there is very little opposition to the monarchy in Holland and why

most Dutch remain firmly attached to their monarchs. It was therefore a shock to many Dutch to witness the violent disturbances in Amsterdam, Rotterdam and Utrecht on April 30, 1980, when the popular 71-year-old Queen Juliana abdicated in favor of her daughter Beatrix. While orange flags and streamers were displayed everywhere and while the mood around the royal palace in Amsterdam was royally festive, elsewhere several thousand protesters waged such violent battles with the police that more than 50 policemen and 100 demonstrators were injured. The slogan of the protesters was "No apartment, no coronation," which referred to the serious housing shortage in the capital city. No doubt some of the protesters wished also to show disapproval of the monarchy and of a family which is among the richest in the world and which draws over $5 million a year from the state treasury to maintain a royal household with 250 servants and other assistants. The area in which the ceremony was held had to be sealed off by the police.

Queen Beatrix was well prepared for her position, having studied law, politics and history at the University of Leiden. She has a pleasantly dimpled smile and is extremely knowledgeable and interested in politics. But she tends to be a strong-willed and impatient person whose manner is often stiff and aristocratic. For a while her manner appealed less to her people than did that of her unpretentious mother Juliana, but the nation's respect

for her has grown considerably since she became queen. It was her mother's enormous popularity that had enabled the family to overcome an extremely embarrassing scandal in the last decade of her reign; it was prompted by revelations that her husband, Prince Bernhard, had accepted payoffs from the Lockheed Aircraft Corporation for his assistance in helping the company to secure lucrative contracts from the Dutch air force.

Beatrix's marriage in 1966 to a German diplomat, Claus, had created quite an uproar at the time, but the marriage became accepted, and Claus proved himself to be an effective promoter of good Dutch relations with developing countries. He acted as an adviser to the Minister of Development. Suffering from Parkinson's Disease, he died in October 2002 at age 76.

Her sons are preparing for their future roles. Johan Friso went to the University of California at Berkeley to study engineering. Crown Prince Willem-Alexander served as a lieutenant on a guided missile frigate, is trained as a pilot and holds the rank of lieutenant-colonel. However, he is not a career soldier. He is a specialist in water management and is on the International Olympic Committee. In 2002 he married Maxima Zorreguieta from Argentina. Since her father had been a cabinet member during the time of Argentina's military dictatorship, he was not permitted to attend the wedding.

Queen Beatrix is extremely hardworking and spends hours preparing for her speeches and meetings, and reading

The Netherlands

The formation of a government out of almost a dozen parties that win parliamentary seats is therefore a very delicate task, requiring a firm but subtle lead on the part of the monarch. She consults numerous party, parliamentary and other political leaders in order to acquaint herself intimately with the political climate. Then, acting entirely independently, she names an *informateur*, who is usually a leading politician, whose task is to advise her of the most promising formula for constructing a government. She then appoints a *formateur*, a person who must seek to form a government in which he himself would probably be the prime minister. He is usually the leader of the party that has won the most seats in the election. His task includes the establishment of a program acceptable to several different parties. Such a broad program is necessarily moderate; no remotely radical program would be acceptable to several parties. The entire process usually takes a very long time, usually two to four months. Fortunately the work is done carefully, and normally results in a government that can survive for at least three years.

In the carefully constructed cabinet, ministerial seats are usually distributed according to the proportion of seats the various governing parties have in the lower house, the most important positions being that of prime minister and minister of finance. Cabinet members, including prime ministers, need not be members of parliament, and some ministers are specialists who had never even run for elective office in their lives.

Crown Princess Maxima and Willem-Alexander

proposed legislation. She was very frank in her inaugural speech about the unromantic side of being Queen: "It is a task no one would ever seek. The glitter is visible, but not the burden and perpetual self-denial." In most matters she is prevented from making any mistakes by the requirement that the appropriate cabinet member also sign all her acts and decrees.

Entangled in a rare scandal in 2003, the Queen was sued for $53 million by her niece, Princess Margarita, who accuses her of abusing royal privilege and behaving like a "tyrant" by bugging her Amsterdam apartment, recording her telephone calls, intercepting her letters and spying on her commoner husband. Responding to evidence that the palace had indeed ordered a surveillance operation without the government's knowledge, Prime Minister Jan Peter Balkenende issued an apology. Claiming that these tactics had ruined her husband's business and amounted to "psychological terror," Margarita's lawyers took the unprecedented action of filing criminal charges against the state and considering calling the Queen to appear in court. Because of a special immunity law of 1840, Beatrix cannot be prosecuted for any crime, but she can be summoned as a witness. The angry niece also took the opportunity to reveal that the Queen's father, Bernhard, had had a secret love affair. Polls in 2003 revealed that 54% of Dutch believe that the revelations have compromised Beatrix, and the percentage of subjects no longer happy with her role as head of state rose from 8% to 28%.

Forming a Parliamentary Government

She is certainly very capable of performing the one public act she is charged to accomplish independently: to coordinate the long coalition talks that are necessary to form a government after a parliamentary election. Because the Netherlands uses the proportional representation electoral system, many parties are able to win seats in the lower house, and no single party can even come close to winning a majority on its own.

The Hague, with the Dutch Parliament in the background

The Netherlands

Compared with other parliamentary systems in which a prime minister is the most important political figure, the Dutch system is almost unique in that it calls for a separation between the executive (cabinet) and the parliament. All cabinet members must resign their seats in parliament, and the new government need not seek the formal approval of the lower house. Nor is there such a thing as a vote of confidence in which a majority in parliament can vote against the government, causing it to fall. The government is, however, always free voluntarily to pose a "question of confidence" to the lower house if it chooses. It is acutely interested in maintaining a majority without which it could not gain approval for important legislation, which is almost always written and submitted by the government, not by members of parliament.

The Parliament

The Dutch Parliament, called the States General, remains powerful in comparison to many other parliaments in Western Europe. One reason is that the lower house has permanent committees that correspond to each ministry. Therefore, parliament members can develop the necessary expertise to question and control the work of the ministries. Further, parties in parliament do not require absolute discipline from their members, who according to the constitution represent the entire nation, not a regional or party constituency. Therefore, the government can never be absolutely sure that its measures will pass in both houses. It must design its legislation in such a way that it would be acceptable to more than a slim majority, and it must work very hard to persuade parliaments to support its programs. Parliament is by no means dominated or overshadowed by the cabinet.

The States General was first established in 1464 by the Burgundian kings as an advisory body. After independence in 1581, it considered itself the keeper of Dutch sovereignty and granted an hereditary official, the *Stadholder*, the right to exercise executive power. The States General is bicameral, and both the First and Second Chambers meet in the Binnenhof (Inner Court) in The Hague. The First Chamber, or upper house, is composed of 75 members elected by the 12 provincial parliaments for six-year terms, with one half of its membership being elected every three years. Since the provincial chambers are elected directly, the upper house usually has roughly the same party composition as the Second Chamber. This First Chamber cannot introduce or amend bills, but it is far more than a mere advisory or delaying chamber as is the British House of

Lords. It has the right to approve or reject all legislation.

The Second Chamber is composed of 150 members elected at least every four years by all citizens 18 years or older. In contrast to most other European countries, elections are not held on Sundays. Nevertheless, voter turnout is high (roughly 75%) in contrast to U.S. presidential elections which are also held on Tuesdays and which now rarely attract more than 60% of the voters. The Second Chamber generally meets three days a week, Tuesday through Thursday, and its members are expected neither to reside in The Hague nor to give up their normal employment while they serve. About a third of its members are women.

Both chambers are regarded as the chief interpreters of the constitution, and together they are empowered to initiate the process to amend the constitution. If a majority in both houses finds a constitutional amendment necessary, then both houses are dissolved, new elections are held, and the amendment can then be accepted by a two-thirds vote in both chambers. No court in Holland has the right to declare a legislative act unconstitutional. The highest court of the land, the Court of Cassation, can only nullify a statute that is in variance with an international agreement. Its chief tasks are to insure the uniform administration of justice and to serve as the court of high appeal for decisions made in lower courts. Presiding over those lower courts are independent judges who apply Dutch law. There are no juries; the Dutch want a professional administration of justice by judges who serve for life and who are as free as possible from popular influences.

Dutch law has its origins in Roman law. However, the Dutch copied and codified the French civil code in the 18th century. After a significant recent reform of its Citizens' Law Book (*Burgelijk Wetboek*), based on a major comparative study in 1992, the Dutch private legal system now functions as a guideline for democratizing countries, such as Estonia.

Assisting the Queen and government as the highest advisory body is the Council of State, which is composed of a crown prince or princess over the age of 18 and no more than 24 persons appointed for life, although they normally step down at the age of 70. They are expected to have political, commercial, trade union, diplomatic or military experience. The Queen officially presides over the Council, although it is actually guided by a vice-president who is selected from among the members. The cabinet can seek expert advice from the Council and is always responsive to any constructive advice it might give.

Political Parties

At all levels of government Dutch political parties play a key role in informing voters about the most important political issues, conducting election campaigns, and then forming coalitions to rule. Dutch political parties have always tended to represent particular subcultures in society, such as Catholicism, various shades of Protestantism, socialism or liberalism. At the same time, they must adjust their aims to those of other parties in order to be able to participate in government, therefore, compromise and mutual adjustment have been their basic rules. In a small country with such a highly homogeneous population, the range of political interests and opinions is somewhat narrower than in a large, multi-racial, multi-lingual and multi-national country. Thus, a consensus regarding the political system and rules of the game has always been relatively easy to maintain in Holland, and this has made it less difficult for such a multi-party state to have such a high degree of parliamentary stability.

It has, however, become increasingly difficult to form coalition governments in Holland, and this results partly from a change which is occurring in party politics. In the past, no Dutch government could ever be formed without the participation of confessional (religious) parties, particularly the Catholic party. Therefore, the secular parties always had to moderate their programs in order to be able to coalesce with them. But as the importance of religion declines in Dutch society, fewer and fewer Dutch vote for a party exclusively for religious reasons. Therefore, the strength of the confessional parties has declined in recent years. Seeing this, the major secular parties have sharpened up their own programs and have moved more clearly to the right or left in order to draw the formerly religiously oriented voters away from the politically heterogeneous religious parties. In other words, the major secular parties often have intentionally tried to polarize Dutch politics in order to attract more votes. They have even publicly stated that they are not interested in entering into any coalition with each other.

A couple dozen parties usually competed for seats. Some of them, such as the Party for the Liquidation of the Netherlands, the God is With Us, the Live or Die Together, and the hard-line Communist Party of the Netherlands (CPN), could not seriously hope to win seats. But profiting from proportional representation, which grants a parliamentary seat for roughly 55,000 votes, several parties manage to win seats.

The Green Left, which rallies radicals, socialists, pacifists, and communists, won

The Netherlands

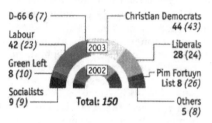

Labour nearly came back

Seats in Dutch lower house, 2003 *(2002)*

D-66 6 *(7)* — Christian Democrats 44 *(43)*

Labour 42 *(23)*

Green Left 8 *(10)* — Liberals 28 *(24)*

Socialists 9 *(9)* — Pim Fortuyn List 8 *(26)*

2003 / **2002** Total: *150* — Others 5 *(8)*

Source: *The Economist*

Prime Minister Peter Jan Balkenende with the picture of Harry Potter

10 seats in 2002 and eight in 2003. Dutch voters are very sensitive to environmental issues. The crowded population, flatness, and the fact that half of it is below sea level make it a first victim to any rise in water levels due to the "greenhouse effect." In fact, in 1989 a Dutch government became the first in Europe to fall in a crisis over the environment. The Socialist Party retained its nine seats in 2003.

The more conservative of the main secular parties is the People's Party for Freedom and Democracy (VVD), headed by Gerrit Zalm. It is usually referred to as the Liberal Party because of its century-long struggle to reduce the influence of the churches in Dutch public life, especially in the schools. Individual freedom is its chief tenet, and it favors lower taxes, an even lower government deficit, a shrinking of the increasingly costly welfare state, higher criminal sentences, and a strengthening of the police in order to curb crime. It supports a free market economy, but it also favors profit sharing with workers. It draws voters particularly from the upper and middle classes. It had done well in the 2002 elections, although it had fallen from 38 to 23 seats. In 2003 it was able to recoup some of its losses, capturing 28 seats. It is in the governing coalition.

The other main secular party is the Labor Party (PvdA), formerly led by Wim Kok, a popular leader, whose relaxed and more moderate, democratic style contrasted strikingly with his predecessor's more autocratic and ideological approach. It is a moderate socialist reform party, which traditionally favors what it calls *Nivellering*, or the elimination of differences in citizens' power, knowledge and income. It supports an increased workers' share of profits and decision-making in the factories. Although the coalition governments Kok had led for eight years had achieved "the Dutch miracle" of low unemployment and solid economic growth, it was rudely thrown out of power in the 2002 elections, declining from 45 to 23 seats.

However, it bounced back vigorously in the 2003 elections, led by a dynamic, telegenic and charismatic young leader,

Wouter Bos. A former Shell manager, Bos had entered parliament only five years earlier at age 34 and had become a junior finance minister in 2000. To shake its aloof image, the party selected its new leader in a rare primary election open to all members, thereby breaking from its former practice of having the party elite decide behind closed doors. Bos spent as much time criticizing his own party for past mistakes as he did his opponents. He also announced that if his party came out on top, it would be Amsterdam's popular mayor, Job Cohen, who would become prime minister, not he. In the 2003 tally the party regained much ground, winning 42 seats and coming within a whisker of the leading Christian Democrats.

The moderately left-wing party called Democrats 66, had been founded in that year in order to present voters with a clear alternative to the established parties, especially the PvdA, whose strong, paternalistic leadership was widely resented at the time. It opposes the ideological approach to politics and sees itself as a prac-

Wouter Bos, Leader of Labor Party

tical, problem-party. It advocates reforms in the society and the constitution, such as the direct election of the prime minister. Once a trendy, intellectual party that appealed mainly to young voters from the upper and middle classes, it has broadened its base considerably. In 2002, it slipped from 14 to seven seats. Its slide continued in 2003 to only six, but it joined the government.

Fighting for its political life until 2002 between the secular parties of the left and right was the Christian Democratic Appeal (CDA). Faced with the gloomy prospect of watching their voters run to the increasingly polarized secular parties, the three major religious political parties, which had long since severed their direct ties with the churches, decided in 1973 to join forces for electoral purposes. In a nostalgic ceremony of prayers and hymn singing in 1980, they went a giant step further by disbanding themselves entirely and becoming full members of the larger CDA.

The merger in 1980 brought birds of many different colors together, which are difficult to control. They all agree basically that Christian principles must be applied in politics and that both a free enterprise economy and the present social welfare system should be defended. The fact that the CDA encompasses a broad political spectrum gives it the advantage that the party can easily form a coalition with almost every other party. Therefore, the CDA has survived the secularization and polarization of Dutch politics and until 1994 was the key party in any coalition. In 2003 three separate fundamentalist Christian parties captured five seats (down from six).

In the May 2002 elections the CDA emerged as the strongest party, advancing

The Netherlands

from 29 to 43 seats. Its leader, Peter Jan Balkenende, became prime minister in a three-party center-right coalition with the Liberals (VVD) and a new party, the List Pim Fortuyn (LPF). Nicknamed "Harry Potter" because of his striking resemblance to the boyish film character, Balkenende is a former professor of Christianity and head of the Christian broadcasting network. He had entered parliament only four years before becoming prime minister. During the electoral campaign, he expressed concerns about his country's euthanasia policy and drug laws and called for more rigorous measures of integrating immigrants, such as required language and culture courses. His short-lived government in 2002 announced plans to put these campaign promises into practice. He thereby turned away from Holland's multicultural approach to immigration.

In the 2003 elections the CDA added a seat and barely nosed out resurgent Labor to remain the country's largest party, 44 seats to Labor's 42. It thereby had the privilege to put together a government after four months of hard negotiations. Unlike all other party leaders, he refused during the 2002 campaign to criticize one of the Netherlands' most colorful and controversial politicians, who was assassinated a week before the elections.

Pim Fortuyn was the antithesis to Dutch consensus politics. An openly gay sociology professor and ex-Marxist, who became a prominent talk-show guest and columnist for the weekly magazine, *Elsevier*, Fortuyn was an effective anti-establishment populist. He dared to express in public his reservations about the effects of burgeoning immigration on Dutch culture and society, something that Dutch political correctness had hitherto forbidden. Even many who did not agree with his views found his directness a breath of fresh air in a stuffy political environment. Three months before the national elections he had been named leader of the Livable Netherlands Party, but he was soon thrown out for violating its nondiscrimination policy. He then formed his List Pim Fortuyn, which immediately captured a stunning 35% of the votes in Rotterdam's municipal elections. He expressed contempt for green politics. He was shot dead by an environmental activist, who in April 2003 was given a shockingly lenient sentence of 18 years in prison, read amidst the boos, curses and sobs of Fortuyn supporters in the courtroom. This shocked his countrymen, who had never imagined that such violence could happen in their well-ordered country.

Led until August 2002 by Mat Herben, a former spokesman for the Freemasons and defense ministry, the party capitalized on this feeling in the May 2002 na-

tional elections, which saw an unusually large turnout: 79%. It won an astounding 26 seats, becoming the second largest party and partner in the ruling coalition. Not since 1945 had a new party won so many seats in its debut. Its success reflected the increasing worry that the political establishment was not in touch with the voters' concerns about a level of immigration that could no longer be absorbed. This eclectic "List" includes a young West African entrepreneur, a former Miss Netherlands beauty queen, and a pig farmer. Almost all were political novices. Dutch politics had been changed dramatically by the LPF.

The list failed miserably as a governing party in Prime Minister Balkenende's ruling coalition, with four novice politicians in ministerial posts. The party's continuous internal feuding and power struggles, culminating in the raucous resignation of two of its ministers in October, blew the three-party government apart after only 87 days in office. Returning to the voters again in January 2003, the Pim Fortuyn List was issued a rude rebuke for their irresponsibility, losing all but eight of their seats. However, the party could take some consolation in the fact that all the established parties adopted much of the Fortuyn platform, calling for tighter immigration policies and the need for more integration.

Unitary System, Regions, Municipalities

The Netherlands is a unitary, not a federal state. There are elected provincial and municipal governments which deal with matters of regional or local concern, but about 90% of their income is channeled to them by the central government. In each of the 12 provinces voters elect by means of proportional representation a Provincial Council. This assembly appoints from among its own members a Provincial Executive who is responsible for the day-to-day administration; retaining a French practice, the central government appoints a Queen's Commissioner, who presides over the Provincial Council and Executive and seeks to insure that nationwide interests will not be overlooked. The Provincial Councils elect the members of the First Chamber in The Hague, a provision which helps insure that provincial interests in turn will not be passed over by the central government.

Considerably more important in Dutch government are the Municipal Councils, which are also elected by proportional representation in the cities and towns. Each Municipal Council appoints Aldermen from their own membership who serve as an executive. Presiding over both the executive and the Council is the *Burgemeester* (mayor), who is appointed by the central government for a six-year term. Although he usually does not come from the city in which he serves, he very often becomes the locality's most effective spokesman in The Hague. Increasingly, several municipalities are joining to form regional authorities to tackle such matters as the location of industry, housing, transport and environment. The need for action on a larger scale than the municipality has

The Royal residence in The Hague: *Palace House in the Woods*

led to a proposal to increase the number of provinces and to allow the new provincial governments to perform such tasks.

Other very important local bodies in the Netherlands and among the oldest form of democratic administration in Europe are the Water Control Boards. Property owners within a board's jurisdiction elect a general council, which in turn elects an executive committee. The central government chooses the executive committee for the most important Water Control Boards. These are responsible for what might be considered the most important task in Holland: defending the land against water.

Housing Shortages

The Dutch government must grapple with some very difficult problems. One of the thorniest is the desperate housing shortage in the *Randstad*. People disagree on how such a shortage arose and how it should be eliminated. The shortage is due in part to changed demands for housing. As young people leave home earlier, as the divorce rate climbs and as an increasingly prosperous people demand larger and better quality housing, the demand for existing housing increases. Like other European countries, the Netherlands is experiencing a dramatic increase in homeless persons. In a controversial effort to help them, Rotterdam began in 1993 distributing tent-shaped waterproof cardboard boxes to the estimated 3,500 homeless in that city.

About half of the Dutch housing stock is owner-occupied. Rotterdam is an exception, where nearly all the land is owned by the city, and 80% of its housing is rented. Private investors are discouraged from building more new apartments because the government forbids the returns on housing investments to exceed the returns paid on state bonds. No government has been able to find a way out of this trap. With low rents, many landlords refuse to pay for the kinds of renewal which much housing needs. According to the Amsterdam municipal council, as much as 60% of the city's housing is in need of renewal. In some districts, three-fourths of the houses have no bathrooms. Thus, rather primitive accommodations are hidden behind many of the stately facades that foreign tourists admire in the capital city.

Social Welfare Problems

The government was confronted with the problem of how to finance the generous social welfare system the country has built up. Unlike many Western European countries, where welfare states were created after 1945 as a compromise between capitalism and socialism, and as an essential ingredient for social peace and political stability, Holland's welfare system (called the *verzorgingsstaat*) was built more on a Christian imperative, rather than on a political necessity. Most observers believe that it has reached the limits of the welfare state and that it must realistically revise downward its earlier version of a new society. The Christian Democrats cut back the welfare system, and the Labor party continued in this direction.

It is understandable why the Dutch want to cling to the social welfare system. Parents receive special allowances for children, and widows and orphans receive special benefits although widows who can work must do so. Health insurance has been privatized, is universal, and includes dental care. It covers treatment and nursing in institutions for the physically and mentally handicapped, nursing homes, hospitals, sanitoria and similar establishments.

Workers who are declared to be fully or partially disabled are entitled to benefits in amounts up to 70% of their wages. Since 1968 when these disability benefits were expanded, the nation's health has seemingly declined rapidly. In that year 5.5% of the work force was considered to be at least partly disabled. By 1991 over 16% were so categorized on the basis of complaints ranging from claustrophobia to chronic backache, and this was swallowing up almost 7% of GDP. In 1988 the average worker called in sick 8.4% of all workdays. In the 1990s this disability scheme (called WAO) was reformed slightly. The qualification criteria were tightened and benefit levels cut to 70% of previous salary. Nevertheless the number of claimants continued to rise, especially after psychological problems and stress were added. By 2002 nearly a million persons qualified for WAO out of a work force of seven million.

All in all, only one out of two adults worked by the 1990s (compared with about 80% in the U.S.), which is one reason why economic growth has lagged behind most industrialized countries for years. Government efforts in 1991 to rein in the runaway costs of the disability benefits scheme by limiting the number of years of entitlement ignited a nation-wide strike. The Kok government toughened the conditions for unemployment benefits and broadened the definition of "suitable work" to prevent people from easily rejecting job proposals. As a further incentive to work, the link between wage and benefit rises was temporarily abolished.

Generous retirement benefits await all employees who contributed to special pension plans. All Dutch who cannot support themselves, including artists, are entitled to state aid. Employers and employees contribute 50-50 to the unemployment and health insurance, but the employers and, in some cases, the state treasury pays for all the other benefits. In 1986, one-fourth of Amsterdam's residents was living from welfare or social security. The Dutch took the steady improvement of welfare provisions so much for granted that it is a small miracle that a majority of voters approved in 1986 of a reduction. Indeed, from 1983 to 1987 welfare support fell by 7.5%. The Dutch grudgingly accepted Lubbers' outlook after his 1986 election: "The role of the government in our society is changing because people are becoming more independent and want to be more responsible for themselves and others."

The luxurious social welfare system grew out of the unpleasant memories of the depression of the 1930s and of the war. At first it was paid for by rising productivity and prosperity, and after large natural gas reserves were discovered in the late 1950s, budget deficits resulting from the social welfare bill were simply paid for by large government revenues derived from the export of natural gas. But the government, wishing to conserve the country's precious supply of natural gas, announced that all export contracts were to be terminated in the 1990s.

The country faced serious choices, with no more gas revenues to look forward to and with a budgetary deficit that has fallen dramatically; in 2002 it was .1% of GDP with total debt at 51% of GDP. Public sector spending is half of GDP. How should the system be financed? By 1991 the combined burden of welfare premiums and taxes was already the second highest in the OECD behind Sweden. The Dutch government believes that the welfare state can be maintained only if it is operated more strictly and efficiently. Therefore, in 1994 it privatized sickness insurance and shifted responsibility for social security from the government to companies. It hopes to improve greatly the ratio of active to inactive persons in a land where almost half the population lives on benefits.

European and Third World Relations

The Netherlands is a founding member of the EU and has long been one of the chief proponents of a more unified Europe. The Hague is the site of several supra-national institutions, including especially the International Court of Justice, which is the supreme UN legal body in theory. This International Court meets in the stately Peace Palace built by money donated by the American steel magnate, Andrew Carnegie. The Hague has, in a way, become the center of a world system of justice. The Balkan war-crimes tribunal, which tried former Serbian President Slobodan Milosevic for war crimes, is there,

The Netherlands

A young Dutch soldier
Royal Netherlands Embassy

as is the new International Criminal Court. The world appears to trust the Dutch sense of justice and fair play.

Holland has especially distinguished itself in development aid. In 1983 it had given 1.5% of its GDP, the highest in the world, but by 1992 this had declined to .88%. It still donates more on a per-capita basis to Third World development than any other country. It is the fourth-largest financial backer of the UN refugee agency, the UNHCR. In 2000 former Prime Minister Ruud Lubbers was appointed the United Nations' High Commissioner for Refugees. One Dutch official commented, "development aid is a breed of sacred cow with us. We carry it out with the zeal formerly reserved for our country's Christian missionaries." By 2002 the Netherlands had also become the second-biggest net contributor to the EU budget (after Germany); in per capita terms it pays more into the EU coffers than any other member.

Defense Policy

Its defense policy is based on its membership in NATO. Dutch troops are well-trained and equipped, and are considered to be among the best-prepared forces in NATO. One unique feature of the Dutch military is that it officially recognizes almost a dozen official personnel associations that function very much like labor unions except that they have no right to strike.

Another unique feature is that the Dutch military was the first in the world to assign to combat units any woman who volunteers and who can satisfy the physical requirements. They also are permitted to serve on all naval vessels and to fly combat aircraft. The Dutch invested several million dollars on such things as developing backpack straps which do not irritate women's breasts, constructing separate quarters and conducting studies to determine how valid the Israeli experience is that military units are more quickly demoralized when women are wounded than when men are hit. In 2001 there were 1,920 women in the Dutch forces, 7.6% of the total. They serve in all branches.

Other armies, including that of the U.S., watched the Dutch experiment closely, as they did Holland's policy since 1974 to allow gays in the military. Gays have their own Foundation for Homosexuality in the Armed Forces (FHAF), which represents gay interests in the services. For example, when Dutch troops serving in the Balkans in 1993 were sent complimentary copies of Playboy, homosexual soldiers were sent issues of a corresponding gay publication. Self-declared homosexuals are officially welcome in the volunteer army although most experience difficulties.

The Dutch have abandoned conscription and created a flexible volunteer army designed to be used in rapid deployment actions and UN peace-keeping operations. The force has been cut 37% from 101,000 to 56,380: 27,000 in the army, 13,800 in the navy, and 11,980 in the air force. They are

backed by 75,000 reservists. Stricter discipline and grooming standards have been introduced. Earrings and ponytails have been curtailed, and the use of cannabis has been banned. The non-saluting policy was not changed.

Some army bases were closed, and 3,000 of the army troops are assigned to a joint German-Dutch corps headquartered across the border in Münster. The command for this joint corps rotates between a German and a Dutch general, and English is the unit's official language.

The air force, which since 1977 has used the American F-16 fighter, has the task of protecting Dutch air space and of contributing to the tactical air forces of the alliance. The navy plays a part in defending the Atlantic, the English Channel and the North Sea. Its most important assignment is to keep the Dutch coast clear of mines and to defend the Dutch ports, which are critical for NATO supply lines. To utilize their assets more rationally, the Dutch and Belgian navies and air forces coordinate some of their operations close to home. Several Dutch naval vessels were sent in 1991 to the Persian Gulf, and missile batteries were deployed to Turkey and Israel. The U.S. had reduced its troop level in the Netherlands from 2,200 to 1,380 by the turn of the century. In 2001 the Dutch entered a treaty with the U.S. allowing American aircraft to use Dutch bases on the Caribbean islands of Aruba and Curacao as staging areas to fight drug trafficking.

In the Balkans Dutch soldiers serve on the ground, in the air, and at sea main-

The Netherlands

taining a naval blockade. Their humanitarian image was badly tarnished by allegations in 1995 that they had stood aside after Srebrenica fell to Bosnian Serbs while 7,000 Moslem men and boys were butchered, while the women and girls were raped and expelled. The troops had been sent into the area under an ill-defined UN mandate, with none of the weaponry necessary to withstand the onslaught of thousands of Serb troops. The Dutch commander on the ground had separately sought air strikes, but failed to get any support from allies, including the U.S. The Dutch government absolved them in 1995 of any wrongdoing in that complicated and tragic situation. However, it commissioned an inquiry, which issued its report in April 2002 that Dutch troops had been sent on an "ill-conceived and virtually impossible mission." Even though the fault lay with the UN and some allies, the incident haunted the Dutch conscience for seven years, and it prompted Prime Minister Wim Kok to resign after the report was issued.

In 1999 it deployed one ship, 16 combat aircraft, and 738 troops in the NATO air war against Yugoslavia to stop ethnic cleansing in Kosovo. A tenth of its peacekeeping forces there is female. Its maintenance of peacekeepers in the Balkans, Cyprus and the Middle East underscores its changed emphasis from home defense to peacekeeping. Following the September 11, 2001, terrorist attacks against the United States, the Netherlands sent troops to Afghanistan both to serve as peacekeepers and to fight alongside American and other allies to root out and destroy the last remnants of Taliban and al-Qaeda fighting forces. In February 2003 it joined hands with Germany to command all peacekeeping forces in Afghanistan for a half year.

During the 2003 American-British war against the regime of Saddam Hussein in Iraq, which most Dutch opposed, the government permitted the American and British allies to move troops, tanks and other military supplies through the Netherlands to the Persian Gulf. This included airspace and airports, rail lines and Rotterdam harbor. Defense Minister Henk Kamp stated, "the Americans are our friends. They are here in Europe to help and protect us." The government also stood by NATO and shipped three of its four Patriot air-defense batteries and 370 soldiers to operate them to Turkey after France, Germany and Belgium had blocked Turkey's request for NATO protection against Iraq. Kamp justified this action by explaining, "we are an independent country. We have certain obligations in NATO and no one can prevent us from honoring them." After the rapid victory in April 2003, the Netherlands agreed to provide troops to help police postwar Iraq.

ECONOMY

The Dutch economy is the fourteenth largest in the world. It is almost entirely in private hands and the government restrains itself from subsidizing or assuming a direct or indirect ownership of Dutch companies. Nor does it engage in compulsory economic planning. The state nonetheless is active in the economy. For example, it is a major participant in the Netherlands Gas Company. The state employs 12% of the nation's work force, and including all social security programs, it spends half of the country's GDP.

The government is also closely tied in with the highly structured Dutch system for dealing with conflicts of economic interests. The labor unions (which have unionized about 40% of employees) send representatives to the Joint Industrial Labor Council, established in 1945; employers, primarily the Federation of Netherlands Industry and the Netherlands Federation of Christian Employers, send an equal number of representatives. The Council not only engages in collective bargaining, but serves as an official advisory body to the government.

Another important body is the Social and Economic Council (SER), which is composed of 45 representatives: 15 each from the labor unions and the employers' organizations, 13 academics, and the heads of the central bank and planning agency. The government is required to ask its opinion on all proposed economic and social legislation, and the Council is free to give unsolicited advice. The cabinet is not required to follow the advice, but if the Council's recommendations are supported by a large majority of its members

it is very difficult for the government to disregard them.

The Netherlands has long since shed its traditional character as an agricultural country. Nevertheless, Dutch agriculture is important. It is very intensive, and farms in Holland, which are predominantly small family operations, are the most productive in all of Western Europe. The Netherlands is the world's third-largest agricultural exporter after the U.S. and France. The percentage of Dutch engaged in agriculture or fishing has dropped by two-thirds in the last three decades to only 3% of the total population, who produce 2.8% of GDP. Since three-quarters of them are unionized and since their representatives sit in all economic advisory organs and political parties, they still can wield considerable political clout.

Over 70% of the land is used for agricultural purposes, of which 62% is used for grassland, 32.5% for cultivation and 5.5% for horticulture. The visitor notices much cultivation under glass. Of course, no one can overlook the most beautiful crop of all: flowers. The Dutch have grown and exported all over the world a wide variety of plants ever since the first tulip bulbs arrived from Central Asia in the 16th century. Their most splendid showpiece is Keukenhof and its environs, which in the months of April and May must surely be the largest and most colorful garden in the world.

The country is heavily industrialized. Its highly diversified industry employs 22% of the work force and accounts for 26.4% of GDP. Some of the most prominent industrial names in the world are based in Holland: Phillips, Unilever and Royal Dutch Shell. In 1993 the giant music company, PolyGram NV, purchased the legendary symbol of African-American music, Motown Records. Services provide employment for 75% of the Dutch and produce 71% of GDP.

Almost 70% of the industrial turnover is in chemicals and petroleum, metals, biotechnology products, food, drink and tobacco. Chemical and petroleum industries, which include the processing of natural gas and the refining of oil, alone account for one-half of all exports. The Netherlands does have some lame industries, such as shipbuilding. It is, however, trying to gear up for future trade competition by exporting such sophisticated products as micro-computers and precision optical equipment. The government is strongly supporting the search for new Dutch markets abroad and does offer export subsidies to Dutch companies.

For centuries this has been a trading country, and today it is the world's seventh largest trading nation. Over half of its GDP is derived from the export not

149

The Netherlands

only of its goods, but also the services (in which sector three-fourths of the Dutch work force is employed). It always has invested heavily abroad, ranking second behind the U.K. in total foreign investment in the U.S. It has always been a particularly important transit country because of its ports and inland waterways.

Of all goods loaded or unloaded in the EU destined for or arriving from overseas, 30% pass through Rotterdam, the world's largest port. The port moves almost half of all cargo entering or leaving ports between Le Havre in France and Hamburg in Germany. In 1996 the Dutch state and city of Rotterdam launched an investment program valued at $6.1 billion to boost the harbor's capacity. It includes building eight new state-of-the-art terminals capable of serving jumbo container ships. Because a deep channel was dug in the bed of the North Sea, the port can accommodate heavy tankers. Over half the cargo tonnage handled by the port now consists of crude or refined oils, and it is the world's chief oil port and "spot market" on which oil is bought and sold on a supply and demand basis. Pipelines have been constructed which can move petroleum to Germany and Belgium. Rotterdam alone provides more than 10% of the country's GDP.

Because of its inland waterways, which include Western Europe's most important rivers, the Dutch ports of Rotterdam and Amsterdam have the capacity to transport goods by water to markets that serve over 200 million persons. Dutch companies are responsible for 40% of the EU's inland waterway transport. About 70% of the transport between the ports and the European hinterlands moves on water, but Holland also has an excellent road and rail net that is connected with those of neighboring countries. Finally, the national airlines, KLM, links Schiphol airport near Amsterdam to cities all over the world. Schiphol is Europe's second biggest airport for goods transport.

Holland's chief customer by far is Germany, whose unity was a powerful stimulus for Dutch goods and which accounts for 26% of exports and 18% of imports. Belgium provides 9.4% of its imports and buys 11.8% of its exports. In all, the EU accounts for 77.3% of its exports and 55.1% of its imports. U.S. trade makes up 10.2% of the Netherlands' imports. But the U.S. is Holland's largest source of private foreign investment; a fifth of American (and a third of British) investment in the EU goes to the Netherlands. The amount of American dollars per capita invested in the Netherlands is larger than in any other European country. The U.S. has 1,100 companies there, including 42 of the top 50 American Fortune 500.

Offshore gas/oil rigs

Energy

The Netherlands must, with a few exceptions, import almost all the raw materials its industries need. It has large salt deposits in the eastern part of the country, and it also is able to produce about 5% of the oil it needs. The principal exception is natural gas. Huge gas reserves were discovered in 1959 in Slochteren in Groningen Province. This is now the largest producing gas field in the world and contains about half of all natural gas reserves in Western Europe. Its gas reserves are the world's fifth largest, after those of Russia, the U.S., Canada and Norway. In energy equivalent, it is equal or superior to Britain's oil reserves in the North Sea. The Slochteren fields produce 84% of the country's gas, the remaining 16% coming from Holland's continental shelf off shore. It exports about one-half of its gas, which is the country's most valuable source of foreign exchange. About 3% of its GDP is generated by oil and gas.

The proceeds from these exports have not only kept its balance of payments in surplus since 1982, but the government, which claims a 90% share of all gas export income, derived about 10% of its revenues from this source. In 1980 Holland renegotiated its ten-year gas sales agreements with its Western European customers in order to bring the price more into line with world energy prices.

When the Dutch first discovered their large gas reserves, they decided to exploit them very quickly because they saw that a rapid worldwide conversion to oil was in process. They foresaw the prospect of atomic plants supplying a high percentage of the industrialized world's needs in the future. Therefore, they rapidly converted 90% of Dutch homes and other buildings to gas heat. They also sought to sell their gas quickly while there was still a market for it. Almost all Dutch now regard this decision to have been a very serious mistake.

In the twenty-first century natural gas accounts for about half of the nation's energy supplies, while oil accounts for 37%, coal 12.6% and nuclear less than 1%. In order to stretch out their gas supplies at least until the year 2000, the Dutch decided to terminate all gas export contracts in the early 1990's, to limit their own gas use to high-priority needs, such as home heating, and to mandate home insulation and the conversion of industry from gas to coal and oil. They also decided to begin buying gas from abroad, especially from Russia. The government negotiated contracts with Moscow whereby Dutch gas companies would provide assistance in helping it extract gas, which would then be sent to Western Europe.

Oil had to take up the energy slack, a fact which not only damaged Holland's balance of payments, but also made it far more vulnerable to an oil boycott such as the nation faced in 1973–4, when the Arab-dominated OPEC nations singled out Holland for its support of Israel. New discoveries in the North Sea enable the Netherlands to supply 20% of its own oil.

The Netherlands

Schiphol Airport

The future reliance on oil can be relieved also by increased use of coal and nuclear power. The Netherlands wanted to raise coal's share of electricity generation from the present 5% to 40% by the end of the century. This is made difficult by the fact that since Holland has already shut down its coalmines, most of the coal will have to be imported. Also, coal has a frightening effect on global warming, a pernicious development that threatens the Dutch almost more than any other nation. Holland has two nuclear power plants, but there is strong opposition to nuclear power generation; a 1990 poll showed 85% opposed building new reactors. The Labor Party even advocated the shutdown of the existing plants. With razor-thin majorities, and with the 1986 Chernobyl nuclear accident in the Ukraine still in people's minds, shaky coalitions can seldom afford to touch such hot potatoes. Holland's energy problems will not be alleviated by nuclear power.

Current Economic Situation

Dutch industry faces several problems. The workweek has fallen to 36 hours. Wage costs are very high, and, if one adds employer contributions to social security, wages are on a par with Belgium. Employers must also pay employees a holiday bonus of 7.5% of their annual pay. Normal wages are not indexed, but pensions and certain benefits are. The trade unions are still moderate, but they are often tempted to seek wage increases that could heat inflation (2.7% in 2003),

and they resist reductions in social welfare benefits.

Despite high wage levels and the maintenance of extensive job protections and cooperation with the unions, unemployment had risen to 4.9% in 2003. Part of the success has been the willingness to create incentives to work by lowering unemployment benefits and to make the labor market less rigid by reducing job security and increasing temporary employment. By deregulating work hours and allowing previously unthinkable part-time and temporary work contracts, these jobs now make up a third of all jobs, the highest proportion in all Europe. Such workers also continue to get benefits like vacation and health insurance, and after six months they begin to accumulate pension rights. Thus the Dutch labor market combines flexibility with protection: workers now accept more uncertainty in return for the reassurance of welfare assistance if all goes wrong.

Unlike most European countries, the Netherlands actually created jobs in the late 1990s, and this is a particular boon to younger Dutch. Success is due in part to the Dutch tradition of consultation and cooperation. It is also a small enough country that all the key political, labor and employer figures know each other and can work together. There is hidden unemployment, such as early retirement and disability payments. Although the criteria have become stiffer, disability is so loosely interpreted that a million in a workforce of seven million

are legally considered to be fully or partially incapacitated.

In the twenty-first century the Netherlands is showing some of the healthiest economic indicators in the EU. Its economy grew faster than that of its neighbors since 1993; its growth in 1997 was twice that of Germany and France and averaged 3.4% between 1996 and 2000; however, in 2002 its growth shrank to zero. Its budget deficit (up to 1.6% of GDP in 2003), government spending and taxes are sinking, while its national debt, at 51% of GDP in 2002, is falling. Its welfare program has become less generous, but unlike most of its EU partners, it faces no "welfare crisis." The Dutch have already tackled most of the economic problems that are now afflicting other EU states.

CULTURE

A largely homogeneous country, the Netherlands has only a small non-white racial minority, and except for about 400,000 in the province of Friesland northeast of Amsterdam who speak a German-Dutch language called Frisian, all whites speak Dutch as their mother tongue. Thus, the country avoids the terrible language problems found in neighboring Belgium. At the same time, the Dutch are very open to the world, and most school children learn English, German, and to a lesser extent French. Visitors who seek information from or contact with the Dutch are relieved that most Dutch have learned these languages rather well: three-fourths speak at least one foreign language, 44% speak two and 12% three or more.

Holland is a very pluralistic country in which diversity is institutionalized in a way that the Dutch used to call *Verzuiling*, or "columnization." This meant the coexistence in political and social life of separate religious organizations which operate parallel to one another, but which aspire to the same goals. Such columnization is no longer relevant, but diversity still is found in education, the mass media, sports and social clubs. Dutch school children are free to attend either state or private (mainly religious) schools, all of which are financed entirely by the government.

Primary schooling lasts six years, and 70% of primary school children attend private schools. Secondary school pupils can choose either to go straight into vocational education, which would lead to careers in the trades, services or sales, or into a general secondary education, which paves the way to the university. Approximately 60% of the secondary school pupils attend private schools. There are 14 universities, four of which are private. Only 3% of Dutch students of

The Netherlands

university age attend them, compared with approximately 50% in the U.S. Over 70% of university students attend state institutions. Many Dutch attend religious schools from the beginning through the university. Aside from some supervision to ensure minimum standards, the government does not attempt to influence the private schools.

Religion

In the Netherlands religion has always been an important force shaping the national character. The Reformation took seed in Holland and it was the attempt of the Spanish king to re-Catholicize Holland that sparked the Dutch rebellion in the 16th century. It remains a tradition for the Dutch royal family to belong to the Protestant Dutch Reformed Church. When the Queen's younger sister Irene left the Netherlands in 1963 to marry Prince Carlos Hugo de Borbon y Parma, a Catholic pretender to the throne of Spain, the very enemy her forefathers fought for almost a hundred years, she threw her family and her country into a rage. But in fact, the Netherlands was never thoroughly converted to the Protestant sect of Calvinism. Even today a third of the population is Catholic, 21% Protestant, 7% Muslim, .5% Hindu, and 40% who profess no belief in religion at all. Still, those observers are to some extent correct when they say that every Dutchman is somewhat a Calvinist.

The Dutch take a very strong moral approach to most human affairs. One sees this in the tone and content of Dutch politics. Moral arguments are invariably made to support many political issues, including social welfare, human rights, nuclear disarmament, environmental protection and aid to developing countries. Some political parties are organized around religious principles. Although Dutch voters are less likely than they once were to vote primarily out of religious considerations, political parties often cannot resist the temptation to sprinkle their appeal with biblical messages, even if practical political considerations far outweigh religious ones. Most radio and television organizations and some newspapers have religious affiliations. Further, despite the fact that church and state are officially separated, the school system offers both religious and secular schools, with the state picking up the bill for both; 70% of these schools are privately owned, often nominally religion-based.

Despite their religious and moral approach to many human affairs and despite the religious strife that one still finds in the country, the Dutch have never practiced the kind of intolerance Calvinists practiced in, for example, the Massachusetts Bay Colony. Most of its people continue to practice some of the tolerance toward other ideas and ways of living for which the Dutch were once famous and without which no democracy can function properly. Some Dutch are increasingly inclined to cast off their tolerance and to attack violently those views they do not accept. For instance, when the Pope visited the Netherlands in 1985, he was greeted by bottles, cans, bombs and such obscene chants as "Kill, kill, kill the Pope!" A majority of Dutch Catholics opposes the Vatican's teachings on contraception, abortion, celibacy and the ordination of women, and

John Paul had gone to Holland in the first place to heal these divisions.

While religion plays a role in many facets of public life, church attendance is actually falling. The importance of religion in everyday affairs is no longer as great as it once was. Polls in 1987 indicated that 27% of Dutch adults attend church regularly (vs. 14% in the U.K. and 12% in France). The fact that both religions draw believers from all occupations prevents them from being linked closely with any particular social class, as is the case in Northern Ireland.

The churches' influence at election time is also declining. In 1963, for instance, 83% of Catholics voted for the Catholic People's Party, but in 1972, only 38% did. Still, there are fewer interfaith marriages than in most European countries.

The Dutch remain a very family-oriented people, who tend to treasure family life and prefer private to public amusement. There is very little outright class discrimination. Nevertheless, there is still a large income gap among citizens, and people of different social classes tend not to mix as frequently and as easily as in the U.S.

Diminishing Tolerance for Minorities

Holland was always a land of refuge. It absorbed religious refugees from England, Belgium and France, and Jews from Spain and Portugal. In fact, because of the tolerant and relatively enlightened and prosperous conditions inside the Netherlands, the Dutch never poured out of their country and colonized foreign lands in great numbers. Presently about 6% of the population is visibly different ethnically from the native Dutch, and the figure in the largest cities of Amsterdam, Rotterdam and The Hague is more than 30%. When Indonesia won its independence from the Netherlands, many people of Indonesian ancestry came to Holland and assimilated rather well. Exceptions were the 15,000 South Moluccans who could not get along with the new rulers and who were permitted to resettle in Holland. Their community has since more than doubled to 40,000. They have borne a deep grudge against the Dutch, for whom these Protestant Christians had fought. They claim to have been led to believe that their homeland would be made independent as a reward for their loyalty and that the Dutch still have an obligation to help them achieve a free South Moluccan republic. They have long refused to integrate into Dutch society, preferring instead to dream of returning to their homeland on their own terms.

In order to publicize their plight in 1975, a group of them besieged both a train in northern Holland and the Indonesian consulate in Amsterdam, actions that result-

A residential area in Amsterdam

ed in several deaths. In 1977 they seized another train and a school. Despite such problems, the Dutch have refused to consider washing their hands of these troublesome guests by simply expelling all of them or even their more violent fringe. In 1986, on the 35th anniversary of their arrival, the Dutch government announced annual tax-free payments of $800 and commemorative medals to 3,000 South Moluccan veterans or their widows, as well as creation of a museum on Moluccan history.

When Suriname became independent in 1975, approximately 140,000 Surinamese left their newly freed country to go to Holland. The Dutch did almost nothing to stop or discourage them. Referring to these Surinamese, who now number 180,000, one Dutch clergyman spoke for many of his countrymen when he said, "they are here because we were there." The Netherlands continued to provide $1.5 billion of aid to Suriname annually.

In the 1960s when the labor-starved Dutch economy was in desperate need of more workers, thousands of guest workers poured in from the Mediterranean area, primarily from Turkey (now 156,000), Morocco (now 112,000), Spain and Italy, and concentrated in the cities of Rotterdam, Amsterdam and the Hague. The influx from non-EU countries has been stopped, but foreign workers and their families already account for about 6% of the Netherlands' population and for 13% of residents in the country's larger cities (a figure which is expected to rise to 20%). This percentage includes neither the Surinamese nor the immigrants from the

Netherlands Antilles, who are continuing to enter Holland.

The foreign workers are a very convenient target for quasi-fascist extremist groups such as the Netherlands People's Union, this latter group can be expected to win very few votes in any Dutch election. Although these minorities are not on an economic or social par with the Dutch, and while unemployment is considerably higher among these groups, the Dutch government bends over backwards to serve them if they stay. For instance, mobile caravan schools have been organized for gypsy children, and all minorities are entitled to the same social welfare benefits as are the native Dutch. The Dutch Broadcasting Foundation beams television shows in five languages with subtitles. In 1986 'outlanders' (as the resident foreigners are called) were permitted to vote or run for office in municipal elections, and 49 were elected to city council posts. A 1998 survey on racism in Europe revealed that about a third of Dutch admit to being "racist" or "fairly racist." This regrettable statistic was nevertheless far below that in Belgium (55%) and France (48%).

In 1992 an Israeli cargo jet crashed into an Amsterdam apartment building filled with illegal aliens, killing 43 and leaving many survivors with chronic health problems. An enquiry in 1999 revealed that the plane had had 600 pounds of depleted uranium and components of deadly Sarin nerve gas on board. This led to accusations against the Dutch government that it had misled parliament on the consequences of the crash. This tragic accident

sparked calls for more rapid expulsion of such illegal residents, who constitute up to 1% of the population. Partly in response, political asylum regulations were tightened to allow faster expulsion of rejected applicants.

Former Prime Minister Lubbers reaped vehement criticism in 1993 when he commented that the Netherlands had reached the 'critical threshold' as far as the number of resident foreigners was concerned. In 1996 the Netherlands adopted a method of dealing with illegal immigrants so harsh that it caused a wave of protests in reception centers. Some foreigners there complained that cells were overcrowded, that they had been denied access to lawyers, and that they had been forced to pose nude for photographs. Prison authorities acknowledged that the policy is intended to discourage further immigration.

The earlier Labor government claimed in 2002 that its tightening up of the rules, especially on asylum, had cut the numbers of new arrivals by 25%. The center-right government under Prime Minister Balkenende announced immediately after its formation in July 2002 the creation of a Ministry of Immigration and Integration and plans for even tougher restrictions. They include admitting fewer immigrants and making it more difficult for ethnic minorities to bring a partner from their home country. Those seeking permanent residency must pay in advance for a compulsory course on integration, and the sum would be reimbursed only upon completion of the course. Illegal immigrants' home countries were put on notice that they would not be eligible for Dutch development aid (.86% of GDP) if they refused to take back subjects whom the Netherlands had refused asylum.

The fact is that many Dutch have never come to terms with the reality that the Netherlands has become an immigrant and multicultural country. Visible ethnic minorities make up 6% of the population, a higher percentage than in France or Britain. At least half of them are Muslim. A minority of Muslim children attend 37 Islamic schools, financed by the state in the Dutch tradition. The secret service recognizes that al Qaeda is succeeding in recruiting young Muslims in mosques, cafes and prisons in the Netherlands for a "holy war" against the U.S. and its allies. In late-2002 two men were accused in a Rotterdam trial of plotting to attack the American embassy in Paris. Nervous Dutch authorities requested the U.S. in 2003 to move its embassy from the middle of The Hague for security reasons.

In Amsterdam and Rotterdam, over a third of the population is non-Dutch, and it is estimated that in 15 to 20 years, half

The Netherlands

Moulin de la Galette by Vincent Van Gogh (1853–1890)

the residents of the four largest cities will be from ethnic minorities. Half the prison population already is. These facts put wind in the sails of politicians, like the late Pim Fortuyn, who reject the traditional political correctness about tolerance and the multiculturalism so many Dutch fear. Many insist that newcomers integrate into Dutch society, learn the Dutch language, and realize that they cannot recreate their old lives at government expense in the midst of one of the world's richest nations.

Sexual Tolerance

The hallmark of modern Netherlands has become to acknowledge common practices and to decriminalize them. An example is prostitution, which has long been legalized. However, brothels were

not. In 2000 parliament passed a law making the 2,000 brothels legal and subjecting them to government regulation and regular inspections. A job category for the 30,000 registered prostitutes was created: "freelance workers." They have employment rights and the right to establish a trade union, a process that began in 2001. Not all "sex workers" like their new legal status because they have to pay taxes. But it has done much to separate their work from organized crime, and it has stimulated a profitable sex tourism industry.

Homosexuals in the Netherlands have wider civil rights than anywhere in Europe. Since 1999 they could register their partnerships in a civil ceremony and receive almost the same rights and obligations as heterosexual couples. In 2000 the

Netherlands became the first country in the world to allow same-sex couples to marry on the same terms as heterosexuals. They can take each other's surname, inherit their property, receive alimony, and enjoy the same tax status. The only restriction is that a homosexual couple may adopt only a Dutch child, not one from abroad. Polls indicate that most Dutch support these reforms. In the words of one of the bill's sponsors, Boris Dittrich: "A person's sex is not important for marriage."

Euthanasia

Another case of legalizing what has been long-standing practice is euthanasia. Passive euthanasia (halting life support systems to allow natural death) was long permitted, and doctors in the 1990s were virtually never prosecuted for assisting in thousands of suicides of terminally ill patients. In 1995, for the first time, a physician was found guilty of murder for ending the life of a deformed newborn who was unable to ask explicitly that a doctor do so. But as a sign of how torn even judges were over this issue, the court ruled that the doctor's actions were justifiable under the Netherlands' tolerant euthanasia laws and refused to punish him. In 1999 alone, there were 2,216 reported cases of euthanasia and assisted suicides.

The Netherlands moved toward permitting voluntary euthanasia ("mercy killing" through fatal injections to hopelessly ill patients); 80% involve cancer patients. One out of every 50 deaths is a mercy killing. Polls have long indicated that three out of four Dutch support this, although the practice remains ethnically troubling and controversial. Dutch courts stopped prosecuting and jailing doctors who, according to a 1993 law (the first of its kind in an industrialized nation), followed a detailed 28-point checklist: the patient had to be terminally ill and in a clear state of mind, and he or she, not family or friends, had to ask repeatedly to die. A second opinion had to be obtained.

In 2000 euthanasia and assisted suicide were decriminalized under certain circumstances: A patient need not be actually dying. People over age 16 who suffer acute and unremitting pain may ask to die. Doctors are not allowed to recommend suicide as an option and must inform the patient of all other alternatives known. They must get a second medical opinion and be sure that the patient's request is well considered and that he has acted voluntarily. In 2001, the Netherlands became the first country in the world to legalize mercy killing for terminally-ill persons with "lasting and unbearable suffering" as long as the volunteer's doctor and an independent consultant approve.

The Netherlands

still technically illegal, but the state taxes the profits from the sale of cannabis, and police put the lowest priority on preventing the sale and use of small amounts of it. Marijuana is so tolerated that 1,200 coffee shops put it on their menus and serve it to customers. There are some legal problems. Dutch law prohibits substances that have been "processed." Does that include mushrooms merely if they have been dried? Authorities are well practiced at turning a blind eye. When ecstasy tablets became popular in the 1980s, they were declared illegal. But the police were told to ignore consumption and to try to curb manufacturing.

Uncomfortable with its reputation as being soft on drug users, Dutch authorities cracked down on the larger-scale commercialization of soft drugs. Neighboring countries put pressure on the Dutch government to enforce stricter laws on drugs. The German government blames it for the vast amount of drugs crossing the German border. The Netherlands is responding to those concerns as Europe moves toward tighter economic and monetary unification.

Cafe owners were put on notice not to call attention to their wares, deal in carry-out quantities, sell more than a sixth of an ounce at a time, or sell cocaine and heroin under the counter. Coffee shops caught selling cannabis to children under age 18 are to be shut down. The new Balkenende government pledged in 2002 to enforce more strictly the criteria governing the coffee shops and not to allow them to be located close to schools or the national borders. One earlier justice ministry spokeswoman had commented: "We want just enough to cater to our own citizens, not to the drug tourists."

Police are cracking down on drug dealing at highway rest stops and parking areas. They have especially gone after the traffic in hard drugs, even though users are not arrested unless they commit other crimes. Such tolerance had been extended to ecstasy use. Although the country produces an estimated 80% of the world's supply, its trafficking and manufacturing are illegal. The government in 2002 pledged a crackdown on ecstasy, summarizing its tougher approach toward drugs: "The production of and trade in drugs in the Netherlands has reached unacceptable levels and must be tackled more firmly." Authorities had believed that their tolerating soft drugs is responsible for the decline in the percentage of young people using hard drugs from 14% in the 1980s to only 1.6% in 1997, compared with 3% in Italy, 2.8% in France, and 1.5% in Germany.

Addicts are steered into treatment and are provided with clean new needles to

Coffee shop, not to be confused with cafe (a bar) or coffee house (for coffee and tea).

Photo by Juliet Bunch

Drug Policies

In the early 1970s, the Dutch had another opportunity to show their toleration when Amsterdam became the favorite destination for longhaired, guitar-toting young people who were called at the time "hippies," as well as other younger people with different lifestyles. While these young people horrified the established citizens almost everywhere they went, the Dutch accepted them with good humor and tried hard to find them temporary shelter and areas where they could meet freely. They also tried to look the other way when the visitors chose to use "soft" drugs or violate the sexual standards of Dutch society.

By the mid-1980s, though, Dutch patience with hard drug trafficking and crime in Amsterdam had visibly begun to wear thin, and neighborhood vigilante groups were organized to protect against

lawbreakers. On the whole, the crime rate remains low compared with the U.S. and many other Western European countries. But street crime has increased dramatically. Some politicians suggest that judges hand out sentences that are too lenient. In 1986, for instance, a punker who stabbed to death a young man outside a disco was sentenced to four years in prison, two of which were suspended. Dutch jails are known throughout Europe to be the hardest to enter and the easiest to leave. Even hardened criminals in prisons are permitted to vote and to have overnight visits with their families, girlfriends or homosexual partners in special rooms with complete privacy. Two-thirds of all prisoners are hard drug addicts, which points to a further problem.

Polls in 1996 showed that only 5% of the population uses cannabis regularly. It is

The Netherlands

prevent AIDS. In 2000 only 10% of AIDS victims in the Netherlands were intravenous drug users, compared with nearly 40% across Europe. The publicly visible use of drugs has caused some Dutch to wonder if their country has indeed become too permissive. Ed van Thijn, former mayor of Amsterdam, confessed that "in the past 15 years tolerance became synonymous with permissiveness and softness on law-and-order." In 1990, the Washington-based Drugs Policy Foundation awarded the Dutch government a prize for "its effective and humanitarian drug policies." Said one senior Amsterdam policeman: "We do not say that our way is right for them [Americans], but we are sure it is right for us."

The Dutch, as a people, are inclined to cling to tradition and to be conservative. At the same time, they are open to new ideas and are relatively tolerant toward all forms of individualism. This is why criticism and protest can be so firmly entrenched in the Dutch tradition, but why the Dutch are at the same time not inclined to be revolutionary. Compromise is a highly developed art in the Netherlands, and protest groups have often been smothered by tolerance. It often saps one's strength to beat one's head against a richly padded, sympathetic wall!

Media and Arts

"Columnization" is also found in the press and electronic media. Newspapers and magazines reflect the opinions of many diverse groups in society, and the average reader expects to find his own opinions expressed in the news he reads. Financial problems have resulted in the concentration of most newspapers in the hands of a few large companies, although 60% of the dailies still manage to take an independent editorial line. To help preserve their independence the government provides financial support to newspapers and magazines that are undergoing reorganization to become profitable again. The major dailies, in order of circulation, are *De Telegraaf* (conservative), *Algemeen Dagblad* (neutral), *De Volkskrant* (progressive), *Het Parool*, (center-left) and *Trouw* (Protestant). Top people tend to prefer the *NRC-Handelsblad* and the *Financiele Dagblad*. The major magazines are *Elseviers Magazine*, *Elseviers Weekblad* and *Vrij Nederland*. In 1990, the first Sunday newspaper, called *De Krant op Zondag*, was introduced in 50 years. It is printed in Belgium to avoid Dutch union laws against working on Sunday. In a study in 2002 by the professional group, Reporters Without Borders, the Netherlands ranked third in the world after Finland and Iceland in terms of press freedom. The U.S. placed 17th.

de Volkskrant

Kroonprins: Máxima brengt enorm offer

Prinses Máxima pinkt zaterdagmiddag in de Nieuwe Kerk een traantje weg bij de tango Adiós Nonino.

Het Huwelijk

De kus, een offer voor hongerige wolven 10

De kleding was ingetogen, de make-up tranenproof 10

Iedereen steekt Máxima een hart onder de riem 11

Langoustinestaartjes en tartelette van knolselderij 11

De sabel en de bruidstaart: het huwelijk in beeld 12, 13

Huwelijksreis voert stel naar de camping 14

PRINS BERNHARD
'Wat een mooie bruid!'

NRC HANDELSBLAD

President Bush in State of the Union:
Bestrijding terreur maar net begonnen

De Amerikaanse president George W. Bush waarschuwde gisteravond, in zijn State of the Union-toespraak tot het Congres, dat de oorlog tegen het terrorisme in Afghanistan getrainde terroristen op vrije voeten zijn, "als tikkende tijdbommen". (Foto Reuters)

There are three public television channels, including a public educational and cultural channel (Nederland 3), and five public radio stations. Also on the air are 400 local radio stations, including a handful that broadcast legally from abroad, especially Luxembourg. Commercial TV channels have operated since 1992. Programming is in the hands of both the state and a variety of private broadcast-

ing organizations that largely operate free of government control. Some of these organizations represent the basic pillars of society. For instance, KRO is Catholic, NCRV is Protestant, VPRO is liberal Protestant and VARA is socialist. Unlike many newspapers, however, the broadcasting companies attempt to broaden their appeals to include all social groups. They are, therefore, actually able to overcome some of the cleavages in Dutch society.

These four private organizations operate within the framework established by the government-related Netherlands Broadcasting Association (NOS). The NOS, a quasi-governmental broadcasting foundation, is charged with producing programs "in the general interest," such as news bulletins. The Ministry of Welfare, Health and Culture is the authority that oversees its operations. The postal service, privatized in 1989, collects fees to finance broadcasting. The NOS also controls the amount of advertising that may be broadcast.

When one thinks of Dutch culture, perhaps the first words that come to mind are the names of painters: Hieronymous Bosch, with his powerful and sometimes terrifying scenes, brought to European art in the 16th century a form of symbolism which reflected the mind of a great visionary. In the 17th century, Rembrandt, Franz Hals and Jan Vermeer established an artistic tradition through their vivid depiction of early Dutch life. In the 19th century J.B. Jongkind became a precursor of impressionism, and Vincent van Gogh, in a short but wild life, helped create the romantic picture that many people have of artists. He sketched the drab and dreary life of persons living in working-class and rural areas in the late 19th century, going later to Paris and southern France where he established his personal style of short brushstrokes in brilliant colors, which pointed the way to a new, expressive style.

In the Dutch artistic tradition of accurately recording the landscape around them, Hendrick Willem Mesdag painted in 1880 the world's largest panoramic painting, portraying Scheveningen, a fishing village on the outskirts of The Hague. Displayed in a museum in The Hague, called the "Panorama Mesdag," the painting completely surrounds the viewer and gives him the most vivid possible impression of Holland in Mesdag's time. Piet Mondrian, the greatest and most consistent renovator of modern Dutch art of the 20th century, began with experimental nature paintings, but gradually he departed from nature and sought harmonious and universal images. His paintings of lines and colors are among the world's most treasured modern art works. Willem De Kooning and M.C. Escher also enjoy worldwide fame.

The Dutch consider art to be so important for the society that they maintain, at public expense, some 3,000 artists who are unable to make a living. Although they must demonstrate that they are full-time and professionally trained artists with talent, once they are selected they merely

Rembrandt, self-portrait

have to deliver a modest number of paintings each year to the state in return for their pay.

Most of the paintings go into storage and are never seen again. Some critics argue that this subsidy lowers the quality of painting and is merely an example of the welfare state run wild, and these funds have been heavily cut. The government also helps to finance experimental theater, orchestra, ballet and film companies. Over 4% of the central government's budget is devoted to supporting the arts. Even Dutch businesses are financing a variety of artistic groups from jazz to chamber music artists in order to improve their image with customers.

Historically, Holland is rich with philosophical and intellectual leaders. Hugo Grotius founded the study of international law. René Descartes, a Frenchman who was living in the Netherlands, developed a new starting point for philosophy when he asserted, "I think, therefore I am." Baruch Spinoza wrote treatises on the relationships between the human intellect, the state and religious belief. Anton van Leeuwenhoek invented the microscope that thereby revolutionized the study of biology. Christian Huygens invented the pendulum clock, and the Dutch have been a very punctual people ever since.

There are more than 20 million people inside and outside the Netherlands who can read Dutch literature in the original, and the Foundation for Promoting the Translation of Dutch Literature seeks to introduce the nation's writings abroad. Before the 16th century, literature was primarily composed of plays, religious literature, folk tales and stories of chivalry. In the 17th century, Joost van den Vondel's writings were read all over Europe. The most noted author of the 19th

century was Multatuli (pseudonym for Douwes Dekker), who worked in the colonies and observed the mistreatment of the native populations. His 1860 novel *Max Havelaar*, attacked colonialism. The works of novelist Louis Couperus evoke the atmosphere of the turn of the century. After 1945, Holland rapidly lost its rural character. The postwar literature of such younger writers as Jan Wolkers, W.F. Hermans, Harry Mulisch and G.K. van't Reve often deals with the problems arising from life in a highly urban and industrial society.

FUTURE

The Dutch are concerned about senseless violence that has stricken their country, and their legendary tolerance and consensus orientation have become somewhat frayed. The "polder model," the popular name for the practice of policymaking by consensus between government, employers and trade unions, still exists. But political correctness has weakened. More and more Dutch were willing to support politicians like Pim Fortuyn, assassinated nine days before the May 15, 2002, elections, who openly defy the old rules of the game and speak openly of problems on many voters' minds, such as crime and immigration.

Conservative Prime Minister Peter Jan Balkenende formed a coalition government in July 2002 with the liberals and list Pim Fortuyn (LPF) that promised to tighten immigration laws, crack down on crime, review drug and euthanasia policies, reduce welfare spending, shorten hospital waiting lines and improve public transportation. Given the number of inexperienced and diverse newcomers in the LPF, one should not have been surprised that their nonstop infighting would make this government unstable and brief; it collapsed after only 87 days. In the January 2003 elections the two traditionally leading parties, CDA and PvdA, reasserted themselves after having taken up some of the popular causes espoused earlier by Fortuyn, whose party plummeted. Balkenende concluded the seemingly interminable task of trying to put together a stable governing coalition in May.

The Netherlands will remain a reliable ally for its NATO partners, as its participation in the wars in Kosovo and Afghanistan and its support of Turkey in 2003 demonstrated. In the first half of 2003 it shared with Germany command over all peacekeeping forces in Afghanistan. It also offered to send peacekeepers to Iraq after the 2003 war to help police the reconstruction of the country. The Netherlands will continue to play an active and constructive role in the world.

The Kingdom of Belgium

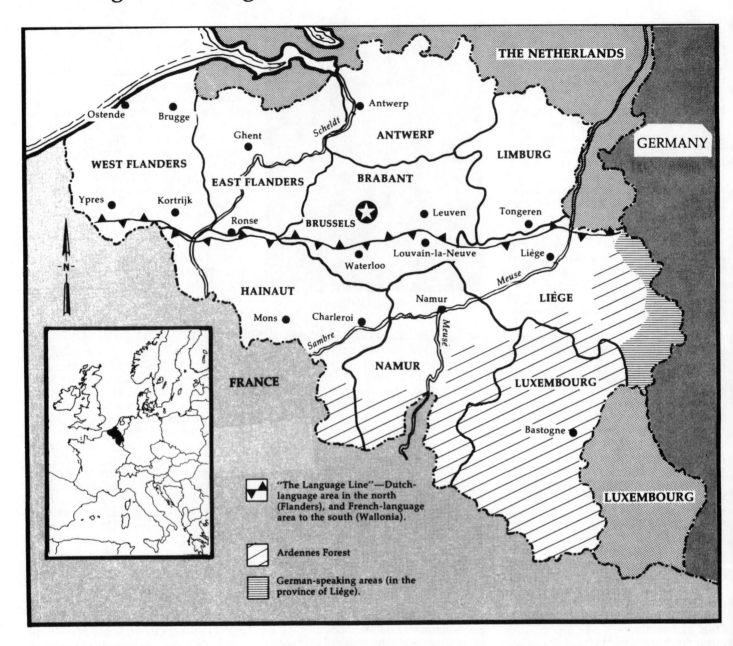

Ostende · Brugge · Ghent · Antwerp
WEST FLANDERS · **EAST FLANDERS** · **ANTWERP** · **LIMBURG** · **BRABANT**
THE NETHERLANDS · **GERMANY**
Scheldt
Ypres · Kortrijk · Ronse · **BRUSSELS** · Leuven · Tongeren
Waterloo · Louvain-la-Neuve · Liège
HAINAUT · Namur · **LIÈGE**
Mons · Charleroi · *Sambre* · *Meuse*
FRANCE · **NAMUR** · **LUXEMBOURG**
Bastogne
LUXEMBOURG
-N-

"The Language Line"—Dutch-language area in the north (Flanders), and French-language area to the south (Wallonia).

Ardennes Forest

German-speaking areas (in the province of Liège).

158

Area: 18,991 sq. mi. (30,562 sq. km., somewhat larger than Maryland and about 200 miles or 320 km. wide, taken from its northwest to southeast points).

Population: 10.2 million (estimated).

Capital City: Brussels (Pop. 1.1 million, estimated).

Climate: Temperate, with rather mild winters and comfortable summers.

Neighboring Countries: Germany (East); the Netherlands (North); France (South); Luxembourg (Southeast); England is about 54 miles (87 km.) away across the English Channel.

Official Languages: Dutch (57%), French (32%), and both languages are spoken by another 10%, principally those living in and around Brussels, 80% of whose citizens are native French speakers. German is the native tongue for 1%.

Ethnic Background: Indo–European, descendants of the Gauls and Franks.

Principal Religion: Roman Catholic (95%).

Main Exports: Metal manufactures, chemicals, steel products, textiles, food products, 70% of the world's cobalt, 60% of the world's diamond dealing and 40% of cutting.

Main Imports: Motor vehicles, chemicals, foodstuffs.

Major Trading Customers: EU 74.2%, France 17.6%, Germany 16.8%, the Netherlands 12.5%, UK 10%.

Currency: Euro.

National Day: July 21st.

Chief of State: His Majesty King Albert II (b. 1934). Ascended the throne on August 9, 1993. Married Paola Ruffo di Calabria (Italy), 1959.

Heir Apparent: His Royal Highness Prince Philippe (b. 1960).

Head of Government: Guy Verhofstadt, Prime Minister (July 12, 1999).

National Flag: Vertical stripes of red, yellow and black, with the black stripe at the pole.

In some ways Belgium is a very unnatural country. It has no natural frontiers, such as a mountain chain or wide river, to set it off from its neighbors. It has therefore always been very vulnerable to foreign invasion. Belgians have no common language and are extremely sensitive about being forced to speak the one not used in their half of the country. Their tradition as a unified country is only a century and a half old and is too weak to give its citizens a strong com-

Belgium

Market Square in Bruges

Photo: Juliet Bunch

mon identity. Unlike the Swiss, many Belgians never really developed the habit of thinking in terms of a single nation.

It sometimes seems that there are just six million Dutch–speaking Flemings and four million French–speaking Walloons, who must try very hard to live with each other. Unfortunately, the forces that once held them together—Roman Catholicism, economic and political opposition to the Dutch—are no longer strong. During the 1970s, the economic prosperity that in the past smoothed over some of the most important lingual and cultural problems was threatened. In short, Belgium appeared almost like a shotgun wedding—like a hopelessly broken marriage which held together only because the partners could find no other place to live.

Such a view is that of a pessimist, who likes to call half–empty a glass that is half–full. For a while, Belgium's language disputes showed signs of cooling. Parties that preach language radicalism are still being demolished at the polls. Economic performance and stable government, as well as language issues, are foremost in Belgians' minds. Belgians have many trumps in their hands as they face the future. They are rather cautious, conservative people, a fact that causes some critics to call Belgium a private, family–centered country. It also means that while their conflicts are often verbally bitter and serious and sometimes erupt in street brawls between the rare hotheads, Belgians are very unlikely to resort to outright violence and terror to accomplish their goals. They have always shown a ge-

nius for compromise by very small steps. Thus, no one expects the community problems, as the language issue is called, to explode into a bloody and tragic Northern Ireland–style conflict. They can still cause a government to collapse.

It still has many valuable economic resources. It has a very skilled work force with a proven willingness to work. Its economy remains highly productive; this has usually kept inflation low and has maintained for Belgians one of the highest standards of living in the world. Its central location in Europe remains a very significant trading advantage for the country. It is an important partner in a unified Europe and in the Atlantic Alliance, and its capital city, Brussels, is in many ways the "capital of Europe," housing the headquarters for both NATO and the EU. One in three residents of Brussels is now non–Belgian. There are an estimated 23,000 foreign EU bureaucrats (dubbed "Eurocrats") and their families in Brussels and perhaps another 10,000 Europeans whose jobs are linked to the EU. Such massive presence and the decision to hold all European summits in Brussels starting in 2002 have prompted the European Commission to consider declaring the city as the "capital of Europe." Some countries, including the United States, even send three ambassadors to this city: one to the King of the Belgians (ie. to the government), one to NATO and one to the EU.

Belgium is a picturesque country with scenery varying from Gothic medieval university cities to countless towns and villages located along winding rivers with

Belgium in NATO

steep bluffs. The country is mainly flat, but it rises toward the south, away from the North Sea coast and toward the Ardennes Forest. The country can be divided roughly into three geographic parts. In the North is the Flemish plain, which extends westward from a 41-mile (60 km.) North Sea coastline, with its sandy beaches and luxurious and expensive resorts. Flanders presents a pastoral landscape with small farms and most of Belgium's agricultural production. With 56% of the Belgian population, it is the most densely populated part of the country which itself is the second most densely populated land in all Europe, behind the Netherlands. Here are the Flemish cities of Bruges (with its many bridges which gave the city its name), Ghent and Antwerp, all three towns filled with cathedrals and other medieval structures. Most of Belgium's newer industries are located

Belgium

in Flanders, which is the country's most economically dynamic section, a fact that greatly riles the Walloons today.

At the center of Belgium are rolling fields of grain and many villages with houses grouped around the parish church. In the middle is Brussels, and below it are heavy industrial centers, clustered around the formerly rich Walloon coalfields, which are now largely exhausted and closed. This was the area of the country's industrial revolution in the 19th century, which occurred in Belgium earlier than almost anywhere else in Europe. It is where such industrial cities as Mons, Charleroi and the ancient and dignified city of Liège are located. South of the Sambre and Meuse rivers is the third area, with no large cities or industries. It is a region of fields and pastures with woods thickening as one travels southward into the Ardennes Forest.

Running west to east just south of Kortrijk, Ronse, Brussels, Leuven (Louvain) and Tongeren is an invisible line established 1,500 years ago and now of far greater significance for contemporary Belgium than the geographic areas mentioned above. This is the language line that separates the Flemings from the Walloons. Along the German border is also the German–speaking minority numbering about 64,500 people. Because most Belgians live on "their" side of the language line, they have fewer language problems, now that Flemish (a language which differs from Dutch about as much as American from British English), French or German is used exclusively in all affairs, including education, law, government and business, within each respective region.

The people in the various sections do not look or act very differently, although some observers claim to notice differences in the people's characters—the Flemings being severe and serious and the Walloons being more outgoing, volatile and fun–loving. In fact, the visitor would scarcely notice any difference at all if it were not for the fact that he hears different languages spoken on the streets and sees different languages on street signs and on billboards. The language separation is greatly complicated by the capital city of Brussels, which has 11% (1.1 million) of the country's population, 90% of whom speak French as a mother tongue. This city is situated uncomfortably north of the language line and is surrounded by Flemish speakers. It is over the hurdle of Brussels that all proponents of regional language reform have tripped.

One would not expect language difficulties to trouble this small, cosmopolitan country which is located at the very crossroads of Europe and which has been

Bilingual signs, Brussels: Flemish, then French

one of the most persistent and constructive proponents of European integration. But it is exactly this problem that has caused many people to wonder how more birthdays this country will be able to celebrate.

HISTORY

Shaky Independence

Belgium proclaimed its independence from the Netherlands in 1830, and its new king took the name of Leopold I. Because the Dutch king refused to recognize Belgian independence until 1839, his most immediate goal was to win recognition for his new state, a goal that was greatly boosted by his marriage to the daughter of Louis–Philippe, King of France from 1830–1848. Having adopted a modern liberal constitution in 1830, Belgium was scarcely affected by the storm of revolution that blew across Europe in 1848 and could turn its attention to economic development.

Following Britain's example, Belgium adopted a policy of free trade and plunged headlong into industrialization, using its large and easily extracted coal resources. This effort was aided by an agreement with the Dutch in 1863 ending tolls for the use of the Scheldt River, which passes through Dutch territory before emptying into the North Sea. This agreement enabled the Belgians to develop fully the port of Antwerp that now plays such a key role in their trade.

The rapid industrial growth also gave birth to an urbanized working class and ultimately to socialism, which along with liberalism and Catholicism became one of the three main political "families" or social cleavages in Belgian society. These divisions still exist, although they are now less hostile to each other than they once were. The liberal and Catholic "families" squabbled throughout the 19th and early 20th centuries over the relations between

church and state, especially insofar as the schools were concerned. Their struggle roughly ended in a draw, and state financial support continues to flow to both secular and denominational schools.

King Leopold II actively engaged in colonial activity. Henry Stanley, the famous Welshman who after emigrating to America fought on both sides of the U.S. Civil War, proceeded on an arduous journey to Africa in search of the Scot missionary, Dr. Livingstone. Leopold summoned him to Belgium and engaged him to explore the Congo area of Africa (not on behalf of Belgium, but on behalf of the king!). Stanley accepted, left for Africa and negotiated many favorable treaties with local chiefs that resulted in the establishment of the Congo Free State. Conditions were harsh, since Leopold reportedly condoned labor and torture as

King Leopold II of Belgium

160

The three arches at the ruins of the monastery at Orval

Courtesy: Jon Markham Morrow

instruments to produce wealth. Some say that about eight million Africans lost their lives during 23 years of Leopold's exploitation. Bowing to strong international pressures after a commission reported that administration of the colony was scandalous, the parliament passed an act in 1908 annexing the Congo state of Belgium. But Leopold had already enriched his treasury with the immense copper deposits in Katanga Province (now Shaba) during his years of possession.

Another problem began to bubble in the 19th century: the conflict between languages. French so dominated the over centralized bureaucracy, the court system, schools and businesses in the entire country that ambitious Flemings felt obligated to observe the rule "French in the parlor, Flemish in the kitchen." In the long run, such suppression of the Flemings'

language, and with it their identity as a people, could not last. In 1898 Belgium officially became a bilingual state, although it was not until 1932 that Flemish could be used in the national administration and not until the 1960s that Flemish became fully equal to French.

Failure of Neutrality and World War I

Since independence, Belgium tried to preserve its neutrality, which had been guaranteed by the great powers in Europe. However, when this was put to a test in 1914, the result was disastrous. Imperial Germany had set its gun sights toward France and demanded the right of free passage through Belgium for its troops. The Belgians refused, and the British announced that they would stand by the treaty of 1839 and support the Belgians to the end. Winston S. Churchill,

the First Lord of the Admiralty, wrote later that the British cabinet had been "overwhelmingly pacific" at the beginning of August 1914, but the direct appeal from the King of the Belgians for French and British aid raised an issue which united an overwhelming majority of ministers."

In a meeting with the British ambassador to Berlin, the German Chancellor, who thought he was speaking off the record, expressed amazement that the British would go to war over a mere "scrap of paper." Of course, the treaty rested on more than paper. It was anchored to the British national interest of preventing the North Sea coasts from being dominated by a hostile power and of preventing any European power from dominating the continent, as would have been the case if the Germans conquered France. The Germans conquered the Belgians in a few weeks, but their bravery against truly insurmountable odds was one of the most important factors in preventing a German victory in World War I.

The German violation of Belgian neutrality conformed with the German "Schliefen Plan," designed to meet the danger of a two–front war in the East and West through a strike at the heart of France on the well–fortified Franco–German frontier, which extended 150 miles (240 km.) from Switzerland to Verdun. German forces were to be concentrated on the right flank, which would sweep through Luxembourg and Belgium into northern France. Paris would be enveloped and the French troops would be pushed back toward the Moselle where they would be met by the German left flank.

By late August 1914 this plan appeared to have succeeded. German troops, which had bypassed Antwerp and the Belgian coast were dangerously close to Paris, with only a retreating French and British army before them. However, the German commanders grew increasingly nervous about the Belgian army, which was in a position to strike at the Germans' right flank and perhaps even to sever their lengthening lines of communication and supply in Belgium. Therefore, some German troops were detached from the main invasion force in order to contain the Belgian army in Antwerp. Seeing a chance to increase the Germans' nervousness, the British sent a brigade of marines (about 3,000 men) to Antwerp and leaked rumors of much more massive British landings and of totally fictitious British–aided Russian landings involving more than 80,000 troops.

This partly contrived danger to the German right flank, along with the Belgian army's refusal to surrender, influenced the German decision to avoid Paris and to

Belgium

Bastogne: winter of 1944

slow down their advance. This interruption of momentum proved to be crucial during the four–day Battle of the Marne in September and turned the tide of the war. The Belgian military effort was an example of how seemingly hopeless defensive operations, when seen in a larger strategic context, can be crucial for overall victory.

The Germans occupied most of Belgium for the remainder of the war although the king and the remains of the Belgian army held out in Ypres on a few square miles of unoccupied Belgian soil on the western tip of the country. This small salient was pulverized by four years of constant bombardment, and by the time the armistice was signed, it resembled a crater–filled lunar landscape.

Initially the Germans found some favor among some Flemings, who saw the possibility of liberation from Walloon control. Such sympathy, which was again manifested in World War II, created great distrust in Wallonia toward the Flemings and has still not been entirely forgotten by Walloons. Further complicating the picture was a feeling on the part of some Walloons that the French had "defaulted" in both World War I and World War II, and that Belgians had to pay a high price in helping pull French irons out of the fire. This strengthened the realization that union with France was unthinkable. Thus, although "estranged," the couple (Walloons and Flemings) had no choice but to remain in the same house.

German plunder of Belgian industry led to high unemployment and the mass deportation of Belgian workers to Germany, creating downright hatred. Even the Ger-

man military commander in Belgium had to protest the policies he was asked to enforce. He remarked sarcastically that "a squeezed–out lemon has no value and a slaughtered cow gives no milk!"

The Inter–War Period and World War II

After World War I, Belgium entered the League of Nations and was given the German–speaking area of Eupen, Malmedy and Saint Vith, as well as a League of Nations mandate over two former German colonies in Africa, now called Rwanda and Burundi. It also abandoned its earlier policy of neutrality and negotiated a military agreement with France and Great Britain. As the clouds of war became more ominous in the 1930s, however, Belgium again proclaimed a policy of neutrality on October 28, 1936. It was thus without allies when on May 10, 1940, German troops again invaded Belgium. After 18 days of bitter fighting the Belgian army was forced to capitulate. The government escaped to London, but the King of the Belgians became a prisoner of the Germans.

Although Belgium was liberated after the Normandy invasion in the summer of 1944, war returned when Hitler threw his last tanks into the Ardennes Forest in order to recapture Antwerp and break the Allied advance. The decisive action took place at the southern Belgian town of Bastogne, where the surrounded U.S. forces under General Anthony McAuliffe refused to surrender. When called upon to recognize the hopelessness of his situation and to give up, he reportedly answered defiantly, "nuts!" It has long been rumored that the general actually used a different expression, but decorous mili-

tary historians chose to report it in the now famous way. Fortunately, foggy weather broke and enabled the necessary air support to preserve the general's position. After the war, Bastogne's main square was renamed "Place McAuliffe." The Bastogne Historical Center was opened to commemorate one of the most important battles of the war, and every December a "Nuts Festival" is held.

Postwar Reconstruction and "The Royal Question"

Belgium's postwar reconstruction was accomplished very rapidly. Partly because it had been liberated so quickly, the country had not been as heavily bombed and shelled as the Netherlands, and Antwerp was virtually undamaged. It adopted a financial policy to strengthen the Belgian franc, which soon became one of the most stable currencies in Europe. It also blocked all bank accounts and levied a high tax on fortunes acquired as a result of collaboration with the Germans.

From 1945 until 1950 Belgium was rocked by the so–called "royal question." King Leopold III, unlike his Dutch and Luxembourg counterparts, refused to leave Belgium when the government fled. He argued that as Commander–in–Chief of the armed forces he was compelled to stay where he could help his people more than by leaving. He did deal with the German occupiers, and some of his countrymen claimed he had actually *collaborated* with them. Shortly before liberation, the Germans moved him to Austria, where he remained until 1950. Until his wartime role could be determined, his brother Charles served as regent. A parliamentary commission appointed in 1947 returned a favorable verdict as far as the king's wartime actions were concerned, but the socialists and communists continued to oppose his return. In an attempt to settle the question once and for all, a referendum was held in 1950 in which 57.7% of all voters approved of the King's return. Significantly, 58% of the Walloons were opposed. When he reentered Belgium in 1950, the resulting disorders were so intense that Leopold felt obligated to abdicate in favor of his eldest son, Prince Baudouin, on July 16, 1951.

Ever since the "royal question" divided the country, the Belgian king has never been able to exercise the considerable influence on Belgian affairs that he formerly had. None of his acts is effective unless the responsible ministers countersign his orders. Baudouin was a popular monarch who restored dignity to the Belgian throne while stripping it of much of its earlier pomposity. The monarch is now expected to be a symbol of the nation, but to perform this role he often

Belgium

Their Majesties King Albert and Queen Paola

Overcoming the Language Barrier

Any discussion of Belgian politics always has to begin with the ever–present language problem. No major issue could be divorced from it, and it exhausted, paralyzed and fractured coalition governments to such an extent that the country was scarcely able to tackle the extremely important economic problems which it increasingly faced. Belgium was seriously distracted.

Flemings have fought hard and successfully for the complete equality of their language and culture, although some of the victories might strike foreign observers as petty and unnecessary. Now cabinet posts must be distributed exactly equally between the French and Flemish speakers. The office of the prime minister technically remains outside of all language quotas or restrictions. However, given the permanent Flemish majority in the country, every prime minister since the 1970s has come from Flanders. All discussions in cabinet meetings are conducted through simultaneous interpreters. All major political parties are formally split along language lines, as are most military units and labor unions.

Even the prestigious medieval Catholic University of Louvain, which had become a bilingual university, had to be split in 1968 because it was located in the Flemish area a few miles north of the language line. The French–speaking part was moved just below the language line and was renamed *Louvain–la–Neuve* ("The New Louvain"). When it came to deciding how to divide the holdings in the famous university library, one of the oldest in Europe, the only solution which was acceptable was that all books with an even file number would remain in Louvain (now called by its Flemish name of Leuven), and all books with an odd file number would be moved to the new campus!

The tension between Flemings and Walloons has been exacerbated by the economic disparities that have developed between them. In the words of ex–premier Leo Tindemans, whose government foundered on the rocks of language regionalization in 1978, "the basic problem is not linguistic. It is the unequal economic development of two regions which speak different languages, have a different mentality and different dynamics, with the jealousy between them that often results and that can be easily exploited by politicians."

The economic inequality was becoming more apparent. By the turn of the century, Wallonia had become one of the richest regions on the continent while Flanders was a poor, rural area. Then the tables turned with a vengeance. Wallonia's coal industry disappeared, and its antiquated steel plants are in desperate need of

has to bend over backward to please the Walloons, whose hatred of grandfather Leopold still smolders. Of course, overt efforts to satisfy the Walloons inevitably stimulate Flemish criticism.

The king must often play a role in facilitating the formation of cabinets, and since more than 30 have been formed since 1945, this is no small task. It is after parliament has been dissolved and a new cabinet is being sought that the king's influence is greatest. The limited nature of his power was again shown in 1981 when he called together 18 political, labor and business leaders in order to appeal to them to end the country's political instability. Some criticized this, accusing the king of going beyond his established powers. Though there is no republican movement in Belgium, the king is truly a very limited monarch.

One of Belgium's most serious and prolonged postwar crises was the painful decolonization of the Belgian Congo, 80 times the size of Belgium with a vastly larger population. Over 100,000 Belgians had settled in the Congo, and Belgium had certainly developed economic interests there, although it sought to avoid mutual economic dependence between the colony and mother country. Belgium opened up the colony to foreign investment and trade. In the 1950s winds of African independence began to reach gale proportions, especially after the new French President, Charles de Gaulle, offered the French colonies in Africa their independence in 1958. A Congolese leader, Patrice Lumumba, emerged as a highly visible proponent of a free Africa. On January 4, 1959, riots broke out in the Congo; 42 persons died in events that deeply shocked the Belgians.

The Congolese had not been prepared for independence. Belgium quickly granted it on June 30, 1960. Unfortunately, a series of bloodbaths ensued, sparked by greed

for power and wealth as well as by tribalism. It was not until seven years later that the Congo became orderly, in part because of vigorous efforts of the Belgians and of UN troops.

In 2002 a parliamentary commission concluded that Belgium shared moral responsibility for the assassination in Katanga province of Patrice Lumumba on 17 January 1961, seven months after being elected to lead Congo. It concluded that the Belgian government and king had known of plans for the police to kill him, but they did nothing to stop the assassination, which occurred in the presence of Belgian police and officials. Belgium's Foreign Minister Louis Michel apologized to the Democratic Republic of the Congo on behalf of the government.

The copper, cobalt and uranium mines in the southern Shaba Province are still of great interest to Belgium. When this province was invaded from Angola in mid–1978, Belgium and France sent paratroopers to evacuate white families and to secure the area. In 1979 the Belgian government again sent paratroopers to join its soldiers in training exercises near Kinshasa, the capital city. Thus, Belgium retains a great interest in its former African colonies, and the great bulk of its relatively large development aid (.35% of its GDP) has gone to the Congo as well as to Rwanda and Burundi, which had been granted their independence in 1962. The Congo is not always a grateful recipient of such aid, and by the end of the 1980s Belgium's importance as a source of trade and aid had declined. In 1989 Belgium halted all development plans there in response to President Mobutu's suspension of payments on Belgian loans. In 1990 it used its diplomatic influence to try to sort out civil unrest in Rwanda, and in 1991 it sent 750 commandos to help evacuate Belgian citizens from the riot–torn country.

Belgium

streamlining and restructuring. Other traditional industries such as textiles lost out to competition from Third–World countries, where labor costs are very low. Thus, unemployment and labor unrest were higher in Wallonia. The EU declared Wallonia a "development area." Unfortunately, because of the psychological shock caused by crossing the linguistic border, unemployed Walloons are not inclined to move to Flanders to find work. Thus, there is little labor mobility.

While Wallonia faced an uncertain economic future, Flanders is experiencing an economic boom, based on future–oriented industries such as chemicals. Output per capita is higher in Flanders than in Wallonia. Because of Antwerp, foreign investments poured into the area. Earlier, most foreign investment went to Wallonia, but by 1975 it received only 20% of the total. By 1979 the figure had dropped to 10%, while Brussels received the same amount and Flanders a gigantic 80%. Distrust made both decisive governmental action and the establishment of some kind of national consensus, so strong in the Netherlands and Luxembourg, almost impossible in Belgium. But since the mid–1980s Wallonia has experienced an economic turn–around. Investment, including high–technology, has flowed in, industrial output has risen, and the economy has shifted from one in which 53% of the gross regional product is derived from industry and 42% from services to one in which 36% comes from industry and 60% from services. Unfortunately services can still not provide sufficient employment; in 2003 Wallonia's jobless rate was still higher than that of Flanders'.

There was general agreement in Belgium that Wallonia and Flanders had to be given more powers to control their own affairs, but there was much haggling on the details. As early as 1963 the two respective languages were given supremacy in the two main regions, and Brussels was declared to be a bilingual city. In 1971 the constitution was revised to permit the establishment of two cultural councils within parliament with authority over certain cultural and linguistic matters. The revision also established the necessity for special majorities (mostly two–thirds) for legislation touching these matters. Such special majorities were demanded by Walloons, whom the Flemish outnumber 60–40 and who have a lower birthrate as well. The amendment called for the establishment of a federal state composed of two lingual communities and three precisely defined regions, each empowered to legislate within carefully drawn limits.

Eight years and a string of cabinet crises later, two–thirds of both houses of Parliament approved an autonomy plan establishing regional assemblies and executives with authority over cultural and family affairs, public health, roads, urban projects, energy, environment, hunting and fishing, water resources, housing and many other matters. In 2000 they gained control over agriculture and in 2001 over much of foreign trade. They receive a total of 10% of the national budget to finance these tasks. However, the central government retains control over national finances, defense and justice. Belgium thereby ceased being a unitary state and became more decentralized.

The new arrangement is messy. Borders differ for "regions," which deal with political, administrative and economic matters within territorial areas, and for "communities," whose competencies relate to language and cultural issues and are linked to persons, not areas. Flemings choose to have one government for both, but Walloons and German-speakers keep them separate. Also, some of the ministries at the federal and regional levels share the same responsibilities. There are seven regional and community governments and parliaments—one federal, one Flemish, one in Brussels, two in Wallonia and two in the German-speaking area. There are a total of 58 ministers and junior ministers. In a country with one of Europe's highest tax rates, this seems wasteful and inefficient. In 1990 the federal government could do little to solve a long teachers' strike in Wallonia because it had lost its former powers over education. To make matters potentially even more complicated, there is an ongoing project to give Belgium a fourth official language: sign-language!

This act of parliament was an important step, and the establishment in 1981 of regional and community institutions has sparked enthusiasm and energies to improve the life in the language regions. Nevertheless, there are still many problems in the two larger regions that must be solved. There are small language enclaves on the wrong side of "the line." In 1987 the Belgian government collapsed over such an issue. Because of its location, the small, predominantly Walloon town of Fourons (or Voeren, depending on where one stands on this dispute!) had been transferred in 1963 to the Flemish province of Limburg. Although most of the inhabitants of the town actually speak a dialect of German among themselves, two–thirds consider themselves French speakers.

They elected as mayor a militant French–language campaigner, José Happart, who refused to speak Flemish or take a Dutch–language test. The Belgian Supreme Court ruled that Happart's appointment was therefore illegal. This village incident mechanically set off reactions which would be possible only in Belgium: Flemish ministers in Prime Minister Martens' cabinet threatened to resign if Happart were not sacked, and their French–speaking colleagues said they

Brussels—carefully bilingual

would leave if he were! Evicted from the mayor's office, Happart won a seat in the European Parliament and remained one of Wallonia's most popular politicians. An exasperated Martens had to resign over the issue, which he and many others considered absurd. He was understandably furious that such a parochial dispute could prevent his government from solving the critical economic challenges facing the country. In 1992 power sharing was introduced to such mixed communities. But Belgians remain acutely aware of the underlying message of the dispute: never underestimate the importance of language factors in Belgian politics!

Belgium's high unemployment rate has created an interesting situation: in the past, the only Belgians who were bilingual were Flemings, since the Walloons traditionally refused to learn Flemish. Brussels' bilingual status has placed a premium in the job market on the ability to speak both official languages, and that means that the Flemings there have a leg up on their Walloon competitors. This economic fact has given rise to a phenomenon which would have been unimaginable even a few years ago: Walloon parents are beginning to send their children to Dutch–language schools in order to improve their employment prospects. In more and more schools in French-speaking communities, some or all subjects are taught in Flemish in order that pupils can become bilingual. This is occurring while fewer Flemish children are learning French.

The three regional governments, along with three additional separate governments of the country's francophone "communities" in both Wallonia and Brussels and of the tiny German-speaking "community" in the east, work alongside the traditional provincial and communal governments in Belgium. The country has always been divided for administrative purposes into nine provinces, each with a provincial council of 50 to 90 members and a governor chosen by the cabinet and officially appointed by the king. Four of the provinces are French-speaking—Hainaut, Namur, Liège and Luxembourg (a large chunk of the Grand Duchy of Luxembourg which was transferred to Belgium in the settlement of 1839). Four are Flemish-speaking—East and West Flanders, Limburg and Antwerp. Brabant, which includes Brussels, is bilingual.

In 1989 parliament passed legislation to devolve further power to the regions, and a special court was created to solve problems stemming from devolution. In 1992 an elected regional government for Brussels was approved, and the following year Belgium became even more federalized. The regional governments were

granted all powers but those of the treasury, defense, and foreign policy. In 1995 their parliaments, as well as local parliamentary bodies, were directly elected for the first time. There are potential problems in foreign affairs because the three regions have the right to sign treaties with other nations. Flanders signed one on water with the Netherlands and set up a network of 70 economic representatives in five continents; it also has its own diplomats in Vienna, The Hague, Washington, Tokyo and Brussels. Such separate foreign ties could diminish the standing of the federal government.

Local governments in Belgium have a long tradition stemming from the Middle Ages and have had much autonomy. Each has an elected council of aldermen, who serve six–year terms. As a holdover of Napoleon's reforms, the mayor (called *burgomaster*) is nominated by the city council, approved by the cabinet and officially appointed by the king. He presides over the city council and is expected to insure that national interests are considered. They very often become skilled defenders of local interests in opposition to the central government.

Since 1971, Brussels is officially a bilingual city, broken down into 19 bilingual and seven Flemish communes and ruled by a metropolitan council elected by proportional representation and a council executive with an equal number of French and Flemish–speaking members. There is nevertheless sufficient language tension in the capital city and its suburbs that the Council of Europe formally rebuked Belgium in 2002 for violating minority rights. The fact that Brussels itself was once predominantly Flemish but is now about 90% francophone makes Flemings all the more determined that only Flemish will be used in the suburbs regardless of the fact that 120,000 Walloons live there. All local council proceedings and all official mailings must be in Flemish. Anyone showing up at a council meeting who cannot speak Flemish must bring interpreters. Local libraries that stock too many French-language books lose their subsidies. Belgium signed the Council of Europe's convention on protecting minorities. However, all seven regional and national parliaments would have to ratify it, and few expect the Flemish parliament ever to agree.

In general, government at the provincial and communal level works rather efficiently and has been able to keep an important part of the governmental machinery running smoothly at times when the central government has been paralyzed. Also, city officials have much influence on the central government; more than three-fourths of the members of the Belgian parliament are at the same time

local government officials, and this fact strengthens the ties between the national and local governments.

The National Government

Belgium is a constitutional monarchy in which the king exercises largely ceremonial powers. The established tradition is that he signs all legislation passed by democratic methods. That is why there was dismay in 1990 when former King Baudouin announced that he could not sign a bill liberalizing abortion within the first 12 weeks of pregnancy. The childless, devoutly Catholic monarch asked: 'Would it be normal that I be the only citizen in Belgium to be forced to act against his conscience? Is freedom of conscience a privilege for all except the King?' The pragmatic Belgians found a way out of this dilemma: invoking Article 79 of the constitution on April 3, the government declared the king 'temporarily incapable of ruling,' and it hurriedly promulgated the abortion law in his absence from the throne. Then on April 5 a joint session of parliament, invoking Article 82, offered him his job back. This bizarre episode prompted some Belgians to question again whether their country really needs a monarch after all.

After reigning for 42 years, King Baudouin died suddenly of a heart attack in Spain on July 31, 1993. Though his official powers were limited, he was popular among both Flemings and Walloons, and many credited him for helping preserve Belgian unity. Childless, he was succeeded by his brother Albert. King Albert II is a relative newcomer to the political world, but he is familiar with the leaders of all three regions and is experienced in business. He had stated that he would step aside and allow his son Philippe to

Prince Philippe and Crown Princess Mathilde with Princess Elisabeth

Belgium

Hon. Wilfried Martens

assume the throne. However, since the king's influence is considered essential to a smooth transition to greater federalism, he was convinced to become king himself "in the interests of continuity."

In December 1999 Philippe married a glamorous speech therapist, Mathilde d'Udekem d'Acoz, who is now in line to become the kingdom's first Belgian-born queen. In 2002 they had a daughter Elisabeth. The royal family's main contribution to Belgium is to be one of the few remaining symbols of unity. Royals now learn Flemish and do a part of their schooling in Flanders. When officials at the Catholic University of Leuven decided in 2002 to award Crown Prince Philippe an honorary doctorate for his service to Belgian unity, 200 scholars signed a petition protesting the degree because of Philippe's earlier poor performance as an engineering student.

Real power is exercised by coalitions of parties that can maintain a majority in the Chamber of Representatives, the lower house of parliament. This is never easy because the proportional representation electoral system enables about a dozen parties to win parliamentary seats. Therefore, Belgian governments tend to be very fragile and seldom last the entire four years for which a parliament is elected.

It is striking that few cabinets are overturned by votes in parliament. Members of Parliament are firmly bound to the party leaders through party discipline, so it is the powerful party leaders who make or unmake governments. Even when cabinets fall, the new governments are usually formed after minor reshuffling of cabinet posts. For example, after 1978 Wilfried

Martens was prime minister in six governments, and they came to be known as Martens I through VII. Thus, there is usually more governmental stability in Belgium than meets the eye. This is particularly so because of the nature of Belgian political parties. Although they are very different ideologically and linguistically, they are normally willing to compromise in order to form a government. This stems in part from the tradition of elite cooperation in Belgium that has always helped to bridge some of the differences in the heterogeneous Belgian society. Nevertheless, the delicate compromises necessary to form and preserve a government make it very difficult to attack the country's pressing problems head–on.

The Parliament

The Belgium parliament is bicameral, and both houses constitutionally have the same powers. However, tradition has made the lower house, the Chamber of Representatives, the more important. Its 150 members (reduced from 212 in 1995) are elected at least every four years by all citizens 18 years or older, who are required to vote. Nevertheless, in the 2003 federal elections 10% of voters abstained in certain areas. The great majority of its members continue to perform their normal jobs and commute to Brussels for parliamentary sessions. Most legislation is discussed first with the major Belgian interest groups and is introduced into the Chamber before being passed on to the upper house.

The Senate accepts about 90% of the laws without change. The 181 senators are elected for four year terms in three different ways. Fifty are elected by the provincial councils, 25 by the Senate itself and the rest directly by Belgian voters. The heir–apparent to the throne, presently Prince Philippe, is always a member, and

the senate almost always has roughly the same party composition as the lower house.

Both houses are empowered to amend the constitution by simple majority in both houses, although a two–thirds majority is now necessary for certain language and cultural legislation. The highest court in the land, the Court of Cassation, whose chief justice is chosen by the government and formally appointed by the king, cannot declare acts of parliament unconstitutional. In the Belgian legal system, which is modeled on the French, there is no provision for judicial review, but the Court of Cassation can rule administrative acts unconstitutional. A separate body, the Council of State, is permitted to give advisory opinions on the legal suitability and constitutionality of major legislation.

Political parties in Belgium follow the cleavages of society. There are specific language parties whose main objective is to preserve or extend the language rights of their particular groups. The three "traditional" parties spring from the three great movements in Belgium during the 19th century: Catholicism, liberalism and socialism. Coalitions always require the participation of at least two of these, and one usually leads the opposition. None of the traditional parties is highly ideologically oriented, and all are rather flexible. These parties have been challenged by three language parties whose demands in behalf of Walloons, Flemings and residents of Brussels have been so appealing that these three language parties have increased their electoral strength enormously in the past two decades. This challenge was so great that all three traditional parties have split into separate French–speaking and Flemish–speaking parties that limit their appeal strictly to their own region. However, they are inclined to cooperate with their former party comrades when it comes to con-

The port of Antwerp from the Scheldt River

Belgium

structing a national governing coalition. There are no major national parties in Belgium today. One can scarcely imagine governing a nation with only regional parties! Energy is expended on the pettiest of issues.

The Christian Parties

Until 1999 the largest twin party was the Christian People's Party (CVP), as it is known in Flanders, or the Christian Social Party (PSC) in Wallonia. Participation of the CVP and PSC was crucial in all coalition governments from 1958 to 1999. Recent prime ministers, Leo Tindemans, Mark Eyskens (son of earlier Prime Minister Gaston Eyskens, who played a key role in the development of a satisfactory regionalization plan) and Wilfried Martens were all from the CVP. Martens was a particularly important integration figure for the party. He started his political career as an ultra-nationalist Flemish radical who painted over signs at the 1958 World's Fair because they were not written in both Flemish and French. He later became a convinced federalist and a model of adaptability. He was one of the few Belgian politicians trusted by both language groups.

Formerly a single Catholic party, it severed all its formal ties with the Catholic Church in 1945 in order to become the two mass parties they are today. Nevertheless, the two parties are still the only ones many Belgian Catholics find acceptable. Their program endorses a policy guided by Christian principles (liberally interpreted), and they have always been staunch proponents of state support for parochial schools. They favor a free market economy and the protection of private property. At the same time, they advocate equality of opportunity, an active state role in the economy and state assistance for those persons who cannot compete successfully in the capitalist economic order. These positions enable them to work sometimes with the Socialist parties. The CVP is relatively stronger in Flanders than the PSC is in Wallonia, where the Christian Socialists have always taken a back seat to the Socialist parties. Both find the bulk of their voters among the middle class, farmers and Catholic labor movement, particularly within the Christian Trade Union Federation (CSC), Belgium's largest trade union. The CVP also attracts upper–class voters, such as prosperous merchants and high–ranking military officers.

In 1992 Jean-Luc Dehaene, who is from the trade union wing of the Flemish Christian Democrats, became prime minister. He was known as the "Bulldozer," "Carthorse," and "Plumber" because of his ability to fix problems. What awaited the new government was a host of difficult

Children during Carnival at Binche, Hainaut Province

decisions, such as direct election of regional and communal assemblies. Dehaene pushed hard to get parliament to accept constitutional reforms devolving additional power to the regions and trimming the large budget deficit to qualify for the Euro.

The CVP was confident as it entered the 1999 parliamentary elections. This was the first in which parties received public financing, freeing them from reliance on bribes; they agreed among themselves to limit campaign spending. But in the week before the elections Belgians were traumatized by evidence that dioxin had gotten into animal feed and thereby poisoned much of their food. With their grocery shelves empty, angry voters threw out the Dehaene government, which had mishandled the crisis. His Christian Democrats fell to 22 seats in Flanders and 10 in Wallonia and were forced into opposition. Led by Stefaan De Clerck, they did no better in 2003 and remained on the opposition benches.

The Socialist Parties

The Socialist parties (SP in Flanders and PS in Wallonia) are a strong twin party nationwide. The Socialist Party is one of the oldest parties in Europe. It was never an extreme left-wing party and always sought to work within the constitutional system. Winning elections always took priority over doctrine. The best-known Belgian Socialist, Paul-Henri Spaak, former prime minister, foreign minister, first president of the UN General Assembly and NATO general secretary, expressed the character of his party this way: "There are two kinds of Socialists—Socialists and real Socialists. Me? I am a Socialist."

Its program presents a parliamentary–reformist path to a socialist society. The party congress of 1974 defined the party's aim as democratic socialism, which gives each individual the possibility for full social, economic and cultural realization. Belgian Socialists seek to change the present capitalist economic system because it allegedly concentrates economic power, dehumanizes the workingman's world and increases global tensions between rich and poor. They favor economic planning, nationalization of certain key economic sectors such as energy and banking, and the establishment of a national

Belgium

health service. They find their voters chiefly among lower level employees and workers, especially those without strong ties to the Catholic Church and those who belong to the second–largest trade union, the Federation of Belgian Labor (FGTB).

The Flemish party is generally less friendly to far–reaching reform than the Walloon party, which must stay left in order to compete in the more socialist Wallonia. The Socialists are considered to be especially useful coalition partners because of their ability to help control the powerful Belgian labor movement. Belgian Socialists are among the very few outside the United States who allow their parliamentary candidates to be chosen by means of party primaries, with all party members entitled to vote.

A scandal scarred the party in 1995. The Flemish party reportedly received kickbacks from an Italian arms firm, Augusta, in a sale of 46 helicopters to the Belgium army. In the wake of the scandal, three ministers resigned, one top military official committed suicide, and two internationally prominent figures, Willy Claes, who was economics minister when the deal was made, and EU Commissioner Karel van Miert, were tarnished. In 1995 Claes had to resign as NATO secretary general.

In 1999 the Socialists dropped to 14 seats in Flanders and 19 in Wallonia. They nevertheless were able to enter the "rainbow" coalition with the Liberals and the Greens. Led by high-profile Foreign Minister Louis Michel, the Socialists won a narrow victory in the Walloon area in 2003 and remained in the governing coalition with the Liberals.

The Liberals

The third traditional party group and currently the leading ruling party is the Party for Freedom and Progress, renamed in Flanders the Flemish Liberals and Democrats. It is called the PRL in Wallonia and Brussels. But both parties are generally referred to as the Liberals. They pursue traditional European liberal policies, such as the limitation of the power of the state in society and the greatest possible freedom for private initiative. They generally want to prevent the socialization of the economy, to reduce taxes and to cut state expenditures. Perhaps the only expressly conservative parties in Belgium, they appeal mainly to middle class voters, especially small businessmen and professionals.

Also divided by regions, the Liberals were the big winners in the 1999 elections and became the country's largest party after being in third place for more than 80 years. This electoral triumph represented the most dramatic turnover in Belgian po-

Prime Minister Guy Verhofstadt

litical history. It repeated its victory in Flanders, narrowly beating out the Flemish Socialists in the 2003 federal elections and remaining the senior member of the governing coalition. The Flemish Liberal leader is Guy Verhofstadt, who in 1981 at age 28 had become the youngest major party leader in Belgian history. At age 32 he was already a vice-premier and budget minister. Over the years he changed his conservative views and moved closer to the political center, especially since he must lead a center-left governing coalition with the Socialists from 1999. He cast his earlier heroine Margaret Thatcher overboard and embraced Tony Blair's "third way." His center-left governing "rainbow" coalition capitalizes on the economic achievements of the previous Duhaene government, which had sharply reduced the country's budget deficit. Bolstered for a while by a growing economy, Verhofstadt could make popular promises, such as across-the-board tax cuts and a more efficient public service. As prime minister in league with the Socialists, he has changed his priorities by showing sympathy with the anti-globalisation movement, legalizing marijuana and gay marriage, becoming the second country, along with the Netherlands, to end the ban on euthanasia, and joining with neighboring France, Germany and Luxembourg to oppose U.S. policy toward Iraq.

Smaller Parties

A relatively new party, which doubled its vote in 1999, is the Greens, which are divided into Flemish and Walloon parties. They do meet together but make decisions separately. As in other European coun-

tries, they find voters among those who are concerned about environmental protection and nuclear dangers. They are convenient parties for expressing discontent and protest. They are the only partner parties whose French and Flemish factions cooperate easily in parliament. In 1999 the Walloon Greens won 11 seats and the Flemish nine. They joined the ruling coalition but had to leave it in 2003 after a disastrous electoral result. Voters had not appreciated the Greens' campaigns against arms exports to Nepal, night flights over Brussels, and tobacco advertising. The latter cost Belgium its Formula One Grand Prix race.

The oldest of the Belgian autonomy parties is the Flemish People's Union (VU), established in 1954. The VU draws almost half its votes from workers and half from the middle and upper classes. It supports a free market economy and Flemish and Wallonian autonomy bound together loosely in a Belgian state. From 1987 to 1991 it was in the ruling coalition. It skidded to five seats in 1995, but jumped back to eight in 1999. It remains in opposition even after the 2003 elections.

The hard-line anti-immigrant law-and-order Flemish Block (*Vlaams Blok*), which also advocates independence for Flanders, did very well in 1999, advancing from 11 Flemish seats to 15. It continued its rise in the 2000 local elections. Marching under the banner, "Our People First!", it is the largest party in Antwerp, where it wins a third of the votes. It also does well in Brussels, where half the newborns are from Arab parents. In the May 2003 federal elections, held five months after serious race riots erupted in Antwerp, it gained 17.9% of the votes in Flanders and 18 seats for its best result in its 25-year history. Its performance was helped by former beauty queen Anke Vandermeersch, who ran for a senate seat and helped soften the Block's edge. However, while beautifying the package somewhat, the message Vandermeersch delivered was the same: "We still are very much against the multicultural society. We need people who emigrate here to adapt. If they don't adapt to our systems, to our laws, to our values, they should go back to where they came from."

Filip Dewinter from Antwerp leads the party. The titles of his three books succinctly express his point of view: *Our People First*, *We Stand Alone*, and *Masters in Our House*. He opposes letting in more non-Europeans and insists that those already in Belgium "assimilate" or leave. Because of its views, no other Belgian party will team up with it, and this keeps it out of office, even in Antwerp. However, by closing ranks against the *Vlaams Blok*, forming what is known as the *cordon sanitaire*, the other parties have provided it with a monopoly on the protest vote. Privately some mainstream politicians sense that this approach is backfiring because it strengthens the *Blok's* image as an anti-establishment party and thus enhances its popularity.

The *Blok's* steady rise has also generated another challenger to the country's respectable parties: an Arab pride movement called the Arab European League, which claims to be the voice for frustrated Muslims in Belgium. Its leader, Dyab Abou Jahjah, a Lebanese-born son of university teachers who speaks five languages, demands affirmative action in schools, the workplace and housing and the elevation of the Arabic language, spoken by the roughly 5% of Belgium's population that is of Middle Eastern descent, to the fourth official language. Calling assimilation "cultural rape," Dyab has become the target not only of the *Vlaams Blok*, which demands that his Belgian citizenship be revoked, but also of Prime Minister Verhofstadt. The latter had tried to avoid discussing the explosive issue of immigration. But after two days of rioting broke out in Antwerp in December 2002 in which a young Moroccan teacher was killed by a deranged elderly white man, the prime minister went on television and blasted the Arab European League as a "threat to our society that thrives on confrontation and provocation."

Whatever one's opinion of Dyab, he has forced Belgians to think more deeply about whether their traditionally tolerant country really welcomes immigrants and who precisely is a Belgian. He has also pointed to a political truth that the *Vlaams Blok* has more influence on mainstream Belgian political parties than many people realize: "*Vlaams Blok* talks about security, so they start talking about security. *Vlaams Blok* talks about assimilation, they speak about assimilation. That's the power of the *Vlaams Blok*."

The Flemish Block's French equivalent is the National Front, which made some in-roads in Wallonia in 2003. In Brussels the Democratic Front of French Speaking Brusselers (FDF), which advocates a redrawing of the boundaries separating Flemish from French speakers, has become the strongest single party. In a 1998 survey on racism, 55% of Belgians admitted to being "racist" or "fairly racist." This was the highest percentage in Europe. In an attempt to reduce the number of illegal immigrants, the government in 2000 offered citizenship to 38,000 illegals in the country, while tightening controls at its borders to prevent such persons residing in other European countries from streaming into Belgium to gain a permanent right of residence.

The Communist Party (KPB in Flanders and PCB in Wallonia) is a small, politically insignificant party that appeals almost exclusively to workers and which is strongest in Wallonia, and Brussels. In 1971 it separated into regional organizations although it did not formally split. Its program is orthodox Marxist. It generally pursued a Moscow-oriented line. For instance, while most Western European communist parties denounced Soviet policy in Poland from 1980 on, the Belgian communists announced that Soviet pressure on Poland to limit or eliminate the free trade unions within the country was "perfectly understandable and exclusively defensive in nature." The party's offer to participate in a ruling coalition has never been accepted. One unique practice observed earlier by the party's representatives in parliament was that each paid his parliamentary salary into the party coffers and accepted in return only a worker's wage from the party. This practice is irrelevant, though, since the communists have been shut out of parliament since 1985.

Foreign and Defense Policy

As a small country, Belgium's foreign policy is anchored in international organizations that seek to maintain peace and prosperity in the world, especially in Europe. The EU continues to give an important boost to this small trading nation, one–half of whose national income is derived from foreign trade.

Belgium is also a founding member of NATO, but in recent years it has been among the alliance's least enthusiastic members, due in great part to its severe financial difficulties and to its preoccupation with its internal problems. Some of its equipment is outdated. It has a total active force of 41,750, including 2,570 women. Its air force of 11,500 troops, including 800 women, modernized its force by purchasing American F–16 combat aircraft. In order to cut costs, Belgium is coordinating some of its naval and air operations with the Dutch. The U.S. maintains approximately 2,000 military personnel in Belgium.

The navy has 2,600 personnel, including 270 women, and is mainly a coastal defense force, composed of four frigates and a dozen minesweepers. In 1987–8 it sent three of those mine sweepers to the Persian Gulf to help in the allied effort to keep that important waterway open to world shipping. In 1991 it again sent four warships, including two mine-sweepers, to the Gulf, and in 1992 its troops were dispatched to the Congo, where violence threatened the lives of Europeans, and Somalia. In Somalia its soldiers were regarded as tough, unforgiving, disciplined (despite several incidents of racism and violence toward the local population) and skilled, traits acquired in previous interventions in Africa.

Belgium has an army of 26,400 soldiers, including 1,500 female troops. They are separated as much as possible into separate language units and divided generally into two armies. The country's reserve force is declining to 62,000. Most soldiers are stationed in Belgium, but 2,100 serve in Germany.

Critics, including high military officers, fear that the drastic cuts deprive Belgium

Bilingual Recruiting Poster

Belgium

Women in armed forces

of the bare minimum needed to defend the country. In 1993 the government decided to participate in the Franco–German Eurocorps, the embryonic European army. This decision provoked criticism in Flanders because Flemish would not one of the languages used. The memory is still alive that Flemish troops sometimes died during the First World War because they could not understand the orders of their overwhelmingly francophone officers.

In the lead-up to the unpopular 2003 war in Iraq, the Belgian government took an aggressively critical stance, which boosted Prime Minister Verhofstadt's and Foreign Minister Louis Michel's popularity before the May 2003 elections. Teaming up with France, which Belgium usually supports unswervingly in NATO, it helped veto a request from Turkey for NATO protection, a decision that was popular with voters but was decried by many Belgian political veterans and business leaders. An editorial in *De Standaard* read: "Belgium is grandiosely overplaying its hand." A couple of weeks later, the government relented, and it supported the assistance to its NATO ally, Turkey.

Following the war, which Belgium vehemently opposed, it joined with France, Germany and Luxembourg to create on paper a joint rapid reaction unit built on the existing French-German brigade. Belgium offered to contribute commandos. In addition, the four said they would set up a multinational headquarters and a separate military center in Belgium in 2004 to command and plan EU military operations when NATO is not involved. Belgium had even recommended that a "hard core" of EU countries form a defense organization entirely distinct from NATO, but that went too far even for its French partners. The four invited other European nations to join their effort, but sensing that

its real purpose was to weaken the transatlantic alliance, none did. Neither Belgium nor the other three pledged to raise their defense spending to cover the costs of these innovations, so it is uncertain whether this initiative will ever get off the ground.

Such a bold foreign policy places Belgium above its usual weight class in world politics. It did not shirk from publicly castigating the United States and such traditional partners as Britain. This daring policy stems in part from the idealism and activism of Foreign Minister Michel, who admitted in 2003 that he now regarded the U.S. as he once did the Soviet Union: "I am beginning to fear the U.S." Disregarding former King Leopold's view of Belgians as a *"petit pays, petits gens"* (small country, small people), Michel takes a "moral stance" in foreign policy and is writing a book titled *The Axis of Good*. His shuttle diplomacy in Africa earned him the nickname, "Louis l'Africain" (Louis the African). He led the ill-fated policy within the EU to freeze relations with Austria when the party of a right-wing politician, Jörg Haider, was invited into the government in 2000. One British scholar, Steven Everts, believes, "Louis Michel is a bull in a china shop, but he does get the country noticed, even if it's often for the wrong reasons."

Perhaps the best example of a small country overstepping good sense and its own influence while seeking a special moral role in the world was a 1993 law granting Belgium "universal jurisdiction"

Politics in the Big Leagues. Louis Michel (2nd from right) with (left to right) Chris Patten, Javier Solana and Colin Powell.   Source: Central Audiovisual Library, European Commission

to try the perpetrators of war crimes, crimes against humanity and genocide even if there is no Belgian connection with the alleged crimes, victims or perpetrators. Ten years later about 30 political leaders, including Palestinian leader Yasser Arafat, Israeli Prime Minister Ariel Sharon, and Cuban President Fidel Castro had been charged under the law. However, the sweeping law became untenable in March 2003 when Iraqis charged former President George Bush, Vice-President Richard Cheney, Secretary of State Colin Powell, and Generals Norman Schwarzkopf and Tommy Franks in Belgium for alleged war crimes in Iraq. Powell issued a stern warning that Belgium's status as an international hub could be jeopardized by such legislation. Realizing that it had overstepped its capacity as a moral force in the world, the Belgian parliament and government amended the law in April 2003 to provide "filters" that allow the judiciary to reject complaints in which there are no victims of Belgian nationality and that authorize the government to reject cases in which the accused are citizens of a democratic country in which they could be tried in their own courts. Nevertheless, at the June 2003 NATO summit U.S. Defense Secretary Donald Rumsfeld questioned whether the alliance could continue to hold meetings in Brussels and whether the U.S. would withhold financing for the new NATO headquarters to be built across the street from the present building if the law remained in place. Under such pressure, Belgium all but scrapped the law especially after

Michel himself was charged for authorizing the sale of machine guns to Nepal.

ECONOMY

Belgium was one of the first countries in the world to become heavily industrialized; this was possible because of large coal, and to a lesser extent, iron ore deposits. The industrialized areas became heavily urbanized, and a well-trained and powerfully organized work force emerged. Today, two–thirds of Belgium's workers are unionized, the high-

est percentage in Western Europe. They are divided almost evenly between socialist and Christian unions.

As in every other Belgian institution, language separations weaken the unity of the unions. The country experienced its first general strike in 58 years in 1993; it was aimed at the austerity program of a shaky government, which beat a tactical retreat. The government can weather many such labor disturbances because the mainly French–speaking socialist unions and the dominant Christian unions in Flanders cannot pull together sufficiently to bring the government down.

Over the years, a highly elaborate system of formal discussions between labor unions, employers and the government has developed. These discussions facilitate the exchange of conflicting views and aim at establishing the framework for agreements in economic matters that would protect the well–being and future of the entire country.

Sometimes this cooperation breaks down, but as a rule, the unions take a constructive, pragmatic approach to economic matters. They have much to show for their high productivity and cooperative policies: wages which, though declining in real terms, remain among the world's highest, one of the world's shortest work weeks (less than 38 hours), pensions and social security benefits which until the 1980s were fully protected from inflation by means of indexing, which means that they were automatically raised to keep step with rises in retail prices. Such indexing took some of the heat out of labor relations, but it invariably contributed to inflation and to government spending deficits.

As many European countries which were left in a condition of devastation and destitution at war's end in 1945, Belgium,

A panorama of industry in Antwerp

Belgium

within a few months, passed sweeping social welfare legislation which could give the people some economic hope for the future. Benefits were continually expanded through the 1970s. For instance, generous unemployment benefits take much of the sting out of losing one's job. The state medical insurance reimburses three-fourths of all medical and pharmaceutical expenses and pays persons with long-term illnesses—60% of their salaries for the first two years and 40% for the next two years. Belgium's social welfare net has attracted many admirers, but such a net became extremely expensive. Its nominal costs multiplied twelve–fold from 1960 to 1980, and the government exhausted domestic sources of credit to pay for them.

After 1978 the government has had to borrow heavily abroad, not merely to finance foreign trade, but to meet the budgetary demands created by what many consider to be an overly generous social welfare program. With its high standard of living and small domestic market Belgium is extremely dependent upon foreign trade; about half of its production must be exported. Of course, it has many foreign trade advantages. Its central location in the middle of major European economic centers and its membership in the EU are very significant. Belgium lies within a 200-mile radius of a market containing 100 million consumers. This includes Holland, the Ruhr area, Paris and London. Three–fourths of its exports go to the EU, and 60% flows to its three neighbors—Germany, France and the Netherlands.

Also, it has the second largest port in Europe and one of the most modern, best equipped, efficiently operated and busiest in the world—Antwerp. This port, which is owned by the city, is located within 250 miles of Frankfurt, Düsseldorf, Lille, Paris, Amsterdam and London. Situated 45 miles (72 km.) inland along the Scheldt River, its access to the open sea was always a problem because the Scheldt passes through Dutch territory before emptying into the North Sea. For centuries the Dutch, wishing to minimize competition for their own port of Rotterdam, limited or prevented traffic heading to Antwerp from passing though their territory. Excellent relations with the Netherlands finally enabled the two countries to sign a treaty eliminating such hindrance, and Antwerp now thrives.

The port has the largest underwater warehouse facilities in the world, and is especially noted for its lightning–fast turn–around time. More than 75,000 are employed by the port or by companies that in some way service the port. The port complex, which covers 27,000 acres, contains entire industrial plants, including factories owned by such multinational companies as General Motors and Bayer. About half of the traffic entering and leaving the port is moved by Belgium's 930 mile (1,500 km.) canal system, which links the port to all major Belgian cities and rivers, which are easily navigable because of their slow current. Most important, the inland waterway plugs into the Rhine River, a link which perhaps entitles Antwerp to call itself the gateway to Europe.

Backing up this inland waterway is a very well developed internal transport system. The first railway in Europe formally opened in Brussels in 1835 and now with its 2,536 miles (over 4,000 km.) the Belgian railway net is the densest in the world. Its international motorways are also plentiful and fully lighted at night. Its deeply indebted national airline, SABENA, fell victim to the drastic reduction in air passengers after the terrorist attacks against the United States on September 11, 2001. It went bankrupt, and in 2002 the SN Brussels Airlines, formed from Delta Air Transport, a regional subsidiary of SABENA, commenced operations.

Many of the factors that once made Belgium an economic powerhouse have now disappeared. Easily extractable coal, traditionally Belgium's only significant raw material, has been almost completely exhausted in the South, where most of the mines are closed. Coal production in the fresher Flemish mines is now eight times higher than in Wallonia. Belgium's steel industry, which grew up around the coalfields, had become inefficient and obsolete; EU policies to reduce European steel production have cost thousands of jobs in Belgium. Steel towns such as Liège, Charleroi and Mons are now economic and political trouble areas. The Belgian government felt compelled to subsidize many lame industries, particularly in the steel and textile sectors. This aid has almost always flowed to Wallonia, which suffered almost 75% of all plant closures in 1979. Such government subsidies only postpone the restructuring of Wallonia's industries necessary to enable them to compete in modern markets. They have also enabled the labor unions to achieve higher wages in the lame industries, especially steel, than those paid in the more productive mills in Flanders. Indeed, the strike record in Wallonia is three times the rate per capita than in Flanders. This only increases resentment toward Wallonia, which many Flemings believe is in essence being subsidized by Flanders.

The world economic turndowns since the oil shocks of 1973–4 struck a hard blow at Belgium's trading position. Four decades ago, Belgium's own coal supplied 90% of the country's energy needs, but that figure has now sunk to about 20%. About 40% of its present energy needs are covered by oil; almost all of it must be imported and most comes from the Middle East. The oil company, Petrofina, provides a small portion of the country's oil through its concession in the U.S., Canada, the Congo and the North Sea. Natural gas provides for 17% of its energy consumption. It hopes to be able to develop on–site gasification of coal, which could have the effect of reviving the lagging coal mining industry. More than a quarter of its energy is produced by seven nuclear power plants. In 2003 the parliament approved a

The Grand Place, Brussels

172

Belgian Cuisine: Mussels and "French" Fries   Photo: Juliet Bunch

law that would shut all of them down between 2015 and 2025, when each had reached the age of 40 years.

A very unpleasant development for Belgium was the slowdown in foreign investment caused, in large part, by the country's high wage costs and dramatic drop in profitability of Belgian firms. American investors, who in the 1960s accounted for 65% of all foreign investment in Belgium, had reduced their share to less than a third by the 1980s, and some of the most visible U.S. firms such as RCA, General Electric and Holiday Inn, have withdrawn altogether. This is a very serious problem because multinational companies control an estimated one–third of all manufacturing jobs and almost one–half of all industrial assets in Belgium. Thus, their confidence in the Belgian economy is crucial.

The government is trying to lure foreign investment by providing subsidies, reducing interest rates and giving capital bonuses and tax breaks, but the results are mixed. The French automaker, Renault, found out in 1997 what can happen in Belgium when it decided to close its plant in Volvoorde and lay off 3,100 Belgian workers. Ex-Prime Minister Dehaene proclaimed the action as "brutal and unacceptable," and a hundred thousand people staged a protest march in Brussels.

Belgium now has approximately 400,000 foreign workers, who with their families number about 900,000. They are eligible for all social security benefits and cannot be deported for economic reasons. They are concentrated primarily in the Wallonian industrial areas and Brussels. The capital city has a particularly visible foreign presence. The thousands of EU bureaucrats, international businessmen and especially foreign laborers now comprise almost 30% of the city's population.

Foreign workers are a convenient target for extreme right–wing groups such as the VMO and Youth Front, but they do face discrimination in the larger society. The extent of the problem of integrating the predominantly African and Mediterranean workers was revealed by the passage of a law in 1981 directed against racism and hatred toward foreigners. It is now forbidden by law to put up signs such as "Foreigners unwanted" or "No entry for North Africans," as once one saw in Belgium. Public services may no longer be denied to foreigners.

Like many other rich Western European countries, Belgium has become a magnet for persons from the Third World seeking asylum. A fourth of Brussels' residents are immigrants, mainly Moroccans and Turks. With the situation worsening monthly, the government became a firm advocate of strict border controls. The government tightened controls on illegal refugees in 1993 and speeded up the application processing and deportation of such foreigners.

Belgian agriculture is still relatively efficient by European standards and provides 80% of the country's food needs. There are problems, however. Farm incomes have stagnated for years, but farmers have managed to stay afloat because of subsidies from the EU's Common Agriculture Program (CAP). Most Belgian farms are mixed, producing grains and raising livestock and, except for Italy, Belgium has the smallest farms in the EU. Therefore, there is a great need for amalgamation and modernization. But with a high unemployment rate in Belgium, the 2% of the population working in agriculture (producing 1.4% of GDP) must be kept on the land until some can be absorbed by industry, which employs 27% of the workforce and produces 24% of GDP, or services, which provide work for 71% and create 74.6% of GDP.

Despite some improvement, Belgium faces economic problems. Although its government deficit had disappeared by 2002, over a quarter of the budget is devoted to paying interest on the national debt. Its public debt, at 125% of GDP, is the highest in the industrialized world. The government's stiff austerity program since the 1980s was partly successful. The government's borrowing, spending and deficit have all been reduced. Unemploy-

School children parading before King. By Jan Verhas, 1878.

Belgium

ment in 2003 was 11.6%, still one of the highest rates in Europe, and inflation 1%. The economy shrank by .8% in 2002, but it was growing again in 2003 by 1.3% on an annual basis. Tax rates continue to be reduced.

One can no longer call the country "the sick man of Europe," as some observers did. The director of the Belgian employers' association could no longer say about his own country, as he did in 1981: "Belgium reminds me of a well-dressed man who inspires confidence until you learn that he has not paid his tailor."

CULTURE

Belgium has more than one culture, and to understand the cultural dimension of this country, one must unravel the strands of Roman, Frankish, Spanish, French, Austrian, German and Dutch influences. With no common culture, there is very little feeling of Belgian national identity, especially among the Flemish. Unlike in Wallonia, there is a vocal separatist movement in Flanders. It is mainly when they are outside of Belgium that many Flemish and Walloons begin to feel like Belgians.

Today, Belgium is secularized, and few Belgians vote primarily along religious sect lines. Also, there is a trend away from doctrinaire religious positions on social and political matters, even among the Roman Catholics. Catholicism is still a significant social force, especially in Flanders. Catholics organize trade unions, youth movements, hospitals, sports clubs, political parties and schools, and these

organizations are thriving. Perhaps this helps partly to explain the conservatism of the Belgians, who remain largely a rather private, family–oriented people.

The best example of the vitality of Catholicism is the separation of the school system into state schools, which accommodate approximately 43% of the pupils, and "free" (chiefly Catholic) schools, which are largely financed by the state and accommodate 57%. The long and emotional dispute over state support for Catholic

schools was finally settled in 1958. The compromise that was reached probably put to rest the last religious dispute that would significantly affect Belgian politics.

Children are now permitted to choose English as their first foreign language, rather than learning French or Dutch. There has been an increasing tendency to use English as the common language between Flemings and Walloons, including in corporate boardrooms. Even José Happart admitted after a fierce TV debate, "after all, everybody will speak English in 20 years." There is, at the same time, an encouraging trend for ambitious francophones to buckle down and learn Flemish. Most educated Flemings continue to speak fluent French although the percentage that can do so is declining. There are many variants of Walloon French, which is closer to the old rather than to the modern Parisian form. There is diversity at the university level. Four universities are Flemish–speaking and four are French–speaking. Some are Catholic, such as Leuven and Louvain–la–Neuve, and some are not, such as the University of Brussels, Ghent and Liège.

The news media uses both languages. The *Radio Television Belge de la Communauté Culturelle Française* (RTBF) and the *Belgische Radio en Televisie* (BRT) are separate public utilities with state financing but without direct state intervention in their management. Both are run by ten–member administrative councils, of which eight are representatives of political parties and are appointed by the parliament. Belgians were pioneers in radio broadcasting and

Pieter Bruegel, the Bethlehem Census

now have one German, three French and three Dutch channels. There is one French and one Dutch–language television channel.

There are newspapers in all three languages. The leading French papers are *La Libre Belgique* (Catholic) and *Le Soir* (independent). Flemish dailies include *Het Laatste Nieuws* (Liberal) and *De Standaard* (Catholic). One daily, *Grenz Echo*, appears in the German language. Most Belgian dailies have a political affiliation and are owned by one of four large chains, although each newspaper has a great measure of autonomy within each group.

Simply by driving through Belgium, one realizes that the country is filled with art treasures. One can see splendid medieval cities such as Bruges, Ghent, Antwerp, Liège, Brussels, Leuven (Louvain), Tongeren, Namur and Tournai, which are filled with castles, abbeys and venerable public buildings. But it is art museums throughout the world that one can best see the impact of Belgian artists.

Painting was the medium in which artists came to be known best of all, and by the 16th century, Flemish painting with its bold personal expression and vitality marked the high point of the northern Renaissance. Jan Van Eyck was the first Flemish master to arouse the admiration of Italian painters, and his brother Hubert Van Eyck also produced masterpieces of lasting value. Pieter Bruegel the Elder combined religious, moral or satirical subjects with vivid descriptions of the Flemish rural environment. He broadened the art of landscape painting through a masterful, sweeping concept of nature.

Peter Paul Reubens became the most famous exponent of Baroque painting; he also was a noted diplomat and worked for Marie de Medici, Philip IV of Spain and Charles I of England. His collaborator, Anthony Van Dyck, became the court painter of the English royal family. David Teniers was a master at painting highly realistic popular scenes. Flemish artists were pioneers in giving depth to painting, instead of rendering a flat appearance. They paid very close attention to detail and to common people. Thus, they gave us the most vivid picture imaginable of their surroundings and have kept their own time alive in the mind of the modern viewer.

Since ancient times, Belgian literature was bilingual. Until the 19th century its painters overshadowed its writers, but after Belgium gained its independence, literature began to bloom. Hendrik Conscience attracted attention to his homeland through his novel *The Lion of Flanders*. Reminiscent of Sir Walter Scott's romantic novels, Conscience rekindled Flemings' pride and interest in their past. He also wrote other delightful novels depicting life in the Flemish countryside and towns that sparked a literary revival. Another great 19th century Flemish figure was the poet, Guido Gezelle, whose poems presented religious sentiment with great eloquence. Karel van Woestijne was also a brilliant poet who wrote about the eternal conflict between body and soul. Perhaps the greatest 20th century authors are Hugo Claus and the late Baron Marnix Gijsen.

Walloon literature was revived under the leadership of Max Weller, whose literary review *La Jeune Belgique* encouraged experimentation and cosmopolitanism in the late 19th century. Charles de Coster wrote *Ulenspiegel* in 1867, a ribald tale so filled with the spirit of liberty that it became a symbol of Belgian resistance in both world wars. Perhaps the greatest French–speaking Belgian writers were Maurice Maeterlinck, who won a Nobel Prize in 1911, Emile Verhaeren and Michel de Ghelderode. Paradoxically, all three were Flemish! With such a composer as Cesar Franck and ballet artist as Maurice Béjart, Belgium has also gained world acclaim in music and dance.

In general, Walloon literature is strongly oriented toward France, while Flemish literature is concerned chiefly with maintaining and broadening Flemish cultural identity, without strong reference to the Netherlands. In order to attempt to establish a Belgian cultural identity, the state has established "Houses of Culture" all over the country. These houses enrich the quality of life of the communities in which they are located, but it is doubtful that they contribute much to welding together two so distinct cultures.

FUTURE

Belgium has begun to overcome its serious economic difficulties. It is still wealthy even by the high European standards. However, it must continue the restructuring of its traditional industries in order to make them competitive in world markets today. Its greatest problems in the future will involve the attempt to control migration into the country, to assimilate refugees and immigrants who are already living there, and to manage the perpetual and exhausting strife that is sparked by the existence of differing language communities that find it difficult to coexist with each other.

Occupying the EU presidency in the second half of 2001, Belgium's leaders played a prominent role in condemning the al-Qaeda terrorist attacks against the World Trade Center and Pentagon on September 11 and in speaking for Europeans in conveying sympathy toward the victims and the United States. Belgium supported the war effort in Afghanistan and was aggressive in arresting al-Qaeda suspects and in backing tough EU measures to combat terrorism in Europe. Its firm decision not to support the United States and Britain in the war against Iraq was cheered by most of its own citizens. But it created ill feeling and resentment within the Atlantic Alliance that will take time to heal. Belgium will be reexamining the kind of world role it can play that befits its own ideals, aspirations and capabilities.

Brussels: The Grand Place provides a backdrop for the flower market.

The Grand Duchy of Luxembourg

Luxembourg's largest castle dominates the village of Vianden

Courtesy: Jon Markham Morrow

Area: 999 sq. mi. (2,586 sq. km., somewhat smaller that Rhode Island).

Population: 450,000, of which more than 125,000 are foreigners (a third of the total population).

Capital City: Luxembourg (Pop. 80,000, estimated).

Climate: Temperate, with mild winters and summers.

Neighboring Countries: Luxembourg is wedged between Belgium (West); Germany (East) and France (South).

Official Languages: Luxembourgish (a Moselle Franconian–German dialect with numerous additions of French words), French and German.

Ethnic Background: Indo–European, Germanic.

Principal Religion: Roman Catholic (94%).

Main Exports: Iron and steel products, chemicals. International banking activities are extremely important.

Main Imports: Minerals, metals, foodstuffs, machinery.

Currency: Euro.

Major Trading Customers: EU countries (84.5%), principally Germany (24%), France (21%), Belgium (13% but source of 37.5% of imports), U.S. (4%).

National Day: June 23rd.

Chief of State: His Royal Highness the Grand Duke Henri, b. 1955. Married in 1981 to Grand Duchess Maria Teresa. He succeeded his father upon his abdication in 2000.

Head of Government: Jean–Claude Juncker, Prime Minister (since 1995).

National Flag: Three horizontal stripes of equal width, red, white, blue (The flag closely resembles that of the Netherlands).

Since the Roman legions came to what is now Luxembourg in 57 B.C., the Luxembourgers have tenaciously clung to their separate existence. Caesar wrote that the Treveri tribesmen who resisted his troops "never submitted to commands except under the compulsion of an army." In the two millenia that followed, the Franks, Burgundians, Dutch and Germans controlled this tiny land. But, unlike most small nations, the Luxembourgers never allowed themselves to be absorbed entirely by another power. They well deserve their national motto: *Mir wolle bleive wat mir sin!* ("We want to remain what we are!").

Luxembourg is the smallest independent state in the EU, encompassing only 999 square miles, less than the state of Rhode Island. It has a growing population of 450,000, fewer than one–third that of Brussels and one–twentieth that of Paris. Nevertheless, it is one of the most prosperous countries in the world, with an industrial productivity and international significance far out of proportion to its size.

The northern half of the country, called Oesling, is a rugged territory of low mountains and forests. It is a continuation of the Ardennes forest area of Belgium. The southern half is within the Lorraine Plain and is rolling, wooded countryside. Because of its lush pastureland and fertile soil, this area is called the Gutland or Bon Pays (Good Land). It also contains most of Luxembourg's industrial centers and its capital city.

With its many international organizations and multilingual citizens the capital is a very cosmopolitan city. Having only about 80,000 inhabitants, it is no metropolis, but it is a charming, almost fairytale city built in the late 16th century in Spanish Renaissance style and remodeled at the end of the 19th century. Two rivers, the Alzette and Petrusse, flow through the city, which is located on a plateau, and through the centuries they have cut deep, narrow valleys with very steep sides dropping 200 feet. The old section of the city is perched on the highest part of the plateau. Located on one of the many narrow, twisting streets of the old city is the Grand Ducal Palace, built in 1573,

176

HISTORY

The Early Period

Luxembourg's independence was established in 963 A.D. Siegfried, the Count of Ardennes, hewed powerful battlements in the cliffs where Luxembourg's capital city is now located. Until it was demolished by international agreement in 1867, this almost impregnable fortress was called the "Gibraltar of the North." In fact, the word Luxembourg meant "little fortress." The visitor can still climb on the ruins of this stronghold and wander in the maze of passages underneath.

Independent Luxembourg was linked to the Holy Roman Empire, and in the beginning of the 14th century Luxembourg's Duke, Henry VII, was crowned Holy Roman Emperor. Luxembourg ultimately provided four Emperors during this heyday of the Duchy's power. Henry's son, John, a man very fond of travel, women, horses and dice, became the King of Bohemia. After losing one eye in battle and the other to disease, he became known as John the Blind. His bravery became legendary in the Battle of Crecy in 1346 against the English. Unable to see, John galloped to the head of his troops by having his steed tied to those of several loyal aides and then ordering them to advance. Not surprisingly, he did not survive the battle.

John's grandson, Charles IV, was also a Holy Roman Emperor and built the beautiful city of Prague, now the capital of Czechoslovakia. The Luxembourger's golden age of power gradually declined, and in 1443 the Duchy was conquered by the Duke of Burgundy; for more than four centuries, foreign powers gave the orders in Luxembourg.

Neutrality and War

Luxembourg evolved into a neutral country in the 19th century, but this lasted less than a half–century. It was violated by German troops in August 1914. The Grand Duchess Marie–Adelheid remained in the country during the entire four–year occupation, and in the opinion of many Luxembourgers she collaborated with the Germans. Whether this was true or not, she felt obliged to abdicate in early 1919, and her popular sister, Charlotte, ascended the throne. A referendum in 1919 confirmed the constitutional monarchy, but proclaimed the people to be sovereign and introduced universal suffrage for men and women. This referendum established a fully democratic parliamentary form of government in the Grand Duchy.

As small countries often do, Luxembourg felt the need to seek a union with a larger power, so in a referendum in 1921, Luxembourgers voted three to one to enter an economic union with France. The latter country, however, advised Luxembourg to enter a close economic relationship with Belgium; both smaller countries agreed to this in 1922.

In 1940 Luxembourg was given another reminder that a policy of neutrality alone cannot guarantee the security of a country. German troops again occupied the tiny state in 1940 and within a few weeks virtually annexed it. In August 1942 Luxembourg was officially incorporated into Hitler's Reich. When the population responded with a strike, about 30,000 Luxembourgers, or about 10% of the population and most of country's young men, were deported. Many were forced to serve in the German army and until liberation the population continued to suffer greatly from a brutal occupation.

Having learned from her sister's mistake in 1914, Grand Duchess Charlotte fled in 1940 with her entire government, first to London and then to Montreal. She worked tirelessly to assure that Luxembourg would be recognized as an independent country at the war's end. Her son, Crown Prince Jean, served as an officer in the British army, and landed with his unit, the Irish Guards, on the beaches of Normandy on June 11, 1944, five days after the first Allied troops had landed. On September 3 his unit entered Brussels and on September 10 it crossed the Luxembourg border between Rodange and Pétange, exactly at the spot where his parents had left the country in 1940. The same afternoon he reached the capital city—his

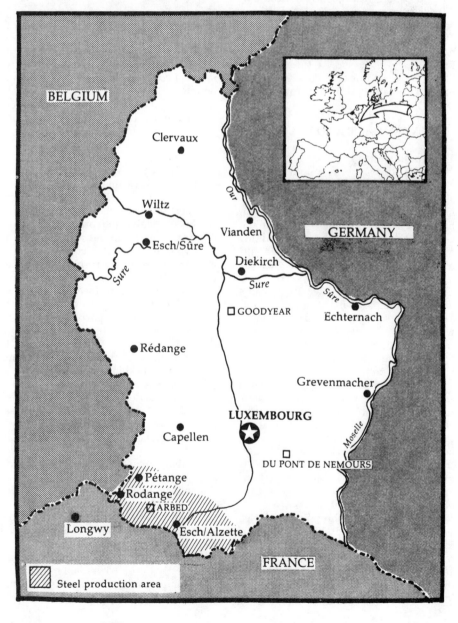

Luxembourg

arrival was hailed by thousands of his countrymen. His father, Felix, had reached the city that morning with an American tank division.

Unfortunately, the war was not yet over for Luxembourg. Hitler's forces made a last offensive at the end of 1944 in order to stop the Allied advance toward Germany. During this Ardennes offensive, known as the Battle of the Bulge, the American commander, General Omar Bradley, made Luxembourg City his headquarters, but a large portion of the Duchy was nevertheless recaptured by German troops. In the fiercely fought Battle of the Bulge such destruction was visited upon the land that it took until 1952 to repair all the material damage. American losses were also very great, as one can see at the American military cemetery in Hamm, located about a mile from Luxembourg Airport. There rest 5,000 American soldiers, including General George Patton, who was killed in a jeep accident in December 1945. Most cities in Luxembourg have a street or square named after Patton, who is hailed as the country's liberator. Ettelbruck in the Ardennes unofficially calls itself Patton Town.

GOVERNMENT AND POLITICS

The Grand Duke

Luxembourg is a constitutional monarchy, whose constitution of 1868 was amended in 1919 to invest sovereignty in the people, rather than in the crown. Executive power is formally vested in the Grand Duke Henri, who assumed his father's legislative powers in 1998 and ascended to the throne in 2000 when his father, Jean, abdicated in his favor. He is the sixth grand duke since 1890. Jean's decision to step down at age 79 followed a precedent set by his mother, Charlotte, who abdicated in 1964. Jean also ordered that Luxembourg's quota of Euro coins, which go into circulation in 2002, bear Henri's head on them. The Grand Duke is a popular monarch, and the Luxembourgers' enthusiastic response to his marriage in 1981 demonstrated this sentiment. Henri met a beautiful and intelligent Cuban exile, Maria Teresa Mestre, while both were studying in Geneva. Although she was not of noble birth, he chose to marry her, and their wedding in the Luxembourg Cathedral drew a large assemblage of European nobility.

The Grand Duke, who takes his duties seriously, has considerable influence in the political process. As all constitutional monarchs, he "reigns but does not rule." To be effective, one or several members of the government, who alone assume political responsibility, must countersign his

Former Royal Highnesses The Grand Duke Jean and Grand Duchess

orders. Nevertheless, he could be an especially important figure in times of national crisis when either the parties are unable to form a government, or the nation desperately needs a symbol of national unity. In normal times his actual powers are limited.

Executive Power

This is actually exercised by the President of the Government (the Prime Minister) and his Council of Government (cabinet). The latter body is composed of eleven or twelve persons, each usually holding several ministerial posts. During the five years between elections, the cabinets are occasionally reshuffled, but the resulting "new" governments are seldom significantly different from the ones they replace. In order to try to create some separation between the parliament and the executive, as mandated by the constitution, all cabinet members are required to resign their parliamentary seats when they assume a cabinet post.

The cabinet drafts and submits legislation, which is debated in parliament. The most important professional organizations, especially the six official groups representing agriculture, handcrafts, commerce, civil servants, private employees and labor, are consulted on legislation affecting their interests. The smallness of the county enables this process to work smoothly. Passage after two rounds of debate is usually a foregone conclusion, since the governing parties' approval had already been reached in advance. Particularly important legislation can be submitted directly to the voters in a referendum if the cabinet and parliament approve, but such referendums occur very seldom.

Legislative Structure and Powers

Although the Grand Duke must formally sign all legislation and appointments, the President and Council of Government are not responsible to the monarch, but to the lower house of parliament, the Chamber of Deputies. Its 60 members (lowered from 64 in 1989 to reflect the declining population) are elected every five years by a system of proportional representation tailored to a small or medium–size country, in which voters live close to the candidates and may even know them personally. Luxembourg is divided into four electoral districts, and seats are distributed to each depending upon population. The largest receives 23 seats and the smallest seven. Each voter is permitted to cast as many votes as there are candidates to be elected and may even cast two votes for the same candidate if he wishes. The seats are then distributed to the candidates who receive the most votes.

Summaries of parliamentary debates and election information are sent to all citizens of voting age, who are required to vote. As in all parliamentary democracies, if the President and Council of Government lost their majority in the Chamber, then the Grand Duke can call new elections, although such early elections are seldom necessary.

Political Parties

Since 1925 no political party has ever been able to win a majority of seats in the Chamber of Deputies, so all governments are coalitions of two or more parties. Luxembourg's three main parties have led Luxembourg for about 50 years and have helped create a democracy based on party cooperation. Although each major party represents a distinct political subculture, they all seek a solution to problems in a way agreeable to all three, no matter which is in government at the moment. All three are willing to form coalitions with each other. Neither ideologies nor historical resentments prevent them from sharing responsibility for their nation's future.

The largest is presently the Christian–Social People's Party (CSV), which represents the bourgeois values of a predominantly Catholic population. Its votes are drawn primarily from practicing Catholics, although the gradual disappearance of church–state issues has greatly reduced the religious component of its program. It does draw votes from the nation's farmers and workers. The party's program calls for support of a social market economy and special attention to the needs of citizens who earn below the national average. It is a middle–of–the–road party which supports the extension of the country's already generous social welfare system. With a loosening of religious bonds and a decrease of the number of farmers, the CSV has begun to lose votes.

The CSV has for years been the key coalition party, and no ruling coalition since World War II has been formed without first trying to win its direct participation. In 1994 it fell to 21 seats, and it maintained its leading role in the governing coalition after the June 1999 elections.

Jean–Claude Juncker replaced as prime minister Jacques Santer, who left office to be EU president from 1995 to 1999. One of seven children of a steelworker and trade union militant, Juncker studied law at the University of Strasbourg. He came from the left of the CSV and joined the cabinet in 1984 at age 29. He quickly gained a reputation as an intelligent, well–connected man in the EU with integrity, a broad mind, and a knack for grasping both practical detail and conceptual problems.

The second largest party is the Democratic Party (DP), usually referred to as the Liberals. Led by popular mayor of Luxembourg City, Lydie–Wurth Polfer, it climbed from 12 seats in 1994. But it remained shut out of the government. In 1999 it continued its growth and replaced the Socialists in the governing coalition with the CSV. The Liberals' support is found primarily in the middle class, professions and skilled working groups. It strongly supports a free market economy and opposes excessive government control over the economy.

The third-largest party is the Luxembourg Socialist Workers Party (LSAP), known generally as the Socialists. Led by Foreign Minister Jacques Poos, it fell from

18 to 17 seats in 1994, but it stayed in a grand coalition with the CSV. This alliance, which in 1994 was reelected for a record third term, broke apart after the 1999 elections, which brought loses to the Socialists and drove them into opposition. The LSAP was founded at the turn of the century to protect workers from the seamy consequences of industrialization. Because it views itself as the party of the working class, it is strongest in the highly industrialized South. In the 1960s it showed signs of broadening its base by weakening the socialist components of its program, but this move was strongly resisted by the left wing of the party. The question of collaboration with communists at the local level prompted the party's right wing to split off and form the Social Democratic Party (SDP), which is insignificant today.

Small parties took a sixth of the votes in the 1994 elections. A one–issue party, calling itself the Five–Sixths Party because it advocates raising all pensions to five–sixths of a person's last salary, as government employees receive, won four seats in 1989. In 1994 it ran under the name Action Committee for Democracy and Pension Justice (ADR) and received five seats. Two Green parties won five seats. Despite turbulent internal politics that have kept the parties split, they wish to reunite and enter the government some day.

The only party that never participates in governing coalitions is the Communist Party of Luxembourg (KPL). It finds its electoral support primarily in the industrialized South. Its electoral support has continuously declined. A major reason is that it has remained relatively immune

Royal Highnesses The Grand Duke Henri and Grand Duchess Maria Teresa

Luxembourg

Prime Minister Jean-Claude Juncker

from the more moderate form of communism known as Eurocommunism, which seeks to respect the democratic process and pursue policies oriented toward the particular needs of their own countries. The KPL's ideological rigidity will probably keep it in the political cold, especially following the collapse of communism in Eastern Europe. It lost its only seat in 1994.

Although the parliament is technically a one–chamber assembly, the 21–member Council of State traditionally functions as an upper house. It is appointed by the Grand Duke, acting upon the advice of the cabinet, Chamber of Deputies and the Council of State itself. Mainly an advisory body, the Council of State must be consulted on all legislation and can actually postpone its enactment. Ultimately, however, the Chamber of Deputies can always override it. Eleven of the Council's members function as the nation's highest administrative court. On the whole, the Council plays an important role in the governing process.

Local Government

For administrative purposes, Luxembourg is divided into three districts: Luxembourg, Diekirch and Grevenmacher, which are further broken down into 12 cantons and 118 communes. Each commune has authority over local affairs and elects a Communal Council every six years. To maintain some measure of national control, the central government appoints a Burgomaster (mayor) to every commune, who presides over the Communal Council. All appointments must, however, enjoy the confidence and support of a majority among the locally

elected members of the Communal Councils; no mayor is ever imposed on a commune. In order to make the system of local government more efficient, the central government has proposed that all the present communes be fused into a total of 30, with none having a population under 3,000. Local resistance so far has prevented the realization of this plan.

Defense and Foreign Policy

Two world wars in the 20th century convinced Luxembourgers that neutrality offered their country no protection whatsoever. Their government–in–exile supported the Allied cause, and in 1949 the country joined NATO. With such a small population, it cannot contribute many troops to the alliance. It abolished its conscript army, created in 1945, in 1967, but it maintains a voluntary army of battalion size (768 troops), including a 60-man band. More importantly, it provides storage sites for NATO equipment. Luxembourg pledged in 2002 that it would purchase an Airbus military transport plane to help provide lift to NATO or EU military units.

In the aftermath of the 2003 Iraq war, which Luxembourg opposed, it joined with France, Germany and Belgium to create a joint rapid reaction unit built on the existing French-German brigade. Luxembourg would contribute a reconnaissance team. In addition, the four said they would set up a multinational headquarters and a separate military center in Belgium in 2004 to command and plan EU military operations when NATO is not involved. The four invited other European

nations to join their effort, but sensing that the real purpose of this effort was to weaken the transatlantic alliance, none did. Neither Luxembourg nor the other three pledged to raise their defense spending to cover the costs of these innovations, so it is uncertain whether this initiative will ever get off the ground.

Luxembourg was also a founding member of the EU, a fact that has greatly enhanced its prestige. It amended its constitution in 1956 to permit the transfer of certain of its sovereign powers to the EU. At first, the EU's founding fathers suggested that tiny Luxembourg, which is the geographic center of the six nations, become a kind of Washington, D.C., for the new United States of Europe. This never happened, but Luxembourg continues to propose it at EU meetings. Now EU officials travel back and forth from Brussels, Strasbourg and Luxembourg, a necessity which many officials and observers find wasteful and irritating. It is now the home of many EU offices and institutions, a large part of which are located in the Europa Center, one of Luxembourg's few skyscrapers. In all, about 7,000 EU employees and even more foreign business executives live in Luxembourg.

Among the EU offices located in the Grand Duchy are the Secretariat for the European Parliament, the ECSC, Euratom, the European Court of Justice, the European Audit Court, the European Investments Bank and the European Currency Union. In 1988 Luxembourg won an important victory in its bid to become the center of the EU's legal operations. A new

Entrance to the Grand Ducal Palace in Luxembourg

Court of First Instance was created there to assume some of the growing workload of the European Court of Justice.

The European Parliament used to meet there sometimes, and a new European parliament building was constructed for these meetings. But in 1979 the parliament decided to hold all sessions in Strasbourg. This decision infuriated Luxembourg, which turned in vain to the European Court of Justice for help. A massive office complex was constructed in Brussels that includes an Assembly Chamber large enough for the European Parliament. Luxembourg tenaciously guards its retention of the parliament's secretariat, a body of about 2,000 European officials who make the parliament work, against Brussels. Most of the parliament's committee work already takes place in Brussels, and all the major political groups within the parliament have established their headquarters there. It has been estimated unofficially that 10% of all retail spending in the city of Luxembourg comes from EU employees and their families. Thus, their disappearance could severely affect retail businesses and property values. Luxembourgers converted their European Parliament building to other purposes, such as an international conference center.

Luxembourg's chief foreign policy goals are to be a significant partner in the defense of Europe and in the building of a politically and economically integrated Europe.

ECONOMY

Luxembourg is a highly industrialized and prosperous country. In 2003 it had the world's highest per capita GDP. Since 1945, it has known a high degree of political and social peace. Its economy has always been based so heavily on iron and steel that it is often said, "Luxembourg is as much a gift of iron as Egypt is a gift of the Nile." This has been especially true since 1877, when the Englishmen Sidney, Thomas and P. Carlyle Gilchrist discovered the Gilchrist Thomas process for removing the phosphorus from Luxembourg's iron ore. Its largest steel company, ARBED, (formerly Europe's third–largest) was partly foreign–owned, but the Luxembourg state became its major stockholder. Only a fifth of ARBED's turnover was in Luxembourg; its operations were worldwide and it had major plants in France, Germany, Belgium, Holland and South Korea. ARBED, Usinor from France and Aceralia from Spain merged to form Arcelor, the world's biggest steel producer with roughly 5% of global output. Only 12% of its revenues came from the U.S. in 2001.

The Château de Berg, Grand Ducal country residence

Luxembourg's reliance on steel is a source of economic vulnerability, as well as of opportunity. The competition among the world's steel producers had become so strong in recent years that production outstripped demand. In response, Luxembourg had to reduce its production. In 1970 the steel industry produced nearly a third of the country's GDP; by 1991 that figure was down to 8%. Steel had fallen by 1991 to a third of manufacturing output, compared with 70% in 1960. This not only led to huge financial losses, but forced the Luxembourg steel industry to restructure itself and ultimately to merge with two other foreign companies. This was also required by the EU, which now seeks to save the European steel industry by requiring it to modernize in member countries.

For Luxembourg this necessitated a gradual reduction of the steel industry's work force from 25,000 in 1974 to 8,000 in 1993 and to 6,000 by 1996. These reductions resulted in a rise in productivity per employee. In order not to disrupt social peace within the country, the reduction was accomplished by retirement of older workers as early as age 57, rather than by massive layoffs. It is this kind of practice which has enabled Luxembourg to hold its unemployment rate to 2.5% in 2003, among the lowest in the world and best in the EU. But it has a labor shortage, and over 80% of new jobs are filled by cross border workers, called "Frontaliers"— approximately 90,000 enter daily to work in Luxembourg, chiefly in the financial services sector. Together with resident aliens, they constituted over 53% of the workforce in 2003; in the financial services sector that figure is two-thirds. Since Luxembourgers grew up speaking French and German, the foreign commuters face no language barriers.

The country's political and economic leaders saw the problem of excessive dependence upon steel and banking well in advance, and, since 1950, they have made a steady effort to diversify the economy. The Goodyear Tire and Rubber Company began building plants in the Grand Duchy

Luxembourg

View of the capital

in 1951 and is now its second largest employer. The program got a particular boost from the industrial diversification law of 1962; this has been renewed regularly and provides state financial assistance for industrial development that contributes to the construction, conversion and rationalization of industries, crafts and commercial operations. The program has greatly stimulated the service industries, which now employ about three-fourths of the workforce, and has attracted over 60 new companies to Luxembourg, which have created employment for more than 11,000 persons. The most important newcomers have been American, such as DuPont.

The program has also helped to attract foreign banks to the country; the number of banks increased from 13 in 1955 to 230 in 1998 and then declined to 185 by 2002. Luxembourg has become one of the financial centers in Europe. When the Eurodollar market (in which Luxembourg had specialized) declined, and London deregulated the British financial industry, Luxembourg shifted deftly to other retail banking services and maintains its place in the world market. This has greatly benefited the country. Banks employ 24,000 and generate over a fifth of the GDP and a third of government revenue. One can almost speak of an economic revolution in the Grand Duchy.

In the 1980s, one job in banking was being created for every job that was disap-

pearing in the steel industry. By 1988 the number of Luxembourgers employed in banking overtook those working in the steel industry, and that gap has continued to widen greatly.

To attract funds to Luxembourg banks, the country has doggedly pursued its right to guarantee bank secrecy, despite pressure from the EU and U.S. to cooperate more closely in cases involving crime, money laundering and tax fraud. Germany suffers most from the capital flight to Luxembourg. Along with other powerful neighbors, it pressured the Duchy to harmonize its low tax regime with its EU partners and abandon its zero withholding tax on foreigners. Because the financial services sector now accounts for more than a fifth of its GDP and employs one in ten persons in the work force, it remains the motor for the country's economic growth. Luxembourg resists these efforts as best it can. However, it pays attention to proposals to reform EU banking policies. In 2003 it agreed, along with Belgium, to levy withholding taxes on foreign accounts and pass them on to other EU governments while keeping the bank secrecy rules in place. It is preparing to expand beyond its traditional banking activities to offer financial services unavailable in other European countries.

The financial services sector has emerged as the economy's largest taxpayer. To keep the economy growing, the government

introduced in 1986 the most sweeping tax reform in the nation's history. Taxes were cut and loopholes were closed. Just over half the cuts are enjoyed by the business sector, prompting some critics of the reform to charge that it is a device primarily to improve the financial environment for bankers.

In 1991 further tax cuts went into effect. Luxembourg was the first EU country in 1997 to meet all the Maastricht treaty convergence criteria for economic and monetary union (EMU). The banks had mixed feelings about the new euro; they quailed at the cost of introducing it, estimated to be 4% of their total revenues. They also feared that the euro could bring with it an EU-wide harmonization of withholding tax, which could be a severe blow to Luxembourg's competitiveness as an offshore financial center. The country's government debt is a mere 6.7% of GDP, its budget shows a 2.5% surplus in 2003, its inflation is steady at 2.2% in 2003 despite wage indexing, and its economic growth at 2.9% in 2002, although down from 6% annually from 1996–2001, is healthy at 2.9% in 2002.

As a tiny but mighty economic dynamo and financial center in the heart of Europe, Luxembourg's influence over the regions it now borders has grown dramatically. It has adapted more successfully to new economic realities than have the German, French and Belgian areas along its borders. Germany's Saarland and Rheinland-Palatinate, France's Lorraine, and Belgium's Wallonia have experienced retarded economic development and have in some ways become economic satellites of Luxembourg. This has been facilitated by the EU's "single market," which promotes the free movement of capital and labor. Employment opportunities in the Duchy help relieve the high rates of unemployment in those neighboring areas. In such a *Grande Région*, as it has been called, the economic, social and cultural ties will continue to deepen, and the borders between them will fade.

With a very small population and a high standard of living, Luxembourg is absolutely dependent upon foreign trade. Exports and imports account for 85% of its GDP, compared with 50% for Belgium, 20% for France and 10% for the U.S. Such dependence indicates why Luxembourg's membership in the EU has been a matter of economic life or death. It sends 85% of its exports to its EU partners and gets 88% of its imports from them. At 4% of its total, Luxembourg's trade with the U.S. remains relatively insignificant. Primary imports are iron ore, coke and all energy sources except hydroelectricity.

Its steel companies own some coalmines in Germany, but its dependence upon imported oil, gas and coal is a major problem. With the highest per capita number of automobiles in Europe, oil is a particularly sensitive import, but by 1991 oil accounted for only 10% of Luxembourg's imports, down from 17% in 1973. To increase its energy supplies, an atomic plant along the Moselle River was planned, which would have supplied most of the power needs until the year 2000. However, the nuclear accident at Harrisburg, Pennsylvania, created political problems that caused the plans for this plant to be dropped. Luxembourg also declined to join with France in developing a nuclear power plant at Cattenom, located only six miles from the Grand Duchy. After the 1986 nuclear accident at Chernobyl in the Soviet Union, the Luxembourg government and, according to polls, 80% of the citizens began to worry more about the safety of the Cattenom plant. However, demonstrations and diplomatic protests have had no influence on the French in this matter.

An important factor in maintaining industrial production in such a small country has been the importation of foreign workers, especially from Portugal, Italy and Spain. Together with their families, they now account for over a third of the population (35.6%) and come from a hundred other countries. This is the highest percentage of foreign workers in the EU. If trends continue, the proportion will be one-half within the lifetimes of most living inhabitants. Over half of Luxembourg City's population is already foreign.

Non-nationals, especially immigrants from Portugal and Italy, hold about half of all jobs in the country. Foreigners provide 52% of the workers in all of Luxembourg's industries, although the percentages differ in the various economic sectors. They account for 85% of the construction workers, 66% of the craftsmen and 35% of the laborers in the iron and steel industry. Their visibility was manifested in a frightening incident in June 2000 when a 39-year-old Tunisian immigrant held dozens of school children captive in the predominantly Portuguese-inhabited village of Wasserbillig, close to the German border. Because so many of the children were of Portuguese origin, the Lisbon government closely monitored the crisis. It ended after 28 hours when a sharpshooter posing as a cameraman shot and killed the hostage-taker with a gun concealed in a TV camera.

Foreign workers and their families are not permitted to participate in the national political life, although they can vote in European parliamentary elections. But even if there is little integration with the native population, they are generally well treated. Unlike in many European countries, there is no seriously destabilizing anti-foreigner sentiment. This is partly explained by the fact that most immigrants share the same Catholic religion with 94% of the native Luxembourgers. In 2000 Luxembourg had the largest percentage of asylum-seekers per capita in the EU (one per 140 inhabitants, compared with one per 830 in Germany and one per 2,600 in France). There was a public protest when 40 of them were deported in 1999.

The dependence upon foreign workers seems irreversible, given Luxembourg's alarmingly low birth rate. Unlike the case in most European countries after 1945, there was no baby boom in Luxembourg, and since 1960 the birth rate has steadily declined to one of the lowest in the world—since 1968 the native population has declined by about 1,000 each year. This is not only a serious problem for the very survival of a small nation, but it creates an increasingly aging population that must be supported by fewer and fewer persons of working age. A fifth is already over 60 years of age, the largest percentage in the EU. This will put increasing pressure on the country's generous pension system.

It is hoped that this unpleasant development can be rendered less serious by automating and modernizing industry. This would establish a productive industrial base that could create a high degree of wealth with fewer workers. The government provides a multitude of inducements to raise the birthrate: increasing family allowances, extending maternity leaves and helping single or divorced women raise children. Few people are optimistic that these measures will reverse the demographic downturn. As one member of parliament worried: "Our country is like an aging couple. We live well, but we don't know what tomorrow brings. We have no grandchildren."

Maintaining economic stability and prosperity will remain a major task for the future. This will require maintaining not only a high level of productivity, but also the labor peace that has prevailed since the end of World War II. There has been scarcely a strike since 1945; this enviable record is due to the well-organized process of consultation among employers, employees and the government, and to the great care taken not to allow the rate of unemployment to increase. In part, this has been successfully accomplished by introducing extensive public works and part-time work schedules with the state paying for the hours not worked.

This daring policy is one that most observers agree will become too costly in the long run. Labor peace was also preserved by indexing incomes and pensions to adjust automatically to inflation although such indexing fans the flames of inflation and damages trade competitiveness. In addition, this desire to maintain purchasing power clashes with the desire to increase social benefits, which already cover virtually the entire population.

Slightly more than half of Luxembourg's land is used for agriculture, of which 54% is used for grazing. A third of the country is planted with forests. Meat and dairy production dominate, accounting for more than 80% of the farm income. Wine production is also important.

Presently fewer than 6% of the population is engaged in agriculture, and this number is steadily declining. Yet even non-farming Luxembourgers are not very far from the natural environment of their rural compatriots. A population density below the EU average, the absence of large cities, and the nearness of wooded areas, together with a relatively unspoiled countryside available for many kinds of relaxation, all contribute to making Luxembourg a pleasant place to live.

CULTURE

Tiny Luxembourg has always been heavily influenced by its neighbors, and nothing shows this quite so clearly as the polyglot of languages that every Luxembourger masters. The everyday language of the people is Luxembourgish, an old Moselle–Frankish dialect of German, which has taken on many altered French expressions, such as *d'fotell* (*le fauteuil*, armchair). The language has become the country's one real symbol of national identity. Even modern Germans have difficulty understanding it.

This native language is spoken at home, in parliament and sometimes in the courts, although documents and formal proceedings are in French. It also has a written form. Despite an official spelling, most Luxembourgers write it phonetically. There are no textbooks clarifying the grammatical rules. Some literature exists in the language, and local publishing houses are producing scores of books in it, spurred by such successful authors as Jhemp Hoscheit, who writes wildly popular children's books in Luxembourgish. Local radio thrives on it. There is a daily one–hour TV news broadcast in it since 1992. The 1990s witnessed a renaissance in interest in written Luxembourgish. A movement has risen to promote the language because many fear it will die in the face of massive migration into the Duchy. The government declared it to be the official language and requires applicants for citizenship to study it. More and more foreign residents are learning to speak and write it as employees are increasingly required to use it on the workplace.

Luxembourg

The German language is primarily used in most primary schools, criminal court proceedings, church, and the press, although it is not uncommon to see articles written in all three national languages on the same page of a newspaper. Finally, French is the language that is used most in administration, civil courts, parliament and secondary education. Since most immigrants living in Luxembourg come from countries (particularly from Portugal, Italy, France and Belgium) where Romance languages or French are spoken, French is an easily learned unifying language that binds the newcomers with native Luxembourgers. Two German invasions in the 20th century caused the elite to align itself more toward France and francophone culture. The country lacks a university. Some persons have noted a positive side of this fact: a source of articulate dissent is exported. Young Luxembourgers do demonstrate, but they usually do so over local issues, and they are seldom violent.

All Luxembourgers are completely trilingual, a fact that spares the country the terrible language conflicts that plague neighboring Belgium. In Luxembourg, culture, including theater, film and literature, is very dependent upon the surrounding French and German worlds, and citizens have realistically accepted this without resentment. Luxembourgers' national identity is so strong and seems so natural that no language issue seems capable of altering it.

Luxembourg introduced Europe's first commercial radio station in 1934. In 1988 it seized the lead in the satellite broadcasting of commercial television when an Ariane rocket placed its Astra satellite into orbit. It has 16 channels that can beam to Britain, France, Germany and the BENELUX and Scandinavian countries.

Radio–Télé–Luxembourg (RTL) broadcasts to 500 million viewers across international borders. It purchased a second satellite doubling capacity to 32 channels. It is the first European country to have an entire satellite system for TV. Some EU members, such as the UK and the Netherlands, oppose such open broadcasting, but Luxembourg is determined that the EU's principle of a "Single Market" should apply to TV viewing. This single market can also have other effects: Ufa, the TV and film subsidiary of the German media giant, Bertelsmann, merged in 1996 with the Compagnie Luxembourgeoise Radiodiffusion (CLR/now CLT), one of the pioneers of the European media industry. RTL is now a majority-owned subsidiary of Bertelsmann and remains Europe's leading broadcasting company with interests in 24 TV channels and 17 radio stations.

THE FUTURE

After a period of rapid economic progress, the economy is growing more slowly. Luxembourg's economic task will be to maintain the productivity, prosperity and social welfare net that it has already achieved. As an exporting nation, it worries about recession in the rest of Europe, especially Germany, and about its increasingly uncompetitive cost structure. It can be expected to maintain the political and social stability that has prevailed since 1945. The Duchy's goal of becoming Europe's capital will remain unfulfilled although its role in Europe is important. Parliamentary elections were held in June 1999. Juncker's Christian Democrats remained in power. But the Liberals overtook the Socialists and replaced them in the governing coalition. Luxembourg is one of a growing number of EU countries that have center-right governments. Next elections will be held in 2004.

The Swiss Confederation (Confoederatio Helvetica)

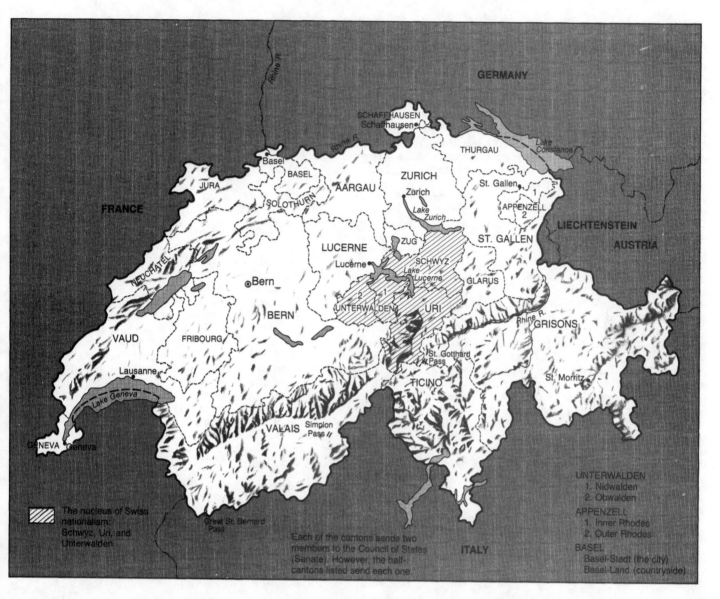

Each of the cantons sends two members to the Council of States (Senate). However, the half-cantons listed send each one.

The nucleus of Swiss nationalism: Schwyz, Uri, and Unterwalden

UNTERWALDEN
1. Nidwalden
2. Obwalden

APPENZELL
1. Inner Rhodes
2. Outer Rhodes

BASEL
Basel-Stadt (the city)
Basel-Land (countryside)

Area: 15,943 sq. mi. (41,292 sq. km.). Roughly the size of Vermont and New Hampshire together.

Population: 7.2 million. Average annual growth rate is .1%. 14.3% of residents are foreigners, primarily Italians, Germans and Spaniards.

Capital City: Bern (Pop. 152,000).

Climate: Owing to great variations in altitude, rapid changes in weather are typical.

Neighboring Countries: France (West); Germany (North); Austria and Liechtenstein (East); Italy (South).

Languages: Swiss nationals—German (64%); French (18%); Italian (8%) Romansch (.5%), Other (9.5%). Total population: German (64%); French (19%); Italian (8%); Romansch (.5%); other (8.5%).

Ethnic Background: Swiss nationals—German (74%); French (20%); Italian (4%); Romansch (1%); other (1%). Total population: German (69%); French (19%); Italian (10%); Romansch (1%); other (1%).

Principal Religion: Swiss Nationals—Protestant (55%); Roman Catholic (43%); Jewish (.2%); other (1.8%). Total population: Protestant (47.8%); Roman Catholic (49.4%); Jewish (.3%); other (2.5%).

Main Exports: Machinery, chemicals, precision instruments, metal products, watches and jewelry, yarn and textiles, dyestuffs, processed foods.

Main Imports: Machinery, chemicals motor vehicles, metal and metal products, foodstuffs, textile fibers and yarns.

Major Trading Partners: EU (60% of exports and 78% of imports)—Germany (22% of exports and 31% of imports); France (9% exports and 11% imports); Italy (7.6% exports and 10% imports); UK (5.4% exports and 4.5% imports), U.S. (11.6% exports and 6.8% of imports).

Currency: Swiss franc.

Independence: August 1291.

National Day: August 1.

Chief of State: A seven–man collegiate Federal Council; ceremonial functions are performed by the Federal President, a member of the Federal Council chosen by Parliament or a one–year term.

Head of Government: The Federal President's position is merely "first among equals" in the Federal Council. Kaspar Villiger (2002), Pascal Couchepin (2003)

National Flag: Square with a white cross on a red field. The flag of the International Red Cross is exactly the same, except that the colors are reversed.

No visitor ever left Switzerland without feeling that he has been in one of the most extraordinary countries in the world. With its stark Jura Mountains, jagged snowcapped Alps with tidy, rustic villages dotting their valleys, clean,

Switzerland

mountain–fed lakes with cosmopolitan, manicured cities such as Geneva, Lausanne, Lucerne, Zurich and Basel on their shores. Switzerland seems to be the epitome of natural beauty, cleanliness, prosperity and stability. Its people speak a polyglot of languages, but such diversity does not threaten the country as it often does elsewhere.

In general, the Swiss are disciplined, thrifty, realistic, cautious, prudent about change and ingenious about using the resources they have at their disposal. They are not an exceptionally outgoing people, but they are renowned for their tolerance. Therefore, Switzerland is a dreamed refuge for political and economic disadvantaged and advantaged from all over the entire world.

A small, land–locked, mountainous country, Switzerland is located in the heart of Western Europe. New Hampshire and Vermont could easily fit into the entire country, and 41 of 50 American states are larger than Switzerland. The Jura mountain chain covers approximately 10% of the country in the west and northwest and separates the city of Basel from the rest of the nation. Of the country's entire land area, 60% is located in the Alpine mountain chain, which runs roughly west to east through the southern part of the country. Often called "the mother of rivers, Switzerland, or more precisely, the Gotthard Massif, is the watershed for some of Western

Europe's most important rivers: the Rhône flows through the canton of Valais, Lake Geneva and France to the Mediterranean Sea. The Rhine forms the border with Liechtenstein, Austria and Germany; it flows through Basel, where because of its large harbor, one has the impression of being closer to the sea than to the Alps. It forms part of the border between Germany and France, and after flowing through the Netherlands, it empties into the distant North Sea. The Ticino River flows into Italy and into the River Po, which ultimately empties into the Adriatic Sea. Finally, the Inn River, rising in the Swiss Engadine Valley flows through Austrian Tirol, the city of Innsbruck and empties into the Danube, which is destined for the Black Sea.

The remaining 30% of Switzerland's land area is composed of the rolling lowlands of the Central Plateau, extending from the northern shore of Lake Geneva (Lac Leman), northeast past Lake Lucerne and Lake Zurich to Lake Constance (Bodensee). This part of Switzerland is one of the most densely populated and heavily industrialized areas in Europe. Here are located three–quarters of the country's population, the bulk of its industry and agricultural crops, and most of its large cities, which by comparison with many other European cities, are relatively small. The largest is Zurich, with only about 720,000 inhabitants, including suburban residents.

Switzerland's central location has made the country a transportation hub for at least 2,000 years. Through it run important arteries connecting Paris with the Balkans, Munich with southeastern France, and northern Europe with Italy. This central location has, throughout the centuries, brought both prosperity and war to the fiercely independent Swiss people. It has presented them with their greatest opportunities and their greatest problems.

HISTORY

The Early Period

Since about 4000 B.C. Celtic tribes settled the fertile plain between the Jura and Alpine mountain ranges. One such tribe, which had moved from the banks of the Rhine, called themselves Helvetians. Scribes at that time described the Helvetians as "wealthy with gold" and as "outdoing all others in martial valor." They also knew how to write, applying the Greek script to their own spoken tongue. These ambitious warriors had been seriously bitten by the restless spirit of the migrations and set their eyes on the lands of the richest empire in the known world: Rome. When they tried to move into what is now southeastern France in 58 B.C., they clashed head on with the legions of Julius Caesar, which decimated

An Alpine village, Château d'Oex, in the canton of Vaud

the Helvetian army. For the next four and one–half centuries, Switzerland was a Roman outpost, an important buffer between the Germanic tribes in the North and the Roman Empire.

The Helvetians prospered under Roman domination. The new masters built cities in which trade, arts and crafts flourished. They secured the mountain passes and opened the Great Saint Bernard Pass for wagon trains in 47 A.D. Thus, military and trade routes between the two halves of Europe separated by the formidable Alpine mountains were created, which proved to be of lasting importance for the future development of Europe. The Roman legions also brought Christianity to Switzerland in the 4th century A.D.

As a Roman rampart and thoroughfare leading to the heart of the Roman Empire, the Helvetians were among the first to face the attacks by northern "barbarian" tribes who were bent on moving south against Rome. By the beginning of the 5th century, the Romans were compelled to withdraw, and the entire area lay open to invading Germanic tribes.

Two Germanic tribes moved to fill the rich vacuum left by the Romans. Christianized Burgundians settled in the western part of the country and gradually adopted Latin as their language. Ultimately their Latin idiom was the source of the French language. Shortly afterwards, the hardy and uncivilized Alemans from north of the Rhine River moved into the central plains and the Alpine area. They refused to give up their Germanic tongue and eventually displaced the Latin language and the Roman culture wherever they settled. Only the Rhaetians, who were firmly settled in the southeastern part of Switzerland (now the canton of Grisons), and the inhabitants of the valleys on the southern slopes of the Alps (now the canton of Ticino) escaped Burgundian or Aleman mastery. They were able to continue speaking Latin, which gradually became vulgarized into Romansch and Italian, respectively. By the 6th century the division of Switzerland into four separate language zones was established—three of Latin origin and the last, spoken by the majority, German.

From the 6th century on, another Germanic tribe, the Franks, established their control over large parts of Europe north of the Alps. During the reign of Charlemagne, who crowned himself Emperor in 800 A.D., the future Switzerland was absorbed into an Empire that scarcely survived his death. Switzerland was partitioned in the 9th and 10th centuries between the Kingdom of Upper Burgundy and the Dukedom of Swabia, both parts of the Holy Roman Empire. Switzerland's

history from then on was closely linked to Germany, particularly to the House of Habsburg in Austria.

Although the new masters tried very hard to impose feudal ties on the Swiss, these attempts were never completely successful. The Helvetians and Alemans both had firm traditions of local autonomy and of personal freedom, traditions clearly visible in Switzerland today. By the 13th century, when Europe's feudal orders had been severely weakened by the crusades, important developments began to take place that ultimately resulted in an independent Switzerland.

In the year 1230 the St. Gotthard Pass was opened. Earlier, only two major, direct roads for crossing the Alps had been open, one in the West and one in the East of Switzerland. The opening of the Gotthard Pass now brought traffic to and from Italy through the heretofore relatively isolated central portion of the land. The great powers of Europe now eyed with much greater interest this valuable piece of territory astride a crucially important trade route.

At the foot of the northern slope of the Gotthard Massif, at opposite ends of Lake Lucerne, are located two small areas: Schwyz (from which Switzerland later got its name) and Uri. Far in advance of their time, these rugged mountain people met in assemblies to elect their leaders and to decide on the administration of common lands. In the 13th century they rebelled against the local dynasties and achieved a semi–independent status linked with the Holy Roman Empire. Schwyz had adopted its own banner, a white cross on a red field, the present Swiss flag.

The Beginning of Independence and Allegiance

The Habsburg ruler Rudolf I died in 1291, and two weeks later, representatives

The Oath of the Three Swiss (18th century)

of Schwyz and Uri, joined by those of a third Swiss area, Unterwalden, which is located on another arm of Lake Lucerne, met on the meadow of Rütli. There they signed a peace alliance in the beginning of August 1291, declaring their right to choose their own judges from among men of their own valleys and pledging reciprocal aid if one of them were wronged by an outside power. Indeed this alliance proved effective in 1315 when a thousand Swiss mountain men trapped and slaughtered two to three thousand knights sent to reestablish full Habsburg control. Although this alliance does not seem very revolutionary today, it was a momentous step at the time and established the cornerstone for modern Switzerland.

What it created was a loose confederation without central authority, army, police, court, or executive. Ultimate power remained with the individual states (called cantons after 1803). Decisions were made in regular meetings among the cantons' leaders, and were made not by majority vote, but by consensus. In other words,

Huge mural in Parliament—Lake Uri where Switzerland was founded

Switzerland

solutions had to be found to which all parties could agree. These principles of reaching agreement for all decisions, known in Switzerland today as "amicable agreement," and of working out problems in a confederal, not centralized way, have become deeply rooted in Swiss democracy.

The legendary William Tell of Uri, immortalized in Friedrich Schiller's drama, remains a symbol for the liberty these three "forest cantons" on the shores of Lake Lucerne pledged to defend. Forced by the tyrannical bailiff Gessler to shoot an apple from the head of his own child, Tell took revenge by shooting a fatal arrow at Gessler himself.

Present–day Switzerland gradually took shape in the following centuries as other cantons or cities joined this original alliance. The major motive for the cantons' joining or remaining in the alliance was usually to defend themselves against the Habsburgs' repeated attempts to regain or tighten control over them. The cities and territories of Lucerne, Zurich, Bern, Glarus and Zug joined in the 14th century. At about the same time Uri conquered the Italian–speaking Levintina, a valley along the Ticino River on the southern slope of the Alps. This was the first time that a non–Germanic speaking area became a part of the Confederation. In 1477 Bern snatched stretches of land in the Vaud from the Duke of Savoy. Again, people who did not speak German were incorporated into the Confederation. Later in joining were Fribourg and Solothurn in 1481, Basel and Schaffhausen in 1501 and Appenzell in 1513. The land between these cantons was gradually purchased or conquered, so that by the early 16th century, Switzerland was a more or less contiguous territory.

Initial Alliance Organization

The terms for each entry were often different, and most maintained their own alliances with outside powers. Thus, Switzerland was at this time a "system of alliances," a patchwork of independent countries with different political systems. What they agreed to do was to assist each other militarily, to consult one another and to hold conventions (Diets) at fixed times and places. Only unanimous decisions were binding. There were certainly powerful disagreements among the members, which sometimes led to wars among themselves. This system of alliances was the first in Europe to combine cities with rural states, and there were persistent disputes stemming from the different interests of town dwellers and peasants. Also, some cantons wanted the Confederation to expand in a westerly direction toward France, while others wanted it to expand in a southerly direction toward Italy.

The Swiss temptation to become a great power through territorial expansion was rapidly extinguished in 1515, when the French decisively defeated the Swiss forces at Marignano. The bravery of highland infantrymen was no match for modern cavalry and artillery in the plain. This disastrous battle, in which only about one–half the cantons chose to participate, made the Swiss realize two things: first, the headless Confederation, with its web of alliances and no overall executive, did not permit ambitious Swiss projects beyond their territory. It decided thenceforth to make key decisions by majority vote, but it was no longer a match for the surrounding monarchies. Second, having eliminated the last vestiges of Habsburg influence from Switzerland in 1499, the Swiss decided to pursue a policy of maximum independence from the alliances and political intrigues of all other European countries. A treaty signed in 1521 with France became the only alliance signed by all the cantons of the Confederation with a foreign power.

Arms, Mercenaries and an Independent Tradition

In return for French protection and the right to trade freely with France, the Swiss obligated themselves to provide soldiers for the French king's infantry. At the same time, the Swiss were permitted to provide military units to other European states. This practice meant that on occasion, Swiss troops faced each other on the battlefield. It was, nevertheless, often economically important for Swiss communities which accepted contracts for the troops. The hiring of mercenaries did not end until 1859, with the one exception of the colorful Swiss guards who still staff the Vatican today.

Due to the outstanding reputation of Swiss troops throughout Europe, these soldiers were very much sought after. Louis XI of France paid Swiss troops premium wages for their services, and when the word got around the Swiss were being paid so well, men from all over the French–speaking world attempted to enlist under the guise of being Swiss. Thereupon, Louis decided that a Swiss was only a person coming from a German–speaking canton, and anyone else who claimed to be Swiss was hanged promptly for "fake advertising."

The excellent Swiss military reputation stemmed from several things. First, Swiss troops served their own cantons' interests, fought under their own cantons' banners, obeyed their own officers and were governed by their own codes. This made them far braver than other mercenaries, who were well known for the speed with which they left the battlefield at crucial times. Swiss troops, with their capacity to stick together and to offer themselves wholly to a collective, were prepared to fight to the last man.

The Swiss soldiers also had certain capabilities that were highly valued. They could march with great rapidity and they could operate very effectively in mountainous areas. Because they could scale cliffs so easily, they could capture fortresses better than any others. Therefore, before heavy artillery was perfected, the best weapon against a fortress was a unit of Swiss troops.

The Swiss infantry units also were the first to use a weapon that was terrifying to knights in armor—the halberd. This hand–wielded weapon, now frequently carried by the Swiss guards at the Vatican, basically stood in the same relationship to a knight's armor as a can–opener now stands to a can. Johannes von Winterthur recorded in his chronicle of a ghastly picture of row after row of dead knights lying on the battlefield, their helmets split wide open.

The Swiss were, and still are, a people in arms. This fact has been a key to Switzerland's survival as an independent country in the heart of Europe. It has also been a key to its establishment very early of an exceptionally high degree of personal freedom for more and more of its own people. Among the first things which European feudal lords did, in order to insure their mastery over serfs, was to disarm them. Thus, in the rest of Europe, fewer persons were armed than in Switzerland. This meant not only that their rulers treated peasants and other citizens of Swiss cantons with greater respect. It underscored the principle that gradually became accepted in Switzerland that the people were sovereign and that no ruler could rule legitimately without their consent.

Although many Swiss did not achieve equality until the 19th century, the ruling nobility in other European countries were well aware after 1291 that a different kind of society existed in some parts of Switzerland, especially in Schwyz, Uri and Unterwalden. They harbored fears that the Swiss example might destabilize the nobility and lead to the liberation of peasants all over Europe. For example the Burgundian King, Charles the Bold, once ordered that all captured Swiss soldiers be exchanged immediately so that they could not infect peasants from elsewhere in Europe with their independent ideas.

While noblemen throughout Europe regarded Swiss progress toward democracy and respect for personal freedom as an ominous development, the Swiss themselves were never crusaders for their own ideas. They satisfied their yearning for freedom neither by trying to spread an abstract idea of justice throughout Europe, as the French did after their revolution, nor by trying to establish a *Pax Helvetia* in the entire known world as the Romans had done. Swiss democracy was always linked with moderation and the willingness to compromise. The Swiss almost always showed common sense by recognizing their own limitations.

The Reformation

Switzerland in the 16th and 17th centuries was shaken and divided by a development that changed the soul of Europe: the Reformation. From Swiss soil the great humanist Erasmus had long criticized the all–too–worldly popes and the many petty clerical abuses, and had advocated a return to the simplicity of the earlier Church. Only two years after Martin Luther had tacked his revolutionary 95 Theses on a cathedral door in Wittenberg, Germany in 1519, Ulrich Zwingli, a priest, army chaplain and humanist known as the "Reformer of Zurich," denounced on his own the abuses of the Catholic Church and began to preach sermons no less inflammatory than Luther's. Several Swiss cities followed his call, but the more rural cantons around Lake Lucerne resisted Zwingli by force. Ultimately he was killed in the violent atmosphere he helped to create. In the Peace of Kappel (1531) the cantons accepted a confessional division of the country into Protestant and Catholic cantons. Thereafter, all citizens in the same canton had to subscribe to the same form of Christianity. Where this was difficult, cantons split into half–cantons, as Appenzell did in 1597.

In another city linked by alliance to the Swiss Confederation, Geneva, a Frenchman named Jean Calvin successfully established in 1541 a strict, Protestant religious government. His pious religious ideas spread quickly to central Europe and across the Netherlands to England and Scotland. Geneva itself became a strict city, where frolicking and frills of all kinds were frowned upon. For example, it was forbidden to wear chains, bracelets, necklaces and gold objects. It became known as the "Protestant Rome." Interestingly, Calvinism as a faith had almost no impact on the rest of Switzerland; its theological radiation was felt chiefly outside the country. It did attract thousands upon thousands of skilled, ingenious, but brutally persecuted French Huguenots into Switzerland during the 17th century. These French Protestants were the first of many waves of immigrants seeking political or religious asylum in Switzerland. The Huguenots also brought skills in banking, trading and manufacturing (especially watch making) which

Statue of Zwingli, Zurich

were of enormous economic benefit to Switzerland.

To its great fortune, Switzerland was able to remain almost completely uninvolved in the confused, bloody conflict known as the Thirty Years War, which ravished parts of Europe from 1618 to 1648. The religious split a century earlier did slow the development of central institutions in the Confederation. Yet, Switzerland was always fortunate to have its internal divisions overlap one another. The many differences among language and religious groups, as well as between urban and rural areas, had and now have the effect of pulling the Swiss back together. For example, two residents of the city of Zurich may belong to different religions, but the fact that they are German–speaking city dwellers means that they have important things in common. A French–speaking and a German–speaking Swiss may both live in a rural environment and belong to the same religion. These overlapping divisions and the traditions of tolerance, moderation and readiness to compromise are important reasons why a multi–lingual, multi–national, multi–religious Swiss state is still able to manage the searing problems of division so well.

Industrialization

Swiss ingenuity and the economic shot in the arm the Huguenots provided were especially crucial in the 17th and 18th centuries because the discovery of America gradually led to a shift in the center of

world trade toward the Atlantic coast. One could almost say that Christopher Columbus had placed severe strains on the economic progress of Switzerland and of many other central European lands. In order to overcome the resultant economic stagnation, the Swiss had to raise capital to develop the country's manufacturing facilities, to expand Swiss banking operations and to build a world-trading network. These efforts later put Switzerland in a position to be one of the first countries on the continent of Europe to undergo an industrial revolution, a fact which has enabled the country to achieve a level of prosperity which is still envied throughout the world.

Democratic Ideals

Switzerland in the 18th century became a cauldron bubbling with explosive democratic political ideas that were to have a dramatic impact all over Europe. One reason for this was that a trend had gathered momentum in Switzerland since the 17th century which saw a narrowing ruling class, rich and often highly cultured, gaining hold over almost all the coveted public offices, monopolies or privileges. Zurich became known as "the little Athens of the North," and after the 1760s Geneva became a magnet for brilliant minds such as Gibbon, Voltaire and Rousseau. Jean–Jacques Rousseau, a citizen of Geneva whose politics made him unwelcome in France, challenged the very legitimacy of all contemporary regimes and societies. His opening to the famous *Social Contract* became a starting point for many revolutionaries, including Karl Marx—"Man was born free, but everywhere he is in chains." In Geneva, which had become known as the "political laboratory of Europe," such ideas helped ignite an unsuccessful revolution in 1782. This was the first in Europe since the American Revolution and seven years before the outbreak of the French Revolution.

As Germany's greatest poet, Goethe, said at that time, "With Rousseau a new world begins. "The momentous events in France after 1789 unleashed aftershocks that ultimately tottered the fragile confederal structure of Switzerland. In 1792 Geneva exploded, and the revolutionary fever spread throughout the Confederation. Republican France intervened openly in Swiss affairs, and in 1798 French troops invaded Switzerland, partly in order to secure the Alpine passes. This was the first time since the Thirty–Years War (1618–48) that the Confederation had been occupied by foreign troops. Further, in 1799 Austrian and Russian troops also entered Swiss territory, but the French drove them out. The ease with which the

Switzerland

well–commanded armies conquered Switzerland was another reminder of its inherent weakness. Such an excessively decentralized Switzerland was completely unable to withstand a determined attack. By the end of 1799 war had ravaged large parts of Switzerland, and the French held the cantons firmly under their control.

The conquerors created a "Helvetic Republic," which was a highly centralized state modeled after France. This new republic was almost the complete opposite of the traditional Swiss Confederation and therefore sparked severe disorders within the country. It was replaced in 1803 by a new constitution drafted by Napoleon and called the Act of Mediation. This document permitted more decentralization, and it drew considerable inspiration from the newly–developed U.S. Constitution in that it combined federalism, separation of powers, popular sovereignty, individual rights and the central government's authority over foreign and military policy. It reestablished the cantons, and to the older ones it added six new ones: French–speaking Vaud, Italian-speaking Ticino, partly Romansch-speaking Grisons and the three German-speaking, St. Gallen, Aargau and Thurgau. Thus, under French influence, Switzerland, which had hitherto been a predominantly German–speaking country, was converted into a truly multi–lingual state.

For the next ten years Switzerland remained a scarcely disguised French protectorate. Much to the disgust of many Swiss, it was compelled to supply a contingent of 16,000 men to the French army. In 1812 Napoleon's dominance of Europe received its fatal blow in the snows of Russia, and in 1813 Napoleon's enemies marched through Switzerland on their way to conquer France. When Napoleon escaped from Elba the following year and attempted to pick up his tattered imperial flag, Switzerland joined France's enemies in burying the Napoleonic Empire once and for all.

It received its reward at the Congress of Vienna, which put Europe back together in 1815. The European powers added three cantons: two French–speaking ones (Neuchâtel and Geneva), and the bilingual Valais, thereby completing the boundaries of present–day Switzerland. The Congress also proclaimed the neutrality and inviolability of Switzerland, and from that date on, Swiss neutrality has been an established principle of international law.

Although the French Revolution had been crushed, its ideals retained their force and popularity in many countries, including Switzerland. Pressure mounted in the cantons to achieve more democracy. Such efforts received a powerful boost at the time of the Paris uprisings in 1830, which prompted some cantons to regenerate themselves by establishing fully elective governments. They were also furthered by the industrial revolution, which created a confident middle class and a growing urban working group. Both demanded greater influence in the political affairs of their cantons. The democratic movement rapidly gained steam, and between 1830 and 1848 conservatives throughout Europe viewed Switzerland as a carrier of dangerous democratic germs that could infect the rest of Europe.

By 1847 proponents of an even more democratic national constitution had won the majority in more than a dozen cantons. As in the U.S., a civil war had to be fought between those insisting upon states' rights and those advocating a stronger federal government. The conflict lasted little more than a month and claimed only about a hundred lives. But the federal victory was necessary for the pact among cantons to be converted into a truly federal constitution with institutions under which Switzerland still lives. A Swiss federal state with a democratic constitution inspired by the American Constitution and the 1803 Act of Mediation was created. This actually occurred before many revolutions had erupted throughout Europe in 1848, all of which ultimately failed. The only consequence of these outbreaks as far as Switzerland was concerned was that the European powers were far too busy with their own domestic problems to interfere in Swiss affairs at this crucial time. From 1848 on, Switzerland has been a democracy in the modern sense of the word. The industrial revolution, with a Swiss emphasis on watch making and fine machine tools and equipment, continued steadily during the balance of the century and the 20th century. Brilliant engineering enabled construction of a comprehensive rail system through the rugged terrain.

Rumblings and Difficulties During World War I

During World War I, tension between the German and French–speaking populations erupted over a scandal involving a high–ranking Swiss military officer who had passed intelligence information to the Germans. Also, thousands of refugees poured into the country; many continued political activity involving other countries from Swiss soil, a practice that threatened the country's neutrality. Perhaps the best known of these was Vladimir Ilyich Lenin. He was living in Zurich in 1917 when the Russian Revolution erupted, and he reportedly screamed in exasperation that he would gladly sell his soul to the devil for the chance to return

The church in Meiringen (Bern canton) has frescoes from the 11th and 12th centuries

190

Switzerland

Scenic valleys in the canton of Bern

to his country to take control of the upheaval. German leaders, desperately wishing to eliminate Russia as a battlefield foe, decided to support the Russian revolutionaries, who promised peace to their war–weary countrymen. Of course, the Swiss authorities were delighted to be rid of him and many other Russian radicals. The Germans provided him passage in a train closed to German officials of all kinds. As Winston Churchill later wrote, Lenin was sent "like a plague bacillus from Switzerland to Russia."

European wars always threaten the markets and raw materials that trade–dependent Switzerland needs in order to survive. Price controls and rationing had to be introduced during World War I, and the Swiss economy suffered greatly. In November 1918 the social discontent created by such setbacks exploded into a general strike with Marxist revolutionary overtones. Timely concessions, such as the introduction of a proportional representation electoral system, enabled the government to end the strike quickly, and thereby to avert the danger of further domestic tensions.

Switzerland made three significant foreign policy decisions in 1920–21. It turned down a request by the Austrians living in the Alpine area of Vorarlberg to become a part of Switzerland. It agreed to form a customs union with its small eastern neighbor, Liechtenstein. Third, it decided to become a member of the League of Nations, whose headquarters had been established in Geneva. Thus, it decided that membership in international organizations did not violate Swiss neutrality so long as (1) the organization publicly recognized Swiss neutrality, (2) Switzerland be permitted to abstain from sanctions against other countries and (3) Switzerland be permitted to maintain its universal economic relations with all countries of the world, a principle which it considers essential for its prosperity.

The Depression and World War II

The great depression of the 1930s inevitably affected Switzerland because of its dependence upon foreign trade. The social unrest the economic shocks helped to create spawned some radical political movements such as the youthful Front groups that demanded a fascist order. Nevertheless, Switzerland managed to preserve its democratic order at a time when most of the democracies in Europe collapsed.

It also managed to remain neutral during World War II, which followed on the heels of the depression. Such neutrality was not entirely a gift of the neighboring fascist dictators. Switzerland mobilized 430,000 soldiers and threatened to destroy all major tunnels and bridges. It declared its determination to fight to the last man if it were invaded, although it was revealed after the war that only the heartland, including the St. Gotthard Pass and the Simplon tunnels, were to be defended to the end. This threat, backed by the Swiss military reputation and determination, helped to dissuade Hitler and Mussolini from attacking the country, which the former scornfully called "the anus of Europe."

But Switzerland did not remain free as a result of military deterrence alone. Faced with the prospect that it could share the fate of other occupied countries, it made compromises with Nazi Germany in the name of "neutrality" that now make it seem to many Swiss and non–Swiss that the country may have bought its freedom at a very high moral price. It continued to trade with Germany and Italy, and some of the products it sold were obviously used for armaments. Further, thousands of Jews and political refugees were denied entry into Switzerland and therefore ended up in prisons or extermination camps. An agreement with Germany in 1938 required Jews to obtain visas and have a special stamp in their passports. Elie Wiesel argues that the idea of stamping German passports with a "J" for "Jewish" came from the Swiss. Police officials who allowed Jews to enter the country illegally were punished.

Recently declassified Allied intelligence documents reveal the extent to which the Swiss also reaped handsome profits by serving as bankers both for the Nazis and their Jewish victims. Prominent Nazis were steady customers of Swiss banks: Hitler reportedly deposited royalties from *Mein Kampf*, and Hermann Goering made regular trips to Zurich to deposit art masterpieces stolen from museums in occupied countries. The banks purchased from the Nazis hundreds of millions of dollars of looted gold, and other looted funds were invested in Swiss enterprises. Bank secrecy was introduced in 1934 to accommodate Jews who wanted to deposit their assets quietly outside of Germany, and then those same secrecy laws were used to prevent the heirs from claiming those assets after the war. Jewish groups estimated in 1996 that the banks hold about $7 billion including interest that belonged to Jews who perished in the Holocaust, in addition to gold and other valuables looted from Jews. After years of denial, the government admitted that the Swiss secretly used some of these funds to compensate their own citizens for property confiscated by the Communists in Poland, Hungary and Czechoslovakia.

Switzerland

The Swiss refusal to discuss or deal with these problems cracked in 1996 under intense pressure from Jewish organizations, the American Senate Banking Committee, and other foreign governments. Attempting to contain this gigantic public relations disaster, it formed one commission, chaired by former U.S. Federal Reserve Chairman Paul A. Volcker, to oversee the search for dormant accounts left by Jews. A second international historical panel was appointed to investigate the extent and fate of Jewish wealth and Nazi loot sent to neutral Switzerland during the war.

A further panel was set up under foreign pressure in 1996, composed of nine international historians with economists, legal experts and researchers to assist them in examining the country's culpability. In 2002 it issued its massive final report that concluded that Switzerland's politicians and businessmen had failed the country on three counts: They contributed to the Holocaust by turning back 20,000 refugees, at times discriminating against Jews, even though they knew what fate awaited them in Germany. They helped the Nazi war machine by going further than necessary in trade and financial support. After the war, banks and art galleries were negligent about restoring property. The end of 2002 the Swiss government supported a proposal to overturn the wartime convictions of people who broke the law by sheltering Jews and others fleeing Nazi Germany.

In 1997 Switzerland agreed for the first time to use the funds in Holocaust victims' unclaimed bank accounts to help survivors. It also set up a separate fund of about $200 million contributed by private banks to distribute to individuals who survived the Holocaust. In 1998 the two largest Swiss banks reached a $1.25 billion settlement of a lawsuit by Holocaust survivors and their descendants. Two major European insurers also reached an accord on life insurance claims for victims. In return, U.S. cities and states canceled an economic boycott against all Swiss banks, institutions and companies, and a $20 billion class–action suit brought against the banks was dropped. Ursula Koch, president of the Socialist party, said, "we have to come to grips with our history."

While few Swiss are proud today of such past policies, Swiss national survival seemed to require them at the time. On the positive side, Switzerland was a base during the war for allied spies, such as Allen Dulles, as well as for international Jewish agencies operating in Europe. It also offered protection to thousands of refugees who would otherwise have joined the many victims of fascism. Switzerland did not entirely escape the destruction meted out in other parts of Europe. In April 1944 U.S. squadrons mistakenly bombed the Swiss city of Schaffhausen, the only major Swiss city located entirely north of the Rhine River. Allied bombers also attacked other localities, such as Basel and Geneva.

In April 1999 the Swiss government disbanded a special crisis task force looking into the country's role in the war. But it will take much longer for the bruised feelings to heal. The myth of wartime Swiss neutrality was exposed. Yet nothing in recent years unified this highly decentralized country as thoroughly as the world's condemnation of its actions during the war. The crisis opened Swiss eyes to their contemporary isolation. Many Swiss believe that their European neighbors and the U.S. had abandoned them by bearing down on them so forcefully over Nazi gold.

POLITICAL SYSTEM

In many countries of the world today, ethnic, lingual and regional diversity often create almost insolvable problems of political and social instability. This has not been the case in Switzerland. Thanks to its tradition of tolerance and compromise, its economic prosperity and its decentralized democratic order tailored to its particular needs, Switzerland enjoys a level of political stability envied in much of the world.

The constitution, adopted in 1848, was considerably revised in 1874 to establish national responsibility for defense, trade and many legal matters. On the whole, it has served Switzerland well. Some Swiss now consider the much–amended constitution to be unwieldy and outdated, and since the 1960s the government studied the possibility of rewriting the document. In April 1999 voters, backed by all the major parties, approved a new constitution that abolished the gold standard for the franc and enshrined new rights in law, including the right to strike and the principle of equal opportunities for the handicapped.

The central elements of Swiss democracy remain unchanged: a federal form of government composed of powerful and confident cantons, jealously protective of their own powers; the participation of all major parties in the national, cantonal and communal governments; a collegial executive elected by, but not responsible to the Parliament, rather than a one–man executive elected directly or responsible to the Parliament; a method of decision–making known as "amicable agreement" involving consensus and respect for minority opinions, rather than the majoritarian approach and, finally, a system of semi–direct democracy at the national, cantonal and communal levels.

Canton Customs and Government

A Swiss person tends to consider himself a citizen of his commune or canton, and secondly of Switzerland. Only communes can grant citizenship, but communal approval is normally a mere formality when the person meets all federal requirements. About 12,000 foreigners become naturalized citizens each year. Federalism, reinforced by strong regional pride, is very much alive in Switzerland, and as a result the 26 Swiss cantons have been considerably more successful in resisting the trend toward government centralization than most other countries, including the U.S. As is nominally true in the U.S., Swiss cantons in reality exercise all powers not explicitly granted to the federal government. In general, they have their own taxing authority, and the Swiss pay most of their income taxes to their cantons. The cantons have the right to

The government procession at Nidwalden

192

manage their own affairs and the responsibility to enforce the law within their own boundaries.

A proposal in 1978 to create a federal police force was rejected in a national referendum. In 1982, 74% of the voters agreed to increased penalties for violent crimes, such as terrorism and hostage-taking, but they also overwhelmingly rejected the creation of a federal anti-terrorist unit. They also have the authority to decide who has the right to vote in cantonal elections.

Because 60% of all voters in a 1981 referendum agreed to amend the constitution in order to give women and men equal rights, it was inevitable that women would ultimately get to vote at every level. In 1990 the Federal Tribunal ruled that Article 4 granting equal rights overrides Article 74 giving cantons the power to decide their own voting rules. Thus, in 1991 the last hold-out, Appenzell–Inner Rhodes, counted women's votes in its open–air assembly. The trend toward full equality for women was continued in a 1985 referendum that granted them equal marriage rights. The husband will no longer be the legal head of the household who could decide where to live, to what schools the children should go or whether the wife could open a bank account or take a job. Since 1971 all women have been allowed to vote in national elections. Cantons also have the right to decide what kind of governments they will have, so long as they are democratic and conform to the federal constitution. All have chosen to have a collegial executive with a unicameral legislature.

On the last Sunday in April and the first Sunday of May the citizens of the five mostly rural Swiss cantons of Obwalden, Nidwalden, Glarus and the two Appenzell half cantons of Inner Rhodes and Outer Rhodes gather in annual open air

assemblies to elect their leaders and judges, vote on important laws, approve the budget and change their constitutions. In the early days attendance at such assemblies, which date back to 1231, was required for all male citizens old enough to fight, which was usually 14 years. Participants came to the assemblies armed. Male citizens in Appenzell must still appear with side arms in order to vote; women were granted an exception to this rule. A large, ornate sword, which is the symbol of cantonal authority, is carried into the assembly area (called the "ring") with great pomp. In Glarus, the presiding official (called the *Landammann*) even wraps his arm around the sword during the entire session. In the past, the people dismissed the *Landammann* by the simple act of taking the sword away from him.

The assemblies begin, proceed and end with ceremony and colorful folklore, which give vivid glimpses into Switzerland's past. Honored participants and guests are led into the ring by full–bearded attendants in long robes, baggy striped pants, fur or pointed hats, or plumed helmets. They carry the cantonal insignias, seals, banners, keys and other relics with them. The leaders stand on a wooden stage surrounded by attendants, while the citizens stand or sit on long wooden benches. In Nidwalden, the assembly is opened by the blowing of a large curled horn, a word from a priest, the introduction of honored guests and an oath of the leaders to respect the constitution.

The visitor is usually so fascinated by the ceremonial aspects of the assembly that he forgets that the citizens have gathered in order to make policy, not to view a parade. There is a serious air, and participants in modern business suits and dresses far outnumber those wearing ornate traditional jackets and bonnets. All

voters receive detailed information in advance on the issues that are to be discussed. Except in Appenzell, where there is no discussion at the assembly, each citizen has a right to speak. Speeches are well–prepared and short, and normal voting is done by raising hands, with officials in red robes judging the results from an elevated platform.

A 1982 vote showed how uncertain the outcomes can be. In Obwalden the president of the federal senate, Jost Dillier, one of Switzerland's leading national politicians, was voted out of office, even though he had no opposing candidate. Newspapers the next day wrote of "an absolute sensation," a "bomb which exploded." The Swiss emphasize continuity and stability so strongly that elected officials have no formal limits on the time they may serve. However, most retire when their terms expire. Dillier had violated two fundamental rules of Swiss politics. He had assumed too many offices in politics and business and thus had too much power in his own hands. Also, he paid more attention to politics in Bern than in his canton. Many said that he personified the "arrogance of power," and in Switzerland there is almost nothing which is more distrusted than obvious political ambition or heavy–handedness.

At the end of the four to six hour assemblies, ceremony again glosses over the differences that arose in the debates. The attendants lead the procession out of the ring and to the church or city hall, where the newly elected leaders are greeted before attending a banquet. The other citizens spend the rest of the day in a holiday manner.

In order to accomplish anything in such annual meetings, the canton must be rather small in size. It must also have a small and homogeneous population. Granting women the right to take part has created a particular problem by doubling the number of participants. Serious divisions between Catholics and Protestants or city and country dwellers have wrecked such annual assemblies. There are many tales of brawls at meetings, even though such disturbances of the peace traditionally carried a higher sentence than at other times. To reduce the likelihood of these outbreaks, the consumption of alcoholic beverages at such meetings has long been strictly forbidden. Success requires concentrating on a few important issues, as well as discipline on the part of the individual citizens. Long–winded speeches would seriously try the patience of the participants, and filibusters would be a catastrophe.

One can call this form of direct democracy antiquated or mere ballast tradition. Yet every form of democracy has its

The vote is taken in Glarus

Switzerland

advantages and disadvantages. This kind of colorful, but serious, gathering brings together several thousand citizens for public debate on political issues immediately affecting their lives. There have been practical reasons why some such assemblies have had to be abolished. But none has ever been cancelled because of lack of public spirit or citizen interest.

Trends Toward Centralization

There is an undeniable trend toward greater governmental centralization because of the many knotty problems of modern life. Such issues as environmental protection, nuclear energy and especially economic matters including unemployment, inflation, foreign trade, currency controls and planning are increasingly seen to be problems with which single cantons cannot easily cope effectively. A rule of thumb is that whenever the Swiss economy is in a slump, there is the strongest demand for shifting more powers to the central government. When the economic picture is rosier, then the resistance to such transfer stiffens.

Over the years the principle has developed that "federal law is superior to cantonal law." The cantons are, nevertheless, far from helpless in the face of this powerful pull toward the federal capital city of Bern. Any constitutional change requires a "double majority" in a national referendum—a majority of all Swiss voters and a majority in more than half the cantons. For instance, in 1973 a majority of Swiss voters supported a proposal to give the national government authority to unify the country's schools, traditionally a cantonal power. However, a majority of the cantons rejected the proposal, so each still maintains its own preferred school system.

The Bicameral Legislature

Both houses of the national Parliament, including the Council of States, must approve all national legislation. This upper house, modeled after the U.S. Senate, is composed of two representatives from each canton regardless of size—and the cantons vary in population from 50,000 to more than a million. The cantons are free to decide how these representatives are chosen; in fact, the 46 members are elected directly by the people in all but four. This Council of States tends to be far more conservative than the lower house of the national Parliament, especially insofar as cantonal prerogatives are concerned. As is true of other Swiss political offices, the title of parliamentarian carries neither great influence nor prestige. Parliament meets for approximately 16 weeks a year divided into four sessions. Deputies are given only a part–time wage

The Swiss Parliament, Bern

for their service and are even freed two days per week during the sessions to perform their regular jobs.

As the United States' leaders saw in the 1780s and as Belgium's leaders realized in the 1970s, federalism is a very important means of enabling a heterogeneous population to live together in harmony; it certainly has been a key ingredient in Switzerland's success as a multi–national, multi–lingual state. Switzerland has had the flexibility to adjust its federal order when a serious problem developed, such as that which emerged in the bilingual canton of Bern. The French–speaking inhabitants in the Jura Mountains that border France sensed discrimination by the canton's German–speaking majority and desired to live in an autonomous canton of Jura. Mass demonstrations were organized, and a few extremists even planted bombs in prominent public places

to underscore this separatist demand. In a national referendum held in 1978, 82% of all voting Swiss and a majority in virtually all cantons approved the creation of a new Jura canton, the first new canton to be created in 130 years. Thus, instead of suffering a festering problem with a separatist minority, Switzerland now has an additional canton exercising all the powers enjoyed by all the other cantons. Again, federalism was able to act as a tranquilizer.

Below the cantons are more than 3,000 communes of greatly differing size. They choose their own system of local government (with approval of the cantons), elect their own officials and assume general responsibility for granting citizenship, administering public lands, such as the forests, and supplying citizens with water, gas, electricity, bridges, city administrative offices, schools, swimming pools, sanitation facilities, fire services and police protection. Swiss communes have to submit to some supervision by cantonal governments, but their right to self-rule is guaranteed by the federal constitution, and they can appeal to the Federal Supreme Court if their autonomy is excessively infringed upon.

Political Parties

At all levels of government in Switzerland, political parties play a key role. In contrast to most other European parties, Swiss parties did not grow out of parliamentary groupings or honorary societies, but were mass parties from the very beginning. This was because Switzerland had introduced universal manhood suffrage as early as 1830. As in the U.S., Swiss parties were, and still are, organized primarily at the communal and cantonal level, and the national parties are little more than umbrella organizations for local parties, some of which even have different names than the larger national parties. As decentralized bodies, the national parties are all able to perform an important integrative function by cutting across most subgroups in Switzerland. The major Swiss parties encompass all language, regional, religious and occupational groups. Decentralization also permits maximum flexibility for local and regional solutions to problems.

Swiss parties have a few other important characteristics. First, organized interest groups are represented formally in the parties to an extent unknown in most other countries. Second, the parties demand almost no "party discipline." Members are left more or less free to vote as they please, and it is therefore often difficult to pin a particular policy to a particular party. Third, conflicts within the parties are settled by the principle of "amicable agreement." The majority tries to find solutions acceptable to the minority rather than merely voting it down. This is widely accepted as the best means of finding a common denominator for all the diverging language, religious and economic interests. At the same time, it makes parties and governments very cautious and deliberate and therefore helps give Swiss government and all major parties their rather conservative hue.

The principal parties' voting strength has remained stable since the end of World War I. In 1919 the four major parties received 88% of the vote; 60 years later they still received approximately 80%. All four strongly support the existing political order in Switzerland, and none sees itself as an opposition party. For this reason, no major party and no government in Switzerland has a firm party or governmental program against which

one could easily evaluate its performance. Because of the proportional representation electoral system, votes for the 200-seat National Council (lower house) seldom produce dramatic shifts in political power. Elections normally renew the governing coalition.

The most traditional and oldest Swiss party is the Radical Democratic Party (FDP), which after the October 1999 federal elections has 43 seats. Founded in the 19th century as a radical (which in the traditional European sense means anticlerical) and liberal (meaning traditionally that it favored an expansion of individual rights and a reduction of governmental power) party, it now defends the economic and social status quo. It has very close connections with private economic groups and influential molders of opinion in the mass media, schools and universities. It is perhaps the most influential party in Switzerland.

The Christian People's Party (CVP) received 35 seats in 1999 and has obtained approximately 20% of the vote since 1919. The bulk of its voters are practicing Catholics. It does recruit members and voters from all language and occupational groups; but although it has attempted to leap beyond the confessional barrier by attracting Protestants, it has not been very successful in doing so. The party sees itself as a "dynamic center" party, with a social policy slightly to the left of the FDP.

Since 1935 the Social Democratic Party (SPS) has received more votes than any other party and now has 52 seats. Founded in 1904, it was originally a working-class party dedicated to the class struggle. But the fascist threat and the economic crises in the 1930's convinced Social Democrats that support of reform policies in the existing Swiss state was its best course. It officially changed its program in 1959 and is now a moderate party which wants to reform the capitalist economic system by expanding the social security net, reforming the tax structure and evening out incomes. Its voters were once found only in the working class, but many intellectuals now support it. It helps to form every government in Switzerland, but it is the only major party that tries to project an image of the "opposition within the government."

For instance, the party pushes hard to relax the bank secrecy laws, which the party believes attracts money to Switzerland from criminals and right-wing dictators. Within the party there are intense conflicts fueled by the violent youth protests of recent years. There is a growing demand within the SPS to present the party as a leftist, anti-capitalist force, even if this means that it cease cooperating with the other parties. The intra-party quarrels have become so serious that the SPS faces

the possibility of a split into a reformist social democratic and less compromising socialist party.

Finally, the Swiss People's Party (SVP) skyrocketed to 22.6% of the votes and 44 seats in 1999. Its increased votes came mainly from the smaller rightist parties. The SVP traditionally tried to represent the interests of farmers, small businessmen and craftsmen. It is traditionally more conservative than the FDP in the sense that it has openly skeptical of any sign of a welfare state and European integration. Its phenomenal electoral success in 1999 not only upset governing traditions, but it threw the entire political landscape into chaos. Led by billionaire industrialist Christoph Blocher, one of the world's richest 300 people, the party appealed to voters worried about high taxes, a flood of illegal immigrants, and closer ties with Europe. It also reflects a continuing reaction to embarrassing disclosures about the country's role as the Nazis' banker during the Second World War. Blocher proclaimed: "As far as Switzerland is concerned, the threat to boycott Swiss banks in America is pure extortion." Many Swiss voters agree. The electoral outcome also calls into question the "magic formula" for distributing seats among the four main parties. As the smallest of the four parties, the SVP always had to be content with only one seat in the Federal Council, the Swiss governing body, while the other three each got two. As the second-largest party now, the SVP demands its share.

A few other parties receive a smattering of seats. The ecologically-oriented Greens continue to gain, winning 12 seats in 1991. The Swiss, who in 1991 had experienced several fire-bombings of dwellings harboring immigrants, woke up to find that 13 right-wing representatives, 11 of whom from the Motorists' Party, demanding curbs on newcomers, had won seats in the lower house; this is the strongest xenophobic contingent in two decades. There is also the Workers Party (PdA), a communist party founded in 1944 to replace the outlawed Swiss Communist Party. Its base is almost exclusively in French and Italian Switzerland. It was traditionally an orthodox Marxist-Leninist, Moscow-oriented party, but it has now advocates a "Swiss way toward socialism" and respect for individual freedoms. It fashions itself as Switzerland's only real opposition party, even though it has become politically irrelevant.

Foreign Workers

The Swiss Democrats, formerly called the National Action for People and Homeland (NA), aims its arrows toward what it sees as a threatening perversion of the

Switzerland

Swiss character caused by foreign workers, rapid urbanization and growing concentration of power in Switzerland. This openly patriotic and nationalist party reached its zenith in 1970 when a majority of Swiss voters was almost persuaded in a referendum to limit the numbers of foreign workers. In the 1990s the less democratic, neo–Nazi Patriotic Front, entered the anti–immigrant scene.

In their opposition to foreign workers the REP and NA unquestionably touch a very sensitive nerve in Switzerland. The country has traditionally been very hospitable to political exiles; for example, it took in 16,000 Hungarians after 1956 and 14,000 Czechoslovaks after 1968. Swiss industry learned very early that high levels of production could be achieved only by attracting foreign workers. No one doubts that the hotel and restaurant industries would never be able to survive without foreign workers. About half of these workers are Italians, followed by Germans and Spaniards. In 2000 foreign workers accounted for 25% of the labor force.

These groups certainly integrate themselves into Swiss society more easily than do Turks in Germany or Arabs in France. While all Swiss are aware of the foreigners' economic indispensability, they are nevertheless uneasy about their very visible presence. This visibility has been especially enhanced by a wave of arrivals: Sri Lankan Tamils, Kurds, Pakistanis and Congolese. In a 1987 referendum, voters accepted by a margin of two–to–one a new law tightening rules even more regarding immigration and political asylum. It extended to peacetime the government's emergency powers to close the border to all refugees. The Swiss government also maintains a fund to send asylum seekers arriving by air back to their homelands on the next flight. As classrooms in Swiss schools sometimes swell with foreign children and as run–down areas with predominantly foreign residents begin to appear in some cities, cultural clashes are inevitable. In fact, this same problem is seriously testing the tolerance of many European countries. In a 1994 referendum, a majority of voters accepted a government ban on all forms of racism, including a belittling of the Holocaust, and 53.6% rejected in 1996 a proposal to tighten regulations over asylum–seekers from Africa and Asia.

In five referenda since 1970, Swiss voters, not wishing to tarnish Switzerland's image as a land of refuge or to harm its economy, rejected proposed laws to limit the percentage of foreigners. A proposal in 2000 to limit the percentage of foreigners to 18% was defeated by 64% of voters in a referendum. For a while, the Swiss government responded to the discontentment by quietly reducing the percentage of foreigners in Switzerland to 17% of the total population. It could do this because, although foreign workers enjoy many rights and social benefits while in the country, many must renew their work permits every year. However, the country's dependence upon such labor is so great that by 2000 the percentage of foreign residents had grown to 19.3% and continues to rise. In 2002 voters rejected by the closest referendum margin since 1891 (50.1%) another proposal to curb the number of asylum–seekers; none of the French- or Italian-speaking cantons approved of the proposition. In the previous year only 12% of asylum applications had been accepted.

A quarter of the work force is foreign; those with permanent work permits, with the same employment rights as Swiss nationals, slightly outnumber those with limited rights. Foreign workers must live in the country four years before they are permitted to bring their families. In one French-speaking canton, Neuchâtel, long-term foreign residents are permitted to vote in local elections.

In 1997, the Swiss Statistical Office calculated that, with declining birth rates, the working population would be reduced by almost a third by 2050 if the level of immigration were kept stable. This means that the foreign population would have to expand to a total of 23% by 2017 if the country's workforce is to be kept stable. It is not easy for some Swiss to face this fact.

The Federal Government

The federal government, with its seat in Bern, is composed of a bicameral parliament similar, in some ways, to the U.S. Congress, and of a powerful seven–man executive elected by parliament. The National Council, elected every four years by male and since 1971 female voters over 18 years of age, represents the interests of all Swiss. Because elections almost never produce significant changes in the parties' strength in Parliament, Swiss elections are never the heated, highly publicized affairs they are in the U.S. and many other European countries.

Both houses have equal powers. Although all bills are now drafted by the government and presented to Parliament, both houses must examine them. Once both have passed a piece of legislation, the executive may not veto it, and the Supreme Court may not declare it unconstitutional. In drafting legislation, the government, by tradition, consults all interested groups inside and outside Parliament. This is a clumsy, time–consuming process, but it helps to ensure better results in that potential objections to the legislation are ironed out in advance; it also reduces the possible danger of a law being overturned in a referendum.

Both houses meet to elect the seven Federal Councilors (*Bundesräte*), who have steadily become more powerful in the Swiss political system. The parties carefully select by on the basis of party membership and political experience at the federal or cantonal level. Highly charismatic figures are very seldom chosen because of the traditional Swiss aversion to a personality cult of any kind. The recommended candidates are almost always elected. Their terms are four years, during which time they cannot be removed by Parliament for any reason. They are traditionally reelected until they voluntarily choose to retire. Thus, strictly speaking, Switzerland does not have a parliamentary system as in most Western democracies.

Since 1959 they have been selected according to a so–called "magic formula": two councilors are chosen from each of the

Former President (1982) Fritz Honegger with the author's two daughters, Katie and Juliet Thompson, April 1982.

three largest parties in the National Council and one from the fourth largest. By 1999, it was no longer clear which party was fourth. The anti–EU Swiss People's Party had caught up with the Christian People's Party in popularity and demanded that it be recognized in the National Council. At least two councilors must be from the French or Italian–speaking sections, and it is usual that one comes from each of the country's three largest cantons—Zurich, Bern and Vaud. Finally, no two councilors may come from the same canton. One can imagine the compromises necessary to satisfy such a "magic formula"!

Each directs one of seven ministries, called departments. Together the seven form the government, and they play the predominant role in drafting legislation, executing laws and dealing with the outside world. They make decisions collectively according to the principle of "amicable agreement." They are nominated by the major parties, but they are expected to cease being "party men" once they are in office. Therefore, they have no coherent government program, and there is no formal opposition either within the government or the parliament. This does not mean that a particular party cannot oppose a particular issue; what it means is that none of the major parties consistently opposes the government with a view to replacing it. In other countries such an "all parties government," also known as "grand coalitions" are formed only in times of national emergency. Switzerland always has them.

The year 1984 saw a break in the tradition of parliament's more or less automatic acceptance of the parties' nominations to the Federal Council. Polls indicated that 64% of citizens thought it was time to have a woman federal councilor, so the Social Democrats nominated Lilian Uchtenhagen, a respected economist. Reportedly grumbling that she was "too emotional," "too elegant," "not enough of a mother figure" and "unable to stand the strain of high office," a majority in the Federal Assembly in a joint meeting of the two chambers rejected her.

The widespread bad feelings caused by Uchtenhagen's rejection no doubt helped Elisabeth Kopp, a lawyer and leading member of the Radical Democratic Party, to win a seat on the Federal Council in 1984. Unfortunately Kopp became implicated in Switzerland's biggest scandal in years. In 1989 she resigned because of accusations that, as justice minister, she had used her influence to protect her lawyer husband against charges of complicity in a major drug money–laundering operation by leaking confidential information to him about the inquiry. She was

Young woman gathers signatures opposing centralization of power

later acquitted of violating the official secrecy laws.

In 1993 it was time for another woman to be named to the Federal Council. She had to be a Social Democrat from a French–speaking canton, and parliamentarian Christiane Brunner fit that bill. However, an overwhelmingly male parliament rejected her, some say for sexist reasons: she was a thrice–married blond who liked flashy clothes, opposed the military, and was said to have had an illegal abortion and posed in the nude. She denied the latter charge. Switzerland had never experienced what followed: thousands of women gathered in front of parliament, spattering paint and eggs, and chanting: "We have lost the first battle, but only the first!" They were right. Ex–trade unionist Ruth Dreifuss of the SPS was promptly elected as interior minister. A close friend of Brunner, she concluded, "I reassure people because I look a little plain." In 1999 she became the country's first female and Jewish president.

Every year the Parliament elects from among the seven a President and a Vice–President for one–year terms. They are not permitted to succeed themselves immediately, and by tradition, the Vice–President is elected President the next year. The President of the Confederation is only a "first among equals," representing the government in ceremonial functions. In times of emergencies he may assume greater powers than the other Councilors. Under no circumstances can he be recalled or impeached.

Swiss presidents are so inconspicuous in comparison to French or America counterparts that most Swiss, when asked, are unable to name their own president in any given year. In a country in which the most glamorous figure is the head of the central bank, the president needs neither bodyguards nor staff cars, and he lives in his own house during his term of office. He goes unguarded to movies or restaurants and probably carries out his own garbage. When Kurt Furgler (1981) traveled to work or around the country, he either drove his own car or went by rail. Only when his schedule was particularly tight was he transported by helicopter. Once, when he was being flown to an appointment, his helicopter developed engine trouble and was forced to make an emergency landing. Undaunted, he merely walked to the nearest road and hitch–hiked the rest of the way.

The Courts

Since the Federal Supreme Court has no power to judge on the constitutionality of federal laws, it does not have the same prestige or importance as does the U.S. Supreme Court. It is chiefly the highest court of appeals for civil and criminal cases. Its judges are selected by both houses of Parliament meeting together for six–year terms and must be chosen from all language and regional groups in order that the entire population be represented. Its seat is not in Bern, but in Lausanne. The administration of justice remains primarily a cantonal affair, but the supreme civil and criminal laws of the land are the federal code of civil law, in force since 1912, and the federal code of penal law, enacted in 1942.

Switzerland

Direct Democracy

Many European democracies permit citizens to vote directly on some particularly important political issues, rather than to leave virtually all such decisions to the Parliament. This is called "direct democracy" because the will of the people is not filtered exclusively through Parliament. In most countries this instrument is used very sparingly, particularly because it has often been a favorite tool for dictators to legitimize their power over a frightened people. The Swiss have never needed to fear such abuse in modern times, and direct democracy is a very important part of the political process at all levels of government. If at least 100,000 voters sign a petition demanding a constitutional change, then such an "initiative" must be submitted to a direct vote of all Swiss. If at least 50,000 demand in a petition that an act of parliament or an international treaty be approved by all the voters, then a "facultative referendum" is held. Parliament can declare an act to be too urgent to allow time for a referendum, but one is mandatory if Parliament adopts any constitutional changes or approves of an international treaty of supranational or security character which affects the country's sovereignty.

Initiatives and referendums are held on an extremely wide range of subjects: abortion, conscientious objection to military service, modernizing the armed services, restructuring civil defense, mandatory wearing of safety belts, increasing federal powers to tax and to control unemployment and inflation, mandatory retirement ages, gun control, bans on automobile driving and on leaded gasoline, daylight savings time, nuclear power, rent controls, euthanasia, worker participation in management, and many more topics.

By threatening to organize an initiative or referendum, interest groups in Switzerland can almost always secure a serious hearing for their concerns within the government or Parliament. This insures that they will not be overlooked in the decision–making process and that the government will try to establish a consensus for all its acts. Still, the problems associated with direct democracy have increasingly become the subject of discussion. The first problem is that the number of referendums and initiatives at all levels has sharply increased. Between 1914 and 1934 there was an average of 8.5 referendums per year. At present, the average has climbed to more than 30, and this includes neither the many referendums at the communal and cantonal level, nor the up to four national initiatives per year. Constitutional changes since 1871 have been made an average of once every 13 months, and the frequency has risen in recent years. Further, the issues on which the people are asked to decide have become more and more complex, and fewer and fewer citizens are able to form a firm opinion about them. From 1971 to 1997 only five of 68 national initiatives passed.

The cost of gathering signatures by convincing enough people of an issue's importance has become very expensive, and the Swiss government must now spend more than four million Swiss francs (about $3 million) to conduct a referendum. The increasing dissatisfaction with this form of democracy is demonstrated by the rapidly decreasing voter participation. Few referenda, initiatives or national parliamentary elections attract more than 50% of the voters, and no one is surprised if only one–third of the eligible voters choose to vote on an issue; the average was 42% by 1998. In fact, Switzerland is the only democracy in the world where voter participation in major elections is now lower than in the U.S. Nevertheless, Switzerland, with only 4.7 million voters, accounts for an estimated half of referendum ballots worldwide.

Drugs

Youth protests died down significantly in the late 1980s. A greater scourge in the 1990s and beyond is drugs. Nowhere in Europe were they as available as in a park (nicknamed "Needle Park") located a few hundred meters from Zurich's main shopping center; on a normal day, 2,000 people, half of whom under age 22, came to buy or sell drugs, and the number doubled on the weekend. Because of the influx of professional dealers and the rising crime and chaos in and around the park, it was closed in 1992. The drug population merely dispersed to other Zurich neighborhoods.

Hard drug use is illegal in Switzerland, but the police almost never arrest anyone for mere possession. In 1997 voters overwhelmingly endorsed their government's liberal drug policies, including state distribution of heroin under doctors' care to longtime addicts. However, in 1998 nearly 74% rejected the legalization of heroin, cocaine and marijuana. The Swiss try hard to find acceptable compromises with the youth because they fear that failure could damage or destroy a very delicate but essential ingredient of Swiss democracy: the inclination and ability to solve serious problems by means of consensus. Without its traditional "rules of the game," which include tolerance and compromise, Swiss democracy would lose much of its uniqueness. In 2001 the government decided to remove penalties for consumption of marijuana and hashish. This drew the wrath of both neighboring countries and some UN agencies, which had already been critical of the program of proving needles and heroin to some addicts. Swiss officials defended themselves by pointing out that the old approach had not worked. Surveys found that a fourth of all Swiss had tried marijuana, and of the 90,000 daily users, a third were teenagers.

Foreign Policy

Swiss foreign policy is based on five main pillars: (1) armed neutrality, (2) universality of diplomatic and economic relations with all countries of the world regardless of regime or foreign policy, (3) the readiness to provide its "good offices" to other countries (for instance, Switzerland represents the U.S. in Cuba and Iran, where no U.S. diplomats are allowed; it also represents Cuba in the U.S., Iran in Egypt, and Israel in Ghana), (4) providing

Young people ("drop–outs") at their favorite hangout

198

Montag, 4. März 2002 · Nr. 52

Der Zürcher Zeitung 223. Jahrgang

Neue Zürcher Zeitung

INTERNATIONALE AUSGABE

Briefadresse von Redaktion und Verlag: Postfach, CH-8021 Zürich, Telefon +41 1 258 11 11, Telefax +41 1 252 13 29, NZZ Online: www.nzz.ch
€ 2.– / £ 1.40 / dKr. 17.– / nKr. 18.– / sKr. 19.– / Tl. 3 000 000.– / zy. £ 1.– / Ft. 400.– / tKr. 62.– / slKr. 100.–

Blutiges Wochenende im Nahen Osten
Über 20 Tote in Israel – Rund 30 palästinensische Opfer

Israel hat ein besonders blutiges Wochenende erlebt. Am Samstagabend riss ein palästinensischer Selbstmordattentäter vor einer Synagoge in Jerusalem neun Personen mit sich in den Tod. Am Sonntagmorgen erschoss ein palästinensischer Scharfschütze zehn israelische Siedler und Soldaten, danach gelang ihm die Flucht.

gsz. Jerusalem, 3. März

Israel kommt aus dem Schrecken der blutigen Ereignisse der letzten Tage nicht heraus. Drei Anschläge haben in kaum 12 Stunden fast 20 Tote und viele Dutzend Verletzte gefordert. Im Weiteren wurde ein Motorradfahrer erschossen, der in Cisjordanien einen Ausflug machte, und zwei Sol-

HEUTE — Umfang 48 Seiten

Woge des Protests gegen Berlusconi
In Rom haben am Wochenende ein paar hunderttausend Personen gegen Ministerpräsident Berlusconi demonstriert. Dieser zeigt erste Zeichen von Nervosität.
INTERNATIONAL 3

Commonwealth-Gipfel in Australien

daten kamen bei Militäraktionen in palästinensischen Flüchtlingslagern ums Leben. Ziel des ersten Anschlages war das von ultraorthodoxen Juden bewohnte Stadtviertel Mea Shearim in Jerusalem. Ein palästinensischer Selbstmordattentäter mischte sich kurz nach Ende des Sabbat-Ruhetages unter die vor einer Synagoge wartende Menschenmenge und brachte einen Sprengsatz, den er auf seinem Körper trug, zur Explosion. Neun Personen, unter ihnen Kinder und zwei Babys, kamen ums Leben, über fünfzig weitere wurden verletzt, einige von ihnen kämpfen noch um ihr Leben. Der Tatort liegt unweit des von Arabern bewohnten Ostteils der Heiligen Stadt. Die Aksa-Brigaden, die Arafats Fatah-Bewegung angehören, beanspruchten laut einem Sprecher die Urheberschaft für das Attentat. Laut palästinensischen Angaben soll ein 19-jähriger Palästinenser aus einem Flüchtlingslager den Terrorakt ausgeführt haben.

Ja zum Uno-Beitritt der Schweiz
Knappes Ständemehr – deutlicheres Ja des Volkes

bre. Die Schweiz wird Vollmitglied der Vereinten Nationen. Volk und Stände haben dem Beitritt zur Uno zugestimmt. Bei der Eidgenössischen Abstimmung vom Wochenende wurde eine knappe Mehrheit von zwölf befürwortenden Kantonen erzielt, während elf Stände die Vorlage ablehnten. 54,6 Prozent der Stimmenden legten ein Ja in die Urne. Damit wird die Schweiz nach dem massiven Nein in der Abstimmung von 1986, als der Beitritt noch von drei Vierteln der Stimmenden und von allen Kantonen verworfen worden war, Vollmitglied der Vereinten Nationen. Die Schweiz wird voraussichtlich im September als 190. Mitglied in die Uno aufgenommen.

Bei einer hohen Stimmbeteiligung von 57,6 Prozent wurde der Uno-Beitritt mit 1 489 062 (54,6 Prozent) Ja zu 1 237 725 (45,4 Prozent) Nein angenommen. Mit zustimmenden Mehrheiten in elf ganzen und in den zwei Basler Halbkantonen wurde das Ständemehr jedoch nur knapp erreicht. Ein geschlossenes Ja kam aus der Westschweiz und aus den beiden Basel. Am deutlichsten zugestimmt wurde der Vorlage im Kanton Genf (66,9 Prozent), wo der europäische Uno-Hauptsitz beheimatet ist. Ebenfalls über der

60-Prozent-Marke lagen die Kantone Neuenburg, Basel-Stadt, Waadt und Jura. Die Kantone Zürich, Freiburg, Basel-Landschaft, Bern und Zug stimmten ebenfalls Ja. Ein eher knappes Ja gab es in den Kantonen Solothurn sowie Luzern und Wallis.

Abgelehnt wurde die Vorlage dagegen von der Mehrzahl der Innerschweizer und Ostschweizer Kantone und dem Tessin. Wie bereits vor 16 Jahren wurde die Beitrittsvorlage am deutlichsten vom Kanton Appenzell Innerrhoden verworfen (67,5 Prozent). Deutlich abgelehnt wurde die Vorlage auch in den Kantonen Schwyz, Glarus, Obwalden, Appenzell Ausserrhoden, Schaffhausen, Graubünden, St. Gallen und Nidwalden befanden sich ebenfalls bei den gegnerischen Ständen. Nur knapp scheiterte die Vorlage im Kanton Aargau.

Die zweite zur Abstimmung gelangte Volksinitiative «für eine kürzere Arbeitszeit» von rund 42 auf 36 Stunden pro Woche wurde in allen Kantonen sowie mit 2 021 078 (74,7 Prozent) gegen 685 002 (25,3 Prozent) Stimmen verworfen.

Analysen und Berichte Seiten 13 bis 15

---

its own territory for international organizations and conferences and (5) solidarity with other peoples of the world, especially when it comes to humanitarian actions.

There are many international organizations with headquarters in Geneva, including many UN specialized agencies such as WHO, ILO, ITU, and WTO. Numerous non–governmental organizations have their headquarters in Geneva, such as the World Council of Churches, the International Committee of the Red Cross (for war emergencies) and the International Federation of Red Cross Societies (for natural disasters and peacetime emergencies). The latter organization was founded in 1864 by the Swiss businessman Henri Dunant, who had been shocked by the carnage he had witnessed on Italian battlefields during the campaigns of Napoleon III. Switzerland's close links to the Red Cross are still symbolized by the latter's use of the Swiss flag with reversed colors. The Red Cross is an important vehicle for international humanitarian actions involving prisoners and refugees.

Switzerland is often criticized for its mediocre record for foreign aid. In 2003 it devoted .37% of its GDP to helping developing countries, compared with 1.04% for Denmark, .86% for the Netherlands, .85% for Norway and less than .13% for the U.S. Yet, the quality of its assistance is very

high, and there is scarcely a people in the world which is more generous in time of crisis.

Switzerland is not a member of NATO, and its and Austria's neutrality separates NATO's northern and southern halves. However, it joined the "Partnership for Peace" within NATO in order to strengthen its cooperation with that alliance. Its citizens also voted in 2001 to allow their soldiers to train with NATO forces. Earlier, its political leaders never publicly commented on foreign political events, such as elections or *coups d'état* or on foreign military actions such as the Soviet Union's invasions of Czechoslovakia in 1968 and of Afghanistan in 1979. This changed in August 1990, when for the first time Switzerland applied the UN sanctions against Iraq, which had invaded Kuwait. However, it staunchly opposed the military action taken by the U.S. and Britain against Iraq in 2003 and closed its airspace to military planes on their way to the front.

Until 2002 the Swiss conception of neutrality had prevented the country from joining the UN. It joined many of the specialized UN organizations, and it pays more than half a billion Swiss francs ($300 million, more than 72 Swiss francs per inhabitant). Geneva is the seat of the UN's European headquarters. It has held that the UN's provision for sanctions against

member states is incompatible with Swiss neutrality. The Swiss Federal Council and Parliament gradually reached the conclusion that Switzerland could no longer remain outside the UN, which they believed would officially take note of Swiss neutrality. They were supported by most university educated Swiss and by the country's most prestigious newspapers.

The Swiss government has steadily nudged the country in the direction of greater international involvement. In a 2002 referendum, a majority (54%) of Swiss finally voted to join the United Nations. They concluded that their country, which sits in the middle of Europe, could no longer remain on the sidelines in an era of global politics and interwoven economics. Support for the move came from the gov-

Switzerland

ernment, most political parties, business and trade unions. Foreign Minister Joseph Deiss noted: "Switzerland needs the world and the world needs our country." The September 11 terrorist attacks against the U.S. boosted the vote because it shattered the Swiss sense that their country could remain outside of and immune from world events. In September 2002 Switzerland became the 190th member of the United Nations. President Kaspar Villiger said: "The people realized that they are no longer an island. We can be neutral—and be a good member of the UN."

Switzerland participates in international peacekeeping missions and helps finance UN peacekeeping operations. In 1989 it took the bold step of actually sending unarmed but uniformed medical personnel, administrators and observers to Namibia, and later to Western Sahara. Since the Swiss constitution forbade sending troops abroad, this was not an ordinary military unit: all were volunteers; a third were women, only a few of whom are members of the country's tiny women's military services (known best for their former work with carrier pigeons that has been abandoned with "Army 95"). Nevertheless, this marked the first deployment of Swiss troops abroad since the Battle of Marignano in 1515. Switzerland also sends officers and aircraft to assist the UN in the Middle East.

Following an unusually bitter campaign preceding a 2001 referendum, a narrow majority (51%) approved of arming Swiss soldiers participating in peacekeeping missions. Heretofore, they had been unarmed in accordance with the policy of neutrality. The government wanted to avoid situations such as in Kosovo, where 160 Swiss peacekeepers had to rely on German and Austrian troops for protection. Opponents had displayed posters showing the battered corpse of an American soldier in Somalia, with the words, "Die for foreign powers?" The country's neutrality continues to prevent its soldiers from performing peace-enforcing operations, as opposed to peacekeeping ones.

In 1996 it broke with its tradition by allowing NATO troops to pass through its territory on their way to implement the peace in Bosnia. By giving sanctuary to 400,000 refugees from former Yugoslavia, it also turned its back on its refugee policy before and during the Second World War. The growing internationalism is strongest in the French– and Italian–speaking parts of the country.

Military Service

The Swiss are armed to the teeth in order to demonstrate their determination to defend their neutrality and in order to dissuade any belligerent in a European war from viewing Swiss territory as a military vacuum and thereby inviting invasion. There is no general staff in peacetime, and parliament creates the rank of general only in wartime. There is only a skeleton standing army. Nevertheless, defense spending claims about 20% of the Confederation's budget and about 2% of the nation's GDP.

The Swiss buy some of the most sophisticated military hardware available, including U.S. fighter aircraft. They also produce a wide range of military equipment that they sell—subject to certain restrictions—to countries as diverse as Australia, Turkey, Egypt, Saudi Arabia, Burma, Guatemala and Angola. It has built a network of bomb shelters that would protect 90% of the population in the event of nuclear attack.

Every Swiss male must serve in the national militia from age 20 to age 42 (age 52 for officers and 62 at the latest for generals). It has been aptly noted that Switzerland "has been in a state of war every weekend since 1945" and that "Switzerland does not have an army, it is an army!" Although there is a civilian service for those citizens who are morally or religiously opposed to all forms of military service, this service lasts 1.5 times longer than the minimum requirement for ordinary military duty. Those who for any legitimate reason cannot perform military service must pay a fee to the Swiss state. If they want to do so, women can also serve in the armed forces, except in combat missions.

After 15 weeks of basic training, soldiers are assigned to militia units and are required to perform three weeks of duty every other year. Special units such as militia pilots and tank formations, serve two weeks each year. Thus, the country could mobilize 400,000 soldiers within 48 hours. The Swiss soldier is permitted to take his equipment, including his assault rifle and five sealed magazines of live ammunition, home with him. He is required to practice his sharp shooting regularly in rifle associations. Former reservists are permitted to buy a weapon for private use.

This policy of having so many weapons in the society came under close scrutiny after a grisly massacre that occurred in 2001. Using a semi-automatic weapon a man burst into the cantonal parliament in Zug and shot dead 14 people and wounded as many more before killing himself. This was the first time in more than 100 years that any Swiss politician had been murdered and was the biggest mass murder in the country in living memory. The man had never been in the military and had probably purchased the gun in a shop that sells semi-automatic weapons legally or from another person, also legally. Although gun laws vary depending upon the canton, any citizen without a criminal record can buy one after an identity check and official approval. One may keep it locked up at home.

The Swiss ability to shoot straight is widely respected. As the Swiss often remind listeners: "William Tell was a man of courage and integrity—and he was a good shot!" The last German Kaiser,

Swiss soldiers

Wilhelm II, was also given a friendly reminder of this. Once, after inspecting a Swiss army unit, he turned to one of the Swiss soldiers and asked what his comrades would do if the German army were to invade Switzerland with twice as many soldiers. The answer: "In that case, each of us would have to fire twice!" In 1989 the government decided to add some American firepower by acquiring several thousand shoulder–fired Stinger anti–aircraft missiles and 34 F/A–18 fighter airplanes.

In 1989 the revered armed forces, which in a country with so many ethnic divisions is one of the few truly national institutions, was seriously buffeted by the winds of détente. In a referendum, in which 68.6% of the eligible voters participated (the largest turnout in 15 years!), 35.6% voted to abolish the military. Although the President at this time, Jean–Pascal Delamuraz, had called the initiative "an idiocy as big as the Matterhorn," (one of the highest and best known mountains in Switzerland), the results severely shook the armed forces. A coalition called Switzerland Without an Army was able to resubmit the question of disbanding the armed forces to the voters in December 2001. It was again overwhelmingly rejected; only 21.9% voted in favor of the initiative. Even though it had survived twice, the votes pointed to resentment against the army's influence in Swiss society.

The army embarked on reform and rehabilitation. Former General Heinz Häsler admitted that "everything must be done to restore the people's confidence that military defense is needed." In 1994 voters were asked to decide on the questions: "Does Switzerland really need an army?" and "Does Switzerland need 34 new fighter airplanes?" Both votes passed by a small majority. By 1995 the Armed Forces were reduced from 600,000 to 400,000 soldiers and converted into a "static force" to a "dynamic force." The professional support comprises about 1,500 instructors, pilots and professional soldiers (to protect the underground installations). As a result of the most extensive armed forces reform since 1907, called "Army 95," the minimum total service time (after basic training) is 295 days for soldiers, 900 days for officers up to the rank of captain, and 1,200 days for colonels.

In May 2003, three-fourths of the voters agreed in a referendum to plans for reducing and professionalizing the military, ignoring arguments that such a reform could undermine the country's traditional neutrality. The number of men in active and reserve service will be cut from 350,000 to 220,000. At the same time, civil defenses would be refocused from war to national catastrophes, and it will be possible for recruits to opt for civil defense duty instead of the armed forces. The Cold War requirement that all residences and businesses have their own nuclear fallout shelters will also be relaxed. The government claims that Switzerland already has sufficient bunker places for almost the entire population.

ECONOMY

The economy is one of the most efficient and prosperous in the world. Its per capita GDP and income is one of the highest in the industrialized world—slightly below the United States and less than that of tiny, neighboring Liechtenstein with its postage stamps and tremendous number of banks. The Swiss work longer than any nationality in the OECD (44.5 hours average per week). The economy is firmly based on the principle of free enterprise.

The public sector accounts for a lower percentage of GDP than in most other European countries, and some public companies, such as telecommunications, are being privatized. There has traditionally been little protection for their industries, so Swiss companies have always been stimulated by international competition to adapt in order to survive. However, as in all modern states, the Swiss state intervenes more and more in the economy. It offers export risk guarantees to exporters who doubt the viability of their customers. But it scorns central planning and other attempts to limit the flexibility of private firms.

The Swiss economy is influenced heavily by several basic factors. First, Switzerland is a very small country with almost no exploitable raw materials. This includes, most importantly, oil. Switzerland meets more than three–fourths of its energy needs with oil, and almost every drop must be imported from as many diverse sources as possible. It must also import natural gas—which constitutes about 4% of its energy consumption—and nuclear fuel for its four nuclear plants, which produce almost 40% of its electricity. In 2003 voters rejected proposals to impose a 10-year moratorium on new atomic plants, to require existing ones to be closed after 40 years of service, or to close nuclear power plants after 30 years. One of its few natural resources is mountainous terrain for waterpower, which provides the country with about 60% of its electricity. The only other natural resource is wood, available because forests cover one–fourth of the country.

Second, Switzerland has insufficient farmable land to feed its population. Since it has pasturelands, much of which is in or at the foot of mountains, it has a productive dairy industry. Milk has always been plentiful, and long ago the Swiss discovered that by converting it to cheese, it could export its milk to the world. This discovery made it famous for cheese. Its sunny hillsides also enable every single canton to produce excellent, mostly light dry white wine, which supplies well over one–half the Swiss market. Unfortunately, there is very little left over for export. Only 6.3% of Switzerland is suitable for grain crops, and this is the chief reason for its excessive dependency upon food imports. In terms of calorie intake, Swiss agriculture produces only 55% of the national requirements, or 45% if one takes into consideration the imported feed component of milk and meat production.

Switzerland is willing to pay a high price to keep farms operating in remote areas of the country in order to reduce the wartime vulnerability of its food supplies. Swiss farmers comprise only 5% of the labor force, compared to 22% prior to World War II, the lowest proportion of any continental European country except Belgium. They produce only 1.6% of the GDP, but they earn an average of 50% more than other European farmers. This is not due entirely to subsidies, but also to heavy mechanization and to the government–sponsored effort to combine more than half the arable land into larger farms more suited to efficient farming.

Third, the lack of raw materials and sufficient home–grown food has forced the Swiss to make the most of their human resources. This means that they have had to industrialize and, above all, to become a trading nation. Almost no European country with such a high standard of living has reached such a high degree of dependence on the world economy. Almost two–thirds of its GDP is derived from foreign trade in goods and services. This high volume of foreign trade is also made necessary both by Switzerland's small domestic market stemming from a small population and by its high level of prosperity.

Germany is its most important trading partner. The lion's share of Switzerland's trade is with European countries, particularly with the members of the EU: 70% of its exports and 80% of its imports. Of course, it benefits from being strategically located at the junction of Europe's main trade routes and from having an excellent road and rail network that plugs into the transportation nets of its neighbors. However, it has faced severe problems with terrible fires in key tunnels that are essential to through-traffic. In 1999 a fire in the Mont Blanc Tunnel, killing 39 people in an inferno, was not reopened with new safety features until 2002. Another fire in the St. Gotthard Tunnel closed it for three months until the end of 2001.

Switzerland

Swiss chocolate factory

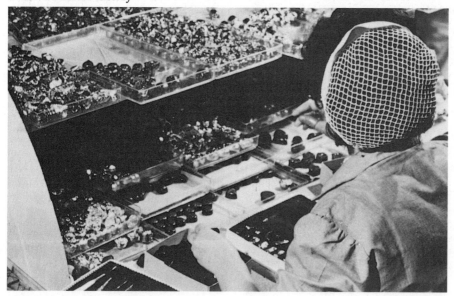

About 30% of Swiss exports are sent outside of Europe, and about 7% of its exports are to the U.S. This points to an almost unique problem for a European trading nation: Switzerland is landlocked. It does have one important port on the Rhine–Basel. It maintains 29 merchant ships on the high seas and is in 50th place among 111 nations that maintain a merchant fleet. However, its lines to its overseas trading partners are very vulnerable.

This was one reason why it maintained its important air link through Swissair, a semi–public corporation that went bankrupt on October 1, 2001, a day the prestigious *Neue Zürcher Zeitung* called "the blackest day in Switzerland's economic history." It was the first collapse of a European flag-carrier, and its demise was a huge blow to Switzerland's image as a solid business and financial center. Already terribly indebted before the September 11 terrorist attacks, it could not secure the funds to continue. It also caused the collapse of Belgium's Sabena, which was partly owned by Swissair. In 2002 the defunct Swissair was combined with Crossair, which flew routes within Europe, to form Swiss International Air Lines, known as "Swiss." It added international flights and used two-thirds of Swissair's planes. Despite the fact that it was Europe's fourth-largest fleet in 2003, its passengers were dwindling, and the company had to lay off workers, ground some planes and cut some routes to stay competitive. The airports at Zurich and Geneva remain among the busiest in the world.

Industrial Sector

Swiss industry, which was fortunate to survive World War II almost unscathed, produces a wide variety of quality, precision goods. It has some heavy–weight multinational corporations, 12 of which are on the Fortune 500 List, led by Nestlé (which ranked number 12). However, most of its factories are by world standards relatively small and widely dispersed throughout the country. About a fourth (26%) of all employed persons work in industry and 69% in services. A third of the GDP is derived from industry, compared with over two–thirds (64.6%) from the growing service sector.

About one–sixth of all employees work in the machine and equipment sector, which provides one–third of Switzerland's exports. It specializes particularly in equipment that does not lend itself to mass production, such as generators and turbines. It produces over 15% of the world's textile machines and roughly 13% of the precision instruments. The country provides about 1% of the world's arms exports. In 1997 three–fourths of voters approved continuing arms sales despite reports that Switzerland had delivered about a fifth of the equipment for Iraq's atomic program. It is also a leading chemical exporter. Three Basel firms alone produce roughly 10% of the world's need for medicines, and Swiss chemical plants provide 13% of the world's production of paint materials.

The chemical industries in the Basel area created great concern and international consternation in November 1986. Accidents at the chemical plants of Sandoz and Ciba–Geigy spilled masses of toxic waste into the Rhine, undoing much of the hard work in the preceding 15 years to revive a river that had been declared ecologically dead. Countries all along the Rhine protested the Swiss handling of these disasters and the fact that informa-

tion about them was withheld for many hours by Swiss authorities. These incidents were also a rude awakening for the Swiss, who had comfortably contended that nothing like this could happen in their country because their technology was too good and they were so careful.

Two of Switzerland's traditionally most important industries, watch making and textiles, have faced serious challenges. The textile industry is a victim of high labor costs and the rising value of the Swiss franc, which has priced many textile products out of the market; they cannot compete with cheaper Asian products.

In 1970, Swiss watchmakers had a third of the world's sales. By 1984 that share had fallen to 10%. Benefiting from the technological spin–offs of space exploration, the U.S. watch industry moved rapidly into the field of digital, electronic and quartz watches regulated by computer chips, and Japan was close behind. Swiss watchmakers responded by restructuring and investing effectively, diversifying into such products as heart pacemakers and by shifting some of the production facilities to foreign countries with low labor costs. To the horror of traditionalists, many "Swiss" watches bear the stamp "Made in Hong Kong under Swiss supervision." Two Swiss firms, (SSIH and Asuag) have also merged to form the world's second largest watch producer—Industrie Horlogère Suisse—and have met the challenge of the electronics revolution by introducing robots to produce such big, mid–price sellers as the "Swatch," which make a lifestyle statement. As a result, the watch making industry has recovered steadily since 1982. It is also making advances in microchips for watches. Switzerland now has a 60% share of the world market. Watches account for 8% of exports, and brands such as Rolex and Omega are among the most coveted in the world.

Strikes in key sectors of the economy were almost unknown since 1937, despite the fact that nominal wage increases are traditionally the lowest of all industrialized countries. This fact is crucial for Switzerland's ability to maintain its international competitiveness. Consensus and conservative continuity are the foundation of the country's stability and steady economic progress. Wage negotiations are conducted at the local level, and the government stays out of them. Nevertheless, 2002 saw the first nationwide strike in Switzerland in 55 years. Construction workers protested their employers' refusal to sign a contract to allow early retirement at age 60.

A chronic problem had been a shortage of labor. This helped insure that Switzerland did not have the unemployment

Cheese–making

Bank's successful policy of restricting the domestic money supply, the high value of the franc has kept Switzerland's inflation rate (.7% in 2003) under control. This is because with its valuable franc, it can buy raw materials abroad more cheaply than it could if its currency were worth less. Of course, the rise in the franc's value can increase the price of Switzerland's exports, thereby hurting Swiss industry. However, the extremely low inflation rate helps keep down the price of Swiss exports and thereby keeps the export industries competitive.

A very important ace which Swiss bankers hold in their hands is the country's bank secrecy laws, which sometimes make their banking system look like the Ali Baba caves. These laws were introduced initially in 1934 to protect Jewish victims of Nazi persecution. They differed from bank secrecy laws in other countries in that bank information was also withheld from revenue authorities, and any breach of banking secrecy was a criminal offense. Yet since 1991 absolute secrecy is no longer possible. Swiss courts can order banks to divulge information or to freeze accounts, as they did when the U.S. Congress began investigating insider trading.

A 1973 treaty with the U.S. permits the divulging of bank information in cases where U.S. authorities can prove that a criminal offense is under investigation. This does not include U.S. tax evasion, which does not violate Swiss laws. After 1983 Swiss authorities were willing to extend legal assistance to other foreign governments seeking evidence to convict persons accused of tax fraud or other penal cases. The code was tightened in 1989 when the laundering of money obtained through illegal activities was made a criminal offense. This law was in part a result of American pressure, as was a 1985 measure dealing with insider stock trading.

The trail leading to the conviction of Ivan Boesky began with a Swiss account. In 1990, the Swiss handed over bank documents on his and his associates' deposits. They froze assets of deposed dictators Nicolae Ceausescu (Romania) and Manuel Noriega (Panama) and of the Medellin drug cartel, and they divulged information on accounts needed in the trial of Elizabeth Kopp. They agreed to cooperate with investigations on unclaimed Jewish assets from the Second World War. In 1997, they for the first time took action against a ruler still in office, Zairian President Mobutu, who by the time of his death was said to hold $4 billion in Swiss bank accounts. In 1998, Switzerland's highest court ordered $500 million in assets belonging the late Philippine ruler Ferdinand Marcos to be returned to the

other European nations face although it rose to 3.9% in 2003. The labor shortage compelled Switzerland to attract foreign workers, who comprise a third of the labor force and are essential to Swiss prosperity. In earlier years the country could cope with the threat of unemployment by simply sending some guest workers home. However, criticism of this policy shamed the government into granting more permanent visas.

Banking

Since the 16th century Switzerland has been among the world's major banking nations. Geneva became an extremely successful banking city, which aroused admiration and exasperation throughout Europe. Voltaire once advised that if one sees a Genevese banker jump out the window, one should jump after him because there is bound to be gold on the pavement! The French novelist, Stendhal, called them "the foremost money men of the continent. In this *metier*, they have the foremost of virtues, that of eating less each day than they earn!" The U.S. also profited from this talent when the scion of a wealthy Geneva family, Albert Gallatin,

was appointed Secretary of the Treasury in 1801. Later, as the U.S. Ambassador to France and Britain, Gallatin adroitly negotiated commercial relations between the U.S. and Europe.

Switzerland has more banks than it has dentists—one per 1,400 residents. They have a reputation for secrecy, security and efficiency. Banks account for more than 10% of GDP. However, they have begun to lose ground to the three big world banking centers of New York, Tokyo and London. A third of its smaller banks have merged or closed. Even two of its largest banks, Union Bank and Swiss Bank, announced a merger, and the three largest banks reported financial losses in 1997. The banks' dealings with the Nazis have also tarnished their reputation. In 1997 California, New York City and other U.S. cities even started boycotting their services.

Swiss banks have profited from Switzerland's political stability and hard currency, which is the most highly treasured in the world. By attracting funds to Switzerland the "Gnomes of Zurich," as the Swiss bankers have been called, in turn help to drive up the value of the franc. Combined with the Swiss National

Switzerland

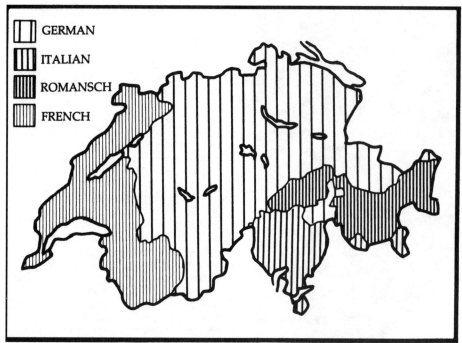

LANGUAGE AREAS

GERMAN
ITALIAN
ROMANSCH
FRENCH

Philippine central bank. In 2001 Switzerland cooperated with the United States' anti-terrorist campaign by freezing 24 bank accounts linked with al-Qaeda. A year later it returned to Nigeria more than $1 billion the late dictator Sani Abacha and his family had embezzled and placed into Swiss accounts.

The Trade Union Federation and the Swiss Socialist Party have long demanded that banking operations be opened even more to public scrutiny, and American law gave strength to these demands. Many other Swiss grew uncomfortable with the notion that their prosperity might partly be based on the huge deposits of dictators and drug kings, especially as drug consumption is a growing problem in Switzerland itself. Finally, in 1991, Switzerland abolished its "Form B" accounts, which allowed clients to conduct bank transactions through intermediaries without revealing their own identities. Banks must now know who is behind each account.

Desiring to ward off dirty money in the first place, Swiss authorities tightened their "know your customer" rules in 1997 and introduced one of the world's strictest money-laundering laws. Bankers must report suspicious deposits or transfers to a special police office, and they must relinquish account details requested in criminal investigations. Legal procedures were streamlined to make it easier for foreign police or prosecutors to get assistance. In 1999-2000, authorities froze more than $1 billion in bank accounts. However, they

need cooperation from foreign governments, which must be willing to prosecute. In 2000, the third Russian prosecutor was fired in Moscow after trying to build a criminal case with the Swiss.

In 2003 Switzerland grudgingly agreed with the European Union that it would discourage citizens from EU countries from using Swiss accounts. The EU is aggressively cracking down on tax evaders, and the trail all too often leads to the Alpine banking center. The drain on Swiss banking assets seems relentless, a very serious problem for a country whose banks manage about a third of the world's private savings (ca. $3 trillion). It reached an agreement with the EU in 2003 to collect taxes for bank account interest and return 75% of it to the country of residence without providing account holders' names.

Tourism and International Organizations

A further essential aspect of the Swiss economy is tourism, which accounts for about 8% of the overall national income, although Swiss tourists re-spend about one-half of that income outside Switzerland. This industry is threatened by the high value of the franc. Anyone who has seen pictures of Switzerland's majestic mountains, its sparkling spring-fed lakes and streams, or its beautiful meadows and valleys has no difficulty understanding why the tourist industry is so successful. It has also been the salvation for rural areas that would have become almost completely depopulated due to the

economic and cultural attractions of the cities. Since the tourist trade is concentrated largely in otherwise economically disadvantaged areas, rural Switzerland has been kept alive and prosperous. Of course, some veteran travelers miss much of the color and folklore of the earlier rustic Switzerland, but they sometimes forget that such folklore often masked great poverty.

Switzerland is a member of several economic international organizations. In addition to the OECD, IEA and the WTO, it has belonged since 1960 to EFTA, which is now largely irrelevant. Although Switzerland signed an agreement with the EU that removed all tariffs on industrial products in 1972, it could not become a full member for three reasons: first, it would have had to relinquish a portion of its sovereignty to the EU; second, its neutrality could be affected; third are economic reasons. For example, the free movement of labor guaranteed within the EU would undermine the Swiss policy of reducing the number of foreign workers. Also, Switzerland gives much higher subsidies to its farmers than the EU allows.

The EU's push toward greater unity stimulated fears in Switzerland that it could be isolated, and in 1992 the Federal Council formally applied for membership. In that year Swiss voters voted to join the IMF and the World Bank. But in December they rejected their country's entry into the European Economic Area (EEA), a link between the EU and EFTA. German-speakers in the large cities said yes, but they were outvoted by rural and small town German-speakers, whose traditional fear of being absorbed by a larger Germany was revived by the EU. By contrast, French-speaking Swiss, who have no fear of France, said yes.

The rejection of the EEA put the application to the EU, for which there is no parliamentary or popular majority, temporarily on ice. In a March 2001 referendum, 77% of the voters in an unusually large turnout again rejected a proposal to enter negotiations to join the EU. French-speaking cantons were most inclined to favor entry. This blocked the government's hopes that talks with the EU could get underway during the 2003-7 legislative session. Thus EU membership is unlikely before 2010. Its laws have already been made "Euro-compatible" in most sectors. If it were ever to enter, it would be the second-biggest financial contributor after Germany. It has negotiated a series of bilateral deals with the EU that give it access to most EU markets without loss of sovereignty. Therefore, it has not suffered economically by not joining.

In a step to align their fiscal policies to the EU and to lower the budget deficit,

Jean Tinguely's *Chaos I* on the commons in Columbus, Indiana   Photo by Claude and Victor Thompson

voters approved in a 1993 referendum the introduction of a Value Added Tax (VAT). Refusal to join the EU hurts some industries, such as chocolate. To retain their market shares in other European countries, chocolate makers are having progressively to shift their production outside of Switzerland, thereby dulling the magic ring of "Swiss chocolate." At least they retain a huge market at home: the average Swiss consumes more than 22 pounds of chocolate per year, more than do Americans (10 pounds) or any nationality.

CULTURE

Switzerland is a multi-lingual country. The most widely used official language is German, spoken by 64% of the citizens. Actually, most German–speaking Swiss speak one of many different dialects of Aleman German, which differs from valley to valley and which is spoken very differently from that which is heard in Berlin. The other official languages are French, spoken in pure form by 18% of the Swiss, and Italian is spoken by about 8%.

A fourth "national language" is Romansch, a collection of five not always mutually intelligible Latin–based dialects spoken mostly in the more isolated valleys of Grisons. Some linguists argue that it is the closest living language to the late Roman Empire vernacular. It is spoken by

about 40,000 (.6%) of the Swiss. That number has been declining as tourism has helped encourage slightly more than half the residents in Grisons to speak Swiss German. To fight against this trend, linguists are busy standardizing the idioms and spelling and translating many texts, including income tax forms, into Romansch. T.V. and radio air–time is also being increased and broadened to include comedians and such local pop groups as Ils Hades ("Hell's Boys"). In 1996 the Swiss voted in a referendum to elevate Romansch to the status of a "semi–official" language, meaning that speakers may use it in dealings with the federal government.

Although only a minority of Swiss is fully multilingual, as are Luxembourgers, the fact that the language groups are separated and largely concentrated in single–language, autonomous cantons prevents the language diversity from being a major problem as in Belgium. It is true, though, that French and Italian–speaking Swiss somewhat resent the dominance of German in the federal institutions in Bern.

In 1998 a new language problem emerged: the most populous canton, Zurich, decided that English, not French, should begin at an early age, perhaps in the first grade. Its officials argued that in the contemporary world pupils need more than the one or two years of English they used to get before age 16, when they

can leave school. Education officials in 11 of 19 other German-speaking cantons want to follow Zurich's lead. This produced an uproar, especially in the French–speaking cantons. Many fear such a change could erode Swiss identity. But with no national ministry of education, it is difficult to establish and maintain one common policy in the cultural field. Federal Interior Minister Ruth Dreifuss argued in 2000 that English "should not be like a steamroller" crushing the country's languages. But she recommended that all Swiss children have a fair command of three languages, including two of Switzerland's official ones.

Switzerland is also multi–religious. While Protestants outnumbered Catholics by nearly three to two in 1900, Catholics, who now comprise 49.4% of the population, presently outnumber the Protestants, who comprise 47.8%. Each canton is free to decide whether or not to have complete separation between church and state, as in Geneva. The federal government does exercise some control over the churches by reserving the right to approve bishoprics and by banning members of the clergy from the National Council. Not until the 1970s did the government permit the Jesuits to resume activities in the country. However, one cannot say that serious tensions exist among religions or between the churches and the state. Religion also plays an insignificant role in Swiss poli-

lontag, 4. Februar 2002 · Nr. 28

Der Zürcher Zeitung 223. Jahrgang

Neue Zürcher Zeitung

INTERNATIONALE AUSGABE

HEUTE — Umfang 40 Seiten

ustizfarce in Tunis
or den Augen von 300 anwesenden internationalen eobachtern hat das Regime in Tunesien demonstriert, ie die Polizei den Justizbehörden Befehle erteilt.
INTERNATIONAL 2

'owell präzisiert «Achse des Bösen»
ussenminister Powell hat Befürchtungen der Bündnisartner zu zerstreuen versucht, die USA könnten ohne onsultationen weitere militärische Angriffe lancieren.
INTERNATIONAL 2

)ifferenzen in Arafats PLO
ie Volksfront zur Befreiung Palästinas (PFLP) hat ren bedingten Rückzug aus dem Exekutivrat von Arats PLO erklärt. Sie verlangt die Freilassung ihres in isjordanien inhaftierten Generalsekretärs Saadat.
INTERNATIONAL 3

ranische Replik auf Bushs Vorwürfe
anische Politiker haben mit Empörung die Vorwürfe on Präsident Bush zurückgewiesen. Die Phase der stiln Kooperation in Afghanistan dürfte zu Ende sein.
INTERNATIONAL 3

tuhige Dorfwahlen in Kambodscha
ı Kambodscha sind erstmals Gemeinderegierungen in emokratischer Wahl neu besetzt worden. Im Wahlampf hatte es viele Gewalttaten gegeben. Der Urnenang selbst scheint friedlich verlaufen zu sein.
INTERNATIONAL 4

ilobalisierungskritik in Porto Alegre
ɪm Weltsozialforum in der brasilianischen Stadt Porto legre diskutieren Bürgerrechtsbewegungen aus Nord nd Süd Alternativen zur Globalisierung.
INTERNATIONAL 4

.indbergh – zwiespältiger Held

Transatlantische Dissonanzen zum Terror

Konferenz über Sicherheitspolitik in München

Meinungsverschiedenheiten zwischen den USA und Europa über das weitere Vorgehen im Krieg gegen den Terrorismus sowie die Beteiligung der Europäer an Entscheidungen der USA dominierten die Sicherheitskonferenz in München. Deutlich wurden auch die international sehr unterschiedlichen Definitionen des Terrorismus.

slz. München, 3. Februar

An der 38. Münchner Konferenz über Sicherheitspolitik haben am Wochenende knapp 300 Teilnehmer aus insgesamt 43 Ländern über eine globale Bekämpfung des Terrorismus debattiert. Während über die Notwendigkeit eines solchen Kampfes rundherum Einigkeit herrschte, traten auch deutliche Meinungsverschiedenheiten über das weitere Vorgehen zutage, vor allem zwischen den Amerikanern und den Europäern. Von allen Konferenzteilnehmern positiv vermerkt wurde die offene Atmosphäre in München, die es gestatte, Differenzen zu formulieren, und die vielfach genutzte Möglichkeit, sich in kleinen Gruppen auszutauschen.

Alleingang der USA?

Die Amerikaner betonten, dass sie sich in einem Krieg befänden. Die Attacken des 11. September seien ohne jeden Zweifel eine ausreichende Berechtigung für jedes weitere militärische Vorgehen gegen Staaten, die laut amerikanischer Einschätzung Terroristen unterstützen. Der amerikanische Senator John McCain nannte dabei an erster Stelle den Irak. Die Europäer hingegen meldeten Bedenken gegen ein militärisches Vorgehen gegen den Irak zum jetzigen Zeitpunkt an und verlangten generell von der Uno mandatierte Einsätze. Doch die Vereinigten Staaten scheinen durchaus zu einem Alleingang willens. Wenn man zwischen der eigenen Verteidigung und einer langen Liste von Freunden wählen müsse, werde auch an den Entscheidungen beteiligt zu werden. Die Amerikaner drückten zwar in warmen Worten ihre Bekenntnisse zur Nato und zu deren genereller Bedeutung aus. Doch McCain machte auch klar, dass für diesen Krieg eine Hightech-Armee benötigt werde, und diese hätten nun einmal nur die USA zur Verfügung. Die Europäer müssten deutlich mehr in ihre Armeen investieren und diese technologisch aufrüsten.

Hier stimmten die europäischen Redner an der Konferenz den Amerikanern geradezu kleinlaut zu. Allseits wurde die «technologische Lücke» zwischen Europa und den USA beklagt und von den eigenen Regierungen mehr Investitionen in diesem Bereich verlangt. Angela Merkel, die Vorsitzende der CDU, forderte darüber hinaus auch eine wesentlich effizientere europäische Verteidigungspolitik. So benötige man einen europäischen Geheimdienst; die Ämter des Hohen Vertreters für die gemeinsame Aussen- und Sicherheitspolitik sowie des EU-Aussenkommissars sollten in Personalunion vergeben werden. Die europäische Rüstungsagentur sollte für eine gemeinsame Beschaffungspolitik zuständig werden.

Doch die Europäer gestanden nicht nur ihre eigenen militärischen Defizite ein. Der Generalsekretär der Nato, Lord Robertson, forderte von den USA mehr Technologietransfer und weniger Exportbeschränkungen auf militärischem Gebiet. Robertson verneinte zudem entschieden, dass der Einsatz in Afghanistan nur eine Aktivität der USA sei. Von europäischer Seite wurde auch auf die

Dutzende von Toten bei Kämpfen in Nigeria?

Gewaltausbruch zwischen zwei Stämmen

Lagos, 3. Febr. (Reuters) Bei Kämpfen zwischen Angehörigen zweier Volksstämme in einem Vorort der nigerianischen Stadt Lagos sind nach Angaben von Einwohnern zahlreiche Menschen getötet worden. Viele Leichen lägen in den Strassen, sagte ein Bewohner Mushins am Sonntag, der vor den Kämpfen zwischen Angehörigen des Yoruba-Volkes und des Haussa-Volkes geflohen war. Aus Mushin war Gewehrfeuer zu hören. Rauch stieg aus brennenden Gebäuden auf. Er habe 12 Leichen mit eigenen Augen gesehen, aber nach verschiedenen Berichten müssten wohl mehr als 45 Menschen gestorben sein, sagte ein weiterer Einwohner. Örtliche Zeitungen berichteten, 10 Menschen seien getötet worden. Das Haussa-Volk kommt aus dem vorwiegend muslimischen Norden Afrikas. Die Yoruba stammen aus der Region südwestlich von Lagos.

Scharping und andere europäische Teilnehmer den Nord-Süd-Konflikt, Armut und Hunger als Ursachen ausmachten, sahen die USA die Wurzeln vor allem in einem «Bürgerkrieg in manchen islamischen Staaten», wie Senator Joseph Lieberman es formulierte. Und Paul Wolfowitz, der stellvertretende Verteidigungsminister der USA, fügte hinzu, bei den momentan weltweit agierenden Terroristengruppen handle es sich mehrheitlich um gut ausgebildete Personen und finanziell gut dotierte Organisationen.

In der internationalen Gemeinschaft ungeklärt war auch die Frage, was eigentlich als Terrorismus definiert werde und wer zu den Terroristen zähle. Vor allem China, Indien und Russland reklamierten, schon immer gegen Terroristen im eigenen Land – wie in Tschetschenien oder in

Seite 27: Afghanistan, Qatar und der Irak: Ein Bericht des Filmers Christian Frei

Basler Zeitung

AZ 4002 Basel

BaZ online: www.baz.ch

Basler Zeitung – Aeschenplatz 7, 4002 Basel, Telefon 061 639 11 11, Fax 061 631 15 82, E-Mail: redaktion@baz.ch – *Abonnements- und Zustelldienst:* Tel. 061 639 13 13, Fax 061 639 12 82, abo@baz.ch, www.baz.ch/abo/ *Inserate:* Publicitas AG, Tel. 061 275 41 41, Fax 061 275 42 42

161. Jahrgang

Montag, 17. März 2003 — Nr. 64

Fr. 2.50 (inkl. MWSt), Elsass/Deutschland: € 1.70, übriges Frankreich/Eurogebiet (A, E, GR, I) € 2.–, Türkei TL 4 250 000, Zypern CYP 1.20

Teil I		Teil II		Teil III		Teil IV		Teil IV
Zweite, Tagesthema	2, 3	Wirtschaft	9, 10	Region Basel, Aktuell	19, 21	Feuilleton	27	Sport
Ausland, Inland	4, 5	Forum	12	Basel	22, 23			
Wetter, Fernsehen/Radio	6, 7	Bestattungen	16, 17	Baselland, Region	24, 25			
Letzte	8			Kultur aktuell	26			

Kein Triumphzug. Proteste gegen die Rückkehr Vittorio Emanueles. **8**

Luftfahrt-Pionier tot. Der Franzose Jean-Luc Lagardère ist gestorben. **9**

«Zürich-Häuser». Ein Gutachten lässt doch mehr Spielraum. **23**

Georges Simenon. Wäre in diesem Jahre 100 Jahre alt geworden. **27**

Fünfmal bezwungen. Der sel verlor in Visp 0:5.

Fürstlicher Sieg

Vaduz. BaZ. Triumph für den liechtensteinischen Fürsten: Fast zwei Drittel der Stimmbürger stellten sich gestern hinter die Verfassung von Hans-Adam II. – bei einer Stimmbeteiligung von 88 Prozent. Die neue Verfassung räumt dem Monarchen das Recht ein, die Regierung zu entlassen, wenn diese sein Vertrauen verliert. Die Verlierer der Abstimmung kündeten bereits eine Beschwerde beim liechtensteinischen Staatsgerichtshof an. **Inland, 5**

Wasser-Forum

Kyoto. BaZ. Rund 1,2 Milliarden Menschen weltweit leben ohne gesicherten Zugang zu sauberem Trinkwasser – und mit zunehmendem Wohlstand wird Wasser auch in Industriestaaten immer knapper. Am dritten Welt-Wasser-Forum, das am Sonntag in der japanischen Stadt Kyoto eröffnet wurde, beraten in dieser Woche rund 10 000 Politiker und Fachleute aus aller Welt darüber, wie die Versorgung mit Wasser sichergestellt werden kann. **Tagesthema, 3**

Weiter abwärts

Basel. F.E. Trotz den kräftigen Avancen Ende letzter Woche dürften die Aktien an den Börsen weiter fallen, sagt Novartis-Finanzchef Raymund Breu im Interview mit der BaZ: «Wir sind der Ansicht, dass die Bewertungskorrektur selbst auf dem heutigen Niveau nicht vorbei ist.» Für das Pharma- und Generikageschäft von Novartis rechnet Breu

Der «Moment der Wahrheit»

Der heutige Montag werde zum «Moment der Wahrheit», hat US-Präsident Bush gestern Abend erklärt. Die USA suchen im UNC heitsrat das letzte diplomatische Gefecht, um anschliessend in den Krieg zu ziehen. Verloren haben sie schon jetzt ihre moralische Aı

Auftritt der Kriegstroika auf den Azoren. Tony Blair, José María Aznar und US-Präsident George W. Bush bekräftigen ihre Entschlossenheit zum Krieg nes Eiland mitten im Atlantik war am Sonntag der einzige Ort, an dem sie vor Massenprotesten sicher sein konnten. Fo

tics today except when such issues as abortion are the subjects of referendums.

The cantons organize their own school systems, and this enables the schools to reflect their religious, lingual and cultural uniqueness. All children enter primary school at age six or seven. After four or five years of primary school, the children enter one of three different kinds of "upper school": an extended primary school makes the lowest academic demands; a second type, called a *Realschule*, prepares pupils for a commercial or technical career and a Gymnasium prepares pupils for the universities. After the mandatory eight or nine years of schooling, pupils can enter an apprenticeship, and roughly 80% do this; or they can continue their general education, aiming toward specialized training or the university. There are seven cantonal universities, one business and social science university in St. Gallen and two federally operated technical universities in Zurich and Lausanne.

Radio and TV operate under government license and are administered by a mixed state and privately owned body, the Swiss Broadcasting and Television Corporation (SRG). The SRG broadcasts in four languages from six radio studios and in German, French and Italian from three television stations. Of course, broadcasts from neighboring countries are also received in most parts of Switzerland. In 1983, the cabinet approved the establishment of Switzerland's first local radio and TV stations, which would supplement the existing national broadcasting network. These new stations will be non–profit, and advertising will be limited. With about 231 newspapers, the country also has the greatest number per capita in Europe, although it has declined by 40% since 1939. Zurich has one of the most highly respected newspapers in Europe, the *Neue Zürcher Zeitung*.

Switzerland has a wealth of folk art and music and a rich cultural tradition of its own. The Swiss foundation, Pro Helvetia, seeks both to preserve and stimulate Swiss cultural activities. Yet the cultural and intellectual life of Switzerland has always been enriched by foreigners who were drawn to it or who sought refuge there. Such towering figures as Hans Holbein the Younger, Germaine de Stäel, Franz Liszt, Richard Wagner, Friedrich Nietzsche, Thomas Mann, Jules Verne, Albert Einstein, Karl Barth, Karl Jaspers and Hermann Hesse chose to live and work part of their lives in Switzerland. The proximity of great cultures that surround the country both stimulates Swiss writers and thinkers and draws their minds away. Any Swiss writer who does not feel himself a German, French or Italian, or who does not share in the intellectual life of the neighboring country where his native language is spoken, risks becoming narrow and provincial. But if he takes a much wider view, his work risks losing its Swiss character. Indeed, many Swiss writers have been frustrated and bored with the narrow confines of the small bourgeois and neutral Switzerland. The Swiss psychoanalyst, C.G. Jung, once described Switzerland as a country "beneath the battle," and two of the 20th century's greatest playwrights, Max Frisch and Friedrich Dürrenmatt, both Swiss, have expressed in their works gruesomeness and disillusionment and have generally debunked the lives of those around them.

Still, many Swiss artists have found great international recognition. Paul Klee, who was brought up in Bern and who later fled Nazi Germany, brought Swiss painting to the world stage. His modern art is represented in the great galleries around the world. The art theoretician and one of the greatest architects in history, Charles–Edouard Jeanneret (better known as Le Corbusier) designed buildings throughout the world, although he built very little in his native Switzerland. The modernist sculptor, Jean Tinguely, with his "free and joyous machines," ranks as one of the world's most inventive contrivers. An ingenious example of his work can be found in the town commons of Columbus, Indiana. Using pieces he had found in the Columbus junkyard, he created his indescribable "Chaos" with such intriguing moving parts that the viewer can neither wholly understand nor forget it.

Without a doubt, one of the most important influences on the Swiss culture has been and always will be nature. Perhaps the greatest pages in its literature and its greatest art focus on the incomparable Swiss landscape. They evoke those magic moments when a person surrenders himself completely to the beauty of the world around him, when a person feels himself included for a moment in a great harmony. Foreign writers could scarcely escape this magic effect of the Alps. Friedrich Nietzsche conceived his *Zarathustra*, which expressed his bold, heroic, over–proportional philosophy in the Alpine Engadine, and Thomas Mann set his *Magic Mountain*, one of the 20th century's greatest novels, in the crisp, sanitary Alpine air above Davos. Perhaps Hermann Hesse, who had been drawn permanently to Switzerland, expressed this magic best: "Everything merges into one, distance vanishes and time is done away with."

FUTURE

In 1991 Switzerland celebrated the 700th anniversary of its birth. In the years that followed, instead of patting themselves on the back for the peace and prosperity they have enjoyed, the Swiss are ruminating about their role in the modern world. Such problems as political scandals, laundering of dirty money, and rising drug use have prompted the country, in the words of a Swiss official, "to redefine Switzerland by examining our internal problems and by looking at our future role in Europe and in the 21st century."

That reexamination has dramatically been extended to the country's wartime dealings with Nazi Germany and the possible misuse of bank secrecy laws to prevent the return of Jewish assets to Holocaust victims. The debate will continue whether Switzerland had paid too high a moral price to remain neutral.

It will continue to enjoy a relatively high degree of domestic stability. It is no longer certain that its industry and banks are sufficiently well–equipped and prepared for increasingly intense international trade competition. The Swiss economy is struggling to reinvent itself. Globalization, the aftermath of the September 11, 2001, terrorist attacks, and a worldwide economic slump are shaking the two legs on which Switzerland's economic stability had always rested: its fiercely competitive companies in highly specialized industries and banks legendary for their privacy. Nevertheless, Switzerland will remain a prosperous country. As a member of the UN since September 2002, its foreign policy will have a much more international orientation, and its policy of neutrality will continue to undergo change.

Distance vanishes and time is done away with.

The Principality of Liechtenstein

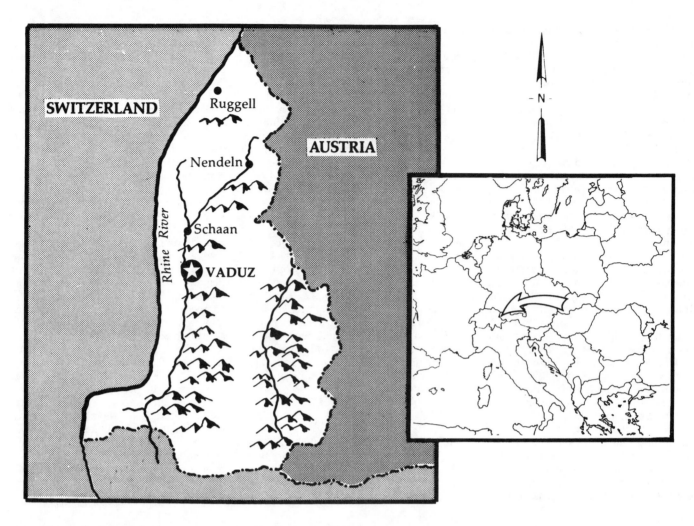

Area: 62 sq. mi. (160 sq. km.)

Population: 33,000, estimated.

Capital City: Vaduz (Pop. 5,000, estimated).

Climate: Alpine, with cool summers and cold winters.

Neighboring Countries: Switzerland (Northwest and South); Austria (Northeast).

Official Language: German (Alemannic dialect).

Ethnic Background: Alemannic German. More than one–third of the residents are foreigners, chiefly Swiss, German, Austrian and Italian.

Official Religion: Roman Catholic (80%).

National Day: August 15 (birthday of Prince Franz Josef II, father of current reigning Prince).

Main Industries: High technology, metal industry, especially production of small machines, textiles, ceramics, chemicals and pharmaceuticals, timber, hydroelectric power, building equipment, processed foods, tourism postage stamps.

Main Customers: EU (45%), EFTA (19%), Switzerland (27.3%).

Currency: Swiss Franc.

Date of Independence: January 23, 1719.

Government: Hereditary constitutional monarchy.

Head of State: His Serene Highness Prince Hans Adam II (b. 1945).

Head of Government: Otmar Hasler (since 2001).

National Flag: Two horizontal bands, blue over red, with a gold crown in the blue field. (The colors of the House of Liechtenstein are gold and red.)

Liechtenstein is an almost unknown Alpine country with a territorial size slightly smaller than the District of Columbia and one–twentieth of that of Rhode Island with a population of only about 31,000. In fact, about the only thing big about this pint–sized state was the name of its late ruler, who died in 1989: Prince Franz Josef II Maria Aloys Alfred Karl Johannes Heinrich Michael Georg Ignatius Benediktus Gerhardus Majella von und zu Liechtenstein, Duke of Troppau and Jägerndorf, Count of Rietberg. It is the last existing intact remnant of the Holy Roman Empire and is the world's only remaining German–speaking monarchy. Its people, who have a strong feeling of independence and tradition, maintain their country's sovereignty without soldiers.

Separated from Switzerland by the Rhine River, a torrent rushing straight down from the mountains which at times threatens the country's fertile valley, Liechtenstein is squeezed between the Swiss cantons of Grisons and St. Gallen to the west and the Austrian province of Vorarlberg to the east. One third of the country, which is approximately fifteen miles (twenty five kilometers) long and an average of four miles (six kilometers) wide, is a rolling, green and fertile area located in the Rhine valley. Most of the country's population, industry and agriculture is located in this area. The remaining two–thirds is composed of the rugged foothills of the Raetian Massif, with peaks ranging from 5,900 feet (1,735 meters) to 8,600 feet (2,599 meters), that form part of the central Alpine chain which runs east and west through the southern half of Switzerland. This forward–looking relic of the past is a land of almost unsurpassed natural beauty, colorful tradition and economic prosperity.

HISTORY

The Early Period

Situated on one of the oldest north–south transit routes in Europe, Liechtenstein was a logical area for continuous settlement since the Stone Ages.

In 15 B.C. the Romans under Caesar Augustus conquered the Celtic inhabitants and established an important highway through the area. This road helped open the land that is now Germany to Roman conquest, trade and administration. Later, it provided good access for German tribes or troops seeking wealth and power in Italy. Liechtenstein also lies astride the Basel–Vienna route, a thoroughfare that also brought soldiers and traders to the area. The remains of Roman villas and the castle in Schaan testify to the former Roman presence. Parts of the Alemannic (Germanic) tribe moved into the region in 264 A.D. Like many other tribes of northern and eastern Europe at the time, the Alemans had pulled up stakes and sought richer territories in western and southern Europe. They drove the Romans out of the area very quickly and have remained ever since. Today's citizens are descendants of these ancient Alemans and still speak their melodic dialect of German, which is also spoken in sections of eastern Switzerland and southern Germany.

The land was subsequently ruled by a variety of noble houses until Prince Hans Adam von Liechtenstein, an Austrian nobleman with a family residence near Vienna, purchased the Lordships of Shellenberg in 1699 and Vaduz in 1712. The calculation of the Prince, who had tried for years to buy territory anywhere between Italy and the Elbe River, was that by purchasing these two independent lordships which were fiefs of the Holy Roman Empire, he could persuade the Austrian Kaiser, Karl VI, to upgrade the united lordships to the status of the Imperial Principality of Liechtenstein. Karl did just this on January 23, 1719, and the House of Liechtenstein, which gave its name to the new Principality, thereby gained a coveted seat in the Imperial Diet of the Holy Roman Empire. Karl's declaration made Liechtenstein the 343rd state in the Empire and gave the Principality its present form. The new ruling family remained in Vienna, caring very little for the small land that had brought it privilege and honor. For 187 years, Liechtenstein was ruled from a distance by an absolute monarch.

Napoleon

In 1806 Napoleon drove out the Austrian troops that had occupied the principality since 1794 and made the country a member of the Confederation of the Rhine. Its ties with the Holy Roman Empire ended with the demise of that long paralyzed conglomerate of states, which, as was often said, was neither holy, Roman, nor an empire. Liechtenstein officially became

Prince Hans–Adam and Princess Marie

a free and sovereign state. Napoleon respected Liechtenstein's independence, which was confirmed later by the Congress of Vienna in 1815. It is, in fact, the only part of the Napoleonic territorial system that survived unchanged to this day.

It is almost inconceivable that a country as small as Liechtenstein could exist without some form of economic union with a greater power. It joined the German Confederation after the fall of Napoleon and in 1852 it joined a customs union with the Austro–Hungarian Empire. From 1876 until 1918, the Principality was a part of an even tighter customs and tax arrangement with the Austrian province of Vorarlberg. Its close ties with Austria made it unavoidable that it lent its support in Austria's feud with Prussia over the future shape of a unified Germany. Nevertheless, Liechtenstein maintained a rather free hand. It resisted all efforts to draw it into the First World War as an ally of Germany–Austria.

After World War I

The links between Liechtenstein and its eastern neighbor were severed in 1918 with the collapse of Austria–Hungary. World War I brought about the collapse of centuries–old dynasties all over Europe in the face of revolution, famine, misery and the widespread evaporation of former ideals. Liechtenstein's partner, Austria–Hungary, had been whittled down to its German core, a mere splinter of the earlier multi–national empire. Such a ruined and chaotic country could no longer offer a promising future to Liechtenstein. In fact, Austria's collapse and dizzying post–war inflation wiped out Liechtenstein's entire savings. Therefore it saw the need for far–reaching changes. It both proclaimed the present democratic constitution on October 5, 1921, and reoriented itself toward its other, more fortunate neighbor: Switzerland. A customs treaty was signed with that nation in 1923, and

this relationship, updated and deepened by subsequent agreements, is now firmly established.

Depression and World War II

In the 1930s Liechtenstein was severely shaken by the economic depression and narrowly escaped being swallowed up by Hitler's Third Reich. Austria was absorbed by Germany in 1938 and the shadow of the swastika was cast over Liechtenstein's border. The 85–year–old monarch, Franz I, was without heirs, and he feared that his death would be the signal for a Nazi takeover of the Principality. He therefore appointed as regent one of his grandnephews, the present monarch's father, Franz Josef II. On July 26, 1938, Franz Josef II ascended the throne. A small minority of Liechtensteiners had actually been attracted to Nazism, and in March 1939 local Nazis attempted unsuccessfully to overthrow the government. This determined minority remained undaunted and continued to publish a semi–weekly Nazi newspaper; a few of them even joined the armed sections of the Nazi SS.

Liechtenstein, which was not included in the Swiss defense system during World War II, miraculously managed to maintain its neutrality throughout the conflict. German troops could have captured the country within a half an hour, especially since the fifty–man auxiliary police corps was under orders to offer no actual or symbolic resistance whatsoever. This corps occupied itself chiefly with trying to control the great number of foreign deserters, conscientious objectors and refugees who streamed into the country.

After Germany's collapse, the border posts were strengthened and a barbed–wire barricade was strung along the entire border with Austria. However, in the night of May 2, 1945, the barricade was trampled and crossed by armed soldiers of the First Russian Army of Liberation,

Liechtenstein

who were fleeing from Red Army units that had been ordered to send them back to the Soviet Union. They were disarmed and interned with thousands of other refugees in camps near Ruggell and Schaan. Despite attempts by a Soviet investigating team that came to Vaduz to demand possession of all Russians, these refugees remained until 1948, when they were permitted to emigrate to Argentina.

POLITICAL SYSTEM

Liechtenstein is a constitutional monarchy in which sovereignty is theoretically shared by the hereditary monarch from the House of Liechtenstein and the people. The Prince's constitutional powers were dramatically increased as a result of a referendum in March 2003, in which 64.3% of voters supported his proposals to strengthen his political prerogatives. Only 35.7% opposed them, with a voter turnout of 87.7%. The reforms made the ruling Prince the most powerful monarch in Europe within his realm. It can no longer be said that this royal "reigns but does not rule." His acquisition of sweeping powers caused concern in the Council of Europe. It set up a commission that concluded that the constitutional revisions are "a serious step backward" and could "lead to the isolation of Liechtenstein within the European community of states." Former Prime Minister Mario Frick agreed: "We have made ourselves an international laughing stock." However, both the Prince and two-thirds of Liechtensteiners waved off these worries. In the Prince's words, "the princely house and the people of Liechtenstein can walk hand in hand into the future."

The country has a 25–member unicameral parliament elected by proportional representation for four–year terms. The voter turnout at elections is quite high, ranging from 76% to 95%, and citizens eighteen years of age or older are permitted to vote. Not until 1984 were women granted the right to vote and to hold public office. Earlier, an antiquated law stripping all locally born women of their citizenship if they married foreigners was repealed. Liechtenstein has ceased being politically a "man's world."

As in Switzerland, the highest executive authority is a collegial board. All five members of the cabinet serve four–year terms. The majority in parliament selects the leading member (called the Head of Government). The Deputy Chief is also chosen in this manner, and by tradition is from an opposition party. Parliament also chooses the remaining members (called Government Councilors). The Prince formally appoints all of them. Since 2003 he can unilaterally dismiss the government,

which is responsible to both parliament and to the Prince.

The Prince must formally approve all legislation, although he has not vetoed a law since the 1960s when he disapproved of the legislature's proposed change in hunting rights. Since 2003 he can kill legislation passed by parliament by not acting on it for six months. He has the right to introduce legislative proposals in the parliament. In time of emergency, he can, with the permission of the Head of Government, decree laws without seeking approval from parliament.

In 1993 he flexed his constitutional muscles by dissolving parliament and calling new elections after the ruling party revolted against its leader, Markus Büchel, whom it accused of incompetence. Such a rejection of a parliamentary no–confidence vote is inconceivable in any other European monarchy. The Prince noted: "There is no majority for a figurehead," and the 2003 referendum confirmed this.

In the past the Prince made no attempt to dominate the political process. How-

ever, in 1997 he demanded and later received the right to approve the appointment of judges. He had said he would pack up his family and move to Vienna if this power were denied him. Even one of his critics in parliament, Peter Wolff, admitted that losing the Prince would be a terrible setback: "The monarchy gives us our national identity." The speaker of Parliament agreed, asserting: "Without the prince, we are nothing." The referendum gave him the power to approve all judges and to be removed from the jurisdiction of the constitutional court.

The Prince found solid support among the political parties and the people. Citizens were divided on his proposed constitutional changes, which some saw as an excessive strengthening of the monarchist element. Some local politicians resent his semi-feudal powers although they want to retain a constitutional monarchy. The constitutional struggle culminated in the 2003 reform, which for the first time grants citizens the right to call a referendum to express any displeasure in the

The Prince and Princess of Liechtenstein with their children—(on the stairs) H.S.H. Princess Tatjana and H.S.H. Prince Maximilian, and (left and right) H.S.H. Prince Constantin, H.S.H. Hereditary Prince Alois.

The Castle at Vaduz, residence of the Reigning Prince of Liechtenstein

Prince's performance. If that were to happen, various males in his extended family could decide whether to replace him. According to custom, the Prince receives no pay from his subjects, although he accepts a token expense allowance of 250,000 Swiss francs. His popularity helps give stability to the country's politics. Having won the referendum after a decade of bickering, the Prince announced that he would begin handing over the reins of power to his son, Alois.

Liechtensteiners generally know how to reconcile their love for the royal dynasty with their right to self–rule. Thus, their traditionally firm attachment to the monarchy was rather surprising to the outsider, considering the facts that the first time their ruler even visited the tiny country was in 1842 and that the rulers declined to live permanently in the land until 1938. Until then, Princes always preferred the splendid family palace, Burg Mödling, near Vienna. But when he ascended the throne in 1938, the quiet and unassuming Prince Franz Josef II, who had been born in 1906 and educated in agriculture and forestry in Vienna, chose to reside in the 100–room medieval castle perched on a high cliff crowning Vaduz. The Prince of Liechtenstein's family possesses an art collection whose estimated value is from $150 million to $500 million.

In 1989 Franz Josef II died, less than one month after the death of his wife, Princess Gina; he collapsed at his wife's bedside and never recovered. The new Prince, Hans–Adam, is an economist who has long administered the family's wealth, estimated at more than $2 billion. This includes a bank with subsidiaries in London and New York, electronics and "software" investments in the U.S., and land holdings in Austria twice the size of Liechtenstein. He is also demanding that the Czech Republic return lands confis-

cated after World War I ten–times the size of the principality. It also owns jointly with the International Paper Company a 75,000–acre farming operation in Texas.

The Prince is married to Prague–born Countess Marie Aglae Kinsky, and they have four children. When Prince Alois was married to Duchess Sophie of Bavaria in 1993, the entire Liechtenstein population was invited to join the festivities.

Political Parties

Except for the Free List (FL), the two main political parties have programs that are difficult to distinguish from each other. They appeal to electors who, not surprisingly in such a small country, are often inclined to vote for the man rather than the party. In the 2001 elections to the 25–seat parliament, the conservative Progressive Citizens' Party (FBP) won 13 seats. The centrist Fatherland Union (VU) won 11 seats and formed a government headed by Otmar Hasler. A left–wing environmentalist group, the Free List, entered parliament, and won one seat.

Liechtenstein has an independent judiciary and a legal system based on Swiss, Austrian and its own law. For administrative purposes, the country is divided into eleven communes, which are governed by mayors and city councils elected locally every three years. A civil service staff of approximately 600 officials administers the government's political decisions.

This is a sovereign state that, because of its extremely small size, has chosen to align itself politically and economically very closely to Switzerland. This places severe limits on its powers, but as a sovereign state, Liechtenstein is free to take back its full powers at any time. It does differ with Switzerland on some diplomatic issues. In 1980 Liechtenstein broke with the Swiss policy and supported the U.S.–led boycott of the Moscow Olympics

to protest Soviet intervention in Afghanistan. Also, it endorsed a high level of European military integration and the creation of a European nuclear deterrent force. As the prince noted, 'We have to think about European stability, even though we are neutral.'

He also announced Liechtenstein's entry into the UN, rather than to wait for the Swiss to make up their minds. In 1992 it announced that it would not enter the EU, even if Switzerland decided to do so. The voters accepted the referendum on the European Economic Area (EEA) treaty in 1992 under the condition that the customs union with Switzerland be maintained. Unlike Switzerland, it joined the EEA in 1995. EEA membership gives it most of the advantages of EU membership and few of the burdens. Prince Hans–Adam called it "the best of all possible worlds for Liechtenstein. We have our cake and eat it too." The greatest beneficiary is its manufacturing sector, which accounts for almost half of the country's 20,000 jobs and which is almost totally dependent upon exporting.

Liechtenstein belongs to several special organizations associated with the UN, such as the International Court of Justice, the International Atomic Energy Agency and the UN Conference on Trade and Development. It belongs to EFTA (to which a substantial amount of its exports go), the OSCE, and the Council of Europe in Strasbourg at which it has taken its turn as chair.

Liechtenstein maintains embassies only in Bern, Switzerland, (which in turn represents its tiny partner throughout the world) and in Austria. It has agreed not to conclude trade or customs treaties with other states, but is bound by most treaties into which Switzerland enters. In general, it avoids any international dealings that would displease Switzerland. It has renounced its right to coin its own money, with the exception of gold coins that have no legal value as currency; Swiss currency has been used since 1921. Swiss officials have full responsibility for all customs questions arising out of the 1924 customs union.

Beautiful postage stamps are printed in Liechtenstein, which it sells profitably throughout the world. In fact, such sales provide 10% of the government's revenues. Switzerland once shared responsibility for the postal, telephone and telegraph systems, although Liechtenstein owned the equipment. In 2000 the principality assumed full control of its postal and telecommunications systems.

Swiss border guards also control Liechtenstein's boundaries. Officially, all able–bodied males to age sixty are required to be ready for military service. However,

Liechtenstein

there has in fact been no army since 1868. Liechtenstein maintains merely a 55–man police force.

ECONOMY

The visitor to Liechtenstein most often remembers the romantic side of this Alpine retreat, which seems to have slumbered almost unnoticed into the modern age. What he often overlooks is the fact that this principality is the second richest, second most industrially productive country in the world when measured in per capita income terms. Only Brunei, with its tremendous oil deposits, earns more per person each year. This economic prosperity tends to change the traditional, overall picture of this nation. Though traditional in so many ways, it has shown itself to be extremely open to progress in research, technology and production. Before World War II more than a third of the population worked on the land, and there were only four factories.

Now only 1.7% of the population is engaged in agriculture, and there are forty-five factories. This leap into the modern industrial age is a result not only of extraordinarily stable political conditions, but also of minimum investment requirements, a very liberal tax policy and strict bank secrecy. The tax laws have encouraged from 20,000 to 30,000 foreign businesses, often called "letter box companies," to maintain nominal headquarters in Liechtenstein. About a third of Liechtenstein's total fiscal revenues are derived from such companies. It is untrue that no individual or company pays taxes there. Income taxes range from 8% to 10% for individuals and 6% to 18% for companies. Property is also taxed.

At the turn of the century, large industrial countries are harshly criticizing small "offshore" countries like Liechtenstein for allegedly catering to persons and groups around the world who want to hide money. Its failure to reform or enforce its bank secrecy laws attracts "dirty" money. In 2000, the French parliament and German intelligence publicized information pointing to funds in the principality linked to Russian and American organized crime, South American drug dealing, and French-German political payola. Such criticism prompted Prince Hans Adam, whose family owns Liechtenstein's largest bank, and the elected government to appoint a financial investigator from Austria to look into corruption. A police raid in May 2000 led to the arrest of a handful of leading citizens, including the brothers of the economics minister and the chief judge. The embarrassed principality amended its laws to facilitate the search for dirty money, dubious deposi-

tors, and other shady individuals who maintain mailbox corporations. In 2002 it was taken off of the OECD's money-laundering blacklist at the cost of loosening its bank secrecy laws. It reached an agreement with the EU in 2003 to collect taxes for bank account interest and return 75% of it to the country of residence without providing account holders' names.

Liechtenstein's industry is very diverse. High technology and the metal industry, which specializes in small machines, are the leading ones, followed by the ceramic, chemical and pharmaceutical industries. The country produces a wide range of goods, including ultra–high vacuum technology, miniature calculators, boilers, textiles, furniture, varnishes, fountains, canned foods, prefabricated houses and protective coatings for spaceship windows and artificial teeth, for which it is one of the world's biggest producers. One of its companies even produced a component for a solar wind experiment that went to the moon with the Apollo astronauts.

Because it has practically no natural resources, Liechtenstein has no heavy industry. The relatively small size of factories and the fact that the firms have been consciously dispersed throughout the country away from urban areas has had the favorable effect of both preventing large industrial plants from dominating the landscape and of preserving the country's environment from the kind of damage that has often accompanied rapid industrialization in other countries. This fortunate situation greatly benefits not only the inhabitants, but also the country's tourist industry, which is the nation's fourth most important source of income. With tourism down in 2003, an innovative "rent-a-state" program was in-

troduced. It offers the whole principality except the Vaduz Castle as a destination for conventions and corporate retreats. For a daily fee of about $320 to $530 per person for groups up to 1,200 people, an organization could reserve entire hotels, restaurants, meeting places and sports facilities and even temporarily put their own logos on buildings.

The thriving economy has enabled the residents to enjoy a high standard of living and a generous social welfare system. It has also brought certain economic and social problems to the country. First, since there is almost no domestic market for its high technology products, Liechtenstein is overwhelmingly dependent upon exporting. It is extremely vulnerable to international developments that might adversely affect world trade. Second, with only 1.7% of its population working in agriculture, it must import 70% of the food needed to nourish its well–fed population. Third, the small size of the domestic work force has necessitated the importation of foreign workers. Approximately 12,000 such workers, who come chiefly from Switzerland, Austria, Germany and Italy, and who are often accompanied by their families, now constitute a third of the country's population. Adding 6,500 commuters who come daily to work, about 60% of the workforce is foreign.

This large percentage of foreigners has placed strains on the highly tolerant and hospitable Liechtensteiners. They can seldom be absorbed into the political life of the country; an ancient practice permits foreigners to become citizens only if the popular assemblies in one of the eleven communes approve them individually. Few of the foreigners ever gain the right to vote. In 2000 a new law was passed to

Liechtenstein princely moments

212

make it easier for foreigners who have been living in the principality for 30 years to become citizens.

Many native Liechtensteiners became concerned about the possibly negative social effects that the presence of so many foreigners might have on the country. Therefore, since 1962 the government has placed severe limits on the influx of foreign workers. This policy has produced undeniable economic difficulties. Without an available pool of labor, Liechtenstein's domestic industry cannot grow. Because of this limitation, almost all of the country's major industries, which need to expand because of the high volume of orders, have begun to transfer substantial portions of their production activities to foreign countries. Unemployment stood at 1% in 1996.

Liechtenstein has a good network of roads, but has no airport and no rail service to the capital city. The railway facilities in the north of the country linking Switzerland and Austria are owned and operated by the Austrian Federal Railways.

CULTURE

As a small country with very few citizens, Liechtenstein is heavily dependent culturally on its German–speaking neighbors. Two German language news-papers appear in the capital city of Vaduz: the *Liechtensteiner Vaterland* published six times weekly by the Fatherland Union, and the *Liechtensteiner Volksblatt*, published six times weekly by the Progressive Citizens Party. Except for a Liechtenstein

station called Radio L, all radio and television programming comes from Switzerland, and the Liechtenstein Postal Ministry pays fees for this service.

Cultural efforts receive generous subsidies from the government. Permanent art collections are maintained in two museums. In the second half of the 1980s a new art museum was supposed to be built in Vaduz to display the bulk of the Prince's collection of paintings, sculptures, old weapons and furniture. However, bickering and red tape held up the construction. Most of these treasures are stored in the royal castle in a five–story depot as large as a medium sized department store. A few can be seen in a new museum that replaced the old Engländerbau in 2000. An impatient Prince Hans–Adam reportedly thought about establishing his own art museum by blasting a huge cavern into the cliff under his castle in Vaduz. The high cost of constructing the new museum was such a political hot potato that it prompted new parliamentary elections in 1989 to try to sort it out. Theater am Kirchplatz in the town of Schaan attracts leading performers from throughout the world.

Liechtenstein's people are 80% Roman Catholic, and in 1999 it finally got its first archbishop. The school system offers kindergarten, elementary and secondary educations, and is modeled largely after the Swiss school system. There is one elite *Gymnasium* (high school) in Vaduz for those pupils who wish to pursue university studies. Students must enter universities outside the country, since none exists locally. The literacy rate among the country's citizens is 100%.

FUTURE

Liechtenstein's close association with Switzerland and its highly advanced and diversified economy will continue to be crucial for its existence as a sovereign micro-state in the modern world. It can be expected to remain politically stable, despite the fact that over one–third of its residents are foreigners. After constitutional reform in 2003, the principality now has Europe's most powerful monarchy. Liechtenstein will remain somewhat vulnerable economically because of its excessive dependence upon exports and its static domestic labor pool. Also, rapid industrialization and sudden wealth can be expected to intensify certain urban problems, such as rapidly increasing land values. In June 1999 Europeans took notice of this minuscule principality when it hosted the small Olympics, held every other year for little European countries.

The Italian Republic (Italy)

Italy

A rainy morning in Rome

Area: 187,176 sq. mi. (301,225 sq. km., about twice the size of California; about 750 miles—1,200 km.—from north to south and from 95 to 155 miles—152 to 248 km. wide).

Population: 57.5 million.

Capital City: Rome (Roma in Italian; Pop. 2.92 million, estimated).

Climate: From late spring to early winter the days are generally sunny and warm. Midsummer is quite hot in all but the North, where in the winter (the rainy season throughout the country) temperatures can sink to below freezing; the South is consistently warm.

Neighboring Countries: France (West); Switzerland and Austria (North); Slovenia (Northeast), with Croatia, Bosnia–Hercegovina, Montenegro (Yugoslavia), and Albania paralleling its eastern coastline across the Adriatic Sea 50 to 100 miles (80 to 160 km.) away.

Official Language: Italian.

Ethnic Background: Indo–European, North African.

Principal Minorities: Predominantly German–speaking people with Austrian culture in South Tirol (Alto Adige); Albanian–speaking people in Calabria and Sicily; Greek–speaking people in Grecia–Salentin (Puglia) and some places in Calabria; French–speaking minority in Aosta–Valley; Slovene-speaking minority in the Trieste–Gorizia area.

Principal Religion: Roman Catholic.

Main Exports: Machinery, textiles and footwear, transport equipment, chemicals foodstuffs.

Main Imports: Machinery and transport equipment, chemicals, energy, textiles and clothing, foodstuffs, ferrous and nonferrous metals.

Major Trading Customers: EU (55%), especially Germany (15%), France (12.6%), U.S. (11%), UK (7%), Spain (6.2%).

Currency: Euro.

National Day: June 5, (1946), Anniversary of the Republic. Actually the first Monday in June is the day celebrated.

Chief of State: Carlo Azeglio Ciampi, President (since May 1999).

Head of Government: Silvio Berlusconi, Prime Minister (since June 2001).

National Flag: From the pole, three equal vertical stripes of red, white and green.

Italy has the second largest population in Western Europe and is easily recognized on every map by its boot shape. This narrow peninsula with the Apennine mountain range as its backbone extends from the Alps almost to the North African coast. It is flanked by the largest islands of the Mediterranean: Sicily (15,500 sq. mi.–25,000 sq. km.) and Sardinia (14,300 sq. mi.–23,000 sq. km.) in the western basin of the Mediterranean. With its own coastline extending almost 5,000 miles (8,000 km.) and its mild climate, Italy has lured people for thousands of years. However, most of its settlers did not come as polite guests with hat–in–hand, but rather as plunderers or conquerors who used force to overrun the land.

In the long course of Italian history, almost all the peoples of Europe have at one time or another either occupied or settled the country. From the ancient Greeks to the Spaniards, from the ancient Germanic tribes and Arab Saracens to the Holy Roman and Austrian emperors, peoples of the world have left their traces in Italy. This almost uninterrupted chain of foreign domination dating back to the classical period has decisively affected the traditions, behavior and mentality of the Italian. At the same time it has provided a basic impulse for Europe. Roman rule, which extended from the Mediterranean area through present day Germany and France as well as all the way to Hadrian's Wall in Britain, and the Renaissance (meaning "rebirth") in the 14th and 15th centuries, decisively shaped western civilization.

Italy

Modern Italy is a country full of contradictions and peculiarities. In the very same state where most of the citizens are Catholic and where the main seat of the Catholic Church is located, one found until the end of the Cold War the strongest and most powerful communist party outside of Eastern Europe. Italy's economy is the sixth largest in the industrialized world, and in northern Italy the visitor witnesses a modern industrial and urban life. But in the South one finds the many typical characteristics of a developing nation with illiteracy, high unemployment and unproductive agriculture.

Whoever takes the so-called "sunny freeway," a gigantic masterpiece of modern highway construction, to a village in the region of Abruzzi in central Italy finds himself in two different worlds: on the one hand steel and concrete construction and on the other hand a medieval mountain village which has had electricity for only 40 years! Old women clothed in black sit in front of their houses and look distrustfully at the stranger who perhaps had come from a demonstration for women's rights in Milan or Rome.

Italy, with its strong, influential unions, has more strikes than almost any other country in Europe. Even by Western European standards, Italy is a prosperous nation. At the same time, one is astonished by the social differences between the rich and poor, and by the frequent servility of the worker and employee toward the boss. Half of the defense budget is swallowed up by the almost 165,000-man army, but the borders must still ultimately be protected either by an ally, such as the U.S., or by neutral states to the north or east. Only one-third of the defense budget is allocated to the navy that has the sobering task of defending the 5,000-mile coastline. Given the strong centrifugal forces of highly diverse regions and countless competing political groups, it is no wonder that Guilio Andreotti wrote in his memoirs that Italy is almost ungovernable.

HISTORY

One of the major contradictions of Italian history is that the heroic epoch that was invoked and emulated by Mussolini, Italy's fascist dictator from 1922 to 1943, is actually not Italian history, but rather the history of a single city, Rome. This city rose to become the ruler of the entire Mediterranean world and, much more, of Europe. At one time, a person could truly say, "All roads lead to Rome." Italians themselves interpret differently the significance of Rome's earlier power and influence. If one were to ask inhabitants of southern Italy, particularly someone from Calabria or Sicily, whether they consider themselves descendants of the Romans, one would immediately receive a vigorously negative response. In contrast to those from the northern and central part of the peninsula, southern Italians view Roman history as the beginning of perpetual foreign or outside control. The present form of this control is the economic predominance of the North over the South.

In a strict sense, Roman history cannot be called Italian national history because the concept of "the nation" was completely unknown in the ancient world. Yet, one cannot understand modern Italy without first viewing some of the principal features of Rome's development. This still vibrant past has had tremendous impact not only upon Italy itself, but also upon Western Europe as a whole. The most evident examples of Roman heritage are found in the Romance languages, which include modern Italian, Spanish, Portuguese, Romanian and French. Without its Latin components, English would never have developed as it did and certainly would be incomprehensible to people today. The grammatical structure and vocabulary of all modern Germanic languages was strongly influenced by Latin (including the old rule that the verb comes last which gives non-Germans so much trouble!). In law, civil administration, literature, art and engineering, ancient Roman civilization established the standards for many centuries.

The Early Period

The history of ancient Rome is long and exceedingly complicated, and is punctuated with magnificent victories and achievements, as well as ignoble failures, corruption and civil war. That history can be divided roughly into three periods: it was ruled by kings from roughly 753 B.C. (according to Roman legend) until 509 B.C., when a revolt led to the establishment of a republic, governed by elected consuls. The Roman Republic lasted until 45 B.C. when Julius Caesar established an empire subsequently ruled by emperors. In 185 A.D. this mighty empire was divided into a Western empire, led from Rome, Milan and Trier in present-day Germany, and an Eastern empire, ruled from Constantinople (now Istanbul) in Turkey. The former empire finally collapsed in 476 A.D., whereas the Eastern one continued to exist for another thousand years.

According to their own legend, the Romans were descendants of a group of Greeks who had accompanied Aeneas, one of the sons of the Trojan King Priam. Aeneas had escaped from the burning city of Troy and had sailed across the Mediterranean Sea before being blown ashore at the mouth of the Tiber River. There he allegedly founded a city called Lavinium. In fact, Italy was settled around 1,200 B.C. by Indo-European tribes which moved into the area from the West, and since the Trojans were Indo-Europeans themselves, there might have been some truth in the Roman belief that they were descended from the Greeks.

The settlers in the Italian peninsula broke up into various warlike tribes: the Etruscans settled around the present city of Viterbo, located about 66 miles (110

Florence: Medieval parade

An Etruscan soldier

kilometers) north of Rome. The Umbrians also settled north of Rome around the present city of Perugia. The Samnites built up their civilization south of Rome, while the Latins were based around the Tiber River. At the bottom of the peninsula and on the island of Sicily, the Greeks and Phoenicians established colonies, which thrived on trade and shipping.

Roman legends tell us that the city of Rome was founded in 753 B.C. by a Latin chief named Romulus, one of the infants allegedly reared by a she-wolf. The new city was situated on a hilly site about 20 miles (32 km.) inland from the former city of Lavinium in order to be out of reach of Phoenician and Greek raiders. Romans believed that Romulus made himself king of Rome and ruled until 716 B.C. He was succeeded by Numa Pomilius, who came from the Sabine tribe and who is said to have introduced Rome's first religious institutions, which were largely copied from those of the Etruscans and Greeks. Many Greek gods were worshipped although the Romans gave them different

names. For instance, Zeus became Jupiter, Hera became Juno, Hermes became Mercury and Athena became Minerva.

Under the rule of the Roman kings, the city's influence and control began to expand beyond the original seven hills, named the Palatine, the Capitoline, the Esquiline, the Aventine, the Caelian, the Quirinal and the Viminal. The most powerful foes were the Etruscans, a fierce, but civilized people, who had perfected the use of iron. The Etruscan leader, Tarquin, reportedly defeated the Romans and became King. Although it still became the leading city of the Latin League, a loose association of cities bound together for purposes of defense, Rome's subsequent kings were of Etruscan descent and were known as "the Tarquins;" they were elected by a small group of noblemen.

Under the Tarquin kings, Rome's class system became more firmly shaped. On top was the patrician class, consisting of free Romans who had the right to attend the assembly of aristocrats who advised the king. Eventually this assembly became open to all Romans who owned property. The plebeian class was composed of freed slaves who had immigrated to the city. The third class was composed of slaves, who had some rights, but who were not citizens. Only patricians and plebeians were allowed to serve in the army—soldiers were at first required to provide their own uniforms, weapons and supplies, and they were paid by being able to share in the booty gained in victorious campaigns.

The last king was also named Tarquin, but his people called him Superbus because of his arrogance. He ruled very badly, involving Rome in expensive wars, arresting and murdering Roman citizens without trial and generally subjecting the city to a reign of terror. Finally in 509 B.C. two patricians staged a successful revolt and drove out the last of the kings, although it was not until 496 B.C. that the final attempt by the Etruscans and Sabines to restore the monarchy in Rome was suppressed.

The Republic

Because the kings had made themselves so hated, the Roman Republic was declared, which was ruled by two consuls elected by the People's Assembly each year for a one-year term. The first two consuls were the leaders of the revolt, Brutus and Collatinus, who were the most important founders of the Republic. Later, officials below the level of consuls were elected in pairs, and the normal career path to the post of consul was through a series of lower offices.

The republican constitution was not wholly democratic in the modern sense

because it granted considerably more power to the patricians than to the plebeians and because most slaves were entirely excluded from politics. Only the election of the civil servants, consuls and judges by the People's Assembly can be regarded as democratic. There can be no doubt that a few influential Roman families wielded a disproportionate amount of power and authority. In general, the nobility and large landowners insured that all political functions were carried out honorably. Yet it was possible for common people with talent to acquire great political prominence and to influence Roman politics. For example, the well-known politician Cicero, who did not come from one of the few influential families in Rome, was the most famous orator of his time. Despite his great influence and fame, he suffered his entire life from an inferiority complex about his humble background.

The Roman constitution succeeded in solving many social crises and enabled Rome to establish and maintain a citizen's army. Realizing that victories were their own, these citizen soldiers were eminently more motivated than the disorderly mercenary armies of oriental dynasties. For the ancient world, the Roman civic virtues such as discipline, obedience and bravery were of great importance—they made their control over other peoples legitimate. Three essential pillars for the Roman state's strength were the exclusively Roman understanding of the commonwealth as *res publica* ("affairs of the people") from which the word "republic" is derived, the right of political participation, which was the highest goal of every distinguished Roman, and the disdain for all purely private matters.

In the Roman Republic important steps toward limited government were made: the very existence of a constitution, so long as it is observed, places limits on rulers' power. The Roman republican constitution, which was unwritten, especially embodied many principles essential for the development of modern democracy and did limit the state's control over citizens in several important ways. It was based on the separation of power between the executive and the legislature. Two consuls, who were elected by the People's Assembly composed of all citizens, provided the executive leadership. However, the electoral system gave more votes to those citizens who paid more taxes. Therefore, upper classes always had a majority of votes. The highest executive authority alternated each day from one consul to the other, although the consul not having the highest authority could veto decisions made by the other except in times of war. The yearly election and the

Italy

mutual control over each other prevented the concentration of power in one person's hands.

The fact that the civilian rulers had command over the military, even in times of crisis, prevented the development of a "state within a state" and the use of war as an end in itself instead of as a political means. The daily alternation of supreme command over the military, however, caused many defeats, the most famous occurring in Cannae in 216 B.C. But these changes helped to prevent a military dictatorship. In time of extreme emergency, the People's Assembly could appoint a dictator to exercise full political powers until the grave dangers to the city had passed. The only exception to such a dictatorship limited in time was Julius Caesar, who at the end of the Roman Republic was appointed dictator for life.

The Senate wielded limited legislative power and had authority over foreign policy, including the declaration of war and ratification of treaties. In domestic policy it had only advisory power. In contrast to the consuls and other civil servants, Senators, who numbered up to three hundred at any one time, were not elected; rather they consisted of retired high government officials, including all former consuls.

To protect themselves in courts of law, the plebeians forced the establishment of Tribunes for the People, elected by the People's Assembly and to whom any plebeian could turn for help whenever he believed that he was being treated unjustly. These People's Tribunes could even veto decisions made by the Senate and they could eventually veto any law. It was considered to be a very serious crime to attack the Tribunes during their term of office. Plebeians won the right for themselves (and for slaves!) to stand for election to all city offices and thereby ultimately to gain seats in the Senate. Plebeians also won the right to marry patricians, thus making class lines less rigid.

Very significantly, the plebeians were able to have a written legal code adopted in 454 B.C. These laws were published on 12 bronze tablets, known as the Twelve Tablets of Law, and were kept in the heart of the city, known as the Forum. Every Roman schoolchild was expected to know them by heart, and they ultimately became the foundation of Roman law and of the legal systems of many modern European nations. Roman laws embodied all the important rules pertaining to contracts, the protection of private property, marriage and divorce and inheritance. Because private property was at the core

of Roman legal thought, offenses were most frequently punished by requiring payment of property. The victims of petty theft and robbery and the families of murder victims were compensated by means of fines and confiscated property. The Romans had no clear–cut criminal law with the exception of a political penal code for corruption, abuse of public office and high treason.

Two important preconditions for the rise of Rome were the still unexplained decline of Etruscan rule over northern and central Italy in the 5th and 4th centuries B.C., as well as the Roman domination of the various tribes in Italy and the Greek cities in the south. Rome had been constantly threatened by various tribes within Italy and by Gauls who poured into the peninsula from the north. Once it was even captured and burned. The city was saved several times by such heroes as Cincinnatus and Camillus.

One Greek city in southern Italy, Tarentum, even sent for the help of Pyrrhus, King of Epirus in northern Greece, who arrived in 280 B.C. with a huge fleet carrying a herd of elephants and 25,000 troops. This army clashed with the Romans outside of Heraclea in 280 B.C.; the Romans fought extremely well, but when Pyrrhus sent his elephants roaring and

Built by the first Tarquin king, the *Circus Maximus*, seating 300,000 Romans, saw the first chariot races

The Roman Senate

screaming against the enemy troops, who had never seen such beasts before, the soldiers panicked and retreated. Though he won the battle, Pyrrhus had lost far more soldiers than had the Romans, and his weakened troops therefore were eventually beaten at Benventum. Today, the words "Pyrrhic victory" refer to any success achieved at too high a price.

Punic Wars

The victory over Pyrrhus, along with other swift and successful campaigns, established Roman domination over the Italian Peninsula in the first part of the 3rd century and permitted them to cast their sights farther for the first time. It is no surprise that Italy hurled a serious challenge against the major naval power in the western Mediterranean at the time: the Phoenician metropolis of Carthage (located a few miles outside the present city of Tunis in North Africa). Carthage had numerous colonies extending all along the coasts of North Africa and Spain, and it dominated Sardinia and the western part of Sicily.

In the first Carthaginian (Punic) War (264 to 241 B.C.) between the land power Rome and the sea power Carthage, Rome demonstrated its unusual adaptability by skillfully utilizing its allies in order to acquire sea power itself and by gaining the three large islands, Sicily, Sardinia and Corsica. From 218 to 202, after the Romans had finally expelled the Gauls from the mainland peninsula, Carthage, which had been provoked by Roman meddling in Spain, sought revenge in a second round of battles known as the Second Punic War.

The Carthaginians, led by a brilliant young general named Hannibal, threatened the very heart of Rome's Italian domain. In 218 B.C. he moved an army of 100,000-foot soldiers, 1,300 cavalry and 40 elephants from Spain over the Pyrenees and Alps right into Italy. But the climate was too cold in the mountains, and he lost all his elephants and many of his troops during this journey. Nevertheless, he was able to assemble an army on its soil in 218 B.C. Although the Romans tried to avoid open battle, except at Cannae, Hannibal's forces succeeded in destroying several Roman armies through skillful maneuvering, but was never able to take Rome; he remained until 203 B.C. when he received word of an end run that the Romans were planning on Carthage itself. He departed hastily to his city's rescue, but to no avail. Roman troops captured the city and destroyed it, salting the soil in the hope that nothing would ever grow again. From this harshness came the expression "a Carthaginian peace." At last, Rome was unchallenged master of the western Mediterranean. (A treaty between Carthage, now outside Tunis, and Rome ending the Punic wars was finally signed in 1987 A.D.!)

Roman Imperialism

Rome could now direct its sights eastward toward Greece. Between 198 and 190 B.C., Rome won victories in Greece, which not only again opened the Roman door wide to Greek cultural influence, but it also gave the Romans a firm foothold in Asia Minor. This was the beginning of Roman imperialism. Hitherto, diplomatic balancing and management of conquered peoples were the primary factors in Roman foreign policy; in the new phase it adopted different methods of power politics. Punitive expeditions against disloyal allies and the destruction of cities like Carthage and Corinth in 115 B.C. revealed the foreign political pattern for the conquest of the eastern Mediterranean area. By 63 B.C. nearly all the countries in the Mediterranean region were paying tribute to Rome.

The burden of constant war and of administering the enormous empire

Italy

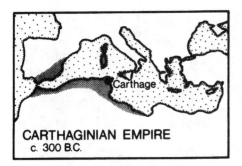

CARTHAGINIAN EMPIRE
c. 300 B.C.

overextended the resources of a small state that started on the banks of the Tiber River at the foot of the Palatine Hill, which had transformed itself into a large and powerful metropolis.

The Romans' encounter with Greece during the conquest of the eastern Mediterranean area influenced Roman life and thought in such a way that the Roman poet Horace could write that the "conquered Greeks conquered their victors." Greek slaves taught the children of the wealthy in the Roman Empire. The Greek language assumed a role during the Republic that in some ways corresponded to that of the French language in the 17th and 18th centuries. On the other hand, the Romans clung to their traditional political and cultural norms and deeply mistrusted foreign influences. They were willing to adopt those technical and institutional achievements of other peoples that the Romans considered worthy of copying. For instance, many weapons systems were patterned after those of the conquered peoples. The critical examination and adoption of that which was considered better, combined with the steadfastness of a self–reliant identity, gave Roman policies their dynamism and flexibility.

After many years the Republican constitution became increasingly incapable of solving the many social problems of such a large realm. The defense of the vast empire, with its many administrative requirements, called for an effective central bureaucracy, but the old Republic did not have such an institution and was therefore unable to perform many essential functions. Numerous military campaigns claimed thousands of casualties and therefore left large tracts of land either to fall fallow or into the hands of the large landowners. Further, following the campaigns, many unemployed soldiers drifted into Rome, thereby adding to the city's mounting problems.

In earlier times no one was permitted to enter the city of Rome with weapons. Standing armies with nothing to do and former peasants who had lost their land to large landowners broke down the old customs that had integrated the army

with the society and the state. At this point, the earlier observation of the Greek philosopher, Aristotle, applied to Rome: masters of weapons are also masters of the state.

The political order in the Roman Republic began slowly to disintegrate, and widespread dissatisfaction, lawlessness and corruption ran riot throughout the realm. The citizens' rights were gradually whittled away; the parties particularly established themselves in the social circles of the later Republic from 133 to 45 B.C. The Senate Party represented the interests of the nobility and the large landowners, while the Popular Party was supported by the masses.

The Republic Falls; The Empire Arises

Early in the 1st century B.C. civil war between these two groups broke out which lasted on and off for most of the remainder of the century. The leading figure in this struggle was Gaius Julius Caesar, the best-known leader within the Popular Party. Born into a patrician's family, but always possessing strong plebeian sentiments, his extraordinary bravery and endurance endeared him with his troops. He was a talented general, politician, orator, poet, historian, mathematician and architect. William Shakespeare called this unique man "the noblest man that ever lived in the tide of times." In 60 B.C. he was elected consul and set about to accomplish his two chief objectives of establishing order in Rome and the empire, and reconciling the conflicting classes. He spent nine years in Gaul (presently France) and Britain, which not only enabled him to win victories for Rome, but to write an eight volume history entitled the *Gallic War*, which remains one of the most important books of ancient history (much to the distress of modern Latin students).

When he wanted to return to Rome in 49 B.C., the Senate informed him that he was to disband his army and to return to Rome alone. Sensing that he was about to be arrested, he decided to cross the Rubicon River and to march his army against Rome itself. For four years he confronted his enemies, including his former friend and son–in–law, Pompey, in battles in Greece, Egypt, North Africa and Spain, before returning in 45 B.C. as master of the entire Roman world.

Julius was acclaimed dictator in 45 B.C. He proceeded to try to restore order and to introduce such measures as founding colonies inside and outside of Italy to provide new lives for Rome's unemployed, providing grain for the hungry, enabling non–Romans to become members of the Senate and making all residents of Italy Roman citizens. He also made no secret of

his conviction that Rome could survive only if it had one ruler with absolute power that included the right to name his successor.

Fearing the restoration of kings, a group of senators let by Brutus and Cassius murdered Caesar in 44 B.C. in the theater of Pompeius, which was being used temporarily as the Senate. This act, vividly dramatized by Shakespeare, again thrust Rome into a civil war that touched every part of the realm. Not until Octavian, Caesar's grandnephew, established order in 31 B.C. did the bloody civil war come to an end. He became the first emperor of Rome, under the name of Augustus (meaning "the revered") and his successors bore the title of "Caesar" in honor of Julius. The Roman Republic was dead, and the Roman Empire had commenced. The Caesars served for life and were selected in many different ways. Most of them were not from the city of Rome. Some even came from Spain, (Trajan), Africa (Lucius Septimius Severus) or from what is now Yugoslavia (Diocletian).

Peace and Prosperity

Augustus restored order and revived trade, and his people again experienced the rare combination of peace and prosperity. He launched a building program in the empire and its capital that enabled him to say toward the end of his life in 14 B.C., "I found Rome a city of brick and am leaving it a city of marble." Despite a string of less capable emperors, his life's work lasted almost two centuries.

There are many preconceived ideas about Roman emperors. They are often portrayed as degenerate beasts who practiced tyranny with Caesarian insanity, only to fall victims to palace revolts or poisonous death. This is only an anecdotal and superficial understanding. It is true that they sometimes directed political cruelty against other members of the noble class who might have presented a threat to them, but the Roman Empire and its citizens drew many benefits from the emperors' efforts.

It was precisely the centralized bureaucracy, which the emperors created, which made the Roman Empire the blooming civilization as we know it today. Some were wise and learned men, such as Marcus Aurelius, whose published volume, Meditations, is still a highly valued philosophical work. Impressive ruins bear eloquent witness to prosperous Roman cities from Germany to the desert sands of the Sahara. The Empire reached its greatest expansion under Emperor Trajan from 98 to 117 A.D. From Iraq to Scotland, from Cologne to Libya, one spoke Latin and lived according to Roman law and customs.

Statue of the Emperor Trajan in Rome

A dark shadow over the cultural splendor of the Roman classical period was the fact that much of the economic prosperity was achieved by means of slave labor. Modern estimations are that at any one time between 300,000 and 500,000 slaves provided a luxurious life for many citizens of Rome, which by the 2nd century A.D. had grown to a city of over a million inhabitants, including slaves. Our present view of humanity inclines us to judge harshly the treatment of the ancient slaves, who without rights or status could be sold or even killed by their masters. Under Roman law they were considered to be nothing more than "animated tools." However, slaves were actually valuable property, especially an educated Greek.

The degree of suppression endured by a slave depended upon his type of work. Naturally, those slaves who served in public office, including the highest administrative offices, or who as scholars instructed the children of wealthy Romans were much better off than those who worked on the large plantations. The exploitation of the latter led to two slave revolts. In 136 B.C. the slaves in Sicily rose up under their leader, Syrer Eunus, and established a short-lived slave republic in the city of Enna. From 73 to 71 Rome trembled before the legendary slave leader, Spartacus, who led 90,000 rebellious slaves in southern Italy.

Very early the conscience of many persons was stirred by the injustice of slavery. In Plautus' comedies the slaves always played the intelligent and superior roles. Stoic philosophy rejected such servitude entirely. In making a judgment against human bondage in the Roman world, one must remember that slavery existed in modern times as well. In addition, the history of human suppression and exploitation is a very long one. To say that a worker during the period of early capitalism in Manchester or a mercenary Hessian soldier bought by the English to fight against Washington's army during the American Revolution was better off than an ancient slave would be deceptive.

The Decline and Fall of the Empire

The emperors considered their main task to be the security of the Empire's extensive borders. However, as the threat of invasion became greater and greater, the ancient Roman world was unable to withstand after the beginning of the 3rd century A.D. the mounted attacks of Germans, Slavs, Huns, Persians, Turks, Mongolians, Berbers and later, of Arabs.

In 284 A.D. Diocletian, the son of a freed slave from Illyria (now in Yugoslavia) became emperor. He realized that the Roman Empire had grown too large to be governed by one man, so in 285 A.D. he divided it into an Eastern and a Western part. He assumed rule over the eastern portion, with its seat in Nicomedia in Asia Minor, and the subsequent Western emperors held court at Milan and Trier. Emperor Constantine, who became sole Emperor of Rome in 324 A.D., continued the reorganization of the Empire initiated by Diocletian. He built a new city on the site of the former Byzantium, a strategically important crossroads between Asia and Europe, and named it after himself: Constantinople. From then on, the Roman Empire was administered from that city and Rome lost much of its significance. There, Roman civilization mingled with that of Greece and of Asia.

Disciples of and converts to Christianity had been circulating amid most parts of the empire since the 1st century A.D., converting many who held the ancient Greek and Roman beliefs in the classical gods to their belief in a single, almighty God. These beliefs and moral teachings were those of a mortal who claimed to be his Son. A gradual Christian penetration of the Roman society and the emergence of Christianity to that of a state religion was not as commonly supposed. They were only persecuted when they directly challenged the traditional classical understanding of a state religion as a form of political loyalty. It would not have been possible for Christian beliefs to spread un-

less there had otherwise been an attitude of relative religious tolerance. In spite of some use of torture and martyrdom, this faith continued inexorably to grow, eventually becoming the most powerful and dominating concept of the western and mid-eastern world (although supplanted by Islam to a large degree in the Middle East after the life of the prophet Mohammed).

Constantine decided to accept Christianity and to make it the Empire's official religion. After his death in 337 A.D. there was less and less cooperation and coordination between the eastern and western parts of the Empire. While Constantinople was a safe distance from the marauding tribes of Europe, the western part became the object of sustained attacks by Goths, Visigoths and Vandals. Rome was temporarily captured and sacked in 410 A.D. and in 476 the East Gothic chief, Odoacer, marched his troops into the city and deposed the last western Roman Emperor, Romulus Augustulus. Thereafter, sheep grazed on the overgrown ruins of the Forum, once the scene of the power behind the heart of the Empire.

Rome Destroyed

The destruction of Rome was without precedent. But many aspects of this great Empire have been salvaged for posterity, including its literature, which was protected in the Christian cloisters, and its law. Further testimonies to the splendor of the Roman past are the unique accomplishments in architecture, such as domes, columns and basilicas, and in engineering, such as bridges, aqueducts and highways. Most of the important European roads today follow the same routes established by the Romans. Therefore, Italy's past is significant not only to Italians, but to all persons touched by western civilization.

The "Middle Ages"

During and after the Middle Ages, Italy was so fragmented into feuding and ever-shifting states, Papal holdings, kingdoms and foreign dominions that even well-educated Italians have difficulty comprehending their own history during that time. In the Middle Ages as well as in modern times, Italy was characterized by foreign domination, inner strife and parochialism of the Catholic Church. Over a span of a thousand years Byzantines, Germanic tribes, Arabs, Germans, Normans (Scandinavians), Frenchmen, Spaniards and Austrians marched across the land and levied taxes or subjugated the dependent minor princes in the peninsula to servitude.

Ideals such as freedom, unity and independence first became political realities in 1861 with the "Resurgence," or unification

Italy

The Roman Empire at its height

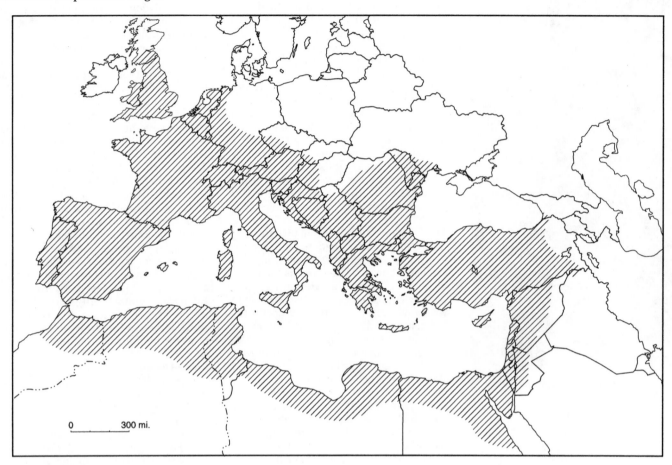

0   300 mi.

movement. With Italy's past in mind, it should be no surprise that Italians' identification with their state developed very slowly. The political culture was stamped with a combined feeling of powerlessness and distrust toward the state.

After the fall of the Roman Empire, centuries of gloom and of alternating domination, particularly by the Germans and Lombards, afflicted the peninsula until the Frankish King Pippin, father of Charlemagne, introduced in the 8th century A.D. a territorial order in Italy. It was divided into a Lombard–Frankish area in the north and a Byzantine area in the south, ruled ultimately from Constantinople. The results of this fateful division continue to be evident in the economic and cultural contrasts between the North and the South right up to the present day.

Along with the division of Italy, the so-called "Pippin Deed" had another extremely far–reaching consequence for the political development of Italy. The Deed assured the Pope an ecclesiastical state in the middle of Italy, which centuries later was the last political entity in the nation that resisted unification with the national Italian state.

Meanwhile during the later Middle Ages, as the North was involved in and profiting from the constant conflict between the German Emperors and the Popes, the South was undergoing an entirely different development. The Byzantines, who were also occupying Sicily, could no longer fend off the attacks of the Moslem Saracens from North Africa.

The Byzantines, who had become Eastern Orthodox Christians, could not count on the Roman Catholic Church for assistance in upholding their occupation. Around 900 Sicily blossomed into a rich and fertile garden under the new Moslem rule. The Saracens, reputed to be blood-thirsty pirates along the coast of Italy, exercised a clever and tolerant reign in which an enormous cultural flowering unfolded. They introduced lemons, oranges, cotton and pistachio nuts, the last being the island's most important agricultural export today. Only an entirely new actor who entered the world scene could put an end to such a rule.

The Power of the Holy "Roman" Empire

In 1080, through a shrewd marriage policy, southern Italy under the Normans (Vikings) became joined with the Holy

Roman (actually German) Empire under Friedrich II of the Staufen dynasty. Known to his contemporaries as "the wonder of the world," Friedrich was an enlightened emperor who was as at home in the world of politics as in the world of scholarship. His reign was the last golden age in Italy before a long period of conservative–clerical foreign domination. Despite their different life–styles, Friedrich succeeded in uniting the original inhabitants of southern Italy, the Byzantine Greeks and the Moslem Saracens, in a life of harmonious co–existence. Under his rule a cultural and economic highpoint was achieved which was unparalleled in Europe at the time.

The new spirit of tolerance as well as the encirclement of the ecclesiastical state by Friedrich's territories did not please the Pope. The long–standing dispute between the German Emperors and the Pope reached a climax with the appeal for a crusade against Friedrich. Many had hoped that divided Italy would develop into a model state under the reign of the House of Staufen. These dreams were shattered, however, when the Frenchman, Charles of Anjou, protégé of the Pope, overthrew Staufen rule in Italy. Southern Italy suf-

Ideal of virility: Tiziano Vecellio, Portrait of a Man ("The Englishman")

Ideal of feminine beauty: Tiziano Vecellio, Portrait of a Young Woman ("La Bella")

The Re–Awakening—(Renaissance)

In the 14th and 15th centuries northern Italy was the cradle of an intellectual and cultural rebirth known as the Renaissance. This reawakening was indirectly stimulated by Venice's refusal to support Constantinople when that city was subjected to a determined Turkish attack. When that last remnant of the Roman Empire finally fell in 1453, many highly cultured Greeks emigrated to Italy from Constantinople and gave the Renaissance movement a significant boost. They helped to reawaken Italian interest in the Greek classical authors. Had it not been for the efforts of the Italian scholars, who laboriously collected and preserved many ancient Greek works, the originals we possess today would have been lost forever.

In the depths of the foaming cauldron of bickering city–states a fundamentally new approach to life was born. Man was no longer the *viator mundi* (pilgrim seeking heavenly salvation) of the Middle Ages, concerned with the universal principle of salvation. He became the *Faber mundi* (the creator and master of the world), who shaped his own destiny. Self–assured individualism and rational thought were reflected in the Renaissance conception of the state. Autonomous states were directed by paid public officials according to the guidelines of "reason of state," and carefully calculated business considerations determined politics and administration. Wars were conducted by mercenary enterprises (known as *condittieri*) that dared to do battle in the same way as one dares to make capital investment, that is, only if a profit is certain. The Florentine, Niccolò Machiavelli, developed the theory of politics that in no way was based upon religious principles.

Correspondingly, scholars who had until that time been considered as *ancillas theologiae* ("slaves of theology") divested themselves of that status and began working independently of theology. Above all, rediscovery of the classical authors advanced this secular conception to that of a rational principle. Spurred on by their Latin predecessors, Dante, Petrarca and Boccaccio, they created new literature in Italian (sometimes intermingled with Latin) but later a total variant of the historic language of Rome.

The universal man with his comprehensive wealth of knowledge represented the new ideal of the Renaissance man. The universal genius, Leonardo da Vinci, was a painter, artist, engineer, doctor, architect and politician and is a particularly prominent example of vast numbers of creative persons who contributed enormously to his culturally rich times. Inspired by the classical model of rounded arches that tied together the central con-

fered terribly under the domination of the Anjou family until 1282, when the mounting hate against the uninhibited French arrogance erupted. The absolute monarchy of the French in southern Italy was consumed with uninterrupted wars, and could not withstand the attacks by the Aragonians from Spain, who, through intrigues, were able to undermine every French military unit.

Disunification

As a result of the disputes between the Pope and the German Emperor, the small and fragmented states and cities in northern Italy were able to achieve a certain degree of political independence. Loyalty to one side or the other varied, depending upon the political advantage at the time of a given battle.

The cities knew well how to exploit to their own economic advantage the disputes of the Popes and the German Emperors and the Crusades, which began at the end of the 11th century. The latter were medieval efforts directed at reclaiming Jerusalem from the Arabs. Of all cities, Venice profited most of all from these efforts. The Venetians did not in any way share the religious fervor or self–sacrifice of the German, French and English knights. The knights and the pilgrims enroute to the Crusades and Jerusalem poured into rival Venice and Genoa in droves.

One of the most notable Crusades was the Fourth, which took place from 1198–

1204. The aged, composed and politically gifted Doge (leader) Dandolo of Venice was able to redirect the course toward Constantinople and agreed to transport the crusaders to their destination on the condition that they stop along the way and plunder Constantinople for Venice. Thus, instead of becoming conquerors of holy cities held by Moslems, the crusaders attacked and plundered a Christian capital city! The Quadriga, a large statue of four horses from the Hippodrome in Constantinople and now above St. Mark's Cathedral in Venice, bears witness to this strange event. In this way, a troublesome trade rival was seriously weakened. Venice was so powerful that it was not even perturbed by the resulting excommunication of the Venetian leaders by the Pope.

Despite the continuing conflict, no other country in Europe achieved at this time the degree of economic development that took place in Italy. One of the most well–known and powerful families of bankers, the Medici, had gained far–reaching political influence in their home city of Florence, as well as in France, where marriage joined Catherine de Medici with King Henry II. In the economically developed cities of northern and central Italy, the transition had been made from a less productive barter economy to a money economy. The bases of this affluence were the development of industry and trade, especially with the Middle and Far East.

Italy

Da Vinci Design and Backward Handwriting

struction, architects developed a totally new concept of space through emphasis on the vertical, with clear, well–formed proportions. Donatello and Michelangelo surpassed their classical predecessors in expression and monumentality. In painting, the central perspective was developed which strove for ideal anatomical proportion that were at the same time more realistic. Masaccio, Botticelli, Raphael and da Vinci, the best-known painters of their time, were the leading lights of an art movement that influenced the entire field of European painting.

Secular–Religious Relations

The Popes themselves were responsible for directing the focus of the Renaissance from the religious realm to the secular princes and scholars. For instance, Pope Julius was Michelangelo's patron. As learned patrons of the arts, the Popes accelerated the inner disintegration of the Church—the reconstruction of St. Peter's Cathedral, sponsored by a member of the Medici family, Pope Leo X, could only be financed by his system of indulgences (paying for forgiveness of sin). This way of raising revenue unleashed the Reformation in the early 16th century. When the Popes became staunch supporters of the counter–Reformation, Italy ceased being the center of the Renaissance, which thereafter found a more congenial setting in France.

In the conflict between the Habsburgs and the French, which was the central problem for the Western European states until the 18th century, the autonomous Italian city–states lost much of their independence. The plunder and devastation caused by the rival French and Habsburg armies, as well as pillaging and destruction by pirates from North African Barbary states, came to dominate life in Italy. The South gradually faded under Spanish domination and became unhinged from developments in the rest of Europe. The war of the Spanish Succession (1701–1713), which endangered the

Dante in Florence

European balance of power between the Habsburgs and France, brought northern Italy under the domination of the Austrians and southern Italy under the control of the Spanish Bourbons. The Popes retained their political hold over much of central Italy. Due to uncontrolled cuttings, the rich forests of Puglia, where Friedrich II had so happily hunted, were reduced to withering grasslands.

It is hardly surprising that the shock waves of the French Revolution of 1789 soon were felt in Italy, where feudal institutions and conditions were still present. French republican forces invaded Savoy and Nice in the fall of 1792 and in March 1796 a concentrated French campaign began in Italy. This resulted not only in temporary French domination of most of northern and central Italy, but also in brilliant victories for a young French general who soon became the leader of France, Napoleon Bonaparte. In early 1798 French forces invaded the Papal States. The Pope fled and a Roman Republic was established. Although the French were temporarily driven out of Italy in the latter part of 1799, Napoleon, who had seized power in late 1799, renewed his Italian conquests and soon secured much of Italy under his control. When Napoleon made himself Emperor of France he also placed an Italian crown on his head, thereby becoming King of Italy, with all of northern and central Italy under his authority. In the spring of 1806 French forces occupied the rest of Italy and on March 30,

1806, Napoleon's brother, Joseph, was proclaimed the King of the Two Sicilies. When Joseph became King of Spain in 1808, a French general, Joachim Murat, was crowned King of Naples.

Exit Napoleon

Although Napoleon's hold on Italy was finally broken in 1815, his legacy remained. He had decreed important reforms in the country. These included the Napoleonic Code, which together with Roman law, remains the foundation of Italian law today. He confiscated much of the Church's property, ended feudal privileges and immunities and improved roads and education. He thereby gave Italians a crucially important impetus for political, social, legal and economic reform.

The restoration of the old regime after the Congress of Vienna reestablished Austrian domination in northern and central Italy. The Pope was granted the Vatican's pre–Napoleonic holdings again and the Bourbon King, Ferdinand I of the Two Sicilies again became ruler of southern Italy. But the spark of the enlightenment, Italian nationalism and the right of Italians to establish a democratic state continued to ferment within a few secret societies of bourgeois intellectuals.

Fragmented Italy

Prince Metternich of Austria stated correctly in 1815 that Italy was not a nation, but rather a "geographic concept." The only state within Italy that played an active role in Europe was Piedmont–Savoy, where the unification movement originated. The remainder of Italy was either under foreign control or ruled by small splinter states. The parochialism that had its roots in Italian history also resisted the liberal ideas of the French Revolution and those of the few "middle and upper–class romantics" who dreamed of Italian national unification. Numerous uprisings, usually started by the secret societies against the established rulers from 1820 to 1831 were all crushed.

The revolutionary movement was not strong enough to overcome Austrian domination without outside help. The major European powers had concluded that the balance of power in Europe was more important than Italian unity. Further, the most important secret resistance movement, the *Carboneria* (literally "Charcoal Burners") had been so loosely organized, so heterogeneous and so unable to define its aims clearly that it was incapable of uniting in crucial moments.

It was these kinds of problems that certain subsequent Italian nationalists tried to avoid. The traveler to Italy notices that in every town, streets and plazas bear the

Scene typical of the Renaissance—Dante in Florence

names of Mazzini, Cavour and Garibaldi. They made up the triple constellation of the "Resurgence," the name they gave to Italian political unification in 1861.

Gradual Unification

In 1831 a young Genoan political thinker, Giuseppe Mazzini, founded the "Young Italy" movement. He had remained the intellectual head and prophet of the unification drive for a free, independent and republican Italy although he was unable to lead that movement to success. He died in 1872 bitterly disappointed about the kind of Italian state that had been created.

In 1848 uprisings again occurred throughout Italy, and the Pope was even temporarily driven out of Rome. But with the aid of French troops, the rebellion was quelled. With its failure, nationalists' eyes turned increasingly toward the Kingdom of Piedmont–Sardinia, whose capital was Turin and which was ruled by one of the oldest ruling families in Europe, the house of Savoy. It had been the only regime in Italy that had fought hard for freedom from Austria.

The new Piedmont king, Victor Emmanuel, who was to become the first king of a united Italy, was a man of rough manners and visible virility. He became a popular focus of attention for those who

wanted change. But he was also a politically shrewd man, which was revealed by his appointment as Piedmontese Prime Minister of a man whom he personally detested: Count Camillo di Cavour, not a brilliant man, but a pragmatic man who was well aware that Italy could never become independent as a result of spontaneous mass uprisings of idealists. The political hold of Austria had to be broken and he knew that Italians would need the help of a foreign power to do this. Therefore, he turned to the new French Emperor, Napoleon III.

The French leader agreed to support Piedmont in any war against Austria under the condition that in the event of victory, France be rewarded with Nice and Savoy. The deal was sealed by the marriage of Victor Emmanuel's 15–year–old daughter, Clotilde, with Napoleon's lecherous cousin, Jerome. With such a commitment tucked away in his breast pocket, Cavour sought a way to bring about war with Austria. Two blunders by the latter country played directly into Cavour's hands. One was Austria's decision to impose military conscription on its dominions of Lombardy and Venetia, a move which drove many draft–dodgers into Piedmont. The tension which arose as a result of Piedmont's refusal to turn these young men over to the Austrian authori-

ties gave Cavour the excuse he needed to begin military preparations.

The second blunder was committed just when the French Emperor was beginning to have second thoughts about the promises he had made earlier to Piedmont. In the spring of 1859 Austria issued an ultimatum to Piedmont, demanding that it either disarm itself or go to war. Cavour, of course, chose the latter, and with Napoleon's assistance faced the powerful but indecisive Austrian Army and defeated it at Magenta on June 4 and at Solferino on June 24 and conquered all Lombardy and Milan.

After these important victories, Napoleon grew weary of the war and concluded an armistice with the Austrians at Villafranca on July 11. Cavour was understandably furious at the French, but the movement toward Italian unity had gained such momentum that it could no longer be stopped. Revolutionary assemblies in Tuscany, Modena, Parma and Romagna voted in August 1859 to unite with Piedmont; France and Britain spoke out against any foreign (i.e. Austrian) intervention to foil these popular decisions. In March 1860, plebiscites in the four areas confirmed the steps taken by the assemblies. True to his earlier promise, Cavour delivered Savoy and Nice to the French.

Italy

A FOREIGN DOMINATED, POLITICALLY FRAGMENTED PENINSULA

1 DUCHY OF SAVOY
2 DUCHY OF MILAN
3 DUCHY OF MANTUA
4 DUCHY OF FERRARA

REPUBLIC OF VENICE

SAN MARINO

THE REPUBLIC OF GENOA

STATES OF THE CHURCH

CORSICA (GENOA)

ROME

THE KINGDOM OF SARDINIA (ARAGON)

THE KINGDOMS OF NAPLES AND SICILY (ARAGON)

5 DUCHY OF MODENA
6 REPUBLIC OF LUCCA
7 REPUBLIC OF FLORENCE
8 REPUBLIC OF SIENA

About 1450

SAVOY
MILAN
PIEDMONT

REPUBLIC OF VENICE

SAN MARINO

REPUBLIC OF GENOA

GRAND DUCHY OF TUSCANY

STATES OF THE CHURCH

CORSICA (GENOA)

ROME

KINGDOM OF SARDINIA

KINGDOM OF NAPLES (AUSTRIA)

KINGDOM OF SICILY (AUSTRIA)

1 MANTUA
2 PARMA AND MODENA

About 1722

NAPOLEON'S "KINGDOM OF ITALY" (1804–13)

FRANCE

SAN MARINO

OCCUPIED BY FRANCE

CORSICA (FRANCE)

ROME

KINGDOM OF NAPLES (France, 1806–13)

KINGDOM OF SARDINIA

KINGDOM OF SICILY

Under Napoleon, 1804–13

LOMBARDY (FROM AUSTRIA)
VENETIA

PIEDMONT

SAN MARINO

GRAND DUCHY OF TUSCANY

STATES OF THE CHURCH

CORSICA (FRANCE)

ROME

KINGDOM OF SARDINIA

NAPLES

KINGDOM OF THE TWO SICILIES (RULED BY SPANISH BOURBONS)

SICILY

1 PARMA
2 MODENA
3 LUCCA

The Unification of Italy, 1849–70

Southern Unification

With most of northern and central Italy now unified, the cauldron of unification began to bubble in the South. In the spring of 1860 revolts broke out in Sicily that gave a highly talented military adventurer his chance to reenter the center stage in Italy—Giuseppe Garibaldi. A former member of Mazzini's "Young Italy" movement, he had spent 13 years as a soldier of fortune in Latin America, where he became a master in the leadership of irregular forces and guerrilla warfare. He had raced back to Italy in 1848 when he heard of the revolutionary activity there. He formed military forces first in Lombardy, then in Venice and finally in Rome, where he served under Mazzini to defend the Roman Republic which had just been created. From April to the end of June 1849, Garibaldi's legion, clad in red shirts and Calabrian hats, had defended the "Eternal City" valiantly against French troops that protected the Pope. Prolonged resistance had proved to be impossible, so Garibaldi fled with his troops to the tiny independent republic of San Marino, where he disbanded his army and went into exile.

Revolts in Sicily in 1860 again drew him into southern Italy and in May he packed his 1,000 irregulars, mostly students, poets and soldiers of fortune, into rickety steamers and set a course directly to Sicily. When he arrived at Marsala, he declared himself dictator of Sicily and proceeded to defeat piecemeal the confused and divided Neapolitan troops that were supposed to defend the island. By mid–July he poised for his strike against the Bourbon Kingdom of the Two Sicilies with its capital in Naples.

Riding a tide of popular enthusiasm, Garibaldi's army, which had swollen to 10,000 men, crossed the Strait of Messina in mid–1860, and his units produced panic among the Neapolitan troops whenever they appeared. On September 7, a jubilant Garibaldi entered the city of Naples far in advance of his troops. In less than five months he had conquered the Kingdom of the Two Sicilies, a country of 11 million inhabitants.

He immediately set his sights again on Rome, which was still defended by French troops. Not wishing to lose entirely the initiative for unifying Italy, Cavour ordered his own troops to march southward into the Papal States. On September 18 they crushed the Pope's forces at Castelfidardo and then defeated a remaining Neapolitan Army at Capua. These successes prompted the Piedmontese parliament to annex southern Italy. In October plebiscites in Naples, Sicily, the Marches and Umbria revealed overwhelming popular support for union with Piedmont. In February 1861 Victor Emmanuel II was proclaimed King of Italy, and a new Italian parliament representing the entire peninsula except Rome and the province of Venetia assembled. Shortly thereafter Florence became Italy's new capital until 1870.

Differences Among the Union

The historical differences between northern and southern Italy were not overcome through the unification and establishment of a monarchy. Despite the initial enthusiasm in southern Italy for joining the newly unified state, the northern rulers considered the southern half of

Garibaldi

the autonomous Italian national state more as a conquered province of the North. They displayed little respect for traditional practices in the South, regarding the people as backward and rural, and merely included it in a highly centralized governmental administration that was imposed on all of Italy. Therefore, the Italian King's popularity in the South disappeared almost overnight, and southerners again began to look northward with distrust and resentment that has yet to disappear.

The new national leaders next turned to the province of Venetia, which was still in the clutches of the Austrian Empire. When the latter entered a war in 1866 against Prussia, however, Italy immediately sided with the victorious Prussians, who granted their allies the prize Italians had wanted. Only Rome remained outside the new Italy.

The End of the Church State

The ecclesiastical state, under the Pope, remained a drop of melancholy in the wine of the unification. The Vatican resented the reduction of its secular power

Monument in Rome commemorating the unification of Italy

Italy

in the unification of Italy. As the new Italian state was officially declared in 1861, it was taboo even to speak of Piedmont and that part of Italy ruled by it. But when France became locked in war against Prussia in 1870, French troops could no longer defend Rome against the rest of Italy. Hence, in September royal Italian troops marched into Rome unchallenged, and the national capital was transferred to the city without delay.

The ecclesiastical state came to an end, and the popes withdrew in bitterness behind the Vatican walls with utter contempt for the Italian kingdom. This Papal rejection of the Italian state nipped in the bud all attempts to integrate Catholic elements in politics, and the Catholic prohibition against political participation gained strength especially in the more independent–minded South. It hardened many Italians' distrust toward their state, a problem that remains today. Leading liberals asserted their strong anticlerical position despite the Church's opposition. Only in the first decade of the 20th century did the Church support a Catholic People's Party (the *Popolari*), a forerunner of the now defunct Christian Democratic Party. Those historians are certainly correct who argue that an earlier integration of moderate Catholic forces would have helped stabilize Italy's political system and would have helped to prevent the later rise of fascism.

Continued Instability

The first years of unification were overshadowed by political instability, social opposition and an ever–growing gap between North and South. The inhabitants of the South continued to be looked down upon as backward, illiterate semi–North Africans. The people were also disadvantaged by the new liberal leaders' dropping of trade barriers, which clearly favored the industrially powerful North.

The one–crop agrarian society of the South bore the full economic weight of foreign grain imports. Malnutrition, health problems and child labor abuse set in motion an enormous emigration wave from the South. From 1886 to 1890 over 200,000 people left their homeland every year, most of whom sought refuge in the United States. Today, 25 million Americans are of Italian and/or Sicilian descent. The fact that most of their ancestors came from southern Italy helps explain why Americans often have a one–sided view of Italy, namely that of the impoverished South rather than the more opulent North.

Parliamentary proceedings degenerated quickly as deputies became so concerned about clinging to their seats that they avoided taking clear-cut stands on the pressing issues of the day. By means of a method which came to be known as *Trasformismo* ("Transformism"), prime ministers and cabinets disregarded party affiliation and made delicate bargains with any interested deputies from the left, right or center in order to patch together a short–lived parliamentary majority. In the process, all political groups became highly fractured, and cabinets changed so constantly that no coherent and consistent governmental policy was possible. Major questions were avoided or postponed, and when domestic pressure for change became too great, governments tended to divert attention from them by taking refuge in such emotional campaigns as anticlericalism or colonialism.

Colonial Ambitions

In order to cope with the problem of a surplus of workers and to divert attention from the domestic political paralysis and tensions, Italy embarked on a colonial policy which was not only unprofitable, but which robbed it of its strength. After a casualty–ridden expedition into the East African coast of Eritrea (formerly in Ethiopia), Italy temporarily conquered this area in 1889–90. A subsequent campaign in Ethiopia ended in catastrophe soon thereafter, costing the lives of 15,000 poorly–equipped soldiers when the Ethiopians drove them out. Italy took Libya and the southeastern Greek islands (Dodecanese) from Turkey, which was in the process of disintegration.

All of these foreign adventures could not distract from the domestic social tensions and conflicts. Rebellions, violent protests, assassinations and bloody reactions against the forces of order became so commonplace by the turn of the century that many observers believed that the young kingdom could not survive.

The most outstanding politician in the early 20th century was Giovanni Giolitti, who tried to fuse the liberal bourgeoisie and socialists who supported the state from 1903 to 1915. He was able to guide some progressive legislation through a highly undisciplined parliament. Factory laws were passed, insurance companies and railways were nationalized, trade unions were legalized, agricultural cooperatives were subsidized and collective bargaining was encouraged. However, he could not overcome the widespread impression among the people that Italy was not only standing still, but was decaying.

Sick and tired of these internal conflicts, a movement of bourgeois intellectuals under the leadership of the poet Gabriele D'Annunzio, and the political thinkers Gaetano Mosca and Vilfredo Pareto gained respect, and practically declared war on the parliamentary system. D'Annunzio called on young Italians to seek fulfillment in violent action that would put an end to parliamentary maneuvering, general mediocrity and dullness that characterized public life. Mosca and Pareto called for a new political elite that understood how to use power and to put an end to materialist values.

A jingoist National Party was created in 1910 under the leadership of Enrico Corradini, who never tired of painting an attractive picture of martial heroism, of total sacrifice of individualism and equality to one's nation, of the need for reestablishing discipline and obedience, of the grandeur and power of ancient Rome and of the personal gratification which comes with living dangerously. Many Italians, who needed only the travails of a long and disappointing war to make a dangerous leap toward fascism, heard its extremist appeals with enthusiasm.

World War I

Although Italy had allied itself with Germany and Austria–Hungary in 1882, it declared its neutrality at the outbreak of World War I in 1914 on the grounds that its allies were waging an aggressive war. For more than ten years it had pursued, under Giolitti's leadership, a policy of peaceful reconciliation in Europe. Italy did, in fact, enter World War I against Austria and Germany in 1915. In Hemingway's *A Farewell to Arms*, one sees that the Italian war against Austria was neither easily won nor advantageous for Italy. It lost 600,000 men in battle, and the Italian economy was wrecked by the war. The public debt swelled, inflation ran out of control and many of the demobilized soldiers left one kind of army for another: that of the unemployed.

To make things worse, the aftermath of the Paris peace settlement following the war never fulfilled Italy's high expectations. Trentino and the city of Trieste became part of the country, as did the Istrian Peninsula (in former Yugoslavia) and the German–speaking part of South Tirol, which even today remains a bone of contention between Austria and Italy.

Postwar Chaos

Italy had entered the post World War I era as a society badly off balance. Without relief, lawlessness in the countryside and towns, strikes in the cities as well as sharp and often violent domestic differences of opinion, polarized the political scene. The war had brought revolution in Russia, and with that revolution a breaking away in Italy and elsewhere of radically revolutionary communists from the more

Italy

moderate socialist parties. The establishment of the Communist Party of Italy (PCI) scared many anti–Marxist Italians, who became sympathetic to the idea of a strong leader who could protect Italy from the communist revolution. This included many wealthy landowners and industrialists.

The war had also frustrated the dreams of many Italian nationalists, who had believed that Italy should become a major Mediterranean and Balkan power. Millions of returning veterans were bitter about the fact that their country seemed to show no appreciation for the suffering and sacrifice they had endured. Even appearing on the streets in uniform was bound to evoke abuse. Finally, the traditional Italian parties and elites were almost wholly incapable of coping with the domestic political situation. Therefore, a vacuum and a constituency were created for a charismatic opportunist with extremely flexible principles and an emotionally appealing, but intellectually fraudulent political theory: Benito Mussolini.

Mussolini and the Fascists

Born the son of a blacksmith and a schoolteacher in 1883, Mussolini had been educated in a seminary, but had been expelled because he reportedly stabbed another student. After teaching school for a few years, he fled to Switzerland in order to avoid military service. He grew tired of exile after a couple of years and returned to Italy to serve in the army, rising like Hitler to the rank of corporal. He then became a journalist, an activity he performed quite effectively and which helped launch a meteoric career in Socialist politics. In 1911 he was jailed briefly for his inflammatory articles against Italy's colonial policy in North Africa, and in 1912 he was named editor–in–chief of the major Socialist Party newspaper, *Avanti!* ("Forward") of Milan. His writings and speeches sometimes took excursions into anarchism, and they were always radical. At the Socialist Party congress at Reggio in mid–1912, he was among those party members who vehemently rejected a moderate course for the party and insisted that socialism must destroy the "bourgeois experiment" of democracy.

He never veered from his bitter opposition to liberal democracy, but after the outbreak of World War I, he revealed how fluid his political convictions really were. Unlike his former socialist comrades, he strongly supported Italy's involvement in the war. He maintained that it was one of the country's finest hours and that the conniving, greedy politicians at home had betrayed the young heroes. He had coined the slogan "war or revolution," which clearly presented the only alternatives as

he saw them. The moving and persuasive eloquence with which he used the Italian language, his undeniable charisma and showmanship and his appearance of raw manliness (although he was in reality often a timid man in times of crisis when daring moves needed to be taken) greatly appealed to the lost, the frightened and the bored.

They flocked to the many loosely–knit *Fasci* (groups) that sprang into existence in imitation of the *Fascio di combattimento* (fighting group), which Mussolini had founded in Milan in 1919. Mussolini wanted to weld a coalition with the non–communist left, but he found little support for such a union. It took a couple of years for him to gain full control of the fascist movement, named after the Latin word *fasces*, which meant a bundle of sticks around an ax, an ancient Roman symbol of state authority. Not until 1921 was the Fascist Party formally created. Mussolini quickly saw that the government's inability or unwillingness to step in and bring the rural and industrial violence under control offered a welcome opportunity for the Fascists to present themselves as the protectors of life, property, law and order.

His *Squadristi* (black–shirted bully squads) roamed the streets unimpeded and intimidated voters and opponents. When the Socialists proclaimed a general strike in August 1922, the Italian public became exasperated with this newest in a series of crippling strikes. It did nothing

as the Fascists sacked or smashed trade union or Socialist party headquarters and presses all over Italy, including those of *Avanti!*, the paper which Mussolini once edited. They also seized control of the city councils in Cremona, Ferrara, Livorno, Parma and Ravenna. These brazen, but unopposed acts were merely the prelude to a Fascist *coup d'état* that had been long–planned.

After delicate negotiations with royalist and Church circles to assure their acquiescence, Mussolini mobilized his Black Shirts for a "March on Rome" on October 22, 1922. Mussolini demonstrated that he was not entirely confident such a seizure of power would succeed by remaining close to the Swiss border in order to be able to escape into exile just in case the march failed. The prime minister tried to persuade King Victor Emmanuel III to sign a declaration of martial law in order to deal with the crisis, but the latter refused. Informed that there would be no resistance whatsoever, Mussolini took a night train to Rome, where the King appointed him prime minister. After so much violence and lawlessness, Rome fell to the Fascists without a shot being fired. This outrageous act of political adventurers would have been foiled if the forces of order had only shown the smallest bit of courage.

Step by step, Mussolini (who named himself Il Duce—"The Leader") transformed Italy into the first European dictatorship outside of Russia. He combined

Benito Mussolini—*Il Duce*

229

Italy

Mussolini and his "Black Shirts"

workers, employers and other groups into organizations called corporations. This corporate structure was intended to convey the mistaken impression that class and other social conflicts had been or were being eliminated. It therefore was used to justify the abolition of trade unions and strikes, which were allegedly no longer necessary to protect workers.

His power was insured through the introduction of censorship, a strict administration, a youth movement led by the state, a sham one–party electoral system, the incarceration of all political opponents and the creation of a feared secret police (OVRA). The slogan *"credere, obbedire, combattere"* ("believe, obey, fight") reflected the new ideal. Although the King remained on the throne and the bicameral parliament was permitted to go through the motions as if it were functioning, all power by 1925 rested with Mussolini and his Fascist Party, whose organization reached from 10,000 *Fasci* (local) party groups all the way up to a Fascist Grand Council of about 20 men. All other parties were outlawed.

Fascist "Theory" and Administration

In the Fascist ideology Mussolini had helped to concoct, freedom had allegedly been created through authoritarianism, and nobility and heroism had been estab-

lished through discipline and sacrifice. The state was glorified, and liberalism, democracy and socialism were condemned. On top of that allegedly well–ordered state stood the leader, Mussolini, a man with a knack for sensationalism, self–dramatization, effective oratory and heavy–handedness toward those who were weaker than he. The subsequent persecution of all opposition forces was restrained in comparison to the terror in Nazi Germany.

The dead–end policies to establish an autarkical (internationally independent) economy corrupted the initial economic successes resulting from protective tariffs and grandiose state-sponsored projects. The antiquated relationships of the property owners toward the peasants in the agrarian South remained unaffected, and the power of the Mafia was temporarily broken. Of far–reaching importance, however, were the Lateran Treaties (Feb. 11, 1929) with the Vatican. Mussolini settled the long–standing dispute with the Church over its role in Italian politics by granting it extensive opportunities to influence political and social affairs within Italy (see Vatican City State).

World War II

Italy was ill prepared for the wars it fought, at first on a small scale against

Ethiopia in 1935, and then later against Germany's enemies in World War II. After Mussolini's attempts to conquer Albania and Greece in 1941 had failed, Italy and the Duce became more dependent upon Hitler than the Italians had intended. Their initial enthusiasm about the adventure of war soon turned to resignation and disappointment. Although Italy was supposedly a "partner" in the Axis, Hitler and the Germans in some ways considered it as much a problem as an asset insofar as the war effort was concerned. Although Mussolini was arrogant and boastful in public, he was rather timid in reality.

Things got worse when the Americans, British and Canadians began to launch successful attacks against the Italian homeland. In mid–1943 British and Canadian forces landed on the east coast of Sicily and took Syracuse, while General George S. Patton's troops landed in the south of the island and took Marsala and Palermo. They then joined the British forces to expel the Germans who were in control of Sicily. The allies next turned toward the Italian mainland and began bombing Rome on July 19.

The sober reality of war right in the city of Rome brought the downfall of Mussolini. The Fascist Grand Council, formerly a malleable tool in Mussolini's

Italy

hands, which had not met since 1939, demanded his resignation, which the King ordered the next day. The former *Duce* was arrested as he left the royal palace, but German paratroopers rescued him later in a daring, precision operation. Totally at the mercy of Germans, Mussolini eked out a temporary existence as head of a puppet fascist state in German–occupied northern Italy until April 28, 1945, when communist partisans murdered him and publicly hanged him and his mistress upside down. A few days later, his protector, Hitler, shot himself and had his body burned in Berlin to escape such ignoble public treatment.

Unfortunately, long, drawn–out negotiations in the summer of 1943 between the Anglo–American allies and the new Italian government under Marshal Pietro Badoglio enabled the Germans to improve their defenses in Italy. Therefore, when an armistice could finally be signed and an amphibious assault could be launched the very same day against the mainland on September 3, 1943, the Germans were well–prepared. The British Eighth Army under General Montgomery landed with little difficulty on the coast of Calabria. By contrast, the American landing at Salerno thereafter was resisted fiercely and almost ended in disaster.

The rugged and hilly Italian terrain, combined with the dogged German resistance under Marshal Kesselring, rendered every mile of northward advance in the Peninsula painful and costly. The Germans had dug in their heels along the so–called Gustav Line, in the center of which was located the almost impregnable 1,700 foot (510 meter) tall Monte Cassino, which guarded the road through the Liri valley toward Rome. In order to try to circumvent these formidable defenses, the Americans made another amphibious landing at Anzio, located only 33 miles (53 km.) south of Rome. But the American troops were pinned to the slopes overlooking the beach under murderous fire for four months until they could finally break free. In April 1944 Monte Cassino finally fell at the cost of thousands of American lives and after the allies had made the much–criticized decision to bomb the Benedictine abbey there, which the Germans were effectively using for observation purposes.

In June 1944 allied troops entered Rome. When seven allied divisions were withdrawn shortly thereafter in order to take part in an amphibious landing in southern France, the possibility of driving the German armies entirely out of Italy quickly disappeared. Italy therefore remained partially occupied by the Germans until the end of the war. On the plus side, the Italian invasion

Uniformed police—*carabinieri*　　　Courtesy: Jon Markham Morrow

diverted German troops which otherwise would have been available elsewhere. Tactically, it was a very costly mistake, since Italy presented no threat, and the very terrain made it a defender's battlefield, not an invader's. This is reflected in the tremendous number of allied casualties.

The Italian resistance to the Axis powers was militarily significant in the course of the war. After the war the resistance became a symbol of solidarity, and it should have helped the Italians to put aside some of their many regional, political and social differences. Unfortunately, the adhesive effect of the resistance proved to be weaker and more transitory than many had hoped.

After the war, Italy found itself again in the strange position of being both the conqueror and the conquered. Regular troops and partisan units had fought against the Germans ever since the fall of Mussolini in mid–1943. However, the fact that this same Italy had been an ally of Nazi Germany and had led attacks against Albania, Yugoslavia and Greece, had not been forgotten. In contrast to Germany, Italy was able to preserve its national unity, but this was due chiefly to the crucial assistance of the influential Italians living in the United States.

The peace treaty that took effect September 15, 1947, required Italy to renounce all claims on Ethiopia and Greece and to cede the Dodecanese Islands back to Greece and five small Alpine areas to France. In addition, the Istrian Peninsula (including Fiume and Pola) was awarded to Yugoslavia. The Trieste area west of the

new Yugoslav territory was made a free city until 1954, when it and a 90–square–mile (135 sq. km.) zone was transferred to Italy and the remainder to Yugoslavia. In addition, Italy was required to pay reparations to the Soviet Union and Albania.

GOVERNMENT

A majority of Italian voters in a national referendum held in June 1946 chose to abolish the monarchy and to establish a democratic republic. Not until 56 years later, in 2002, did parliament agree that the ban against Italy's male royalty from entering the country would be lifted. Victor Emmanual, who left Italy at age nine, pledged allegiance to the Italian republic. He and his son Emmanuel Filiberto, live in Switzerland.

With the unpleasant memories of a dictator and a rigid one–party state fresh in their minds, the framers of the post–war constitution made two important decisions which have made it difficult for the country's political institutions to cope with some of Italy's festering economic and social problems. First, they greatly curtailed the powers of the head of government in order to make the reemergence of a dictator almost impossible. Second, they adopted the proportional representation system of voting that gave parliamentary seats to as many parties as possible.

Italy is a highly centralized, unitary state. As in France, the prefect in each of the 106 provinces is appointed by and accountable to the central government. The 20 regions each elect regional parliaments and wield limited political power,

231

Italy

but they still are chiefly administrative units for the central government. Five of these regions have had special statutes for a long time: Sicily, Sardinia, Valle d'Aosta, Friuli–Venezia Giulia, and Trentino–Alto Adige. Within the latter region are two partly German-speaking special provinces, Trento and Bolzano, that enjoy autonomy. The other 15 were created in 1970. This broadening of regional government led an actual decentralization of political power in Italy. In 2001 there was further devolution of power in the regions, approved in a referendum. The reform made the 20 regions responsible for everything, including raising taxes, not constitutionally granted to the central government in Rome.

Political Crisis

A political earthquake is occurring in Italy that has brought about profound changes in the country's parliamentary system and party politics. Italians have always known that there was corruption in high places, but what they have now learned is taking their breaths away. It began in 1991 with the arrest of a Socialist Party official in Milan (Mario Chiesa) who was caught taking bribes on a cleaning contract in a home for the elderly. But it developed into an explosion that is demolishing the nation's entire political order.

Investigations (called "Operation Clean Hands") into embezzlement, illicit bribes, and kick–backs to political parties and politicians in return for public–works contracts have produced the greatest public corruption scandal in modern European history. The estimated $11 billion in annual rip-offs was equivalent to the government's annual deficit. The investigations also uncovered possible evidence that the Mafia and top government leaders might have been cooperating for years. None of the traditional parties escaped unharmed; all were discredited.

Until the collapse of communism in Europe, Italians had grudgingly tolerated misgovernment by leaders mainly preoccupied with party intrigue and devious fund–raising because it seemed like the alternative would have been rule by the Communist Party of Italy, which had discomforting links with the Soviet Union. With that danger gone, most Italians see no reason not to confront head on the rot in the political establishment. By mid-1993, more than 2,600 persons in the political and business elite, including top corporate executives, party chairmen, and three former prime ministers, had either been arrested or were under investigation. Entire regional and local governments had been jailed or forced to resign.

Voters' disgust came to a head in an historic referendum on April 18–19, 1993.

Voting on eight separate questions, over 90% voted to abolish state financing of political parties, and 83% chose to scrap the system of proportional representation in the Senate. Designed in the post–fascist era to prevent another single party, such as Mussolini's, from gaining power, this system created government by weak coalitions of quarrelsome partners and by an oligarchy of often corrupt party leaders. In a 1999 referendum, 91% voted to abolish the proportional representation system used to distribute 25% of the seats in the lower house, the Chamber of Deputies. But since only 49.6% turned out to vote, just shy of the 50% required, the balloting was not valid. Many of the more than 40 parties that compete for seats were pleased with the result. The same happened in May 2000 when only 32% of voters turned out for seven referenda, including one to abolish proportional representation. This disappointing outcome raised questions anew about the effectiveness of trying to break the country's long-standing political gridlock through a direct appeal to voters.

Voters abolished the ministries of industry, agriculture and tourism, as well as political appointments of state savings–bank directors; all had been favorite conduits of patronage. The 1993 referendum was a stunning rebuke to politicians and their machinery of power. Operation Clean Hands officially came to an end in 2003. However, in the preceding decade all of the institutions and parties discussed below had been changed or influenced by the rage and determination that had been and still are being expressed.

Parliament

Italy is a parliamentary democracy with a bicameral legislature. The Chamber of Deputies is composed of 630 members elected until 1994 by proportional representation in 32 electoral districts at least every five years. The Senate is composed of 315 members. Every five years members representing the 20 regions (the exceptions being the valley of Aosta, which sends a senator and the province of Molise, which sends two) are elected. Beginning in 1994, 75% in both houses are elected directly, while a fourth enter under the old system of proportional representation. In contrast to the Chamber of Deputies, the Senate contains some non–elected members. Every ex–president of the republic is a senator for life, and five other senators are appointed for life.

Both houses have identical powers. Both function and make decisions independently, and both must pass a bill before it is forwarded to the largely ceremonial president of the Republic for signature. The legislative system is slow

and cumbersome, making passage of laws difficult. Because of the electoral system, almost the same constellation of parties is represented in both chambers with the same proportion of parties in the standing committees. The Senate has 11 such committees and the Chamber of Deputies 14. In both houses party politics determines all aspects of the legislative process.

Since 1988 party discipline is easier to maintain because of the elimination of secret voting, which had permitted dissidents to vote anonymously against their own parties and bring down their own governments; the result was perennially weak government. Secret balloting had been one stumbling block to efficient rule under a constitution that had been designed four decades ago primarily to prevent another Mussolini from coming to power. From 1968 to 1996-2001 no Italian legislature had lived its full five–year life.

Presidency

The president, who is elected by the members of both houses of parliament for a seven–year term, can veto a law, but a simple majority in both houses can override his veto. The *immobilismo* of the party system and the inability to form governing majorities to handle Italy's ever–increasing problems prompted suggestions that the constitution be changed in order to create a presidential democracy on the French model.

The presidency is gaining in influence even without constitutional change. In 1991 Francesco Cossiga grew tired of his figure–head role and proclaimed his intention "to shake a few pebbles out of my shoes." He startled the nation by becoming more involved in everyday politics. His moves were highly unorthodox and caused a storm of controversy. In 1992 he decided to give "a shock to the polit-

President Carlo Azeglio Ciampi

ical classes" by resigning two months before his term ended. He charged that Italy's traditional politicians had ignored the electorate's reform message in the parliamentary elections that month. Facing a crisis which had paralyzed Italy's major parties, his successor, Oscar Luigi Scalfaro, broke long–standing practices in 1993 by not consulting the ruling parties before selecting the first prime minister not to belong to a political party: Carlo Azeglio Ciampi, a respected civil servant and head of the independent Bank of Italy. Scalfaro charged Ciampi with enacting sweeping political reform, trimming the budget, and then bowing out after early elections. In the past, party leaders dictated the political direction to president. But in 1993 it was President Scalfaro who delivered the marching orders to the party chiefs. In May 1999 Ciampi, whose hobby is German literature, became president.

Normally the most delicate political act in which the president is fully involved is the formation of a cabinet. A prospective candidate for the prime ministerial post is charged by the president to form a government. The prospective candidate suggests the composition of the new government after extensive consultations with the possible coalition partners. Whether the prime minister can win and maintain a majority for his cabinet in both chambers is always the decisive question.

Political Parties and Alliances

In June 2001 Italy installed its fifty-ninth government since World War II. The average duration of each has been seven months, although things improved in the 1980s insofar as longevity was concerned. All governments have been coalitions that are forever shifting, with disagreement on a single point bringing down an administration. To understand why Italian governments are so unstable, one must examine the basic party structure and the consequences of the electoral system.

The multi–party system is highly fragmented, but for the 1996 elections many of the numerous parties grouped themselves into two loose alliances, which the *Washington Post* aptly described as "not coalitions but collages, fragments of political movements thrown together without a cogent denominator other than the aim of power. As such they are prone to instability."

On the political right are the parties that formed the Freedom Alliance, which had won the 1994 elections, but declined in 1996 from 366 to 246 seats in the Chamber of Deputies and 155 to 116 in the Senate. They are the totally new Forza Italia ("Go, Italy!"), the National Alliance (formerly

the neo–fascist Italian Social Movement—MSI), the Christian Democratic Center Party, a breakaway minority from the former ruling Christian Democrats, and the Northern League. In April/May 2001 this alliance ran as the House of Freedoms and won the elections by capturing 367 seats. Silvio Berlusconi's Forza Italia alone increased its vote to 30%, while the National Alliance fell to 12%.

In the center are the Italian Popular Party (PPI, formerly the Christian Democrats—DC), the Italian Republican Party (PRI), the Italian Liberal Party (PLI), the Social Democratic Party of Italy (PSDI) and Italian Renewal. In 1994 most had formed an electoral alliance called Pact for Italy, which won only 16% of the votes. In 2001 it ceased to be relevant.

On the left are the Democratic Party of the Left (PDS, formerly the Communist Party of Italy—PCI—and renamed Democrats of the Left—DS), The *Margherita* (Daisy) led by Francesco Rutelli (a former Green Mayor of Rome), the hard-line Refounded Communist Party, the small Italian Communists Party, that broke off from the preceding party in 1998, Socialist Unity, formerly part of the Socialist Party of Italy—PSI), the Socialist Party of Proletarian Unity (PSIUP), the anti-Mafia party in Sicily, La Rete (the Network), and the Greens. For the 1994 elections the leftist parties formed the Progressive bloc, which won a third of the votes.

In 1996 the center and left combined forces to form an "Olive Tree" coalition, a patchwork of ex-Communists, liberals, greens, some former Christian Democrats, and a few independents. Together they made history. By capturing 40% of the votes in April 1996, they became Italy's first leftist government, under the PPI's Romano Prodi. They broke a long-standing taboo by including nine former Communists from the DS in the ruling coalition,

Prime Minister Silvio Berlusconi

more than from any other party. The Communists have not always been easy partners. In 2001 Olive Tree dropped to 39% of the total votes and 248 seats. DS won 16% of the votes and Rutelli's Daisy 14.5%.

By 2003 the center-left was in disarray, and it lacked a single recognized leader. It was unable to capitalize on the government's support of a 2003 U.S.-British war in Iraq that most Italians opposed. It was also divided over the question of whether to send 1,000 Alpine troops to Afghanistan for peacekeeping duties. Nor can it agree on reforming the country's pension system, which swallows 16% of Italy's GDP and is still growing as the birth rate falls. All groups in the left have their own daily newspapers in which they passionately debate issues in which the average voters have little or no interest.

Until 1993, when the entire political landscape began to change, the political fronts in Italy were polarized and somewhat rigid. The problem was that parties cornering roughly a third of the vote—the DS and the MSI—were unacceptable as coalition partners, leaving only two–thirds within which to find a majority. Neither of the two largest parties was capable of winning a majority. No governing coalition could be formed without the participation of the Christian Democrats and the Socialists. Together with the Social Democrats, the Liberals and sometimes the Republicans, these two parties could paste together a wobbly temporary majority in parliament composed of five parties (called the *Pentapartito*), which were generally more interested in their own survival and in delivering maximum benefits to their own special constituencies than in providing stable government capable of dealing with Italy's pressing problems.

The DC and the Socialists were never natural partners, for reasons of ideology and strategy. Any coalition between them was by nature unstable because the partners were fierce competitors. The DC could not win a majority by itself, and most Italians did not accept the Communists as ready for a place in the government. Thus, about a dozen small parties held the balance. This insured incoherence and produced a string of short–lived governments with narrow attention spans.

Even elections could not always produce a government; they could produce only the raw materials for one. They seldom settled questions; they merely deferred them. Following elections, an acceptable coalition, composed almost invariably of the same parties which were in the last one, was hammered together only after a drawn–out process of bargaining. It could take weeks or months until the many demands of powerful party

Italy

The Italian Chamber of Deputies (630 members)

APRIL 1996 ELECTIONS

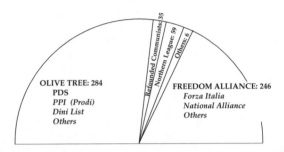

OLIVE TREE: 284
PDS
PPI (Prodi)
Dini List
Others

Refounded Communists: 35
Northern League: 59
Others: 6

FREEDOM ALLIANCE: 246
Forza Italia
National Alliance
Others

APRIL 2001 ELECTIONS

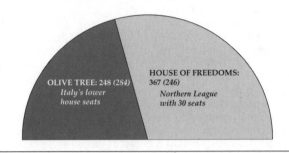

OLIVE TREE: 248 *(284)*
*Italy's lower
house seats*

HOUSE OF FREEDOMS:
367 *(246)*
*Northern League
with 30 seats*

> The Chamber of Deputies is confusingly composed of shifting political party alliances, sometimes, as in 1996, blending right and left. A perfect example is the *Olive Tree*. In order to secure the prime ministership, Prodi's *Italian Popular Party* (formerly called *Christian Democrats*) had to draw from both sides of the political spectrum.

and factional leaders had been satisfied and balanced. While there was a certain stability inherent in this process, the damage to the political system is clear. Widespread corruption and cynicism toward rulers flourished in a fragmented political scene in which politicians were well entrenched with little possibility of being displaced. Nobody expected major changes. One voter remarked before the 1992 polling, "we all know that when the vote is counted we will be right back where we started." The same could certainly not be said of the 1994 elections.

THE RIGHT

Forza Italia

The historic 1994 elections not only produced a parliament in which nearly 80% of the members had never served before and a cabinet in which most members had no previous ministerial experience, they resulted in a governing coalition composed of a party which had not existed six months earlier, a federalist regional group from the North dedicated to weakening the central government, and a former fascist pariah organization which had been carefully excluded from power in Rome for a half century.

None is a conventional political party. Apart from their populist streaks and opposition to the left, they have little in common. The essential prerequisite for this dramatic turnabout was the two–year corruption investigation involving kickbacks from government contracts that ensnared most of Italy's political elite and discredited the Christian Democrats and their traditional ruling partners.

Forza Italia's name was derived from a soccer slogan, "Go, Italy!" At the head of this movement is one of Italy's richest men, Silvio Berlusconi, a entrepre-

neurial superstar whose business empire, Fininvest, includes three TV networks dominating commercial television, Italy's largest department store chain, the top–selling newsmagazine, and an array of other investments, including the AC Milan soccer club, which has become one of the world's best. His opponents charge that he misused his three TV networks, which control 45% of the Italian audience, to propagandize voters. They also claim that a politician with such vast and varied investments cannot escape from conflicts of interest. A man with telegenic good looks, enormous energy and determination, and an excellent business brain, he called for "a new Italian miracle" which would flow from his program of fostering private enterprise, slashing red tape and debt, introducing a flat–rate tax system, and creating a million new jobs.

Like most of the party's office–holders, Berlusconi had never even run for public office before. He claimed to have been forced into politics "to keep my country from falling into the hands of the communists." Centrist reformers had failed to organize an effective bloc to the powerful momentum the communists had displayed in the 1993 municipal elections. Despite inexperience, Forza Italia won about a fourth of the votes and did especially well among young voters. After the elections Berlusconi said: "I know the young generation well. They grew up seeing America through the television shows that I brought to Europe. They have come to believe in the meritocratic philosophy that will help us develop a more liberal and free–market society without losing our cultural roots or traditions."

Its deputies tend to be young, ambitious professionals and business people who helped change the character of the parliament by lowering the average age (40%

under age 50 and 25% under 40), raising the percentage of university graduates to 75, and increasing the number of women representatives from 51 to 93 (of whom 47 are from the three conservative ruling parties). Forza Italia found itself sandwiched between the autonomy–seeking Northern League, with its roots in the rich and industrialized Lombardy region around Milan (Berlusconi's home town), and the National Alliance, whose voters are concentrated in the impoverished South and who advocate a strong central government.

This heterogeneous coalition could not give Italy what has eluded it for more than four decades: stable government. In December 1994 it collapsed after only eight months when the Northern League walked out. Berlusconi had refused to separate himself from his business empire. In June he had accused the three state–owned RAI TV channels of hostile editorial policy and forced the RAI board to resign. When he was formally placed under investigation for his business dealings, including tax fraud and corruption, he could no longer survive as prime minister.

His quarrelsome government was replaced by one of non–elected technocrats, with Lamberto Dini, a taciturn ex–banker and treasury minister under Berlusconi, with no party affiliation, as prime minister. Dini promised to introduce reforms, especially of the under funded pension system, and to cut government spending, and then to call new elections. In the 1996 elections, Forza Italia slipped only slightly, from 21% to 20.6% of the votes, but the larger Freedom Alliance lost 120 of its 366 lower house seats and won only 116 of 315 Senate seats. In 2001 Berlusconi's House of Freedoms bloc shot up to 367 lower-house seats.

Berlusconi was convicted in 1997 for false accounting (though his 16–month sentence was commuted), and he faced five more trials on counts ranging from bribing tax inspectors who were auditing his businesses to illicit soccer transfers. In 1998 he was sentenced to two years and nine months in prison for bribery although his parliamentary immunity and the appeals process keep him out of jail. In 2000 a Milan judge threw out the charge that he had bribed judges, but allegations of corruption and false accounting were still pending as he entered the May 2001 elections. Two years on, he was still struggling to free himself from legal entanglements. In May 2003 he became the first sitting Italian prime minister to be called to give testimony as a criminal defendant in his own bribery trial. Afterwards he sent agents of the state-controlled TV network, RAI, to question its staff for allegedly mocking him during his embarrassing trial by broadcasting the insults of a protester. His close friend and former defense minister, Cesare Previti, was sentenced to 11 years in prison for bribing judges to favor Berlusconi's business empire. He used his majority in parliament to pass laws that make prosecuting corruption cases more difficult. They include a retroactive measure to restrict the use of evidence gathered abroad, especially secret bank account records, the decriminalizing of false bookkeeping convictions, amnesty for illegal transfer of funds outside Italy, change of venue for trials away from judges who are "legitimately suspected" of bias, and immunity for the country's top five posts from facing trial while they hold office. As of mid-2003 he had not yet enacted a law to deal with his conflicts of interest, and his family had still not divested itself of the nation's three largest private TV channels. In any other democratic country he would probably have been forced to step down, but not in Italy. Not only has his popularity not suffered, but a poll published in *Corriere delle Sera*, revealed that only a third of Italians trust the judicial system.

He was confident that he could put into practice the prescriptions he described in his book: *The Italy I Have in Mind*. He was not disappointed. His House of Freedoms coalition won solid majorities in both the lower house and the Senate. His own Forza Italia jumped to 30% of votes in 2001. Two years later, the economy had slowed, his main reforms had stalled, and his legal problems had not gone away. His chief advantage is that the center-left opposition is divided and ineffective.

National Alliance

Until 1994 the neo–fascist Italian Social Movement–National Right (MSI–DN) could be found at the outer right fringe of the party spectrum. It understood how to capitalize on the disadvantaged population of southern Italy. Protest against the establishment and disappointment over the center–left governments increased its percentage of votes to 6.8% in 1983, but their support in 1992 fell to 5.4% and 34 seats. Alessandra Mussolini, granddaughter of the fascist dictator and niece of actress Sophia Loren took one of them. In terms of a political program, the MSI maintained entirely the tradition of Italian fascism.

But then came a new and intelligent young leader, Gianfranco Fini, who steered the party away from the corporatism and exaggerated nationalism of old fascism and gave it a new program (which he calls "post–fascism") and a more respectable name: National Alliance. The MSI was dissolved in 1995. He studiously avoided contacts with extreme–rightist groups elsewhere in Europe and condemned anti–Semitism, attacks against foreigners, and skinhead violence. Emphasizing clean government, law and order (including reintroduction of the death penalty), stricter immigration controls, family values, and the preservation of Italian unity, he transformed the party into a broad–based mainstream conservative political force, modeled on the French Gaullists, and a major player in Italian politics.

Having been excluded from government for a half century, it could not be blamed for corruption and poor performance, as could Italy's traditional parties. Fini declared during the campaign: "Italy no longer divides itself between fascists and anti–fascists, but between thieves and those with clean hands!"

The reward came in the 1994 elections: it more than doubled its previous electoral score, capturing 13.5% of the votes and five seats in the cabinet. It did especially well among the young, who are the most adversely affected by Italy's frighteningly high unemployment. It captured 23% of the votes from Italians under age 25, versus only 13% for the former Communists, now called PDS. Capitalizing on the dramatic decline of the former Christian Democrats, who had long dominated the South, the National Alliance became the strongest political force in the southern half of Italy, including Rome. But the party lost badly in 1996, capturing only 16% of the vote, and it fell further to 12% in 2001. But it reentered the government.

Not everyone is persuaded that the party's transformation is genuine. Fini himself reinforced the skeptics shortly after the elections by describing Mussolini as "the greatest statesman of the century." Some party members demand

The National Alliance's Gianfranco Fini

that Italian claims on parts of Istria and Dalmatia in the present Slovenia and Croatia be resurrected, but Fini assured the public that his party would not press this issue. Most Italians, who are accustomed to seeing neo–fascists in every post–war Italian parliament, are not alarmed.

But in other European countries, which must deal with menacing right–wing movements on the rise, there was near–panic. The hostile foreign reaction prompted former President Scalfaro to warn: "Italy does not need to take lessons in democracy from anybody!" Also Berlusconi asserted, "fascists do not exist in my government." Citing polls showing that less than 1% of Italians identify themselves as "fascists," he asked, "so how can this be considered dangerous?"

Northern League

In the 1990s all of Italy's established parties anxiously witnessed the rise of leagues seeking regional autonomy in the North. The most successful within this *Lega Nord* (Northern League) is the Lombard League, led by Umberto Bossi. The Northern League rocketed to 19% of the vote in that region's 1990 elections. In the 1992 national elections it won more than a fifth of the votes in Lombardy and 8.7% nationally, jumping from one to 55 seats in parliament. In 1994 it entered the ruling coalition and claimed five cabinet posts. But Bossi terminated its cooperation with Berlusconi in December 1994, causing a serious split in the party. It captured a respectable 10% of the national vote and 59 lower house seats. In the process it became the largest party north of the River Po, winning up to 40% of the votes in some northern regions. However, in 2001 it fell to under 4% of the

Italy

The Northern League's Umberto Bossi and family

votes under the threshold for getting seats distributed by proportional representation.

The League stands for federalism and devolution of power to the regions. It capitalizes on local dissatisfaction against what is seen as misrule by Rome, which does not seem to act vigorously enough to stem the wave of immigrants and to reverse Northern Italy's subsidizing of the South. It charges, with considerable justification, that too much of those funds end up in the pockets of Mafia contractors. A clean–government party, the Northern League benefitted from the country's massive corruption scandal. Its spokesman, Roberto Maroni, announced, "our purpose of breaking up Italy is not linked to ethnic or religious identities, but to economic issues."

Emboldened by its strong election showing in 1996, the League proclaimed northern Italy an "independent and sovereign" republic called "Padania" (for the River Po) and called on the United Nations to recognize its right of self–determination. Unlike the Basque country in Spain and France, Padania has never existed before. Nevertheless, its supporters are playing government. They moved their 15 "ministers" into a Renaissance building in Venice and swore in a self–nominated "parliament" in their "capital city" of Mantua. In 1997 they held unofficial parliamentary elections and charged the assembly with writing a new constitution that would make Padania either independent or loosely confederated with Italy. Advocates wave their own flag, wear green shirts and call themselves "citizens of the North." They call on northerners to refuse to pay their taxes to Rome.

Despite these trappings, opinion polls suggest that most northerners oppose secession although many agree with some of the League's criticisms. Bossi did not help his cause in 1997 by referring to the Pope as a "foreigner" and saying that the Italian flag belongs in the toilet. This remark brought a million Italians into the streets in Milan and Venice to demonstrate for national unity.

THE CENTER

Italian Popular Party

Until 1994 the Christian Democrats (DC) had been the dominant party since 1945, and as such was hit the hardest by the political storm that is raging in Italy. It had placed in office all prime ministers until the Republican, Giovanni Spadolini, held the office from 1981 to 1982. The DC formed coalitions with all parties except the PDS and MSI. Also, in 1983, 64% of all mayors, 57% of city councilors, 90% of the managers of state–operated businesses, 94% of all savings and loan presidents and 58% of all bank presidents were members of the DC. In addition to the broad spectrum of closely related organizations in all sectors of the society in which the DC party exercises influence, the party receives special support from the Catholic Church. Two–thirds of the DC's 1,200 sections were founded in 1946 at the insistence and under the influence of local clerics.

Ideologically, the DC built upon the two larger middle class parties of the pre–fascist period. The Catholicism of the old Popular Party and the economic liberalism of the old Liberal Party were the pillars for the DC's political conception. In accordance with the Manifesto of Milan of 1943, the DC defined itself as

a "Catholic People's Party" encompassing all classes. It had no binding party program. Instead, it was the classical example of the "catch–all party."

The DC's adaptability and its openness to coalitions toward both the right and the left were reasons why for so long it survived political and economic crises without suffering large electoral losses. However, it refused to agree to a "historical compromise" (*Compromesso storico*) with the Communists. Its heterogeneity helped it to stabilize Italian society and guarantee the proper functioning of the parliamentary system.

Shaken by scandals that left few of its talented leaders untainted, the party not only suffered election losses, but was affected by the liberalization of Catholicism. The first appearance of erosion became evident with the divorce referendum of 1974, in which the DC and the Catholic Church sought to abolish the 1972 laws permitting Italians to divorce. At least 3 million women, up to that point the party's most loyal supporters, helped defeat the suggestion to repeal the divorce laws. An even harder nut to crack was the referendum in 1985 to abolish the abortion law that had been passed in 1980, permitting abortion under specific circumstances; the DC supported the law, but 70% of the voters opposed it.

The party had failed to take into account the extensive sympathy for the Pope, who had just recovered from an attack on his life, and who was very opposed to the abortion act. Pope John Paul II, who is Polish, generally takes very little interest in Italian politics, a fact that has removed much of the spiritual underpinnings for the DC, which the party has in the past known how to exploit. In 1985 the Italian government revised the 55–year–old concordat with the Vatican ending the status of Roman Catholicism as the state religion. The Church accepted the civil court's right to decide on marital annulments, previously the exclusive right of the Church, and it agreed that religious instruction in public schools would be optional.

The DC had been further threatened by the continuous economic crises, for which it, as the major governing party, had to bear responsibility. Many workers and employers lost confidence in the party. It experienced a sharp fall in the 1992 elections, winning only 29.7% of the votes and 206 seats in the Chamber of Deputies. This ignited an intra–party crisis. Mario Segni, a former Christian Democrat who organized the drive for electoral reform in 1993, broke away and formed a new party, Democratic Alliance, aiming to attract a wide spectrum of reform supporters from all parties.

Hon. Romano Prodi
President, European Commission

Staring electoral disaster in the face, DC party leader, Mino Martinazzoli, led the move in 1994 to rename the party, Italian Popular Party (PPI) in order to try to improve its image and appeal. The "new" name was designed to signal a return to the Catholic values of Luigi Sturzo, the priest who had founded the Popular Party in 1919. The 1994 election results indicated that voters were not willing to accept this cosmetic change. Under a new leader, Romano Prodi, an unassuming economics professor and political neo-

phyte, the party itself won only 6.8% of the votes in 1996. But Prodi was the architect of the Olive Tree coalition, which formed the center–left government and brought most parties of the center and left under its umbrella. In October 1998 the Prodi government fell when its ally, the Communist Refoundation Party, voted to oppose the budget. Prodi was named president of the European Commission in Brussels the following year.

A minority refused to stay in the Popular Party, forming instead the Christian Democratic Center Party, which garnered 5.8% of the votes in 1996. To gain some name recognition, it recruited actress Gina Lollobrigida to be a candidate for the 1999 European Parliament elections.

The Republicans

Despite its voter appeal of only 4.4% and 27 seats in 1992, the Italian Republican Party (PRI) maintained a noticeable position at the center of the party spectrum through its pragmatically–oriented political goals. The Republicans' role consisted in overcoming the lack of innovation in the DC's economic policy through constructive criticism aimed at increasing efficiency. Known as the party of "enlightened capitalism," the PRI has come to represent especially the interests of the export–oriented companies of northern Italy. For example, Fiat boss Agnelli is a registered member of the PRI. The reason for the small percentage of voters is the fact that the party appears too anti–clerical for small farmers, too closely tied to large industry for the workers and too

progressive for the conservative element within the middle class.

The Social Democrats

The PSDI formed the left wing among the center parties and is a strictly anti–communist leftist party. Despite its low voter strength of about 5% from 1947 to 1976, the Social Democrats have participated in over half of the cabinets. Due to the increasing concentration on the large parties, the percentage of PSDI votes sank to 2.7% and 16 seats in 1992. Because of its declining fortunes, it has leaned more heavily toward the left. Workers make up 24% of the PSDI's electorate, while housewives remain the strongest group among its voters, with 27%.

The Liberal Party

The Italian Liberal Party (PLI) was originally the ruling party from the founding of the Italian State in 1861 until World War I. However, the party's strong anti–clerical position and its function as the right wing of the centrist governing coalitions cost it much popularity.

Italian Renewal

A new party created in 1996 by former central banker and prime minister, Lamberto Dini, Italian Renewal won 4.3% of the votes and barely cleared the threshold for winning seats in parliament. They were enough to clinch victory for Olive Tree, and Dini became foreign minister in the government.

THE LEFT

The Communists

The Democrats of the Left (DS, formerly PDS) is the largest party on the left with 1.5 million members. It emerged from the 1996 elections as Italy's largest political party, having captured 21.1% of the votes. It overcame its political and social isolation of the 1950s and 1960s because it was able to reach beyond its traditional base in the industrial working class and to gain new voters from the middle class. A traditionally atheistic party, it can exist in a country closely associated with the Catholic Church because it quietly dropped atheism as a part of its platform. It also ceased being a Marxist–Leninist cadre party and instead became simply a leftist worker's party. It rejected the concept of its first post-war leader, Palmiro Togliatti, who wanted to introduce socialism into Italy through revolution. History had proven that efforts to change Italian society through revolution simply helped to drive an uncertain middle class into the arms of the fascists.

In the 1960s the DS was the first Western European communist party publicly to reject the Leninist doctrine of a

Secretary of State Madeleine Albright with former Prime Minister Prodi

Italy

Ex-Foreign Minister Lamberto Dini

revolutionary seizure of power followed by a dictatorship of the proletariat. That is, it turned down the model of the Soviet Union and sought its own path to socialism.

This enabled the DS to accept Italian membership in NATO and the EU, and as Western Europe's largest communist party, to become the leader of so–called "Eurocommunism," a movement which discards Marxist–Leninist orthodoxy as the basis of its ideology. The movement recognizes parliamentary democracy as a prerequisite for socialism, which, it believes, could be achieved through a wide consensus of reform–oriented forces. It also rejects the planned economies found in Eastern Europe, although this rejection does not imply total acceptance of a free market economy. Economically and politically the DS advocates an unclear course which tries to combine overall economic planning by the state with individual economic decisions.

It is no surprise that these policies led to tensions with the Soviet Union. The DS criticized Moscow because of the Soviet occupation of Afghanistan in 1979 and because of the introduction of martial law in Poland in 1981. Other Italian parties cautiously welcomed such criticism, although the DC recognized that the DS's anti–Moscow course made it difficult for Christian Democrats to reap electoral hay by presenting themselves as bulwarks against communism.

In contrast to that of its voters, the social structure of the party members has not basically changed. The reservoir of the party is still industrial workers, who make up approximately three–fourths of its membership. An important lever for accomplishing party goals is the largest union in Italy, the CGIL, with 4.316 million members. One thing that has weakened the party is that the number of

industrial workers has declined in Italy's modernizing economy. Also, the growth of the service and white-collar sectors reduced the power of trade unions, and that has adversely affected the DS. The new groups in which the party was able to attract voters and members, such as the intellectual and technical elites as well as the civil service workers, remain under–represented in the overall party membership. However, just the opposite can be seen in the party's leadership organs. In the 36–member party directorate, a majority has full university credentials.

To hold on to the votes of young and well–educated people, the DS has loosened the leaders' grip on the rank and file by making public criticism of the party no longer grounds for expulsion and by permitting elections to the party's central committee to be held in public. The formerly closed way of making party decisions has been replaced by free and open votes in all party committees, from the national to the local level. It has formally embraced the market economy and has not opposed the privatization of national-ized industries. It accepts NATO and American nuclear bases in Italy, and it rejects unilateral nuclear disarmament.

In order to escape from its political isolation, the DS abandoned all hope for a coalition with the DC and sought links with other leftist parties, including the Socialists. This course brought frustration and danger. Just how unreliable the Socialists were for the DS was revealed in a string of municipal elections in 1985–86. Since the 1970s, the Communists had ruled or co–ruled most large Italian cities.

Along with the trade union movement (whose membership is decreasing), city government was a pillar of Communist power. There they could prove that they were efficient and largely incorruptible, and therefore capable of participating in national government. However, when the Socialists began to ally with the center par-ties at the local as well as the national lev-el, Communist mayors were thrown out of city halls all over Italy: Venice, Milan, Turin, Parma, and, most galling to the DS, Rome. Only the traditional stronghold of Bologna remained secure for the DS.

In an attempt to stem the party's decline, the DS, after open and heated debate, replaced the tired and gray Alessandro Natta in 1988 with a more youthful leader: Achille Occhetto, who rep-resents a more open–minded generation within the party. Occhetto adopted a new language: the words "Marxist" and "Eu-rocommunism" have vanished, to be re-placed by "progressive" and "Euroleft." "Our party isn't a member of a particular political–ideological camp. It's not part of the so–called communist camp. On the contrary, I maintain that there is no longer a real communist movement, and the traditions we represent in Italy are our own." He was replaced in 1994 by another pragmatist, Massimo D'Alema, who later passed the party leadership on to Piero Fassino.

In 1991, the DS cast off both its name and hammer and sickle symbol and sought membership in the Socialist Inter-national. Occhetto argued that "shatter-ing events" in Eastern Europe had left the party with no choice. One member admit-

Demonstration by largest union, the CGIL

238

Former Prime Minister Massimo D'Alema, *DS*

ted, "in terms of Italian politics, this is our Berlin Wall that has come crashing down." The new insignia is a spreading tree, with the hammer–and–sickle practically hidden in the roots. But the difficulty in transforming this party was shown when Occhetto temporarily lost his job as party secretary; reformers deserted him when he backed the hard–liners' demands that Italy withdraw its air and naval forces from the Gulf War against Iraq.

With the total collapse of Moscow–led communism in Europe, the other parties have lost their rationale for excluding the DS from government. The communists are now in a position to enter a governing coalition with any major party. The DS has become an especially potent political force in central Italy. The DS was the main pillar of the Olive Tree coalition with nine ministers in the cabinet. Olive Tree lost power in the 2001 elections, but DS captured an impressive 16% of the votes.

In October 1998, DS leader Massimo D'Alema became the first ex–Communist to form an Italian government, the country's 56th. A pensive former editor of Italy's largest leftist newspaper, *L'Unità*, and author of many books, the most recent of which is aptly entitled *La Grande Occasione* (The Big Chance), D'Alema admires Tony Blair's style of reform and has attacked irresponsible trade unionists. He broke a record by bringing nine parties into his government, sarcastically dubbed "the first center–left government of the center–right open to the radical left." It included Communists, ex–Communists, various Greens, centrists, and a new party, Francesco Cossiga's Democratic Union for the Republic, which had

been a part of the conservative opposition. This government fell in April 2000 because of disastrous DS losses in municipal elections throughout Italy. It captured 16% of the votes in 2001.

Refounded Communist Party

Hardliners broke from the DS and formed a separate party, Refounded Communist Party, led by Fausto Bertinotti. The leader demands that Italy withdraw from NATO and opt out of further European integration. He also calls for a restoration of inflation indexing for wages. The party refused to join the Olive Tree coalition, which, in Bertinotti's opinion, was too "heavily weighted on the side of centrists and moderates." But its 35 lower house seats, won through 8.6% of the votes, were crucial for the survival of the government. In 2001, its share of the votes sank to 5% and 11 seats.

The Socialists

Former leader Bettino Craxi, who in 1983 became both the first Socialist and youngest prime minister of Italy since 1945, moved the party more toward the political right and replaced the hammer and sickle as the party's symbol with a red rose. The Socialists advocate a reformed market economy including returning some state enterprises to private hands, closing highly inefficient state–owned businesses and trimming payrolls in the over manned nationalized firms. They also staunchly support the Western alliance. Since the beginning of the 1960s they have changed structurally from a

working–class party to one which is led by intellectuals, and whose electorate is composed of middle class voters.

Craxi was one of the first politicians implicated in the kickback scandal that has shaken Italian politics at the roots. The first revelations were made in his power base, Milan. Craxi aroused indignation in 1993 when he refused to relinquish his parliamentary immunity and to answer the corruption charges against him and his party. His successor as party leader, Giorgio Benvenuto, resigned in disgust, charging that political bosses are resisting surrendering their influence and power. His resignation demonstrated how difficult it was for reformers to purge the old political elite, despite the unmistakable message sent by voters in the April 1993 referendum. In parting, Benvenuto said: "Socialism has a future in Italy, but I don't know whether this party can survive."

In early 1994 the party split, and the party sank to irrelevance after the 1994 elections. Facing 20 different graft investigations in 1994, Craxi refused to surrender his passport to magistrates in Milan and fled to Tunisia. He died in 2000. His former protegé, Giuliano Amato, became prime minister for the second time in April 2000. A clever, diminutive man whose nickname is "Topolino," Italy's version of Mickey Mouse, he constructed a 12-party stopgap coalition that includes former Communists, ex-Christian Democrats, Greens and others. It is fragile, did poorly in the 2001 elections and is unlikely to survive long.

Former President Scalfaro addresses the Chamber of Deputies

Italy

Other Parties and Politicians

Benefiting from the yearning for clean government are the Greens, who won 2.5% of the votes in 1996 and entered the governing Olive Tree coalition. The party had once gained some notoriety through one of the most colorful advocates of environmentalist causes, who stimulated both excitement and embarrassment in the Italian parliament—the erotic Hungarian–born porno star, Ilona Staller, known as "Cicciolina" (meaning "little fleshy one"). Her position: "more pornography equals knowledge and nonviolence." To buttress her rhetoric in public appearances, she gave her campaign speeches topless. Her bare breasts in public rallies seemed to underscore how little else there was to think about in some past elections. In 1988 she lost her parliamentary immunity, which had protected her from counts of public indecency. She had gone out in Venice "clad" only in a see–through skirt. In 1989 she was again censured because of her continued public stripping. It is little wonder that the U.S. was reluctant to issue her an official visa to air her views in this country.

Surprisingly, her legislative record became more serious: she introduced bills banning furs and taxing cars to raise funds for planting trees. As she philosophized: "It's better to come up with strong bills than to show off your boobs." She added: "I don't undress in parliament anymore." But she did try her hand at diplomacy in 1990, offering her body to Iraqi dictator Saddam Hussein in exchange for hostages. After he rebuffed that tempting offer, she married and divorced American artist Jeff Koons, whose art, like his wife, blends business with pornography. In 1998 a Rome court ruled that because of her "excessive permissiveness" she was unfit for motherhood. It granted custody of their child to Koons.

Uncivic Culture

When considering Italian government, it must be remembered that the society has often been characterized as an "uncivic culture." According to studies made by Almond and Verba in the late 1950s, two–thirds of the Italians refused to have anything to do with politics or to discuss the subject with anyone. Only 3% were proud of their state institutions, and only 10% approved of political participation.

An updated version of this study in 1980 revealed that Italians have become much more inclined to engage in direct political action, especially in the form of demonstrations, strikes, blocking of railroads or highways or even political violence. Many Italians cling to the view that laws have been made to be evaded, that taxes are hostile acts of the state against the individual, and that one who does not successfully embezzle the government when one has the opportunity is considered a fool. Public institutions were long regarded with an unparalleled carefree air. The citizen's contempt and irritation toward his state was almost nihilistic, as is manifested in the widely used expression *piove, governo ladro* ("It's raining on this corrupt state"). The political revolution in the 1990s has shown that toleration of corruption and indifference toward elected representatives have dramatically changed.

Government Under Constant Challenge

The bad state of government affairs is not simply a result of the continuous public scandals that have brought down many governments and have helped paralyze the bureaucracy. For instance, in 1981 the Cossiga government fell because of an affair centered around an ultra–secret Masonic Lodge named P2 in which many of the country's leading politicians, industrialists and tax officials were closely linked in a scandal. This is rather the result of an historically developed behavioral pattern. For centuries the state meant nothing more to Italians than suppression by foreigners of subordination to the Doge princes, who themselves were dependent upon others. It has been difficult for Italians to believe that the state is working for their interests. One Italian expressed this in 1993: "We expect little of our politicians, and that's what we get."

The permanent crisis of the modern democratic state in Italy is scarcely suitable for developing a stronger sense of public spirit among its citizens. The work of many heterogeneous factions organized into many groups has made the establishment of a political consensus difficult. In Rome alone, over 25,000 politically active organizations have been counted. Some of these groups refuse to observe the democratic rules of the game and have become parts of the powerful terrorist movements that seek to achieve their political goals through violence. Terrorists on the extreme right have tried to upset the political system by means of countless indiscriminate bomb attacks. They have not been brought entirely under control.

The extreme leftists, the Red Brigades, posed a great problem for Italian domestic security through their precisely planned and executed attacks and kidnappings of high–ranking personalities. Their objective is to undermine the state and then to provoke a fascist reaction, which, they hope, would be the prelude to a "proletarian" revolution, although the working class in Italy shows almost no sympathy for such aims. U.S. Brigadier General James L. Dozier, the highest ranking American general stationed in Italy, was kidnapped from his Verona apartment in 1981 and freed by a highly-trained Italian anti–terrorist unit in a daring and brilliant raid in 1982 after he had been held prisoner for over 40 days.

This spectacular kidnapping was intended to be the opening act for a carefully planned spree of further kidnappings, commando–style raids on jails to free arrested terrorists, and as a final bloody crescendo, the massacre of the entire Christian Democratic leadership at a DC gathering in Rome. Yet this campaign was foiled by the absolute determination of the Italian government to put an end to left–wing terrorism. The government was greatly aided by the crack anti–terrorist units, which had been created in order to achieve the same level of expertise as that of the astonishingly well–informed, well–armed and well–trained terrorists.

In 1982 almost a thousand suspected terrorists were arrested, including many of their known leaders. Bases, conspiratorial apartments and arms dumps were raided. The police and courts also made effective use of a temporary law permitting more lenient sentences for terrorists who tell on their former comrades. The state thus made a significant strike at left–wing terrorism. Very importantly, it did this without abandoning democracy or an observance of civil rights. But the causes of such violence remain: an immobile political system, a corruption-ridden bureaucracy, and the bleak economic outlook for many young Italians. In 1999 there was a frightening reminder of Red Brigade terrorism when one of the government's top advisers, Massimo D'Antona, was gunned down as he walked to work. Prime Minister D'Alema vowed: "We are faced with a terrorist band that the state intends to find and to hit."

Italians' worries about violence in their midst were fueled again in 2001 by the radical Islamic terrorist strikes in New York and Washington on September 11. Police authorities determined that al-Qaeda cells were operating in Italy and were planning violent attacks against such targets as the U.S. embassy. Police made many arrests of suspected terrorists. For example, in September 2002 they followed a tip from U.S. naval intelligence and seized a ship carrying 15 suspected terrorists. They also raided a farmhouse near Venice in January 2003 and arrested five Moroccans in position of explosives and chemicals, plus maps of NATO bases in Italy and the London underground. Police have shut down money-transfer operations suspected of financing terrorist groups and concluded that Italy was being used by internationalist terrorist groups as a transit and logistics center.

In March 2002 another more familiar brand of terrorism reemerged. A top economic adviser who was helping the government draft controversial changes to the labor laws, making it easier to lay off workers, Marco Biagi, was murdered in Bologna. Authorities had ignored Biagi's pleas for protection. Forensic tests indicated that the assassination was the work of the Red Brigades. A Red Brigade member arrested a year later admitted that the assassination had been part of the group's strategy to derail the government's plans to reform Italy's labor laws.

The Mafia

Organized crime, particularly the Sicilian Cosa Nostra, whose power extends from Sicily to Rome and the industrialized area further north, and its competitors, *Ndrangheta* from Calabria, responsible for the kidnapping of the young American heir, John Paul Getty, Jr., and Camorra from Naples, is the country's number one plague. The Mafia accumulated enormous wealth from lucrative bogus public works contracts, "protection," and international drug traffic, of which Sicily became the European center following the severance of the "French Connection" in the 1970s. The Mafia lost ground in the global drug trade, supplying only an estimated 5% of the American market in 1993. Italian mobsters also face competition from ruthless imitators from Russia, Colombia, and other countries. Italy is not merely a transit point for drugs, which increasingly flow into the veins of Italians themselves, it gives the country the shameful distinction of having the largest number of addicts on the Continent.

With its wealth the Mafia has shifted its emphasis to becoming an entrepreneur, although protection rackets still extort $4.7 billion dollars each year from small businesses alone. A 1996 survey revealed that 23% of businesses paid racketeers an average of 10.7% of their annual sales. The Mafia bought into countless businesses and penetrated a portion of the Italian banking system, which it needs to "launder" its "hot" money. Whereas the Mafia's main profits were once from the drug trade, they are now from government contracts and extortion. In 1996 the Italian trade association, *Confcommercio*, estimated that a fifth of all trade and construction enterprises in Italy are controlled by organized crime and that the authorities discover no more than 8% of illegal businesses.

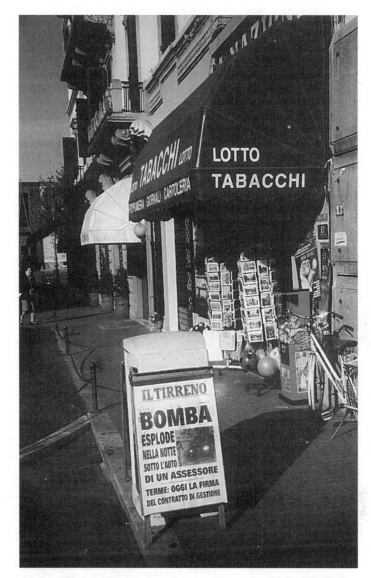

Report of car-bombing

The competition among Mafia families for larger shares of the drug trade unleashed ruthless gang wars that left the streets and countryside strewn with hundreds of bloody corpses. It also led the Mafia to aim its ugly pistol against the political process itself. In 1979 it began liquidating top Italian political officials in Sicily who stood in its way. The government responded to this deadly challenge by making membership in a Mafia clan a crime, by legalizing the confiscation of suspects' estates if they cannot demonstrate that their income was legally acquired, and by sending the new leader of the secret services to Sicily as that island's regional prefect. In 1987 courageous judges and prosecutors in Palermo, relying heavily on testimony from 14 Mafia members who broke the code of silence, convicted 338 Mafiosi of crimes

ranging from murder to drug trafficking in the biggest Mafia trial in Italian history. For the first time, the leading mobster bosses received the stiffest sentences.

In the 1980s and 1990s the Mafiosi maintained a steady wave of killings, not only among themselves, but against the Italian state. In 1988 they murdered an active judge for the first time. The government cooperated with U.S. officials to crack a powerful transatlantic drug ring. Despite the scores of bosses arrested, all agree that only the tip of the iceberg had been shattered. Authorities are able to prosecute criminals more quickly because of a 1989 judicial reform aimed at streamlining the system. As one headline read: "Perry Mason has finally entered Italy's old and decrepit courtrooms."

The criminal families not only expanded their operations into northern Italian

Italy

cities, but began influencing municipal and regional elections by murdering or intimidating candidates. In 1991 five persons, including a member of a city council, were shot; one victim was even beheaded; his head was used for target practice. This horrified the Italian public and prompted the government to assume the authority to dissolve any city council or local authority infiltrated by the Mafia and to send judges, even against their will, to man under–staffed courts in the three regions most plagued by gangs: Calabria, Sicily, and Campania. The government created in 1991 a special post, dubbed the Italian "FBI," within the Attorney General's office to coordinate the fight against organized crime.

Like some Latin American countries, Italy is fighting to prevent itself from falling under the control of un-elected international criminals. At stake is the freedom of Italians to be ruled by leaders they elect, rather than by those who reap undreamed profits from feeding human vices. After the Mafia murdered two top anti–Mafia officials (Giovanni Falcone and Paolo Borsellino) in 1992, the government deployed 7,000 soldiers to Sicily in July to crack down on the mob. This was the most drastic step taken since 1945 against a domestic disorder and the first time troops were used in a large–scale crackdown on the Sicilian mobsters. Also in 1992 law–enforcement officials joined Spanish, British, and American police to arrest Italians working with the Cali (Colombia) cocaine cartel. In November the biggest organized crime sweep in almost ten years put scores of Mafia suspects in jail, including several mayors and three members of parliament.

Armed with strengthened antiracketeering laws permitting wider use of phone taps, property searches, confiscation of property of convicted or suspected Mafia people, state reimbursement to businesses which suffer for defying the racketeers, and guarantees of protection for state witnesses, police maintained this momentum in 1993. A startling development occurred when the Pope broke the Church's long tradition of silence on Mafia matters and lashed out against organized crime. The Mafia's two top leaders, Salvatore ("Nitto") Riina and Benedetto Santapaola, as well as the only women known to have headed an Italian crime syndicate (the Camorra around Naples), Rosario Cutolo, were captured. In 1996 one of the most powerful and ruthless bosses in the history of the Corleone clan, Giovanni Brusca (nicknamed "the Pig"), who had masterminded the murder of Falcone and Borsellino, was captured by 200 black–hooded special police troops.

The key has been a crumbling of the long–standing code of silence. By 1997 more than 1,200 arrested Mafiosi were collaborating with investigators. The growing number of *pentiti* ("penitents") has prompted Mafia organizations to retaliate brutally, departing from the older code of honor not to attack women, children, judges, government officials, and innocent bystanders. It has also been expensive for the taxpayer to take care of more than 6,000 people, including families, who need escorts, protection, money and shelter, special schools and churches. But organized crime really does seem to be on the run.

The resulting confessions of these *pentiti* led not only to the dramatic arrests of Mafia leaders. They opened perhaps the most explosive chapter in Italy's mega–corruption scandal: that top Christian Democratic leaders, especially seven-time prime minister, Giulio Andreotti, may have cooperated with and protected the Mafia. No Italian politician had as many revealing nicknames as he: "Machiavelli," "Mephistopheles," and "the Fox." Prosecutors claim that the Mafia had guaranteed his party votes and political control in Sicily in return for government contracts for Mafia–controlled companies and protection from police crackdowns. Andreotti denied the charges but agreed to have his senatorial immunity lifted in order to clear his name in court.

Commencing in 1995, this trial was a humiliating ordeal for Andreotti; two-thirds of respondents in a 1995 poll think he did indeed have a "relationship" with Mafia. The press called it "the trial of the century." In 1999 he was acquitted on charges that he had associated with the Mafia and had ordered it to kill an investigative journalist (Mauro De Navro) in 1979. The court decisions did not dispel all doubts about his activities, and in November 2002 this verdict was overturned in a court of appeals, and Andreotti was sentenced to 24 years in jail. He quickly appealed this reversal, as the country was aghast at this never-ending ordeal based on the testimony of a Mafia turncoat.

In May 2003 he was absolved from another charge of having connections to the Mafia, but his continued legal entanglement ignited attacks on the controversial use of over 1,100 *pentiti*, on whose testimony all his cases had been based. This questioning became a furious public debate in May 2003 when a mobster convicted of a grisly murder was released from prison after only seven years behind bars. Enzo Brusca had kidnapped an 11-year-old boy and held him captive before strangling him and dissolving his body in acid. In 2001 parliament had already toughened the *pentiti* law by limiting the

window for providing information and requiring them to serve at least 10 years of a life sentence.

Many Italians now believe that organized crime can finally be defeated. No longer able to act with impunity inside Italy, the Mafia and other organized crime groups are increasingly expanding their operations into other European countries. In 1998 one of the new generation's top bosses in Sicily, Vito Vitale, was arrested. Declaring the anti–Mafia crackdown to have been successful, the government moved to pull 7,000 army troops out of Palermo and the rest of Sicily. Many Sicilian politicians found this move too hasty. Despite the fact that many bosses and their underlings are behind bars, the Mafia is far from destroyed. No part of Sicily is free of its influence, and extortion and protection rackets remain commonplace.

The Italian Family

Despite the complicated historical development and the division into numerous interest groups, the Italian family has traditionally been responsible for Italy's national identity and strength. It is the most important institution and focal point of Italian life. Its significance has changed due to the modernization that accompanies industrial life. Italy reached zero population growth in 1987, and by 1998 the average mother produced only 1.2 children, compared with 2.7 in 1964.

In most years now, deaths outnumber births, and only immigration somewhat stabilizes the population. Among western European countries, only women in Catholic Spain bear fewer children. But in contrast to most northern European nations, only 6% of Italian babies are born out of wedlock. The worsening age distribution presents a time bomb for the pension system. In 2001 pensions claimed 60% of welfare spending, compared to an EU average of 45%, and by 2003 the annual pension bill was 16% of GDP and rising. It is estimated that by 2030 about 42% of Italians will be pensioners, the highest proportion in Europe.

An opinion poll in the 1970s revealed that nearly half the women between the ages of 25 and 35 no longer considered motherhood as their most important goal in life. Earlier, Italians would have been shocked by such a result. Because of Italians' desire for higher living standards, the emancipation of women, and the declining influence of the Catholic Church, the birth rate has fallen dramatically, especially in the North of Italy.

The Bureaucracy

Because many political decisions are made within the various interest groups

The Galdino Barella family of Paina, near Milan

Photo by John M. Morrow

rather than in the official political channels, the Italians have a good understanding for the term "under government" (*sotto-governo*). Italian bureaucracy, with 1.7 million civil servants, has been reproached for its general inefficiency, inflexibility and corruption. Government employees have alarming absenteeism, and far too many who report for work either do nothing or use their time to do outside work in order to have a second income.

Government officials are, for the most part, recruited from the South, where an administrative position is for many the only opportunity for a job. The emphasis on authority, exaggerated bureaucracy and official government patronage and nepotism which characterizes public offices, can be traced back historically to the behavioral patterns of the pre–capitalistic feudal states of the South. It is a curious phenomenon that in this land of contradictions the North conquered the South during the "Resurgence" partly through its economic predominance; however, the South conquered the North through the Italian bureaucracy.

The South

The main domestic problem remains the structurally underdeveloped South. When describing the Italian social and economic situation, one can speak of an industrialized state that has some characteristics of an underdeveloped country. Four–fifths of the industry is concentrated in the Turin–Milan–Genoa triangle.

Although roughly one–third of the population is concentrated in the South, two–fifths of Italy's unemployed live there. In 2003 the jobless rate in the South was 20% vs. 7% in the North. The problem is bound to get worse because the birth rate and illiteracy are considerably higher in the South. The average income per capita in the South is 70% of the Italian average, and it is widening. The per capita productivity in the South is 40% to 60% under that of the North. In the 21ˢᵗ century most of the gaps in the labor market in the dynamic North of Italy are being filled by workers from Central and Eastern Europe, no longer by immigrants from the South of Italy. There are, of course, significant differences between regions within the South. For instance, Calabria and Campania are very depressed, while such areas as Abruzzi and Molise are catching up with the North. Clearly prosperity is not being shared equally throughout Italy.

The traveler coming from the modern, industrialized North to Calabria or the Basilicata in the South has the feeling that he has left a highly developed country and has landed in an underdeveloped one. In order to compensate for this historical disadvantage, a governmental agency called the *Cassa per il Mezzogiorno* was established in 1950 to channel resources to the South and thus stimulate improvements. The *Cassa* has accounted for a few worthwhile projects, including a turnpike from Milan to Palermo, which opened up the South to tourism. However, overall results have proved to be

disappointing. Profit–seekers in the North benefited excessively from road construction, favorable state credits, as well as cheap, unskilled labor available in and from the South. The Mafia and the Ndrangheta also earned through fraud a massive fortune from the money provided by the *Cassa*.

In order to fill the industrial gap, the government financed a petrochemical and iron works, which achieved high rates of production, but which *Corriere della Sera* called the "cathedral in the desert." This capital–intensive plant employed few persons, contaminated large areas of land and failed to stimulate an economic base around it. The best example of a grandiose government–subsidized project that failed, though, is the mammoth ironworks in Calabria's Gioia Tauro. This made little economic sense because its superfluous steel could hardly be sold in the saturated world market. However, an entire citrus producing area was destroyed in order to build this plant. To transport the steel products, a nearby port was dredged despite the fact that the southern Italian coast was rich with natural bays. Many millions were spent for this project, but much of the money landed in the pockets of the Mafia. Therefore Rome decided to terminate the plant's production.

The culmination point for misery in the South is Naples, the "capital of poverty," as the Turin newspaper *La Stampa* described it. The city, with its 1.3 million inhabitants, among which over 100,000 are unemployed, is practically incompre-

Italy

hensible. Speculation on construction projects has been boundless. Also, the absence of a sewage system has transformed the once renowned gulf into a cesspool that is five times more polluted than Italy's other coastal waters. Neapolitan newspapers read many days like a hair–raising chronicle of crime and catastrophe. The number of stolen vehicles is estimated at 40,000 annually. There are not enough orphans' homes to accommodate the deserted children of desperate parents living in a city known traditionally to be family–conscious. It is surprising that Naples has not collapsed under the pressure of such massive problems.

Foreign Relations and Defense

Italy joined the UN in 1955, but the two main pillars of its foreign policy are membership in the EU, of which it was a founding member, and NATO. It has 265,500 men under arms, almost half (126,100) of whom are doing their basic 10-month military service. In 2000 the first female volunteers entered the military. Italy's forces are supplemented by more then 10,400 U.S. ground and air force troops, mainly in northern Italy, and more than 4,000 U.S. naval personnel in the 6th fleet based in Naples. Although it occupies a strategically important position on NATO's southern flank, its defense spending accounts for less than 2% of its GDP. This has dire consequences for the Italian navy, which must leave the defense of Italy's extensive coastline to the army and the air force, which are concentrated in the North. The navy is capable of defending only merchant vessels in the Mediterranean.

NATO membership for a country that had the largest communist party in Western Europe caused some tensions. However, as the PCI moved steadily away from Moscow and renamed itself the PDS (then DS), it increasingly accepted national defense within NATO. The dilemma still gives Italian foreign policy one of its major characteristics: it is normally conducted quietly and with the utmost of discretion in order not to allow foreign policy to become part of the always heated domestic cauldron.

A dramatic exception occurred in 1990 when the prime minister admitted that in 1956 the government, aided by the CIA, had set up a clandestine paramilitary network (code name: *Gladio*, Latin for "sword") to resist a possible Communist occupation. Weapons and explosives were hidden in 139 caches. Communists were incensed that they were the targets, and a national scandal ensued when suspicions were aired that renegade *Gladio* agents might have used some of the explosives to make right–wing terrorist attacks in the

The Italian aircraft carrier *Giuseppe Garibaldi* is inspected by former Prime Minister Craxi

1960s and 1970s, a charge which the government vehemently denied. The revelations also stirred debate in other NATO countries, especially Belgium, where right–wing terrorists might have gotten their weapons from similar caches.

Italy has long sought to play a more assertive role in the world, especially in Mediterranean affairs. It became the first European NATO ally to accept, without condition, U.S. medium–range cruise missiles, which began to be deployed at Comiso, Sicily, in 1983. Italian willingness to contribute to strengthening NATO was again shown in 1988 when its government termed the eviction of American F16 fighter aircraft from Spain as "disastrous" and agreed to their being based in Southern Italy. The end of the Cold War made that relocation unnecessary.

Rome's concern for stability in the area is expressed in the 1990s by its support for a Council for Security and Cooperation in the Mediterranean (CSCM), modeled on the OSCE, to include countries on all shores of the Mediterranean. It is worried that its confused domestic politics, its difficulty in meeting the criteria by 1998 for a unified European currency, and the emergence of a dominant Paris–Bonn/Berlin axis might relegate it to second–class status in the EU. To demonstrate that her country cannot be taken for granted, ex-Foreign Minister Susanna Agnelli temporarily refused an American request in 1995 to deploy F–117 "stealth" fighter–bombers in Italy for use in NATO's Bosnian campaign.

Italy was the first European country to join the multi–national peacekeeping force in the Sinai Peninsula to help pre-

serve the peace between Israel and Egypt, and in 1982 its troops joined the French and Americans in overseeing the withdrawal of the PLO and other foreign belligerents from the war–torn city of Beirut, Lebanon. It is willing to guarantee Malta's neutrality. In 1991 it sent ten Tornado aircraft and five naval vessels to the Persian Gulf to support its allies' war effort against Iraq. In 1993 Italy was one of the first countries to send troops on the UN humanitarian mission to Somalia, part of which had been ruled by Italy until 1960. Links with Somalia remained strong. Most educated Somalis still speak Italian, and many studied in Italy.

When NATO launched an air war against Serbia in 1999 to try to stop ethnic cleansing in Kosovo, Italy stuck with the alliance. Although its own aircraft were not involved, it sent 2,000 troops to Albania to administer humanitarian aid, and it permitted NATO pilots to use 14 bases in Italy, including especially Aviano in the Northeast. Although some parties, such as the Northern League and the United Communists opposed the air strikes, Prime Minister D'Alema, a former Communist, declared, "we'll be loyal to the end."

American flights from Aviano had become an emotional public issue in 1998–9 when a low–flying Marine Corps EA–6B Prowler aircraft passing through Aviano clipped the cable of a gondola killing 20 skiers. Anti–American and anti–NATO feelings were inflamed when an American military court acquitted the pilot on charges of negligence. However, he was found guilty of obstruction of justice for destroying a video taped record, and the Americans agreed to tighten restrictions and accountability for training flights in Italy.

The Italian government responded without hesitation when radical Middle Eastern terrorists attacked the World Trade Center in New York and the Pentagon in Washington on September 11, 2001. It offered the aircraft carrier Garibaldi, two frigates, Harrier jump jets and Tornado aircraft, a supply ship, and 2,700 troops including 150 paratroopers. It also organized a rally in Rome called "USA day" on November 10. On the same day leftists organized a peace rally. This reflected the ambivalence and division within Italian society over the issue of going to war in Afghanistan. Opinion polls revealed only a slight majority favoring such participation. In the heat of the debate, Prime Minister Silvio Berlusconi made unfortunate statements about Islam: "We must be aware of the superiority of our civilization." He added that the West "will continue to conquer peoples, like it conquered Communist," even if that meant confronting "another civilization, the Islamic one, stuck where was 1,400 years ago." Having forgotten that Moslem countries were also engaged in the struggle against terrorism, he apologized.

When the U.S. and Britain went to war in Iraq to unseat dictator Saddam Hussein in March 2003, most Italians opposed the conflict. But the Berlusconi government backed the Anglo-Saxon allies by offering Italian airspace, ports, highways and bases, provided that they were not used for actually launching attacks against the enemy. After the three-week conflict was over, Italy joined several other European allies in agreeing to send 3,000 soldiers to help humanitarian efforts in Baghdad. Along with his new foreign minister, Franco Frattini, an intelligent Forza Italia politician who, at 45, was the youngest person in postwar Italy to be given the post, Berlusconi declared that his government will use its six-month EU presidency to try to help heal the wide transatlantic rift that had developed over the Iraq crisis. "Italy will make the Euro-Atlantic relationship a priority."

Immigration and Balkans

One of Italy's thorniest future foreign policy problems is immigration. By 1999 legal immigrants living there numbered around one million. About 800,000 illegal ones had slipped in, and loopholes in the law made it difficult to deport them. Many Italians fear that some of these illegals are involved in prostitution and drug rings in the major cities. Other European countries fear that Italy could be a gateway into the EU now that Italy has become a member of the EU's Schengen

group, which lifts border controls for those persons already inside an EU country. Until recently Italy was a land of emigration, but its long coastline facing North Africa has made it a natural bridge between the burgeoning populations of Africa and the rich nations of Europe. Not wishing to damage its good relations with its Arab neighbors on the other side of the Mediterranean and Adriatic Seas, Italy has not wanted to impose quotas. To

encourage its growing number of illegal residents to register with the authorities, it offered its generous welfare benefits to non–EU citizens, but this merely stimulated even greater immigration.

In a country that thought it was above racism, daily headlines now report racial strife. Nowhere was that more visible than in Florence, where the presence of hundreds of North African street vendors sparked protest marches to decry the

Italy

influx. Gangs of white rowdies set upon the newcomers with baseball bats and iron bars.

To the East, the collapsed communist regimes in Albania and Yugoslavia have enhanced the specter of an immigration flood. Waves of Albanians, traveling across the Adriatic Sea in overcrowded boats, were washed ashore in 1991, only to be penned into coal docks and a local soccer stadium, which they proceeded to wreck out of anger toward their reception. One Caritas relief worker complained, "the police threw food at them like in a zoo."

Stung by the criticism, the government adopted a new policy to prevent the exodus of impoverished Albanians. Italian naval vessels help Albania patrol its shores. It also established a large emergency aid program within Albania itself. Italian soldiers distribute food and advice on improving the infrastructure, as a forerunner to a longer–term program to help stabilize the Balkan country's ailing economy. By 2003 the main immigration route into Italy had changed. Instead of coming from the east into the southeastern region of Apulia, more immigrants now come north from Africa and land on the southern and southwestern shores. Italy also adopted a tougher law in 2002 making it harder for new immigrants to obtain residency permits. It made it easier for law enforcement authorities to expel those who do not have the right papers or consistent employment, to levy higher fines and criminal sentences, and to mete out stiffer penalties for employers and immigrants who violate the regulations. Non-EU immigrants must now be fingerprinted upon arrival in Italy.

In 1997, for the first time since the Second World War, Italy led a multinational force, including 6,000 of its own soldiers, into Albania to restore order. Violence and anarchy had broken out when thousands of people lost their savings in shady financial pyramid schemes. By the end of the year, order had been restored, and thousands of the Albanian refugees began to be deported. In 2001 it

still had 1,100 troops in Albania and the second-largest contingent (4,900) in Kosovo after the United States. In the Balkans as a whole, Italy deploys approximately 8,000 peacekeepers, second only to France. The Balkans are simply too close and too unstable not to warrant Italy's full attention. In the words of Lucio Caracciolo, editor of Limes magazine, they "have become our top foreign policy priority."

ECONOMY

The motor which keeps the country operating despite all of the crises, scandals, strikes, poverty and natural catastrophes, is the Italians' ability to improvise and adapt to existing conditions. Such extraordinary resilience and resourcefulness have taken shape through centuries of foreign domination and of continuous threats along the coastline from pirates and conquerors. The every–day problems merely stimulate these qualities and enable one to understand why so many informed commentators on the state of Italian affairs are inclined to say with confidence that "the situation is desperate, but not hopeless."

Italy has a private enterprise economy, although the government has a controlling interest in some large commercial and industrial firms. Electricity, transportation, telephone and telegraph are largely owned by the state. Three TV channels are dominated by the state RAI network, although voters in a 1995 referendum chose to allow private shareholders to buy a stake in them. Silvio Berlusconi's Fininvest owns three other channels, with 65% of the advertising market, and voters in 1995 decided that he should not be forced to give up control of two of them.

The changes in wage indexation and the remarkable improvement in labor productivity have stabilized inflation (2.7% in 2003), despite a VAT of 19%. In the 1990s its economy was growing at an annual rate of about 4%; in 2003 growth had declined by .8%, one of the slowest of all large European countries. Tourism dropped by a quarter after the September 11 terrorist attacks and the discovery of al-Qaeda cells in Italy. Italy has a modern economy: 62% of the work force is employed in services, who produce 65.3% of the GDP, while 33% is employed in industry, who produce 31.9% of GDP.

Italian firms have invested heavily in the latest technology and have some of the most productive factories in Europe. Its companies are also actively investing outside the country. Northern Italy shows particular dynamism. Of Italy's 20 regions, the three northern ones—Lombardy, Veneto and Piedmont—produce almost 40% of

Prosperous shoppers in Florence

the GDP. Lombardy alone generates 30% of the country's exports.

Prodded by its strong desire to join the EU's single currency (euro), Italy has made spectacular economic progress since 1992. By 2003 the budget deficit has declined to 2.4% of GDP, even though its total national debt is equal to 111% of its GDP. Servicing that debt consumes a tenth of its GDP and a fifth of government spending. Fortunately, 90% of Italy's debt is funded domestically, thanks largely to Italians' fetish for saving: they save 15% of their earnings, the highest rate in the EU. Much of it is in government securities. Thus, most of the interest payments are recycled into the economy.

Partly because of the shaky ruling coalitions that require expensive concessions to keep all partners satisfied, it has not been easy for any government to make big cuts in government spending and borrowing. The country's financial system both in banking and the stock market must be further modernized. Obstacles to business exist, such as rigid hiring and firing laws, high employers' social security contributions, and widespread price controls. These raise unemployment, which stood at 9% in 2003. Half have been out of work for more than a year, and a third of adults under 25 have no job. Joblessness is higher in the South (20%, and about 60% for youths) than in the North (7%). It is also higher for women.

The South will get an economic boost from the construction of a bridge over the strait of Messina linking Sicily with the mainland beginning in 2005 and scheduled for completion in 2010. It will stretch 2 miles, three times longer than the Golden Gate bridge, and have 12 lanes for cars, trucks and trains. Its towers will soar 1,230 feet above sea level. The megaproject could create 10,000 jobs. The failure to build this long-discussed bridge had become a symbol of the country's inability to modernize its road and rail infrastructure.

A further problem is Italy's lag in innovation. A 2003 survey revealed that it holds a mere 1.8% of the world's high-tech patents, compared with Germany's 15% and France's 7.3%. Its citizens' scientific knowledge, internet use, and vocational training are low compared with many other European countries, and the resources it allots to research and higher education are inadequate. As many as 5% of its university graduates leave the country to work elsewhere. This is why the education ministry announced plans in 2003 to improve schools, to have pupils begin school at an earlier age, to study computers and English from the start, and to stay in school for a minimum of 12 years, two years more than before.

Nevertheless, Italy remains a visibly prosperous country. A reflection of such prosperity is the fact that almost two-thirds of the adult population were homeowners by the end of the 1980s, and one Italian family in four has a second home.

Italian students celebrating end of course.

One explanation of such economic well-being which defies the gloomy statistics is the celebrated "submerged economy," a parallel unofficial economy, mainly behind the backs of government statisticians and tax collectors. In 2002 the IMF estimated that about 27% of Italy's GDP is generated by the black labor market. Tax revenues equal about 41% of GDP (which is below the EU average), and it is conservatively estimated that tax evasion amounts to around 15% of GDP. This kind of economic activity is done at home, in the streets or on the job, while the boss is looking the other way.

If the production of goods and services from such a submerged economy were able to be included in the official economic figures, an estimated 10% to 30% would have to be added to the national wealth. This "black economy" makes the country's double-digit unemployment figure less serious politically than in many other Western European nations. Also, whereas unemployment prevails in large parts of the South and in some cities in the industrial North, there are other regions where the demand for jobs must be filled with guest workers such as Tunisians in Sicily and Yugoslavs in Trieste.

Italy's dependence upon oil and raw material imports is excessive. It has almost no domestic energy sources except small amounts of natural gas (chiefly in the Po Valley) and very few other raw materials. Domestic oil production meets only 3.6% of needs. Government plans to expand nuclear power production were dealt a severe blow in a 1987 referendum vote which stopped the building of atomic power stations. Italy still has only three functioning nuclear plants, which produce only 1% of the country's energy needs. As a result, it must continue to import 80% of its energy needs, twice the Western European average. Such extreme dependence on energy imports explains its determination in 1982 to defy President Reagan's embargo on the sale of gas

Chatting at the market

Italy

The frenzy of last–minute Christmas shopping in a Rome food market

pipeline equipment to the Soviet Union. Russia pays for such equipment by delivering large quantities of natural gas to Italy and other Western European countries. Also, it explains the heavy Italian investment in a trans–Mediterranean gas pipeline, which began in 1982 to bring Algerian gas to the economically depressed southern Italy.

The country's periodic trade deficit results mainly from the import of consumer goods and even agricultural products which Italy itself produces. It is only 80% self–sufficient in food. It does have impressive trade successes, though, in clothing, shoes and mechanical goods; 90% of its total exports are manufactures. Over half its trade is with its EU partners.

Agriculture

The percentage employed in agriculture has dropped over the years from 38% in 1951 to 5% in 2003. Italy's agricultural population generates only 2.8% of GDP. The rather unproductive Italian agriculture suffers from the small size of farms and the advanced age of farmers. Also,

about a fourth of the farmland is underutilized and about a tenth is not used at all.

A major agricultural obstacle is, of course, the problem of hill farming. More than 40% of Italy is classified as hilly, and such terrain merely intensifies the country's other agricultural problems of fragmentation and low productivity. Only about 23% of the land is classified as plain, most of it in the fertile Po Valley in the North, the Pontine Valley south of Rome and parts of Puglia in the South, although the latter is strapped by severe irrigation problems. The Po Valley is Italy's breadbasket, producing cereals, dairy products and sugar beets. In the South, Mediterranean produce predominates, such as citrus fruits, olive oil, wine and tomatoes. But Italy is faced with a particular dilemma as far as this latter farming is concerned. On the one hand, it is inefficient. Yet, if farming in the South were reorganized, many agricultural workers would lose jobs.

Government–Owned Enterprises

Italy's enormous budget deficits in the past can be partly explained by the huge

losses by some of the businesses that are wholly or partially owned by the state, the almost uncontrollable system of social expenditures, and the hostile attitude of the citizens toward taxes. The state's hand in the economy is large. In contrast to many other European countries, where left–wing governments once nationalized many companies, such work was done in Italy by Mussolini. The three large state–owned industrial groups—IRI, ENI and EFIM—account for about 10% of GDP. Some of the firms controlled by these huge holding companies are not profitable. These debt–ridden enterprises are an economic burden in a country in which most private concerns report a profit.

Therefore, the government decided to reduce the state's ownership in the economy. It is in no great hurry to privatize, and it has made no commitment to divest itself totally. The reason is political. Few of the country's leaders were convinced that privatization was a good way to improve the economy. But the former "Olive Tree" coalition pledged to get the process started. During the 1990s the proportion of the banking system in state hands declined from 70% to 20%. Nevertheless, Italy is less inclined than most other European countries to reform its economy.

Unions

In the view of many analysts, it is an encouraging sign that the Italian trade unions, which in 2002 organized 35.4% of Italy's work force (down from 39.2% in 1990), have lost a considerable portion of their power and influence. In the past the unions had made the Italian worker one of the most protected in Europe, and they had gained a practical veto power over the country's economic and social policies.

The reversal in trade unionists' fortunes has come since the Communists have lost votes in successive parliamentary elections, and since a massive strike against the Fiat automotive company collapsed in the fall of 1980. Fiat had to keep its overseas prices competitive with those of other countries. Now only 30% of Fiat's work force is unionized. Italy enjoys better industrial relations as a result: from 1984–8, only 40 million man hours of work were lost each year, compared to an annual average of 130 million in the previous decade. Enhanced competitiveness enabled production and export of a somewhat unique item: subway riders on Washington D.C.'s Metro are now riding in cars of Italian manufacture.

The heavy political involvement of the unions has caused them to lose touch with the rank–and–file members, who are more interested in bread–and–butter economic

Coming home from school past the *Piazza San Marco*, Venice

Photo by Vincent Campi

issues. In the midst of a recession, more and more Italians have also come to the conclusion that private enterprise and market–oriented management are necessary if the country's prosperity is to be maintained. Further, the unions were forced to budge on wage indexation, which had kept the motor of inflation well lubricated. The result is a generally favorable economic outlook. At the same time, despite the fact that things Italian miraculously turn out to be less serious than they are usually predicted, the country continues to face some serious economic challenges.

CULTURE

No other country has both profited and been stifled by the wealth of its historical inheritance as has Italy. This inheritance has attracted educated tourists for over 200 years. Annually, 26 million tourists exchange their currencies in Italy in order to see its incomparable art treasures and to enjoy the usually mild climate. In addition, approximately 80 million individual pieces of art await restoration. The most dramatic reappearance in 1999 was Leonardo Da Vinci's "Last Supper," which had undergone a meticulous 21–year restoration in Milan. Italy possesses 30,000 churches, 20,000 castles, 3,000 archaeological sites that are of value to art historians and shelters in its 712 museums countless important works of art. According to one UNESCO estimate, Italy possesses more than two-thirds of western civilization.

Only one who understands the ambivalent attitude of the Italian toward his history and state can excuse the fact that the money used by the state to maintain the irreplaceable wealth of arts corresponds to the amount needed to construct 18 miles of freeway. Since 1909 the immeasurable cultural inheritance has been administered by a small group of 284 highly–placed civil servants. However, Italy alone cannot be expected to bear the burden history has placed upon it; the entire civilized world is also, to some extent, responsible for the vast historical wealth.

UNESCO provided a considerable contribution in order to save Venice, which was threatened by uninhibited industrial exploitation of the hinterlands. In 2003 one of the largest public works projects in a long time was launched to save Venice, which is threatened by rising sea levels and the sinking of the city itself, which had been built on a soggy foundation. A series of 79 sea gates are being constructed to rise from the ocean floor if high tides in the Adriatic threaten to swell the lagoon in which Venice is located.

Many European and American organizations provided aid to cover damages caused by the catastrophic flood in Florence in 1966. It continues to face flooding, with the low–lying parts of the city inundated about every three years. Florence was again shaken in 1993, when terrorists exploded a car bomb in front of the 16th century Uffizi Gallery, which houses the world's most important collection of classic Italian art, including priceless paintings by Leonardo da Vinci, Michelangelo, Raphael, and Titian, and which is visited by more than a million persons each year. Six people died, three paintings and many medieval manuscripts in the library were destroyed, and 21 canvases and three statues were damaged.

The Uffizi's cash flow problem was dramatized in 2002 when the state electric company threatened to cut off its power if it did not pay its long overdue quarter of a million euro bill. This was symptomatic of a larger problem: the state spends much too little on maintaining the country's cultural treasures: only .18% of GDP. Since there are no tax deductions for private donations, the private sector lacks an incentive to step in and help. The Berlusconi government introduced an experiment to see if some of Italy's treasure trove could be privatized. A new state agency, Patrimonio dello Stato, was created to evaluate Italy's cultural patrimony and decide what could be sold or leased in order to generate income. The government promised not to sell off any treasures that are part of the country's national identity, such as the Colosseum, the leaning tower of Pisa, or the Uffizi. Nor would private owners ever possess a majority stake or hold leases longer than five years. The government also announced in 2002 that it would return to Ethiopia the prized Obelisk of Axum, looted by Mussolini's soldiers in 1937. Italy's past reluctance over its repatriation stemmed from a worry shared by many European countries: once such repatriation of antiquities begins, where does it stop?

The unique Byzantine churches of Ravenna are threatened, the cathedral in Milan is unstable and there is danger that the Palatine Hill in Rome will collapse. Unfortunately, the international contribution has never been used in full because of competition and disputes among the different bureaucracies. The burden of history has not only left its imprint on the political culture and on the problem of

Italy

Lucca

southern Italy (*Mezzogiorno*) but also literally threatens to slip out of the Italian state's control.

Italy's extraordinary significance for the development of western civilization from antiquity through the Middle Ages and the Renaissance in the areas of science, the arts, architecture and finance is well known. The Italians have also accomplished much in more recent times. The recognition of Italian as the language of music indicates the influence it had on the developing years. During the Baroque period (17th/18th centuries), composers such as Domenico Scarlatti, Antonio Vivaldi and Luigi Boccherini, just to name the most important figures, were prominent; (Bach was a great admirer of Vivaldi's works). The 19th century also produced world-renowned composers, such as Gioacchino Rossini, Giuseppe Verdi, Gaetano Donizetti and Giacomo Puccini. Even today, Italian composers such as Luigi Dallapiccola, Bruno Maderna and Luigi Mono are conspicuous. No singer of opera is a star until he performs at the incomparable La Scala in Milan.

Without even taking into account the countless artists of the 15th, 16th and 17th centuries, Italian artists include modern painters such as Amadeo Modigliani and Giorgio de Chirico and sculptor Marino Marini, who have maintained Italy's reputation in the international art world. In 1906 and 1936 respectively Giosuè Carducci and Grazia Deledda received Nobel prizes for literature. Significant writers such as the novelist Giovanni Verga and the romantic poet, Gabriele D'Annunzio, lead a long list of splendid literary figures. In lyric poetry, Giuseppe

Composer Puccini in his hometown, Lucca

Ungaretti, Eugenio Montale and Salvatore Quasimodo (who won a Nobel prize in 1959) have made important contributions. Dramatist Luigi Pirandello and novelists Curzio Malaparte, Cesare Pavese, Tomasi di Lampedusa, Ignazio Silone and Alberto Moravia dominated the Italian literary scene until after World War II. The critical realist, Italo Calvino, enjoys postwar popularity.

International film, opera and theater festivals, as well as modern art exhibits reflect the ever–vibrant cultural life of Italy. In terms of cinema, Rome is to Italy what Hollywood means to the U.S.A. Italian directors have been and still are the leading film figures in Europe. Names such as Vittorio de Sica, Federico Fellini, Luchino Visconti and Pier Paolo Pasolini have decisively affected European films. With his commercial Italian Western (often referred to jokingly as "spaghetti Western") director Sergio Leone captivated masses of movie–goers all over the world. Italian cinema's stellar position was shown in 1999 by Roberto Benigni's "Life is Beautiful," which won two Oscars, including the best foreign–language film, and the Grand Jury Prize at the Cannes Film Festival. Italians continue to see many American feature films, and in 1999 two–thirds of its foreign TV programs were purchased from the United States.

In the natural sciences, the Italians have also distinguished themselves—Galileo Galilei, Luigi Galvani and Alessandro Volta played a prominent role in the research of electricity. Guglielmo Marconi won a Nobel price in 1909 for his discovery of the wireless telegraph. One cannot overlook another Nobel Prize winner, Enrico Fermi, who investigated the peaceful use of the atom.

The Spanish Steps, Rome

250

TRUSSARDI JEANS

la Repubblica

Fondatore Eugenio Scalfari

Direttore Ezio Mauro

TRUSSARDI SPORT

Anno 27 - Numero 38 · € 1,19 L. 2300 in Italia

venerdì 15 febbraio 2002

INTERNET www.repubblica.it

F

L'ex presidente ha parlato per tre ore mostrando un video sulla guerra. "Contro di me un oceano di bugie"

L'autodifesa di Milosevic "Ecco le stragi della Nato"

Milosevic nell'aula del Tribunale ripreso mentre punta il dito verso Carla Del Ponte

L'ILLUSIONISTA

GUIDO RAMPOLDI

ET VOILÀ, torna in scena il prestigiatore di cadaveri. Destrezza e sapienza: è nel mestiere da dieci anni. Con l'assistenza della sua tv, Milosevic trasformava cadaveri di musulmani in salme di serbi ufficialmente uccisi dalla Bestia islamica. Complice la sua polizia, più tardi fece sparire centinaia di albanesi, ammazzati e sepolti in segreto alla periferia di Belgrado.

SEGUE A PAGINA 16

L'AJA — Dopo Slobodan Milosevic si difende attaccando: di fronte al Tribunale penale internazionale l'ex dittatore ha parlato per 3 ore, contestando il ruolo di Carla Del Ponte e ha accusato la Nato. Per l'ex "uomo forte" dei Balcani la pulizia etnica contro i kosovari era «lotta antiterrorismo», le prove delle atrocità «solo un oceano di bugie». Milosevic ha anche mostrato un video sugli effetti dei bombardamenti dell'Alleanza: i massacri di civili non erano errori, ma stragi cercate e volute.

MILELLA e VERONESE
ALLE PAGINE 8 e 9

Volevano partire per la Mecca

Ministro linciato dai pellegrini a Kabul

RENATO CAPRILE
A PAGINA 19

Casini: sulla tv pubblica si decide la prossima settimana. Giustizia, il Senato vara la riforma del Consiglio superiore

Ciampi: basta con le risse

Ma le nomine Rai tornano in alto mare. Ed è scontro sul Csm

I VETI DEI NUOVI GHINO DI TACCO

CURZIO MALTESE

A PRIMA vista, la rissa sulle poltrone Rai, censurata ieri dal presidente Ciampi, riporta l'orologio della storia agli anni grotteschi della prima Repubblica, al periodico scannarsi nel pentapartito per i posti migliori in viale Mazzini. Una vecchia commedia con nuovi interpreti. La Lega, già movimento «rivoluzionario» contro «Roma ladrona», s'è ridotta a minacciare la crisi se gli verrà negata una poltrona nel consiglio, come neppure il Psdi di Nicolazzi. Fini e An, ex partito delle mani pulite», rilanciano il ricatto di Ghino di Tacco: o ci date più posti o di qui non si passa. Forza Italia applica alla virgola il manuale Cencelli della lottizzazione, cercando di trovare l'accordo con tutti, ma conservando la presidenza e/o la direzione generale, come la Dc di Andreotti.

Archiviata la stagione delle speranze e del «nuovismo», sembrano tornati gli Anni Ottanta. Il nuovo ceto politico imita alla perfezione il vecchio, ma con una dose maggiore di aggressività, come una specie animale sopravvissuta a una catastrofe. È significativo che l'unico attore di questa farsa che si sia preoccupato del salvaguardare un minimo di forma sia stato il democristiano Casini, nel ricordo di un'epoca in cui, pur mangiando parecchio, il ceto politico sapeva almeno stare a tavola.

Ma la farsa che si ripete ha un elemento nuovo, che la peggiora di molto. Ed è il conflitto d'interessi. Questa non è una lottizzazione come le prece-

L'organo di autogoverno dei magistrati ridotto a 21 membri L'Ulivo: Stato di diritto violato I giudici: vogliono asservirci

ROMA — Dopo lo scontro sulle nomine Rai, arriva il richiamo ai partiti del presidente della Repubblica Ciampi, che a Grosseto dice ai politici locali: «Non prendete esempio dal palcoscenico nazionale, basta con le risse». Ma nonostante l'appello, non si placano le polemiche sul rinnovo dei vertici della tv pubblica. Il presidente della Camera, Casini, avverte: «Se ne riparla al mio ritorno dalla Grecia, la prossima settimana». E anche al Senato va in scena un altro scontro durissimo. La maggioranza ha approvato a Palazzo Madama la nuova composizione del Csm, che passa da trenta a ventuno componenti. L'Ulivo insorge: attaccano lo Stato di diritto. I magistrati: vogliono asservirci.

ALLE PAGINE 2, 3, 4, 10 e 11

Il governo rinvia la scadenza di 2 mesi e mezzo

Scudo fiscale prorogato fino al 15 maggio il rientro dei capitali

FABIO MASSIMO SIGNORETTI
A PAGINA 33

Accordo dopo i blitz degli addetti alle pulizie. Arrivano nuove agitazioni

Stop alla protesta delle stazioni oggi scioperano scuola e trasporti

La stazione di Milano invasa dai rifiuti
A PAGINA 13

LE IDEE

Tony Blair il fascino di un hobbit moderno

TIMOTHY GARTON ASH

I PRODOTTI culturali britannici più esportati dello scorso anno, mi riferisco, ovviamente, a Harry Potter, Frodo Baggins e Tony Blair, hanno tutti qualcosa in comune. Avvolta in una confezione ultramoderna, tecnologica e cinematografica, troviamo una tradizionalissima inglesità.

Ne "La compagnia dell'anello" lo "Shire" di Tolkien è un idillio in chiave fantasy della campagna inglese com'era prima del 1914. Così milioni di spettatori in tutto il mondo all'inizio del ventunesimo secolo si trovano trasportati in un ambiente agreste «very English» di un continuo di anni prima. Il piccolo hobbit dall'animo audace Frodo Baggins, in marcia verso Mordor è un fante inglese che va alla guerra contro il Kaiser, o Hitler, o forse Stalin, il rosso Sauron. Un elfo ci viene in aiuto spiegandoci che i suoi compagni sono scelti tra "i popoli liberi del mondo". I valori celebrati da Tolkien sono lealtà, coraggio, cameratismo, patriottismo, estremo sacrificio. Ancor più singolare è il caso di "Harry Potter e la Pietra Filosofale". Se togliamo la magia, ci appare il racconto d'altri tempi della vita in un collegio, una public school, secondo la fuorviante definizione inglese, che vuole "pubblica" la scuola privata.

SEGUE A PAGINA 17

Da "Cucchiaio blu" a "Enduring Freedom", così vengono scelti i nomi delle operazioni militari

Datemi un logo, farò la guerra

ANTONIO POLITO

CON REPUBBLICA
La Biblioteca del '900
In edicola

L E PAROLE contano, più dei fatti che descrivono. Le grandi fedi sono "logos": l'Antico testamento, Cristo, il Corano. Il capitalismo globale è "logo". La rivoluzione antiglo-

FRANCESCO ALBERONI

L'ARTE

For the first time since Italy's creation, the press is no longer controlled by political power and parties, but by the normal business groups in the Italian economy. Major dailies include Rome's *La Repubblica* and *Il Messaggero*, Milan's *Corriere della Sera*, *Il Giornale*, and *Il Sole 24 Ore* (important financial newspaper) and Turin's *La Stampa*. *Il Foglio* is a clever four–page daily. The Communist *L'Unita* is no longer widely read. Italians buy no more dailies than they did in the 1930s—six million, compared with 22 million in the UK. The major newsweeklies include *L'Espresso* and *Panorama*.

Despite its problems, Italy remains a prosperous, democratic country, in which civil rights are protected far better than in most countries of the world. It sometimes looks maddeningly chaotic, but the Italian brand of chaos has a certain refreshing sweetness to it which is precisely why millions of non–Italians are fervent admirers, even lovers of this country and its basically friendly people. Perhaps a touch of chaos is essential to the renowned Italian dolce vita ("sweet life").

251

Italy

FUTURE

That Italy will not collapse or capitulate under the weight of its multi–faceted ordeals is due largely to the fact that the Italians have an unshakable ability to adapt to existing circumstances with imagination and practicality. Some tendencies toward integrating the otherwise centrifugal political forces are evident in the widespread rejection and struggle against corruption, terrorism and organized crime.

Pressure for reform of the political system continues. Corruption is no longer as integral a part of political life as it once was. Pressure on the Mafia is being maintained. Since there are allegations that the Mafia and part of the political elite collaborated in the past, the "Clean Hands" campaign had some success because it proceeded on both fronts. It is unlikely that the Mafia now has protectors at the heart of government. Referring to the country's biggest corruption scandal and shake–up since 1945, Italy's most famous living novelist, Umberto Eco, stated in 1993, "we are living through our own 14th of July 1789." The difference, he noted, is that newspapers and television, not by a guillotine, are chopping off the heads of the political elite.

Electoral reform was supposed to clarify political choices and allow voters, not parliamentary intriguers, to choose who would govern. Governments were supposed to last longer. But the new election law intended to diminish the number of parties did not have the desired effect. Until 2001 only shaky governing coali-

tions resulted; cobbled alliances remained the Italian way. The political landscape is fragmented, with two communist and one ex–communist parties, three former socialist parties, four ex–Christian Democratic parties (three on the left and one on the right), one ex–fascist and one currently fascist party. Despite such fragmentation, Italy's politicians succeeded until 2001 in making the new system work more or less like the old one. In the May 2001 elections Silvio Berlusconi's House of Freedoms coalition won solid majorities in both the lower house and senate. No wonder the prime minister basked in victory: "Italy has turned a page."

Repeated massive demonstrations to protest the government's proposed changes to the pension and labor laws reveal how difficult and politically dangerous reform of these two explosive issues is. In March 2002 Red Brigades murdered the consultant advising the government on how to make it easier to lay off workers, Marco Biagi, after the government disregarded Biagi pleas for more protection. Berlusconi accused the largest labor union (CGIL) of creating an atmosphere of violence in its effort to stop the reform. Questions about Berlusconi's own probity and conflicts of interest will continue to nag him throughout his rule. He made anti-Muslim remarks after the September 11 terrorist attacks that embarrassed many Italians. When he and some of his cabinet ministers seemed to be resisting further European integration, his foreign minister, Renato Ruggiero, resigned. For ten months Berlusconi himself took over that

portfolio promising to support the EU and the euro while defending Italian national interests more strongly.

Nevertheless, his popularity remains intact, and his policies meet widespread approval. He increased child benefits, raised salaries for teachers, policemen and soldiers, gave tax breaks to companies in the South that hired young people, and presided over a further devolution of power in the regions, approved in a referendum in October 2001. The reform made the 20 regions responsible for everything, including raising taxes, not constitutionally granted to the central government in Rome. It is a sign of how confident and stable the republic has become that the Senate and Chamber of Deputies voted in 2002 to permit the heirs to the Italian throne to return to Italy for the first time since 1946. The ranking royal promised loyalty to the republican constitution.

Prime Minister Berlusconi, who supported the U.S.-British war against Iraq in 2003 in the face of overwhelming opposition at home, declared that his government would use its six-month EU presidency, which began July 1, 2003, to try to help heal the wide transatlantic rift that had developed over the Iraq crisis. "Italy will make the Euro-Atlantic relationship a priority." He was less kind with the Germans. In his first speech before the European Parliament he compared a German deputy to a concentration camp commandant. His deputy tourist minister called them "beer-guzzling chauvinistic boors." An irate Chancellor Schröder cancelled his Italian holiday in protest.

Lovers in a sunlit piazza in Florence

Photo by Jon M. Morrow

The Republic of San Marino

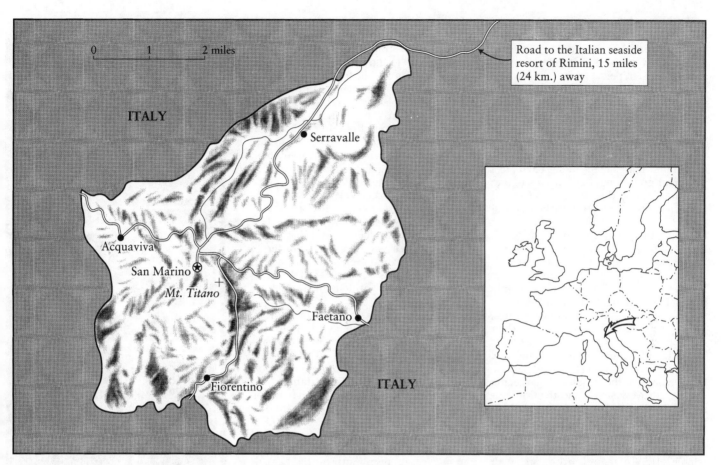

Road to the Italian seaside resort of Rimini, 15 miles (24 km.) away

ITALY

Serravalle

Acquaviva

San Marino ✪

Mt. Titano

Faetano

Fiorentino

ITALY

0   1   2 miles

Area: 23.5 sq. mi. (62 sq. km.)

Population: 24,300 (estimated).

Capital City: San Marino (Pop. 4,500, estimated).

Climate: Mild and temperate.

Official Language: Italian.

Ethnic Background: Italian.

Principal Religion: Roman Catholic.

Main Industries: Postage stamps, tourism, cotton textiles, brick, tile, cement.

Main Customer: Italy.

Currency: Euro.

Independence: Fourth Century A.D.

Government: Republic.

Chiefs of State: Two Captains Regent, selected every six months.

Heads of Government: Secretary of State for Foreign and Political Affairs and for Information, Secretary of State for Internal Affairs and Justice.

National Flag: Two horizontal stripes, one white on the top and one blue on the bottom.

National Holidays: April 1, October 1.

Known today chiefly to collectors, who prize this tiny country's beautiful postage stamps, the most serene Republic of San Marino is a historical curiosity situated on the slopes of Monte Titano in the eastern part of central Italy, to which it is linked by a customs union and a treaty of friendship. The last remaining relic of the self–governing Italian city-states, San Marino is the smallest republic in the world, and it always has wanted to stay that way. Its residents once refused Napoleon's offer of more territory on the grounds that the country's small size and poverty were the greatest guarantors of its independence. It has an irregular rectangular form with a maximum length of eight miles (13 km.) The country's setting is dominated by the 2,424 feet high (739 meters) Monte Titano, whose three summits are crowned by ancient fortifications. The medieval–looking capital city with its red–roofed stone houses is located directly below one of these fortifications and is surrounded by triple walls. Of its 23,400 residents, roughly 3,000 are non–citizens, mainly Italians. An additional 20,000 of the people (known as Sanmarinese) reside abroad, principally in Italy.

San Marino traces its origin to 301 A.D. when St. Marinus (from whom the country derives its name) and a small group of Christians fled to Monte Titano to escape religious persecution. In memory of their founder, the San Marinese do not date years according to Christ's life, but instead begin counting the years from 301 A.D. For instance, the year 2004 in San Marino is 1703! By the 12th century this tiny territory had become self-ruling. It has always managed to maintain its independence chiefly

thanks to its geographic isolation, its mountain fortresses and its skill in playing rival noble families against one another. By the 15th century, it was a republic ruled by a Grand Council composed of 60 men from San Marino's leading families.

During the Italian unification struggles in the 19th century, San Marino offered asylum to revolutionaries, including the hero Giuseppe Garibaldi. This assistance enabled it to gain a guarantee of independence from the Kingdom of Italy in 1862. San Marino remained neutral in World War II until September 1943, and in November of that year it was temporarily occupied by German troops. In June 1944 it was damaged by British bomber pilots who were attempting to dislodge the occupiers.

The Statutes of 1600, enlarged in 1926 and revised in 1939, serve as a constitution. They established a parliament, the Great and General Council, with 60 members elected every five years by universal suffrage since 1960. This Council in turn elects two Captains Regent, largely ceremonial figures who formally exercise executive power for a period of six months. During their semi–annual investitures on April 1 and October 1, the Noble Guard and Great and General Councilors all dress in brightly colored uniforms and parade through the capital's streets. The Captains Regent cannot be elected for a second term

The Republic of San Marino

until three years have elapsed. In 1981 for the first time in the country's history, a woman, Maria Lea Pedini Angelini, was chosen. The Council also elects from among its members ten persons who serve as secretaries of state in the Council of State, the principal organ of executive power. These secretaries of state each head a government administrative department.

The Secretary of State for Foreign Affairs and the Secretary of State for Internal Affairs are in fact the highest and most powerful government executives of San Marino. Finally, the Great and General Council elects a supreme appellate judicial body, the Council of Twelve, which hears appeals from the decisions of San Marino's two full–time judges, who need not be citizens. These judges decide on the basis of San Marino's own civil and criminal legal system, which has understandably been influenced greatly by Italian law.

The country has many political parties, which are heavily influenced by their much larger counterpart parties in Italy. These include the Christian Democratic Party (DCS), the Socialist Party (PSS), the Left Democrats, the People's Alliance, the Democratic Movement, and the Communists. Like their Italian counterparts, these parties are not rigidly bound to doctrine. In the June 2001 elections the Christian Democrats continued their dominance, winning 41.5% of the votes, compared with 24% for the anti-Marxist Socialist Party.

A unique election feature is that the state pays 75% of the return fare for any Sanmarinese living abroad to come home and vote in general elections. Over 5,400 did just that in 1988, returning from as far as Detroit, where many Sanmarinese live.

This tiny mouse roars against the United States if it gets an urge to do so. In 1982 its parliament voted to "deplore" American policy in El Salvador and authorized a symbolic $4,500 contribution to the rebel forces in that Central American nation.

All parties in San Marino favor a broad social security system that, among other things, provides health care from state funds. Children up to the age of 12 receive a guaranteed summer holiday on the seaside, and up to the age of 14 a free public education. Those wishing to study further are eligible for state scholarships to Italian high schools and universities. Finally, the state of San Marino finds work for all citizens who cannot obtain employment privately. If no work at all can be found, then the state provides unemployment benefits amounting to 60% of the person's normal salary.

This country has no army because Italy provides for its defense. It does have a military corps that performs parade duty during national celebrations. It has a gendarmerie that maintains public order. In 1988 San Marino entered the Council of Europe, and in 1992 it joined the United Nations. It sends athletes to the winter Olympics since 1976.

There are utterly no natural resources, so earnings must be made from farming (chiefly wheat and grapes), livestock raising, light manufacturing (chiefly cotton textiles, brick and tile, cement and pottery), the sale of postage stamps and tourism. Diplomatic relations between the EU and San Marino were opened in 1983. Its goods have free access to the EU. It not only adopted the euro in 2002, but it was permitted to mint its own euro coins with its own motif on the back. It began to attract capital by being a tax haven. However, in 2000 it joined five other small states in agreeing to cooperate with international efforts to curb abusive and criminal tax-avoidance schemes. It reached an agreement with the EU in 2003 to collect taxes for bank account interest and return 75% of it to the country of residence without providing account holders' names.

During the summer months, from 20,000 to 30,000 foreign tourists visit San Marino each day. Unfortunately, the Sanmarinese welcome these tourists with solid rows of souvenir shops on both sides of the principal streets. Without doubt, it has more tourist stands and shops per capita than does any other country in the world. This creates an excessively commercialized air in this naturally beautiful mountain–top republic. But several handsome hotels and restaurants have appeared in recent years, relieving this monotony. There is no radio broadcasting or television of its own, and there are no railroad or airport facilities.

FUTURE

Although legally independent, San Marino has always been very vulnerable to pressure from the Italian government, political parties and trade unions. This situation will certainly continue. Its beautiful setting and the curiosity this tiny republic stimulates will help assure that tourism will continue to be a lucrative source of income. However, a shortage of energy will continue to exist, and San Marino will have great difficulty finding the necessary funds to finance badly needed expanded water and electric power systems.

Monte Titano dominates San Marino

254

The Vatican City State

St. Peter's Square

Area: .15 sq. mi. (.40 sq. km.)
Population: 1,000 (estimated).
Climate: Temperate.
Neighboring Countries: Italy.
Official Language: Latin. Italian is the working language at the Vatican.
Religion: Roman Catholic.
Currency: Vatican Lira, interchangeable with euro.
National Day: June 30.
Chief of State: His Holiness Pope John Paul II (formerly Karol Cardinal Wojtyla), elected Pope October 16, 1978.
Suffrage: Limited to cardinals less than 80 years of age, who elect a Pope for life.
National Flag: Yellow and white stripes parallel to the staff, with the papal insignia on a white field.

Vatican City is the world's second smallest state. One can leisurely stroll around the full length of its borders in less than one hour. Located in the heart of Rome, near the west bank of the Tiber River, and surrounded by medieval walls and the Church of St. Peter, this tiny dot on the Rome city map is often said to wield more influence in the world than the entire nation of Italy. The reason is that this is the headquarters of the Roman Catholic Church, the largest body of Christians in the world. Building began in the 8th century to create a residence for the popes. By the Middle Ages the Vatican had come to control a large part of Italy and was one of the most important and influential powers in European politics. In 1870 the government of the newly founded Italian state annexed the extensive Papal States throughout Italy. The pontiffs rejected all offers of financial compensation, choosing instead to withdraw behind the Vatican's walls in defiance.

In 1929 the Pope chose to sign the Lateran Treaty with the then fascist government of Italy. This treaty established the independence and sovereignty of the State of Vatican City, fixed the relationship between the Italian government and the Catholic Church and set a cash payment for the earlier seizure of papal property. A revision of this treaty in 1984 ended the status of Roman Catholicism as Italy's state religion. Despite the loss of much of its property, the Vatican has very extensive investments throughout the world, especially in Italy.

The Church's wealth is widely assumed to be massive. Financial operations are handled by the Institute for Religious Agencies, better known as the "Vatican Bank," whose depositors are Catholic religious orders, Vatican employees and clergymen. For 2,000 years until 1987 the Vatican kept its financial operations strictly secret. However, an inspection of the books of the bankrupt Milan–based Banco Ambrosiano and the mysterious suicide of that bank's president in 1982 revealed deep Vatican entanglement in questionable financial dealings. The Church hierarchy was so seriously embarrassed by this scandal that the Pope ordered an end to the Holy See's dependence upon investment and speculation for its funds. It would rely instead on "the spontaneous contributions of the faithful and of other men of good will." The bank scandal made it more difficult to raise money.

In 1987 an Italian court issued an arrest warrant against the head of the "Vatican Bank," American Archbishop Paul Marcinkus, as "accessory to fraudulent bankruptcy." Because the Archbishop, who the Vatican insisted was innocent, had moved inside the Vatican walls, Italian authorities could not arrest him; Italy has no extradition treaty with the Vatican.

There were no precedents for such a complex legal standoff between the two sovereign states. According to Article 22 of the Lateran Treaty, the Vatican is

Vatican City

obligated to surrender to Italian custody anyone who enters its grounds in order to escape from Italian law. However, Article 11 states, "central bodies of the Catholic Church are free from every interference on the part of the Italian state." During the Second World War, even the Mussolini government did not try to get possession of Jews and political refugees who had hidden within the Vatican's walls. Italy's highest court annulled the arrest warrant, and Marcinkus retired from papal service in 1991 and returned to Chicago as a parish priest. Supervision of the bank passed to an international board of five Catholic lay directors.

The Lateran Treaty established extraterritorial status, but technically not papal sovereignty, for 13 areas outside Vatican City. These are chiefly the major Catholic churches in Rome and the Pope's summer residence of Castel Gandolfo. In an agreement of 1951, the Vatican's radio station (*Stazione Radio Città del Vaticano*) also was placed under Vatican jurisdiction. This created tensions in 2001 when citizens charged that the electromagnetic emissions from the Vatican Radio's large towers on the outskirts of Rome cause cancer.

Insofar as the purely political functions of the Vatican are concerned, all executive, legislative and judicial authority is vested in the Pope. He appoints a governor and organs to administer the Vatican. The College of Cardinals serves as the chief papal advisers, and the Roman Curia carries on the central administration of the Roman Catholic Church's religious affairs.

Within the Vatican live fewer than 1,000 persons, all of whom have Vatican documents, rather than other passports. They are chiefly permanent Vatican employees, the largest number being priests and nuns. Cardinals are considered to be Vatican residents whenever they are in Rome.

His Holiness Pope John Paul II

When a citizen of the Vatican leaves the city limits of Rome, he automatically becomes a citizen of his original nationality (or of Italy if the original nationality does not permit dual citizenship).

Vatican City has within its borders its own telephone system, a post office (which uses the Vatican's own stamps), a radio station, a pharmacy, several stores, and a banking system with its own coins and the only cash machines in the world with instructions in Latin. It was also granted permission to mint its own euro coins with Pope John Paul's profile on the back. In addition to the Church of St. Peter and the Vatican Apostolic Palace (which was expanded in the 15th and 16th centuries to become the largest palace in the world) with all its museums and library, the Vatican contains a score of administrative and ecclesiastical buildings, a "village" of apartments and the beautiful Vatican gardens. There is a small railroad station at the perimeter of the Vatican that is connected by 300 meters of track to the Italian state railway station.

Permanent diplomatic representatives (known as *nuncios*) in capitals throughout the world conduct the Vatican's dealings with the outside world. By tradition, papal nuncios are granted the first rank at those diplomatic ceremonies that they attend. In 1984 the United States became the 107th nation to establish full diplomatic relations with the Vatican, which also has permanent observer status at the United Nations. It established official ties with the Palestinian Liberation Organization (PLO) in 1994.

Sensitive to allegations that the Vatican had done little to condemn the holocaust or help Jews during the Second World War, the Vatican intervened to support the relocation of a cloister located on the edge of the Auschwitz death camp in Poland. The Holy See's relations with Jews had been strained for 2,000 years. But in 1965 the Vatican repudiated the doctrine of collective Jewish guilt for the death of Jesus. This was documented in "Nostra Aetate" ("In Our Time") published in 2002. The Vatican official in charge of Jewish relations, Cardinal Walter Kasper, stated in that year that Catholics and Jews may still disagree on some things, but they do so as brothers. In 1993 it signed an accord with Israel leading to full diplomatic relations the following year, and in 1994 it published a document acknowledging its past mistakes that had contributed to anti–Semitism.

In 1997 the Pope condemned the actions of many Christians before and during the Holocaust, saying that they contributed to the rise of anti–Semitism and then failed to help as Jews were being eradicated. Jewish groups criticized the fact that this

Fresco in the Sistine Chapel

strong statement fell short of an apology, which they have been demanding. In 1998 the Church, while defending the actions of Pope Pius XII as having been a quieter form of resistance against the Nazis, officially apologized for failing to take a more active role in stopping Nazi persecution of Jews. It also declared Edith Stein, an Orthodox Jew who had converted to Christianity and died at Auschwitz in 1942, to be a saint.

Until 1975 the foreign diplomatic representatives to the Vatican had to be men. When the West Germans sent a woman counselor to its mission, they were reminded of the Vatican's "tradition that forbids Vatican officials from having business contacts with ladies." Finally the former African dictator of Uganda, Idi Amin, forced the Vatican to accept a female mission chief. The Church's ban on women priests is under increasing attack by Catholics. In 1987 it was revealed that a priest who had served in southern Italy for 25 years had undergone a sex change and become a woman. Church practice holds that an ordained priest remains one whatever his transgressions might be. Therefore, the Church granted her early retirement with the usual pension. The Church often acts slowly: in 1992 it formally rehabilitated Galileo Galilei, whom the Inquisition had condemned in 1633 for daring to prove that the Earth orbited the sun, rather than the other way around.

Italy assumes responsibility for defending the Vatican and for patrolling St. Peter's Square. When the Turkish gunman who shot the Pope in May 1981 was captured, he was taken initially to the Commissariato Borgo, the Vatican police headquarters. He was then bundled very quickly into an armored car and driven to central police headquarters in downtown Rome. There was inconclusive evidence that Soviet or Eastern European intelligence agencies, operating through Bulgaria, were involved with this attempted murder. The Pope requested clemency for Agca, and Italian President Carlo Ciampi pardoned him in 2000. He was extradited to Turkey to serve a sentence for a prior crime.

By the end of the decade, though, Mikhail Gorbachëv's *Glasnost* had led to better relations between the Holy See and Eastern Europe, and the Pope launched a campaign for a "Europe without spiritual frontiers." The reconciliation between communism and Christianity was crowned by Gorbachev's historic audience with the Pope (whom he addressed as "Your Holiness"!) in 1989. Said a Vatican diplomat: "Catholicism and communism are ideologies that cannot be reconciled. But there is space for common endeavor in the social, cultural and humanitarian fields." Gorbachev expressed interest in the Pope's call for a third road between capitalism and socialism, a new social order that would combine social justice with economic efficiency and political pluralism. The USSR wanted to be a full partner in a common European civilization, and the Pope holds one of the keys to that community. In 1991 he named spiritual leaders for Soviet Catholics, published a social doctrine for societies returning to capitalism, and convened an unprecedented synod of bishops from the two halves of Europe to meet in Rome.

In 1996 Pope John Paul II received one of the world's last Communist leaders, Fidel Castro. In return, the Cuban dictator renewed his country's invitation of the Pontiff; Cuba was the only Latin American nation the pope had not yet visited. The Pope arrived in Cuba in 1998 to large and enthusiastic crowds. One million Cubans assembled to hear him read mass at Revolutionary Square. The political importance and influence of the Pope were visible in the easing by Castro (who for the first time as president wore civilian clothes in his own country) of religious intolerance before the Pontiff arrived and his public composure while the Pope admonished the Cuban church to fight for "the recognition of human rights and social justice" and to take "courageous and prophetic stands in the face of the corruption of political and economic power." The Pope also won the release of 299 prisoners. However, in 2003 he decried the harsh sentences against dissidents meted out by the Castro regime, as well as the execution of three men who had seized a ferry in an ill-fated attempt to escape to the United States.

In 2001 the Pope apologized to China for errors of the colonial past and pleaded for diplomatic relations, broken in 1951, in order to protect Chinese Roman Catholics from continued persecution. This is made difficult because the Vatican maintains diplomatic relations with Taiwan.

The Church also clashed with Russia's Orthodox church in 2002 when it created four new dioceses in that country, which has an estimated 1.3 million Catholics. Or-

thodox leaders charged that Rome seeks to poach converts. On his 100th foreign trip during his papacy in June 2003, he reached out to leaders of the Orthodox Church and called on the Catholic majority in Croatia to seek reconciliation with Orthodox Serbs.

Order within the small state is provided by a colorfully dressed regular army of Swiss guards. Recruitment is held in the cantons of Freiburg, St. Gallen and Lucerne; the men must be between 20 and 30 years old. They carry old-fashioned halberds, but they always have machine guns hidden close by. Perhaps former Soviet Foreign Minister Andrei Gromyko was wrong in calling them "the world's least frightening army"! Plain-clothes Swiss guards and agents from the papal gendarmes always accompany the Pope everywhere when he confronts audiences and crowds within the Vatican, just as Secret Service men accompany the President of the United States. One difference is that the agents never turn completely away from the Pope in order to scan for potential troublemakers. Paul VI ruled that it was disrespectful for the guards to turn their backs on the Pontiff. In 1998 a disgruntled guard fatally shot his commander and wife and then killed himself. This was the first time in 150 years that this had occurred, and it prompted the Vatican to review its recruiting procedures and administer psychological exams for new guards.

The Vatican possesses priceless cultural treasures, including the Vatican Museums, the frescoes by Michelangelo in the Sistine Chapel, frescoes by Pinturicchio in the Borgia Apartment, Raphael's Stanze and the Church of St. Peter, where such art treasures as Michelangelo's "La Pietà" are displayed. In 1983 more than 200 of these irreplaceable art works toured the United States, where they were viewed by millions of Americans in New York, Chicago and San Francisco. The Vatican Library contains a valuable collection of manuscripts from the pre-Christian era to the present. It also publishes an influential daily newspaper, *L'Osservatore Romano*.

The Vatican owns a press that publishes books and pamphlets in all languages of the world. In 2003 it published the latest edition of a two-volume Latin dictionary containing 15,000 modernized Latin words. The Vatican's Latin Foundation, set up in the 1970s to keep Latin alive in the Church after it had been decreed that mass could be celebrated in local languages, is behind the project. Although Italian is the working language of the Vatican, Latin remains the Church's official language, and an up-to-date dictionary is needed for encyclicals and other scientific documents. It is not easy to keep

Reprinted with special permission of King Features Syndicate

Vatican City

Latin alive after more than two millennia, and many of the dictionary's new words are compounds of existing Latin words. For example, "dishwasher" is *"escariorum lavator"* and "disco" is *"orbium phonographicorum theca."*

FUTURE

Because of the failing health of the formerly active and charismatic Pope John Paul II, who suffers from Parkinson's disease and near-crippling arthritis and who almost always needs a wheelchair, there is a danger that the influence of the Roman Catholic Church, and therefore of the Vatican could decline. Since the Vatican Law does not cover the possibility of incapacitation, an ill Pope could leave the Church rudderless or in the hands of aides who act in his name. The last Pope to resign willingly was in 1294. John Paul II's reign is already the fifth longest in history, and he vows to serve "until the end of the

mission with which Christ entrusted me." There are signs that his clout is weakening, as was shown by the election of a former Communist as president in his native Poland and by referenda in Ireland permitting divorce and abortion under certain circumstances. In 2003 The Vatican expressed surprise and disappointment that the convention drafting a constitution for the EU ignored the Pope's repeated appeals that the document recognize Europe's Christian heritage in the preamble. It no longer swings much political weight in Spain. Its former political influence in Italy was greatly diminished by the collapse of the Christian Democracy party. Nevertheless, the Pope gave a historic address to the Italian parliament in November 2002, the first time this had ever happened. Appealing to Italians to meet the "crisis of the birth rate," he received a standing ovation, which was in part a tribute to his physical perseverance. The appearance was a sign that the turbulent re-

lationship between Italy and the Church was becoming warmer.

Its role in Europe has not yet been reduced to trying to influence only social issues. Even this is difficult in the face of so many persons who describe themselves as "cultural Catholics" while blithely ignoring the Pope's teaching when it does not suit them. In Poland many analysts credit a pastoral letter from the Pope for persuading the required number of people (50%) to vote in a June 2003 referendum that approved the country's entry into the EU. His letter, which was read in churches across Poland the weekend before the voting, called EU membership "an act of historical justice." The Holy See, which claims over a billion believers or 17.3% of the world's population, now faces a major challenge over the ordination of women. It is not surprising that the Vatican looked forward to a grandiose diversion to celebrate the dawning of the third Christian millennium in 2000. More than 30 million visitors journeyed to Rome for the event.

Fearing that this celebration would be marred, the Vatican suggested that it would have been a "matter of common sense" for Italian officials to ban a World Gay Pride parade in Rome in July. Many persons were offended by posters highlighting God's hand touching Adam's private parts in Michelangelo's masterpiece in the Vatican's Sistine Chapel. However, the Holy See took no formal steps to stop the parade, especially since the most recent concordat between the Vatican and the Italian state, signed in 1984, deprives Rome of the "holy status" Mussolini granted it in 1929. The event drew 70,000 participants, according to the police (200,000 according to organizers). The Pope bitterly denounced it as an insult and an offense to Christian values, saying that homosexual acts are "contrary to natural law." A Vatican glossary of sexual terms that appeared in 2003 asserts that homosexuals are not normal and that the increasingly large number of countries that allow gay marriages are inhabited by people with "profoundly disordered minds." Nevertheless, the Pope argues that gays should be treated with "respect, compassion, and delicacy" because homosexuality is a "disorder."

The Church has sexual problems of its own as its clergy are charged in many countries, including the U.S., of sexually abusing believers. All American cardinals were called to Rome in April 2002 to be lectured on the impermissibility of such behavior. However, when the United States Conference of Catholic Bishops approved of a zero-tolerance policy on sexually abusive priests in October 2002, the Vatican demanded major revisions.

Federigo Il Da Montefeltro, 15th century

The Sovereign Military Order of Malta

(The Roman Catholic *Sovereign Military Hospitaler Order of St. John of Jerusalem, of Rhodes and of Malta)*

Area: The Malta Palace (Palazzo di Malta) and the Villa Malta, about three acres.

Population: International membership in the Order is about 9,600, all of whom retain their own nationality.

Neighboring Countries: Located in Rome, Italy.

Religion: Roman Catholicism.

Chief of State (Head of the Order): The Prince and Grand Master (since 1988), His Most Eminent Highness Frà Andrew Bertie (b. 1929).

Flag of State: A plain white cross on a red field, (of the Grand Master)—The white Maltese Cross on a red field.

Only with a magnifying glass can one see the world's smallest country on a Rome city map. Completely surrounded by a wall and with a territorial size equivalent to half a football field, The Sovereign Military Order of Malta (SMOM) is the only country in the world which has *no* citizens whatsoever and which is small enough to be assigned a street address: 68 Via Condotti, a very elegant street just a stone's throw from Rome's famous

Spanish Steps. By peeping through the keyhole of the main gate of Villa Malta on the Aventine Hill, a palace which is also part of SMOM, one can gain the kind of view normally available only to astronauts: one can see three sovereign countries, namely the SMOM, Italy and the Vatican.

The Prince and Grand Master was elected in 1988 by the Council Complete of State and was duly confirmed by the Pope. Today this ancient entity maintains diplomatic relations with the Holy See, on which it depends as a religious Order, but not as a sovereign, and with 48 nations (but not with the United States). It has delegations to the Council of Europe and UNESCO. It sent a delegate to the UN Millennium Summit in New York, September 2000, who was imaginative in getting himself and his sovereign order noticed. Publication of the official photograph of world leaders was delayed because a man in the photo could not be identified. It turned out that he was Count Carlos Maruulo di Condojanni, Grand Chancellor of the Sovereign Military

Order of Malta, who somehow slipped past security into history.

It enjoys the same status of extra–territoriality that the Italian government grants to any embassy; that is, it is considered to be foreign soil. On January 28, 1961, the Civil Courts of Rome declared the Order an " international sovereign society." Issuing its own passports and conducting its affairs without interference, this tiny state is truly an oddity in the contemporary world.

The hospital–infirmary dedicated to St. John the Baptist was founded in Jerusalem about the middle of the 11th century. It was administered by a monastic community, originally connected with the Benedictines but later independent, which was dedicated to the care for those Christians who fell ill during their pilgrimages to the Holy Land.

In the same century Pope Urban II urged the formation of a great crusade in order to sweep the Moslems from the cradle of Christianity and to expand the reach of the Roman Catholic Church. A growing army, led by French knights and

The Sovereign Military Order of Malta

joined by noblemen and simple folk from many nations, in 1096 progressed on horseback and foot across Europe and toward the Holy Land. The crusader knights were young, ranging from 16 to 30 years, and they were brimming with enthusiasm, self–confidence, a strong taste for adventure and (for many) visions of riches. They seized Jerusalem in 1099 and surrounding areas in a series of bloody battles. During the first years the hospital's prior installed some of them into the Order of St. John of Jerusalem as defenders. To confirm their intense

dedication at the time of their induction they held out their swords, which were blessed under flickering torches.

In 1113 the community of the Hospital of St. John was recognized by the Pope as a religious Order of the Church, free from all lay interference. This was the germ of the Order's sovereignty. In the 1130s, because of the need to protect the sick, the pilgrims and the Christian settlements in the Holy Land, the Order acquired the additional military character and became a monastic–chivalric Order, in which monks were knights and knights took the

H.M.E.H. The Prince and Grand Master

The Malta Palace, 68 Via Condotti

monastic vows. The Order's military edge was first felt in 1118 when its knights did more than protect; they openly attacked the Moslems. Stories of their bravery made them living legends, and new recruits continued to join their ranks every year.

In 1187 the overwhelming forces of Saladin, Sultan of Egypt and Syria, drove the Knights, who suffered terrible losses, from the Latin Kingdom of Jerusalem. All of them were at least wounded, and only a handful survived, including the Grand Master. Those who remained escaped. The Kingdom and the Order continued at Acre (Akka). In even greater numbers than before, knights came from all over Europe to join the struggle against the "infidels." There were eight crusades until 1291, but each grew weaker. The crusaders were never permanently able to wrest Jerusalem from Moslem control. The Moslems wiped the Kingdom out in 1291, and the order moved to Cyprus. But the Knights of St. John remained dedicated to their task of defending Christianity.

They used Cyprus as a base for the next 120 years, continuing to battle the Moslems on or around the Mediterranean Sea. The island was never considered ideal for their purposes because the coastline was too extensive to defend adequately. In 1310 the Knights attacked and captured Rhodes, a beautiful island of meadowlands and forests lying some 25 miles (40 km.) off the southwestern coast of Turkey. Establishing their headquarters there, they continued to expand their navy and constructed a watchtower on the nearly

The Sovereign Military Order of Malta

islet of Simi in order to foil any naval attack.

In the following years their control extended over most of the islands off the western coast of Turkey, some little more than outcroppings of jagged rock. Their activity excited admiration throughout Europe because the Knights could effectively challenge Turkish domination in the Mediterranean Sea. In recognition of this role, Pope Nicholas V recognized the Grand Master of the Order as the Sovereign Prince of Rhodes in 1446.

The Turks overran Asia Minor and were moving into Europe—in 1453 they put an end to the Byzantine Empire and proceeded to launch attacks on Rhodes. Over and over the Turks made massive attacks against the island, but not until 1532 did they succeed in overwhelming the Knights and forced them to leave. During the following eight years the Knights were homeless, but in 1530 the Holy Roman Emperor, Charles V, gave the Order the island of Malta, on which they built the finest hospital in Europe at that time. Included were the nearby islands, as well as the African mainland fortress–city, Tripoli, a city which the Knights soon abandoned.

During the next 268 years they vigilantly patrolled the waters to protect trade routes for Christian merchants. They continued to raid Turkish ships and those of Barbary pirates (see The Republic of Malta).

The Prince Grand Master of the Order, who since 1630 has the rank equal to that of a Cardinal, was the undisputed ruler of Malta and was a sovereign who entered into treaties with other nations and enjoyed the usual rights accorded to a chief of state. Of course, the Order's very existence, powers, privileges and immunities remained under the protective umbrella of the Roman Catholic Church, and these were therefore respected throughout Christendom. Splendid architectural monuments, churches, public buildings and fortifications still bear witness to the Order's sovereign rule in Malta.

It took periodic interest in acquiring territory in the New World. In 1653 Louis XIV of France gave the Order four Caribbean islands—St. Kitts, St. Martin, St. Croix and St. Barthélemy—but the Order later decided to sell these small islands to the French West India Company.

In 1794 it approached James Monroe, the U.S. Ambassador to France, with an offer of ports, provisions and protection for American sailors in the Mediterranean in return for lands in America. Monroe responded that the Order was welcome to purchase land, but that such property could not become a part of another sovereign government and would have to remain under the jurisdiction of the United States. Although the Order was not interested in buying under these terms, its personal ties with the United States have remained strong—approximately 1,500 out of 9,600 of the Order's knights are presently living in the U.S., and they include such prominent American Catholics as former Treasury Secretary William E. Simon, the late Clare Boothe Luce, William F. Buckley, Jr., and the late Terrence Cardinal Cooke, Archbishop of New York. However, Americans can never ascend to the highest ranks of the Order because only persons of long–standing nobility are admitted to high leadership positions.

Napoleon's forces, engaged in a campaign against Egypt, occupied the island of Malta in 1798 and drove out the Order. The knights were overwhelmingly French and were reportedly somewhat sympathetic to the French general. But they again found themselves without a home. This was followed by what has been called the Russian *coup d'état* (1798–1803).

Tsar Paul I of Russia was a bitter opponent of the French Revolution and also had hopes of setting up a Russian naval base in the Mediterranean. He had shown

Interior courtyard of the Malta Palace

The Sovereign Military Order of Malta

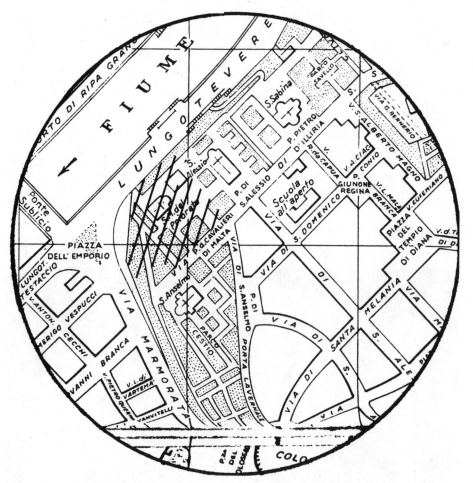

Location and grounds of the Villa Malta on the Aventine Hill

rule the island until it became independent in 1964. Surviving knights scattered throughout Europe attempted after 1802 to persuade European powers once again to give the Order a base. Various islands were considered, but no nation seemed interested in donating even a small one to what they considered to be a fading order of knighthood. The Sovereign Order's headquarters moved to Sicily and then to Ferrara. Finally, in 1834 the 16th century Malta Palace in Rome, which had been the Order's embassy to the Papal State since the early 1600s, became the Order's headquarters and remains so to the present time.

Maintaining health institutions throughout the world, from small dispensaries and leper colonies to ten hospitals, the Order has returned to its original mission of caring for the sick. Yet those persons who dismiss The Sovereign Military Order of Malta as being neither sovereign nor military are only half right. It no longer performs a military function, despite the shining swords that the Knights still bear on festive occasions. It does perform an admirable humanitarian function in a world that, in many places, is still largely gripped by disease and misery. And it is a sovereign entity by international recognition, even if it only has three acres in Rome to call its very own.

himself as a friend of the Order. He now had himself proclaimed Grand Master by a handful of knights who had gone to live in Russia, instead of the Grand Master Frà Ferdinand von Hompesch, who had abandoned Malta to the French. This proclamation of a married non–Catholic as head of a Catholic religious order was wholly illegal and void; the Holy See never recognized it, which was a necessary condition for legitimacy. Accordingly, Paul I, who was nevertheless accepted by many knights and a number of governments, can only be regarded as a Grand Master *de facto*, never one *de jure*. This was only a brief interlude. Paul was murdered in 1801 and was succeeded by his 24–year–old son, Alexander I. The new Tsar helped the Order to return to legitimate rule. In 1803 Frà Giovanni Battista Tommasi was elected Grand Master.

In the meantime, the British, who had seized the island of Malta from Napoleon in 1801, specified in the 1802 Treaty of Amiens with France that Malta must be restored to the Order. This never happened, though, and Britain continued to

262

The Republic of Malta

Mdina—old capital of Malta

Courtesy: Alexandra Schaerrer

Area: 122 sq. mi. (316 sq. km., one–tenth the size of Rhode Island).

Population: 392,000.

Capital City: Valletta (Pop. 21,000, estimated).

Climate: Mild and sunny Mediterranean.

Neighboring Countries: Italy lies to the north, Libya to the south.

Official Languages: Maltese, English. Italian is also widely spoken.

Other Principal Tongues: Italian is understood.

Ethnic Background: Mixture of Phoenician, Carthaginian, Arab, Sicilian, Norman, Spanish, Italian, British.

Principal Religion: Roman Catholic (98%).

Main Exports: Tourism, ship repair, clothing, food manufacturing and processing, textiles.

Main Customers: Italy (40%), Germany (15%), France (9%), UK (6%); EU (70%).

Currency: Maltese Lira.

Former Colonial Status: British Crown Colony.

Independence Day: September 21, 1964, within the British Commonwealth of Nations; Republic declared on December 13, 1974. Government: Parliamentary democracy.

Chief of State: Guido De Marco, President (since April 1999).

Head of Government: Eddie Fenech Adami, Prime Minister (since September 1998).

National Holiday: Republic Day, December 13.

National Flag: Two large vertical white and red stripes with a gray cross in the upper left–hand corner.

Malta is a small but historically and strategically important group of five islands (two of which are uninhabited) in the central Mediterranean Sea 60 miles (96 km.) south of Sicily and 180 miles (290 km.) north of Libya. For centuries Malta, with its well–sheltered anchorage, has been squarely in the middle of the many struggles to control the Mediterranean Sea and with that, the traffic between Europe, Africa and the Middle East. Because of its strategic importance and small size, Malta has always been dependent upon exterior powers.

Malta's people and culture today clearly reflect the influence of the many conquerors who have dominated the islands. Ethnically, the Maltese people are predominantly of Carthaginian and Phoenician origin. The latter named the islands "Maleth," meaning "hiding place," from which the country's present name is derived. The Maltese culture is a mixture of Italian and Arabic traditions. Maltese is a Semitic language arising from the mixture of Arabic and Sicilian Italian. It is the only Semitic language that is written in Latin script, and to the stranger it sounds very much like Arabic. The official language since 1934, Maltese is the most widely used medium of communication. It is also the language of instruction in the schools, which are patterned on the British educational system, and is used by one television and nine radio networks. Scholars disagree whether the European or the Arabic component predominates in the Maltese character and nature, but they do agree that the Maltese have a distinct culture and identity of their own.

HISTORY

The Early Period

Archaeologists have uncovered evidence of Neolithic cave dwellers from approximately 3800 B.C. on Malta, and it is probable that the islands were a center of Mediterranean civilization before Crete was. Between the 9th and 6th centuries B.C. the Phoenicians, Greeks and Carthaginians established colonies in Malta and the islands' inhabitants came into contact with Semitic cultures along the southern and eastern rim of the Mediterranean. In 218 B.C. the islands fell under Roman control.

Christian Beginnings

According to Biblical legend, a Roman ship carrying St. Paul crashed on offshore rocks in 60 A.D., and Paul saved himself by swimming shore. The Maltese still use the favorite saying when everything seems to go wrong: "Don't forget that even St. Paul was shipwrecked on Malta!" He wasted no time in converting the population, and the majority of Malta's population has been Christian ever since.

Arabs and Normans

When the Roman Empire approached total collapse in the 4th century A.D., Malta fell under the domination of Constantinople. Until the 16th century the islands were ruled successively by Arabs, who came in 870 A.D. and placed their indelible stamp on the Maltese, by Normans, who displaced the Arabs in 1000 A.D. and who improved Maltese political and legal structures, and later by other European nations.

Control by the Knights

In 1520 Malta came under the control of the Order of the Hospital of St. John of Jerusalem (otherwise known as the "Knights Hospitalers," or the "Maltese Knights"), a Roman Catholic religious order. It had been founded in Jerusalem before the Crusades in order to protect Christian pilgrims. Later, it had established its headquarters on the Greek island of Rhodes before being driven out by the Turks. The Holy Roman Emperor of the time, Charles V, granted Malta to the Knights, which they turned into a fortress against Islam.

Their military mission was to keep the Turks out of the western Mediterranean and to clear the southern Mediterranean of pirates. Their raids on the immense Ottoman Empire so enraged the Turkish Sultan that he sent a huge army of 40,000 men and a navy of 200 ships against the heavily fortified islands. The four–month Turkish siege was one of the bloodiest in history, and of 9,000 Maltese Knights and soldiers, fewer than 1,000 survived unwounded. But their valor, under Grand Master Jean de La Valette, a shrewd military tactician after whom Malta's present capital city was named, forced the Turks to withdraw. Never again did the Turks attempt to penetrate the western Mediterranean.

The victorious and prosperous Knights began to build the capital city of Valleta on a rocky headland. They built innumerable splendid baroque palaces, churches and public buildings, financed primarily by booty from their naval adventures against the Turks. Many of these structures still survive and testify to the great prosperity of that time. The famed Sacra Infermeria Hospital, whose construction began in 1571, was recently converted to a magnificent and modern Mediterranean conference center in an attempt to make Malta a major trade center.

The Republic of Malta

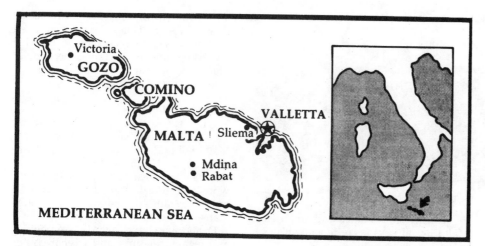

Napoleon and British Rule

Napoleon Bonaparte seized the islands in 1798. Because of sympathetic French Knights, his troops scarcely had to fire a shot. However, realizing that he would be unable to defend the islands against the British Navy, he decided to return them to the Knights soon thereafter. Not wishing this to happen, a sizable number of Maltese rebelled and demanded to be placed under British sovereignty. Always attentive to the strategic needs of its empire and navy, and bracing itself for a bitter struggle against Napoleonic France, Britain gladly accepted in 1800. The Treaty of Paris confirmed British sovereignty over Malta in 1814. The Maltese Knights never returned to the islands as rulers, but each June they return from all over the world in full regalia for the Feast of St. John at St. John's Cathedral.

Throughout the 19th century, a British governor ruled Malta, and its economy grew almost entirely dependent upon the proceeds from British military facilities on the islands, a dependence which Malta has never been able to overcome successfully. Immediately following World War I the British granted internal autonomy to the Maltese, but the experiment failed and in 1933 Malta reverted to its status of a Crown Colony. During World War II, this "unsinkable aircraft carrier," as Winston S. Churchill called it, heroically resisted brutal German bombing and refused to surrender even though the islands were frequently cut off from supplies for months at a time. Malta played an extremely significant role in the successful Allied efforts in North Africa, Sicily and southern Europe. In 1947 the islands were again granted self–government, but a British–appointed governor maintained control over foreign affairs, defense and currency.

In 1955 the Maltese Labor Party won a parliamentary majority and made a radical proposal for full integration of Malta into the United Kingdom. This proposal, which now appears highly surprising in view of the party's later stand on independence, received the support of three–fourths of the voters in a referendum in 1956. However, negotiations to work out such integration broke down two years later, and by 1960 the Maltese support for the tie had disappeared. Independence, not integration, became the new goal, and the Nationalist Party, which had won the 1964 parliamentary elections, achieved this the same year.

GOVERNMENT

The constitution of 1964, which had made Malta an independent parliamentary monarchy within the British Commonwealth, was revised in 1974 to create a republican parliamentary democracy. A 65–member unicameral parliament, called the House of Representatives, is selected by universal suffrage of all citizens over the age of 18 on the basis of proportional representation (PR) at least every five years. Since 1987 any party that wins more than 50% of the popular vote is assured a majority of parliamentary seats, despite PR. In deference to the country's Catholic majority and past, all members of parliament take the constitutional oath of loyalty in the traditional manner, by kissing a cross held out to them. The majority party appoints the prime minister and cabinet, who exercise executive power, but who remain responsible to the House of Representatives. An indirectly elected, largely ceremonial president serves as the head of state for a five–year term.

The government of the country is highly centralized in the capital city although Sliema is actually the country's largest city. There is little established local government. The major exception to this is the island of Gozo, which has a locally-elected Civic Council which rules that small island in conjunction with a commissioner appointed by the central government in Valletta. Malta has an independent judicial system consisting of lower courts and a Constitutional Court, a Superior Court and a Court of Appeal.

POLITICS

Only two political parties have a significant number of seats in the House of Representatives or play an important role in Maltese politics. The opposition Labour Party (LP) sees itself as a socialist party and depends upon the support of workers and the powerful trade unions. From 1961 until 1971 the LP was embroiled in such a bitter struggle with the Catholic Church that the Church declared any vote or other active support for this party to be sufficient grounds for excommunication. The lifting of this ban in 1971 enabled the party to maintain its position.

For many years the character of the LP was shaped by the personality of its mercurial former leader, Dom Mintoff, who stepped down as prime minister in 1984. His hand–picked successor, Carmelo Mifsud–Bonnici, succeeded him. The LP favored an independent and neutral Malta playing the role of bridge between Europe and the Arab world and an anti–colonialist foreign policy involving close ties with the "Third World." To strengthen its European credentials, it joined the Council of Europe in 1965.

The LP advocates foreign investment and economic help to industrialize the islands. At the same time, it seeks the redistribution of property and income in order to create a more egalitarian society. In many ways, these last two objectives are in conflict with one another. Under Mintoff's premiership the government took over broadcasting, telecommunications, oil and gas and a full or majority interest in all banks. It also established a

Hon. Alfred Sant
Leader, *Labour Party*

national airline and shipping line, and his government introduced a minimum wage, a 40–hour workweek and mandatory wage increases to keep pace with inflation.

The LP clashed with the Catholic Church because of his decision to nationalize hospitals and schools. Mintoff expelled all nuns and doctors who refused to comply with the state takeover of the hospitals. He refused all state assistance to the country's private (mainly Catholic) schools, which educate about a third of all Maltese children. The government's campaign against Catholic schools was stepped up in 1984 when it was announced that private schools could no longer charge tuition. This move was followed by widespread violence, including a raid on Catholic Church headquarters, reportedly led by Mifsud–Bonnici. Hostility between the Church and the LP had been intensified when the latter introduced a bill to authorize state seizure of about three–fourths of the Church's property in Malta. Not surprisingly, Vatican spokesmen warned that such action would have "predictable repercussions on religious peace." But in 1985 Mifsud–Bonnici signed an agreement with the Vatican designed to end the controversy over government control of Catholic schools. The Church remains influential in Malta, where 98% are Catholics. Divorce and abortion are illegal. When the Pope visited the country in 1990, half the entire population gathered in a large square to see him.

Under the leadership since 1992 of Alfred Sant, a pragmatic Harvard PhD in business administration and former diplomat in Brussels, the party shook off its confrontational socialist image. He severed

Prime Minister Eddie Fenech Adami Leader, *Nationalist Party*

the party's formal links with the trade unions and admits that economic liberalization has benefited Malta. Not all LP militants supported these changes, but they paid off in the 1996 elections. At the end of a spirited campaign opposing Maltese entry into the EU, a 15% value added tax (VAT) required by the EU, and gun controls that were unpopular in this country with a strong hunting tradition, the LP won 50.7% of the votes and 35 parliamentary seats, giving it a narrow one–seat majority. But the Labour was brought down by disloyalty within its own ranks. The fiery Dom Mintoff opposed his party's plan to lease state land to an American consortium to build a new yacht marina. When he voted against his government, it fell and lost the September 1998 elections. In the April 2003 elections it lost again, receiving less than 48% of the votes.

The ruling Nationalist Party (NP), led by Prime Minister Eddie Fenech Adami, stands much closer to the Catholic Church and to the Maltese middle class. It wishes to safeguard Malta's Catholic Church and European traditions. The NP advocates Malta's following the example of other minute European states, such as Andorra, Monaco and Liechtenstein, in lowering taxes so that foreign wealth and business enterprises are attracted to the islands. This reduces the island's dependence on financial handouts from other countries and brings prosperity to Malta. The NP advocates closer relations with Europe and the U.S.

The NP ruled from 1987 to 1996. The transition of power in 1987 went more smoothly than many observers had feared. Fenech Adami vowed that his government would work to bring about national reconciliation in a land bitterly polarized in many ways: labor unions based in the dockyards versus the middle class; clans with generations of hostility; villages divided in their loyalty to competing saints; townships torn by rivalry between clubs which parade on holy days; males by their rooting for Italian or British soccer teams. The transition from violent confrontational politics succeeded. Party allegiance no longer dominates every issue, and the pervasive tension is gone. In 1996 the NP captured 47.8% of the votes and 34 seats. In 1998 it regained the reins of power. In the April 2003 parliamentary election that revolved around the question of joining the EU, the pro–membership NP won almost 52% of the votes and carried the day.

A third party, the Democratic Alternative, won only 1.46% of the votes in 1996. It is politically active, but it is irrelevant in the House of Representatives. It describes itself as "green–progressive" and focuses on corruption and social and environmen-

Advertising for tourists in Germany

tal issues. It publishes a monthly newspaper, *XPRESS*.

Foreign and Defense Policy

Malta had difficulty solving its major long–standing economic and foreign policy problem: how to survive economically without the rental fees paid by Britain for use of Maltese defense facilities. In 1971 the strong–willed Mintoff abrogated the Mutual Defense and Assistance Agreement of 1964; after months of difficult negotiations a new seven–year agreement was reached tripling the rental fees Britain was required to pay. He again demanded an increase in 1973. Britain finally decided it could live without Malta's base facilities and withdrew from the island in 1979, after 179 years of military presence there. Mintoff hailed this as "the day of light, freedom day, the day of the new Malta."

The economic problems caused by the loss of more than $70 million in revenue were not solved by that freedom. Mintoff's attempts to obtain a quadripartite guarantee of Maltese neutrality and a five–year budgetary subsidy (financial gift with no strings attached) from France, Italy, Algeria and Libya were rejected. Mintoff ridiculed Italy's offer of a loan amounting roughly to $5 million at low interest as "crumbs which no government can accept that wants to be taken seriously." Nor was Britain inclined to help Mintoff.

A modest amount of development assistance the People's Republic of China

The Republic of Malta

had given Malta since 1971 to construct a dry dock to handle tankers was much too small to solve Malta's problems. Therefore, Mintoff turned to that oil–rich state to the south, whose leader had shown himself willing to support practically any state or group whose policies are directed against the industrialized west: Libya. Mintoff announced in 1979, "Europe showed us the cold shoulder, but Libya heartily and spontaneously accepted our suggestions for collaboration." Libya's flamboyant and erratic leader, Col. Moamer al Ghadafi, took a 500–man delegation to the ceremony in Malta marking the British withdrawal, and promised the country unlimited aid.

Ghadafi delivered oil and gasoline to Malta almost without charge, and the Maltese government was able to derive even greater profit from this gift by imposing a stiff local consumption tax on the petroleum. Libya also invested approximately $150 million in the islands, entered a defense pact with Malta and provided helicopters and coastal patrol boats. Ghadafi proudly proclaimed Malta as the "northern outpost of the Arabic world" and even aspired to introduction of pure Arabic as Malta's official language (Arabic is no longer compulsory in secondary schools.). Such pronouncements merely aggravated many Maltese who from the beginning had misgivings toward this strange marriage of convenience. NP leaders called it an exchange of "one type of colonialism for another."

The marriage was scarcely a year old when a disagreement erupted. Both governments claimed oil rights in the waters between the two states. An angry Mintoff declared Libya "a danger to peace in the Mediterranean" and expelled as "security risks" 50 Libyan military personnel who had been sent to train Maltese helicopter pilots. By 1984 differences with Libya were settled. Both countries agreed to submit their dispute over oil rights in the sea to the International Court of Justice, which rendered a decision satisfactory to both parties. They signed a military cooperation treaty under which Libya would help to train and supply the Maltese forces and help to protect Malta "in case of threats or acts of aggression." In 1981 Malta had signed an agreement with the Soviet Union, which pledged to respect Malta's neutrality in return for the right to store up to 300,000 tons of oil on the islands. Mintoff claimed that the Soviet Union was not committed to defend the island if Maltese territory were violated.

Under Fenech Adami, Malta steered a more pro–Western course. The NP has a tradition of strong sympathies with Italy. Under Labour rule, Malta had already secured assistance from its nearest north-

ern neighbor. Arguing that Maltese neutrality was in Italy's and NATO's interest and threatening to allow the Soviet navy to use the harbor of Valletta, it persuaded Italy to support Malta. The Italian government rather liked the idea of assuming greater responsibility in the Mediterranean area. In 1980 it promised Malta technical assistance and financial support. Until 1994 Italy covered a third of Malta's budget deficit, enabling that shortfall to remain below 4% of GDP.

The islands, which for five years had maintained a consultative arrangement with NATO, received in 1981 military guarantees from Italy, which stations 47 air force personnel in Malta to operate two helicopters. In exchange, Malta formally declared neutrality and promised not to allow any foreign military bases. In 1987 the Maltese constitution was changed in order to entrench both non-alignment and neutrality and to forbid foreign military bases.

In 1986 the former LP prime minister admitted having tipped off Ghadafi minutes before the American bombing raid on Libya, thereby possibly saving the Libyan leader's life. The NP government did not show such "even–handedness." Malta maintained economic ties with Libya and renegotiated its friendship treaty with it. But Fenech Adami emphasized that he had widened the political distance with Ghadafi and that the military clauses, which had obligated Malta to warn Libya of American air strikes, had been removed. Fenech Adami's government severed air links with Libya and honored the UN embargo imposed after Libya's complicity in the bombing of a Pan Am plane over Lockerbie, Scotland, appeared obvious.

In 1996 former Prime Minister Sant informed Brussels that he had put Malta's application for EU membership on hold because joining was supposedly not in the tiny country's interest. After the 1998 election, the new NP government renewed the country's EU application. In one of his first acts, Sant formally withdrew Malta from NATO's Partnership for Peace program "because it contradicts our constitutional neutrality. . ." Malta allots about 3.5% ($29 million) of its budget to the maintenance of its small army, navy and air force of 2,140 troops. There are also 47 Italian air force personnel stationed in Malta flying two AB-212 aircraft. However, it could never defend itself alone.

ECONOMY

Malta is a highly over–crowded mini–state with four–tenths of a million people on only 122 square miles (316 sq. km). Only one-third the size of New York City,

it has one vehicle for every two residents, making it Europe's most traffic-congested nation. It has no natural resources except limestone, and its terrain is very unsuited to agriculture. It can supply only about 20% of its food needs, and only 6% of its population can find employment in agriculture. Its major agricultural products are potatoes, cauliflower, grapes, wheat, barley, tomatoes, citrus fruit, cut flowers, hogs, poultry and eggs. Desalination plants provide half of Malta's fresh water.

Its major industry, thanks to its deep-water harbors, is ship repair. This provides 5% of total employment, although it has fallen on hard times. The government's efforts since independence to diversify the economy have had modest success, and Malta now has some light manufacturing enterprises in the clothing, textile, building and food processing sectors. Foreign investments contributed significantly to this success, but they have meant that more than half of Malta's industrial production is in foreign hands. Maltese industry will be lucky if it can continue employing a fourth of the workforce. Not wanting to compete as a low-wage economy, it faces a particular obstacle in that it must import so many raw materials in order to export finished products at a profit.

An Achilles heel is the fact that more than half of its exports are textile products. In the industrialized nations to which it exports, there are increasingly loud demands to erect barriers against textile imports in order to protect their own clothing industries. Malta must still import most consumer and industrial needs, including fuels and raw materials.

A fourth of its GDP is derived from tourism, its biggest revenue earner. The number of foreign tourists who visit Malta is more than twice as large as the country's population. The government believes that with a million tourists every year (predominantly Britons) the three islands have reached the saturation point. Therefore, it aims to restructure the industry to attract more up-market tourists. This would bring more income from fewer visitors. They arrive at the country's two usable airfields, one major and two minor harbors.

In order to try to overcome Malta's economic stagnation, the former NP government liberalized the economy, which was over–protected and state–dominated. Through "tax holidays" it lured foreign investment from the West. Some other countries and the OECD criticized its status as a tax haven. Therefore, in June 2000 it joined five other small states in agreeing to cooperate with international efforts to curb abusive and criminal tax-avoidance schemes. It largely completed its first priority of improving the infrastructure by overhauling the telecommunications network and building a new power station, desalination plants, and a second airport terminal. It attracted some higher-skill and technology industries to replace traditional ones, like textiles, which are threatened by low-cost competition from north Africa and Asia.

In 2003 Malta could look back on a decade and a half of robust annual economic growth and a 7.5% unemployment rate (up from 3% in 1997). Its public-sector finances are solid, with an overall public debt of 36% of GDP, lower than any EU country except Luxembourg. In 1993 employment in the service sector overtook private direct production for the first time. Malta's per capita income exceeds that of Portugal and Greece. Its inflation rate in 2003 was 2.2%, and its prices were 87% of those in EU member states, the highest among the EU 10 accession states. With one or more cars per family, there is an air of prosperity in the country. Growing wealth has created the same phenomenon in Malta as in other developed European countries: a lowering of the fertility rate to only 1.5 (2.1 is needed to maintain the population level). The feeling that Malta is already performing rather well was an important reason why many voters did not view EU entry as an urgent necessity.

Since 1971 Malta has had a special trade relationship with the EU, to which it sent 68% of its exports and from which it bought 78% of its imports in 1990, the year in which it applied for full membership. The NP government drafted all its legislation with eventual EU membership in mind. Prime Minister Fenech Adami had announced, "Malta is a European country. To us, this will be a homecoming." Voters saw it differently in 1996, but they changed their minds in September 1998. Malta's EU application was renewed. In December 1999 the EU invited Malta back to formal talks leading to membership.

The talks went well, and in March 2003 the Nationalist Party government was ready to put the emotional question of membership to the voters. Rallies for and against joining drew thousands of people. Many Maltese feared that Europe would take away the hard-earned independence they had finally won in 1964. As the least populous country in the EU, Malta risked being overshadowed by the large EU nations and might not have a voice that would be listened to. The Labour Party led the charge against EU membership. However, arguing that membership is vital for Malta's economy and international credibility, the government prevailed. In the March 9 referendum, 53.6% supported accession, while 46.4% said no. Malta's constitution required that the referendum be confirmed by a general election, which took place April 12. Interest was at such a high pitch that plane loads of Maltese returned to vote, benefiting from reduced fares by state-owned Air Malta. In an election whose central issue was the EU, the government won almost 52%. Four days later Prime Minister Adami traveled to Athens to sign the EU accession treaty, with formal membership following in May 2004. The accession of Malta and Cyprus will undoubtedly strengthen the EU's Mediterranean dimension.

To create a sense of urgency to spur reform of the economy in order to qualify for the EU, Finance Minister John Dalli had released to the media in May 2001 a report by Moody's Investors Service that presented a negative outlook for Malta if it did not act. It warned that Malta's indecision on EU membership was a major worry for the island's economic prospects and discouraged investment. It contended that real growth had remained strong in recent years and that unemployment and inflation had stayed low. It identified as problems the large public sector debt and internal market rigidities that weakened competition and deterred productive investment. Malta should reform its pension system and deregulate and privatize its economy, but these matters remain contentious in the domestic political context.

FUTURE

With a Nationalist government and prime minister and with economic optimism in the air, Malta looks into a future of prosperous alignment with Europe and in the EU. Prospects for the tiny island nation are good.

Source: BBC

Source: BBC

Maltese celebrating EU referendum victory

Iberian Peninsula

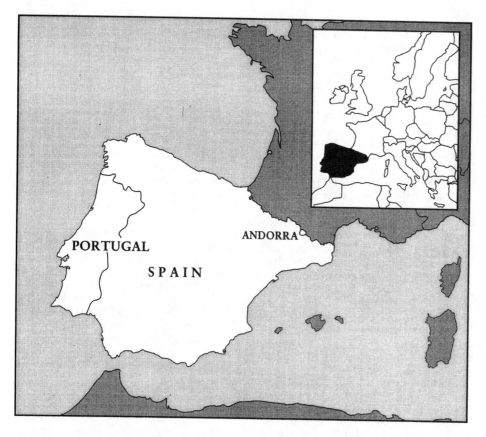

Contemporary Mutual Relations

The Iberian Peninsula is located at the southwest periphery of Europe, separated from the rest of the Continent by the high Pyrenees Mountains. Most of the population is settled around the coastal areas, with certain prominent exceptions, most notably Madrid, where a third of Spain's inland population is concentrated. The land area is distributed very unevenly among the three countries on the Peninsula; Spain occupies about 85% of the space, and Portugal occupies most of the rest. Tiny Andorra has a very small chunk of mountainous land in the Northeast, and Britain still controls a strategically important toehold on the rock of Gibraltar at the southern tip of Spain.

Spain and Portugal do not have identical characteristics and problems. But they undeniably have very much in common. Perhaps most obviously, if one casts a quick glance at the globe, are their strategically significant locations. They are placed between the continents of Europe and Africa and face the Atlantic and, in the case of Spain, the Mediterranean Sea.

They possess islands in the Atlantic Ocean that are important links between the Western and Eastern Hemispheres: the Canary Islands are Spanish, and the Azores and Madeira are Portuguese. The Spanish also possess the Balearic Islands in the Mediterranean, the largest of which is the tourist Mecca of Majorca. Spain also owns a few islands off the Moroccan coast and the cities of Ceuta and Melilla on the northern coast of Morocco. In 1987 the Portuguese agreed to relinquish to China their small enclave of Macao on the southern coast of China. It was their highly valuable strategic positions which enabled Spain and Portugal to escape prolonged international isolation and to regain a status of relative respectability after 1945, despite the fact that until the mid–1970s they had authoritarian political systems which were repugnant to most persons in the democratic countries of the world.

These lands were formerly mighty colonial powers that spread their languages and cultures to colonies in Latin America and Africa, which were many times greater in size and population than the mother countries. Their empires have by now almost completely disappeared. The process of de-colonization brought the fascist regime to its knees in Portugal in 1974 and was a consequence of the collapse of fascism in Spain in 1975.

Portuguese and Spaniards speak languages which are derived from Latin and which are very similar to each other. Although their words are spelled and pronounced somewhat differently, they understand the gist of what each other is saying. However, the Spaniard, except in Galicia, generally has more trouble understanding Portuguese than *vice versa*. Both countries are also predominantly Roman Catholic, and the Catholic Church has traditionally wielded considerable power and influence in them.

Both countries have similar political backgrounds, traditions, institutions and problems. They had monarchies that collapsed in the first third of the 20th century because of chronic political turmoil and violence. In neither country did experiments with republican and democratic forms of government go well, and in 1926 in Portugal and 1936 in Spain the military seized power. Such seizure was quick and bloodless in Portugal, but painful and bloody in Spain. The carnage that lasted for three years in Spain was portrayed with great force by Picasso's unforgettable painting, *Guernica*, and by Ernest Hemingway's moving novel, *For Whom the Bell Tolls*.

Both countries lived under fascism for several decades. In the mid–1970s they reemerged from fascism, but experienced different transitions. Portugal dived headlong into revolutionary and democratic government and passed through two tense years of political experimentalism and uncertainty until it could gain its balance in the political center. By contrast, Spain experienced in 1975 a long and carefully planned entry into democracy and a restoration of the monarchy, which has proven to be one of the major bulwarks of democracy.

During the last decade and a half of fascist rule, Spain underwent rapid and extensive industrialization. By contrast, Portugal did not, and it entered its new democratic era as the poorest country in Western Europe. Although Spain was one of Western Europe's poorest countries, its economic head start over Portugal strengthened the inclination of Spaniards to regard the poorer, smaller Portugal in a condescending, patronizing way. In the 21st century, both are experiencing an economic boom.

In 1983 the Spanish prime minister traveled to Portugal for a summit conference designed to bury "historical ghosts." He called for "a new era in our relations." His Portuguese counterpart responded by announcing, "the mistrust and reservations which many Portuguese continue to feel toward Spain are no longer justified. Portugal has survived eight centuries of independence and nation identity, and Spain, a great country, has respected and will continue to respect our independence." Clichés remain, though. Some Portuguese still see Spaniards as explosively talkative, opinionated, aggressive, arrogant, sociable and dressed beyond their means, with a barely concealed contempt for Portugal, while the Portuguese are quieter, more reserved and self–deprecating.

In 1986 they again pledged closer cooperation and agreed on frequent and regular meetings between the heads of their governments. As a symbol of closer ties, they agreed to have a bridge built over the Guadiana River frontier. In 1989 they adapted their narrow–gauged railway systems to the one used in the rest of Europe so that rail cars will not need to be changed at Iberia's frontier with the rest of Europe. Portugal launched a major effort to streamline and modernize its rail system and highways toward Spain.

The results of their cooperation are clear: Between 1985 and 1989 trade trebled between them, and it doubled again in the 1990s; 9.4% of Spain's foreign trade in 2003 was with Portugal, and it is Portugal's largest supplier and its biggest market. By 2003 Portugal bought a quarter of its imports from Spain, more than from any other country. Portugal sends 19% of its exports to its eastern neighbor. Spain trades more with it than with all of Latin America. Spain is now the world's largest investor in Latin America, and it invests more heavily in Portugal than anywhere else in Europe. By 2003 there were over 2,500 Spanish firms in Portugal, compared with only 400 in 1989. Spanish banks control about one-sixth of Portugal's banking. Many multinational corporations deal with Portugal through their headquarters in Madrid. About two–thirds of foreigners visiting Portugal are Spanish.

Portugal has about 300 companies operating in Spain. Its income per capita was half that of Spain in 1991, but by 1996 its per capita GDP, adjusted for purchasing power, had increased to $13,100, compared with $14,954 in Spain.

The relationship is asymmetrical, partly because of the different size and partly because of their past: Spain began encouraging competition and entrepreneurship during the Franco years, while Portugal did not. Spain was also largely free of the costly colonial wars, disruptive revolution and political upheaval that set Portugal back. Some Portuguese worry about the Spain's economic influence on them. In 2003, 40 Portuguese economists and business leaders published an open letter entitled "Patriots' Manifesto," warning against the steady move of their country's economic decision-making centers abroad.

Portugal and Spain have long traditions of military intervention into politics. Since the 19th century, soldiers in the Peninsula have viewed themselves as the guarantors of their nations' sovereignty and integrity. Although soldiers in both lands symbolically show their loyalty to the state by kissing the respective national flags at ceremonial occasions, their commitment to democracy was not entirely certain, as the attempted *coup d'etat* in 1981 by elements within the Spanish military revealed. In the constitution of Spain, the military as an institution is granted explicit political powers. In Portugal from the 1974 revolu-

tion until 1986 the highest political office, the presidency, was occupied by high–ranking officers. The potential political activity of the military sets these nations off from the rest of Western European nations, where the military is indisputably subordinate to the elected political leadership. Nevertheless, by the 1990s democracy had set deep roots in both countries, and the danger of military intervention had diminished significantly. This adjustment to the Western European norm was strengthened by Spain's entry into NATO in 1982 (Portugal was a founding member), as well as by both lands joining the EU in 1986 and the WEU in 1988.

The Early Period

Many things that Portugal and Spain have in common stem from 2,000 years of shared history. It is likely that the first settlers began arriving on the Iberian Peninsula from 3,000 to 2,000 B.C., and were followed by waves of Celts, Phoenicians, Greeks and Carthaginians from the rest of Europe and Africa. Most of the settlers were firmly unified under Roman rule by 19 B.C., although individual tribes and cultures in the interior and northern parts of the Peninsula continued to exist. Tensions between the center and the periphery have continued to plague Spain and Portugal to the present day, although they are certainly less significant in contemporary Portugal than in Spain. The Romans brought the Latin language to the Peninsula, from which both modern Spanish and Portuguese developed. They also brought Roman law and administrative practices, and in the 4th century they introduced Christianity to the area. From the important Roman cities in the South

and East of the Peninsula came many of the Roman Empire's great leaders, such as Hadrian, Lucan, Marcus Aurelius, Seneca and Trajan.

Visigoth and Moslem Rule

The collapse of Rome in the 5th century A.D. was followed by three centuries of rule in Spain by the Visigoths, who had stormed the Peninsula by force. Taking advantage of divisions and quarrels among the Visigoth leaders, Moors from North Africa began crossing the Strait of Gibraltar in 711 A.D. Within a very short time Mohammedans controlled virtually all the Roman cities in the South and East of the Peninsula. Iberian art and commerce bloomed under the new Moslem rule, which was, on the whole, very tolerant toward Jews and Christians.

Christians ensconced in strongholds in northwestern Spain hammered away at the Mohammedan realm in Iberia. It was further weakened by quarrels and intrigues among the Moslem rulers themselves, whose grip on the Peninsula began to loosen. The newly emerging Kingdom of Castile, which combined with Leon and whose military prowess is symbolized by its hero El Cid, and the Kingdom of Aragon, which in 1137 combined with Catalonia, slowly but steadily pushed back the Mohammedans. Moslem rule in most of the Peninsula had been broken by the mid 13th century, although a small Moslem kingdom hung on in Granada until 1492.

Moslem Decline; Portugal and Spain Separate

While the re-conquest of the Peninsula from the Moslems was taking place, Por-

Spain under Roman rule

Iberian Peninsula

The Iberian Peninsula about 1150

tugal began to sever its ties with Leon and to establish itself as an independent country. In 1095 Count Henri of the House of Burgundy became the direct ruler over Portugal, and in 1140, after a nine–year rebellion against the King of Leon–Castile, Henri's son, Alfonso Henriques, declared himself to be the King of Portugal. The Burgundians ruled Portugal until 1383, during which time Portugal's borders were expanded from the original Oporto and Coimbra. Lisbon was snatched from the Moslems in 1147. Since the second half of the 13th century, Portugal's boundaries have been the same as today, with the exception of the district of Olivenca, which Spain took in 1801 and continues to hold.

Portuguese Exploration and Conquest

As a country facing the sea, Portuguese sights were always directed outward, and the bulk of the population was attracted to the coast because of this maritime and external commercial orientation. By 1337 their mariners had already landed on the Canary Islands. Overseas exploration was particularly encouraged by Prince Henry the Navigator (1394–1460), a far–sighted and imaginative man who established a maritime school to assemble and extend his country's knowledge of the sea. Portuguese mariners explored the African coast, and in 1488 Bartolemeu Dias rounded the Cape of Good Hope and

reached East Africa. In 1497 Vasco da Gama set sail for India. He not only reached it, but he returned to describe the land to a receptive and curious Europe. Pedro Alvares Cabral landed in Brazil in 1500.

Such activity stimulated important advances in cartography and astronomy and also helped redirect the attention of Europe outward toward the larger world. It enabled Portugal to build up a massive empire which included Mozambique, Angola and Guinea–Bissau in Africa, Brazil in South America, East Timor, Macao (which the Chinese gave to Portugal as a reward for its fight against pirates), and Portuguese India (with its capital of Goa) in South and Southeastern Asia, and the Atlantic islands of the Azores and Madeira. Portuguese naval squadrons were stationed permanently in strongholds in or around the Atlantic and Indian Oceans. The Portuguese also began to send settlers to some of these imperial holdings, especially to the Azores, Madeira and Brazil.

These colonial activities brought definite advantages to Portugal, as it did to Spain. It provided it with gold and other precious stones, silks and spices, which were treasured in Europe at that time, and needed foodstuffs, especially wheat. It also provided an occupation for those portions of the feudal nobility that could no longer be supported by domestic agricultural production. Settlement in the

colonies offered many Portuguese the hope for a better life. Finally, the desire to convert the peoples of the world to Roman Catholicism furnished the entire enterprise with a spirit of crusade and gave it a religious and spiritual justification.

Spanish Colonial Activities

Portugal's most avid competitor was its only neighbor—Spain. Spanish attention had remained largely focused on Iberia until 1492, which was a very significant date. In that year the Spanish captured Granada, the last Moslem foothold on Spanish soil. The triumphant entry into that city of Ferdinand and Isabella, whose marriage had sealed the unity of Aragon and Castile, signified the end of the seven and one–half century re-conquest of the Iberian Peninsula. Thus, Spain took shape as a unified kingdom over an ethnically diverse area three and a half centuries after Portugal. The re-conquest sparked a flourish of Spanish literature and artistic achievement that lasted at least two centuries. It also allowed Spaniards to concentrate their energy on overseas expansion and exploration.

As every American school child knows, the year 1492 was significant for another event: Christopher Columbus, a native of Genoa (Italy) working for the Spanish, sailed west in search of India, but instead bumped into the island of Santo Domingo in the Caribbean. His discovery opened the eyes of Europeans to an entirely new part of their world and launched an era of Spanish colonialism that spread Hispanic culture and languages to dozens of modern–day countries.

In order to minimize a potentially dangerous rivalry between Spain and Portugal in the wake of Columbus' discovery, the sovereigns of the two countries agreed in the Treaty of Tordesillas (1494) to divide the world in such a way that Spain would receive the Philippines (named after the Spanish king) and most of the Western Hemisphere (including large chunks of the contemporary U.S., such as California, the Southwest and Florida) with Portugal receiving what is now Brazil, and parts of Africa and Asia. Both countries continued generally to observe this agreement, which had the Pope's approval, but to their consternation, other interested powers, especially Britain, France and the Netherlands, did not.

As Portugal, Spain had several different motives for establishing and maintaining an empire. Dominican and Franciscan friars were always close on the heels of the *conquistadores* in order to convert and educate the native populations. Also, the *conquistadores*, the royal court and the private companies that stood behind them clearly sought wealth, status and power. The Spanish kings insisted that all trade

---

with the colonies be conducted through Seville and be reserved for Castile, although most of the trade was actually organized by Genoese and southern German merchants.

The Spanish kings also claimed one–fifth of all precious metals imported from the New World. Such metals greatly enriched the Spanish treasury, but they also heated inflation within Spain and created serious economic distortions. This wealth was used to add glitter to the royal and noble courts, to finance massive Spanish imports, and also to finance Spanish armies and navies. These military forces were constantly embroiled abroad maintaining an empire which encompassed the present–day BENELUX countries, Italy and, through the Hapsburg throne, all of the Austrian Empire. Throughout the 17th century Spanish money and troops also supported the Catholic struggle against Protestantism. Since almost none of its wealth was invested in productive facilities within the home country itself, Spain remained poor despite its temporary wealth.

Temporary Unity

The 16th century had been Portugal's "Golden Age," but it was dealt a devastating blow in the aftermath of events in Morocco, where King Sabastião and much of the nobility were slain while trying to protect the kingdom's holdings there. Spain claimed the Portuguese throne on the grounds that the mother of King Philip II of Spain was descended from Portuguese nobility. Thus, in 1580 the two countries were united in a dual monarchy, which was supposed to leave the Portuguese with domestic autonomy. In fact, Spaniards were appointed to Portuguese offices.

Despite initial economic advantages that Portugal gained through a dropping of customs barriers between the two lands, it was compelled to enter and to help finance through heavy taxes a costly and protracted war against England. This not only cost Portugal most of its lucrative markets in the Orient, but the bulk of its fleet as well. Both consequences directly benefited England and the Netherlands. Disillusioned about Spanish rule, and taking advantage of a revolt in Catalonia, the Portuguese also revolted. French support helped the rebellion to succeed in 1640, when the House of Bragança was established as the Portuguese ruling family (which it remained until the monarchy fell in 1910). The Portuguese still mark the anniversary of this revolt that ended Spanish rule, and much of their subsequent history can be summarized as a struggle against absorption by its big neighbor. The Spanish did not accept Portuguese independence without a fight, though,

and until 1668 they struggled unsuccessfully to win back the country. As late as the early 20th century, King Alfonso XIII, grandfather of currently reigning King Juan Carlos, was considering the annexation of Portugal.

In order to guarantee that it would never again fall under Spanish domination, Portugal entered an alliance with the sea power, Britain, which always had a sharp strategic eye for coastal countries that could be useful allies. This alliance lasted into the 20th century. The struggle against Spain affirmed and strengthened Portuguese national identity, which still defines itself most clearly in terms of its distinctiveness from the Spanish nation. The loss of many of its colonies and markets in the Orient necessitated a shift of Portugal's colonial attention from the Indian Ocean to Brazil. The revenues from Brazilian sugar, coffee, diamonds, gold and other minerals became extremely important to the Portuguese economy.

Separation

The separation of Portugal from Spain was, for the latter, merely one of a series of foreign political setbacks following the destruction of the Spanish Armada, a mighty fleet sent to subdue England in 1588. Spain squandered its wealth on endless wars on the European Continent, and its European holdings were gradually whittled away. The last blow was the War of the Spanish Succession that erupted after the death in 1700 of Charles II, the last of the Hapsburg rulers in Spain. This conflict ended in the establishment of a Bourbon dynasty in Spain. In practical terms, this meant French domination of Spain's foreign policy. Occasionally Spain seemed to be about able to rear its proud head once again and to assert primacy in its own affairs. However, any chance of Spain's restoring its former imperial

grandeur and power was undercut by that social and political convulsion which changed Europe irrevocably—the French Revolution and the accompanying French military conquest of most of Europe.

French troops invaded Spain, and in 1808 Napoleon placed his brother, Joseph, on the Spanish throne. Many Spaniards valiantly resisted this foreign invasion, as Goya's powerful paintings portray. The Grand Army was nevertheless able to conquer most of the Peninsula by 1809. Yet its hold on Spain was only temporary. The English Duke of Wellington supported by Spanish guerrillas advanced from Portugal and delivered crushing defeats at Talavera in 1809 and Vitoria in June 1813.

As an ally of England, Portugal intervened much earlier, in 1793, in the war against revolutionary France. In 1807 the French invaded Portugal, prompting the royal court to flee to Brazil. By 1811, however, the French had been driven out again by British troops and by Portuguese soldiers who had been placed under the command of an English general, Lord Beresford, who in the Portuguese King's absence continued to dominate Portuguese politics long after Napoleon's troops had departed.

Both Spain and Portugal faced the post–Napoleonic era with restored monarchies but with the liberal ideas of the French Revolution in the heads of many of their citizens. These ideas would not permit a quiet return to the authoritarian government of earlier years. Also, these new notions, combined with the long rupture in reliable communication with their American colonies, spelled the end of their empires in the Western Hemisphere. The Spanish and Portuguese had fought heroically for their national independence. Now their American colonies decided to do the same.

Driving the Moors from Spain

The Kingdom of Spain

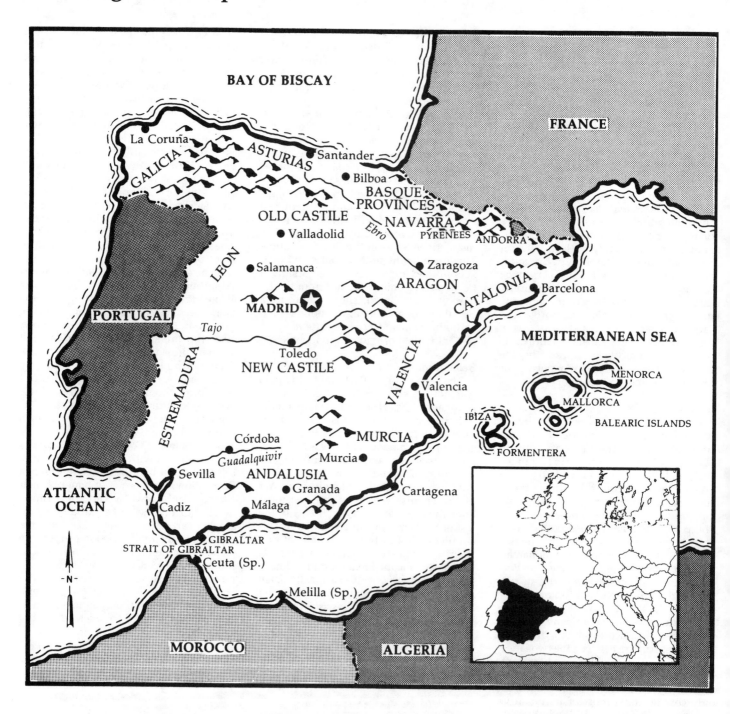

Area: 194,897 sq. mi. (504,750 sq. km.), some 640 miles (1,034 km.) from east to west, 530 miles (848 km.) from north to south.

Population: 40,000,000 (estimated).

Capital City: Madrid (Pop. 4.1 million, estimated).

Climate: Varying from Madrid's 2,000-foot (610 meters) elevation, making the area cold in winter and hot and dry in summer, to the Mediterranean coast that is hot in summer, mild in winter.

Neighboring Countries: France, Andorra (North); Portugal (West); Morocco lies

only eight and a half miles across the Strait of Gibraltar.

Languages: Spanish (primarily the Castilian dialect), with Catalan, Basque, Galician, Valencian, regional languages which are once again flourishing and compose an important part of the tongues spoken every day.

Ethnic Background: Indo–European, North African, Arab.

Principal Religion: Roman Catholic.

Chief Commercial Exports: Machinery, iron and steel, fruits and vegetables, footwear, textiles.

Major Customers: EU (70.6%), France (19.4%), Germany (12.4%), Portugal (9.4%), Italy (8.8%), UK (8.3%), U.S. (6%).

Currency: Euro.

National Holiday: October 12 (1492)—*Dia de la Raza* (Columbus Day).

Chief of State: His Majesty King Juan Carlos I (b. 1938). Married Princess Sophia of Greece, 1962. Proclaimed King of Spain, November 22, 1975.

Heir Apparent: His Royal Highness Crown Prince Felipe, Prince of the Asturias (b. 1968).

Head of Government: José María Aznar, Prime Minister (since April 1996).

National Flag: Three horizontal stripes of red, yellow, and red, with the center yellow stripe twice as wide as the red ones. The Spanish royal crest is set off center on the left of the flag.

For as long as most people could remember, Spain was, by European standards, a poor, thinly populated country on the edge of the Continent and separated from the rest of Europe by more than the high peaks of the Pyrenees Mountains. Its people had produced a language and a high culture which had been spread to most countries in the New World, but in politics it appeared excessively passionate, polarized, and generally ungovernable by any other means than authoritarianism. The Spanish Kings had never thoroughly integrated this heterogeneous country, and at times it threatened to split apart, with the Basque and Catalonian provinces in the Northeast leading the way. Unceasing political instability prevailed, punctuated by longer or shorter periods of authoritarian rule. The last such interlude lasted until the end of 1975 and was guided by a diminutive general named Francisco Franco, called *El Caudillo* (the Leader). His fascist regime made Spain an embarrassment to and, for a long time, an outcast in Western Europe.

After Franco's death Spain began to move in a different direction. Indeed, he would scarcely recognize the land he claimed to have "saved" in 1939. Wishing both to create a parliamentary democratic order and to avoid a bloody repeat of the turmoil and civil war of the 1930s, the major contenders for political power have displayed a remarkable willingness to cooperate with each other and to moderate their political demands.

Spain's regions have been offered autonomy statutes that reduce Madrid's hold on the country's politics. Communist and Socialist–led trade unions operate freely and act with moderation and responsibility. Many political parties compete for seats in the national Parliament, but Spanish voters have overwhelmingly supported the moderate democratic parties in the political center, despite a shaky economy whose performance has disappointed many Spaniards' hopes. A king, picked and trained by Franco, has shown unswerving determination to create and to preserve a democratic order and has therefore won the admiration of most of his countrymen. Spain also moved into Western Europe by joining NATO and by entering the EU, which enjoys a broad consensus within the country.

It is true that every November the anniversary of Franco's death still brings some Spaniards out into the streets to wear and wave fascist paraphernalia and to hear inflammatory speeches against the new democratic order. There is also a diminishing minority within the army which has learned little and which vents its dissatisfaction with the new Spain often enough to keep Spain's democrats nervous and willing to go more than an extra mile in order not to provoke the military. But to many people's surprise, democracy in Spain, as well as in Portugal, is working. The Pyrenees are no longer the edge of Europe.

CONTEMPORARY HISTORY

The Post–Napoleonic Period

The liberation of Spain from French occupation and the restoration of the Bourbon dynasty by no means brought the country peace and stability. Spain's isolation from its American colonies during the Napoleonic wars had loosened its grip and had given Latin American leaders a taste of local rule they liked. They therefore revolted. Again, the Spanish treasury was drained by protracted war far from its own territory. After the disastrous Spanish defeat at the battle of Ayacucho in 1825, the vast and mighty Spanish empire had been reduced to the islands of Cuba, Puerto Rico, Guam and the Philippines.

Spanish domestic politics was marred by almost continuous political, social and economic crises. This turmoil began with the King's revocation in 1814 of the admirably liberal Cadiz Constitution, which had been approved in 1812. By 1820 the dim–witted Ferdinand VII had alienated many important groups, especially the liberals and the military, and in the midst of widespread demonstrations and riots throughout the country, the military revolted. In an unsuccessful attempt to salvage his throne, the King allowed the Cadiz Constitution to be proclaimed again, but it was exactly such democratic constitutions which most of the conservative monarchs of Europe could not tolerate. Therefore, in April 1823 French armies again invaded Spain on behalf of most other European powers. (with the notable exception of England) and restored Ferdinand VII to power.

The next decade and a half were filled with reaction and unrest, followed by another quarter century of rule by generals and a scandal–ridden Queen Isabella II, who was finally deposed in 1868 by military officers. When they tried to appoint a Prussian Hohenzollern to the throne, they provided the spark for a war between France and Prussia in 1870, which resulted in German unification (See Germany). A brief and unsuccessful republican experiment ended again in military intervention and the restoration in 1874 of the monarchy under Alfonso XII, the son of Isabella II. A parliament (*Cortés*), for which only property owners could vote, was also created. In order to achieve some measure of stability, the Conservative and Liberal parties agreed to alternate power. However, this system of *turno político* had broken down by the end of the 19th century.

The Spanish–American War and Ensuing Turbulence

Spain was badly shaken in 1898 by its war against the United States. This conflict was sparked by an explosion of dubious origin on a U. S. vessel, the Maine, which was anchored in Havana harbor. American soldiers, including those led by Theodore Roosevelt's "Roughriders," entered the battlefield with the cry, "Remember the Maine!" The war left Spain with 200,000 dead in Cuba, a sorely humiliated officer corps, an empty treasury, and a denuded empire. The U. S took Cuba, Puerto Rico, Guam and the Philippines, and Spain retained only a smattering of holdings in West Africa and Morocco.

Wide–spread domestic dissatisfaction increasingly began to manifest itself again, urban workers began to be attracted to Marxism and syndicalism (radically political trade unionism), and anarchism infected the downtrodden workers in Barcelona and the peasants in southern Spain. Also, corruption and inefficiency in Madrid stimulated separatist sentiments in the Basque and Catalonian regions. Political violence became commonplace, and Spanish politics was in a state of utter confusion. Between 1902 and 1923 the country averaged one government every 18 months.

Spain managed to remain neutral in World War I, but in 1921 it experienced such a stinging military reversal at the hands of the Moors at Anual in North Africa that public pressure forced the government to conduct an investigation of that institution which had never contented itself with mere military matters—the army. However, before the investigation could be completed, the military's rage at such "impudence" boiled over. The army seized power in 1923 and formed a government under General Miguel Primo de Rivera. Primo de Rivera's government banned all opposition parties, slapped severe controls on the press and the universities and openly expressed great admiration for the kind of fascist political order that Mussolini was establishing in Italy.

The new Spanish leader did launch an extensive public works program and, with the help of the French, ended the war in

Spain

Morocco in 1926. But without the support of the masses or of the youth or intelligentsia, Primo de Rivera's authoritarian government could not survive the jolt which the world–wide depression gave to Spain and most other European countries at the end of the 1920s. He therefore resigned in January 1930. Demonstrations in favor of a republic became so intense that King Alfonso XIII was forced to flee the country April 13, 1931. The almost immediate proclamation of the Second Republic (the first being in the early 1870s) unleashed such enthusiasm from its supporters that 200 churches were burned to the ground!

Many Spaniards today look back very carefully to Spain's entry into democracy in 1931 in order to try to insure that earlier mistakes which helped lead to the downfall of the democratic republic would not be repeated. The new constitution of December 1931 legalized all political parties and created a unicameral *Cortés* (Parliament) to which the government was responsible. The constitution declared Spain to be "a workers' republic," and the new government under Manuel Azaña launched a full–scale attack on the old ruling pillars: the Church, the army and the wealthy. The Jesuit order was expelled, and fully state schools were established in order to eliminate religious influence over education. Large estates were confiscated, and the beginnings of a land reform were introduced. Railroads and the Bank of Spain were nationalized, the eight–hour workday introduced, and, perhaps most disastrously, the army officer corps was reduced by almost half.

It soon became clear that many of the new government's reforms were unrealistic. Both the delay in their implementation and the fear that they might actually be implemented brought peasants, workers, anarchists, fascists and monarchists out into the streets. Spain was bubbling with conspiracies and intrigues. It experienced one government after the other; in the five years of the Republic, there were 18 different governments! This came to a head shortly after the beginning of 1936 when a Popular Front on the French model, composed of Socialists, Communists, Anarcho–Syndicalists, and Basque and Catalan nationalists, was formed and won an electoral victory. The assassination on July 13, 1936, of the former finance minister under Primo de Rivera, Calvo Sotelo, was the cue for the army to launch a long–planned coup against the Republic.

Civil War

On July 18, 1936, a diminutive general, Francisco Franco, flew to Morocco from the Canary Islands and drew his sword against the Republic. Within a few days the revolt spread to garrisons within metropolitan Spain, and within ten days troops were flown in German planes from Morocco to secure strategically important positions. Unlike early military rebellions, which usually succeeded very quickly, this one thrust Spain into a savage three–year civil war that not only destroyed democracy and liberty in Spain, but temporarily moved the country into the center of the world political conflict between the proponents and opponents of fascist dictatorship.

The revolt was successful in certain parts of Spain, but not in such key cities as Madrid. Also, the provinces of Catalonia and Basque strongly supported the Republic because the latter had guaranteed them a large measure of autonomy. Further, Franco did not have the support of the navy, the air force and part of the army.

It is probable that the *coup* would have collapsed within a few months if Franco had not received crucial military assistance from fascist Germany and Italy. The Italians sent more than a thousand planes, four infantry divisions, tanks, artillery and other military equipment. The German contribution was smaller but highly effective. The Germans sent a tank battalion. The major contribution was the Condor Legion, composed of four fighter–bombers, four fighters, one reconnaissance, and two seaplane squadrons. The German aerial bombing of the city of Guernica on April 26, 1937, out-raged world opinion and prompted an indignant Pablo Picasso to paint his famous *Guernica*. Sixty years later Germany agreed to donate almost $2 million to the city in symbolic compensation for the destruction.

Franco and Fascism

The Republic called for help, but France and Britain refused to respond to its calls and limited their reactions to verbal protests. It did have on its side some loyal army and naval units, as well as units hastily formed with trade unionists, students, and Catalan and Basque nationalists. In addition, several thousand generally poorly equipped and insufficiently trained international volunteers organized in such units as the Abraham Lincoln and Ernst Thälmann brigades came to fight for the Republic. This conflict inspired to action many idealistic young people throughout Europe and the United States, who saw in Spain the only determined struggle against fascism. The Soviet Union also sent limited aid in the form of advisers, technicians, tanks and aircraft. However, the Soviet Union itself was in the grips of a terrifying purge at home, which spilled over to communist units fighting in Spain. In such a state of paralysis, the Soviets withdrew their aid to the Republic a year before the end of the war.

Ultimately the military balance tipped in favor of Franco's fascists. In the spring of 1939 armed resistance in Catalonia was broken, and soon thereafter Franco's

A victim of the civil war amidst the ruins of her home

forces entered the severely bombed and starving capital of Madrid. The human costs of this brutal civil war were extremely high: approximately a million Spaniards were either killed or forced to emigrate. The war left most Spaniards with an intense fear of another such armed conflict on their own territory.

Despite Hitler's pressure and threats, Franco did maintain an official policy of neutrality during World War II, although he openly sympathized with Germany and Italy. He even sent a "Blue Division" of volunteers to fight on Germany's side against the Soviet Union from 1941–43. But Franco was always sensitive to the direction political winds blew, and after disastrous German setbacks on the Eastern front in 1943, he decided to maintain his official policy of neutrality more strictly.

Franco created an authoritarian, fascist regime, supported by the army and, initially, by the Catholic Church. This regime remained fundamentally unchanged until his death in November 1975. He always was skillful in playing different groups against each other, but he did not dare create any democratic institutions. The *Cortés* was restructured so that it could not effectively challenge Franco; in reality it was a cheerleader for the rulers. The news media were subjected to close censorship. This was by no means a new phenomenon, since information had been controlled in Spain since the 15th century, except for a brief interlude during the Second Republic. Franco abolished all political parties except his own *Movimiento Nacional* (National Movement).

The right–wing Falangist Movement, which had elaborated fascist ideals for Franco in the early days, gradually declined in influence and ultimately became strictly an agency to administer the bureaucracy. The Catholic Church's support of the regime gradually waned as the years went on, but the Catholic lay organization, *Opus Dei*, did grow in influence, especially within the educational and economic spheres. The *Opus Dei* became more open to progressive ideas and was a force behind Spain's rapid industrialization and robust economic growth that began in the 1960s.

Although Franco was the undisputed dictator from the very beginning, in 1947 he officially made himself chief of state for life, with the right to appoint his own successor. He declared Spain to be a monarchy, but not until 1969 did he name Prince Juan Carlos of Bourbon, whom he had educated and groomed for years to prepare him for his new role, to be the new king upon his death.

Isolation and Economic Progress

Because of Franco's open sympathy with Germany and Italy during World War II, the victorious allies initially isolated Spain in the international community and for years refused to allow it to enter the UN. But the Cold War brought many former enemies onto better terms with each other, and Spain was no exception. The emerging hostilities between the Soviet Union and the nations in the Atlantic Alliance greatly enhanced the value of Spain's strategic location. Therefore, in 1953 the U. S. reached an agreement with Franco providing for American financial assistance in return for the right to establish four air and naval bases in Spain. This agreement was of great military significance for the U. S., but Franco's many opponents never regarded it kindly. The present Socialist leader, Felipe González, for instance, admitted that his attitude toward the U. S. had always been negative, in large part because the picture of former President Dwight D. Eisenhower smilingly shaking hands with Franco had remained firmly etched in his memory.

All in all, the fascist movement failed to stimulate much mass enthusiasm in Spain. It rested on widespread apathy fed by most Spaniards' intense desire for order after the Civil War. Franco had created a panoply of corporatist organizations, which were designed to mobilize and control the diverse elements of society. But as years passed, dissatisfaction and unrest began to manifest themselves since Spain's fundamental problems had by no means been solved. Labor and student unrest, high inflation, growing opposition with the Church, increasing Basque extremism and revolutionary events in neighboring Portugal, beginning in 1974, continually chipped away at the foundations of the fascist state. Yet only one event could wipe away the trappings of fascism and set the process of democracy in motion: the death of Franco, which finally occurred in November 1975.

King Juan Carlos

The most visible sign for a new democratic spirit of reconciliation and national unity quickly became King Juan Carlos de Borbón y Borbón. Even former Communist Party chief, Santiago Carrillo, had to admit, "without Juan Carlos, Spaniards would probably be fighting each other again." Few persons had expected that the monarch would become a major linchpin for democracy in Spain.

Franco had chosen Juan Carlos (the grandson of former King Alfonso XIII) over the head of his father, Don Juan, who lived in Portuguese exile and who had always been an outspoken critic of Franco. From his father, Juan Carlos had learned several very important lessons: to install a democracy in Spain, to shun the everyday dealings of political parties, and never to play the army against the people.

Young Juan Carlos was an uninspiring pupil and rather introverted, especially after accidentally shooting his brother with an air gun at age 16. Remembering a suggestion the Italian fascist leader, Benito Mussolini, had once made to him, Franco brought the nine–year old Juan Carlos back to Spain in 1947 and had him educated under his watchful eye. The boy was sent to the army, navy and air force academies in Zaragoza, Martín and San Javier, respectively. He enjoyed his life at these academies, making contacts within the military that later were to be important to him as King. He had plenty of time for his favorite hobbies of athletics, ham radios and fast motorcycles. He also became a jet pilot, and he still flies himself around Spain for official visits.

Prince Juan Carlos as a schoolboy

Spain

When Franco decided in 1964 that the young Prince had had enough education, he entered a very trying phase in his life waiting for a task. He married Sophia, the sister of the former Greek King Constantine, who is one of the King's few close friends (and who now is a public relations agent in London). Not until 1969 was he officially proclaimed the crown prince after he had sworn allegiance to Franco's basic principles before the Parliament and after he had had a serious argument with his own father over his decision to accept the Spanish crown from Franco's own hand. He was therefore distrusted by Don Juan and by many Spanish democrats, who thought that the Prince had become *El Caudillo's* stooge.

Many in Franco's coterie also distrusted him because he did not ingratiate himself to them. Their suspicions were fed by the fact that Juan Carlos began establishing contacts with political opponents of the Franco regime, including, through an intermediary, communist leaders in Paris. With Franco on his death bed in late 1975, Juan Carlos gave a revealing glimpse of his sentiments by flying to Spanish Sahara and telling the troops there that they would have to withdraw because Spanish colonialism had come to an end.

He was installed as King after Franco's death, but he proceeded cautiously. In fact, the Spanish experiment of making a step–by–step transition from a dictatorship to a parliamentary democracy, while continuing to observe the existing laws of the land, was unique in European history. He temporarily retained Franco's last prime minister, Carlos Arias Navarro. Through wise appointments, he gained influence over the Council of the Realm, a small body whose only clear function was to insure that the new regime would remain within the bounds of Francoism. By the summer of 1976 he was able to have Arias eased out of office and to have a man with reformist designs, Adolfo Suárez, appointed in his place. The King gave Suárez unmistakable instructions to proceed as rapidly as possible toward the goal which Juan Carlos shared with most of his countrymen: "to restore sovereignty to the Spanish people."

As King, Juan Carlos set about to demonstrate that the bitter controversies of the past could be ended. When he visited Mexico three years after becoming King, he requested that veteran republicans who had fled from Franco's rule be invited to the Spanish Embassy, where he received them with demonstrative cordiality. Also, in a public speech he called the Civil War a fratricidal tragedy; Franco had always referred to it as a "glorious crusade."

He chooses to live in the relatively small Zarzuela Palace outside of Madrid, rather than the stately palace his ancestors had built in the middle of the capital. He prevents anything like a palace clique to congeal around him. Realizing that most Spaniards are not ardent monarchists, he keeps protocol to a minimum and leads a relatively austere private life. But his patience, tact, shrewdness and courage in guiding the nation have won him respect from even those Spaniards who had always considered the very word "monarchist" an insult.

Seeds of Democracy

The National Movement (*Movimiento Nacional*), which Franco had formed out of various political movements, was withering on the vine. The best-known component of the National Movement was the fascist–oriented *Falange*, named after the infantry formations which Alexander the Great had called phalanx. The trappings of fascist salutes, paramilitary youth organizations and the calls to revitalize Spain through order, authority and hierarchy remained, but membership in the National Movement had for most Spaniards become a mere formal prerequisite for a government job. In fact, many of Spain's foremost reformers after Franco's death, including Adolfo Suárez, under whose

The ancient city of Toledo, capital of Spain under Roman rule and home of the illustrious artist El Greco

premiership Spain became a modern parliamentary democracy in the second half of the 1970s, had attained political prominence within the National Movement.

Spain felt its way slowly and nervously out of the authoritarian political order created and maintained by Franco. Many Spaniards looked back uneasily to the 1930s, and they saw certain parallels between that period and the 1970s. At both times political parties were legalized after dictatorships had ended, and the Communist Party supported the young democracy both times. At the beginning of the two democracies the vast majority of Spaniards voted for the moderate parties of the center. Also, world economic crises—the latest in the 1970s—set in at the inception of both Spanish democracies. Basque and Catalonian nationalists demanded autonomy, and a fraction of their numbers resorted to grisly violence to provoke the military and press for their aims. Thus, in both eras, Spanish democratic leaders had to face a declining economy, a wave of strikes and demands for better wages, and extremist violence, while creating a political order which would later be, in the words of King Juan Carlos, "a just order, equal for all," supported by "public activity as much as private activity, under legal safeguards."

Economic Progress

Despite the parallels between the 1930s and the 1970s, one must notice also the many significant differences between Spanish society in the heyday of Franco's rule and in the 1970s. One difference is the evolution of the Church in Spain, traditionally one of the most conservative in the entire Catholic world. This evolution will be discussed in the culture section of this chapter.

A further development that favored the post–Franco democratic experiment was economic progress. The recession of the 1970s was not nearly as deep as that of the 1930s and did not shake the democratic foundations of the European countries as was the case earlier. Most important, Spain's economic structure has changed drastically since Franco seized power. *El Caudillo* sought to establish complete Spanish self–reliance, which amounted to sealing Spain off economically from the rest of the world. As an international outcast after World War II, Spain was not permitted to receive Marshall Plan assistance. This greatly widened the gap between Spain and most of the rest of Western Europe. But in 1950 the UN lifted the trade boycott against Spain, and capital and modern production and business ideas began to enter the country.

The result was a doubling of industrial production in the course of the 1950s. This upswing did bring a doubling of prices, which stimulated labor unrest, but it also gave Spanish technocrats the courage to draw up a Stabilization Plan in 1959. This significant plan devalued the peseta to a level that would favor Spanish exports, began to eliminate some unnecessary economic controls, buried the old economic isolation policy (known as autarky) in theory as well as practice, and headed Spain in a dynamic capitalist direction. This new direction was not only good for the living standards of the people, but also for the later stabilizing of democracy. In the last decade of Franco's rule economic growth in Spain was an enviable 7% per year, one of the highest in Western Europe.

Spain's rapid economic growth not only increased the size of the middle class and gradually began to level out class differences, but it changed the country's outlook and demography. As Spaniards' economic expectations grew, their eyes turned more toward Western Europe, where democracy and prosperity were linked. Their contact with other Europeans was enormously increased by the lightning expansion of the Spanish tourist industry, which soon made Spain the number one tourist country in all of Europe. Although the bulk of Spain's tourists flock to the beaches, seldom venturing into the interior, they brought millions of Spanish into direct contact with Western Europeans and their ideas and spending habits.

Many Spaniards themselves began to pull up stakes and seek a better economic life elsewhere. In the 1960s more than three million Spaniards moved from the poorer countryside into the country's major industrial areas, especially Madrid, Catalonia and the Basque country. Well over two million Spaniards left the rural areas for industrialized countries north of the Pyrenees, especially to France, West Germany and Switzerland, sending much–needed foreign currency remittances back to Spain. Entire villages were deserted.

The new trend greatly reduced the number of Spaniards engaging in agriculture and left many pockets of rural poverty, especially in the South and in the province of Galicia. Such rapid industrial growth also left more polluted air, sea, rivers and tap water in Spain. It transformed quiet, picturesque fishing villages into loud, overcrowded mass tourist places with tasteless and cheaply constructed hotels, an army of souvenir vendors and thieves, and much higher prices. Large parts of the beautiful coastline were scarred with factories, chemical

and power plants and blocks of apartments. Also, many of the suburbs around industrial cities shot up almost overnight and were often built without paved streets, or medical, educational and leisure facilities. All too often they became slums and centers for delinquency and crime. Spain paid a high price for its industrialization.

Yet Spain's social base had changed significantly. Workers increasingly began to own their own homes or apartments. They also began to buy cars and take vacations far from home. Although Franco had tried to keep them by and large politically apathetic, more and more Spaniards began under Franco to make public demands on the political system through strikes and demonstrations. Workers began to support the illegal trade union movement that grew out of the 1950s. Workers' Committees (*Comisiones Obreras*) emerged in larger factories to represent workers in negotiations with the management. By the 1970s they had successfully infiltrated the official unions, thereby weakening that prop of the Francoist system. In 1967 workers acquired the right to strike as long as such strikes were peaceful and strictly non–political.

The changes in the Catholic Church, the economy and the social structure had already eaten away at the roots of Francoism long before *El Caudillo* had closed his eyes for the last time. But the main reason why Spain's second attempt at democracy had a better chance to succeed was that Spaniards had a good memory. They remembered that four decades earlier one half of Spain conquered the other after untold suffering and grief and that years of authoritarianism had followed. This time, Spaniards were ready for reconciliation with each other. This willingness to ignore the things they once fought over has been referred to as a *pacto de olvida*, an agreement to forget. For example, after more than a dozen years of Socialist rule, many plazas still bear Franco's name, and almost all monuments and memorials one-sidedly honor Franco's rebels. In 1977, two years after his death, an amnesty was granted to his collaborators, and unlike in several other European countries, there has never been a collective declaration of guilt or rejection of the past even though hundreds of thousands of Franco's opponents had been killed, sent to concentration camps, or forced into exile.

In 1980 the new democratic regime dared to sponsor the first balanced exhibition of the Civil War. Videotapes, old news films, and tapes of the songs of both sides were played. Documents, flags, weapons, posters and newspapers were shown. Rather than rekindling old pas-

Spain

sions, the exhibition seemed to strengthen a very powerful sentiment in contemporary Spain—*never again civil war*.

By 2002, nearly 40% of Spaniards either had not been born when Franco ruled or are too young to remember him. Democracy has been firmly established and reinforced by EU membership, and it now seems less dangerous for the country's cohesion to glance backwards into Spain's past. A flood of books on the Franco era has appeared, as well as a major exhibition (officially opened by the king) on the history of those were forced into exile, and an extremely popular TV series, *"Cuentame, como paso"* ("Tell me how it happened"), based on the day-to-day life of an ordinary Madrid family as Spain began to change in the 1960s. About 60 communal graves of Republican fighters and sympathizers have been located for excavation and transformation into memorials. Retrospection is no longer taboo in Spain.

GOVERNMENT

Monarch as Head of State

The King works hard and is informed about the minutest details of his country's policies. However, unlike Franco, he does not attend cabinet meetings, and he usually keeps himself aloof from day-to-day political affairs. He preserves his real political authority for critical issues and times. Some Spaniards were critical of his outspoken support of joining NATO's integrated command structure and the EU's single currency. But communist leader Julio Anguita's demand in 1996 that the king resign unleashed a public furor.

The king operates under strong constitutional constraints. However, he is able to influence the complexion of the government, and he is the supreme commander

General Francisco Franco

of the armed forces. Unlike any other monarch in Europe, he deals directly with the political and military leaders in his own country. He is without question Europe's most powerful and influential monarch although he probably is the one with the least personal wealth. He performs all the ceremonial duties of a chief-of-state, but because of his guiding role in Spanish politics, he is a far more important conversation partner for foreign leaders than are most heads of state in Western Europe.

A 1990 poll showed that Juan Carlos is more popular than the institution of the monarchy: 82% that he had made a significant contribution to democratic stability, but 42% found the monarchy "out-of-date." Nevertheless, polls in 1996 revealed that the monarchy is Spain's most highly rated institution. By the 21st century it was probably respected more than it was at any time since 1800.

The King influences the selection of the prime minister and the cabinet, and he formally appoints both. The cabinet is technically not responsible to the *Cortés*. However, according to recent practice, a government is expected to have a majority in the Chamber of Deputies.

Parliament

A national referendum in December 1976 established a bicameral parliament, and in another referendum in December 1978, 87.8% of all voting Spaniards approved of a new constitution, which contained few traces of Francoism. The upper house of the *Cortés*, the 248-seat Senate, is the less important chamber. In an electoral system that gives each voter four votes, each province elects the four candidates with the highest number. All provinces send four senators regardless of population. This is designed to protect the interests of the smaller provinces and is one indication of the extent to which Spain had become a federal state. The islands and the two Moroccan enclaves send seven senators, and the King is permitted to appoint as many as 41 additional senators.

The 350 members of the lower house, the Chamber of Deputies, are elected by a modified form of proportional representation by which voters choose from a list established by each party. Independent candidates are forbidden to run for election unless they can combine to form a list. Seats are distributed to the various provinces according to population, with the smallest province receiving at least three seats.

The electoral system is designed to favor the large parties at the expense of the smaller ones. The parties are strengthened further by their power to take away

a parliamentary seat occupied by any of its members and give it to another. This possibility hardens members' loyalty toward their parties and also makes parliamentary speeches predictable and rather dull. One can only marvel, though, at the way the Spanish, who were not permitted to vote in free elections for more than 40 years, can competently sort their way through more than 60 parties and groups, using two different electoral systems at the same time, and produce a similar result in both houses of the *Cortés*.

Political Parties

In 1977 Spain's major parties signed the Moncloa Pact with each other, named after the small governmental palace in Madrid. By signing this pact, the parties agreed to drop their party dogma for the good of the country. The voters appreciated the major parties' moderation. In the first free elections since 1936, the Spanish showed their preference for the parties that are unmistakably in favor of the democratic order. The more radical parties of the left and right found themselves represented in Parliament, but without anything close to a majority.

Political parties entered the post-Franco era with well-founded nervousness. In Spain's past, parties were always plagued by division. Spain was the only country in Europe to experience a civil war in the 20th century, and the political parties had been in the thick of that tragic struggle. From 1939 to 1975 they had been unable to operate freely, and most of them had been driven underground or into exile, where their members were often isolated from each other, and where their leaders had great problems in establishing and maintaining unity. They also had difficulty following political developments within Spain.

When Franco died, the parties had to organize themselves very quickly. Fortunately Spain had an intelligent and able King who could stabilize the transition while the democratic parties prepared themselves. Portugal had not been so fortunate and had to experience two years of chaos before the moderate democratic parties could gain their footing.

Socialists

Only two of the major parties existed before 1975. The Spanish Socialist Labor Party (PSOE) which, together with the Catalan Socialist Party and the Basque Socialist Party, is generally referred to as The Socialists. Founded in 1879, it is the oldest Spanish party. Yet it acquired a young image after a thorough change of leadership in the early 1970s.

Its former leader, Felipe González, was an attractive and charismatic man, who

The Spanish Royal Family: (l. to r.) Princess Elena, Crown Prince Felipe, Queen Sophia, King Juan Carlos I, and Princess Cristina.

was a labor lawyer and who had engaged in anti–Francoist underground activity. He and the other leaders were able to lead the PSOE from a radical leftist Marxist stance during the Franco era to a pragmatic political course that sought to open the party toward the political center. He is a master of compromise, tactics and organization.

A majority within the PSOE decided in 1976 to call itself Marxist, over the urgent protest of González. The latter argued that the party should return to the ethical and un-dogmatic socialism of the party's founders and consider Marxism merely as "an interesting intellectual exercise, but not the holy writ." He, himself, publicly declared that he is not a Marxist. González resigned in protest, and as a result the popularity of the party plummeted. Therefore a special party congress was called in 1979 to vote by 86% to reinstate him as head of a moderate party executive committee. The PSOE is still a party with a broad political spectrum, but González brought the left–wing within the party largely under control. The PSOE calls for a classless, pluralistic, democratic and decentralized Spain with a market economy. Its slogan is: "Socialism is freedom!"

The party is strong in industrial centers, and many large cities have Socialist mayors. It is also strong in the agricultural region of Andalusia. It is the only socialist party in southern Europe that has strong support from a significant independent

trade union, the UGT. It also has a well–developed local base, so it is the only Spanish party with solid roots in the factories, local neighborhoods and national and regional parliaments.

One of the PSOE's major advantages had always been its unity in the face of opposing parties' disunity. But that ended as fighting within González's party erupted over the question of what a socialist government should do. One faction, the *renovadores* (renewers), supported González's pragmatic free market policies, aimed at opening up monopolies, curbing the budget deficit, and creating conditions favorable for job creation and business. The *Guerristas*, named after their leader, Alfonso Guerra, regard themselves as orthodox socialists. The government's economic austerity fueled such strong discontent on the labor front that the unions called several 24–hour general strikes in 1988, 1992, and 1994. The 1988 work stoppage was the first successful general strike in Spain since 1934.

González was sometimes accused of abandoning socialist principles by failing to redistribute wealth. The charge is not entirely fair. During his four terms, education spending rose, as the school–leaving age was raised to 16 and the number of university students doubled. Health services and pension rights were extended to the entire population, and a nation–wide unemployment benefit scheme was created. Overall social spending rose from 27% of GDP in 1977 to 45%

in 1997. The magnitude of these expenditures was reflected in the budget deficit, which in 1996 stood at 4.4% of GDP; when he left office in 1996 the overall national debt was a little over 60% of GDP.

His victory in 1993 left him the only socialist ruler in any major Western European country and the only leader in any European country to win a fourth term. In contrast to other Western European socialist parties, his moderate, pragmatic party still personified Spain's post–Franco modernization.

González's government found itself embroiled in a series of scandals that severely dented his credibility. Early elections in 1996 resulted in the defeat of the incumbent by a narrow margin. In opposition, González stepped down as leader in 1997 and was replaced by Joaquín Almunia, his close associate. Almunia proved to be an uninspiring leader and resigned after his party was defeated in the March 2000 elections. Its electoral alliance with the Communist-led United Left frightened many voters. It dropped from 38% to 34% of the votes and from 141 to 125 seats. It got a new leader in 2000: José Luis Rodríguez Zapatero, a 39-year-old lawyer from northern Castile. The old guard has been largely swept out. Even Gonzáles occupies no post of any kind, even ceremonial.

At the end of González's era, Spaniards reflected on the dramatic transformation their country had undergone during his rule, which lasted longer than any other

Spain

contemporary Western European leader except former German Chancellor Helmut Kohl: Spain is solidly democratic. Franco-ism has lost its force even though old Francoists have suffered little persecution. The army no longer intervenes in politics. The country is more decentralized, with more power having passed to the regions. The nature of Spanish socialism has changed to the extent that most now refer to themselves as "social democrats," and the middle class is no longer hostile to Socialists.

Economically, González championed the free market, was often firm with the trade unions, and privatized some state enterprises. He made Spain look modern, and in 1995 the UN ranked Spain ninth in the world for its "quality of life." In for-eign affairs, he led Spain into the EU and NATO, and he permitted the U.S. to retain its military bases in the country.

The Communists

The other party with deep historical roots is the Spanish Communist Party (PCE). Founded in 1920, it was heavily involved in the Spanish Civil War on the Republican side. The Communists worked closely with the Soviet Union's participants in the Civil War. This collabo-ration was too close and gave Spanish Communists a clear look at Marxist–Leninist practices. This fact helps to ex-plain why the exiled party was the first communist party in Europe to reject the Soviet model of communism and the no-tion of the dictatorship of the proletariat. It condemned the Warsaw Pact invasion of Czechoslovakia in 1968, as well as sim-ilar actions against Afghanistan and Poland in 1979 and 1981. In 1977 former party chief Santiago Carrillo published a book, Eurocommunism and the State, in which he repeated his contention that the Soviet model had so discredited itself that it was beyond rescue. The party's present leader, Julio Anguita, is continuing this moderate, independent course.

The party's operations within Spain began again long before the death of Franco. It built up party cells in the facto-ries, neighborhoods, youth groups, hos-pitals and even in the government min-istries. It is still the most disciplined and best organized mass party in Spain, despite factional splits. The working class provides 80% of its voters, who are predominantly male. Its strongest areas are in the indus-trialized zones of Madrid and Catalonia.

Despite its turn from Stalinism and despite its pragmatic approach and sup-port for the democratic regime, it had little electoral success. In the 1979 national parliamentary elections, it received only about 10% of the votes, and in the 1982 elections its vote plummeted to 3.8% and

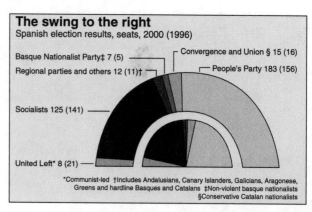

The swing to the right
Spanish election results, seats, 2000 (1996)

Basque Nationalist Party‡ 7 (5)
Regional parties and others 12 (11)†
Socialists 125 (141)
United Left* 8 (21)
Convergence and Union § 15 (16)
People's Party 183 (156)

*Communist-led †Includes Andalusians, Canary Islanders, Galicians, Aragonese, Greens and hardline Basques and Catalans ‡Non-violent basque nationalists §Conservative Catalan nationalists

Source: *The Economist*

four seats. Combining forces with other elements of the old Marxist left under the banner, United Left (IU), it and its allies dropped from 10.6% of the votes in 1996 to 6% in 2000 and from 21 to only 8 seats. It has become almost irrelevant in Span-ish politics. While its cells are well entrenched in numerous organizations in the country, it lacks popular support. Its membership had fallen to about 62,000 from its peak of 200,000 in 1978. Although it is firmly supported by the Workers' Commissions, this most powerful trade union federation is losing ground to the Socialist-dominated UGT.

Many Spanish are still aware of the remorseless and cunning tactics that the Communists used during the Civil War to bring the Socialists and leftist Republicans under their control. Their heavy–handed-ness caused many Spanish to forget their more moderate actions during the Popu-lar Front days before the outbreak of hos-tilities. Although the PCE now advocates a "peaceful road to socialism," there are several other ultra–left and violent groups in Spain that call themselves "commu-nist." They therefore help keep alive the inclination of many Spaniards to associate communism with unrest and violence.

Another problem is that although the PCE publicly supports democracy, there is still too little democracy within the party. Despite periodic purges, there are still wings within the PCE which struggle for domination and which are treated harshly by the party leadership. Former leader Carrillo failed in his attempt to win more popular support by breaking away. The party has difficulties with a younger group that calls itself "renovators" and demands the introduction of gen-uine intra–party democracy and the disavowal of "democratic centralism," which requires absolute obedience after decisions have been made. By 1989 there was even talk of plans to turn the United Left into a non–Communist party.

The hardest nut for the splintered PCE to crack, though, is the presence of an attractive Socialist Party for Spanish vot-ers who want a moderate, democratic leftist-oriented party. In fact, the Commu-nist Party faces a dilemma: it knows that no party in Spain has a chance without a democratic program and policy. But the more the PCE moderates itself and embraces democracy, the more it becomes indistinguishable from the PSOE. Thus, there is little reason to vote for the PCE.

The Political Right

The existence of two parties on the political left which could together capture about half of the votes presented a serious challenge to the more conservative politi-cal forces. The die–hard supporters of the Franco dictatorship had to learn through stinging electoral defeats that Francoism could not survive in Spain without *El Caudillo* himself.

The fact that the two dominant parties in Spain today—the PSOE and the People's Party (PP, until 1989 called the Popular Alliance or AP)—support the democratic order makes the present political situation far different from the early 1930s. Indeed, the emergence of a basically two–party sys-tem strengthens Spanish democracy.

The most conservative of the major par-ties, the People's Party, was re-founded, renamed and revamped in 1989. At first it thought it could win votes by hammering against crime and the alleged Marxist danger and by thereby polarizing the society. Young thugs identifying them-selves as AP adherents roamed the streets with sticks and bicycle chains attacking persons wearing socialist badges. The re-sult was a miserable showing in the 1977 elections.

In post–Franco Spain, the word "right" is still a red flag for many voters, who want to see any conservative policies advocated from the center–right. The party decided to move closer to the politi-cal center and to draw a clear line between itself and the anti–regime parties on the right. It rejects violence, supports the monarchy, advocates reforms and a "social market economy," and opposes monopolies. It seeks a broad alliance of voters.

Its former leader was Manuel Fraga Iribarne, one of Spain's most colorful politicians. As almost all earlier leaders of the party, he was a high functionary in the earlier regime. But he became a strong proponent of parliamentary democracy. He was such a skilled and hard–hitting speaker that he even scared some people in his own party. Campaigning energetically on a platform of lower taxes, protection of Spanish business, law and order and strong support for the military, his party became Spain's second largest political force, despite its lingering associations with the Franco era. Fraga left the national scene to become head of Galicia's regional government. This left the party free to construct a more modern alternative to the Socialist government. In the October 2001 regional elections PP won over 50% of the votes ensuring Fraga his fourth consecutive term as premier.

The party is led by Prime Minister José Maria Aznar, who was able to do what other conservative leaders had failed to accomplish: unite former Francoists, Christian Democrats, and free–market liberals. A master of consensus politics, he insists, "I am a centrist." He narrowly escaped an assassination attempt in 1995. The People's Party has the fewest members of any other major party and is well represented only in the upper civil service and the army. Its views are expressed by the important conservative Madrid daily, *ABC*, which the party controls.

It is particularly strong in small towns and predominantly rural areas. Its chief problem was that González's pragmatic socialism left little room for a conservative party beyond tax cutting. But it benefited from his difficulties.

The PP entered the 1996 elections confident it would take power. It captured 38.8% of the votes. But with only 156 seats in the 350-seat lower house, it fell 20 seats short of an absolute majority. Aznar had to negotiate with the regional parties, especially Pujol's Catalans (CIU, with 16 seats) and the moderate Basques (PNV, with five seats), to scrape together a minority government. The price was another generous increase in regional autonomy. He committed his government to "fully implementing the 1979 statute of autonomy" and to raising the percentage of tax revenues the regions can keep for themselves.

In the March 2000 parliamentary elections a rightist party, albeit one that now calls itself the "reformist center," won for the first time an outright majority of seats in democratic elections. Capturing also for the first time the majority of votes from young Spaniards and from voters

Prime Minister José Maria Aznar

in the industrial quarters in Madrid and performing very well in the Catalonia and the Basque region, Aznar's PP captured 183 seats.

The fact that post–Franco Spain has undergone two peaceful transfers of power, from the center to the left and now from the left to the right, demonstrates that democracy has come of age. In another way Aznar's government represents a *Second Transition* (the title of his 1994 book): it brings to power a new generation of leaders in their thirties and forties who were students when Franco died in 1975. The PP's leadership has allayed Spanish fears that the old Francoist right would dismantle the welfare state and that fascist intolerance might return to Spain. Aznar, who by temperament prefers politics by accommodation, has a powerful historical motive to operate by consensus. Indeed, most of his policies—privatization of industries, full integration with NATO, and fiscal austerity to qualify for European Monetary Union (EMU)—continue rather than break with the Socialists' program.

Aznar, who has repeatedly announced that he will not serve more than two terms as prime minister, benefited from a booming economy and from his brand of cautious and consensual government which has purged the authoritarian reputation that once haunted the country's conservatives. His governance has not provoked the trade unions or the students, and street violence has been practically unknown on his watch. He has gradually withdrawn subsidies from ailing industries, privatized the steel industry and made it competitive, closed the shipyards

in Cadiz, lowered top tax rates from 56% to 48% and loosened the rigid labor market. He has strengthened the delicate consensus that has maintained stability in Spanish politics since Franco's death. This was not endangered by his party's abstention from a parliamentary vote in 1999 officially condemning Franco's 1936 rebellion that sparked the civil war. Aznar has directed the country's politics into the center.

Aznar has also challenged nationalists' holds in the regions, and his party has done well in elections there. His policy is one of national unity. He stresses that the constitution mandates that Spain remain one country. He refuses to grant the Basques a referendum on self-determination or to talk to ETA terrorists until they renounce violence.

In the 2000 elections regional parties won 33 seats in the *Cortés*, up from 29. A conservative Catalan coalition called Convergence and Union (CiU) fell from 16 to 15 seats. The Basque Nationalists (PNV) gained two seats for a total of seven. The Canary Coalition (CC) retained its four seats, and the Galicia Nationalists (BNG) increased their number from two to three. Other regional parties captured a total of five seats.

The Military and Politics

While Spain's parties are doing much to pull Spain's democratic forces together, there are certain elements which place strains on the Spanish constitutional order: the military, regional separatists and a governmental bureaucracy in need of reform.

After Franco's death the civilians carefully removed the 40,000-man National Police from military control and gave the Ministry of the Interior coequal power with the military over the 75,000-man Civil Guard. The latter troops, highly efficient, proud and dressed in dull-green uniforms and black patent-leather tricorn hats, have been used since 1844 as an internal security force by the central government and under Franco as an apparatus of repression. No country can ever make an absolutely clean break with its past, and an essential fact of Spain's past is the military's arrogation to itself of special political responsibility. Every officer takes an oath "to preserve the unity of Spain," and Article 8 of the constitution names the military as ultimate arbiter of Spanish sovereignty and constitutional rights.

Most of Spain's officers are politically conservative and highly disciplined. Most will obey whoever is in power. Since the inception of democracy many officers have openly grumbled about the new kind of politics, which, they say, gives free

Spain

rein to criminals, terrorists, opponents of a unified Spain, bickering political parties and assertive trade unions. They also resented what they saw as politically motivated military promotions and neglect of the military's needs. By the end of the 1980s only about 9% of the central government's budget was spent on defense.

Soldiers have also criticized the civilian government's failure to cope with domestic terrorism. These groups include the Basque separatists (ETA), a leftist–sounding GRAPO (the Spanish initials for "Groups of Antifascist Resistance First of October"), the rightist Apostolic Alliance and the Warriors of Christ the King. All aim to destroy confidence in the government, polarize society and provoke the armed forces to take over power and establish a dictatorship. Their motives are, of course, different.

The ultra–rightists want a dictatorship for its own sake, and the ultra–leftists want one as a prelude to some kind of Marxist paradise. It cannot be denied that these terrorists know their country's history very well. Domestic violence has time and again destroyed the constitutional order and provoked the establishment of dictatorships to restore order.

The 1981 Attempted Coup

One event especially showed that the essential political issues of parliamentary supremacy and civilian control over the military had not yet been entirely solved. On February 23, 1981, only three weeks after Prime Minister Suárez had announced his resignation thereby plunging Spain into a parliamentary crisis, a colonel in the Civil Guard, Antonio Tejero Molina, led 200 guardsmen into the ornate Chamber of Deputies and held the Parliament and the Cabinet hostage for 18 hours. It was the most outrageous event in the *Cortés* since 1874, when General Manuel Pavia rode his horse up the steps of Parliament and dismissed the horrified deputies.

The intruders roughed up Deputy Prime Minister Manuel Gutierrez Mellado, a liberal general in the army, and unleashed bursts of machine gun fire toward the ceiling, forcing most deputies to take cover under their desks. Since the plotters forgot that the session was being televised, Spaniards outside the *Cortés* were able to witness the shameful spectacle. Tejero, who had received a slap on the wrist only a year earlier for his part in a harebrained plot to kidnap the Cabinet, was not acting alone. Other officers were also involved. The regional commander in Valencia put his troops on alert and sent his tanks into the streets, and all but two of the nine regional commanders hesi-

Col. Tejero brandishes a pistol on the podium of the Cortés

tated to do anything while waiting to see if the coup (called *el golpe* in Spain) would succeed.

It was at this critical juncture that Juan Carlos, who had fortunately canceled a long–planned trip to the U.S. in order to be in Madrid during the political crisis, acted to save Spanish democracy. He ordered the creation of a "governmental commission" composed of ministerial undersecretaries to assume provisional civilian governmental power while the cabinet was in captivity. He skillfully turned one of the highest–ranking plotters, his military tutor in the 1950s and chief military adviser since 1975, General Alfonso Armada Comyn, away from the venture by declaring that the plotters would "have to put two bullets in me before they take over" and then dispatching Armada to help suppress the uprising.

The King then turned to his many contacts within the army to assure them that he opposed the coup and would die to defend Spain's democracy. Ironically, one can thank Franco for having sent the King to the military academies and thereby having provided Juan Carlos with so many friends within the armed forces. He persuaded the officers of the elite Brunete armored division on the outskirts of Madrid to keep their tanks in the camp and out of the streets of Madrid. If the capital city had become filled with tanks, it is likely that the *coup* would have acquired uncontrollable momentum. The King phoned all the captains–general in the nine military districts to coax or pressure them into supporting him.

Finally, at 1:15 A.M. he went on national television, wearing a general's uniform

and sitting in front of the royal coat of arms, to announce that "the crown, symbol of the permanence and unity of the nation, cannot tolerate, in any form, actions or attitudes attempting to interrupt the democratic process." This announcement was a tremendous comfort to a people that places great importance on symbols. The next morning Tejero saw that he was alone and gave up.

One Socialist deputy announced with relief that "the time of *coups* is over," but centrist politician Antonio Garrigues Walker was more correct in declaring "Thank you Señor Tejero, for pointing out that our democracy is fragile and incomplete." It is true that Spanish democracy had passed an important test. According to opinion polls, only 4% of Spaniards wanted the coup to succeed, while 76% were hostile to it. Most soldiers had supported their civilian rulers, but some had revealed that they were divided and hesitant about such support. Clearly, some soldiers still have little faith in parliamentary democracy, and the military still plays an important role in politics and cannot be overlooked. Only hours after the abortive coup, the King met with political leaders and warned: "I invite all to reflect and reconsider postures that might lead to greater unity in Spain and more agreement among the Spanish people."

All democratic forces thereafter had to be more cautious and to strive much harder to adopt policies and wage settlements that rest on a consensus, which would include the military. Reforms were slowed down, and a conscientious effort was made to woo the military. For the first time, the army was given an actual role in a stepped–up campaign against Basque terrorism by being deployed along the French border. The *Cortés* passed a law defining states of alarm, siege and emergency, during which times certain civil rights dealing with press freedom, search and detention could be revoked. Finally, Juan Carlos, whose prestige within Spain had soared, had to recognize that his bold actions had alienated him from some elements within the military and that his capacity to prevent another coup had probably been reduced.

Treatment of the Plotters

Spain's political leaders were faced with a dilemma as to what to do with the plotters. If they cracked down too hard, they might provoke an unfortunate military response. Spanish history clearly shows that nothing is more dangerous than a humiliated military. However, if the *coup* leaders were not given stiff sentences, then they might be encouraged to try again. After all, most of the key figures in the coup had been given the mildest suspended sentences for their part in earlier attempts to overthrow the government.

One year after the coup attempt, 32 officers and one civilian were brought to trial before a military tribunal. Tejero had in the meantime become the darling of Spain's ultra–right. In custody, he had enjoyed what he had described as "five–star–hotel treatment" and had received up to 50 admiring visitors each day. Photo books, collections of his jokes (most directed against the new order), and flamenco songs praising him were circulating, and he gave widely published interviews and worked on his memoirs. In his trial in a handsomely furnished hall with soft chairs for the defendants, he supported the slander campaign against the King, which insinuated that Juan Carlos had actually given his advance approval for the *coup*. He also joined other defendants to implicate as many political and military figures as possible in the plot.

Defense attorneys unashamedly cited the many precedents for military intervention in politics. In the closing statements no defendant showed the slightest regret or guilt for his actions, and instead all stressed their love for Spain, their honor as officers and their wish to save the motherland. Tejero probably best expressed the standpoint of a person who learns nothing and understands even less: "I would like to express my utter contempt for those high–ranking officers who have betrayed their motherland." He and the other major conspirator, General Milan del Bosch, were sentenced to thirty years in jail.

The potential strength of the far right was demonstrated by the *Fuerza Nueva* ("New Force"), which had wanted to turn back the wheel of history. Although this and other ultra–right groups never got many votes, they were visible and audible. The leader was Blas Piñar, a highly skilled demagogue who was at his best in rallies complete with outstretched arms giving the fascist salute, fascist paraphernalia everywhere, and the sounds of Franco's hymn, "Cara al Sol" (Face the Sun) blaring in the background. At one time this group could mobilize 300,000 Spaniards in the streets of Madrid every November to honor their dead idol, and their bullies roamed the streets menacingly. The *Fuerza Nueva* idolized the military, especially those soldiers who seized Parliament in 1981, and it promised to help establish a "free Spain." Few Spaniards cared much for its notion of freedom. It was scrapped because it had been ignored by those it had hoped to protect: the Church, conservatives and the military.

González bent over backwards to quiet the soldiers' nerves. Shortly after assuming office, he visited the crack Brunete armored division, which had been deeply implicated in the 1981 plot. He picked up on the initiatives of his predecessor to modernize the army by streamlining and professionalizing it and by giving it better equipment. In 1983 the government moved to tighten control over the military by appointing a single chief of defense responsible to the defense minister. It sought to reduce the number of military regions from eight to six and to move the

Brunete armored division to Extremadura on the Portuguese border, policies which took a long time to be carried out because officers could refuse to be sent to an uncongenial region.

It reduced the number and rank of Spain's most senior officers. In 1985 the defense minister abolished the guarantee that every officer would be promoted at least to the rank of brigadier general before retirement. But he had to concede the right that all would be made colonels, a policy unheard–of in any other Western army. In 1989 Spain introduced promotions based on merit, and those who cannot perform satisfactorily are retired early. These are important steps toward greater professionalization.

Regionalization and Decentralization

A second element that places a heavy strain on the democratic regime is the attempt to decentralize Spanish government and to grant a satisfactory measure of autonomy to the regions. For reasons related to the Moslem conquest, the prolonged expulsion of them and the vast overextension of imperial power, Spain was never a fully integrated country. Madrid was a somewhat artificial creation, surrounded like a bull's–eye by the harsh, sparsely– populated, mainly Castilian Meseta. Around this tableland is the more densely populated and highly diverse periphery.

Tension between the center and the periphery has always been a constant factor in politics. Even today, a fourth of all citizens speak a language other than

West of Madrid in the foothills of the bleak Sierra de Guadarrama stands El Escorial, the brooding, magnificent blue-gray slate and stone symbol of the unchangeable spirit of Spain. Combining a royal palace, basilica, monestery and art gallery, it was built by Philip II, heir to the boundless riches of the New World, the most powerful monarch of the 16th century.

Spain

Castilian Spanish. There are economic disparities. For example, Catalonia, the Basque area and Madrid produce half of Spain's GDP, while almost half the population in Galicia and a third in Estremadura and Castile still work on the land, compared to only 6% in Catalonia and the Basque region. New industries and tourism have helped narrow the gap between these rich and poor regions.

Most Spaniards note regional idiosyncrasies, and many clichés are current: Cordobans are stoic; Galicians are stubborn and moody; Catalans and Valencians are artistic and entrepreneurial; Andalusians are a bit wild and Moorish; and Castilians are austere and noble. Yet all benefit from being a part of the larger Spanish economy and are held together by such strong common interests that no region would vote for secession.

The regions particularly were suppressed under Franco, who in part justified his military *coup* and subsequent rule as the preservation of unity. Franco gained the lasting hatred of the Basques after ordering the devastating bombing of Guernica on April 26, 1937. This situation did not change immediately after Franco's death, and in the Basque country there were some regrettable incidents involving the suppression of cultural events. But in modern Spanish history transitions to greater freedom and democracy were always accompanied by demands for more home rule in the regions, and the post– Franco era was no exception. Fortunately the new leaders had pluralist political sentiments and were therefore willing to make many compromises.

Spain introduced in 1979 the most ambitious plan to decentralize political power since the foundation of the Federal Republic of Germany in 1949. It has already become one of Europe's most decentralized states. Between 1994 and 2000, the central government has 45,000 fewer employees, and the regions have 235,000 more. There are 17 autonomous regions, each with its own government and parliament, though with differing degrees of power. For example, the Basque country and Navarra collect their own taxes and pay Madrid for the services they receive. Other regions live on funds and grants from Madrid. Regional governments dispense about 40% of all public spending, and local governments spend another 20%. The center handles only approximately 40%. About a third of the income tax collected in the regions returns to them.

Ultimately Spain is to have a fully federal system, with the central government reserving for itself the exclusive right to conduct foreign, defense, monetary, customs and strategic industrial policy,

Spanish Provinces

as well as full responsibility over the national police and criminal law. Health, welfare, local administration, local roads, and education were gradually transferred to the regions, but that transfer varies in degree and was still incomplete as Spain entered the new century. The central government negotiates with each of the 17 regions on the powers that should be granted to each. The system has to be renegotiated between the regions and Madrid every five years.

Since the death of Franco, regional languages and history has been emphasized. Madrid was forced to back down in 1997 when a committee of experts drew up a list of 100 teaching points to be used in history classes all over Spain. Regional minorities, especially in Catalonia and the Basque area, considered the idea that Spain had a unified history to be reactionary and intolerable. However, the question was not put to rest. Government education officials in Madrid argued in 2000 that Castile should regain its place at the heart of Spanish history and as the source of the country's main language. The central government has the ultimate authority to inspect and supervise schools although the regions have input. Regions establish a large part of the curriculum and approve textbooks before they are published. The result is that children learn

widely varying things in different parts of the country. Noting reports that a quarter of high school graduates are illiterate and unable to count, the Aznar government also favors a return to the basics.

Relations with the demanding regions are never easy for Madrid. Four regions—Catalonia, the Basque Country, Galicia and Andalusia—have more autonomy than the others. As a price for Catalán support for the Aznar minority government in 1996, the central government agreed to increase the proportion of locally raised income taxes the Catalans may keep from 15% to 30% over five years. This percentage differs in each region, so Spain in effect has 17 different tax systems. In 1998, the central government controlled only 58% of public spending, the regions 27% and local governments 15%.

The *coup* attempt in February 1981 prompted the major parties to hammer out a law (called LOAPA) in June 1981 which would help ensure that the military would not object to the process of devolving roughly half of the central government's administrative and budget responsibilities to the regions. Actual transfer of powers was gradually to take place over years. LOAPA established a clearing fund to help reduce economic differences among the regions. It also contained elements that aroused some suspicion, especially in the

284

Basque and Catalan regions. It placed limits on the regional legislative and executive powers, and, some argue, practically eliminated the concept of exclusive regional jurisdiction over certain matters.

Basque Separatism

Basque nationalism remains the Achilles heel of Spanish democracy, and it was the leading argument of the plotters who tried to overturn Spain's democracy in 1981. There are 2.1 million Basques in Spain (just 5% of the country's population) and about 200,000 in France, which declared in 1981 that it would no longer permit its territory to be used as a base for illegal operations in Spain. The relative prosperity of the Basque area had long attracted immigrants from poorer Spanish regions. The result is that half of the residents are not Basque, and only 30% of the people speak Basque.

An ancient people of obscure origins and speaking a language which is unrelated to any language of Europe and which almost no outsiders speak, the Basques have always been sharply aware of their separate identity. This awareness was greatly enhanced by the suppression of things Basque during the Franco era. People were forced to adopt Spanish names, and local administration and police work was placed in the hands of non–Basques who had no comprehension or sympathy with the local language or culture.

Acting more like an army of occupation than a protector of public safety, the Civil Guard antagonized the local population to such an extent that the latter could not help from sympathizing with a group of Basque Catholic nationalists which took shape in 1952 under the name of *Euskadi ta Askatasuna* ("Basque Country and Freedom," or ETA). In 1968 ETA began resorting to violence to accomplish its aims. This caused it to split into a militant, hyper–nationalist wing, called *ETA–Militar*, staffed by predominantly young, well–educated Basques from middle and working class background and a more moderate wing which now disavows violence. Since 1968 ETA was directly responsible for almost 800 deaths by the late–1990s.

ETA–Militar reportedly receives training and material support from Libya, Cuba, Yemen and from Palestinian terrorist organizations. It is closely linked to the only Basque party which opposed regional autonomy in 1980, *Herri Batasuna* ("Popular Unity"), renamed *Euskal Herritarok* (EH) in 1998, which climbed to 18% of the Basques' votes in the 1998 regional elections, winning 14 of the 75 seats in parliament. Its parliamentary successes or failures were once irrelevant because it

boycotted the national and regional parliaments. That policy changed after ETA declared a ceasefire in September 1998, a few weeks before the elections. The large electoral turnout indicated voters' approval of the decision to renounce violence and seek a political path to independence.

Both organizations demand a revision of the Spanish constitution that would be a prelude for an independent *Euskadi*, based on the right of self–determination. Only a third of Basque voters had supported Spain's new constitution in 1978. That document declares Spain's unity to be forever indivisible, and most parties outside of the Basque region consider that wording to preclude any form of referendum on self-determination. However, that is precisely what all Basque nationalists, including the majority that renounces violence, demand. Opponents retort that any tampering with that clause would lead quickly to the unraveling of Spain.

Short of amending the constitution, there is little else Madrid can offer Basques. They already have wide autonomy, a parliament, the power to raise taxes, control over most aspects of education, health, transport, and local police (although anti-terrorism is a federal matter). Nor are Basques the victims of discrimination. In fact, the reverse is more likely correct. They man the police force and otherwise have good jobs. Their language is spreading and is used in the schools.

EH gave signals that it would like to negotiate with the Spanish government in order to escape from the cycle of violence. But until November 1998 the government refused publicly to enter into such negotiations. The other radical nationalist coalition in *Euskadi*, the more moderate *Euskadiko Ezkerra* ("Basque Left"), fused with the Basque Communist Party and publicly disavowed violence.

The major political force in *Euskadi* is the more conservative Basque Nationalist Party (PNV), led by Xabier Arzalluz. It is rural, conservative and Catholic. It captured 28% of the votes and 21 seats in 1998. A party calling itself *Euska Alkartasuna* (EA) broke away from PNV, thereby dividing the moderate Basques. The Basque subsidiary of the Socialist party is the *Partido Socialista de Euskadi* (PSE), which regards itself as progressive, modern, and secular; it appeals mainly to non–nationalists. More and more Basques are political moderates. They are no longer so afraid to speak out against ETA. The Basque branch of the People's Party, which rules in Madrid, rose sharply in 1998 to 16 seats.

The central government has recognized their specific needs by granting Basques the right to raise their own taxes and pay none to the federal treasury, as well as to

form an all–Basque police force of 6,000 to replace the Civil Guards and national police. Schools, roads, courts and police are all run by the Basques themselves. There are three types of schooling available: in Spanish, Basque, or a mixture of both languages. Fewer than 15% of the schools teach only in Spanish. A 2000 poll determined that almost two-thirds of Basques feel both Basque and Spanish. A groundswell of opinion sees violence as futile and profoundly damaging to the Basque economy. ETA and EH supporters came to realize that their extremism was so unpopular that it undermined their cause.

The autonomy measures cut into public support for the separatist alternative. Also, the anti–terrorist campaign by the Spanish police increased French cooperation, and disillusionment among many Basques with the brutality shown by ETA reduced the number of terrorist attacks and paved the way to the ceasefire in 1998. Spaniards were greatly relieved that ETA terrorists had not disrupted the Barcelona Olympics in 1992. Prior to the games the Spanish and French authorities had launched a determined campaign against ETA.

In 1992 ETA's top leaders were arrested, but authorities found the organization to be more complex than had previously been imagined. Its fighters are equipped with advanced technology, weapons, lots of money, and a back–up leadership ready to take over in case the top members were arrested, as was the case. ETA traditionally bases its command and support structures in southwest France. There its armed units are equipped and trained and then sent across the border into Spain to make its bloody strikes.

In 1993 the police delivered a knockout blow by seizing in Bayonne, France, an arms cache of pistols, automatic weapons and plastic explosives so huge that much of it must have been destined for export. One week later, the head of ETA's vast operations, Rafael Caride Simón, was seized while sipping a beer in a Toulouse bar. By that time more than 500 ETA terrorists were behind bars, dispersed in groups of fewer than 15 in jails all over Spain to encourage them to cooperate with police and to prevent them from continuing their operations during incarceration.

As ETA became more isolated, it attacked higher–profile targets. In 1995 José Maria Aznar, who became prime minister in 1996, barely escaped death when a car bomb went off near his home. ETA also failed in an attempt to assassinate King Juan Carlos in 1995. A year later the mastermind of this abortive plot, Julián Atxurra Egurola, was arrested in France, whose three southwest depart-

Spain

Plaza de Colón, Madrid

ments, together with the four northern Spanish regions, the Basque terrorists claim for the independent Basque country they dream of. The house in which Egurola was captured was a true arsenal, containing explosives, timers, grenade launchers, antitank rockets, machine guns, pistols and ammunition.

The 1997 killing of a town councilor from the ruling People's Party wiped out any remaining support for *Herri Batasuna* outside the Basque area and caused revulsion across Europe and massive protests throughout Spain. In December the entire 23–member leadership of *Herri Batasuna* was sentenced to seven years in prison for helping ETA guerrillas. Losing support steadily, the ETA declared a ceasefire in 1998.

Madrid kept up its pressure in 1999, arresting ETA's top guerrilla in Paris and rounding up one of its main commando units. ETA protested that these actions broke a tacit truce. It also claimed that the non-violent Basque National Party had reneged on an agreement to cut off relations with Madrid and cooperate with ETA and *Herri Batasuna* to win Basque independence. Prime Minister Aznar stuck to his government's policy of seeking a political solution to the problem, while continuing to rule out the Basque nationalists' long-standing demand for a "right

to self-determination" to be expressed in a referendum. This would require an alteration of the 1978 constitution that declares Spain to be indissoluble.

The government released more than 130 Basque prisoners and transferred dozens more to jails closer to their families in the Basque region. But this was not enough for ETA, which ended its 14-month truce in December 1999. By the end of 2000 it had murdered 19 victims since calling off its ceasefire at the beginning of the year. This sparked protest marches and condemnations throughout both the region and Spain involving both the mainstream Basque Nationalist Party, the PP and other parties. Prime Minister Aznar concluded that the ceasefire had been a ruse to give ETA guerrillas a breathing space.

The September 11, 2001, terrorist attacks were a shock to Spaniards and created more backing for the prime minister's tough stand against ETA. The government reacted by arresting many al-Qaeda suspects, sharing intelligence with the U.S. and other allies, and cooperating with police authorities in France and elsewhere. The Americans responded by putting 21 ETA names on their "wanted" list. A series of ETA attacks in 2002 persuaded Aznar that it was time to outlaw its political arm, Batasuna, and the Cortés approved in June 2002. The Spanish Su-

preme Court agreed to this in March 2003 under a new law allowing political parties to be banned if they do not condemn terrorism. Two months later the United States and EU acceded to Spain's request to add Batasuna to their list of terrorist organizations.

In February 2003 the Spanish government had closed down the only newspaper printed in the Basque language, *Euskaldunon Egunkaria*, for allegedly aiding ETA. This did not dissuade the more moderate PNV regional government under Juan José Ibarretxe from declaring that sometime in 2003 it would submit to the regional assembly a plan for a referendum to determine whether the Basque region should become a "free state associated with Spain," perhaps sharing the monarchy. Aznar regards this as a mortal threat to Spain's territorial integrity. The PNV's triumph in local elections in May 2003 strengthened Ibarretxe's hand and indicated that many Basques like the idea of even greater autonomy.

Catalonia

Viewed from Madrid, Catalonia appears almost as the model of civic responsibility, when compared with its Basque neighbors. Catalans are Spain's richest and culturally most illustrious minority. The architect Antoni Gaudi, cellist Pablo

Catalonian separatist symbol

Marketplace, Granada   Photo by Eugenia Elseth

Casals, and painters Joan Miró and Salvador Dali were all from this region. In the past its literature and language, spoken by about 4 million persons, was suppressed, and under Franco one could be put in jail for singing "El Cant dels Segadors," the Catalan national anthem. But the Catalans are a pragmatic and patient people, who are inclined to wait for more promising times, rather than to revolt. As one Castilian observer noted, "the difference between the Basque and Catalan nationalists is that the Basques want to leave Spain, and the Catalans want to run it." Catalan nationalists do not want to secede; they want Catalonia accepted as a nation within Spain, with its own lan-

guage, traditions and history. In 1992, the Olympic Games were held in Barcelona 500 years after Columbus's discovery of America. They were a source of great pride for independently–minded Catalans. All events and results were announced first in the Catalan language, and then in Spanish, English and French.

Since 1979 Catalonia has had an autonomy statute similar to that of the Basque country. However, by the time it was able to manage many of its own affairs, an important change had taken place. The region's dynamic industry and commerce had attracted so many immigrants from the poorer Spanish regions that nearly half of the region's population was no

longer of Catalan origin. A minority of the newcomers refused to learn the Catalan language or to adjust to the cultural traditions in the area. Some become enthusiastic Catalans. After years of teaching it in schools, almost everybody now speaks Catalan. Catalonia had a struggle to define its own identity within the Spanish nation. But by the end of the century the Catalan language had revived remarkably. About 95% of the residents can use it.

In 1993 and 1996 its clout in Madrid was dramatically increased by the fact that both the Socialist and PP governments became dependent on the seats of the two-party alliance, Convergence and Union's (CIU), to have a majority. The skillful Catalan leader, Jordi Pujol, had by 2000 won six regional elections by proclaiming both Catalan nationalism and loyalty to Spain, something that nearly all Catalans want. He knew how to use the CIU's leverage. With the Socialists, he negotiated a measure of fiscal autonomy for the Catalan government to keep 15% of the income tax raised in the region. In 1996 he forced the newly elected Aznar to raise that to 30% within five years. He also stepped up the campaign, supported by all parties, to make Catalan the language used in the schools. When the blockbuster film, "Harry Potter," premiered in 2001, he insisted that it be dubbed in Catalan, not in Castilian Spanish. He kept his focus on his central ambition: a loosely federated Spain in which the King of Spain would become the "King of the Spains." In 2000 Pujol lost his leverage in Madrid when Aznar's party won an absolute majority of seats in the *Cortés*. He announced plans to step down in 2003 and hand over the reins to his number two, Artur Mas.

Catalonia is booming economically, and its six million people generate 20% of Spain's GDP. Pujol's favorite statistics are that Catalonia, which his government calls "a country within Spain," has 6% of Spain's territory, 13% of its population, 25% of its exports, and 38% of its industrial exports. Barcelona is still Spain's industrial heart. Foreign investment poured in, but in the 1990s it was increasingly directed toward other regions, especially

The sign was written in both languages—Spanish and Catalan. The Spanish was crossed out, leaving only the Catalan with the added comment: "In Catalonia, in Catalan," meaning that in Catalonia, it has to be written in Catalan

Spain

Madrid. Catalonia receives $50 million each year in EU grants and has its own seat in such international bodies as UNESCO.

Other Regions

The other Spanish regions are also making their way toward one form of autonomy or the other. In Navarra, many residents speak Basque, but waves of immigrants from the Spanish interior have made a great majority of its residents hostile to any form of integration with *Euskadi*. About half the inhabitants of Pais Valencia (the provinces of Valencia, Castellon and Alicante) speak Catalan. However, the majority is in favor of autonomy, while remaining consciously within the Catalan cultural community, which also embraces the Balearic Islands, Andorra and Roussillon in France.

Spain's largest region, Andalusia, approved its autonomous statute in the fall of 1981. It is one of Spain's poorest regions, with an illiteracy rate estimated at 30%, but accounting for half of Spain's population growth. Its per capita GDP in 1992 was only 55% of the EU average, compared with 77% for the rest of Spain and 100% for Madrid; a third of its workforce is unemployed. It needs all the financial assistance it can get from the wealthier regions and the EU.

In order to stimulate the region's economy and build up its infrastructure, its capital, Seville, hosted "Expo 92," 500 years since Columbus set foot on Santo Domingo. Visitors saw the pavilions around the 15–century Santa Maria de la Cuevas, where Columbus planned his last voyage to America and where he is buried. His voyages were retraced by reproductions of the Niña and Pinta and two of the Santa Maria, which sailed to San Salvador and New York, where three of the ships will remain as part of the Metropolitan Museum's permanent collection. The second Santa Maria proceeded through the Panama Canal and on to Japan, where Columbus had hoped to arrive.

In Galicia, 28.4% of eligible voters went to the polls to approve overwhelmingly its autonomy statute. In the 1996 national elections two candidates of a Galician party won seats in the *Cortés*. Aragon, Asturias and other regions are also moving toward limited self–government. A Valencian party captured one *Cortés* seat in 1996. In the Canary islands the separatist Union of the Canary People, which is discreetly supported by Algeria, won four *Cortés* seats in the 1996 national elections and continues to gain adherents. Although in the minority, this group demands self–determination for the islands and the removal of the Spanish army. To show its free spirit, the islands at

first refused in 1989 to lower their tariffs on EU manufactured goods until seven tense weeks of negotiations between the regional government and Madrid brought a peaceful settlement. In 1990 the Canaries decided to adjust its economy to the EU.

Bureaucracy Reform

A third major problem facing Spain is to reform the bureaucracy while maintaining a reasonable level of services. Large numbers of state employees have had some trouble adjusting to the new democratic environment, where public servants are really expected to serve the public. Many functionaries have long regarded their positions as practically their own property, and many old usages have persisted, such as the right of each department to collect fees for the services it performs. Also, financial inspectors expected to receive a percentage of the taxes they collected.

Each department still has a strong sense of self–interest and internal loyalty, which often take priority over serving the public. They are often inefficient and excruciatingly slow, especially when it comes to paying money they owe. They are also greatly overstaffed. This is made worse by such measures as the requirement that the government bureaucracy absorb 35,000 members of Franco's now disbanded *sindicatos*, or state–controlled unions. Work had to be created for this vast unproductive group, and there is understandably lots of sitting or standing around in many of the departments.

González moved quickly to create the kind of civil service appropriate to a democratic and modern Spanish state. His government began immediately to enforce the conflict–of–interest law passed by the *Cortés* in 1982. Civil servants, cabinet ministers, members of Parliament and top executives of state companies are now allowed to have only one job and one salary. Civil servants, who had become accustomed to a 26 to 28–hour work week, are now required to be at work at 8 A.M. and to work eight and one–half hours, with a half hour lunch break. Also, the first Spanish ombudsman was appointed, with the task of looking into complaints of abuses and neglects inflicted on the people by ministers, administrative authorities or public servants.

Foreign Policy

Franco's death enabled Spain to modify its course in foreign policy. In February 1976 Spain relinquished Spanish Sahara, with its rich phosphate deposits, to Morocco and Mauritania, with the hope that the inhabitants could determine their own future. Algeria greatly resented this solution, and a bloody struggle occurred

over control of this colony. Morocco simply annexed the former colony.

The major change in Spain's foreign policy, however, was that it turned its primary attention toward Europe. Spain was the only country in Western Europe that did not belong either to the EU, EFTA or NATO. It had been permitted to join the UN in 1950 and eventually became a member of virtually all world bodies. In 1987 a Spaniard, Frederico Mayor Zaragoza, was named as director of UNESCO.

Spain's entry into Western Europe signaled certain other foreign policy changes. Franco established a special relationship with Latin America, where there were many authoritarian regimes similar to his own. Now Spaniards openly condemn most Latin American dictatorships. The King left no doubt when he was awarded a prize in Germany for his work toward European unity that although Spain is rooted in Europe, it is also a part of the Hispanic world. Spain's policy during the Falkland Islands conflict underscored this fact.

The earlier Socialist government showed its special interest in helping to bring about peace talks in Central America, if Spain had been asked to do so. During a visit to Cuba in 1986, Cuban leader, Fidel Castro, referred to González as "dear friend Felipe" and pinned Cuba's highest distinction, the order of José Martí, on his lapel. In the mid-1990s Spain became the leading investor and a key Western economic and diplomatic intermediary for Cuba, which, unlike the Philippines, still exerts an emotional pull on Spaniards. Relations cooled after Aznar and the PP came to power. But in November 1999 King Juan Carlos became the first Spanish monarch to visit Cuba, joining the leaders of 14 Latin American countries and Portugal for an Ibero-American summit.

Despite the importance that Spain places on *Hispanidad*, its growing European focus weakens its ties with Latin America. Its historical links with its colonies were severed much earlier than were those of Britain and France, and unlike France, Spain is not the senior member of a currency zone. Its trade with Latin America is also insignificant; the latter provided only 6.2% of Spain's imports and took only 4.3% of its exports in 1987, the major partners being Venezuela and Mexico. Spain is the leading foreign investor in Latin America, and this is visible in Cuba, where Spanish hotels are everywhere on the island. The Spanish could never really dominate Latin America; the size of its economy is roughly the same as Brazil's and only about twice the size of Mexico's. Since 1991 both Spain and Por-

Seaside town of Salobreña on the southern coast   Photo by Eugenia Elseth

tugal maintain formal ties with Latin America and the Caribbean through annual summits, bringing together the leaders of 21 countries and 489 million people. This is merely a forum for discussion.

In 1992, Spain had hoped to celebrate in grand style the 500th anniversary of Columbus' voyage. But it found at a meeting in Madrid of 19 presidential guests from Latin America and Portugal that the New World now has mixed feelings about that explorer who sailed under the Spanish flag.

Spaniards gave strong support to their most famous investigating judge, Baltasar Garzón, who in 1998 demanded the extradition of one of Latin America's most notorious former military rulers, Chile's Augusto Pinochet, who was in London for medical treatment. The charges against him were torture, deaths and disappearances of 94 people. Garzón issued arrest warrants the end of 1999 for 48 members of Argentina's 1976–1983 military dictatorship. In March 2000, after almost 17 months of house arrest in London, Pinochet was freed to leave the UK on grounds of ill health. In December, Garzón again found himself in a delicate situation when he was picked to deal with a Russian extradition order involving media magnate Vladimir Gusinsky, whom Spanish police had arrested after Moscow issued a warrant through Interpol. In April 2001, a Spanish court refused to extradite Gusinsky.

Franco also established another special relationship with the Arab states. Until 1986 Spain did not recognize Israel, for instance. But since Franco's death the Arab states have shown little gratitude for this long–standing policy. Morocco has refused to help implement self–determination for the almost totally nomadic residents of former Spanish Sahara.

With the backing of Arab states, Morocco periodically revives its claims to Ceuta (where 15,000 out of a total population of 70,000 are Muslims, and which is located only 14 kilometers from the Spanish mainland) and Melilla (where 27,000 Moroccans and 45,000 Spaniards, including 15,000 soldiers, live). These are the remnants of a string of fortresses Spain built in North Africa after Andalusia was re-conquered. These bases have lost most of their strategic importance, and the Spanish and Moroccan militaries exercise and interact with each other quite well. There is tension there between Arab residents (many of whom are illegal) and Spaniards, who show no signs of wanting to be ruled by Morocco. In 1997, Spain

Source: *The Economist*

fenced off the enclaves to prevent illegal immigrants from using them to gain access to Europe. The reason is that Spain's per capita GDP is 12 times higher than that of Morocco. However, these 2.5-meter high barriers are easy to breach and have not prevented the enclaves from becoming centers for illegal immigration to southern Europe. Although Ceuta is only a 90-minute boat-ride from mainland Spain, it is a dangerous trip. In 2001 alone, about 710 persons drowned in the attempt to reach Europe from North Africa. One Moroccan association in Spain claims that about 4,000 persons perished in this way from 1997 to 2003. Arabs in the enclaves do not have rights as Spanish citizens. Muslim leaders negotiated with local Spanish officials to improve their social and political conditions, but resistance to their demands remains strong within the Spanish majority.

Perhaps in order to press its sovereignty claim over the enclaves, a group of Moroccan gendarmes occupied on July 11, 2002, the tiny, uninhabited island of Perejil (Parsley, but known in Arabic as Leila) located 200 meters off the North African coast and claimed by both Spain and Morocco. Moroccan marines quickly replaced them, and escalation followed rapidly. The Spanish government dispatched five warships, a submarine, and helicopters and other aircraft to the area and put the 7,000 troops of Spain's Foreign Legion, who defend the two enclaves, on alert. On July 17 Spanish commandos recaptured the island without firing a shot, and a Foreign Legion unit moved in to hold it. Moroccans accused Spain of hypocrisy for demanding that Britain hand over Gibraltar while refusing to talk to them about doing the same for the enclaves. U.S. Secretary of State Colin Powell was asked to mediate the crisis. After he made an estimated three dozen phone calls to both parties, a deal was reached to return the island to its previous demilitarized status. Spanish troops left, and both sides agreed not to send troops there again.

Algeria also has intrigued in the Canary Islands to try to lead them away from Spain, and Libya, Yemen and some Palestinian organizations have helped the ETA terrorists. Largely because of the proximity and near total dependence on Arab oil, Madrid is still more sensitive to Arab sentiments than are most other Western European countries. It forbade the U.S. from using its two bases in Spain to supply Israel, Saudi Arabia or Egypt. In 1986 it also refused to allow U.S. planes to fly over Spain on their way to make a retaliatory anti–terrorist raid on Libya.

Finally, Franco's successors ended the policy of not recognizing the Soviet Union

Spain

and other Eastern European countries. The King paid a visit to the Soviet Union. However, the opening of diplomatic and commercial links brought in its wake such a high incidence of Soviet espionage in Spain that numerous Soviet officials had to be expelled. Also, in 1979 former Soviet Foreign Minister Andrei Gromyko offered to help the Spanish end terrorism in their country in return for Spain's refusal to join NATO. He also insinuated that Spanish entry would lead to even greater terrorist activity. This clumsy hint led many Spanish politicians and intelligence officials to conclude that Moscow was actually helping the ETA. In 1990, President Gorbachëv visited Spain and advocated closer economic ties.

Defense Policy and NATO

Spain's strategic location brought it into an indirect relationship with NATO through a series of bilateral defense agreements with the U.S. beginning in 1953. According to the provisions of this agreement, the U.S. would provide military assistance to the Spanish armed forces in return for the right to have air bases in Torrejon and Zaragoza, a naval base in Rota, and scattered communications installations throughout the country. About 10,000 U.S. troops are stationed in Spain. The periodic renegotiation of these agreements has never been pleasant or easy.

In 1982 Spain became the first country to enter NATO since Germany did so in 1956. Although a majority within the *Cortés* approved membership, the PSOE and PCE opposed it, and public opinion polls indicated that more Spaniards were against NATO membership than for it. There is an undercurrent of neutralism in Spain. Nevertheless the earlier government pressed on without a referendum on the issue in order, in the words of the former defense minister, "to bring us back into European and democratic circles and to strengthen the democratic system in Spain."

Thus, not only would Spanish defense be boosted, but its officers would be brought into closer contact with foreign officers who are committed to democracy and civilian rule. Army officers would have to learn foreign languages, travel to other NATO countries and acquire modern military skills. They would have to accept a promotion system based not on mere seniority but on professional competence, as was already the case for young officers in the Spanish air force and navy.

Modernization is also desirable for strictly military reasons. The army is poorly equipped and has very few mobile units that are up to NATO standards. The air force is competent, but it is scarcely

large enough to provide for Spain's own air defense needs. Therefore, the government decided to purchase 72 American–made F18A fighter planes. It also acquired an aircraft carrier, called the *Príncipe de Asturias*, equipped with a dozen vertical take–off Sea Harrier jets and leading a task force that will include four new anti–submarine frigates. Still, Spanish studies concluded that Spain has half the necessary capability for defending its own airspace; the U.S. provided the other half from its bases in Zaragoza and Torrejon (now vacated).

The armed forces had been reduced to 186,500 active duty forces by 2000 (120,000 army, 36,950 navy and 29,100 air force), including 3,800 women. About 103,000 young men are selected annually by lottery to do nine months in the military (down from 24 months under Franco and 18 months when the Socialists first came to power in 1982). Soldiers are no longer required to perform nonmilitary duties, such as serving as chauffeur of officers' wives, doing laundry or making house

repairs with the commanders taking payment on the black market. Also, serving better food lifted morale. When possible, recruits serve near their homes, and they are never posted outside of Spain. The Aznar government announced plans in 1996 to phase out conscription in favor of a smaller, better-equipped professional army, and steady progress has been made. It is to be paid for by raising defense spending from 1.5% of GDP in 1997 to over 2%, but this had actually declined to only 1.4% by 2000. Nevertheless, Spain is one of the few EU countries that is increasing its defense spending in the twenty-first century.

NATO, of course, also derives important advantages from Spain's entry. This large country can serve as a rear base for stockpiling material and for a strategic withdrawal for troops and aircraft in the event that Western Europe is overrun. It is well–situated for re-supply from the U.S. Ever since France withdrew from the NATO integrated command in 1967, the alliance has lacked the capacity for

Secluded, elegant entrances to several Spanish homes

290

"defense in depth." Spain also provides important bases and surveillance posts to protect Mediterranean and Atlantic shipping routes, and it can help deny the exit of enemy ships from the Mediterranean into the Atlantic. It offered in 1988 to take responsibility for a stretch of sea extending from the Balearic Islands, through the Strait of Gibraltar, and as far as the Canaries. It also offered Spanish territory for reinforcements and supplies needed on the central front.

The Spanish navy is reputed to be a highly professional fighting force, but some NATO observers have doubts that it could perform all its chosen tasks. In 1990 Spain proposed the establishment of a permanent Conference on Security and Cooperation in the Mediterranean (CSCM) as a way of controlling the effects of growing economic imbalances between the northern Mediterranean states and the impoverished North African states. Like most other European countries, Spain fears uncontrollable illegal immigration.

NATO must accept some restrictions. Spain retains a veto on the stationing of nuclear weapons on Spanish soil. In 1966 a U.S. plane carrying four unarmed hydrogen bombs crashed in the village of Palomares. In 1979 the Spanish required the U.S. to withdraw its nuclear weapons from Rota. This does not necessarily mean that Spain will never create its own nuclear weapons. The country has sufficient technology to manufacture nuclear weapons, but Spain decided in 1987 to sign the nuclear nonproliferation treaty. It had sometimes been reported that Spain might need nuclear weapons in order to protect the enclaves in Morocco—Ceuta and Melilla—which are not included by the NATO nuclear umbrella. The Organization of African Unity has already issued a resolution supporting independence for these enclaves, as well as for the Canary Islands. Partly for that reason, the Spanish have declared the latter to be out of bounds for NATO facilities.

Spain also insists that Spanish officers command all units on Spanish territory. Until January 1, 1999, Spain remained outside NATO's integrated military command structure. It is an active NATO member. It sits on the Atlantic Council and in the defense planning committees; it also has observers in the nuclear planning group. In 1988 it further increased its involvement with Western European defense. It joined the Western European Union, which tries to coordinate a stronger "European pillar." It also concluded an agreement with NATO pledging to defend Spain's territory, airspace and waters, including the Strait of Gibraltar, and allowing its soil to be used for NATO logistics and as a staging platform.

Despite his 1982 electoral rhetoric, González became more pragmatic about his party's opposition to NATO. He brought it to accept the view that Spain's democracy and political stability, as well as its commitment to Europe, would be best served if Spain remained inside of NATO. He considered it the "logical consequence" of Spain's entry into the EU, which took place on January 1, 1986.

Nevertheless, in March 1986, he fulfilled his earlier promise to allow Spaniards to express their opinion in a referendum. This was the first time that a member of either NATO or the Warsaw Pact permitted a popular vote on continued membership. Polls had indicated that a majority was against remaining in NATO. To sweeten the pill, González set terms: Spain would not join the integrated command structure, would not permit the entry or stockpiling of nuclear weapons on its territory, and would negotiate the progressive reduction of the U.S. military presence in Spain.

Sensing that a "yes" vote would be interpreted as a great boost for the Socialists, the opposition parties recommended abstention, or, in the case of the communists, rejection. The results stunned many anxious observers: 52.5% voted in favor of continued membership, while fewer than 40% voted for withdrawal. An earlier opponent, Socialist Foreign Minister Javier Solana, was named NATO secretary-general in 1995. The opposition parties were left shocked and divided, while González' moderate and pragmatic brand of socialism was reinforced. More important, Spain had finally and dramatically ended centuries of isolation. No longer would the French be able to joke that Africa begins at the Pyrenees!

In 1988 González carried through with his promise to reduce American military forces in the country. No reductions were sought at Rota, which plays a key role in supporting the U.S. 6th Fleet, nor at 11 other key U.S. military installations. But the 5,000 American servicemen and 72 F16 fighters of the 401st Tactical Air Wing at Torrejon, which is located only 12 miles from Madrid and had become a convenient symbol for anti–U.S. protesters, were ordered to leave by 1991. González argued that U.S. use of Torrejon stimulated anti–Americanism and anti–NATO feeling in Spain. This order was the first unilateral reduction of American forces ordered by a European ally since France ordered them out in 1966.

The U.S. and Spain also reached an agreement in 1988 extending for eight years the American lease on four other military bases, including Rota. The major obstacle—Spain's prohibition of nuclear weapons on its territory—was cleared away by the Spanish government's tacit agreement not to inspect American ships in Spanish ports to see whether nuclear weapons are on board. Spain also gave up all the guarantees of specific levels

EL PAIS

SÁBADO 15 DE MARZO DE 2003   DIARIO INDEPENDIENTE DE LA MAÑANA   EDICIÓN EUROPA
Año XXVIII. Número 9.421   www.elpais.es

Bush, Blair y Aznar se reúnen en Azores para sacar adelante el ultimátum a Irak

La Casa Blanca afirma que la cumbre significa el "fin de la vía diplomática"

El presidente estadounidense, George W. Bush; el primer ministro británico, Tony Blair, y el presidente del Gobierno español, José María Aznar, tienen previsto reunirse mañana en las islas portuguesas de Azores, en mitad del Atlántico, para abordar la crisis iraquí. Los tres líderes, invitados por el primer ministro portugués, José Manuel Durão Barroso, se verán a medio camino entre EE UU y Europa para discutir la estrategia ante la práctica imposibilidad de conseguir el apoyo del Consejo de Seguridad de Naciones Unidas.

La Casa Blanca calificó la cumbre de "esfuerzo de último minuto" en el proceso diplomático para encontrar una salida pacífica a la crisis iraquí. La asesora de Seguridad de Bush, Condoleezza Rice, lo resumió así: "Ha llegado el momento de la verdad".

Los tres copatrocinadores de la segunda resolución de Naciones Unidas, que da un ultimátum al régimen de Irak para que ofrezca garantías de desarme superiores a las certificadas por los inspectores de la ONU, han comprobado que no tienen votos suficientes.

Schröder propone recortes en las ayudas sociales para salir de la crisis

El canciller alemán anunció ayer en la presentación de los presupuestos medidas "dolorosas" y recortes sociales para superar la crisis.
INTERNACIONAL. **Página 10**
Editorial en la **página 16**

El embajador de España en la ONU, Inocencio Arias, ayer, en la sede de Nueva York. / REUTERS

España subordinó sus decisiones en la ONU a la "aquiescencia" de EE UU

Spain

of U.S. aid contained in previous lease agreements. The bilateral defense agreement in effect since 1953 was renewed in 2001 allowing full use of the naval base in Rota and the nearby Moron Air Base. Torrejon could be used for fuel stops.

Spain's government made a crucial decision during the 1991 Gulf war against Iraq to support its allies actively. Before the fighting began it sent three warships to the Persian Gulf to help enforce the UN embargo against Iraq. When the air war commenced, Spain permitted the Americans to launch B–52 bombing raids escorted by Spanish fighter planes from Moron air base near Seville, a base jointly used by both air forces. It ferried bombs to the U.S. planes and even supplied ordnance from its own stocks when the Americans ran low. At first, this was highly unnerving and unpopular in a country whose last war outside its borders was in 1898, when Cuba was lost to the Americans. However, public opinion swung around when reports of Iraqi atrocities in Kuwait began arriving.

It was an enormous political risk for González, but it paid off handsomely. He said: "That is what allies are for," and "for the first time in modern history, Spain has stood where it should be." It marked a defining moment in Spain's effort to end its long isolation and shoulder more international responsibility. It buoyed Spanish confidence and helped sweep away memories of neutrality in the First World War and fascist sympathies in the Second.

In 1992–3 Spain again demonstrated its expanded role in international affairs and the increased professionalism of its military by deploying the Spanish Legion to war–torn Bosnia. This elite unit had been formed in 1920 as a colonial force for Africa and gained a fearsome reputation in the Civil War on Franco's side.

Spanish troops participate in the international force sent to Bosnia in 1995 to implement the peace agreement. The contingent in Bosnia is the largest Spanish force to be deployed outside the country since the Blue Division fought in Russia on the side of Nazi Germany. In 1996 González led an OSCE investigative team to Serbia, which ordered that the country's communist president recognize opposition victories in local elections. In 1999 Spain sent four F–18 fighter aircraft to join NATO's air war against Yugoslavia that aimed to stop ethnic cleansing in Kosovo, and it permitted American military aircraft to stop over at bases across Spain. Public opinion was mixed concerning this action, especially after the Spanish ambassador's residence in Belgrade had been mistakenly damaged in a bombing raid. It sent peacekeeping forces to Bosnia and Kosovo. It also offered in 2000 to provide 10% of its military personnel to a future EU rapid-reaction force.

Following the September 11, 2001, terrorist attacks against the United States, Spain offered unhesitating support to its ally and sent troops to Afghanistan to participate in the peacekeeping effort after the defeat of the Taliban. In May 2003 Spaniards mourned the death of 62 of their peacekeepers on their way home after a four-month tour in Afghanistan. The 15-year old Ukrainian Yak-42 plane, chartered by a NATO agency, crashed into a mountain in bad weather while trying to land in Turkey. It was the worst accident in Spanish military history. Severe criticism was directed against the government for having troops transported in what many considered to be poorly maintained second-rate planes, and Spain suspended all troop transport flights on such equipment.

Spain occupied the EU presidency the first half of 2002, and it served on the UN Security Council during the Iraq war in 2003. The Spanish government and prime minister worked hard to strengthen the strategic relationship between Europe and the U.S. He opposed any signs of resurging anti-Americanism: "We don't always have to agree on everything. But I don't see what's to be gained by beating the drums every time there is a divergence." President George W. Bush appreciated this consideration. In his maiden trip to Europe in 2001, he made his first stop in Spain, and his description of Aznar was sincere: "José María is a man of principle and a man of courage."

The prime minister had a dramatic opportunity to display this in the 2003 crisis in Iraq. While polls indicated that as many as 90% of his countrymen opposed war against Saddam Hussein's regime, he steadfastly supported the U.S. and UK. Although he sent no combat troops to Iraq, he dispatched 200 soldiers to help defend Turkey within the NATO framework, a hospital ship with 900 personnel on board, a frigate, an oiler, and mine-clearing and chemical weapons decontamination units. After the war he agreed to send as many as 1,500 troops to participate in the postwar stabilization force in Iraq although he forbade them from engaging in combat missions; a Spanish brigade of 1,100 soldiers serves in a division with Ukrainian forces, led by Poland, and a Spanish officer is the deputy commander. Spain utilizes its traditionally close ties with Arab nations to help mediate between the U.S. and the Arab world. He emphasized his conviction that "Europe and the United States have to act together. Any weakening of the Atlantic alliance is directly opposed to Europe's interests." When France and Germany moved to block U.S. policy in Iraq, Aznar enlisted seven other like-minded European leaders to sign an open letter praising a strong U.S.-European relationship.

However, his deeper motives were to put an end to Spain's peripheral position in Europe and within the EU and to move it into the center of continental foreign policy, heretofore dominated by France and Germany. As one of his aide's put it, he hopes to make Spain "one of the few and not one of the many." He himself said: "Spain can no longer be just a nice country. It has to assume its responsibilities." By siding with the U.S. and the UK, he furthered his twin goals of raising his country's international profile and gaining American support for his government's fight against Basque terrorists. This policy is fraught with domestic political dangers because not all Spaniards are convinced that a prominent international role is good for them. Since the civil war and Franco's military dictatorship, they are distrustful of military displays. Some were also convinced that the prime minister had degraded himself to being a yes-man for the American president. But there is no doubt that Spain's international stature and visibility have increased.

Gibraltar

The Spanish government also hopes that NATO membership will prepare the way for Spanish sovereignty over Gibraltar, a piece of rock three and a half square miles (6 sq. km.) in size, where a Muslim army under Tarik ibn Zeyad (thus the Arab name for the rock, *gib al–Tarik*) landed an army from North Africa in 711 to begin the conquest of Spain. England snatched the rock during the War of the Spanish Succession in 1704 and has held it ever since.

The 32,000 Gibraltarians are not of Spanish descent, although they tend to speak more Spanish among themselves than English. Their habits are more English, though. They lunch at noon, not in mid–afternoon, and eat and drink more British fare. They read English newspapers, and their currency is sterling, albeit Gibraltar sterling. They are descendants of various Mediterranean immigrants brought to Gibraltar and include Genoese, Catalans, Jews, Portuguese and Maltese. The Spanish maintain that the population is artificial and the mere remnant of a foreign naval base and is therefore not entitled to self–determination in the de-colonization process. The UN has upheld this claim.

Britain, on the other hand, maintains that no change in the status of Gibraltar could be legitimate without the approval of the population. The preamble to Gibraltar's 1969 constitution reads that Britain

Spain

View of the port of Gibraltar

Photo by Eugenia Elseth

"will never enter into arrangements under which the people of Gibraltar would pass under the sovereignty of another state against their freely and democratically expressed wishes." Gibraltarians remain ardently pro–British and profoundly suspicious of Spain. They have their own miniature Westminster–style democracy, and the attempted coup in Madrid in 1981 helped confirm their preference, expressed in a 1967 referendum, when 12,138 voted to remain British subjects; only 44 voted against it.

In 1969 Spain sealed the border between the mainland and the rock. In 1980 Britain agreed to negotiate a settlement. When Prince Charles and his bride decided to visit Gibraltar during their honeymoon cruise, Juan Carlos refused to attend the wedding in London. Also, the Falkland Islands conflict in the spring of 1982 caused further delays. Spain was the only West European land not to support the British in the crisis, and many Spanish see parallels between the Argentines' claim to the islands and the Spanish claim to Gibraltar. Nevertheless, both sides continue to profess the desire to settle their differences. During the Falklands war, Spain did prevent a number of Argentines from launching an attack on Gibraltar from Spanish territory.

Spain made a goodwill gesture in 1982 by opening the border to pedestrians. In 1985 it was opened to vehicular traffic. Britain and Spain reached an agreement in 1988 to share Gibraltar's airport although Spain maintains restrictions on airlines approaching Gibraltar. There are no direct flights, ferry, or ship service

between Spain and the Rock. Common NATO, WEU and EU membership no doubt aids in this, as does the fact that Gibraltar no longer has the enormous strategic value it once had. The area is so small that its airstrip cannot accommodate large aircraft. Also mines, long–range missiles and nuclear weapons make it far easier to block the strait of Gibraltar than to keep it open. The Rock does contain 30 miles of underground tunnels, a hidden strategic command center and berths for atomic submarines, all of which are important for NATO.

On a visit to London in 1991 González called Gibraltar an "anachronism" and noted that for the British, discussions with Spain about it are like an annual visit to the dentist, while for Spain it is like a permanent stone in its shoe. In 1997 Spain proposed "shared sovereignty" of the Rock. Although the British rejected it, they noted that the Spanish no longer rule out the idea of Gibraltar's independence, only that "independence will never be granted against Spanish wishes." That is not the same as insisting that the Rock must one day be Spanish.

The concept of "shared sovereignty" was central to the talks that recommenced in 2002. It will be at the heart of any agreement even though Chief Minister Caruana, who refused an invitation to attend the talks unless he were granted a veto, rejects the concept, as did 99% of the rock's population (with 85% voting) in a November 2002 referendum on the single question: "Do you approve of the principle that Britain and Spain should share sovereignty over Gibraltar?" London refused to rec-

ognize this polling, which was an effort of the Gibraltar government to thwart British plans for a compromise with Spain. It complicates the British government's effort to settle this lingering sore point with Spain once and for all.

The UK's interest in holding on to the colony has waned, and it would like to be rid of it. In 1991 it withdrew the last of its ground forces stationed there. That was an economic blow since spending by British soldiers and their dependents amounted to 18% of Gibraltar's revenues and provided a fourth of the jobs. Tourists will replace some of the losses. Their numbers leaped from 600,000 in 1984, the last full year of the Spanish siege, to more than 3 million annually in the 1990s. In 2000 the OECD named Gibraltar as an unfair tax haven.

In 1996 Gibraltarians elected a new chief minister, a young pro–business lawyer, Peter Caruana. His Social Democrats captured 52% of the votes and eight of 15 seats in the House of Assembly. He tries to improve diplomatic relations with Madrid, while maintaining the Rock's colonial relationship with British. The British welcome this approach, after the more abrasive style of his predecessor, Joe Bossano, whose dream was for the Rock to be independent of both Britain and Spain. Nevertheless, tensions remain. On a visit to EU headquarters in Brussels in 1997, Caruana accused Spain of trying to exclude Gibraltar from EU matters. Spanish leaders are always wary of any moves by Gibraltar to represent itself on the international stage, insisting that it operate through the British foreign office. However, in 2000 Spain and the UK agreed to allow banking and insurance firms based in Gibraltar to sell products across the EU and to have identity cards issued in Gibraltar recognized throughout the EU.

Hon. Peter Caruana

293

Spain

ECONOMY

At one time, Spain was a country with a layer of wealthy persons stretched thin over a large population that lived in varying degrees of poverty. Its industry was small, highly protected, un-aggressive and suffering from a general mental inertia. Its agriculture was unproductive, by comparison with other Western European nations north of the Pyrenees. The chronically unstable political conditions in the 19th and 20th centuries always hampered economic development and delayed the industrial revolution. In the 1940s Spain's national income had fallen to the level of 1906–07, and not until 1954 was the 1936 level reached.

Much of that has changed by now. The Spanish are now modestly prosperous, and they have the fifth largest economy in the EU. In the cities the shops are filled with luxuries and necessities, which most people have enough money in their pock-

ets to buy. There are plenty of cars on the roads, and 60% of Spanish families own or are buying their own homes (compared with slightly over one–half in Britain and France). It cannot be denied that Spain has come a very long way since the 1950s. Spain's economy grew by a fifth from 1996 to 2000, at a rate of 3.5% in 2000; in 2002 it fell to 2%, its lowest in nine years. Per capita GDP had climbed to 85% of the EU average in 2003, up from 78% in 1975.

Economic prosperity in Spain is distributed geographically unequally. In Catalonia, the Basque country and Madrid, incomes are 25% higher than the national average, and in most of Andalusia, Estremadura, Galicia and New Castile, incomes are 30% below the national average. In 2003 unemployment stood at 11.4%, one of the highest in Western Europe even though it had declined dramatically from 23% in 1996. Although the economy had grown almost threefold in the 30 years prior to 1998 and the popula-

tion had risen by a quarter, there were few more jobs than there had been in 1964.

As in all Mediterranean countries, Spain has a sizable "submerged economy," which accounts for an estimated one–fifth of GDP. Perhaps as many as one–third of the unemployed has an income from unofficial work. Taking this into account, the real unemployment figure is lower. Joblessness is also unevenly distributed. For instance, in Andalusia and Extremadura, almost one–third of those of working age have no jobs, and almost a fourth of Basques are out of work. For those under age 25, the jobless rate is over 40%. It is a testimony to the resilience of the extended family–based society that the Spanish can bear such joblessness. Only 35% of Spanish women between the ages of 16 and 65 were employed or were seeking a job in 1994, but the fact that 70% of women under age 30 have or are seeking jobs indicates the future trend.

In an attempt to maintain Spanish firms' economic competitiveness, the Socialist government introduced the concept of "temporary contracts" in 1984, followed by other labor market reforms in 1994 hoping to make it easier for companies to hire and fire. These measures antagonized labor unions and voters, who had grown accustomed since the Franco era to life–time job guarantees. But enough obstacles remain to make Spain's labor market one of the world's most rigid. Employers must pay 20 days salary for each year of employment to workers "fairly" dismissed, and 45 days to those "unfairly" dismissed. The courts almost always rule that dismissal is "unfair."

Not wishing to hire full–time employees who would receive this kind of protection, employers can, since 1984, hire them on "temporary contracts," which provide no job security. Thus, a two–tier labor market has developed: one for older workers with such protection that they have little incentive to be productive or to restrain their pay demands, and younger ones who stagger from one short–term contract to the other without building real careers. In 1996 fully 97% of all new jobs were in the "temporary" category, and by 2000 a third of all workers (and three-fourths of young people under 25) had such contracts.

To make matters worse, nationwide collective–bargaining agreements are negotiated for each industry, making it hard for individual firms to adjust their employment conditions to their own particular economic circumstances. The result is chronic high unemployment. Fearing the general strikes that plagued the Socialist government, Prime Minister Aznar cannot attack this problem head–on,

Días 15 y 16 agosto 1987 - 7 tarde

se celebrarán, si el tiempo no lo impide,

UNA GRAN NOVILLADA SIN PICADORES y UNA SOBERBIA CORRIDA DE TOROS

SABADO 15   NOVILLADA SIN PICADORES

SEIS soberbios novillos SEIS, de
DON VICTOR LOPEZ CHAVES
de SALAMANCA, para los   ESPADAS
JOSE   JULIAN   DENIS
MAREGIL - MARTINEZ - LORE
DOMINGO 16   GRAN CORRIDA DE TOROS

SEIS bravos toros, SEIS, de
«BRANCO NUNCIO.»   (BN)
de EVORA (Portugal), para los ESPADAS

Carlos Escolar **FRASCUELO**
FERNANDO GALINDO
SANCHEZ CUBERO

PLAZA DE TOROS **LAS VENTAS**

COMUNIDAD DE MADRID TOROS MADRID, S. A.

Spain

The seaside resort of Torremolinos on Spain's southeastern coast

Courtesy: Minnie Lee Wilt

despite his proclamation of 1997 a "employment year."

Inflation fell from 14% in 1981 to 3.1% in 2003, still higher than the EU average. During most of the Franco era, workers and employees were forced to work long hours for low pay. Not until the early 1970's did the lid on the enforced "labor peace" threaten to blow off, so Franco permitted wages to rise in order to buy labor peace. After El Caudillo's death, pay continued to rise. Wage settlements above the Western European average, which fed inflation, ceased to make Spain a country with low labor costs and eliminated some of Spain's competitive advantages.

González decided to change this. He viewed inflation as a bigger problem than unemployment and reduced the rise of prices by means of tight fiscal, monetary and wage policies. The austerity policy was not popular, as general strikes in 1988, 1992, 1994 and 1996 revealed. But it worked. Under his successor, the economy is growing, investment is high, and foreign capital pours in. By 2003 the budget deficit had fallen to .4% of GDP, and the total national debt was 63% of GDP. Madrid annually receives about $7.5 billion in EU regional, social and "cohesion" funds, plus $6.75 billion from the EU's Common Agriculture Policy (CAP). After subtracting Spain's $6.4 billion in annual payments into the EU budget, it chalks up a net gain of almost $8 billion each year. The Spanish government rejected any suggestion that it accept fewer subsidies when poorer Central European countries enter the EU even though current EU

guidelines would still permit subsidies to three of the 11 Spanish regions. By 2002 its per capita GDP was 80% of the EU average, compared with Poland's 35% and Latvia's 27%.

It is no wonder that two out of three Spaniards in 2000 thought that membership in the EU was both beneficial and good. It has brought prosperity; per capita income has risen to above 80% of the EU average. But belonging to the EU was never primarily a matter of money for Spain. It was a symbol of European norms of social progress, democracy and freedom. It is also a context within which Spain's strength and size can count. In all the discussions about how a larger EU will govern itself, Spain insists that, whatever the details, its status as on of Europe's big five countries must be assured. Prime Minister Aznar's vision for his nation to be "one of the EU's major countries."

That inflation is under control is partially due to the largely responsible way in which the major labor unions, the communist–controlled Confederation of Workers' Commissions (CCOO) and the Socialist–dominated General Workers' Union (UGT), which work closely together, responded to the economic challenges facing the country. Only one worker in seven (15%) belongs to a union. Yet Spain has the EU's second worst record for days lost in strikes, after Greece.

As in all European countries, the rapid rise in energy prices in the 1970s exacerbated the country's economic problems. Spain is dependent on imported oil for about 60% of its total energy needs. It is

only able to produce domestically 2% of the oil it uses. It receives 60% of its natural gas from Algeria. In years of normal rainfall Spain can provide 15% of its power generation through hydroelectricity. It has had modest success in relieving its excessive reliance on imported oil by increasing its use of this resource, coal and nuclear power. Local opposition to atomic power has caused Spain's nuclear ambitions to be revised downward. Nevertheless, in 1997 nuclear power was generating 30% of Spain's electricity. In 1998 the American energy giant Enron became the first U.S. company to compete in Spain's energy market by building a power station in the South.

Spanish industry under Franco was the most tightly controlled in all of Western Europe. Through his bureaucracy he decreed subsidies, economic privileges, and penalties in a way that created distortions in the economy from which the country still suffers. Yet, while economic competition was tightly controlled, there was precious little control over some things, such as health standards.

Spain now has a modern economy, with 31% of the workforce employed in industry (producing 30.5% of GDP) and 62% in services (turning out 65.9% of GDP). Its industries are, as a rule, much smaller than in most EU countries. It has few multinational corporations. Of the FT–500 top European companies, only 24 are Spanish. Businesses tend not to be as high–tech as in some competitor countries; Spain spends only 1% of GDP on research and development, half the OECD average. Half of Spain's biggest companies (including all the auto industry—Europe's third biggest—and nine out of ten top exporters) are owned by foreign companies, 12% by banks, and 30% by the gigantic Spanish state holding company, the National Institute of Industry (INI). INI owns or controls more than 60 enterprises and has partial ownership in another 200 or so. It was created by the Franco regime in order to establish industries that could back up Spain's defense and economic self–sufficiency, and it was often forced to rescue lame duck enterprises. INI now encompasses Iberia Airlines, as well as steel, ship–building, chemicals, power production, oil–prospecting, news agencies and banks.

To this list of nationalized industries, the former Socialist government added only the crisis–ridden Rumasa group. But it sold some profitable state–owned assets. The state automobile manufacturer, Seat, was sold to Volkswagen, but in 1993 VW announced the closure of the outdated Seat plant in Barcelona. In 1989 the state–owned oil company, Repsol, was partially privatized in Spain's biggest

Spain

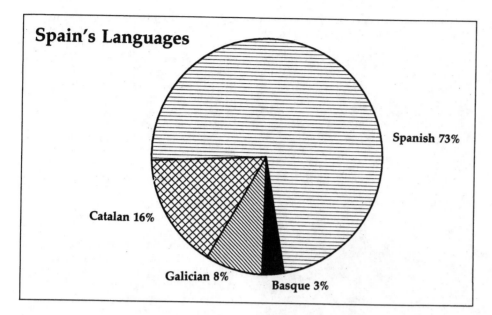

Spain's Languages

Spanish 73%

Catalan 16%

Galician 8%

Basque 3%

stock offering ever. Privatization has proceeded slowly and timidly. The state still accounts for 45% of GDP.

In spite of the many "social" and "national" obligations that compel them to receive subsidies and borrow heavily, most INI firms are economically viable. Also the government is trying to force automation on firms as a price for state subsidies. The state maintains monopolies over petroleum through Campsa, telephones through Telefónica, and tobacco through Tabacalera.

Foreign trade accounts for 38% of Spain's economy, and the emphasis is on Europe; over two–thirds of total Spanish merchandise exports go to the EU, up from half in 1985; 60% of its imports are from the EU, compared with 37% in 1985. Thanks in part to incentives for investment, Spain attracted needed foreign investments. Favorite sectors for their foreign investors are in the auto and chemical industries, financial institutions and the hotel business. But a major problem which continues to cool the enthusiasm of foreign investors and which seriously burdens the economy in certain areas of Spain is the terrorist activity, especially in the Basque country, traditionally one of the most industrialized and economically dynamic regions in Spain. There the ETA has forced "revolutionary taxes" on the companies and has kidnapped and even killed some leading industrialists and engineers. These tactics have prompted other businessmen to leave with their families. In short, Spain will not be wholly attractive for business activity and investments until regional terrorism has ended.

About 7% of the Spanish are employed in agriculture, forestry and fishing. This "primary sector" produces 3.6% of the country's GDP and under 20% of its

exports. Its horticulture, poultry farming, wine and fruit growing are highly productive, but its meat and cereal production is low. Despite the large size of its territory and agricultural population, Spain is not entirely self–sufficient in food.

It needs to reorganize its agricultural production. But the results of such improvement would be to increase rural unemployment and thus stimulate the flight into the cities and industrialized countries. Among the rural problems which must be solved in order to improve the country's agricultural output are insufficient water supplies, forest and brush fires, soil erosion, the preponderance of small, uneconomical farms in the North and the West and the existence of large underutilized estates in the South.

A Spaniard eats an estimated three times more fish than the average West European. To supply this immense seafood appetite, the country has built up the largest fishing fleet in the EU and the third largest in the world. This caused concern over Spain's entry into the EU, and members fight bitterly over fishing quotas. Spain accounts for a fifth of the EU's catch. In 1988 a French coast guard vessel fired on Basque fishing boats who were exceeding Spain's quota. Canada captured a Spanish vessel over fishing off its coast in 1994 and found on board doctored records and illegal nets designed to catch undersized fish. Despite being caught red–handed, Spanish public opinion was enflamed by this "act of piracy." One of its diplomats proclaimed: "We may not be big in anything else, but in fish we are a superpower."

Two of Spain's major economic assets have been the sun and the sea, and since the 1960s Spain has been one of Euro-

peans' favorite tourist countries. In 1996 it temporarily overtook France as Europe's leader in terms of tourist earnings. Only the U.S. exceeds its income from tourism. With 52 million overnight foreign tourists in 2002, it is an important source of income and employment; it is Spain's biggest earner of foreign exchange. However, the tourist industry is vulnerable to recession in the rest of Europe and to international terrorism. It had only one million American tourists in 2002. Not only do Americans spend more money on vacation, but they are more likely than Europeans to visit cultural sites in the interior of the country as opposed to sunning themselves on Spain's beaches.

For a long time, Spain relied on its beaches and good weather to attract tourists, but as the euro hardens, prices have risen, and many tourists look elsewhere. This presents challenges to the industry. In order to stimulate both tourism and its economy in general, Spain decided in 1988 to modernize its railroad, which is one of Europe's oldest, slowest and financially troubled. It adapted its narrow-gauge railway system to the one used by the rest of Europe and introduced its first high-speed train (known as AVE) between Madrid and Seville in 1992. Travel time is less than two and one-hours, and its AVE trains are punctual, clean, safe and highly profitable. The project to create a similar AVE line from Madrid to Barcelona had by 2003 gone only as far as the Catalan town of Lerida. Optimists looked to 2004 as the year of completion, with the possibility of future links to France, which would require an eight-kilometer tunnel through the Pyrenees.

Spain has had to make some painful adjustments after its entry into the EU. It caught up with many other Western European countries in terms of social welfare benefits. Almost a third of its unemployed receive some form of assistance, and the social security system (known as "SS") is able to provide free or cheap medical care, although its facilities are often overcrowded. The SS provides pensions, welfare and other social assistance. From 80% to 85% of its funds are provided by a payroll tax on employees. This tax increases labor costs, though, by about 35%.

There can be no doubt that Spain's economy has benefited from EU membership. Trade is booming, and foreign investment pours in. At the same time Spain has surpassed the United States as the largest foreign investor in Latin America. It has also been a net recipient of structural funds from Brussels. It has overtaken Italy as the EU's major receiver of regional development funds. *The Economist* estimated in 2000 that about 3% of

Goya's epic painting *El 3 de mayo de 1808,* which hangs in the Prado Museum in Madrid, commemorates the French invasion which placed Napoleon's brother, Joseph, on the Spanish Throne.

Spain's annual GDP comes from these monies and from the EU's Common Agricultural Program (CAP). Perhaps most significantly, the historical phenomenon in Spain of disinterest or lack of prestige accorded to business activity has almost disappeared.

CULTURE

Languages

Spain's culture and language have taken root far beyond its own borders. In fact, 300 million speak Spanish as a mother tongue, making it the only real challenger to English as a world language. Spanish is the favorite foreign language in American high schools and universities, and as many as 20 million citizens and residents of the U.S. speak Spanish as a mother tongue. The official language in Spain is the Castilian dialect of Spanish, which differs in some respect from the many different dialects of Spanish spoken in South and Central America. The most audible difference is that the "s" or soft "c" sound sounds in Castilian Spanish like the English "th" sound.

There are, of course, many languages spoken within Spain itself, and three are especially important. In Galicia one speaks Gallego, which is more similar to Portuguese than are other Spanish languages. In Catalonia, Valencia and the Balearic Islands, a separate language called Catalán is spoken. It is a Romance language closely related to Provençal and Languedoc, spoken in France. It has a rich written literature and has always been a crucially important cultural tool for preserving Catalán national identity. Cataláns requested that the EU recognize their tongue as an official language. Basque, a language with neither Romance nor other Indo–European roots, is spoken mainly in the villages of the Basque country and is seldom heard in the two major Basque cities of Bilbao and San Sabastian. It remains, however, a very important vehicle for Basque identity.

Literature and Arts

Spain was always a crossroads between the European and Islamic Oriental cultures. Indeed, some of Europe's greatest writers wrote in Spanish. During the "Golden Age" of the 16th and 17th centuries, Cervantes wrote his classic, Don Quixote, a humorous story of chivalry and lofty, idealistic aspirations beyond all human capacity to achieve. Today, the word "Quixotic" is used in English to refer to any naive venture which, because of hopeless odds, is doomed to failure from the very start. In the 20th century, Spain has produced several internationally renowned poets, most notably Juan Ramón Jiménez, who won a Nobel Prize in 1956, and Federico García Lorca, who was murdered during the Civil War. Its novelists, such as Ricardo Vásquez Montalban and Soledad Puertolas, have international reputations. In 1989, Camilo José Cela was awarded the Nobel Prize for Literature. Author of 60 disturbing and powerful books, Cela lived an exciting, risky and iconoclastic life, disdaining authority in all forms. His regular newspaper columns and television appearances also helped make him a living legend in Spain.

In art Spain has also distinguished itself. El Greco (words which mean "the Greek" and applied to Kyriakos Theotokopoulos, who lived and worked in Toledo) established his own characteristic style in the 16th century. Diego Rodríguez de Silva Velázquez painted revealing and astonishingly uncomplimentary portraits of the Spanish court during the 17th cen-

Spain

Philip II by Sánchez Coello 1531–88

tury, and Francisco José de Goya painted powerful portrayals of revolution and resistance in the 18th and 19th centuries.

In the 20th century, Salvador Dalí, Joan Miró and Pablo Picasso have inalterably influenced modern painting. Because of political disagreements, these artists lived a part of their working lives outside of Spain. Dalí's personalized museum in the former theater of his Catalan hometown of Figueres, just south of the French border, is unforgettable.

The most ringing protest against Franco, and of course, against war itself, was Picasso's *Guernica*, which he painted for the Spanish pavilion of the Paris World Fair in 1937 in order to invoke the memory of the German bombing of the Basque city of Guernica. He then lent the painting to the Museum of Modern Art in New York and ordered that it not be returned to Spain until democracy had been restored in his homeland. In 1980, after a long legal wrangle with Picasso's heirs, the painting was finally returned to the magnificent Prado Museum in Madrid. In 1992 it was moved to the new modern art museum, Centro de Arte Reina Sofia. Spanish viewers, who often chatter and exclaim in museums, are hushed when face to face with the shrieking victims portrayed in this stark mural.

A major addition to Spanish culture is the Guggenheim Museum in Bilbao, opened in 1997. Costing $171 million to build, this is the anchor project in an effort to preempt Basque violence by emphasizing national pride and culture in a positive way. Basque officials requested that *Guernica*, the work of art most symbolic of the region, be moved or lent to the museum, which is located only 12 miles from the town of Guernica. Citing the

painting's deteriorating condition and concerns over its safety in the Basque area, the request was turned down. This decision sparked fierce controversy. Nevertheless, the experiment of stimulating the entire Basque region through this art magnet is a smashing success. In its first 18 months, tourism in the Basque country increased by 28%, most of it attributable to the museum. It has become a symbol of the area's economic and cultural resurgence that could be secured by the permanent end of separatist violence.

Cinema

Over four–fifths of all films shown in Spain are foreign, especially American. Spanish directors have created some very good ones. Luis Buñuel, who for decades lived in exile in France, Hollywood and Mexico, was especially acclaimed for his playful and charming films. He aims his subtle but deadly arrows toward the Spanish bourgeoisie, from which he himself descended.

In 2000, Spanish director Pedro Almodovar's film, "All About My Mother," won the Academy Award for best foreign-language film. He comes from a poor village in La Mancha to the south of Madrid, and his loyalty to his roots, despite past criticism of some aspects of Spain, endeared him to most of his compatriots. Two cabinet ministers accompanied him to Hollywood, and in accepting his statue he dedicated the prize "to Spain and Spaniards." The entire country cheered, and King Juan Carlos and Prime Minister José María Aznar sent him congratulatory telegrams.

The kinds of Spanish films which have won international acclaim are facing almost impossible domestic competition from another kind of movie which has sprung alive after 1975—pornography. Of course, pornography is in the eye of the beholder: one man's treat is another man's horror. But even the most tolerant must be horrified to see a film entitled "Would you like to be my husband's lover?" being shown in a Granada movie house named Isabel la Católica (Isabel the Catholic). The main problem is that such films have driven away family audiences from the cinemas, and movie attendance has fallen. By 1978, only 42% of the Spanish regularly went to the cinema, compared to 87% who regularly watched television.

The conservative government announced plans in 1996 to reexamine subsidies to the film industry and to lift screen quotas that had offered some protection for Spanish films against American competitors; 80% of all films shown in Spain were already American. Two–thirds of the foreign TV films purchased are from the U.S. Only slightly more than 10% of Span-

iards go to the theater, despite heavy state subsidies of theater tickets. Many more follow bull fighting closely: 40% according to polls, although a small minority is deeply opposed to the sport. It employs about 1% of the entire workforce and nets over one billion dollars every year.

Media

Spain's newsstands have also become inundated with pornographic literature since the repeal of the pornography law. On TV Spaniards can watch programs with such titles as "Let's Talk about Sex," "Erotic Saturday Nights," and "Marriage and Something More." But the lifting of censorship in Spain has also brought a flowering daily and weekly press, even though newspaper readership remains low. Only about 8% of Spaniards buy a newspaper, which is half as many as in France and a fifth as many as in Britain. One in seven young adults claims to read any printed medium at all. Three of the best papers in Europe now come from Spain: *Cambio*, a weekly which was modeled on *Time*, the conservative daily, *Vanguardia* (circulation 198,000), and the liberal broadly pro-Socialist daily, *El Pais*, which is unloved by the police, army, and Church, and which has become the most courageous and intelligent watchdog of the new constitution. *El Pais* is the leading daily with a circulation of 434,000 copies. *El Mundo* (312,000) is its livelier conservative rival. *La Razón* (149,000) is another voice on the right. Even the right–wing dailies, *ABC* (279,000) and the Catholic-oriented *Ya* have greatly improved their standards and have converted to democracy. However, most papers are partisan in one-way or the other. The weekly newspaper, *El Independiente*, is close to the Social and Democratic Center Party.

There are some black spots in Spanish journalism. The government inherited 30 state–owned newspapers from the Franco era which cannot be abolished suddenly. Also, there are some newspapers which rail against the new order. The most influential is the ultra–right daily, *El Alcazar*, which is named after the famed fortress in Toledo. This fortress became a legend during the Civil War by surviving a two–month Republican siege before being relieved by Franco's troops on September 28, 1936. The newspaper began as a newsletter for Franco's troops and became a mouth–piece for the fascist leadership.

The most regrettable black spot, though, is that the Spanish press still fears to work as freely as in most other Western European countries. For instance, it is still a serious offense to question the honor of the royal family or the legitimacy of the monarchy or the unity of Spain. The press

The horror of April 26, 1937, in Guernica . . .

. . . and Picasso's stark depiction—*Guernica*

Spain

is also forbidden to challenge the honor of the armed forces, including the paramilitary police. The Spanish military is still the most publicly flattered in all of Western Europe. Despite these continuing limitations on the freedom of the press, it should not be forgotten that for the first time in Spanish history people can generally speak and write about politics and religion without fear of being jailed. Only about 8% of Spaniards buy a daily newspaper.

Television is the real molder of society. Polls indicate that about two–thirds of adults form their political opinions from television, which 87% watch daily. The state remains a large owner and voice in the media. It appoints the heads of state TV and radio, as well as of the national news agency, EFE. Critics say this limits the objectivity and selection of images and news. Others argue that the private sector provides an adequate balance. The autonomous governments also run regional channels, but only in Catalonia do they find a large viewer audience. In 1991 private TV was established. Two central and seven regional public-sector channels, two private channels, a subscription company called Canal Plus, and the state's main channel—TVE-1—get about 25% of the viewership. The private channels, Antena 3 and Tele-5, receive about 20% apiece.

Catholic Church

The Church had been one of Franco's chief supporters, and he repaid the favor by restoring its role in the schools, and by granting it generous state subsidies. He effectively had the power to appoint bishops, a prerogative which Juan Carlos eliminated. On Spanish coins Franco was called "leader of Spain by God's grace."

In the 1960s, though, the Church's support for El Caudillo began to change. Many Spanish priests adopted the ethic of social justice. They formed social action groups and spoke out in support of disadvantaged workers and peasants. Priests in the Basque country, Spain's most fervently Catholic area, sometimes publicly supported the Basque nationalists.

In the 1960s the Catholic lay organization, Opus Dei (Latin for "God's Work"), which began its existence in 1928 as a highly conservative effort to become firmly rooted in the society's elite, changed its thinking. It became an important force for rationalizing the economy, improving workers' living standards and taking cautious steps toward political democracy. From a force for reaction, Opus Dei became one of Spain's most important forces for innovation. Although it had largely lost its influence on public policy by the end of the 1980s, its membership

had by 2003 grown to 84,000. Pope John Paul II ordered in 1982 that Opus Dei become a "personal" bishopric, meaning that its members owe spiritual allegiance to its head, not to the local bishop. In 2003 he canonized its founder, Josemaria Escriva de Balaguer, who died only in 1975.

By 1972 most of Spain's bishops were moderate. Franco's displeasure was demonstrated by his government's threat in 1974 to cancel the Concordat (treaty) with the Vatican. Most Spaniards favored maintaining this Concordat with Rome; it provides the state with a voice in appointing bishops, while the Church receives a modest subsidy. The Church had changed from a major foundation for the Franco regime to a skeptical semi-opponent. Although it speaks out on social issues like abortion, it now stays out of party politics. Nevertheless, it decided in 2000 not to plead forgiveness for siding with Franco after the Civil War.

In the 1980s, the Church accepted the Socialist Party's law permitting the sale of contraceptives. But it fought hard to prevent the full legalization of abortion and divorce, problems that cannot be so easily hidden in the medicine cabinet. An estimated 300,000 Spanish women each year have abortions either abroad or illegally in back rooms. It is understandable why many Spanish supported the Socialist government's reform to de-penalize abortion in cases such as rape or where the mother's life is in danger.

The Church hierarchy and the conservative opposition expressed outrage and are helpless against Europe's steepest drop in the birth rate, from 19 births per 1,000 Spaniards in 1975 to 11 by 1989. By 2002 the average Spanish woman had become the least reproductive in the EU, with a birth rate of only 1.22 children, down from 2.8 in 1975. Italy and Greece were close behind with 1.25 and 1.3 respectively. This is well below the 2.1% needed to keep a population steady. Spain's overall population is expected to begin declining around 2010. This is influenced by the fact that a third of Spanish women are already in the workforce, and 70% under age 30 have or are seeking employment. Although Spanish families are still cohesive and close, they will continue to become less male–dominated than they once were.

The changed environment in Spain is reflected by opinion polls, which indicated that fewer than 15% of Spaniards considered marriage to be indissoluble. Yet the roots of social conservatism in Spain were also revealed in the fact that it took six years after Franco's death to pass a liberal divorce law, which permits civil divorce by mutual consent one year after the couple has been legally separated. The

EL PAIS

DIARIO INDEPENDIENTE DE LA MAÑANA

VIERNES 1 DE FEBRERO DE 2002
Año XXVII. Número 9.017

EDICIÓN EUROPA
www.elpais.es

Los líderes mundiales analizan la crisis en un Nueva York en estado de sitio

Globalización y antiterrorismo dominan los debates del Foro Económico

Después de 31 años de reuniones en la localidad suiza de Davos, la élite política, empresarial y cultural del mundo se dio cita ayer en Nueva York —símbolo de su respaldo a la ciudad golpeada el 11 de septiembre—

La decisión de elegir un marco especial para el Foro Económico Mundial es excelente, en opinión de su antiguo alcalde y héroe del 11 de septiembre, Rudolph Giuliani: "Nueva York es la capital del mundo". En el centro auténticamente militarizado de la ciudad, más de 4.000 policías y cientos de agentes del Servicio Secreto, ayudados por perros, barreras de cemento y camiones de arena, empezaron ya ayer a controlar a miles de manifestantes antiglobalización y a proteger a los casi 3.000 asistentes a la reunión. Entre ellos se cuentan grandes empresarios como Bill Gates, presidente de Microsoft, o el inversor internacional George Soros; líderes políticos como el canciller alemán, Gerhard Schröder; el secretario de Estado, Colin Powell, y el del Tesoro, Paul O'Neill, y dirigentes culturales, religiosos y sociales.

En la primera jornada de un encuentro que se celebra bajo el lema "El liderazgo en tiempos de fragilidad", los expertos pronosticaron un futuro a corto plazo con más incertidumbre política y más riesgos económicos, en el marco de una globalización en la que no disminuyen, sino al contrario, las desigualdades entre pobres y ricos. Entre los debates que apuestan por la recuperación de la economía estadounidense: "No veo que (...) sea factible este año, o incluso más adelante; el mundo tendrá que buscar otra locomotora", según Stephen Roach

para debatir los problemas internacionales más acuciantes: los cambios tras los atentados de Al Qaeda y la guerra antiterrorista, la crisis económica y el abismo que separa a los sectores acomodados de los desesperados del mundo.

dos del mundo. La reunión, que durará hasta el lunes, se celebra en uno de los hoteles más famosos de Nueva York, el Waldorf Astoria, defendido por un ejército de policías para controlar las manifestaciones.

Miles de activistas antiglobalización inician su cumbre paralela en Brasil

Miles de activistas del movimiento   mo y la globalización. La crisis en   Alegre y será uno de los temas que

Cuatro policías neoyorquinos forman durante unos ejercicios antidisturbios. / EPA

La policía francesa detiene a seis supuestos etarras preparados para atentar en España

España y Francia estrenaron ayer su equipo policial conjunto contra el terrorismo con la detención de seis supuestos etarras en Burdeos. Los terroristas integraban un grupo de reserva listo para entrar en España y cometer atentados, según el Ministerio del Interior. Uno de los detenidos, Ángel María Cruz Arróspide, pertenecía al comando Donosti y ahora se encargaba de acoger y formar a los reservistas. Los agentes franceses encontraron cinco pistolas, tres subfusiles, un fusil de asalto y diversos explosivos en el piso donde se produjeron las detenciones. Desde que el pasado 10 de octubre Francia y España firmaron un acuerdo de colaboración contra ETA, los agentes franceses han detenido a 18 supuestos terroristas, desarticulado el grupo de adiestramiento de etarras y desmantelado el mayor arsenal de la banda en Francia.   **Página 15**

Redondo pide tiempo a Zapatero para decidir sobre su futuro en la ejecutiva socialista

Nicolás Redondo, ex secretario general de los socialistas vascos, se reunió ayer con Rodríguez Zapatero y le pidió tiempo para decidir si continúa en la ejecutiva. Algunos sectores del partido tienen previsto plantear hoy a Zapatero la necesidad de ejercer una oposición más contundente.
ESPAÑA. Página 22

LONDRES y Madrid aplicarán en Gibraltar la misma estrategia que llevó a la paz al Ulster
ESPAÑA. Página 20

As only the Spanish can dance it—*El Flamenco*

debate exasperated Church leaders so much that they told Spanish Catholics that the law does not apply to them.

The Church's stand on this issue is not likely to persuade many Spaniards, 80% of whom consider themselves to be "culturally Catholic" and are members of the Church. In his May 2003 visit to Spain, the Pope pleaded with the people: "Do not break with your Christian roots!" He claimed, "the Christian and Catholic faith constitutes the identity of the Spanish people." That appears no longer to be the case. A 2003 poll revealed that only a minority confessed to being practicing Catholics (with varying degrees of intensity). In 1975, 61% claimed to go to church regularly; by 2003 that figure had fallen to 19% (less in urban areas); 46% of those saying they are Catholic admit that they "almost never go." Even the clergy is shrinking. In 1952 Spain had 77,800 priests and 7,050 seminarians studying for the priesthood; today the figures are 18,500 and 1,800. From 10–15% of parishes have no priest at all. Since 1979, Spaniards can choose to give a half percent (.52%) of their income tax to the Church by checking a box on their tax returns. Only a third (32%) do so.

Far more Spaniards go to soccer games regularly than to Church. In fact, the Association for the Defense of Animal Rights, with 5,000 members in 1986, would like even more Spaniards to give

up bullfight entertainment for soccer; it has issued stickers saying: *Toros no. Futbol sí.* Noting that 24,000 bulls die every year in the spectacle, it maintains, "torture is neither art nor culture." It even launched Spain's first–ever protest march against bullfighting. Although the sport provides employment for 150,000 people and earns more than $100 million per year, most Spaniards do not like it. A survey taken in 1986 found that more than half actively dislike bullfighting, while only a third said they liked it.

Education

The role of the Church in contemporary Spanish society is not a burning political issue. It has turned away from active intervention in politics. But it does raise its voice on certain issues, such as private education, culture and the information media. The Church energetically defends its influence on parochial schools, which 40% of all Spanish schoolchildren attend (twice the figure even of the Franco years) and which are reputed to be academically better than the public schools. The Church is willing to accept some standards and guidelines by the state, such as teacher training and financial accountability. It is also understandably interested in continuing to receive state financial assistance, which reportedly accounts for about 30% of the Church's income. But it wishes to avoid any state control over the content of

education in its schools, which it insists must remain religious.

The Socialists aroused the ire of the Church by passing legislation guaranteeing the right to free secular education and thereby reducing the Church's influence in the schools. The government also announced that for the first time, books and teaching materials would be distributed free of charge to some 200,000 school children attending rural public and private schools. The school–leaving age was lifted to 16.

When the government tried to raise university tuition slightly in 1987 and to tighten university admissions and academic standards, thousands of students rushed into the streets to protest. Some were concerned that the door might be closing on the accessibility of a university degree, the traditional path to a good job and financial security. Others added that frustration stemming from youth unemployment of more than 40% for ages 16 to 24 and from a crackdown on drugs fueled the flames. One hears criticism that there is too little rigor in the educational system and that some universities have grown too large to be effective. For instance, Madrid's Complutense University has 86,000 enrolled.

Drugs and Immigration

Spain has replaced the Netherlands as the most important conduit into Europe for illegal drugs. European addicts now receive 40% of their cocaine via Spain. In part this is explained by the more open borders to other EU partners, the congenial Spanish–speaking environment for Latin American drug–runners, and the 1983 decriminalization of possession of small quantities of soft or hard drugs for personal use. The González government had made the country's drug laws among the most lax in Europe, and the rapid spread of drug abuse brought a reaction. Spain has Europe's highest incidence of drug abuse and AIDS. It is faced with an epidemic: it has an estimated 100,000 heroin addicts, and cocaine use has spread into the middle–class. It is reckoned that 1.5 million smoke marijuana often. Most of Spain's heavy drug–users are young. The Socialist govern-ment tried to fight back by increasing maximum prison sentences, fines and indictments for drug traffickers, but critics called these measures too little, too late.

Also a shock for Spaniards is racial violence, despite polls that suggest that they are more tolerant of outsiders than are most other Europeans. By the 1990s, more than a quarter million legal and 300,000 illegal immigrants were pouring into Spain each year. At the beginning of the 21st century about a million foreigners, or

Spain

2.5% of the total population, lived in Spain, far fewer than in most EU states. Former Foreign Minister Javier Solana said, "Spain is a country where others have always been taken in with great generosity and solidarity." To try to demonstrate this, the conservative government adopted a law in 1996 giving the two million legal foreign residents the right both to vote and to run for office in municipal elections starting in 1999. Another law in 1999 made it possible for 70,000 illegal immigrants to have residence permits and to bring their dependents into Spain. Nearly a quarter million applied. This was advertised as one of Europe's most liberal immigration policies. The following year the government announced the creation of a department for integrating immigrants. By 2000 Spain had 750,000 legal immigrants and many more illegals. Most immigrants live along the southern coast and in the main cities. Demography experts calculate that Spain will need 12 million immigrants until 2030 in order to prevent the population from shrinking below its 2000 level.

Yet a spate of attacks against foreigners in Catalonia and elsewhere reminded Spaniards of the magnitude of the problem. In El Ejido, a town of 50,000 people including 11,000 totally segregated immigrants, mainly Moroccans, the worst case of racial violence in modern Spain occurred in February 2000. In response to reports that Moroccans had murdered three Spaniards, youths rampaged through the streets, stoning immigrants and burning down their shacks. Five hundred riot police restored peace after three days.

FUTURE

Spain's future is promising. It has a democratic constitution and a King who has shown that he is willing to die to defend democracy. Spanish voters avoid extremist parties, trade unions show responsibility and moderation, and politicians cooperate with each other. Time has dampened passions over the Civil War, fears of military coups, and emotions over NATO. Its stability and democratic confidence allow it to reexamine its Franco past without tearing the nation apart. Separatist terrorism in the Basque region continues, but has suffered setbacks. In 2003 Batasuna, the political arm of ETA, was banned with the support of the Spanish Supreme Court, the U.S. and the EU. The liberal, parliamentary order has definitely sunk its roots deeply, and it has already long outlived the earlier Republic, during which 18 governments fell before Franco took full control.

Aznar's government delivered on its promises. The economy is buoyant, and the budget deficit has fallen to .4% of GDP and the national debt to 63% of GDP. Success enabled Spain to qualify for the euro, which became the country's currency in 2002. Aznar pressed on to reform the welfare and tax systems and to reduce the size of the bureaucracy. He and his People's Party were rewarded with an absolute majority in the March 2000 elections. His plans to reform the laws on hiring and firing and on unemployment benefits were met by a general strike on June 20, 2002. It was reminder that the unions are a force to be reckoned with. The government was widely criticized for its handling of an oil spill in December 2002, when the rickety tanker, Prestige, broke in two and sank off the northwest shore, fouling 700 beaches and throwing thousands of fishermen and others out of work. Half of the Prestige's oil is still inside the ship 2.5 miles under the sea.

Aznar's support of the war in Iraq was extremely unpopular at home. Nevertheless, his Popular Party escaped disaster in the May 2003 municipal and regional elections, which the opposition Socialist Party had hoped would be a referendum on the government's Iraq policy. Although the Socialists got more votes (34.7% to 33.8%) than the Popular Party for the first time in a decade and took control of the Madrid regional government, PP captured more seats in regional and local parliaments and held on to the city governments of Madrid and Valencia. Aznar has announced that he will step down as prime minister when his current term is finished. New elections must be held by March 2004 at the latest. Given his party's good showing in May 2003, it has a fair chance of hanging on to power.

Meadows blossom beneath the towering Pyrenees Mountains in the north

The Republic of Portugal

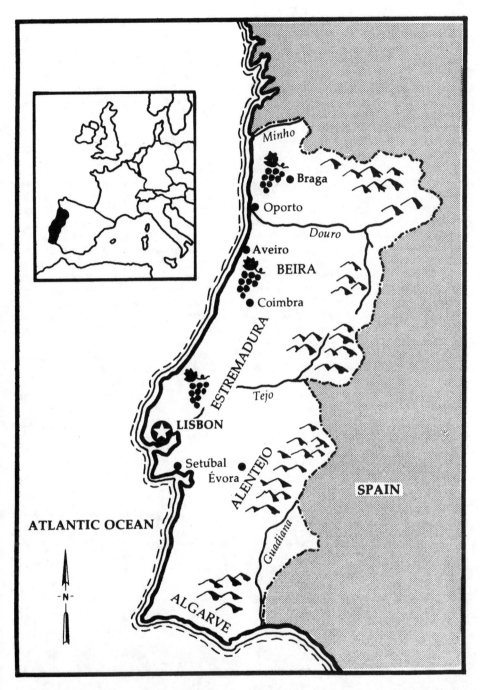

Chief of State: Jorge Sampaio, President (since 1996).

Head of Government: Jose Manuel Durão Barroso, Prime Minister (since April 2002).

National Flag: From the hoist, green and red vertical fields, the green being somewhat less than half of the flag. The Portuguese coat–of–arms is imposed where the two fields meet.

Portugal entered the 1970s as a conservative, industrially underdeveloped country at the bottom of Western Europe's economic barrel. It had a authoritarian political order that suppressed all signs of genuine opposition, and which therefore was an embarrassment to its NATO allies, which sought to defend democracy on both sides of the Atlantic. It was embroiled in a multitude of hopeless colonial wars in an attempt to maintain control over an empire more than 20 times the size of the mother country.

Yet by the 1980s Portugal offered an almost entirely different picture. It had undergone a revolution that, though claiming almost no lives, drastically altered many aspects of the country. It is now a thriving democracy in which persons of all persuasions can speak and act openly. Although it is one of Western Europe's poorest nations, with the continent's highest infant mortality and illiteracy rates, it was willing to accept the economic challenge of entering the EU. It is a country now entirely stripped of its colonial empire, but it is much healthier and stronger as a result. It is a democratically ruled member of NATO with an army radically reduced in size but with military facilities of great strategic importance for the alliance.

The Portuguese are tolerant, friendly, polite and patient, and form a relatively cohesive society. Without these qualities, the Portuguese would not have survived so well the radical changes that have occurred in the country since 1974. The population is largely homogeneous. But there are about 100,000 blacks from the former African colonies; 10% of Lisbon's population is black, some of whom have been the targets of racist attacks in recent years. There are also about 90,000 gypsies, who have not integrated as well in Portugal as they have in Spain.

Few European countries have such a large portion of its population living abroad as does Portugal. Since the 15th century the Portuguese have emigrated in large numbers, first toward Brazil, and then after Brazilian independence, to such destinations as North America, Venezuela, Angola and Mozambique. However, after 1955 the greatest number of Portuguese emigrants, two–thirds of whom left

Area: 35,553 sq. mi. (92,082 sq. km.), not counting the Azores or Madeira; (about the size and general shape of Indiana—380 miles north to south, and 140 miles at its widest point).

Population: 10 million (estimated).

Capital City: Lisbon (Pop. 2.3 million). *Lisboa* in Portuguese, pronounced Lee's–boa.

Climate: Mild and rainy weather in late fall and early winter, but cold and snowy in the mountains. From June to September the days are hot, but the air is rather dry.

Neighboring Countries: Spain (North and East); Morocco lies 140 miles across the ocean to the southeast.

Language: Portuguese

Ethnic Background: Indo–European (predominantly Mediterranean type).

Principal Religion: Roman Catholic.

Chief Commercial Exports: Cork, textiles, clothing and footwear, wood and wood products, wine, canned fish, tomato paste, olive oil, machinery and transport equipment.

Major Customers: EU (79.4%), principally Spain (19.2%), Germany (17.6%), France (12.5%), UK (10.7%), U.S. (6%).

Currency: Euro.

National Holiday: June 10 (Luiz de Camões Day, and Day of the Portuguese Communities).

Portugal

agricultural areas in Portugal, went to industrialized Western European countries, especially France and Germany, in order to find employment. From 1960 until 1972 a million and a half Portuguese left the country, mainly in the direction of other West European nations. That the number of emigrants to the rest of Western Europe has slowed down considerably is due to the restrictions those countries have erected since the world recession began in 1974.

The U.S. and Venezuela have become again the favorite destination for Portuguese. The U.S. is now the single country that accepts the greatest annual number of Portuguese emigrants. Indeed, more than a million Portuguese now live there, most of whom are from the Azores. By 1987 the total number of Portuguese living abroad was more than four million—roughly 40% of the country's total population. They send back more than $2 billion in remittances every year, which in 1986 accounted for 13% of Portugal's GDP and more than offset its trade deficit. From 30,000 to 40,000 are returning every year. This intensifies the housing shortage in a country where thousands of impatient residents have already constructed homes without waiting for a building permit.

Portugal is a rectangular–shaped country, a little larger than the state of Maine, but with ten times as many inhabitants.

It has a long Atlantic coastline, along which most of the country's inhabitants live, and it has only one neighbor: Spain. The country is separated into northern and southern halves by the Tejo River. The north is cooler and more mountainous, with small family farms and three–fourths of the entire population. The south is hotter and drier, with rolling plains and large farms, called *latifundios*.

Astride the line between the two halves is Lisbon, where the Tejo empties into the Atlantic Ocean. The capital city is located on seven hills and still reflects a physical character shaped by its Moorish past. It is very much the heart of a highly centralized country and has all too often in the past looked down upon the rest of the country and has seemed to be uninterested in the fate and welfare of the regions. With all its suburbs it counts more than a million and a half inhabitants. It and greater Oporto, which is Portugal's only other major city and which has 800,000 residents, have attracted three–fourths of the population which is active in the industrial and service sectors of the economy. Unfortunately a fire in 1988 seriously scarred Lisbon's historic central shopping district.

Portugal has three main rivers: the Douro in the north, which empties near Oporto, the Tejo in the middle, and the Guadiana, which forms part of the border with Spain and then empties into the Gulf

of Cadiz. All originate in Spain, but almost none is navigable between the two countries. Indeed, the transportation links between Spain and Portugal remain very difficult. This is a major reason why both countries have stood for so long with their backs practically toward each other facing somewhat different directions.

CONTEMPORARY HISTORY

In 1834 Portugal became a constitutional monarchy in a setting of bitter power struggles and intrigues among rival claimants to the throne and between conservatives, who supported the Catholic Church and the nobility, and liberals, who wished to reduce the power of those groups. Except for a relatively brief respite between 1851 and 1910, the century preceding the military takeover of power in 1926 was an era of restlessness, discontent and civil disturbances. It was peppered by wars and revolts which so shook the land that conservatives and liberals finally agreed to avoid bloodshed by alternating power in a system called *rotativismo*.

This rotation system could not prevent the steady erosion of support for the monarchy, caused by financial and colonial difficulties and by the rising political ambitions of the middle class, which wanted a greater share in political power. In February 1908 King Carlos I, a man of absolutist inclinations and a lust for

The Avenida da Liberdade, Lisbon

Lisbon from the Tejo River

personal gratification, and the Crown Prince, were both assassinated, and, after a spell of uncontrollable political turbulence, the monarchy fell in October 1910. As usual, the military was heavily involved in this overthrow.

The monarchy was replaced by a parliamentary republic, whose main accomplishments were to separate Church and state, to end Catholicism's status as the official state religion, and to terminate religious instruction in state schools and state aid to religious schools. But the republic could not find solutions for the country's economic problems or the political factionalism, extremism, terrorism, anarchy, riots, strikes and attempted *coups d'etat*, which continued to be a part of daily political life. The republic was further weakened by Portugal's participation in World War I, which in no way unified the many leading groups behind a common objective.

Not only were many politicians corrupt and incompetent, but the rapid turnover of governments prevented any policy continuity. Portugal had a average of three governments per year until 1926, when the military stepped in again and took political power into its own hands Because the years of political havoc had not thoroughly polarized Portuguese society, as had been the case in Spain, and because Portugal has, in general, a more homogeneous, less fragmented society than does its neighbor, the military takeover was not followed by a bloody civil war, as in Spain a decade later.

Military–Fascist Rule

In order to attack the financial problems, especially inflation, which the years of chaos had exacerbated, the generals, in 1928, named an economics professor from the University of Coimbra, Dr. Antonio Oliveira Salazar, as finance minister. In 1932 he became leader of the only legal party and prime minister, the post that until 1974 remained the heart of political power in Portugal. He established a fascist state, called the *Estado Novo* ("New State"), which he guided until his incapacitation in 1968. In 1933 a constitution was promulgated which had a few trappings of parliamentary government, such as a unicameral National Assembly and a directly elected president.

The corporatist character of the new constitution was embodied in an advisory organ called the Corporative Chamber. This allegedly united all classes by bringing together representatives of diverse economic and professional groups in order to evaluate all legislation. Also, over the years other organizations were established to encompass workers, employers, craftsmen, landowners, rural laborers,

fishermen, women and youth, in order to lock all citizens tightly into a bundle of groups, all directed from the top by Salazar. There was only one legal political party, the *União Nacional* ("National Union"), which never played a central role in Portugal, as did the Nazi or Fascist parties in Germany and Italy.

The Portuguese political system was complicated in theory, but it was rather simple in practice. Salazar, with the advice of trusted cronies from industry, the military and the Church, made all crucial political decisions. Freedom of press and assembly were curtailed, and all written and electronic communications were censored. Critical professors were dismissed, and strikes were outlawed. As every Portuguese knew, the secret police (PIDE) was ever–present. It is estimated that one in 400 Portuguese were paid informants.

When the Spanish civil war broke out in 1936, Salazar ordered the creation of a "Portuguese Legion" to fight on Gen. Francisco Franco's side, and about 6,000 Portuguese fought against the Spanish Republic. Portugal also tolerated the transport of munitions from France across its territory until mid–1937, when the British, Portugal's closest ally for three centuries, pressured Salazar into closing its borders to such war material. On March 17, 1939, Franco and Salazar signed a non–aggression and friendship pact,

which was amended on July 29, 1940, to obligate both governments to discuss their mutual security interests with one another whenever the "independence or security" of one of the countries is endangered. That pact still remains valid.

Portugal, like Spain, did not become linked militarily and diplomatically with Germany and Italy before and during World War II. Portugal even profited from its neutrality; the country became one of Europe's major centers for spies from all belligerent countries. However, Salazar's sympathies were revealed when he ordered a day of national mourning after Germany's Hitler had committed suicide.

Portugal's valuable strategic position and long–standing relationship with Britain enabled it to become a founding member of NATO, and in 1955 Portugal was admitted to the UN. However, Portugal remained in an economic, social and political condition of stagnation and immobility, ruled and administered by an aging dictator, and a tight clique of generals, admirals and bureaucrats, who, through a swarm of spies, rendered the population submissive, but increasingly dissatisfied and restless.

In 1968 a law professor, Dr. Marcelo Caetano, assumed leadership over this regime, which was in the process of rapid decay. He had high hopes of reforming and liberalizing the authoritarian system

Salazar greeting Spain's Franco

Portugal

War in Angola: troop carrier swerves to avoid a road trap

which his predecessor had created, but it had become far too late for such reform. Portugal had just about reached the exploding point, and all that was needed was a spark. That spark came in 1974 from the same institution which had stepped into the Portuguese political sphere many times before and which had established the half–century dictatorship in the first place in 1926—the military.

Colonial Problems

The last straw was the seemingly endless wars in Portugal's African colonies, which the Portuguese preferred to call Ultramar (overseas territories). The Portuguese settlers had always mingled more easily with non–white native populations than did the British, French and Belgian colonizers. One still sees the results of this in Brazil, where blacks and whites seem to live together relatively harmoniously (albeit under a predominantly white elite). Also, nothing resembling an apartheid ("separateness") policy ever developed in the Portuguese colonies, such as in formerly British and Dutch South Africa.

A certain conviction that Portuguese rule was both good and tolerable for the subject peoples, combined with the economic importance for Portugal and with the fact that there were over a million Portuguese living in the colonies, led Portugal to hang on to its empire long after the other European nations had decided to relinquish theirs. Foreign Minister Franco Nogueira even wrote in 1967 that the Portuguese considered themselves "to be an African nation." The obvious point,

however, was that the bulk of the native populations in the colonies did not consider themselves to be *Portuguese*!

In 1961 India simply invaded and annexed the mini–territories of Goa, Damão and Diu. Since 1913 the Portuguese had had to quell occasional native uprisings in Africa. In 1961 these uprisings re-erupted, first in Angola around such groups as the Popular Movement for the Liberation of Angola (MPLA), the Angolan National Liberation Front (FNLA) and the National Union for Total Angolan Independence, (UNITA), then in 1963 in Mozambique (led by the Front for the Liberation of Mozambique) and in Guinea–Bissau. The Portuguese government decided to hold on to the African colonies at all costs, fearing that their loss would spell the doom of the Portuguese state. In fact, it was this decision more than any other that led to the ultimate downfall of the Portuguese fascist regime.

Military Unrest

By 1974 there were 170,000 men in the Portuguese army, 135,000 of whom were stationed in Africa. The lion's share of these troops were four–year conscripts, who increasingly resented their role in quelling native rebellions against a regime which fewer and fewer Portuguese wished to preserve. The need to expand the size of the army to cope with the African wars brought many young men from the lower classes and the universities into the officers' corps. These groups had earlier been largely excluded from the officers' ranks and were more inclined to

sympathize with the rebels' aims. These young officers gradually lost faith in the kinds of arguments that had long been used to justify the protracted colonial struggle. Many became inspired by the revolutionary ideas espoused by their African adversaries. They grew to dislike strongly their more traditional military superiors. These radicalized lower–ranking officers formed the illegal Movement of the Armed Forces (MFA), which became the core of opposition to the regime.

Their convictions and confidence were enormously strengthened by the appearance in February 1974 of a book which must be considered one of the most significant in modern Portuguese history: *Portugal and the Future*. It was written by the monacled General António de Spínola, the former commander in Guinea–Bissau, whose legendary bravery in battle had won him the admiration of the lower ranks. Spínola advocated a political solution to the colonial question and the establishment of a sort of Portuguese commonwealth of nations, similar to that of the British. It is not surprising that Dr. Caetano reportedly could not sleep the night after he had read the book!

The "Carnation Revolution"

Plotters in the MFA went to work on a plan to overthrow the regime. In the night of April 25, 1974, troops numbering about 5,000 occupied Lisbon in a well–planned operation. Since most officers had become indifferent to the survival of the regime, there was no resistance to the surprise coup. Some nervous PIDE agents, (which the underground press had called "Gestaportuguese"!) who had fled to their headquarters in panic, had reportedly fired on a crowd of a few persons (reports differ, but the total casualties did not exceed four). Except for these, not a shot was fired to defend a fascist regime that had ruled Portugal for about a half century. Rarely in history has such a fundamental political change occurred with so little loss of life.

The plotters formed a "Junta of National Salvation," which abolished the PIDE and announced that the colonies would be granted the right of self–determination and that political exiles would be permitted to return to Portugal. Political enthusiasm burst into life, and public debates, rallies and street demonstrations seized a nation in which such things had been forbidden for 48 years.

For two years Portugal was rocked by a succession of provisional governments and confusing revolutionary turmoil. While this turmoil was fired by much emotion, it occurred in the traditional Portuguese style of little actual bloodshed.

The military *coup*, April 25, 1974

The new leaders were in such a hurry to cut their former colonies totally loose that they made little effort to try at least to introduce a stable transfer of power in the colonies to groups that might have been willing to legitimize their rule through democratic elections. The MFA's strong Marxist bias inclined it to hand over power in the colonies to like–minded revolutionaries.

Decolonization and Internal Turmoil

The rapid Portuguese withdrawal from the African territories and Timor in the Far East reduced overnight most of Portugal's land area and its world–wide population by 65%. This created a particularly great refugee problem for the home country. Between 1974 and 1976 at least a half million refugees poured into Portugal, mainly from Angola. In March 1977 the new Marxist leader ordered the expulsion of all persons holding Portuguese passports, so a new wave of expellees began to pour in. The U.S. helped pay for the airlift of the *retornados* (a term Portuguese dislike today because it implies the returnees were not welcome) and gave Portugal more than $1 billion over five years to help cope with the financial crisis.

The returnees arrived in a chaotic Portugal with few possessions and with currencies that were not accepted in Portugal. Many were convinced that their home government had sold out to revolutionary terrorists and were therefore deeply embittered and inclined toward active, anti–communist and conservative politics. Their bitterness was also stimulated by the facts that there were almost no jobs for them in Portugal and that the government could provide only meager financial assistance. Many only found shelter in shantytowns that cropped up everywhere. In some places, especially in Algarve, the government commandeered luxury hotels for the returnees, a logical and humanitarian action which, however, almost bankrupted the country and deprived one of Portugal's most important industries, tourism, of many needed facilities. Ultimately the returnees were dispersed more evenly throughout the country and slowly began to find work. But the initial problems for the shaken country were immense.

There were moderates within the ruling MFA, such as General Spínola, whom the MFA had appointed immediately as provisional president, who believed that the

new leaders had moved too far to the left. As a result of unsuccessful countercoups against the leftist elements within the leadership in September 1974 and again in March 1975, the moderate elements within the government were purged and, in some cases such as Spínola himself, were driven into exile.

Those leaders who remained were highly critical of what they derided as "bourgeois democracy." The avowedly pro–Communist Colonel Vasco Gonçalves advocated the creation of Soviet–style "committees for the defense of the Revolution," and the swaggering admirer of Fidel Castro, General Otelo Saraiva de Carvalho, championed the notion of "people's power" to replace the political parties. These leaders, along with a more pliant presidential replacement for Spínola, General Costa Gomes, allowed the Communists and the far left to assume control of the trade unions, the news media and local governments.

They ordered the soldiers not to intervene when left–wing mobs broke up socialist and conservative political gatherings. They nationalized major industries, insurance companies and banks, and they looked on approvingly as workers seized

Portugal

factories and as peasants took over land in the central and southern provinces. Roughly a fourth of Portugal's forest and croplands were seized and most of them were converted to forms of collectively owned farms. But these new farms, especially in the province of Alentejo, where farming had traditionally been done on large estates called *latifundios*, were so inefficient that by the end of the 1970s Alentejo produced about a third to half of the grain and livestock it had supplied before the revolution.

The MFA's revolutionary economic experiments were devastating for the country, and they aroused intense opposition. It almost seemed that Portugal was going to return to the political havoc that had stricken the country before 1926. But the politically naive and inexperienced captains, who suddenly wore colonels' and generals' brass on their shoulders, lost sight of one important factor: the Portuguese voter.

They had announced that they intended to hold power for three years, but they did not prevent the holding of elections in April 1975 for an assembly that would produce a new constitution. They dismissed the elections casually as a mere opinion poll that could not possibly lessen their grip on political power. However, the results stunned them. In the first free election in a half-century, 92% of eligible voters turned out to give a massive vote of non–confidence to the heavy–handed, revolutionary–authoritarian rulers. Over 70% of the voters supported the three moderate democratic parties, and only 17% supported the soldiers' only friends, the Communists and their allies.

When the officers in power made it clear that they had no intention of honoring the results of the election and instead moved to eliminate entirely the freedom of the press, the supporters of the democratic parties poured into the streets to show their disapproval. Beginning in July 1975 anti–Communist riots erupted in the North in reaction to a Communist bombing campaign there. This massive resistance jolted the majority of military officers out of their state of indifference. When far–left paratroopers supporting General Otelo tried to seize full power for themselves on November 25, 1975, Lt. Col. Ramalho Eanes, who had heretofore been almost unknown, led a crack commando force to foil the uprising. Eanes took the revolution back to its democratic purpose. In the aftermath, all Communists and extreme leftists were purged from the MFA and from all governing bodies, and the Communists' hopes of taking command over a radical revolution were dashed.

A decade later, Otelo was put on trial for his continuing support for leftist revolution. The press dubbed it the "trial of the century," and it lasted 19 months. He was convicted in 1987 of belonging to a terrorist organization, Popular Forces of April 25 (FP–25), which is suspected of being responsible for at least 15 assassinations of businessmen and landowners and for attacks against the U.S. embassy, NATO warships and the residences of German airmen. Forty–seven co–defendants were also convicted. In April 2001 a Lisbon court acquitted Otelo of terrorism charges.

In the mid–1970s foreign observers were left dizzy by all the fundamental shifts, from right to left and then back to center, where Portugal was to stay. Most Portuguese had wanted a revolution, but they had wanted a moderate democratic revolution, one that would bring them a stable and just political order, protection of individual rights, and ultimately economic prosperity. The last 50 years had brought them enough tyranny and extremist politics. Within a year and a half, the Portuguese revolution had been tamed.

In February 1976 the MFA signed a pact with the political parties that greatly restricted the political role of the military. In April 1976 the assembly that had been elected a year earlier to write a new constitution completed its job. Elections in the same month produced another victory for the moderate democratic parties. Eanes, who had been promoted to the rank of general, was elected president in June 1976, an office he occupied for a decade. One month later he swore in Portugal's first truly democratic government since 1926. Within a few months the radically revolutionary military officers disappeared from the political stage. In 1996, Portugal's first contemporary history museum, charting the transition from dictatorship to democracy, was opened in Leiria. It contains official archives of the 1974 armed forces revolt.

GOVERNMENT

The Arrival of Democracy

One of the most astonishing aspects of Portuguese events after April 25, 1974, often called the "carnation revolution" because of its bloodless character, was the speed with which the Marxist flirtation

Former President Eanes

Lisbon: panoramic view of the *25th of April Bridge,* showing the Christ the King monument

expired and the extent to which the revolution became tamed. Within two years, the swaggering officers who had seized power and set Portugal on the fast track toward a radical socialist state had disappeared almost completely, and the rigidly orthodox Portuguese Communist Party (PCP) saw much of its electoral support evaporate. Within two years the moderate democratic parties could claim the support of more than 80% of the voters. Also, a president was in office who had snatched the revolution out of the clutches of the extreme left, even though he has moderate leftist sympathies and sees the revolution as something more than the mere establishment of a politically democratic system. He had left no doubt whatsoever that he would support democracy in Portugal with all the vigor that his serious and ram-rod frame could muster.

Of course, the salvation of democracy in Portugal was greatly aided by other important factors. First, the extremists were effectively challenged by a democratically oriented Portuguese Socialist Party (PS), led by Mario Soares, one of the most respected Portuguese political figures. His popularity within Portugal helped him counter the Communist grab for power by presenting a responsible, socialist, democratic alternative to the Stalinist, heavy-handed, Moscow-oriented PCP. Also, his immense prestige abroad helped bind Portugal's untried democracy to the West. The PS was also aided by the existence of attractive social democratic models in other Western European countries, such as Germany.

A second factor was U.S. financial assistance to Portugal. In addition to helping to finance the return of many refugees from Africa to metropolitan Portugal, the U.S. from 1975 to 1980 granted $1.5 billion in economic assistance to Portugal. This was the largest contribution by any single nation to the $2.3 billion worth of aid given to Portugal by Western countries and institutions during that period. The U.S. also provided Portugal with long-term, low interest credit to purchase grain and animal feeds. This example of enlightened self-interest reflected the earlier insights of the Marshall Plan in the rest of Europe after World War II—the best policy against Marxist appeals is economic success. The U.S. held itself aloof from Portugal's domestic battles and thus enabled the democratic forces to expose the blatant Communist attempts to seize power, backed by money from the Soviet Union.

A final factor, and perhaps the most important, was the fact that the Portuguese were tired of 50 years of dictatorship and wanted desperately an effective economy to scrape the country out of the bottom of the Western European economic barrel and to set it on the path to stability and prosperity.

In spite of the success in grabbing the revolution out of the eager hands of the extremists, there were significant visible traces of revolutionary enthusiasm left in the constitution and the political and economic system, which could only gradually be erased. One was the far-reaching nationalization of much of the economy; Article 10 of the constitution called for

"the collectivization of the main means of production." Second, the constitution of 1976 ruled out the idea of a market economy and placed severe limitations on any non-socialist government.

It read like a "Third World" manifesto. For example, Article 1 called for "Portugal's... transformation into a society without classes." Article 2 obligated the nation's leaders to "assure the transition to socialism through the creation of conditions for the democratic exercise of power by the working classes." A third remnant was the relegation of the Revolutionary Council, the governing body of the old Armed Forces Movement, as a kind of watchdog of the revolution. Article 273 of the constitution gave the army the duty to "secure the continuation of the revolution." This body was composed of 14 military officers chosen among themselves, the heads of the three branches of the armed services, and the president of the republic, who was chairman of the Council. It had the power to block or even to veto parliamentary legislation, a power it was not afraid to exercise.

A New Constitution

A fourth remnant is the strong presidency, elected every five years by direct, universal suffrage. A president may be reelected only once. The president relinquished in 1981 the post of supreme commander, and he can no longer control promotions within the armed forces. He lost his power to appoint and dismiss the government. According to the new 1982

Portugal

constitution, the government is responsible only to the Parliament, and not to the president. The latter can dismiss a government only after consulting the constitutional committee. Although the president's formal powers are limited, his influence is considerable. The reason is that with so many changes in governments (by 1987 there had been 17 in 13 years), the presidency has been the center of political continuity.

The former president, General António Ramalho Eanes, can undeniably take more credit than anyone else for establishing order and discipline among the country's highly politicized military officers and for purging the leftist extremists within the army. In February 1976 he signed a pact with the leaders of the major political parties that demoted the army to a less direct political role. He ruled as a quiet, shy, serious and very hard–working man from a peasant background. Although he is a man who has seldom been seen smiling, he was unquestionably the most popular man in Portuguese politics at the time. This is very important in Portugal, where, as in many young democracies, politics is highly personalized. Names tend to be more important than programs.

The winner of the 1986 presidential election was the Socialist, Mario Soares, who jubilantly proclaimed that his election marked "the end of Portugal's transition to a genuine democracy." The event was a watershed in Portuguese politics in that none of the candidates was a military man. It signaled the definite return of the soldiers from politics to the barracks. Unlike Eanes, who was always locking horns with the government, Soares went out of his way to get along with the prime

minister, despite ideological differences. In fact, he even left his Socialist Party and declared himself president of all Portuguese, regardless of their politics. In 1991 he easily won reelection with 70% of the votes, the widest margin since 1974.

Soares relinquished the presidency in 1996 to fellow Socialist, Jorge Sampaio, a lawyer and former Lisbon mayor who defeated ex–Prime Minister Cavaco Silva 53.8% to 46.2%. This was the first time since 1974 that voters chose a president from the same ranks as the ruling party. Sampaio speaks excellent English, having spent part of his boyhood in Baltimore and London. He was comfortably reelected in January 2001.

Changes in Government Structure

There are some institutions, policies and trends that have steadily reduced the revolutionary stamp on political life. One is the unicameral parliament, called the Assembly of the Republic, with 230 seats elected for four–year terms by proportional representation. At the head of the majority within the assembly is a relatively strong prime minister. Since 1974 regional governors or parliaments have not been able to block either the prime minister's or the president's powers since Portugal is a highly centralized, unitary state. It has also developed a stable political system. From 1975 to 1985, the average life of a government was only ten months. Since 1987, every government has served out its full four-year term.

For administrative purposes Portugal is divided into 18 districts, each with a governor appointed by the Ministry of Internal Administration upon the approval of the prime minister and his cabinet. A plan to devolve more power to the regions failed in November 1998 when an overwhelming 64% of voters in a referendum rejected it; the majority feared that it would destroy national unity, undermine budgetary discipline, and create another wasteful layer of bureaucracy. A few months earlier only a third of voters turned out to express their opinion on the country's strict abortion laws; since a majority did not vote, the results were invalid. This had been Portugal's first–ever referendum, a device whose introduction a year earlier had been hailed as the completion of a finely balanced constitution.

All institutionalized control by the military over the civilian government was eliminated, and military officers were banned from politics. This does not mean that all military influence in Portuguese politics will vanish. Indeed, military intervention in politics has historical roots too deep in Portugal to disappear completely. But it did mean that a civilian Council

of State and Constitutional Council, appointed jointly by the parliament, the government and the president replaced the Revolutionary Council. The adoption of the new constitution in 1982 marked the formal end of the "carnation revolution" and the coming of age of Portugal's parliamentary democracy.

A further move to strengthen the Portuguese incentive to remain on the road of democracy was the decision in 1976 to seek entry into the EC and thereby to tighten the links that bind Portugal to the older democracies of Western Europe. Perhaps the most important trend that has reduced the revolutionary stamp on public life in Portugal has been the string of electoral victories for the moderate democratic political parties. This is particularly significant for a country in which all earlier attempts at democratic rule collapsed partly because of a paralyzing multi–party system.

POLITICAL PARTIES

Social Democratic Party (PSD)

The ruling Social Democratic Party (PSD) changed its name from the People's Democratic Party (PPD), in order to give itself a sharper programmatic definition. It is a moderate, progressive and organizationally decentralized party without a rigid ideological position. It is an avowedly anti–Marxist party which supports basic democratic freedoms and the market economy. It draws its voters mainly from the middle class in small and medium sized towns, from the independent professions and from mid- and upper–level technical cadres. It is traditionally strongest in the Azores and Madeira archipelagos and in northern and central Portugal.

Under former leader Aníbal Cavaco Silva it became in 1987 the first party since 1974 to win a majority of either votes or seats. It was also the first time that the parties of the left did not win most of the votes. Cavaco Silva's immense appeal and his message of economic modernization through private enterprise had paid off.

The 1991 elections demonstrated the steadiness of his free market policies, economic privatization, and encouragement of private initiative and foreign investment. For the first time since the founding of the republic 81 years earlier, a democratically elected party won two consecutive absolute majorities. This was a stunning change for a country whose only previous periods of political stability were under fascist dictatorship.

The PSD was defeated in the 1995 parliamentary elections. The same thing happened in 1999 under its new leader, Manuel Durão Barroso, when it fell 12

President Jorge Sampaio

Prime Minister Manuel Durão Barroso

percentage points behind the Socialists. Its fortunes changed in the March 2002 elections, when it captured 40.1% of the votes and 102 of the 230 seats, a gain of 21 seats since the 1999 elections. Barroso, a former foreign minister who had lived seven years in the U.S., became prime minister. In order to rule, he had to form a coalition government with the People's Party and rules with a narrow majority in parliament. Barroso promised to give the anemic economy a "fiscal shock" by cutting corporation taxes over time from 28% to 20%.

The People's Party

The People's Party (PP, formerly called the Democratic and Social Center—CDS or Christian Democrats) is the newest and most conservative of Portugal's four major parties. It has an anti–Marxist, Euroskeptic, Christian and humanistic orientation and a politically moderate leadership. It is the only major party that rejects socialism as a goal. It finds its members and voters chiefly among industrial management, the service industries, independent farmers and the *retornados* from the former colonies. Women also vote disproportionately for it. The party is strongest in the north, where the influence of the Catholic Church has not sunk as rapidly after 1974 as in Lisbon and the south.

It is decentralized and organizationally weaker than the other major parties. It does have the backing of the major industrialists' association, the CIP, but this organization's influence is considerably less than one might think because of the fact that most of Portugal's larger industries had been nationalized. Led by Paulo Portas, the party did well in the 2002 elections, winning 8.8% and 14 seats on a program of limiting immigration, fighting

crime more aggressively, and introducing the national anthem in schools. By entering the coalition government with the PSD, it got three cabinet posts, and Portas became defense minister. This was difficult for Prime Minister Barroso, who had not gotten along well with Portas in the past. Also Portas has more charisma and tends to outshine the prime minister.

Socialist Party (PS)

The Socialist Party (PS), is led by Ferro Rodrigues, who replaced former Prime Minister Antonio Guterres shortly before the 2002 elections. Along with some close associates, Mario Soares had founded the PS in Münstereifel, Germany, in 1973, with the helping hand of the then ruling Social Democratic Party of Germany. When the Portuguese revolution erupted in 1974, Soares rushed back from his Paris exile, and the PS was thrust into the forefront of the turbulent events without having time to become well organized for its new role. The PS and Soares certainly share much of the credit for channeling the revolution into a democratic direction. But after being the country's most important political party for a few years, its extreme fragmentation and organizational difficulties, along with the widespread unsatisfied economic expectations of the Portuguese, caused it to suffer a string of election failures, which shook the party's confidence.

The party is organized in a democratic and decentralized way. Unlike all other Portuguese parties, its voting strength is spread fairly evenly over the entire country and is found primarily in the working and lower middle classes. It is backed by the moderate General Union of Workers, (UGT), which, since January 1979, has increasingly challenged Communist domination of the organized labor movement. The party program is officially Marxist, but both the economic crisis and existence of a rigid and stubborn Communist Party to its left, with which the PS refuses to form any coalition, have pushed the party more toward the political center. In the minds of most politically active Portuguese, the desire to overcome Portugal's economic difficulties has replaced earlier aspirations of establishing socialism. This nation–wide change of priorities has understandably forced the PS to change its own priorities as well. It now admits that the introduction of socialism in Portugal could only follow a very long transition period.

The Socialists ruled Portugal from 1995 to 2002. When the party under former Prime Minister Antonio Guterres lost a majority of municipalities, including most of the large cities, in local elections in December 2001, he regarded this as a vote

of no confidence and stepped down. Voters had reacted to the economic slowdown and sharp cuts in public spending. Without a parliamentary majority, his government did not proceed with his promised reforms. His successor, Ferro Rodrigues, led the party into the March 2002 elections. PS garnered 37.9% of the votes and 95 seats and is the main opposition party.

Portuguese Communist Party (PCP)

The final major party is the Portuguese Communist Party (PCP), once led by Alvaro Cunhal and now by Carlos Carvalhas, whose second in command is Octavio Teixeira. The PCP is still fairly orthodox. Indeed, it is the most Stalinist Communist party in all of Western Europe. Perhaps this is not surprising when one considers the fact that during the fascist rule many of its leading functionaries were either in prison or in exile in the Soviet Union. Cunhal himself was in prison eight years and is too bitter and frozen in his thinking to change now. It is Portugal's oldest party and is the only one with roots in the first republic from 1910 to 1926. This is also the country's best-organized party. It was a tight, clandestine group during the fascist period, and when the revolution came in 1974 it was immediately prepared to jump into the political fray and attempt to take all the reins of power in its own hands.

Its major base of power since the summer of 1975, when its patrons within the army lost most of their own power, was the landless farmers in the Alentejo region, where the party helped organize collectivized agricultural enterprises (UCP), and the trade unions, especially the powerful General Confederation of Portuguese Workers (CGTP–*Intersindical*) which organizes almost three–fourths of all trade union leaders. The PCP has also attracted some intellectuals. Geographically the party's electoral fortresses were the agricultural area of Alentejo and the industrial zone around Lisbon. In the north, it faced almost complete rejection, except in the city of Oporto. The disillusioned, more educated party members are defecting in droves. Among the party's problems are a general de-radicalization of the working class and the rise of a younger wing within the PCP that advocates less dogmatic policies. In 2002 it forged an electoral alliance with the Greens, but its support dived to 7% and 12 seats, down from 17 in 1999.

Foreign and Defense Policies

Portugal's defense policy has long been based on its membership in NATO. As a traditional ally of Great Britain, it was a founding member of the Atlantic Alliance. In fact, its historical partnership with the

Portugal

UK is the longest-standing pact in Europe. In 1988 it joined the WEU. Portugal's major contribution to the alliance has never been in the form of combat troops. During the decade and a half preceding the 1974 revolution, Portugal's army was bogged down in colonial wars, but between September 1974 and November 1975 these millstones were cast off one by one: first Portuguese Guinea (now Guinea–Bissau), then Mozambique, Angola, the Cape Verde Islands, São Tomé and Príncipe. In 1996 Portugal and its six former colonies, including Brazil, fulfilled a long–held ambition by uniting their 200 million people (of whom 162 million are Brazilians) in the Community of Portuguese–Speaking Countries (CPLP). Its task is to protect their common language and promote cooperation. The post of secretary general is rotated alphabetically every two years.

Macau

The only actual colony that remained until the end of the century was Macau, a tiny (six sq. miles) outpost on the southern coast of the People's Republic of China, 40 miles (64 km.) across the Canton River Estuary from Hong Kong. Only about 10,000 of the estimated 427,000 are Portuguese, although 110,000 hold Portuguese passports and can therefore live and work anywhere in the EU if they choose. Few of the Chinese who live there speak Portuguese. In fact, English is used far more than Portuguese. After the 1974 revolution, Lisbon wanted to give up the colony, which is an important trade outlet and source of foreign capital for Beijing. In 1979 officials from both countries met secretly in Paris, where the Portuguese acknowledged Chinese sovereignty over the territory and agreed to administer it until China wanted it back. China assumed full control on December 19, 1999, after 442 years of Portuguese rule.

Even if the Chinese Communists are not directly involved in Macau's main industry, gambling, they always derived considerable profits from Macau. Although nominally under Portuguese administration until the end of 1999, Portuguese officials made no pretense of being in charge. Indeed, all it would have taken for the Chinese to regain control of the colony earlier was a phone call from Beijing. There is little popular agitation for greater democracy, as in Hong Kong. The Chinese promised to respect Macau's western, capitalist society and economy until at least 2050 and leave it with considerable autonomy in local affairs. The Portuguese were a bit nostalgic. Fernando Lima, a journalist and author of several books on Macau, wrote: "At least Portuguese can look back with some pride. We created a special culture you don't find anywhere else in the world, a melting pot of people of mixed-European, Indian, and Asian descent."

East Timor

Technically speaking, Portugal still has another colony, namely Portuguese Timor. Neither Portugal nor the UN ever officially recognized the annexation of this half of the Timor Island by Indonesia on July 17, 1976. Almost half of East Timor's population died as a result of Indonesia's invasion and a native independence movement still resists Indonesian authority. The situation recaptured the world's attention in 1991, when Indonesian soldiers and police opened fire on peaceful demonstrators, killing dozens in front of Western journalists' cameras. All over Portugal, flags were flown at half-mast, newspapers appeared with black bands, and ceremonies and church vigils were held. Portugal's talks with Indonesia on this issue in 1992 ended with no concrete results.

In 1996 the Nobel Peace Prize was awarded to José Ramos–Horta, a U.S.–educated human rights activist whose leftist Portuguese father had been deported to East Timor, and to Roman Catholic Bishop Carlos Filipe Ximenes Belo, a native of Timor, who had studied in missionary schools in Portugal and Rome. President Jorge Sampaio, whose country had provided refuge for many East Timorese dissidents and had conducted the UN–sponsored negotiations with Indonesia for 12 years, called the award "a wonderful surprise" that reflects the two men's "indefatigable work in the service of human rights and peace in the territory." Portugal was rewarded by being given a two–year seat on the UN Security Council in 1997. In the words of ex-Prime Minister Guterres, this recognizes the "prestige and influence of Portugal in the world."

The situation changed dramatically in 1998 when the Indonesian government of longtime ruler Suharto was overthrown, and the new leaders offered the 800,000 Timorese the opportunity to choose autonomy or independence. In May 1999, following more than 15 years of UN-sponsored negotiations in which the Portuguese were more closely involved than any other nation, Portugal signed an agreement with Indonesia calling for a referendum on August 8. A majority voted for independence, but violence continued. Portugal dispatched 1,000 troops to help reestablish and keep the peace.

The UN decision to make Portuguese the official language of independent East Timor ignited an intense protest and debate about what it means to be East Timorese. Only 10%, most of them older people, speak it. Proponents, like resistance fighter Joao Carrascaló, argue, "we have a strong and long link with Portugal. They were benevolent colonialists. It makes sense for us to speak the language." Opponents, such as youth leader Nino Pereira, disagree: "If that [Portuguese] is what they want to speak, how are we supposed to be involved in the new government? The old people have this nostalgia with Portugal, but they have to realize that we are moving forward. The colonial days are over." In August 2001 voters elected a constituent assembly that produced a constitution. In 2002 East Timor became an independent state.

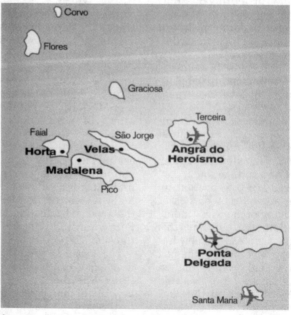

Azores

312

The Azores

The Azores, nine mountainous and beautiful islands of volcanic origin which are located about 1,000 miles (1,600 km.) west of Lisbon, are a vital stepping stone for NATO airborne forces moving toward the Mediterranean, Middle East, Persian Gulf or Africa. Former President Eanes was certainly correct in calling them "a pillar of support in the defense of Europe." American Air Force General Larry Wright underscored this: "Whoever controls the Azores controls the Atlantic."

Of particular importance is the U.S. air base at Lajes on the island of Terceiram, which the U.S. leases from Portugal, renewable every five years. Lajes is a refueling station, and about 250 U.S. aircraft touch down each month. It is also a base for P–3 Orion maritime surveillance planes that patrol 2.5 million square miles in the North Atlantic.

A serious financial dispute arose in 1988 when the U.S. announced that it would provide less aid. The prime minister noted, "expectations are not being met." Many of his countrymen had the impression that Portugal was being taken for granted, now that democracy had been stabilized. Unlike the situation in Spain concerning Torrejon Air Base, where the issue was political, not financial, there is no public resentment over the American military presence at Lajes. In 1988 the Portuguese government announced that it did not want the F16 fighter-bombers that were being evicted from Spain to be redeployed in Portugal. It called for a formal review of the base agreement, and a solution was found in 1989: the U.S. supplied the Portuguese armed forces with 20 F16s, as well as a battery of Hawk ground–to-air missiles, 57 antisubmarine, combat and utility helicopters, air defense radar, and a hydrographic vessel. U.S. financial aid for 1989 was set at $150 million, down from $208 million in 1985. All this assistance enables Portugal to shift its military emphasis in NATO from leasing bases to a more active antisubmarine role in the mid–Atlantic.

In the 1990s the U.S. pulled some of its military assets out of the Azores after Soviet activity in the Atlantic had ended. The U.S., which maintains 1,800 military personnel and 1,900 dependents on the island, also has an underwater terminal on the island of Santa Maria to monitor submarine movements in the Atlantic and a network of underground supply areas throughout the islands whose contents can be airlifted to any transatlantic area within hours. France also operates a missile tracking station on the island of Flores. Because of its need for a rapid deployment capability for the Middle East and elsewhere, the U.S. con-

Wine-growing country around the Douro River Valley

ducted a major buildup of its military facilities here, aimed at providing a "viable support base" eastward and southward.

When, in 1975, the leftist Portuguese government allowed Cuban planes carrying troops to Angola to use Santa Maria for refueling stops, a pro–American Azores separatist movement sprang up, but it withered again when more moderate leaders came to power in Lisbon. This movement indicated the basic strength of the ties between the 200,000 residents of the Azores and the U.S., where more than 600,000 Azoreans now live, mainly on the east and west coasts.

A dispute in 1986 over the elevation of the Azorean flag and anthem to equal

Portugal

status with those of the motherland served as a reminder of local pride. They had been waved and played in official ceremonies since 1980. Nevertheless, because of the symbolic importance, President Soares vetoed the islands' revised autonomy statue, which had been approved by the Portuguese parliament. This was the first use of the presidential veto under the 1976 constitution, and it indicated how a flag and anthem question can revive Lisbon's fears of possible Azorean separatism.

The Madeira Archipelago

The Madeira Archipelago is not only the home of a desirable aperitif wine, which rivals sherry for popularity. It guards the southern approaches to Europe and the Strait of Gibraltar and is the southernmost NATO territory. The island of Porto Santo has excellent airport and deep–water port facilities, which at times has been used for military purposes, such as in 1978 when it was used as a refueling stop for aircraft carrying Belgian troops to Zaire. NATO military planners are very interested in Madeira because the Spanish made it clear that their Canary Islands, which lie only 300 miles (480 km.) south of Madeira, would not be considered NATO territory once Spain entered the Atlantic Alliance.

Portugal is very wary about allowing Madeira to become a military bastion like the Azores. A major reason is that this could create a conflict with the Organization of African Unity, in which voices have long been raised that the Madeira archipelago is colonized African territory and should therefore be liberated. After all, Madeira lies only 350 miles (560 km.) west of Morocco. Lisbon is trying to forge closer links with its former African colonies in order to regain some of their lucrative markets and to send them some of their excess work force.

Mozambique and Angola

Both Mozambique and Angola, the two richest of the former colonies, have realized the benefits the more skilled Portuguese could bring to their countries and have asked the Portuguese to return under a new guise. This reconciliation with its former colonies has been made politically easier since Portugal supported the Black African position toward South Africa. One–seventh of the white South Africans are of Portuguese origin.

In 1991 Portugal mediated the "Estoril Accord," ending Angola's 16–year civil war. It also participated, along with American, Russian and Angolan observers, in the political–military commission to supervise the truce and prepare for elections. It also sent peacekeeping forces to Mozambique in the early 1990s. Portugal supported peaceful change in part because it wants to avoid the kind of refugee flood it experienced in the 1970s. Emotional ties with Africa are still strong, but economic links have become much weaker. By the 1990s only about 1% of Portugal's foreign trade was with Angola and Mozambique.

Immigrants from Portugal's former colonies have changed the face of Portuguese society and made it much more heterogeneous. Historically the Portuguese were an emigrant people, settling all corners of the globe. By the end of the 20th century, the flow had reversed, and Portugal has become a net importer of labor. By 1997 there were 175,000 foreigners in the country, more than half of whom from Africa. An increasing number comes from Central and Eastern Europe. Unlike in some other European countries, this ethnic mixing has not been accompanied by serious racial tension.

Defense

After the 1974 revolution had been tamed, Portugal could afford neither politically nor economically to continue maintaining a large land army. Therefore the size of the armed forces was cut from nearly a half million to about 49,700 politically obedient troops (25,650 army; 16,600 navy; 7,445 air force) in 2000, including 2,300 female volunteers. Compulsory service dropped to 4-12 months, depending on the service. It disappears altogether in 2003 as Portugal shifts to a professional army with modern rapid reaction capability. The military's share in the budget fell from 50% in 1970 to less than 10% by 2000. What Portugal can contribute to NATO is the use of strategically important facilities on the mainland, where NATO has naval and air facilities, and in the Azores and Madeira island groups, which are autonomous parts of Portugal.

In 1991 it supported its allies' war to dislodge the Iraqi aggressors from Ku–wait. It sent 900 troops to Bosnia to help NATO implement the 1995 Dayton Peace Accord. In 2000 it still maintained peacekeeping forces in both Bosnia and Kosovo. Its diplomatic support for the U.S. is not due exclusively to the fact that the U.S. provides Portugal economic and military aid. The two nations now share democratic values and common interests and therefore have a solid foundation for good relations.

Portugal is trying to improve its relations with the nations of the Middle East.

Picking grapes in Estremadura

Stripping cork

Portugal was the first ally to heed President Carter's call in 1979 for sanctions against Iran when Iranian mobs had seized the U.S. embassy. It also levied sanctions against the Soviet Union when it invaded Afghanistan, although President Soares' visit to Moscow in 1987 signaled a normalization of relations with Russia.

Portugal supported the U.S., UK and Spain in the 2003 war in Iraq although it supplied no troops or military aid. It hosted in the Azores a summit meeting of the leaders of these three allies on March 16, 2003, that culminated in a final 24-hour notice to the UN Security Council to act, or a decision to take military action would be made without the UN. President Bush said: "Tomorrow is the day that we will determine whether or not diplomacy can work." After the war, Portugal turned to Washington for help in rebuilding its neglected armed forces. At its June 2003 summit, NATO decided to locate a sea-based joint task force in Portugal.

ECONOMY

Under fascist rule, Portugal's economy was relatively isolated and sheltered from the rest of Europe. Its industry was primarily in the hands of rather inefficient family businesses, which were protected from stiff Western European competition and which had a comfortable export and import monopoly with their country's African colonies. A third of the Portuguese worked in agriculture. After 1974 much of Portugal's economic situation changed for the better.

The 1974 revolution did, however, create additional economic problems, beyond the temporary scaring away of tourists and their much–needed foreign currencies. Most of the earlier large private industrial and financial groups were broken down, and a wide range of economic activities that were not foreign owned was brought under state control. These included banks, insurance, airlines, railways, electricity, oil, gas, petrochemicals, cement, breweries, tobacco, wood pulp, steel, shipping and ship–building, urban transit, trucking, metallurgy, chemicals, food processing and textiles. Many of these sectors were combined in a huge publicly–owned conglomerate called Quimigal.

In all, 60% of Portugal's industry was nationalized after 1974. These nationalized industries exacerbated Portugal's problems. In 1991 the state still accounted for 40% of GDP. Although many firms escaped the sword of nationalization because of their small size, it is not surprising that an immediate result of this policy was that investment capital was scared away. Productivity dropped and, because wages were doubled after 1974, inflation soared. Such nationalizations merely added to the weight of Portugal's already cumbersome bureaucracy. The state–owned companies also sap up the lion's share of the government's economic subsidies, but these funds are insufficient to convert them into efficient companies able to compete well in international markets.

The Cavaco Silva government vowed in 1985 to end state domination of the economy, which he blamed for keeping Portuguese living standards so far below the Western European average. His reelection in 1987 boosted his program to begin gradually selling off most industries and financial institutions nationalized after 1974. Cavaco Silva noted, "the state should control only companies of particular importance to public service," such as power, water and public–transport utilities. The government's extensive media holdings, including newspapers, are also earmarked for sale, save one television and radio channel. "The era of state paternalism will soon be over." Progress on this privatization program has been slow. One problem is that there are too few large Portuguese groups with enough money to buy what is up for sale. Not wishing to sell most of these assets to foreigners, rigid, but ineffective, limits on how much foreigners can buy were established. Beginning in 1993 foreigners could buy control in state firms on a case–by–case basis.

A welcome reform after the 1974 revolution was the lifting of the ban against strikes and independent trade unions. However, in the heady days after the revolution the well–organized Communists seized control of the major labor union, the CGTP–Intersindical. This union drives an extremely hard bargain and became accustomed to getting what it demands. It is highly politicized and is able to threaten the government through potentially crippling strikes. In 1988 it sought by means of a 24–hour strike to preserve the stringent dismissal law from 1975 that makes it virtually impossible to fire a worker from his job. For the first time, communist and socialist labor federations united, and factories, airports and banks across the country were shut down, as hundreds of thousands of workers staged the biggest industrial action in Portuguese history. But Cavaco Silva, refused to change a single line of his legislation to make it easier for businesses to fire workers, on the grounds that it is crucial for attracting investment and modernizing the economy.

The decolonization of Portugal's empire forced Portugal to compete with other nations for markets and brought close to a million bitter and penniless *retornados* to the motherland. What was worse, it cut off the country's most important sources of raw materials, especially energy. Even though Portugal has the lowest per capita energy consumption in Western Europe and also the lowest ownership of automobiles per inhabitant (although the number of cars doubled between 1985 and 1990, causing congestion in Lisbon), it can produce only about 20% of the energy it needs. The country

Portugal

must import all of its oil and 83% of its coal. It is usually able to meet 60% of its electricity demand through its own hydro–electricity, but recurrent droughts make this source uncertain. Therefore, it imports substantial amounts of electricity from Spain and France.

Portugal must spend about 10% of its GDP in energy imports, compared with only 1% in 1973, and most analysts expect energy demand to rise, as Portugal expands its industry. Perhaps there will be no alternative to using its one untapped energy source, namely the 8,000 tons of proven uranium reserves, mostly located in the northern area of Urgerica, to produce nuclear energy. In the meantime, Portugal will have great difficulty paying for oil, especially since it has a limited range of competitive exports. Therefore, its large trade deficits will probably continue.

Agriculture and Fishing

Portuguese agriculture is traditionally inefficient, and 13% of all Portuguese are engaged in agriculture (down from 44% in 1960). Farming contributes only 3.8% of Portugal's GDP; if one adds fishing and forestry, that figure would be about double that. Portugal continues to have proportionately the EU's largest agricultural sector. The country must still import half of its food and animal feeds. Food makes up one–fifth of the nation's total imports.

It has the lowest per capita productivity in Western Europe. In fact, its productivity is only a fourth to a third of the EU average and two–thirds that of Spain and Greece. This is due to several factors, including the rocky, hilly soil, the low level of mechanization, the inefficient collective farms in the South, the insufficient size of family farms in the North, and the farmers' general resistance to change. About 30% of Portugal's rural population is estimated to be illiterate, compared with 13% of all Portuguese over age 15. Portuguese farmers' inability to compete successfully within a single European market has left a majority of them living at subsistence levels on incomes a third as big as their Spanish counterparts.

The revolution of 1974 by no means created Portugal's agricultural problems. However, the initial leaders' fervor created particular problems in the south, where the land conquered from the Moors in the 13th century was distributed in large tracts to Portuguese nobility. These large land–owners often lived in Lisbon and had their large estates worked by low–paid agricultural laborers. These large estates were ripe for picking in revolutionary times.

The Communists, supported by the ruling leftist military leaders, seized many of the estates and converted them into large collective farms. In other cases, they forced the owners to hire more workers than could be employed profitably. By the 1990s more than half the seized estates had been returned to their original owners, and all owners have received some compensation for their former holdings. Nevertheless, about one–fifth of Portugal's forest and cropland remains collectivized. But these collectively–owned farms have, on the whole, been poorly managed. They therefore now produce only a third to a half of the grain and livestock that they supplied before the revolution. Because of legal tangles, the Cavaco Silva government did not move as fast to de–collectivize farming in the South as it had hoped.

Portugal faces a problem of what to do about its inefficient farming and antiquated fishing fleet that is already unable to withstand competition in its home waters. Also, it has few agricultural products that can compete in the EU. The ones that can are wines, tomato concentrate and cork. The heart of its wine growing is in the Douro River Valley, from which port wine (named for the city of Oporto) comes. Also, the world's largest exporter of a single brand of wine, Mateus Rose, comes from Portugal, the largest importer being the U.S. Actually, the Portuguese seldom drink Mateus Rose, preferring their own dry whites from northern and central Portugal. It is understandable that they prefer not to export these fine wines and, instead, to keep their limited supply for themselves.

Portugal's fishing fleet is the oldest and least productive in all of Western Europe. Many of its vessels have no engines. Portugal leads the world in ship repair; its repair yards are the world's biggest and handle more tonnage than their top four competitors together. In 1969 the Portuguese government granted Spain, which has a fishing fleet that is larger than that of all 15 EU countries combined, unrestricted rights to fish in Portugal's waters. Most leaders in Lisbon now view that decision as a cardinal error and have been trying hard to undo it.

Portugal's chief export is cork, of which it supplies half of the world's supply (most of the rest comes from Spain.) and 85% of the wine corks. The industry creates 3% of the country's GDP, but it is threatened by the rising popularity of synthetic corks, estimated to have captured 5-10% of the world market already. This substance is the bark that is stripped off the cork oak trees every 11 years, a process which leaves the trees a bright red color. Cork production suffered a setback in the mid–1970s, when following the seizure of large estates in Alentejo thousands of cork trees were uprooted to make way for wheat, a crop unsuited for the region. The Communist–inspired wheat drive at least temporarily destroyed cork–growing there.

In order to irrigate more than 272,000 acres in the Alentejo region, the government adopted a plan to close the giant Alqueva dam in order to create the largest artificial lake in Western Europe. When filled it would submerge the village of Luz, a million trees and hundreds of Stone Age rock drawings. Environmentalists decried the damage this project does to nature.

Membership in EU

Portugal's political leaders, supported by a large majority of the population, chose a formidable challenge to prepare their country for a more prosperous future—entry into the EU. Before becoming a full member in 1986, it was a member of EFTA. In 1972 Portugal had entered an agreement with the EU providing free

Cork strips ready for transport

The National Theater, Lisbon

trade of industrial products. Its leaders, as well as those in the EU member countries, hoped that such entry would help solidify the democratic foundations in Portugal, as well as provide a mighty boost for the country's economy. By 2003, 79.4% of its exports went to Europe (the largest market being Spain, followed by Germany), more than double the proportion a decade earlier. The most dramatic change is with Spain, to which it sends 19.2% of its exports and from which it purchases 25.3% of its imports.

Portugal has developed a modern economy that employs 35% of its workforce in industry (which produce 30.5% of GDP) and 52% in services (creating 65.7% of GDP). The introduction of greater incentives through a reform of personal taxation, which some observers described as the most punitive in all of Western Europe, stimulated the economy. Portuguese industry enjoys other advantages. Its smallness and fragmented nature lend it some flexibility. The Portuguese could not bear much more poverty. Their poor remain the poorest in Western Europe, and a third of all households still have no running water.

Its basic strength is in the cheapness of labor, the lowest in Western Europe; average wages are only a third of EU average. At $5.60 per hour in 1996, its manufacturing pay was two–thirds lower than in the U.S., three–fourths lower than in Germany, and 60% less than in Spain and Ireland, economies at a similar level of

development. The Portuguese labor force, on the whole, works conscientiously and acquires new skills quickly. Of course, there are considerable domestic dangers involved with relying on cheap labor to maintain international competitiveness. It could stimulate even more labor unrest than already exists. Also, it cannot be long maintained given the chronic shortage of labor by the turn of the century.

Portugal exports textiles and footwear and faces stiff competition not only in the EU, but also from Third World countries. Portugal is already dependent on the Americans for a large portion of food–stuffs, including 90% of its wheat.

Entry into the EU brought needed social and regional funds to Portugal; from 3% to 4% of its GDP is derived from financial transfers from Brussels, a total of $30 billion between 1986 and 2003. Those funds will end in 2006, and new ones are likely to go to new members in Central Europe. However, these monies have made a real economic difference. One can see this in Portugal's infrastructure. In 1987 it had only 240 kilometers (144 miles) of freeways; by 1998, it had 840 kilometers (504 miles).

This country, which was so successful in establishing a democratic political order despite enormous problems and the absence of a democratic tradition, is meeting the economic challenges associated with becoming a full economic partner in Western Europe. By bringing its budget deficit down to 1.5% of GDP and its total

national debt to 66% of GDP by 2000, it met the most important qualifications to enter the European Monetary Union (EMU) in 1999, and it adopted the Euro. In the first half of 2000 it assumed the EU presidency. In 2001 Portugal became the first country to exceed the limit for a budget deficit by reaching 4% of GDP. It was compelled to impose painful cuts that sparked widespread strikes among civil servants, who protested against the government's required austerity drive to meet the EU's tough rules on public spending. In 2003 it was able to announce that it was below its target of 2.8% of GDP.

Portugal is experiencing slackening economic growth (less than 1% in 2002). Inflation, at 3.5% in 2002, is high by Western European standards, but its 5% unemployment rate in 2003 is far below the EU average. Living standards have risen fast. Since it joined the EC (now EU) in 1986, they have risen from about half the EU average to 78% in 2002. Tourism is booming with about 20 million guests in 1992, primarily British and Spanish; it accounts for 6% to 8% of its GDP. Foreign investment is pouring in, and two-thirds of it comes from the EU. With 75% of its GDP derived from foreign trade, Portugal is one of the most open countries in Europe. It is therefore natural that it became a part of the world's largest economic market, and it is doing quite well. Its huge Autoeuropa car plant, owned by Volkswagen, accounts for 12% of Portugal's exports. The U.S. is one of the country's leading investors, and

Portugal

among the major American firms active in Portugal are Ford, General Motors, Microsoft, Texas Instruments, Compaq, Johnson and Johnson, Unisys, Citibank and Chase Manhattan. The U.S. purchases 13% of Portugal's exports and provides 30% of its imports from non-EU countries. An active American Chamber of Commerce in Portugal promotes this important bilateral trade.

Since the 1990s the state has been selling off its interests in oil, gasoline, natural gas, electricity, banks and telecommunications companies. In 2000 it unloaded an additional 20% of the national power company, Electricidade de Portugal. It sold most of its remaining interest in Portugal Telecom (PT). However, the government maintains close ties with formerly state-owned firms. It keeps "golden shares" that allow it to veto mergers, even when it retains only a minority stake in a company.

The existence of a lively "submerged economy" makes it more difficult to get an exact picture of Portugal's economic condition. This kind of activity is done at home, in the streets, or on the job while the boss is looking the other way. It takes place behind the backs of government statisticians and tax collectors. If the production of goods and services from such an invisible economy were able to be included in the official economic figures, an estimated 10% to 25% would have to be added to the GDP, and real unemployment would be below the official figures.

CULTURE

Portugal is a nation whose cultural influence extends far beyond its own borders. Today nearly 200 million people speak Portuguese. Its outward–looking orientation was beautifully reflected in its greatest literary figure, Luiz de Camões (1524–80), who wrote poetry and dramatic comedies. In 1572 he published perhaps the greatest piece of Portuguese literature, *Os Lusíadas* ("The Lusitanians"), a long epic poem celebrating Portuguese history and heroes. His story is linked with that of Vasco da Gama's voyage to India and is infused with much Greek mythology. In general, Portuguese today are nostalgic about their country's great past, and they have a term for this yearning: *saudade*.

Portuguese culture has also been enriched by experiences or influences from abroad. For instance, the novelist, John Dos Passos, and the undisputed king of march music, John Philip Sousa, were both sons of Portuguese emigrants and received their artistic inspiration in the U.S.

In 1998 a Portuguese writer won the Nobel Prize for literature for the first time.

Jose Samarago was born into a home with no books, grew up in poverty, never went to the university, and toiled as a metalworker until the fall of dictator Antonio Salazar enabled him, an active Communist, to publish his first novel in 1974. The best known of his imaginative novels are *Baltasar and Blimunda* and *The Year of the Death of Ricardo Reis*.

He expressed his hope on receiving the honor that "Portuguese will become more visible and more audible." Earlier in the century Egas Moniz had won the Nobel Prize for medicine.

Influence of Brazil

Perhaps the greatest foreign cultural influence comes from Brazil. For years after 1974 one of the most popular television serials in Portugal was a sort of soap opera from Brazil called "Gabriela." Set in Rio de Janeiro and using an all–Brazilian cast, this *telenovela* (T.V. serial) filled Portugal's air waves with Brazilian slang, songs, accents and dress. Many other such series have subsequently been brought in from Brazil to be aired on Portugal's two state–owned and run

channels, RTP 1 and 2, and on its two newer private commercial channels, SIC and TV1.

Chiefly because of its small size and high degree of centralization, there are few different dialects spoken within Portugal, except in Miranda do Douro in the northeast. But of the 150 million persons in the world who speak Portuguese as a native language, only 10 million live in the mother country. At newsstands one finds many Brazilian publications mixed with Portuguese ones: Lisbon alone has five morning and four afternoon papers, the most popular being the tabloid *Correio da Manha*. In 1991 the last state–owned daily newspaper, *Diario de Noticias*, established in 1864, was sold into private hands; it is respected as a serious but rather dull paper, but its look is being modernized. There are also hot-selling weeklies, such as *Expresso*, *O Jornal*, *Semanario* and *Independente*.

It is not surprising that the Portuguese spoken out side, especially in Brazil is changing the language spoken in this small country. Oral expression is being strongly penetrated by Brazilian words

Portugese student

nize this fact and negotiate a linguistic agreement with Brazil and other former colonies. Proponents argue that a common structure of the language must be preserved and that the constant evolution of the language should be incorporated in the mother country. Critics decry the "crime against the patrimony of the Portuguese language" and "a disgusting resignation to Brazil's economic interests." It cannot be expected that, in the long run, any effort to erect a barrier against the flood of foreign cultural influences could succeed in a country like Portugal that is adapting itself so quickly to the changing world it faces. Millions of Portuguese really want no such barrier anyway. Nevertheless, the government established tough requirements that by 1995 40% of all TV shows must be in Portuguese, three–fourths of which must be produced in Portugal.

and idiomatic phrases. The economic prowess of Brazil has meant that the Portuguese being learned by foreigners abroad is now primarily Brazilian. Most magazines on Portugal's newsstands are from Brazil.

A passionate debate began in 1986 over whether Portugal should simply recog-

Education

Post–revolutionary Portugal inherited considerable educational problems. These included a shortage of schools and teachers, a clear and discriminatory separation of the elite lycée (high school) from the trade schools, a poor geographic distribution of educational facilities throughout the country, and especially the concentration of higher education along the coast. Just before the revolution, the progressive minister of education, Mr. Veiga Simão announced a comprehensive reform, which would have combined all the various educational tracks into one, opened up the path to the universities at Evora,

Braga, Aveiro and Lisbon, in addition to the existing universities at Coimbra, Oporto, and Lisbon (where there are two). By the 1990s there were 12 state universities, 14 polytechnic schools, and a growing number of private universities.

Simão was swept out of office along with the entire *ancien regime*, and for a couple years, the educational system became the wet clay in the hands of leftist and Marxist teachers and reformers. Many Marxist textbooks replaced the out–dated books from the Salazar era, schools were taken over by management committees which excluded most parental influence in the schools, and pupils were examined on their "collective work" and even had a voice in the grades they received.

When the Socialist Party finally gained a firm grip on the reins of government in the second half of 1975, the textbooks were changed again to reflect the more moderate and pluralistic character of the new leadership. Parents were again given some say in the school system, the former strict grading system was reintroduced, and hundreds of leftists were removed from the schools and the ministry of education. With order restored in the schools, the education system was more or less back where it had been in 1974, but the ground had been laid for important changes.

In 1977 a system of pre–school instruction was introduced, and the pre–university schooling was established at 11 years, with the possibility of a twelfth year later. All pupils in Portugal now

Portuguese students help Belgian cooks prepare a Portuguese meal at the College of Europe, Bruges.

Photo by Nuno Quieros

Portugal

receive six years of elementary education, which is obligatory, and some secondary schooling. Those who wish to stay in school have six years of secondary school, which over half finish.

All children must remain in school until age 14. This is a real strain on the system when one considers that Portugal has one of Europe's youngest populations: almost a fourth is under age 15. After the one–year transition class, qualified students can enter the university for a "short advanced education" of two to three years, or for the "diverse superior courses" of four or five years. The number of students is still low with only one in five going on to higher education. But the number is eight times higher than in 1974. In 1998 many of those students participated in a one–day strike to protest the raising of their annual tuition from $7 to $330.

The educational system remains a matter of concern. Only a third of people age 25-34 had completed 12 years of school, compared with an average of three-fourths in the rest of the OECD. It does spend 5.7% of its national income on public schools and universities, a relatively high proportion by OECD standards. It also spends more per student in secondary education than most countries, in part because its teachers' salaries are relatively high.

All kinds of scholarly and cultural endeavors are generously supported in Portugal by the Gulbenkian Foundation, established and richly funded by a foreign oil magnate who made Portugal his home. Since the foundation is massively involved in supporting a wide range of cultural activities, is private and has carefully steered clear of government control, it was able to support research with critical political implications, which the politicians in power viewed with some distrust. The Luso-American Foundation sponsors scholarships for American students of Portuguese descent and provides funding for hiring American professors at MBA programs at Portuguese universities.

Cultural activity also got a boost in late 1986 with a new law (called the "Maecenas Law") that concedes tax breaks to corporations that support cultural initiatives. Up to 60% of any "cultural financing" costs can be written off taxes. Since only about 1% of the national budget is allotted to culture, and public support is very scarce, this new measure is most welcome.

Religion

Portuguese society has experienced some social transformation in the past decade and a half, but religion has not changed as much as in many other Western European countries. Divorce was permitted after the revolution. The Catholic Church continued to oppose birth control, but Portuguese of child–bearing age are inclined to ignore that opposition.

Despite bitter protests by the Catholic Church, Parliament voted in 1984 to permit abortions following rape, or whenever medically advisable. Nevertheless, it has the strictest abortion laws of any EU country except Ireland. Nevertheless, legal abortion is rare today, and illegal abortions continue. It was estimated in 2002 that as many as 40,000 women a year have them. One 23-year-old female journalist stated, "I would say 60% of the women I know have had abortions. If they're rich, they go to Spain, and if they're not, they go to midwives, often in really bad conditions." The trial and conviction in 2002 of a female abortionist who performed illegal operations in a clean, modern clinic provoked outrage among pro-choice groups.

Religious superstitions and symbols remain strong. One sees "Our Lady of …" various things everywhere. A popular cult is the shrine of Our Lady of Fatima, where the virgin reportedly appeared to three shepherd children in 1917. Hundreds of thousands of pilgrims attend candlelight masses at the rural shrine twice a year. Portuguese are conscientious church–goers, by European standards. Although only about a third of all Catholics attend regularly, this compares with less than a fifth in Spain and a sixth in France. About two out of three choose to get married in a church, compared with nine out of ten in 1960. The divorce rate has shot up to approximately 14,000 a year, from only a few hundred before the 1974 revolution. A fifth of all babies are born out of wedlock, compared with one in 14 in 1970.

Perhaps the greatest social change involves women. Before 1974, a woman had to get her husband's permission to go into higher education, take a job, or get a passport. In 1960, only about a fifth of women in working age had paying jobs. Now the proportion is 63%, at the top end of the EU range. Women account for 60% of university students and graduates, up from a fourth in 1960. As a result of increased education and employment possibilities, fertility rates have plummeted from the highest in Europe to among the lowest.

Reflecting a shifting attitude in Europe, Portugal adopted in 2002 a new approach to the problem of drug addiction by decriminalizing all drug use. Users (now officially called "consumers") are no longer viewed as criminals, but as victims of a drug culture that tough laws cannot control.

FUTURE

Since 1974, Portugal has established a democratic political order that has shown itself capable of surviving. Its extrication from costly colonial wars not only aided its own economy, but it enabled Portugal to concentrate its military attention on common NATO objectives. With the continued need for the U.S. and its allies to be able to project their military presence into the Mediterranean and Middle Eastern regions, Portugal's Azores and Madeira

A final view of Porto

archipelagos in the Atlantic Ocean will continue to have strategic importance. Portugal has benefited from stable, energetic government.

Portugal has undergone a dramatic transformation since joining the EU in 1986. The economy experienced an unprecedented boom and has been modernized and liberalized. Despite poverty that still exists, standards of living have been raised, unemployment is among the lowest in the EU, and most Portuguese have experienced progress. One sees manifestations of economic progress in the construction boom, huge shopping malls, and the emergence of a new technocratic class, although the success is uneven throughout the country. Two showcases of the country's economic development in 1998 were the world exposition in Lisbon, which commemorated the 500th anniversary of Vasco da Gama's first voyage to Brazil and drew millions of visitors, and the opening of the 11–mile Vasco da Gama Bridge spanning the Tejo River.

Former Prime Minister Guterres succeeded in reducing the budget deficit from 4.2% in 1997 to 2.2% in 2002; it was 2.8% in 2003, below the 3% required for the European currency union, which Portugal joined. The euro began circulation in 2002. Prime Minister Jose Manuel Durrao Barroso was able to capitalize on the previous government's failings and the bad will they created in the minds of voters. His coalition government, formed with Paulo Portas' People's Party, has a narrow parliamentary majority to tackle the country's problems. Such a slim margin is not an ideal situation for a coalition dependent upon a forceful and volatile junior partner like the PP. It is uncertain that the government will survive a full four years.

Portuguese will seize the European spotlight in 2004 when they will host the European soccer championships. To get ready, the new Barroso government is replacing Lisbon's present airport on the edge of the city with a more modern one farther away.

Portugal's democratic constitution has been reformed and strengthened, and Portuguese have rediscovered a sense of national pride. In April 2004 they will celebrate the 20th anniversary of the "Carnation Revolution." They can look with satisfaction on the legacies of that revolution: a stable parliamentary democracy, membership in the EU, and sustained economic growth that has raised living standards.

Andorra

The church Sant Cristòfol d'Anyós high in the Andorran Pyrenees dates from the 12th century

Area: 188 sq. mi. (487 sq. km.)

Population: 65,844. More than 80% are foreigners.

Capital City: Andorra la Vella, population with adjoining Encamp, 22,000.

Climate: Cool, dry summer and snowy, mountain winter climate.

Official Language: Catalan; Spanish and French are also widely spoken.

Ethnic Background: Catalan stock; ca. 15% of residents are native Andorrans, 61% Spanish, 6% French.

Principal Religion: Roman Catholic

Major Industries: Tourism, free port for consumer goods, tobacco products, hydroelectric power, timber.

Major Customers: France, Spain, Germany, Japan.

Currency: Euro.

Year of Independence: 1278.

Government: Since 1993 a self-ruling sovereign state.

Chiefs of State: Figurehead Co-Princes are the President of the French Republic and the Spanish Bishop of Seo de Urgel, who are represented locally by officials called Veguers.

Head of Government: Marc Forné Molné, Prime Minister (since 1994).

National Flag: Three vertical bands of blue, yellow, and red with the national coat of arms in the center.

Perched high in the Pyrenees Mountains is the largest of Europe's six microscopic independent states: Andorra. Mountain peaks rising to 9,000 feet (2,743 meters) overlook six deep valleys on the

southern slopes of the Pyrenees. Bordering on France to the north and on Spain to the South, Andorra, with its ruggedly beautiful landscape, is a geographic blend of glacial valleys, lakes, fresh water springs and Alpine meadows. Abundant rainfall and snow give this tiny land a green, rich look half the year and a white mountain look the other half. In the 58 villages and hamlets in the highlands, with their typically granite, wood and slate houses, live many of the native Andorrans, who now comprise only about 15% of the population.

They have a strong affinity with the region of Catalonia in Northern Spain. They speak Catalan, a rich romance language related to Provencal, spoken by approximately six million persons in the region that encompasses French and Spanish Catalonia. In the age of the automobile, Andorra has been ripped from the

Middle Ages, and its dizzying economic advancement has attracted thousands of Spaniards and French, who now comprise 61% and 6% of Andorra's residents respectively. These developments have made Andorrans a minority in their own country, but they have also given the land a prosperous, international character.

There is evidence of human settlements in Andorra dating many thousands of years ago, and the first written records date from the third century B.C. It is a local legend that the mountain people in these valleys helped a grateful Charlemagne drive the Moors from the area in 806 A.D. Charlemagne's son, Louis the Pious, granted the six valleys to the Spanish Bishop of Seo de Urgel in 819 A.D. In 1278 the French Count of Foix and the Bishop recognized each other as Co-Princes of Andorra. Over the years, the Count of Foix's claims passed to the King of Navarre, then to the King of France, and finally to the President of the French Republic. Except for a brief period during the French Revolution, when the French occupied Andorra and declared it a republic, it has retained to the present day its co-allegiance to France and the Bishop of Seo de Urgel.

Until 1993 the co-allegiance was formally acknowledged by a token annual tribute (*questia*) of 960 French francs (about $190) to France and 460 Spanish pesetas (about $15) to Spain in alternating years. Because of this tribute and because the country existed as a result of a feudal grant, Andorra was technically not a state,

Andorra

according either to international law or to its own statutes. It was a fief, a feudal carry–over from the Middle Ages with no equivalence in modern Europe.

POLITICAL SYSTEM

In 1990 reformer Josep Maria Beal was elected Sindic, pledging to modernize the country's institutions to enable it to survive in the new Europe. With the support of his successor, Jordi Farras, and other Andorran leaders, such as Oscar Ribas Reig, his pledge was fulfilled. In 1993 the tiny country adopted its first–ever constitution. With three–quarters of the eligible voters participating, 74.2% opted for sovereignty. By choosing self–rule, they acquired the right to have their own judicial system and foreign policy.

Andorrans are now completely free to establish political parties. Traditionally, all Andorran candidates ran as independents. In 1976 Andorra's first political party, the Andorran Democratic Association, was formed. In the February 1997 elections for the 28 seats in the General Council, the Unio Lliberal surged to 18 seats. The center–right Agrupament Nacional Democratic fell from eight to six seats. Nova Democracia dropped from five to only two seats. A National Democratic Initiative won the two remaining seats.

The right to vote is very restricted. Only the 10,000 or Andorrans whose families have had Andorran citizenship for three generations are permitted to vote. This amounts to only 15% of the population. Women citizens were granted suffrage in 1970. Over time the new constitution is

THE CO-PRINCES OF ANDORRA

His Excellency
The Honorable Jacques Chirac
President of the French Republic

His Excellency
The Most Reverend Joan Martí Alanis
Bishop of Seo de Urgel

bound to affect every preexisting political institution in the country.

The President of France and the Bishop of Seo de Urgel are figurehead Co–Princes of Andorra and until 1993 had full executive, legislative and judicial power. In practice, *Veguers* (their designated representatives) and *Battles* (magistrates) represented them in the country. These feudal offices were combined with more modern elected offices.

The country had no constitution before 1993, but a "Plan of Reform," adopted in

1866. It established the groundwork for a General Council of 28 members (at least four of whom are elected from each of the six Parishes in the six valleys—Andorra, Canillo, Encamp, La Massana, Ordino, and Sant Julià). Each member is elected to a four–year term, and half the members were elected every two years. Before the new constitution was implemented, the General Council had no formal legislative power, but it was the supreme administrative body. It elected for three–year terms a Sindic (manager) and Sub–Sindic

Hon. Marc Forné Molné

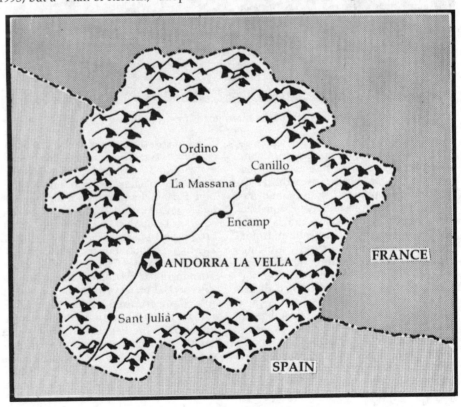

Andorra

Statue in front of the main government building

to implement its decisions. There was usually tension within the General Council between the four representatives from the capital city, where two–thirds of the country's population lives, and the remaining 20 representatives from the more rural parishes. When the capital's four representatives request funds for facilities needed by the rapidly growing capital city, the remaining members are inclined to demand similar facilities for their parishes. This often created deadlocks on important issues.

The judicial system is now independent. It is based on French secular and Spanish Ecclesiastical law. That such a hybrid legal system could function in Andorra is demonstrated by the fact that the entire country maintains only six jail cells, most of which usually are empty.

The constitution emboldened the judiciary in 1993 to arrest the director of state security and president of the Olympic committee in a new effort to fight corruption. Earlier, the country's main families had been powerful enough to suppress scandals through their dominance of the French and Spanish courts in Andorra. The tiny mountainous land has sent athletes to the Winter Olympics since 1976.

Andorra has no defense forces, but all able–bodied men between the ages of 16 and 60 are required to arm themselves and be ready to serve without pay or uniforms in the People's Militia, which has not fought in a war for 700 years. This strange, unorganized army regards all its "soldiers" as officers. In practice, France and Spain provide for Andorra's defense, and the Barcelona police and French

gendarmerie alternate year by year in assisting the 32–man Andorran police to maintain order within the country.

Andorra is a member of UNESCO, but until 1993 France played the primary role in handling its diplomatic affairs, the Bishop of Seo de Urgel having no official international status. Its 1993 constitution permits Andorra to conduct its own foreign policy. It immediately joined the UN as a full member, entered the Council of Europe in 1994, and tightened its ties with the EU. The United States' relations with Andorra have traditionally been conducted through its consulate in Barcelona.

ECONOMY

Since only 4% of the country's land can be cultivated, most of its food must be imported. It owes its livelihood to tourism and to its status as a free port (duty–free marketplace) for manufactured goods from many industrialized nations. This duty–free status makes Andorra one of the most active smuggling centers of Europe, an activity which French and Spanish customs officials have difficulty controlling due to the country's remote and rugged frontier, and due also to the impossibility of checking all the thousands of automobiles which cross its borders daily. Andorra refuses to make smuggling a penal offense. Therefore, dealing in contraband, by either organized criminals or legal merchants, thrives. So do money laundering and the hiding of assets. In 2000 the OECD placed Andorra on a list of unfair tax havens. It reached an agreement with the EU in 2003 to collect taxes for bank account interest and return 75% of it to the country of residence without providing account holders' names.

This tiny country absorbs 12 million visitors each year—two–thirds of them from Spain. What awaits this throng of visitors are good bargains at gaudy shops, but also long traffic jams, tight parking, exhaust–filled air, shoulder–to–shoulder walking, and almost interminable waiting at the border. For export, it manufactures cigars and cigarettes, matches, anisette liqueur and sandals. It also produces for sale that customary product of micro-states: beautiful postage stamps, although no postage whatsoever is required for mail *within* the country. In January 2002 the euro became the official currency.

Both France and Spain want to limit Andorra's duty–free business. Many Andorrans fear that the attractiveness of a shopping trip to their country will decline in the future. Andorra's favorable trade agreements with Spain and France give it legal trade outlets to the entire EU. In 1990, for the first time 700 years, Andorra signed an international treaty, approving a trade agreement with the EU. It makes Andorra a member of the EU customs union. It permits industrial goods to flow freely to and from the EU and obligates Andorra to apply the EU's external tariffs on such goods to third countries. Full EU membership must wait. Spain insists that Andorra introduce adequate labor and social security laws for the 20,000 Spaniards who work in Andorra, mainly in tourism, before the tiny country is considered for EU membership. Andorra's 1993 constitution permits the establishment of labor unions, hitherto banned.

It has a hydroelectric plant at Escaldes, which provides electricity for Andorra and which exports a modest amount of power to the northern part of Barcelona province and to southern France. Residents of Andorra pay no personal income taxes.

The 1993 constitution grants freedom of religion although Roman Catholicism remains the established church. Andorra's school system is a cumbersome combination of French secular schools and Spanish parochial schools, financed and staffed by France and Spain, and terminating educational possibilities within Andorra at age 14. Because there is no university, young Andorrans go to France or Spain for higher education. Only half of them return, in part because the exorbitant property prices, which have spiraled to Parisian levels, keep them away.

Andorra has one daily newspaper, *Pople Andorra* and one monthly, *Andorra Magazine*. Radio service is provided by the Spanish–owned *Radio Andorra* and the French–owned *Sud Radio*, and Andorrans can receive one Spanish and two French television stations. There are no railroad or airport facilities, but good roads tie the country to Spain and, except in the winter months, to France.

FUTURE

Andorra has undergone great social, economic, and political changes, from a traditional pastoral and farming fiefdom and economy to a sovereign mini–state thriving on commerce and tourism. This process, which has led to a quadrupling of Andorra's population in 25 years, brings both promise and problems to the future Andorra. Population density has become and will remain very high. Tourism is expected to provide prosperity for years to come, but it is uncertain whether such tourism will destroy Andorra's traditions and mountain tranquility. Western Europe's newest sovereign state, with a new constitution and its first general elections in 1993, Andorra can face the future with confidence.

Web Sites and Bibliography of Key English-Language Books

WEB SITES

Useful Web Sites on the UN, EU, OECD, NATO and other:

www.un.org (Web site for United Nations. Many links.)

www.unsystem.or (Official UN website)

http://europa.eu.int (EU server site)

http://ue.eu.int (The Council of European Union site)

http://europa.eu.int/comm (European Commission site)

http://www.euobserver.com (EU news)

http://www.euractiv.com (European news)

www.EU-Values.org (Site maintained by students and staff of the College of Europe, Bruges)

http://www.europarl.eu.int (European Parliament)

http://european-convention.EU.int/ (Site for EU constitutional convention)

www.euractiv.com (Diverse news on EU and Europe)

www.aktion-euro.de (Site for the euro currency)

www.europeanaccess.co.uk (Links to various subjects)

www.eurunion.org (EU delegation of the European Commission to the U.S.)

www.oecd.org/daf/cmis/fdi/statist.htm (OECD site)

www.osce.org (Site of OSCE)

www.nato.int/structur/nids/nids.htm (NATO documentation, NATO Review)

www.nato.org and www.NATO.int (Web sites for NATO. Many links.)

www.wto.org (World Trade Organization site)

www.worldbank.org/html/Welcome.html (World Bank news, publications with links to other financial institutions)

www.ceip.org (Carnegie Endowment for International Peace, using a fully integrated Web-database system)

www.cia.gov/index.html (Central Intelligence Agency)

www.odci.gov/cia (Includes useful CIA publications, such as The World Factbook and maps)

www.state.gov/www/ind.html (U.S. Department of State, including country reports)

lcweb2.loc.gov/frd/cs/cshome.html (Library of Congress with coverage of over 100 countries)

Newspapers, Journals and Television with good coverage on European affairs:

www.chicagotribune.com (Named best overall US newspaper online service for newspapers with circulation over 100,000.)

www.csmonitor.com (Respected U.S. newspaper, *Christian Science Monitor*. Named best overall US newspaper on-line service for newspapers with circulation under 100,000.)

www.economist.com (British weekly news magazine)

www.nytimes.com (Respected U.S. newspaper, *The New York Times*)

www.washingtonpost.com

www.IHT.com (*International Herald Tribune*, published and distributed in Europe)

www.Europeanvoice.com (Weekly newspaper with EU and European news)

www.timeeurope.com (European edition of *Time*)

www.foreignaffairs.org (One of best-known international affairs journal)

www.cnn.com (Latest news with external links)

www.news.BBC.co.uk (British Broadcasting Corporation site)

www.c-span.org (Includes C-SPAN International)

Country Web Sites:

www.embassy.org (This website contains links to all embassies in Washington)

www.britain-info.org (British press reports with links)

http://www.european-defence.co.uk (UK defense)

www.fco.gov.UK (British Foreign and Commonwealth Office site)

www.mod.uk (British Ministry of Defence site)

www.irlgov.ie/frmain.htm (Irish government cite)

www.info-france-usa.org (French culture and government)

www.NBT.nl (Netherlands, with links to many subjects)

www.parlement.nl (Dutch parliamentary site)

www.expatica.com (Dutch news)

www.Belgium.fgov.be (Cite of Belgian government)

www.vlaanderen.be (Flemish Community in Belgium)

www.cfwb.be (French Community in Belgium)

www.wallonie.org (Walloon Region in Belgium)

www.europeonline.com/bel/index_gb.htm (Belgian cite)

www.restena.lu/luxembourg/(various topics with links)

www.admin.ch (Swiss cite)

www.firstlink.li (Liechtenstein site)

www.news.li (news of Liechtenstein)

www.tourismus.li (Liechtenstein tourism)

www.mi.cnr.it/WOI/ (Italian history and cities)

http://cca.imediata.pt (American Chamber of Commerce in Portugal)

www.vatican.va/ (Vatican site)

http://searchmalta.com (Malta)

http://www.magnet .mt (Malta's government website)

www.timesofmalta.com

www.independent.com.mt (Maltese newspaper in English)

http://inthenet.sm/rsm/intro.htm (San Marino)

GENERAL

Barzini, Luigi. *The Europeans*. New York: Simon Schuster, 1983.

Bell, David S. *Western European Communists and the Collapse of Communism*. Oxford: Berg, 1993.

Black, Cyril E., et al. *Rebirth. A History of Europe Since World War II*. Boulder, CO: Westview, 1992.

Calleo, David P. *Rethinking Europe's Future*. Princeton: Princeton University Press, 2001.

Cole, John and Francis. *The Geography of the European Community*. New York: Routledge, 1993.

Craig, Gordon A. *Europe Since 1815*. 3rd ed. New York: Holt, Rinehart Winston, 1971.

Curtis, Michael. *Western European Government and Politics*. New York: Longman, 1997.

Dinan, Desmond, ed. *Encyclopedia of the European Union*. Updated ed. Boulder, CO: Lynne Reinner, 2000.

———. *Ever Closer Union: An Introduction to European Integration*. 2d ed. Boulder, CO: Lynne Reinner, 1999.

Dragnich, Alex N., Rasmussen, Jorgen S, and Moses, Joel C. *Major European Governments*. 9th ed. Chicago: The Dorsey Press, 1994.

Dunkerley, David et al. *Changing Europe. Identitites, Nations and Citizens*. NY: Routledge, 2002.

Dyker, David. *The European Economy*. New York: Longman, 1992.

———. *The National Economies of Europe*. New York: Longman, 1992.

Dyson, Kenneth, and Featherstone, Kevin. *The Road to Maastricht. Negotiating Economic and Monetary Union*. New York: Oxford University, 2000.

Duroselle, Jean–Baptiste. *Europe: A History of its Peoples*. New York: Viking, 1990.

Gallagher, Michael, et al. *Representative Government in Western Europe*. 3d ed. New York: McGraw Hill, 2001.

Gärtner, Heinz et al. *Europe's New Security Challenges*. Boulder, CO: Lynne Rienner, 2001.

George, Stephen and Ian Bache. *Politics in the European Union*. New York: Oxford, 2001.

Giustino, David de. *A Reader in European Integration. A selection of key documents*. New York: Longman, 1996.

Goodby, James, et al. *A Strategy for Stable Peace. Toward a Euroatlantic Security Community*. Washington: Association for Diplomatic Studies and Training, 2002.

Hancock, M. Donald, et al. *Politics in Western Europe*. 2d ed. Chatham, NJ: Chatham House, 1998.

Hitchcock, William I. *The Struggle for Europe: The Turbulent History of a Divided Continent 1945–2002*. NY: Doubleday, 2003.

Hix, Simon. *The Political System of the European Union*. New York: St. Martin's Press, 1999.

Hunter, Robert E. *The European Security and Defense Policy. NATO's Companion—or Competitor?* Santa Monica, CA: Rand, 2002.

Jones, Robert A. *The Politics and Economics of the European Union*. Williston, VT: Edger Elgar, 1996.

Kagan, Robert. *Of Paradise and Power. America and Europe in the New World Order*. NY: Alfred A. Knopf, 2003.

Kesselman, Mark, et al. *European Politics in Transition*, 4th ed. New York: Houghton Mifflin, 2002.

Kramer, Jane. *Europeans*. New York: Penguin, 1992.

Lane, Jan–Erik and Ersson, Svante O. *European Politics*. 4th ed. Beverly Hills: Sage, 1998.

Laqueur, Walter. *Europe in Our Time. A History, 1945–1992*. New York: Penguin, 1993.

Mahncke, Dieter and Wayne C. Thompson and Wyn Rees. *The Challenges of Change: Redefining Transatlantic Relations*. Manchester, UK: Manchester University Press, 2003.

Mair, Peter, ed. *The Western Europe Party System*. Oxford: Oxford University Press, 1990.

McCormick, John. *Understanding the European Union. A Concise Introduction*, 2d ed. NY: Palgrave, 2002.

Miller, Steven L., ed. *European Unification: A Conceptual Guide for Educators*. Bloomington, IN: ERIC Clearing House for Social Studies, 1995.

Nugent, Neill. *The Government and Politics of the European Union*. 4th ed. Durham, NC: Duke University, 1999.

Pells, Richard. *Not Like Us. How Europeans Have Loved, Hated and Transformed American Culture Since World War II*. New York: Basic Books, 1997.

Pinder, John. *European Community. The Building of a Union*. 3d ed. Oxford: Oxford University Press, 1998.

Perry, Marvin. *An Intellectual History of Modern Europe*. Boston: Houghton Mifflin, 1993.

Peterson, John and Michael Shackleton. *The Institutions of the European Union*. New York: Oxford University Press, 2002.

Pond, Elizabeth. *The Rebirth of Europe*, 2d ed. Washington D.C.: Brookings, 2002.

Roberts, Geoffrey and Hogwood, Patricia. *European Politics Today*. New York: St. Martin's, 1997.

Salmon, Trevor C. and Alistair Shepherd. *Toward a European Army: A Military Power in the Making?* Boulder, CO: Lynne Rienner, 2003.

Sloan, Stanley R. *NATO, The European Union, and the Atlantic Community. The Transatlantic Bargain Reconsidered*. Lanham, MD: Rowman & Littlefield, 2003.

Slomp, Hans. *European Politics into the Twenty-First Century. Integration and Division*. Westport, CT: Greenwood, 2000.

Steiner, Jürg. *European Democracies*. 2d ed. NY: Longman, 1991.

Tsoukalis, Loukas. *The New European Economy*. 3d ed. New York: Oxford University Press, 1996.

Urwin, Derek W. *Western Europe since 1945. A Political History*. 5th ed. New York: Longman, 1997.

———. *The Community of Europe. A History of European Integration since 1945*. New York: Longman, 1991.

———. *Dictionary of European History and Politics Since 1945*. New York: Longman, 1996.

Warmenhoven, Henri J. *Western Europe*. Guilford, CT: Dushkin, annually updated.

Young, John W. *Cold War Europe. 1945–1989*. New York: Routledge, 1991.

Great Britain

Adolino, Jessica R. *Ethnic Minorities, Electoral Politics, and Political Integration in Britain*. Herndon, VA: Cassell, 1998.

Ascherson, Neal. *Stone Voices: The Search for Scotland*. NY: Hill and Wang, 2003.

Baylis, John. *Anglo–American Relations Since the Second World War*. New York: St. Martin's, 1997.

Blair, Tony. *New Britain*. Boulder, CO: Westview, 1997.

Bartlett, C.J. *The Special Relationship. A Political History of Anglo–American Relations since 1945*. New York: Longman, 1992.

Beer, Samuel H. *Britain Against Itself*. New York: Norton, 1982.

———. *Modern British Politics. Parties and Pressure Groups in the Collectivist Age*. rev. ed. New York: Norton, 1982.

Birch, Anthony H. *The British System of Government*. 8th ed. New York: Routledge, 1990.

Briggs, Asa. *A Social History of England*. London: Weidenfeld Nicolson, 1983.

Budge, Ian, and McKay, David, et al. *The Changing British Political System. Into the 1990s*. New York: Longman, 1988.

Butler, David and Sloman, Anne, eds. *British Political Facts, 1900–1979*. 5th ed. New York: St. Martin's Press, 1980.

Cashmore, E. Ellis. *United Kingdom? Class, Race, and Gender since the War*. Winchester: Unwin Hyman, 1989.

Childs, David. *Britain since 1945*. 3d ed. New York: Routledge, 1992.

Clarke Michael. *British External Policy-making in the 1990s*. Washington, D.C.: Brookings, 1992.

Colley, Linda. *Britons. Forging the Nation, 1707–1837*. New Haven, CT: Yale University Press, 1992.

Croft, Stuart. *British Security Policy. The Thatcher Years and the End of the Cold War*. New York: Routledge, 1992.

Crossman, R. H. S. *Introduction to Bagehot's English Constitution*. London: Fontana, 1963.

Davies, John. *A History of Wales*. New York: Penguin, 2000.

Davis, Charlotte. *Welsh Nationalism in the Twentieth Century*. Westport, CT: Praeger, 1989.

Devine, T.M. *The Scottish Nation. 1700–2000*. New York: Penguin, 2000.

Edgell, Stephen and Duke, Vic. A Measure of Thatcherism. *A Sociology of Britain in the 1980s*. New York: Routledge, 1991.

Evans, Eric J. *Thatcher and Thatcherism*, 2d ed. NY: Routledge, 2002.

Forman, F.N. *Constitutional Change in the United Kingdom*. NY: Routledge, 2002.

Forster, Anthony. *Euroscepticism in British Politics*. NY: Routledge, 2002.

Freedman, Lawrence. *Britain and the Falklands War*. Cambridge, MA: Basil Blackwell, 1988.

Garner, Robert and Richard Kelly. *British Political Parties Today*. 2d ed. Manchester: Manchester University Press, 1998.

Hardie, Frank. *The Political Influence of the British Monarchy, 1868–1952*. London: Batsford, 1970.

Harvie, Christopher. *Scotland and Nationalism. Scottish Society and Politics 1707–1994*. New York: Routledge, 1994.

Havighurst, Alfred F. *Britain in Transition: the Twentieth Century*. Chicago: University of Chicago Press, 1979.

Holliday, Ian, ed. *Fundamentals in British Politics*. New York: St. Martin's, 1999.

Irwin, John. *Modern Britain. An Introduction*. 3d ed. New York: Routledge, 1994.

James, Simon. *British Cabinet Government*. New York: Routledge, 1992.

Jones, R. Brinley, ed. *The Anatomy of Wales*. Peterson–super–Hy: Gwerin, 1972.

Kavanagh, Dennis A. *British Politics*. Oxford: 3d ed. Oxford University Press, 1996.

———. *Thatcherism and British Politics. The End of Consensus?* 2d ed. Oxford: Oxford University Press, 1990.

King, Anthony, et al. *Britain at the Polls, 1992*. Chatham, NJ: Chatham House, 1992.

Bibliography

———. et al. *New Labour Triumphs: Britain at the Polls*. Chatham, NJ: Chatham House, 1998.

Kirk, Russell. *America's British Culture*. New Brunswick, NJ: Transaction, 1992.

Krieger, Joel. Reagan, *Thatcher, and the Politics of Decline*. New York: Oxford University Press, 1986.

Major, John. *John Major: The Autobiography*. London: HarperCollins, 1999.

Marwick, Arthur. *Culture in Britain Since 1945*. Cambridge, MA: Basil Blackwell, 1991.

Major, John. *John Major: The Autobiography*. London: HarperCollins, 1999.

McCrone, David. *Understanding Scotland. The Sociology of a Nation*. NY: Routledge, 2001.

Mitchinson, John, and Merullo, Annabil. *British Greats*. London: Cassell, 2000.

Morgan, Kenneth O. *Labour People*. Oxford: Oxford University Press, 1987.

———. ed. *The Oxford History of Britain*. Rev. ed. New York: Oxford University, 1999.

Norton, Philip. *The British Polity*. 3d ed. New York: Longman, 1994.

Paterson, Alan. *The Law Lords*. London: Macmillan, 1982.

Pearce, Malcolm and Stewart, Geoff. British *Political History 1867–1990*. New York: Routledge, 1992.

Pilkington, Colin. *Representative Democracy in Britain Today*. Manchester: Manchester University Press, 1997.

Rasmussen, Jorgen S. *British Politics*. Belmont, CA: Wadsworth, 1993.

Reitan, Earl A. Tory Radicalism. *Margaret Thatcher, John Major, and the Transformation of Modern Britain*. Lanham, MD: Rowman & Littlefield, 1997.

Rentoul, John. *Tony Blair: Prime Minister*. Boston: Little, Brown, 2001.

Riddell, Peter. *The Thatcher Decade. How Britain has Changed During the 1980s*. Cambridge, MA: Basil Blackwell, 1989.

Robbins, Keith. *Nineteenth–Century Britain. England, Scotland and Wales: The Making of a Nation*. Oxford: Oxford University Press, 1988.

Rose, Richard. *Politics in England*. 5th ed. New York: Harper Collins, 1989.

Royle, Edward. *Modern Britain. A Social History, 1750–1997*. 2d ed. New York: Oxford University, 1997.

Särlvik, Bo and Crewe, Ivor. *Decade of Dealignment: The Conservative Victory of 1979 and Electoral Trends in the 1970s*. Cambridge: Cambridge University Press, 1983.

Seitz, Raymond. *Over Here*. London: Phoenix, 1998.

Seldon, Anthony, ed. *Conservative Century. The Conservative Party Since 1900*. Oxford: Oxford University, 1994.

Shaw, Eric. *The Labour Party Since 1979. Crisis and Transformation*. New York: Routledge, 1994.

Shell, Donald and Beamish, David, eds. *The House of Lords at Work*. Oxford: Oxford University, 1993.

Sked, Alan and Chris Cook. *Post-War Britain: A Political History*. 2d ed. New York: Penquin, 1990.

Skidelsky, Robert, ed. *Thatcherism*. Cambridge, MA: Basil Blackwell, 1990.

Smith, Julie and Mariana Tsatsas. *The New bilateralism. The UK's Relations within the EU*. Washington, D.C.: Brookings, 2002.

Smith, Martin J. and Spear, Joanna. *The Changing Labour Party*. New York: Routledge, 1992.

Thatcher, Margaret. *The Path to Power and Downing Street Years*. 2 vols. New York: HarperCollins, 1993, 1995.

———. *Statecraft: Strategies for a Changing World*. New York: HarperCollins, 2002.

Thompson, Juliet S. and Wayne C. Margaret Thatcher. *Prime Minister Indomitable*. Boulder, CO: Westview, 1994.

Trevelyan, G. M. *History of England*. London: Longmans, 1963.

White, Brian. *Britain, Detente and Chaning East–West Relations*. New York: Routledge, 1992.

Williams, Glyn and Ramsden, John. *Ruling Britannia. A Political History of Britain 1688–1988*. New York: Longman, 1990.

Young, Hugo. *The Iron Lady. A Biography of Margaret Thatcher*. New York: Farrar Straus and Giroux, 1989.

Young, John W. *Britain and the World in the Twentieth Century*. New York: Oxford University, 1997.

Northern Ireland

Arthur, Paul. *Government and Politics of Northern Ireland*. Second Edition. New York: Longman, 1984.

———. and Jeffery, Keith. *Northern Ireland Since 1968*. Cambridge, MA: Basil Blackwell, 1988.

Aughey, A. and Morrow, D. *Northern Ireland Politics*. New York: Longman, 1997.

Barton, Brian and Patrick J. Roche. *The Northern Ireland Question*. Brookfield, VT: Ashgate, 1999.

Bew, Paul, et al. *The Political Future of Northern Ireland*. Vancouver: University of British Columbia Press, 1993.

Boyle, Keven and Tom Hadden. *Northern Ireland: The Choice*. New York: Praeger, 1998.

Bruce, Steve. *God Save Ulster! The Religion and Politics of Paisleyism*. Oxford: Oxford University Press, 1989.

———. *The Edge of the Union. The Ulster Loyalist Political Vision*. Oxford: Oxford University, 1994.

Elliott, Marianne. *The Catholics of Ulster. A History*. NY: Basic Books, 2002.

Farren, Sean, and Mulvihill, Robert F. *Paths to a Settlement in Northern Ireland*. New York: Oxford University, 2000.

Feeney, Brian. *Sinn Fein. A Hundred Turbulent Years*. Madison: University of Wisconsin Press, nd.

Gaffikin, Frank and Morrissey, Mike. *Northern Ireland. The Thatcher Years*. Atlantic Highlands, NJ: Humanities Press, 1990.

Geraghty, Tony. *The Irish War. The Hidden Conflict between the IRA and British Intelligence*. Baltimore: Johns Hopkins University, 2000.

Hull, R. H. *Irish Triangle*. Princeton: Princeton University Press, n.d.

Irvine, Maurice. *Northern Ireland*. Faith and Faction. New York: Routledge, 1991.

McGarry, John, ed. *The Future of Northern Ireland*. Oxford: Oxford University Press, 1991.

Mitchell, Paul and Rick Wilford, eds. *Politics in Northern Ireland*. Boulder, CO: Westview, 1998.

Ruane, Joseph and Todd, Jennifer. *The Dynamics of Conflict in Northern Ireland*. New York: Cambridge University Press, 1996.

Whyte, John and Fitzgerald, Garret. *Interpreting Northern Ireland*. Oxford: Oxford University Press, 1991.

Wichert, Sabine. *Northern Ireland since 1945*. New York: Longman, 1991.

Wilson, Tom. *Ulster. Conflict and Consent*. Cambridge, MA: Basil Blackwell, 1989.

Republic of Ireland

Ardagh, John. *Ireland and the Irish. Portrait of a Changing Society*. New York: Penguin, 1998.

Boyce, D. George. *Nationalism in Ireland*. 2d ed. New York: Routledge, 1991.

Busteed, M.A. *Voting Behavior in the Republic of Ireland*. Oxford: Oxford University Press, 1991.

Carter, R.W. and Parker, A.J. Ireland. *Contemporary Perspectives on a Land and its People*. New York: Routledge, 1990.

Chubb, Basil. *The Government and Politics of Ireland*. 3d ed. New York: Longman, 1992.

Collins, Neil and McCann, Frank. *Irish Politics Today*. 3d. ed. New York: St. Martin's, 1997.

Curtis, Edmund. *A History of Ireland*. London: Methuen, 1961.

Fitzgerald, Garret. *All in a Life*. London: Macmillan, 1991.

Foster, R.F., ed. *The Oxford History of Ireland*. New York: Oxford University, 1992.

Fulton, John. *The Tragedy of Belief. Division, Politics, and Religion in Ireland.* Oxford: Oxford University Press, 1991.

Keatinge, Patrick. *Ireland and EC Membership Evaluated.* New York: St. Martin's, 1992.

Macardle, Dorothy. *The Irish Republic.* Dublin: Irish Press, 1951.

Mallie, Eamonn and David McKittrick. *Endgame in Ireland.* Hodder & Stoughton, 2001.

McCaffrey, Lawrence J. *Ireland from Colony to Nation–State.* Englewood Cliffs, NJ: Prentice–Hall, 1977.

Munck, Ronnie. *The Irish Economy.* Boulder, CO: Westview Press, 1993.

Tanner, Marcus. *Ireland's Holy Wars: The Struggle for a Nation's Soul, 1500–2000.* New Haven: Yale University Press, 2001.

Townshend, Charles. *Political Violence in Ireland.* Oxford: Oxford University Press, 1985.

———. *Ireland. The 20th Century.* New York: Oxford University, 1999.

Uris, Leon. *Trinity.* New York: Doubleday, 1975.

France

Adams, William James. *Restructuring the French Economy: Government and the Rise of Market Competition Since World War II.* Washington, D.C.: Brookings, 1989.

Alexander, Martin S. *French History Since Napoleon.* New York: Oxford University, 1999.

Ardagh, John. *France Today.* rev. ed. New York: Penguin, 1991.

Bell, David S. *The French Socialist Party.* Oxford: Oxford University Press, 1988.

———. and Criddle, Byron. *The French Communist Party in the Fifth Republic.* Oxford: Oxford University, 1994.

Bernstein, Richard. *Fragile Glory. A Portrait of France and the French.* New York: Alfred A. Knopf, 1990.

Braudel, Fernand. *The Identity of France: History and Environment.* New York: Harper and Collins, 1989.

Brenner, Michael and Guillaume Parmentier. *Reconcilable Differences. U.S.-French Relations in the New Era.* Washington D.C.: Brookings, 2002.

Bridgford, Jeff. *The Politics of French Trade Unionism.* New York: St. Martin's, 1992.

Brogan, D. W. *France Under the Republic (1870–1939).* New York: Harper and Row, 1940.

Cole, Alistair. *François Mitterrand. A Study in Political Leadership.* New York: Routledge, 1994.

Cross, Maire and Sheila Perry. *Population and Social Policy in France.* Herndon, VA: Cassell, 1997.

Davies, Peter. *The Extreme Right in France, 1789 to the Present. From De Maistre to Le Pen.* NY: Routledge, 2002.

De Gaulle, Charles. *The War Memoirs of Charles de Gaulle.* 3 vols. New York: Simon Schuster, 1960.

———. *Memoirs of Hope and Endeavor.* New York: Simon Schuster, 1970.

Doyle, William. *The Oxford History of the French Revolution.* Oxford: Oxford University Press, 1990.

Ehrmann, Henry and Schain, Martin A. *Politics in France.* 5th ed. New York: Harper Collins, 1992.

Friend, Julius W. *The Long Presidency: France in the Mitterrand Years, 1981–1995.* Boulder, CO: Westview, 1999.

_____. *Unequal Partners. French-German Relations, 1989–2000.* Washington: CSIS Press, 2001.

Gaffney, John. *The French Left and the Fifth Republic: The Discourses of Communism and Socialism in Contemporary France.* New York: St. Martin's, 1989.

Gildea, Robert. *France Since 1945.* Oxford: Oxford University Press, 1996.

Gopnik, Adam. *Paris to the Moon.* New York: Random House, 2000.

Gordon, Philip H. *A Certain Idea of France. French Security Policy and the Gaullist Legacy.* Princeton: Princeton University Press, 1993.

_____ and Sophie Meunier. *The French Challenge. Adapting to Globalization.* Washington D.C.: Brookings, 2001.

Hanley, David. *Party, Society, Government. Republican Democracy in France.* New York: Berghahn, 2001.

Hazareesingh, Sudhir. *Political Traditions in Modern France.* Oxford: Oxford University, 1994.

Higonnet, Patrice. *Paris: Capital of the World.* NY: Belknap, 2002.

Hirschfeld, Gerhard. *Collaboration in France. Politics and Culture during the Nazi Occupation, 1940–1944.* Oxford: Berg, 1989.

Hoffmann, Stanley and Ross, George, eds. *Continuity and Change in Mitterrand's France.* New York: Oxford University Press, 1987.

Hollifield, James F. and Ross, George, eds. *Searching for the New France.* New York: Routledge, 1992.

Holman, Valerie, ed. *France at War in the Twentieth Century. Propaganda, Myth and Metaphor.* New York: Berghahn, 2000.

Horne, Alistair. *Seven Ages of Paris: Portrait of a City.* NY: Alfred A. Knopf, 2002.

Jackson, Julian. *France: The Dark Years, 1940–1944.* Oxford: Oxford University Press, 2001.

Jones, Colin. *The Great Nation: France from Louis XV to Napoleon, 1715–99.* NY: Allen Lane/The Penguin Press, 2002.

Keiger, John. *France and the World in the Twentieth Century.* New York: Oxford University, 2000.

Larkin, Maurice. *France Since the Popular Front. Government and People, 1936–1986.* Oxford: Oxford University Press, 1988.

Lewis–Beck, ed. *How France Votes.* Chatham, NJ: Chatham House, 1999.

May, Catherine. *The Black and the Red.* (Biography of Mitterrand). NY: Harcourt Brace Jovanovich, 1987.

McMillan, James F. *Twentieth Century France. Politics and Society in France, 1898–1991.* New York: Routledge, 1992.

Morris, Peter. *French Politics Today.* New York: St. Martin's, 1994.

Northcutt, Wayne. Mitterrand. *A Political Biography.* New York: Holmes and Meier, 1992.

Perry, Sheila. *Voices of France. Social, Political and Cultural Identity.* Herndon, VA: Cassell, 1997.

Safran, William. *The French Polity.* 3d ed. New York: Longman, 1991.

Schoenbrun, David. *Soldiers of the Night: The Story of the French Resistance.* New York: New American Library, 1981.

Stevens, Anne. *The Government and Politics of France.* New York: St. Martin's, 1992.

Tilly, Charles. *The Contentious French: Four Centuries of Popular Struggle.* Cambridge: Harvard University Press, 1986.

Tocqueville, Alexis de. *The Old Regime and the French Revolution.* New York: Doubleday Anchor, 1955.

Védrine, Hubert with Dominique Moisi. *France in an Age of Globalization.* Washington: Brookings Institution, 2001.

Wahl, Nicholas, ed. *DeGaulle and the United States, 1930–1970.* Oxford: Berg, 1992.

Wall, Irwin M. *France, The United States, and the Algerian War.* Ithaca, NY: Cornell University Press, 2001.

Wright, Vincent. *The Government and Politics of France.* 4th ed. New York: Routledge, 1994.

Zeldin, Theodore. *The French.* New York: Pantheon Books, 1982.

The BENELUX Countries

General

Eych, F. Gunther. *The Benelux Countries: An Historical Survey.* Princeton: Van Nostrand, 1959.

Kossman, E. H. *The Low Countries, 1780–1940.* Oxford: Oxford Univ. Press, 1978.

Stein, George J. *Benelux Security Cooperation.* Boulder, CO: Westview, 1990.

Weil, Gordon L. *The Benelux Nations: The Politics of Small–Country Democracies.* New York: Holt, Rinehart Winston, 1970.

Bibliography

The Netherlands

Anderweg, Rudi B. and Galen A. Irwin. *Governance and Politics of the Netherlands*. New York: Palgrave Macmillan, 2002.

Bakvis, Herman. *Catholic Power in the Netherlands*. Toronto: McGill–Queen's Univ. Press, 1981.

Cox, Robert H. *The Development of the Dutch Welfare State*. Pittsburgh: University of Pittsburgh Press, 1993.

Daalder, Hans and Irwin, Galen A. *Politics in the Netherlands. How much change?* Portland, OR: Frank Cass, 1989.

Gladdish, Ken. *Governing from the Center. Politics and Policy–Making in the Netherlands*. DeKalb, IL: Northern Illinois University Press, 1992.

Israel, Jonathan I. *Dutch Primacy in World Trade, 1585–1740*. Oxford: Oxford University Press, 1990.

Lijphart, Arend. *The Politics of Accommodation: Pluralism and Democracy in the Netherlands*. Berkeley: University of California Press, 1968.

Mak, Geert. *Amsterdam*. Cambridge, MA: Harvard University Press, 2000.

Wolters, Menno and Coffey, Peter. *The Netherlands and EC Membership Evaluated*. New York: St. Martin's, 1990.

Belgium

Belgium: A State of Mind. (ISBN: 9020244649). Lannoo, 2001.

Boudart, Marina, et al. *Modern Belgium*. Palo Alto, CA: SPOSS, 1990.

Cowie, Donald. Belgium: *The Land and the People*. Cranbury, NJ: A. S. Barnes, 1977.

Fox, Renée. *In the Belgian Chateau. The Spirit and Culture of a European Society in an Age of Change*. Chicago: Ivan R. Dee, nd.

Hochschild, Adam. *King Leopold's Ghost. A Story of Greed, Terror, and Heroism in Colonial Africa*. New York: Houghton Mifflin. A Mariner Book, 1998.

Hooghe, Liesbet. *A Leap in the Dark. Nationalist Conflict and Federal Reform in Belgium*. Ithaca, NY: Cornell University Press, 1993.

Fitzmaurice, J. *Politics of Belgium. Crisis and Compromise in a Plural Society*. New York: St. Martin's Press, 1983.

Lijphart, Arend, ed. *Conflict and Coexistence in Belgium*. Berkeley: University of California Press, 1980.

Meerhaeghe, M.A.G. van. *Belgium and EC Membership Evaluated*. New York: St. Martin's, 1992.

Meeus, Adrien de. *History of the Belgians*. New York: Praeger, 1962.

Strikwerda, Carl. *A House Divided. Catholics, Socialists, and Flemish Nationalists in Nineteenth Century Belgium*. Lanham, MD: Rowman and Littlefield, 1998.

Luxembourg

Barteau, Harry C. *Historical Dictionary of Luxembourg*. Metuchen, NJ: Scarecrow Press, 1996.

Majerus, Pierre. *The Institutions of the Grand Duchy of Luxembourg*. Luxembourg: Ministry of State Press and Information Service, 1976.

Margue, Paul. *A Short History of Luxembourg*. Luxembourg: Ministry of State Press and Information Service, 1976.

Switzerland

Bonjour, E., et al. *A Short History of Switzerland*. Oxford: Clarendon, 1972.

Bradfield, B. *The Making of Switzerland: From Ice Age to Common Market*. Zurich: Schweizer Spiegel Verlag, 1964.

Craig, Gordon A. *The Triumph of Liberalism: Zurich in the Golden Age, 1830–1869*. New York: Collier, 1990.

Gstöhl, Sieglinde. *Reluctant Europeans: Norway, Sweden, and Switzerland in the Process of Integration*. Boulder, CO: Lynn Rienner, 2002.

Hilowitz, Janet Eve. *Switzerland in Perspective*. Westport, CT: Greenwood, 1990.

Kieser, Rolf and Spillman, Kurt R., eds. *The New Switzerland. Problems and Policies*. Palo Alto, CA: SPROSS, 1996.

Linder, Wolf. *Swiss Democracy*. New York: St. Martin's, 1994.

Luck, Murray J. *History of Switzerland: The First Hundred Thousand Years From Before the Beginning to the Days of the Present*. Palo Alto, CA: SPROSS, 1985.

McPhee, John. *La Place de la Concorde Suisse*. New York: Farrar/Straus/ Giroux, 1983.

Milivojevic, Marko, and Mauerer, Pierre. *Swiss Neutrality and Security. Armed Forces, National Defence and Foreign Policy*. New York: St. Martin's, 1991.

Remak, Joachim. *A Very Civil War. The Swiss Sonderbund War of 1847*. Boulder, CO: Westview, 1993.

Sorell, Walter. *The Swiss*. New York: Bobbs–Merrill, 1972.

Steinberg, J. *Why Switzerland*. 2d ed. Cambridge: Cambridge University Press, 1996.

Steiner, Jürg. *Amicable Agreement Versus Majority Rule: Conflict Resolution in Switzerland*. Chapel Hill: University of North Carolina Press, 1974.

———. *Conscience in Politics*. Levittown, PA: Garland, 1996.

Liechtenstein

Kranz, Walter, ed. *The Principality of Liechtenstein: A Documentary Handbook*. Schaan: Lingg, 1973.

Raton, Pierre. *Liechtenstein: History and Institutions of the Principality*. Vaduz: Liechtenstein Verlag, 1970.

Schlapp, Manfred. *This is Liechtenstein*. Stuttgart: Seewald, n.d.

Mediterranean Europe

General

Aliboni, Roberto, ed. *Southern European Security in the 1990s*. New York: St. Martin's, 1992.

Chilcote, Ronald H., et al. *Transitions from Dictatorship to Democracy: Comparative Studies of Spain, Portugal and Greece*. Bristol, PA: Crane Russak, 1990.

Kurth, James, and Petras, James. *Mediterranean Paradoxes. The Politics and Social Structure of Southern Europe*. Oxford: Berg, 1992.

Liebert, Ulrike and Cotta, Maurizio, eds. *Parliament and Democratic Consolidation in Southern Europe. Italy, Spain, Portugal, Greece and Turkey in Comparison*. New York: Columbia University Press, 1990.

Italy

Barkan, Joanne. *Visions of Emancipation: The Italian Workers' Movement Since 1945*. New York: Praeger, 1984.

Barzini, Luigi. *The Italians*. New York: Atheneum, 1977.

Bull, Martin and Martin Rhodes, eds. *Crisis and Transition in Italian Politics*. Portland, OR: Frank Cass, 1997.

Burnett, Stanton H. and Luca Mantovani. *The Italian Guillotine: Operation Clean Hands and the Overthrow of Italy's First Republic*. Washington D.C.: CSIS, 1998

Catanzaro, Raimondo, ed. *The Red Brigades and Left–Wing Terrorism in Italy*. New York: St. Martin's, 1991.

Caesar, Michael, and Hainsworth, Peter, eds. *Writers and Society in Contemporary Italy*. 2d rev. ed. Oxford: Berg, 1993.

Chubb, Judith. *Patronage, Power and Poverty in Southern Italy: A Tale of Two Cities*. Cambridge: Cambridge University Press, 1982.

D'Alimonte, Roberto and David Nelken, eds. *Italian Politics. The Center–Left in Power*. Boulder, CO: Westview, 1997.

DiScala, Spencer M. Italy. *From Revolution to Republic. 1700 to the Present*. Boulder, CO: Westview, 1998.

Duggan, Christopher and Wagstaff, Christopher, eds. *Italy in the Cold War. Politics, Culture and Society 1948–1958*. Oxford: Berg, 1993.

Farneti, Paolo. *The Italian Party System*. London: Frances Pinter, 1985.

Francioni, Francesco, ed. *Italy and EC Membership Evaluated*. New York: St. Martin's, 1992.

Furlong, Paul. Modern Italy. *Representation and Reform*. New York: Routledge, 1994.

Giammanco, Rosanna Mulazzi. *The Catholic–Communist Dialogue in Italy: 1944 to the Present*. Westport, CT: Praeger, 1989.

Gilbert, Mark. *The Italian Revolution. The End of Politics, Italian Style?* Boulder, CO: Westview, 1995.

Ginsborg, Paul. *A History of Contemporary Italy. Society and Politics 1943–1988.* New York: Palgrave Macmillan, 2003.

_____. *Italy and its Disontents: 1980–2001.* New York: Penguin, 2002.

Hearder, Harry. *Italy: A Short History.* Cambridge: Cambridge University Press, 1990.

Hibbert, Christopher. *Rome: The Biography of a City.* New York: Viking, n.d.

Hine, David. *Governing Italy. The Politics of Bargained Pluralism.* Oxford: Oxford University Press, 1993.

Kertzer, David I. *Comrades and Christians. Religion and Political Struggle in Communist Italy.* Prospect Heights, IL: Waveland, 1992.

Kogan, Norman H. *Political History of Postwar Italy: From the Old to the New Center Left.* New York: Praeger, 1981.

Levy, Carl, ed. *Italian Regionalism. History, Identity and Politics.* New York: Berg, 1996.

Locke, Richard M. *Remaking the Italian Economy.* Ithaca, NY: Cornell University Press, 1997.

Leonardi, Robert and Wertman, Douglas A. *Italian Christian Democracy.* New York: St. Martin's, 1989.

McCarthy, Patrick. *The Crisis of the Italian State.* New York: St. Martin's, 1997.

Moss, David. *The Politics of Left–Wing Violence in Italy, 1969–85.* New York: St. Martin's, 1990.

Mountjoy, Alan B. *The Mezzogiorno.* New York: Oxford University Press, 1973.

Partridge, Hillary. *Italian Politics Today.* New York: St. Martin's, 1998.

Pasquino, Gianfranco and McCarthy, Patrick. *Elections in a Changing Italy.* Boulder, CO: Westview Press, 1993.

Pinter Publishers, *Italian Politics, A Review.* New York: Columbia University Press, annual updated editions.

Pridham, Geoffrey. *Political Parties and Coalitional Behavior in Italy.* New York: Routledge, 1988.

Procacci, Giuliano. *History of the Italian People.* Hammondsworth, UK: Penguin Books, 1973.

Putnam, Robert D. *Making Democracy Work. Civic Traditions in Modern Italy.* Princeton: Princeton University Press, 1993.

Richards, Charles. *The New Italians.* New York: Penguin, 1995.

Sassoon, Donald. *Contemporary Italy. Politics, Economy Society since 1945.* New York: Longman, 1986.

De Scala, Spencer, M. *Renewing Italian Socialism. Nenni to Craxi.* Oxford: Oxford University Press, 1988.

Sciascia, Leonardo. *The Moro Affair.* Granta Books, 2002.

Spotts, Frederic and Theodor Wieser. *Italy. A Difficult Democracy. A Survey of Italian Politics.* New York: Cambridge University Press, 1986.

Trevelyan, J. O. *A Short History of the Italian People.* London: Allen and Unwin, 1956.

Weinberg, Leonard. *The Transformation of Italian Communism.* New Brunswick, NJ: Transaction, 1995.

San Marino

Bent, James T. *A Freak of Freedom or the Republic of San Marino.* Port Washington, NY: Kennikat, 1970.

Rossi, Giuseppe. *San Marino.* San Marino: Governmental Tourist Body Sport and Spectacle, n.d.

_____. *A Short History of the Republic of San Marino.* San Marino: Poligrafico Artioli–Modena, n.d.

San Marino. Milan: Ediz. Garami (Garanzini Milano), 1977.

Vatican City

Bernstein, Carl and Marco Politi. *His Holiness. John Paul II and the Hidden History of our Time.* New York: Bandam Doubleday Dell, 1996.

Flamini, Roland. *Pope, Premier, President.* New York: Macmillan, 1980.

Kreutz, Andres. *Vatican Policy on the Palestinian–Israeli Conflict: The Struggle for the Holy Land.* Westport, CT: Greenwood, 1990.

La Bello, Nina. *Vatican Empire.* Frieside: SS, 1970.

Nichols, Peter. *The Pope's Divisions.* New York: Holt, Rinehart and Winston, 1981.

Partner, Peter. *The Lands of St. Peter: The Papal State in the Middle Ages and the Early Renaissance.* London: Methuen, 1972.

Walsh, Michael J. *Vatican City State.* Santa Barbara: ABC–Clio, 1983.

Malta

Berg, Warren G. *Historical Dictionary of Malta.* Metuchen, NJ: Scarecrow Press, 1995.

Blouet, Brian. *The Story of Malta.* Rev. ed. London: Faber Faber, 1972.

Sire, H. J. A. *The Knights of Malta.* New Haven, CT: Yale University Press, 1996.

Iberian Peninsula

General

Baklonoff, Eric N. *The Economic Transformation of Spain and Portugal.* New York: Praeger, 1978.

Kohler, Beate. *Political Forces in Spain, Greece and Portugal.* Woburn, MA: Butterworth, 1982.

Mar–Molinero, Clare and Angel Smith. *Nationalism and the Nation in the Iberian Peninsula. Competing and Conflicting Identities.* New York: Berg, 1996.

Michener, James. *Iberia.* New York: Random House, 1968.

Payne, Stanley G. *A History of Spain and Portugal.* 2 vols. Madison: University of Wisconsin Press, 1973.

Tovias, Alfred. *Foreign Economic Relations of the European Community: The Impact of Spain and Portugal.* Boulder, CO: Lynne Rienner, 1990.

Wiarda, Howard J. *Politics in Iberia. The Political Systems of Spain and Portugal.* New York: HarperCollins, 1993.

_____. *Iberia and Latin America. New Democracies, New Policies.* Lanham, MD: Rowman & Littlefield, 1996.

Spain

Alba, Victor. *The Transition in Spain: From Franco to Democracy.* New Brunswick, NJ: Transaction Books, 1978.

_____. *The Communist Party in Spain.* New Brunswick, NJ: Transaction Books, 1983.

Ampara, Almarcha and Ortega, Alfonso, eds. *Spain and EC Membership Evaluated.* New York: St. Martin's, 1993.

Arango, R. *The Spanish Political System.* Boulder, CO: Westview, 1982.

Bertrand, Louis, and Petrie, Sir Charles. *The History of Spain. From the Musulmans to Franco.* New York: Collier Books, 1971.

Carr, Raymond, and Fusi, Juan Pablo. *Spain: Dictatorship to Democracy.* 2nd ed. Winchester, MA: Allen and Unwin, 1981.

_____. *Spain: 1808–1975.* 2nd ed. New York: Oxford Univ. Press, 1982.

Castro, Americo. *The Spaniards: An Introduction to Their History.* Berkeley: University of California Press, 1985.

Collins, Roger. *The Basques.* London: Blackwell, 1987.

Conversi, Daniele. *Nationalist Mobilization in Catalonia and the Basque Country.* Reno: University of Nevada, 1995.

Eaton, Samuel D. *The Forces of Freedom in Spain, 1974–1979.* Palo Alto: Hoover, 1981.

Fusi, J. *Franco: A Biography.* New York: Harper and Row, n.d.

Gil, Federico G. and Tulchin, Joseph S., eds. *Spain's Entry Into NATO.* Boulder, CO: Lynne Rienner, 1988.

Gillespie, Richard. *The Spanish Socialist Party. A History of Factionalism.* Oxford: Oxford University Press, 1989.

_____ and Richard Youngs, eds. *Spain. The European and International Challenges.* Portland, OR: Frank Cass, 2003.

Gilmour, David. The *Transformation of Spain.* Topsfield, MA: Quartet, 1986.

_____. *Cities of Spain.* Chicago: Ivan R. Dee, nd.

Bibliography

Grugel, Jean and Tim Rees. *Franco's Spain.* New York: St. Martin's, 1997.

Gunther, Richard, ed. *Politics, Society, and Democracy. The Case of Spain.* Boulder, CO: Westview Press, 1993.

———. et al. *Spain After Franco: The Making of a Competitive Party System.* Berkeley: University of California Press, 1988.

Holguin, Sandie. *Creating Spaniards. Culture and National Identity in Republican Spain.* Madison: University of Wisconsin Press, nd.

Hooper, John. *The New Spaniards.* Rev. ed. New York: Penguin, 1995.

Hunt, Rosemary. *Get to Know Spain.* New York: Heineman, 1979.

Jackson, Gabriel. *The Spanish Republic and the Civil War, 1931–1939.* Princeton: Princeton University Press, 1965.

Kenwood, Alun, ed. *The Spanish Civil War. A Cultural and Historical Reader.* Oxford: Berg, 1992.

Kurlansky, Mark. *The Basque History of the World.* New York: Penguin 1999.

Lancaster, Thomas D. and Prevost, Gary. *Politics and Change in Spain.* New York: Praeger, 1985.

Maravall, Jose. *The Transition to Democracy in Spain.* New York: St. Martin's Press, 1983.

Maxwell, Kenneth, ed. *Spanish Foreign and Defense Policy.* Boulder, CO: Westview Press, 1991.

———. and Steven Spiegel. *The New Spain. From Isolation to Influence.* New York: Council on Foreign Relations, 1994.

McRoberts, Kenneth. *Catalonia.* New York: Oxford University, 2000.

Newton, Michael T. *Institutions of Modern Spain: a Political and Economic Guide.* New York: Cambridge University, 1997.

Parry, J.H. *The Spanish Seaborne Empire.* Berkeley: University of California Press, 1990.

Payne, Stanley G. *Basque Nationalism.* Reno: University of Nevada Press, 1975.

Pilar, Ortuño Anaya. *European Socialists and Spain. The Transition to Democracy, 1959–77.* New York: Palgrave, 2002.

Preston, Paul, ed. *Spain in Crisis: The Evolution and Decline of the Franco Regime.* London: Harvester Press, 1976.

———. *The Triumph of Democracy in Spain.* Methuen, 1986.

———. *The Politics of Revenge. Fascism and the Military in 20th Century Spain.* New York: Harper Collins, 1990.

Rodosh, Ronald, et al, eds. *Spain Betrayed. The Soviet Union in the Spanish Civil War.*

New Haven: Yale University Press, 2001.

Salmon, Keith. *The Modern Spanish Economy. Transformation and Integration into Europe.* New York: Columbia University Press, 1991.

Shubert, Adrian. *A Social History of Modern Spain.* New York: Harper Collins, 1990.

Sullivan, J.L. *ETA and Basque Nationalism. The Fight for Euskadi 1890–1986.* Kent: Croom Helm, 1988.

Tortella, Gabriel. *The Development of Modern Spain. An Economic History of the Nineteenth and Twentieth Centuries.* Cambridge, MA: Harvard University Press, 2000.

Vilar, Pierre. *Spain. A Brief History.* 2nd ed. New York: Pergamon, 1980.

Williams, Mark. *The Story of Spain,* 3d ed. Fuengirola, Spain: Santana Books, 2000.

Woolard, Kathryn A. *Double Talk. Bilingualism and the Politics of Ethnicity in Catalonia.* Palo Alto, CA: Stanford University Press, 1989.

Portugal

Birmingham, David. *A Concise History of Portugal.* Cambridge: Cambridge University Press, 1993.

Bruce, N. *Portugal, The Last Empire.* New York: Wiley, 1975.

Bruneau, Thomas C. *Politics and Nationhood. Post–Revolutionary Portugal.* New York: Praeger, 1984.

———. *Political Parties and Democracy in Portugal.* Boulder, CO: Westview, 1997.

———. and Macleod, Alex. *Politics in Contemporary Portugal: Parties and the Consolidation of Democracy.* Boulder, CO: Lynne Rienner, 1986.

Crollen, L. *Portugal, the U.S. and NATO.* Leuven, Leuven University Press, 1973.

dos Passos, John. *The Portugal Story: Three Centuries of Exploration and Discovery.* New York: Doubleday, 1969.

Figueiredo, Antonio de. *Portugal: 50 Years of Dictatorship.* London: Penguin, 1975.

Graham, Lawrence. *The Portuguese Military and the State.* Boulder, CO: Westview Press, 1993.

———. and Makler, Henry, eds. *Contemporary Portugal: The Revolution and its Antecedents.* Austin: Univ. of Texas Press, 1979.

Hamilton, Kimberly A. *Lusophone Africa, Portugal, and the United States.* Boulder, CO: Westview Press, 1992.

Harsgor, Michael. *Portugal in Revolution. The Washington Papers,* Vol. III, No. 32. Beverly Hills: Sage, 1976.

Harvey, Robert. *Portugal: Birth of Democracy.* New York: St. Martin's Press, 1978.

Janitschek, Hans. *Mario Soares. Portrait of a Hero.* New York: St. Martins, 1986.

Livermore, H. V. *Portugal: A Short History.* Princeton: Scholar's Bookshelf, n.d.

MacDonald, Scott B. *European Destiny, Atlantic Transformations. Portuguese Foreign Policy under the Second Republic, 1974–1992.* New Brunswick, NJ: Transaction, 1993.

Magone, José M. *European Portugal: the Difficult Road to Sustainable Democracy.* New York: St. Martin's, 1997.

Marques, Antonio H. *History of Portugal.* 2 vols. New York: Columbia University Press, 1972.

Maxwell, Kenneth. *The Making of Portuguese Democracy.* New York: Cambridge University Press, 1995.

Nataf, Daniel. *Democratization and Social Settlement. The Politics of Change in Contemporary Portugal.* Albany, NY: SUNY, 1995.

Opello, Walter C., Jr. *Portugal. From Monarchy to Pluralist Democracy.* Boulder, CO: Westview Press, 1991.

Pinto, António Costa, ed. *Introducing Modern Portugal.* Palo Alto, CA: SPOSS, 1998.

———. *Salazar's Dictatorship and European Fascism.* New York: Columbia University Press, 1996.

Porch, Douglas. *The Portuguese Armed Forces and the Revolution.* Palo Alto, CA: Hoover Institution, 1991.

Raby, D.L. *Fascism and Resistance in Portugal: Communists, Liberals and Military Dissidents in the Opposition to Salazar, 1941–1974.* New York: St. Martin's, 1988.

Silva Lopes, José de, ed. *Portugal and EC Membership Evaluated.* New York: St. Martin's, 1994.

Wheeler, Douglas L. *Historical Dictionary of Portugal.* Metuchen, NJ: Scarecrow Press, 1993.

Andorra

Cameron, Peter. *Andorra.* New York: Ferrar Straus Giroux, 1997.

Carter, Youngman. *On to Andorra.* New York: Norton, 1964.

Deane, Shirley. *The Road to Andorra.* New York: Morrow, 1961.

Morgan, Bryan. *Andorra, the Country in Between.* Nottingham, U.K.: Palmer, 1964.

EU summit in Nice

Courtesy: Central audiovisual Library, European Commision